HANDBOOK OF THE
UNDERGRADUATE CURRICULUM

Association of American Colleges and Universities

The Association of American Colleges and Universities is the only institutional-membership higher education association whose primary mission is to improve undergraduate liberal education. Founded in 1915, AAC&U serves more than 650 higher education institutions of all types through its Annual Meeting, national grant initiatives, publications, workshops, conferences, and consultative services that (1) address vital issues affecting students' undergraduate intellectual experiences, (2) create opportunities for engagement between national networks of administrators and faculty members focusing on improving students' learning, (3) involve campus teams of administrators and faculty members in curricular development, and (4) represent and model liberal learning to the higher education community and the public.

Internationally renowned for its work on curriculum reform and substantive publications, AAC&U has led the way in guiding curricular reform and intellectual thought through such landmark publications as *Integrity in the College Curriculum* and the more recent *Strong Foundations: Twelve Principles for Effective General Education Programs.* The late educational leader and reformer Ernest Boyer said of AAC&U, "I know of no association in the United States that has more consistently kept its message clearly focused on the central issue of excellence."

AAC&U's current strategic planning efforts will guide its mission into the twenty-first century and develop important organizing principles that center college- and university-wide planning deeply in the institutions' educational purposes and values.

The National Center on Postsecondary Teaching, Learning, and Assessment

The National Center on Postsecondary Teaching, Learning, and Assessment (NCTLA) is a research, development, and dissemination center devoted to studying teaching and learning, the improvement of educational practice, and the advancement of theory and practice in the assessment of student and institutional performance. NCTLA is a consortium housed at The Pennsylvania State University and includes The University of Illinois at Chicago, Syracuse University, Northwestern University, The University of Southern California, and Michigan State University. Its four research programs and longitudinal panel study all focus on three policy issues: (1) the experiences and learning outcomes of underrepresented groups, (2) the educational impacts of different kinds of institutions, and (3) the need for credible means of assessing student learning, educational progress, and institutional effectiveness.

HANDBOOK OF THE UNDERGRADUATE CURRICULUM

A Comprehensive Guide to Purposes, Structures, Practices, and Change

Jerry G. Gaff,
James L. Ratcliff, and
Associates

Jossey-Bass Publishers
San Francisco

In Chapter Seven, the summary of the literature on what constitutes "good practice" in undergraduate education is reprinted by permission of the National Center for Higher Education Management Systems (NCHEMS), from *Indicators of "Good Practice" in Undergraduate Education: A Handbook for Development and Implementation*. Boulder, Colo.: NCHEMS, 1991.

In Chapter Fifteen, Levi's "list of 'universal questions' for any literature whatsoever" is reprinted with permission from "Literature as a Humanity" by A. W. Levi in *Aesthetics and Arts Education*, edited by R. A. Smith and A. Simpson, University of Illinois Press, 1991.

In Chapter Sixteen, the list of goals for a program of professional relicensure is reprinted with permission from "Increasing Pressures for Recertification" by J. J. Norcini and J. A. Shea in *Educating Professionals: Responding to New Expectations for Competence and Accountability*, by L. Curry, J. F. Wergin, and Associates, Jossey-Bass, 1993. The list of six goals that should be part of each professional curriculum is reprinted with permission from "Building Awareness of Ethical Standards and Conduct" by D. T. Ozar, also in *Educating Professionals*, by Curry, Wergin, and Associates, Jossey-Bass, 1993.

In Chapter Twenty-Two, the conclusion of the report on longitudinal studies conducted to evaluate the impact of collaborative pedagogies and learning communities on student learning and persistence is reprinted with permission from *Building Learning Communities for New College Students: A Summary of Research Findings of the Collaborative Learning Project* by V. Tinto, A. G. Love, and P. Russo, National Center on Postsecondary Teaching, Learning, and Assessment, Syracuse University, 1994.

In Chapter Thirty-Three, the list of substantial gains experienced by institutions with major faculty development programs is reprinted with permission from *New Life for the College Curriculum: Assessing Achievements and Furthering Progress in the Reform of General Education* by J. G. Gaff, Jossey-Bass, 1991.

 Manufactured in the United States of America on Lyons Falls Turin Book. This paper is acid-free and 100 percent totally chlorine-free.

Library of Congress Cataloging-in-Publication Data

Handbook of the undergraduate curriculum : a comprehensive guide to
   purposes, structures, practices, and change / Jerry G. Gaff, James
L. Ratcliff, editors.
      p. cm.—(The Jossey-Bass higher and adult education series)
   ISBN 0-7879-0289-6
   1. Education, Higher—United States—Curricula—Handbooks,
manuals, etc. 2. Curriculum change—United States—Handbooks,
manuals, etc. 3. Curriculum evaluation—United States—Handbooks,
manuals, etc. I. Gaff, Jerry G. II. Ratcliff, James L.
III. Series.
LB2361.5.H35 1996
378.1'99'0973 dc20   96-16111

HB Printing 10 9 8 7 6 5 4 3 2   FIRST EDITION

THE JOSSEY-BASS

HIGHER AND ADULT EDUCATION SERIES

CONTENTS

PREFACE

The last two decades have been a time for serious thought about undergraduate education, particularly the nature of the curriculum, teaching, learning, and assessment. Large numbers of colleges and universities have made significant changes in their academic programs. Innovation, experimentation, and reform have been the order of the day.

The purpose of this book is to provide in a single volume an overview of the debates and reforms now swirling around the undergraduate curriculum. This volume is comprehensive, including all aspects of the curriculum—its purposes, origins, practices, trends, outcomes, obstacles, and prospects. It is intended to be a compendium of the best ideas, analyses, and practices described by leading figures in the field. It stresses a variety of initiatives for improving undergraduate education, both those currently in progress and those needed in the future. The book is practical, offering realistic frameworks, useful advice, workable strategies, and helpful cautions to those who wish to understand better the intricacies of the undergraduate curriculum and those striving to make improvements.

Although issues of teaching, learning, and assessment are closely related, this book keeps the spotlight on the curriculum. Indeed, we argue that the curriculum should be driven primarily by a concern for student learning; several authors touch on the implications of various curricula for teaching and learning; and we include chapters on assessment. Throughout, however, the focus is on the curriculum.

Colleges and universities are seeking ways to make better and more targeted, enriching, and engaging curricula. In the 1990s, very few institutions have either the human resources or the financial latitude to allow the unbridled growth of courses and programs. The emphases on enhancing quality and cutting costs often drive curricular decisions for conciseness and coherence in colleges and universities. Different types of undergraduate curricula require different approaches to reform and renewal. This volume catalogues and describes the different philosophies, frameworks, program designs, instructional strategies, and assessment methods being employed to strengthen and transform the curriculum.

When provosts, deans, department chairs, or curriculum committees set out to review or revise the curriculum, they typically seek a curriculum that is more engaging, inviting, and effective. They need designs distinctive to their institutional setting, including their particular mission, social context, educational philosophy, students, and faculty. While academic leaders may sense the need for significant and fundamental curricular change, they usually also wish to preserve those qualities of the undergraduate program that have drawn students to the institution or program in the past. This handbook allows such efforts to select appropriate curricula and strategies for change to be based on evidence, experience, and broad intellectual perspectives rather than on folk wisdom and anecdote.

Major Thesis

Although there are thirty-four chapters in this volume, virtually all of them written independently of each other by practitioners and experts, this book has a general thesis running through it. Stripped to its essentials, it is this: the history of the undergraduate curriculum is marked by the growth of specialization and proliferation of programs and courses, and while this specialization has generated a vast richness of scholarship, it has often led to disconnected bits of information, fragmentation of the learning experience of students, and disintegration of the academic community. We are in the midst of a historic reversal of this trend because it is not conducive to good education for students, academic community for faculty and campuses, or continued financial support from the public. This is thus a time ripe with innovation and experimentation, and such innovation cannot proceed effectively in the absence of sound assessments of student growth, development, and attainment. Although the outlines of the future are not very clear, we can be sure it will be different from the present.

Obviously, not all of the fifty-seven authors of these chapters are of one mind on these matters. But the book was conceptualized and chapters were commissioned to show the richness of historical and contemporary perspectives on these issues. We particularly wanted to show the creativity to be found within the different domains of knowledge and the various innovations that span the academic disciplines.

A corollary of this general thesis is that while it is important to understand and analyze the curriculum, it is also important to change it. We have worked with literally hundreds of colleges and universities of all types as they try to increase the quality and coherence of their courses of study and to assess the impact of those courses on students. We have tried to make this volume useful to the leaders of such institutions.

The style of each chapter reflects the approaches taken by its authors. Some serve as guides to a topic, others are personal essays, others review promising innovations, and still others focus on illustrative patterns of thought or advocate specific changes. In many ways, this diversity of topics and approaches mirrors the variety of concerns and ideas found on college campuses today. In addition to reflecting the diversity of campus voices, we hope the chapters help academic leaders negotiate such differences by finding shared educational principles on which to construct a meaningful curriculum.

How This Book Is Organized

This book is structured in six parts. This preface gives a brief overview of the logic behind the organization of the handbook and what one may expect to find in each part, then provides some sample road maps for those undertaking analysis of an undergraduate curriculum or seeking to better understand its components. While we urge those using the handbook to turn to those chapters most appropriate to their needs, we provide a sequential plan for gaining a comprehensive understanding of what the undergraduate curriculum is all about.

Part One deals with the purposes and objectives of undergraduate education. It looks at pivotal historical developments, illustrates how the curriculum changes in response to social and historical forces, explores traditional and innovative philosophies, discusses how those philosophies are given shape in operational programs, and looks at current social forces impacting the undergraduate curriculum.

Part Two focuses on the central aims of undergraduate education: the knowledge, skills, and attitudes expected of all students. General education is the largest and most contested academic program at most institutions, and this section of the book analyzes the issues of quality and coherence embedded in that part of the curriculum. It also discusses the issues involved in learning various intellectual skills, thinking about cultural differences and dealing with diversity, and helping at-risk students succeed with these common tasks.

In Part Three, we look at specialized learning and the academic disciplines that are central features of almost all curricula. The chapters here deal with intellectual developments and educational innovations in college majors, and in the humanities, the natural sciences and mathematics, the social sciences, the arts, and professional and occupational programs.

Part Four details curricular innovations that span the academic disciplines and fields of specialization and point the way to further curriculum change. Included are teaching writing and other subjects across the curriculum, establishing inter-disciplinary studies programs, internationalizing the curriculum, incorporating cultural diversity into the curriculum, developing learning communities, and using the expanding array of technologies.

Part Five examines the topics of administration, assessment, and institutional support. Forms of administrative structures, strategies for developing community while containing costs, ways to develop efficient as well as effective curricula, and procedures to facilitate transfer between institutions are examined. Other chapters look at evaluating learning in courses, assessing whole programs, and developing indicators of quality within and between institutions.

The process of changing the curriculum is discussed in Part Six. Various strategies for change—including both what to do and what to avoid—are offered, along with discussion of the kinds of support faculty need to make significant change.

The final chapter synthesizes much of the earlier material and explores the nature of a curriculum for the twenty-first century. It argues that traditional curriculum structures dating from the end of the nineteenth century are experiencing increased stress and that new curricula will be needed for the future.

Road Map to Reform

The handbook is designed to be a useful operating manual and desk reference for individuals with responsibility for, or interest in, the curriculum. As such, it contains both conceptual and practical information about organizing and operating a curriculum; research, effective practices, and the opinions of leaders in the field are presented. It directs readers to the essential publications in the field; key reference lists accompany each chapter. It presents state-of-the-art knowledge about many of the multiple dimensions of undergraduate curricula. It specifies unresolved issues and gaps in the knowledge base about effective undergraduate studies, seeking to lay aside common myths and unsubstantiated practices. In the process, it also describes exemplary programs and practices to highlight the very best in undergraduate studies at all types of institutions—from community colleges to research universities, in America and abroad.

Who should read this book? The audience is the usual broad one reached by Jossey-Bass books. It includes academic administrators, faculty leaders, curriculum committee members, libraries, and staff from the instructional development center, faculty development center, and learning assistance center. It should also interest state policy makers, legislators on education committees, boards of trustees, staffs of accrediting agencies and educational organizations, foundation program officers concerned with higher education, and journalists whose beat is education. It may also serve as a text for courses on the undergraduate curriculum or as a reference for students of higher education as a field of study.

The practical applications for using this handbook are as varied as are the audiences for this book. We suggest that, rather than reading the book cover to cover, readers create their own road maps to understanding and reforming the curriculum. The three examples presented here give an idea of how to use the book as a tool.

Route One: General Education Curriculum Review Committee

This committee is typically composed of faculty members from various disciplines who differ in their educational views, concerns, and exposure to different curricula. Individuals hold competing educational philosophies, curricular models, and ideas about how to proceed—and worse, these differences are often implicit and unspoken. At the outset, the group needs to study and learn about substantive curricular issues—problems, trends, analyses, and models—and to become sophisticated thinkers so as to lead their colleagues through the many conceptual tangles that can thwart meaningful change. In addition, the committee should realize that what most often jeopardizes proposed change is a failure of process and procedure. They should confront at the outset the reality that they are seeking serious change in the organization and become sophisticated strategists in designing and managing their change process.

The committee will need to find a common language and understanding of curricula, and reading Chapters One and Four, which discuss the nature of a curriculum and the philosophies and aims which go into its construction, may help. Committee members should be asking some major questions: What knowledge, skills, and values should graduates of this institution possess, regardless of major, minor, or field of specialization? What is the educational philosophy guiding our selection of general education goals? Without asking such questions and seeking common language and purpose, the pathway to curricular change may be as clear as peering through a bar of chocolate (and as potentially bittersweet).

To start getting a grip on their own process, it would be helpful to read and discuss at an early time the implications of Chapter Thirty-One, which provides a good introduction to contrasting strategies and procedures for orchestrating academic change. It can help the group devise its own winning process. The other chapters in Part Six should also be read early for their cautions, suggestions, and practical advice. Curricula are reflections of social and historical forces, and the historical material in Chapters Two and Three as well as the contemporary social pressures discussed in Chapter Six may sensitize the committee members to their own societal context. Chapter Seven may be useful as the committee considers approaches to general education, including the knotty issues of quality and coherence. Chapter Twelve may help the group to clarify its thinking about the development of key intellectual skills and the mechanisms that can be employed to help students acquire them.

The committee will doubtless give specific attention to the academic disciplines and applied fields of specialization. Chapters Eleven through Seventeen examine the broad disciplinary groups comprising the curriculum—the humanities, the arts, the social sciences, and the natural sciences, mathematics, and professional and occupational education. The presentation of recent trends and issues in curricular design and development as well as examples of programs and practices will help the group decide how best to structure these subjects for the non-majors, students who may never take another course in the field.

The curriculum committee may wish to review the chapters that describe a range of innovations that cut across disciplines. Taken up in Part Five are reviews of innovations in writing across the curriculum, interdisciplinary studies, internationalizing the curriculum, incorporating cultural diversity, developing learning communities, and using technology in the curriculum.

Once the committee agrees on a framework for the curriculum, it will need to develop an implementation and operating plan, as well as establish procedures to assess the effectiveness of the curriculum. Toward this end Chapter Twenty-Four, on curriculum administration, and Chapters Twenty-Eight to Thirty, on assessing an academic program, may be particularly helpful. Also, if the college or university accepts substantial numbers of transfer students, the newly revised curriculum will need to be articulated carefully with those colleges that provide the majority of transfer students, a process discussed in Chapter Twenty-Seven.

Thus, by following this road map, the general education curriculum committee can chart an effective course for improvement using this handbook as a reference.

Route Two: Departmental Review of a Major Program

Reviewing the sequences, requirements, and assessment mechanisms for an academic major may appear at first to be easier than overhauling the general education program of the institution. But getting a group of faculty members, even in the same department, to agree on shared goals and principles is not as easy as it might seem. The department review committee might enhance its deliberations by studying what others are thinking and doing. It can be valuable to start by having the group read Chapter Eleven, on academic majors in general, Chapter Eight, on the development of intellectual skills, and whichever chapter in Part Three applies most directly to the major under review.

The chapters of Part Four focus on a variety of curricular issues and trends that cut across disciplinary boundaries. Each member of the committee could review one of these, and then a meeting could be devoted solely to the development of writing skills across the curriculum (Chapter Eighteen), incorporating international perspectives (Chapter Twenty), or establishing learning communities (Chapter Twenty-Two). If the department finds an increasing number of students selecting the major field without sufficient knowledge, skills, or abilities to readily succeed, the committee may wish to consult Chapter Ten, which addresses the question of at-risk students. Similarly, if the program or major is going to be offered at a distance or substantially increase its use of instructional technology, then Chapter Twenty-Three may be just the ticket.

With the increasing attention given to assessment by accrediting bodies and state agencies, it is advisable to have the departmental review committee consider (or establish) the means and methods for assessing student learning within the major. This should not be undertaken until the committee has set clearly articulated goals for the major that describe the student learning that is to accrue from the program. There should be a direct and clear relationship between the goals and the coursework prescribed or recommended to attain the goals. If the departmental review committee decides that a history major should learn critical thinking skills relative to broad themes and interpretations of historical works, then there should be clear curricular sequences that attain that goal. The committee should carefully examine course syllabi and text selections to ensure that learning toward the goal is incorporated in each course in the sequence supporting the goal. Here it may be helpful to review Chapters Twenty-Eight and Twenty-Nine, which relate to evaluating learning in courses and academic programs. A four-year college or university department reviewing its academic majors would also be well advised to consult Chapter Twenty-Seven to ensure that the revised curriculum incorporates in an effective and efficient manner the prior learning of students taking coursework at neighboring community colleges.

The chapters in any of the other parts of the book can enrich understanding and practice in a department. The chapters in Part One, on historical, philosophical, and social perspectives; in Part Five, on administrative, financial, and transfer issues; or in Part Six, on curriculum change, may help put a department's program into a broader context.

Route Three: Higher Education Graduate Course

Those studying the curriculum as part of higher education as a field of study may wish to reflect on the organization of this book. Indeed, one of us used a draft of this manuscript in a graduate course on the curriculum. The students gained a good overview of the field and made many suggestions that improved its use as a text. Each part represents a major component of the curriculum. Part One discusses the structure, history, and philosophies undergirding undergraduate education. The key components of the undergraduate curriculum—general education, the major, and professional or occupational programs—are all reviewed in various chapters, as are current issues and innovations in the academic disciplines. The chapters in Part Four highlight writing and teaching across the curriculum, interdisciplinary studies, global studies, cultural pluralism, learning communities, and technology, implying curricular structures and instructional practices that cut across disciplines and specialization. Successive sections deal with administrative and fiscal issues, transfer, assessment, and the process of curriculum change.

Origins of This Book

The Association of American Colleges and Universities (AAC&U) was established in 1915 to advocate and advance the cause of liberal and general learning in American colleges and universities. It came into being to a large degree in response to the rise of research universities, the importation of German ideals for research and the advancement of knowledge as the primary purpose of university studies, and the ensuing attacks on the quality and direction of liberal learning. During the ensuing decades, the AAC&U came to serve all kinds of colleges and universities. Its mission is to promote quality undergraduate education, particularly liberal learning. It has 660 institutional members, which it serves by means of publications, meetings, research, and funded projects to develop model educational programs. Given AAC&U's history, it was appropriate and logical that Gale Erlandson, senior editor at Jossey-Bass, invited AAC&U to sponsor this comprehensive study of the curriculum. She wrote:

> There has not been a substantive comprehensive book on the college curriculum since Arthur Levine's 1978 *Handbook on Undergraduate Curriculum,* sponsored by the Carnegie Council on Policy Studies in Higher Education. Over those years the curriculum has become a battleground of special interests, a "supermarket" responding to personal tastes of student consumers, and a focus for much-needed comprehensive, coherently developed discussion of the undergraduate curriculum.
>
> AAC&U is to my mind the only group in a position to bring together the best thinking on the curriculum, and to offer an authoritative, unbiased, and

critical analysis of what has been going on in the name of undergraduate education.

AAC&U represents the heart of undergraduate education, and has the best view of the many diverse forces that bear on today's curriculum.

As Paula Brownlee, president of AAC&U, signed the contract for this book with Jossey-Bass, she and Erlandson asked Jerry Gaff, AAC&U vice president, to serve as editor of the new volume. In addition to heading several of AAC&U's national projects, Gaff is the author of several books and many articles on general education and curricular change, including *General Education Today* (1983) and *New Life for the College Curriculum* (1991).

While Erlandson saw AAC&U's special position and role in identifying the best practices, emerging trends, and persistent issues in undergraduate curriculum, she also recognized that there was a growing body of research guiding the improvement of curricular aims, design, and assessment. The National Center on Postsecondary Teaching, Learning, and Assessment (NCTLA), first supported by a grant from the U.S. Department of Education, conducts research on those forces and factors that contribute to (or hinder) undergraduate student learning. NCTLA research focuses on the specific ways that colleges and universities can better promote effective teaching and learning for historically underrepresented groups and for those attending part-time or commuting to campus, and ways they can reframe assessment to better inform teaching effectiveness, curricular design, faculty development, and student advisement. Given NCTLA's purview of research on the undergraduate curriculum, Erlandson and Gaff asked James Ratcliff, the center's director, to coedit this work.

A professor and senior scientist at the Pennsylvania State University, Ratcliff directs the highly acclaimed Center for the Study of Higher Education, as well as the eighteen researchers in the six universities that make up the NCTLA consortium. In addition to his several publications and research reports on linking assessment to curricular reform, he edits the *Journal of General Education*.

In closing, it is perhaps best to reiterate that this is not a book designed to be read cover to cover. While we have provided what we believe to be a logical progression of topics for one seeking to better understand the curriculum, we urge those with more immediate and pragmatic needs to draw upon the chapters most relevant to their agenda. Collectively, the thirty-four chapters provide a wealth of knowledge and analysis that should prove useful for individuals dipping into selected sections, as well as those seeking to cover the landscape. We hope that you will find this handbook a useful reference and resource to design, carry out, and assess high-quality, coherent, and engaging courses of study for undergraduate students in the coming decade and century.

Acknowledgments

Publishing any book is an act of collaboration, and for the size and complexity of this book, the collaboration was extensive. Apart from the ideas and educational principles—which are difficult enough—this undertaking was a constant logistical challenge. Completion of this work has depended on the support and encouragement of the following people, and we are grateful for their assistance:

- Gale Erlandson and her colleagues at Jossey-Bass for conceiving of the need for this volume, inviting AAC&U to sponsor the book, selecting the editors, working with them to conceptualize the volume, and, with the aid of Rachel Livsey, providing editorial support throughout the process.

- Our colleagues at AAC&U—Paula Brownlee, Carol Schneider, Joseph Johnston, Jr., Jane Spalding, Caryn McTighe Musil—who supported sponsorship of the book, advised in conceptualizing the book and selecting authors, wrote chapters, or reviewed early drafts; and Audrey Jones, Erik Ledbetter, and Lee Harper, who helped smooth a complex process and assemble the completed manuscript.

- Our colleagues at the National Center on Postsecondary Teaching, Learning, and Assessment—Trudy Banta, Peter Ewell, Donald Farmer, Faith Gabelnick, Mildred Garcia, Jean MacGregor, Roberta Matthews, Michael Reardon, Judith Ramaley, Barbara Leigh Smith—who contributed to and were associated with the various research and dissemination activities of the center. This association led us to seek their counsel and inclusion in this volume. A special thank you to Ruth Sinton, who assembled the glossary, assisted with the selection of the terms indexed, and verified references; to Sherry Casamento, Nadine Lamb, Sheila Petrosky, and Sally Kelley—the secretarial staff—who carried forward the preparation of drafts, versions, and revisions to their fruition; and to Ben Click, Barbara Gibson-Benninger, Patricia Yaeger, and Karla Sanders, who assisted with editing text drafts.

- All the authors who gave of their time and shared their insight and wisdom—and mostly met deadlines imposed on them—with good spirits.

- Joanne Gainen and Ann Ferren, who assisted the editors with last-minute review and revision of several chapters.

Without their cheerful willingness to work together, this book literally could not have been completed. We thank them all.

August 1996

Jerry G. Gaff
Washington, D.C.

James L. Ratcliff
State College, Pennsylvania

THE AUTHORS

Jerry G. Gaff is vice president of the Association of American Colleges and Universities. He received an A.B. degree from DePaul University and a Ph.D. degree in psychology from Syracuse University. He served on the faculties of five institutions, conducted research at the Center for Research and Development in Higher Education at the University of California, Berkeley, and was dean of the College of Liberal Arts and acting president of Hamline University.

Through his research, writing, direction of national projects, consulting, and speaking, Gaff contributed to several different movements to improve undergraduate education. During the 1960s, he compiled a book on experimental colleges and aided the establishment of such innovations elsewhere. During the 1970s, Gaff helped redefine the meaning of faculty development to include development not only as a researcher but also as a teacher and citizen of the academic community; he directed projects that established centers and programs to support faculty at dozens of colleges and universities. During the 1980s, he assisted scores of institutions in strengthening their general education programs.

Currently he directs the Preparing Future Faculty program, which is developing new ways to socialize graduate students to the values of undergraduate education. This program works with doctoral universities and clusters of diverse undergraduate institutions to incorporate preparation for teaching and service roles into graduate programs. His previous Jossey-Bass books include *The Cluster College* (1970), *Toward Faculty Renewal* (1975), *General Education Today* (1983), and *New*

Life for the College Curriculum (1991). He has served on several boards, received various awards and honors, and is a frequent speaker at conferences and events.

James L. Ratcliff is professor of higher education and director of the Center for the Study of Higher Education (CSHE) at Pennsylvania State University. CSHE is one of the oldest, largest, and most recognized interdisciplinary research centers devoted exclusively to analysis of policy and practice in higher education. Ratcliff is also director of the National Center on Postsecondary Teaching, Learning, and Assessment (NCTLA), a consortium of higher education researchers at Pennsylvania State University, Arizona State University, Northwestern University, Syracuse University, the University of Illinois-Chicago, and the University of Southern California. As the primary research and development center of the U.S. Department of Education, from 1991 to 1996 NCTLA sponsored more than eighteen national studies of the effect of college on student learning, hosted dozens of workshops, seminars, and symposia to facilitate the adoption and adaptation of its research to the improvement of practice, and worked with more than 120 colleges and universities directly in the improvement of undergraduate education.

Ratcliff attended Raymond College at the University of the Pacific (where Gaff began his faculty career). He received his B.A. degree from Utah State University in history and political science, his M.A. degree in history from Washington State University, and his Ph.D. in higher education administration from Washington State University. He is past president and has received the Distinguished Service Award of the College and University Council of the American Association of Community Colleges.

Ratcliff edits the *Journal of General Education,* and is author of *Realizing the Potential: Improving Postsecondary Teaching, Learning, and Assessment* (1995), *Community Colleges* (1994), and *Assessment and Reform of the Undergraduate Curriculum* (1992). He has consulted with hundreds of colleges and universities, several state higher education agencies, and national ministries of education on five continents regarding curriculum development, assessment, community colleges, and academic policy.

Gordon Arnold is associate professor of social sciences and chairperson of liberal arts at Montserrat College of Art. He has been a research associate at the New England Resource Center for Higher Education at the University of Massachusetts Boston, adjunct research associate at the Center for Policy Analysis at the University of Massachusetts Dartmouth, and associate dean of academic affairs at Montserrat College of Art. He received his B.A. degree (1976) in fine arts from Clark University, his M.L.S. degree (1982) from the University of Rhode Island, and his Ph.D. degree (1994) in higher education from Boston College.

James Chenevert is associate professor of music at Alverno College and is also coordinator of the Department of Music. He is a member of the Department of Aesthetic Responsiveness, an interdisciplinary ability-based department. Since 1993 he has codirected a program for the advancement of interdisciplinary teaching and learning in the humanities and fine arts. He received his B.A. and M.A. degrees from the University of Minnesota, and his Ph.D. degree from the University of Wisconsin, Madison.

Jan T. Civian is director of policy research for the Office of Institutional Research at Wellesley College. She is a senior associate at the New England Resource Center for Higher Education at the University of Massachusetts, Boston, and a research associate at the Derek Bok Center for Teaching and Learning at Harvard University. She currently directs Pathways for Women in the Sciences, a five-year study sponsored by the Sloan Foundation and located at the Center for Research on Women at Wellesley College. She received her B.A. degree (1979) in sociology from Wellesley College, A.M. degree (1980) in education from Stanford University, and Ed.D. degree (1990) in administration, planning, and social policy from the Graduate School of Education at Harvard University.

Darrel A. Clowes has taught and administered in community colleges in New York and Florida for eight years, with a specialty in curriculum and critical theory in education. Before that he taught in universities for twenty years, most of them at Virginia Polytechnic Institute and State University. He served in the Peace Corps; edited and wrote numerous books, chapters, articles and reports—mostly on community colleges; edited a journal on community services; served on numerous editorial and review boards; and was a radio sports analyst this past year. He is now an emeritus faculty member at Virginia Polytechnic Institute and State University.

Lynn Curry founded the consulting firms of Seratus and CurryCorp in 1990. Seratus coordinates expertise in health system reform; CurryCorp provides services in evaluation, planning, and organizational redesign. She held graduate faculty positions at the University of North Carolina, Chapel Hill, and Dalhousie University, and concluded her full-time academic career as Rosenstadt Professor at the University of Toronto. She authored and (with Jon Wergin) coedited *Educating Professionals: Responding to New Expectations for Competence and Accountability*, (Jossey-Bass, 1993). She received her Ph.D. degree (1974) in educational psychology from Stanford University, and a diploma in higher education administration (1982) from Bryn Mawr College.

Austin Doherty is vice president for academic affairs at Alverno College. She received her B.A. degree in history from Alverno College, and her M.A. and Ph.D. degrees in psychology from Loyola University, Chicago. As a faculty member in the Department of Psychology, she was a participant in the original development of Alverno's ability-based learning program in the early 1970s. She is particularly interested in the impact on higher education of new trends in psychology.

Judith S. Eaton is chancellor of the Minnesota State Colleges and Universities. Prior to her appointment in Minnesota, she was president of the Council for Aid to Education in New York City, and a vice president at the American Council on Education in Washington, D.C. She has published several books and has edited numerous publications. She received her B.A. degree and M.A. degree from the University of Michigan and her Ph.D. degree from Wayne State University.

Peter T. Ewell is a senior associate at the National Center for Higher Education Management Systems (NCHEMS), a research and development center founded to improve the management effectiveness of colleges and universities, where he focuses on assessing institutional effectiveness and the outcomes of the college, and takes part in both research and direct consulting. Prior to NCHEMS, he was coordinator for long-range planning at Governors State University and was also on the faculty of the University of Chicago. He received his Ph.D. degree from Yale University.

D. W. Farmer is vice president for academic affairs and professor of history at King's College, Pennsylvania. He is a member of the advisory committee on assessment for the Commission on Higher Education of the Middle States Association. He received his B.A. degree (1959) in history and modern languages from Trinity College and his M.A. (1961) and Ph.D. (1965) degrees in history from Georgetown University. He was the recipient of an International Administrators Fulbright Award (1990) to conduct a study of higher education in Japan.

James Farmer is a senior researcher at Systems Research Inc., a Washington, D.C., higher education consulting firm. He has contributed to texts on higher education financing and has designed information systems for state agencies and for colleges and universities. He taught higher education courses at Harvard University's Graduate School of Education and economics courses at California State University, Northridge. He received a B.S. degree (1956) in mathematics from the University of Oklahoma, an S.M. degree (1961) in applied mathematics from Harvard University, and an M.B.A. degree (1962) from the University of California, Los Angeles.

Ann S. Ferren is vice president for academic affairs at Radford University. Previously she was at American University, where she held positions as associate professor of education, associate dean of faculties, director of general education, vice provost for academic development, and interim provost. She was honored for her work on undergraduate curriculum by the National Center for the Study of the First Year Experience. Her research on curriculum, instruction, and faculty development has been published in the *Journal of General Education, College Teaching, To Improve the Academy,* and *Liberal Education.* She received her A.B. degree (1961) in economics from Radcliffe College, her M.A.T. degree (1962) from Harvard Graduate School of Education, and her Ed.D. degree (1971) from Boston University.

Barbara S. Fuhrmann is associate dean and professor of education in the College of Education at Louisiana State University. She received her B.A. degree (1962) in English from Beloit College, her M.S.Ed. degree (1969) in counseling and guidance from Wisconsin State University, and her Ed.D. degree (1973) in teacher education from the University of Massachusetts.

Faith Gabelnick is president of Pacific University in Forest Grove, Oregon. She is the former provost and dean of the faculty at Mills College and has held positions as dean of the Lee Honors College, Western Michigan University and associate director, university honors program, University of Maryland, College Park. Her books, presentations, and articles focus on designing educational environments and on the psychological aspects of leadership. She earned her B.A. degree from Douglass College, Rutgers University, her M.A. degree from the University of Massachusetts at Amherst, and her Ph.D. degree from American University.

Zelda F. Gamson is professor of education and founding director of the New England Resource Center for Higher Education at the University of Massachusetts, Boston. She has published widely on organizational change, innovation, and policy issues in higher education. Her books include *Liberating Education* (1984) and *Higher Education and the Real World* (1989), and she is a coauthor of the forthcoming *Revitalizing General Education in a Time of Scarcity.* Gamson holds an M.A. degree (1959) in sociology from the University of Michigan and a Ph.D. degree (1965) in sociology from Harvard University.

Mildred García is currently assistant vice president for academic affairs at Montclair State University and president of the American Association of University Administrators. She has been a visiting scholar and research associate at Pennsylvania State University and a visiting professor at Teachers College, Columbia University. She is coauthor of "Reflecting Inclusiveness in the College Curriculum" and

Diversity in Higher Education, and *Affirmative Action's Testament of Hope: Strategies for a New Era* is forthcoming in 1996.

Joan S. Girgus is professor of psychology and chair of the psychology department at Princeton University, where she has chaired the faculty committee on the course of study, examinations and standing, undergraduate admission, and financial aid. As a member of the president's cabinet, she was Princeton's representative to the Polity Committee of the Council of Ivy Group Presidents. She directs the Pew Science Program in Undergraduate Education for The Pew Charitable Trusts, and is one of the principal organizers of the Pew Higher Education Roundtable. She received her B.A. degree from Sarah Lawrence College and both her M.A. and Ph.D. degrees in psychology from the Graduate Faculty of the New School for Social Research in New York.

Ellen T. Harris is professor of music at the Massachusetts Institute of Technology, where she was the Institute's first associate provost for the arts (1989–1995). Her extensive publications in music include two books from Oxford University Press and numerous articles and reviews. Articles on policy issues concerning arts education and art censorship have appeared in the *Chronicle of Higher Education* and the *Aspen Institute Quarterly.* She has received fellowships from the American Council of Learned Societies and the National Endowment for the Humanities; for the 1995–96 academic year, she was a fellow at the Mary Ingraham Bunting Institute of Radcliffe College at Harvard University.

Elizabeth M. Hawthorne is director of academic affairs at Pennsylvania State University, Berks Campus, and associate professor of higher education and affiliate in the Center for the Study of Higher Education. She received her B.S. degree (1965) in child study from Tufts University, her M.S. degree (1971) in educational psychology from Temple University, her A.M. degree (1981) in political science, and her Ph.D. degree (1985) in higher education from the University of Michigan.

Anne Barnhardt Hendershott is chair of the Department of Sociology and coordinator of urban studies at the University of San Diego. Formerly director of the Center for Social Research at the University of Hartford, Hendershott's research and publications focus on inequality. She has taught in the areas of research methods, urban social problems, crime and delinquency, and work and family.

John B. Hinni is dean of the School of University Studies at Southeast Missouri State University, where he is a professor of biology. He is the founding president of the executive board of the Council for Administration for General and Liberal

Studies, a newly created national organization designed to support general education programs. He received his B.S. degree (1958) and Ph.D. degree (1963) in biological sciences from Northwestern University.

Philo A. Hutcheson is assistant professor of educational policy studies at Georgia State University, where he has also served as faculty coordinator of the higher education doctoral program. He received his B.A. degree (1969) in French and English from Carroll College, in Wisconsin, and his Ph.D. degree (1991) in higher education from the University of Chicago.

Frederick T. Janzow is director of the Center for Scholarship in Teaching and Learning at Southeast Missouri State University, where he is a professor of biology. He received his B.S. degree (1967) in biology from Concordia Teachers College and his M.S. (1972) and Ph.D. (1978) degrees in biology from Oklahoma State University.

Jacqueline R. Johnson is professor of sociology at Grand Valley State University, where she also chairs the Department of Anthropology and Sociology. Her research interests and writings are in the areas of comparative political sociology and student resistance in higher education. She received her B.A. degree (1968) in sociology from Macalester College and her M.S. (1971) and Ph.D. (1974) degrees from Purdue University.

Joseph S. Johnston, Jr., is vice president of programs at the Association of American Colleges and Universities, where he designs, secures external funding for, and directs projects. He has directed projects with a focus on improvement of undergraduate education, strengthening international education, and establishing ties with higher education systems abroad. He has organized international conferences in Russia and a curriculum development project with the National Universities of Japan. He received his M.B.A. degree from the Wharton School of the University of Pennsylvania and his Ph.D. degree in English Language and Literature from the University of Chicago.

Sandra Kanter is an associate professor and core faculty member of the doctoral program in higher education at the University of Massachusetts, Boston. The author of a number of articles in general education, she has consulted widely with colleges and universities on their general education curriculum. She is a coauthor of the forthcoming book *Revitalizing General Education in a Time of Scarcity.* Kanter attended Connecticut College, the University of Pennsylvania, and the Massachusetts Institute of Technology, and was a Loeb Fellow at Harvard University.

Julie Thompson Klein is professor of humanities at Wayne State University. She received her B.A. (1967), M.A. (1968), D.A. (1970), and Ph.D. (1971) degrees in English from the University of Oregon. She publishes widely on interdisciplinarity and has represented the United States at OECD- and UNESCO-sponsored international symposia on interdisciplinary issues. A former president of the Association for Integrative Studies and former editor of *Issues in Integrative Studies,* she has also been visiting foreign professor at Shimane University in Japan, a Fulbright lecturer and an academic specialist in Nepal, and a University of Auckland foundation visitor in New Zealand.

Arthur Levine is president and professor of education at Teachers College, Columbia University. Prior to Teachers College, he served as chair of the higher education program and chair of the institute for educational management at the Harvard Graduate School of Education. He was also president of Bradford College and senior fellow at The Carnegie Foundation and Carnegie Council for Policy Studies in Higher Education. He has served as consultant to many colleges and universities and is the author of numerous books, articles, and reviews, including the *Handbook on Undergraduate Curriculum* (Jossey-Bass, 1978). He received his B.A. degree from Brandeis University and his Ph.D. from State University of New York, Buffalo.

Jack Lindquist was one of the early specialists in organizational change in general, and in the process of academic change in particular. He was an English teacher, debate coach, student dean, and residence hall director, as well as an influential scholar, writer, and consultant. After receiving a doctorate at the University of Michigan, he directed several national educational improvement projects, including the W. K. Kellogg Foundation's Use of Innovations Project. He consulted with hundreds of colleges and universities; served as president (1981–1989) of Goddard College, an experimental college in the progressive tradition; and advised countless academic leaders about how to make their dreams of improving undergraduate education come true. He died in April 1991.

Howard B. London is professor of sociology at Bridgewater State College, and senior associate at the New England Resource Center for Higher Education at the University of Massachusetts, Boston. He received his B.A. degree (1969) in sociology from Bowdoin College, and his M.A. (1972) and Ph.D. degrees (1976) in sociology from Boston College. In 1987 he received a clinical M.S.W. degree from Simmons College. He is the author of several books, articles, and reports on higher education, including the forthcoming *Revitalizing General Education in a Time of Scarcity* with Sandra Kanter and Zelda Gamson. He currently directs a study of community colleges whose students transfer in unusually high numbers to baccalaureate institutions.

Barbara Lounsberry is professor in the Department of English Language and Literature at the University of Northern Iowa, where she has received both the distinguished scholar award and the Regents' award for faculty excellence in teaching, research, and service. She also has served as chair of the Faculty Senate and chair of the faculty at UNI. She received her B.A. (1969) and M.A. (1971) degrees in English from the University of Northern Iowa and her Ph.D. degree (1978) in English from the University of Iowa.

Jean MacGregor is codirector of the Washington Center for Improving the Quality of Undergraduate Education, a consortium of forty-six colleges headquartered at the Evergreen State College, where she is also an adjunct faculty member. She has coauthored several books on learning communities, and she is a practitioner of collaborative learning approaches, both in community-based organizations and in formal classrooms. She received her B.S. degree (1967) in natural resources and her M.S. degree (1971) in resource planning and conservation from the University of Michigan.

Elaine P. Maimon is provost and professor of English at Arizona State University–West. Previously she was professor of English and dean of experimental programs at Queens College of the City University of New York. She was also associate dean of the college at Brown University and a professor at Beaver College, where she created and administered one of the nation's first programs in writing across the curriculum. An Elaine P. Maimon Award for Excellence in Writing was created at Beaver in her honor. She has authored several publications, *Writing in the Arts and Sciences, Readings in the Arts and Sciences,* and *Thinking, Reasoning, and Writing,* as well as numerous articles and essays. She received her B.A. degree (1966), M.A. degree (1967), and Ph.D. degree (1970) in English from the University of Pennsylvania.

Roberta S. Matthews is provost at Marymount College, Tarrytown. A professor of English, she formerly was associate dean for academic affairs at LaGuardia Community College, City University of New York. She has published and coauthored several books on learning communities and collaborative learning, and she is a member of the board of directors of the American Association for Higher Education. She received her B.A. degree from Smith College (1965), M.A. degree from Columbia University (1966), and her Ph.D. degree in modern English and Irish literature from the State University of New York, Stony Brook (1973).

Dennis McGrath is professor of sociology at the Community College of Philadelphia. He received his B.A. degree (1969) in sociology from La Salle College and his Ph.D. degree (1980) in sociology from the New School for Social Research. His current research interests include the qualitative assessment of large-scale educational reform and the role of social capital in education.

Rhoda R. Miller is associate professor of psychology at Alverno College and is also coordinator of the Department of Psychology. She is a member of the Department of Global Perspectives, an interdisciplinary ability-based department. She received her B.A. degree (1970) from Doane College, her M.A. degree (1972) in educational psychology from the University of Northern Colorado, and her Ph.D. degree (1987) in counseling psychology from the University of Wisconsin.

Caryn McTighe Musil is a senior research associate at the Association of American Colleges and Universities where she is associate director of their campus diversity initiative, "American Commitments: Diversity, Democracy, and Liberal Learning," and director of their program on the status and education of women. She received her B.A. degree (1966) in English from Duke University and her M.A. (1967) and Ph.D. (1974) degrees in English from Northwestern University. From 1984 through 1990 she was executive director of the National Women's Studies Association. Editor of *The Courage to Question: Women's Studies and Student Learning* and *Students at the Center: Feminist Assessment,* she coauthored *Diversity in Higher Education: A Work in Progress.*

Edmund A. Napieralski is professor of English at King's College where he has also served as coordinator for the core curriculum and assessment. He received his B.A. degree (1961) in English from Canisius College and his Ph.D. degree (1967) in English from Loyola University of Chicago.

William H. Newell is professor of interdisciplinary studies and director of the Institute in Integrative Studies at Miami University. He received his A.B. degree (1965) in philosophy from Amherst College and his Ph.D. degree (1971) in economics from the University of Pennsylvania. The founding president of the Association for Integrative Studies in 1979, he has served as its secretary-treasurer and newsletter editor and then executive director since 1983. He has consulted, served as external evaluator, or given keynote addresses on interdisciplinary studies for many colleges and universities. He has published extensively on interdisciplinary higher education as well as in economic and social history.

Jana Nidiffer is visiting assistant professor of higher education at the University of Massachusetts, Amherst, where she is preparing a manuscript tracing the development of the first administrative positions held by women at coeducational universities. Prior to this position, she taught the history of higher education at the Harvard Graduate School of Education and the University of Massachusetts at Boston. She was also the assistant dean of the college and coordinator of women's studies at Brandeis University. Nidiffer received her B.S. and M.A. degrees (1982) from Indiana University and her Ph.D. degree (1994) in higher education from the Harvard Graduate School of Education.

Enrique "Rick" Olguin teaches ethnic studies and is technology director for the Teaching and Learning Center at North Seattle Community College, where he has authored articles on the philosophical implications of ethnic studies as a discipline and conducted numerous workshops and seminars on teaching cultural pluralism in the undergraduate curriculum. He received his A.A. degree (1978) from Orange Coast Community College, his B.A. degree (1978) in history and political science from the University of California, Los Angeles, and his Ph.D. degree (1986) in political science from Stanford University.

Judith A. Ramaley is president of Portland State University and professor of biology. Previously she was the chief academic officer and acting president of State University of New York, Albany. She has also served as executive vice chancellor of the University of Kansas, Lawrence, and has held administrative and faculty positions at the University of Nebraska, Omaha, and at the University of Nebraska Medical Center, where she was an American Council of Education fellow. She has also chaired major committees for the National Association of State Universities and Land Grant Colleges, and the American Council on Education. Ramaley received her B.A. degree (1963) in zoology from Swarthmore College and her Ph.D. degree (1966) in anatomy from the University of California, Los Angeles.

Michael F. Reardon is provost of Portland State University, where he teaches courses on the development of disciplinary knowledge and on the culture of the professions. He has a particular interest in curricular reform, and has been encouraging major changes in undergraduate education and in various national associations. At Portland State University he has also served as chair of the history department, director of the honors program, associate dean of the College of Arts and Sciences, and vice provost for academic affairs. He received his B.A. degree (1960) in international relations from Georgetown University and his M.A. (1961) and Ph.D. (1965) degrees in history from Indiana University.

James L. Roth is professor of history at Alverno College, where he was formerly head of the college's division of arts and humanities. He is also a member of the Aesthetic Responsiveness Department, an interdisciplinary ability-based department. His research interests include the history of women and the teaching of critical thinking. He received his B.A. degree (1967) from Northwestern University, and his M.A. (1968) and Ph.D. (1979) degrees in history from the University of California, Berkeley.

Betty Schmitz is director of the curriculum transformation project in the Office of Undergraduate Education at the University of Washington, where she has been involved in curriculum transformation projects. Prior to that, she developed and directed long-term faculty development projects and institutes at several major colleges and universities. She received her Ph.D. degree (1977) in French from the University of Wisconsin.

Carol Geary Schneider is executive vice president of the Association of American Colleges and Universities. She holds a B.A. degree (1966) from Mount Holyoke College and a Ph.D. degree (1985) in early modern history from Harvard University. She has taught at the University of Chicago, DePaul University, Chicago State University, and Boston University. At the University of Chicago and at AAC&U, she has headed a series of national initiatives to improve undergraduate teaching, learning, and curriculum. Currently she leads a multimillion dollar project titled "American Commitments: Diversity, Democracy, and Liberal Learning."

G. Roger Sell is director of the Center for the Enhancement of Teaching at the University of Northern Iowa, where he is also associate professor in the Department of Curriculum and Instruction. He has served as program chair for the Professional and Organizational Development Network in Higher Education. He received his B.A. degree (1967) in economics and psychology from the University of Denver and his Ph.D. degree (1975) in educational administration from the University of California, Santa Barbara.

Barbara Leigh Smith is provost and academic vice president at the Evergreen State College. She is author and coauthor of numerous works on learning communities, interdisciplinary education, and education reform. She is winner of the Meiklejohn Innovation Award and is the recipient of a certificate of excellence for the faculty development work with the Washington Center for Improving the Quality of Undergraduate Education (which she founded), and is a member of various associations of higher education. She received her B.A. degree from Lawrence University, and her M.A. and Ph.D. degrees from the University of Oregon.

Jane R. Spalding is director of programs at the Association of American Colleges and Universities. Formerly an instructor of French and German, she has assisted in designing and conducting AAC&U's international initiatives, including a series of national and regional conferences and grants competitions to foster cooperation among liberal arts and business programs in internationalizing their curricula; she has also served as consultant to educational institutions and government agencies. She received her B.A. degree (1974) in German language and literature from Boston University.

Barbara K. Townsend is professor of higher education and chair of the Department of Leadership at the University of Memphis. She received her B.A. degree (1965) and M.A. degree (1967) in English from State University of New York, Albany, and her Ed.D. degree (1983) from the College of William and Mary. She has previously taught developmental English at Thomas Nelson Community College.

Leona C. Truchan is professor of biology at Alverno College. She is a member of an interdisciplinary committee studying and implementing experiential education across the curriculum. She received her B.A. degree in biology from Alverno College, her M.S. degree in biological sciences from DePaul University, and her Ph.D. degree in biology from Northwestern University. A former head of Alverno's division of natural sciences, mathematics, and technology, she is also a member of an interdisciplinary committee studying and implementing experiential education across the curriculum. She is a regional and national leader in K–16 articulation efforts, relating science teaching and learning to assessment.

Jon F. Wergin is professor of educational studies at Virginia Commonwealth University. His primary research interests center on evaluation and change in higher education. He is the author or coauthor of five other books, including *Educating Professionals: Responding to New Expectations for Competence and Accountability,* published in 1993 by Jossey-Bass. Wergin has been a consultant for many colleges and consortia, and has served as the external evaluator for numerous projects. Wergin is a former divisional vice president of the American Educational Research Association and a senior associate at the American Association for Higher Education, where he helped inaugurate the AAHE Forum on Faculty Roles and Rewards.

Lyn Maxwell White is in the Office of Challenge Grants at the National Endowment for the Humanities. She worked with curriculum and faculty development grants in the humanities for two decades, managing NEH's Higher Education in the Humanities Program. Prior to joining NEH, she was an instructor at North Carolina State University and an instructor at the University of North Carolina, Chapel Hill, where she received her Ph.D. degree in English and American literature. In 1984–85, she was special assistant to the academic vice president and a visiting associate professor of English at Catholic University of America. She was a Phi Beta Kappa graduate of Agnes Scott College. Her chapter does not necessarily reflect the views of the National Endowment for the Humanities.

Barbara D. Wright holds a Ph.D. degree from the University of California, Berkeley, and is associate professor of German at the University of Connecticut, Storrs. Her scholarly interests include German literature and culture of the early twentieth century and language pedagogy. Over the years, however, she has also worked in the areas of women's studies, curriculum reform, general education, and assessment. From 1990 to 1992, she served as director of the Assessment Forum at the American Association for Higher Education.

Sheila Phelan Wright is vice provost for undergraduate studies and campus life at the University of Denver and an associate professor in the School of Education. She holds a Ph.D. degree in higher education administration from the University of Connecticut. Her academic interests cut across interdisciplinary boundaries and her research interests include interdisciplinary teaching and learning, general education, and intellectual development.

Gene G. Wubbels is senior vice chancellor for academic affairs and professor of chemistry at the University of Nebraska, Kearney. He has served as a program director in the Division of Undergraduate Education of the National Science Foundation while on leave from academic appointments at Grinnell and Washington Colleges. Gene served on the original executive committee of Project Kaleidoscope in the capacity of lead writer. He received his B.S. degree (1964) in chemistry from Hamline University and Ph.D. degree (1968) in organic chemistry from Northwestern University.

PART ONE

HISTORICAL, PHILOSOPHICAL, AND SOCIAL PERSPECTIVES

Nearly twenty years ago, Clark Kerr declared, "In the final analysis, the curriculum is nothing less than the statement a college makes about what, out of the totality of . . . constantly growing knowledge and experience, is considered useful, appropriate, or relevant to the lives of educated men and women at a certain point of time" (Rudolph, 1977, p. ix). What an eloquent statement. The concept of the curriculum sounds so clear and definite. Although the expression of a curriculum may change with circumstances, the idea of a curriculum seemed set twenty years ago.

Since then, we have learned that the concept of the undergraduate curriculum is fraught with ambiguity. The curriculum is an intellectually rich concept that may be viewed and analyzed from many different vantage points. One can look at purposes, experiences, or outcomes of the curriculum. There is the formal curriculum and the informal, or hidden, curriculum. The political left and right have made the curriculum a veritable battleground with their divergent analyses. There is the curriculum offered by the college, taught by the faculty, and learned by the students. Ideally, all these various views of the curriculum would be similar, but, alas, it is not necessarily so.

For nearly two decades, the undergraduate curriculum has received a great deal of national scrutiny. It has been a time of strident criticism of the curriculum, laments that students are not learning what they should, proposals for change, studies and analyses of alternative curricula, development of new knowledge and approaches to knowledge, innovations in curricular offerings, and assessments of student achievement. Indeed, we are in the midst of a fertile time for thinking and experimenting with the undergraduate curriculum.

Part One of this handbook provides some ways of understanding this complexity and diverse perspectives concerning the curriculum. In Chapter One, James Ratcliff points to the multiple contexts, levels, and meanings associated with the term *curriculum* and with the influences of the academic disciplines, students, and social forces on its purposes. He discusses key issues in curricular design and assessment, concluding with the observation that the curriculum is a powerful tool of educational and social policy.

Elizabeth Hawthorne's Chapter Two provides a brief history of the undergraduate curriculum. She argues that when this nation needed change in the undergraduate course of study, it tended to create new institutions and new types of institutions. Following Rudolph's statement (1977, p. 2) that ". . . there is no such thing as *the* curriculum," Hawthorne discusses significant social currents affecting the curriculum. Then she traces the emergence of five types of institutions and their associated curricula: the liberal arts college built on the shoulders of the classical colonial colleges; normal schools to provide teachers for expanding public school systems; land-grant universities to emphasize science, agriculture, and technology; special-purpose institutions to serve women and African Americans; and two-year community colleges to expand access and

serve various career and academic purposes based on local needs. While each type of institution remains identifiable, today the missions and curricula of each are much less distinct than when they were created. Indeed, the diffusion of innovations from institution to institution, from one type to another, and from one region to another has created curricula of colleges and universities that are often more similar than they are different.

In Chapter Three, Arthur Levine and Jana Nidiffer point out that our current pattern of undergraduate education derives from almost 2,500 years of historical evolution. After analyzing some of the most notable influences from abroad, they focus on the American experience and assert that higher education here has developed through a process of addition and accretion. They illustrate their thesis with a chronology of significant events that helped shape the undergraduate curriculum.

Barbara Fuhrmann in Chapter Four discusses the variety of educational philosophies—and philosophers—that have influenced the undergraduate curriculum. She captures the complex of philosophical premises that were pervasive in the colonial period, the nineteenth century, and the twentieth century—and those called for in the twenty-first century. She highlights various purposes and aims of education, including the ideal of liberal education, the importance of research in American curricula, the incorporation of developmental psychology, and the goals touted by educational reformers of the 1960s and

1970s. She concludes with an analysis of the recent debate about higher education, much of which focuses on the content of the curriculum and the education that students most need.

Philo Hutcheson in Chapter Five focuses on the organization of the curriculum. He starts with a discussion of degrees, credits, and structures of the curriculum and follows with an analysis of the impact of specialization on the curriculum. Subsequent sections deal with general education reform efforts in the twentieth century and with examples of institutional innovations that have succeeded and failed. The chapter illustrates the difficulty of translating high-minded ideals, purposes, and philosophies into organizational form at colleges and universities.

In Chapter Six, Mildred García and James Ratcliff, starting with the proposition that the curriculum is a social construction, analyze the demographic, social, political, economic, technological, and global forces that are creating the environment for the undergraduate curriculum. They conclude that the undergraduate curriculum is a malleable, dynamic entity undergoing transmutation in response to external forces and factors.

Collectively, these chapters offer a solid perspective for considering the undergraduate curriculum.

Reference

Rudolph, F. *Curriculum: A History of the American Undergraduate Course of Study Since 1636.* San Francisco: Jossey-Bass, 1977.

CHAPTER ONE

WHAT IS A CURRICULUM
AND WHAT SHOULD IT BE?

James L. Ratcliff

When a committee, a dean, or a department chair contemplates changing the curriculum, it is dangerously easy to make an assumption that everyone agrees on what a curriculum is. Familiarity *does* breed contempt. Since faculties regularly work with the curriculum, it is deceptively simple to assume that everyone agrees on what it is or should be. Making this leap of faith can lead to unnecessary disputes over nomenclature, and worse, aborted attempts at fundamental change. The committee may fail to recognize that the vision of what is a curriculum is heavily shaped by disciplinary values, educational philosophy, the diversity or homogeneity of students enrolled, and the social and institutional context. Answering what a curriculum is and what it should be is fundamental to understanding and improvement.

Beyond problems of nomenclature, folk wisdom says that reforming undergraduate education is a troublesome, tumultuous, and difficult assignment. Actually, changing the curriculum is easy. The faculty does it every term in thousands of courses. Estimates from research conducted at the National Center on Postsecondary Teaching, Learning, and Assessment indicate that about 5 percent of courses appearing on student transcripts for any one year were not listed in the formal college catalogue or university bulletin for that year (Ratcliff, 1993a). These often are new, experimental courses or one-time offerings. Some become part of next year's catalogue, while many others are dropped. A university of fifteen thousand students might well list more than three thousand courses in its catalogue, from which an undergraduate might choose thirty-five to forty-five to complete a baccalaureate degree. At such a university, there would be seventy-five new courses each year (2.5 percent of three thousand), or as many credits as two undergraduates would need to complete their entire program of study! While this represents a substantial amount of curricular innovation, change, and expansion, it is atomistic, course-by-course change. It often involves a single faculty member constructing an innovative outline for a new upper division course or seminar. While such innovation often goes largely unrecognized in the curriculum reform literature, it challenges conventional wisdom that college and university curricula are difficult to change.

What is difficult is getting a group of faculty from many different perspectives and prior institutional and educational experiences to work together to design or change a curriculum to be cogent, coherent, and meaningful to students. A department often finds it difficult to agree on a common core of purposes, a set of required and elective courses, and a sequence of curricular and extracurricular experiences that develop student talents. Even more difficult is revising the general education curriculum, because it involves people from many different disciplines, with differing educational philosophies and diverse prior experiences. It is easy for any individual to design his or her favorite curriculum, but it is hard to get a group to find common ground on what constitutes an effective program of study for a department or institution. That, perhaps, is why academic folklore tells us that it is harder to change the curriculum than it is to move a cemetery.

In the typical undergraduate curriculum of the 1990s, courses in the catalogue are like so many logs on a stack of firewood from which the students select a few to ignite the flames of intellectual inquiry associated with general, specialized, and liberal learning. Unfortunately, it takes more than logs to build a fire. Certain kindling is necessary, and someone needs to light the match. Equally important is the way the logs are arranged. And there are different theories of how best to arrange the logs to produce a quick-starting and heart-warming blaze. Currently, there is much debate as to what should be the purpose, content, and structure of the undergraduate curriculum—and often, it all hangs on what people mean by the word *curriculum*.

Curriculum Definition and Change

An *undergraduate curriculum* is the formal academic experience of students' pursuing baccalaureate and less than baccalaureate degrees. Such a curriculum is formalized into courses or programs of study including workshops, seminars, colloquia, lecture series, laboratory work, internships, and field experiences. Here, the term *course* is used generically, to designate a formal unit of undergraduate curriculum. Faculty members most often design and teach these courses singularly. However, there are many instances of team-teaching, teaching in turn, and the use of teaching assistants, student peer tutors, and guest lecturers. Faculty organizing and conducting a course generally control its purpose, process, and content. The role of a course in the curriculum at the inception is largely determined through a review by colleagues, first within the faculty of the home department and division. Subsequent reviews may be conducted at the school, college, or institutional level. The focus of these reviews is often to determine the overlap and duplication of the proposed course with others. The presumption is that if the new course does not substantially duplicate others, it must have merit as a contribution to and representation of the expanding knowledge base. Thus, in contemporary colleges and universities, faculty members individually, independently, and often unilaterally design and conduct the learning experiences that are referred to collectively and generically as the curriculum. What we call an undergraduate curriculum tends to be a universe of courses, each with its own purpose and environment (Levine, 1978; Ratcliff, 1990; Veysey, 1965).

The term *curriculum* can refer to the educational plan of an institution, school, college, or a department, or to a program or course. At the program level of analysis, undergraduate curricula typically consist of three to four components: general or liberal studies, major specialization, minor specializations, and elective studies (Levine, 1978; Toombs, Fairweather, Amey, and Chen, 1989). The content of general or liberal studies is often set institution-wide by the faculty, while major and minor are prescribed by the department or program offering the particular specialization. The major and minor fields may, in turn, be governed by curricular prescriptions of a professional field represented, by guidelines extended by the disciplinary association, or by state licensure requirements or professional board examinations. While enrollment in elective courses nominally is left to student discretion, a prescribed range of electives may be set by the departmental major or minor.

Prescription or election? A major fulcrum of an undergraduate curriculum is whether the course of study should be determined by the student or by the faculty. The German or Humboldtian philosophy underpinning the research university (described in Chapter Four) presumes that students do not enroll unless they are prepared to take responsibility for their learning, and that they are not admitted unless they have the appropriate prior education to make sound educational choices and to decide upon the direction of their advanced studies. These assumptions support the practice of expecting the student to choose major, minor, and electives and to make sound choices among arrays of options in the general education curriculum. The philosophy of liberal education presumes that students enter undergraduate study for intellectual, personal, and social development; that the faculty have the expertise to and should provide direct guidance to students in that development; and that certain subjects in the curriculum provide essential knowledge, skills, and abilities toward those aims.

The liberal arts assumptions promote the establishment of prescribed core curricula in general and liberal studies, prerequisite courses in the major and minor, and limitations on the range and timing of electives. For example, consider a hypothetical African Dance course at a liberal arts college. Our course bears the department and course number Dance 123, and is offered for two credits. Its 100 series number signifies a first-year course; at this college, its course credits apply to the humanities and fine arts requirements of the general education curriculum. However, Dance 123 is cross-listed with Anthropology 123, signaling that it can qualify toward the social science requirements in general education as well. The general education curriculum committee at this institution regularly debates whether taking Dance 123 or Anthropology 123 should be double counted; that is, should the same credits be applied to both the humanities and social science requirements, or should students be allowed to apply the credits to only one category, and if so, does that render these categorical requirements of the curriculum meaningless? While the faculty struggle to reach an agreement on this matter, the unfortunate students merely trying to navigate the maze may miss the meaningful goals and purposes of the program.

To make matters more complex, general education and major curricula often overlap as well. At our college, there is a three-credit course, Dance 323, African Dance, which is the same as Dance 123 except that it is offered for an additional credit containing a studio component. Dance 323 is numbered as a 300-series course to signify as an upper division or third-year course; its credits may apply to the major requirements in Dance. There is, of course, a corresponding Anthropology 323 with similar expectations. Again, the faculty debate whether a course in the major can also count as a course in general education, and the students scratch their heads in wonder and confusion. The college catalogue grows ever more baroque and bureaucratic. Student decision making about what to study is constrained by a vast array of rules, lists, prerequisites, and course sequences. These too are part of the intentional curriculum. Reform of such curriculum requires questioning who decides when and why the curriculum should be prescribed or elective in nature. How does Dance 123 (or Anthropology 123) help students attain any of the institution's general education goals? Faculty should be asked, in a nonrhetorical manner, "Why should students be required to take these courses?" Answers typically vary according to differing faculty views as to what students should be free to take and what they should be required to take.

External representation. At the macro level, the undergraduate curriculum of a particular college implicitly represents the philosophy and educational aims of that institution. It in effect is its academic policy. The educational program of the institution reflects the norms, values, and behavior of the organizational culture. Those in turn communicate an institutional image to various external constituencies, including prospective students, alumni, and civic and political leaders. Similarly, the curriculum articulates educational content, process, and standards for attainment to state, regional, disciplinary, and programmatic agencies, organizations, and associations. *All* are forms of a prescribed curriculum. *All* implicitly assume the hypothesis that students with different social and educational backgrounds experience different undergraduate curricular experiences and show different resulting rates and types of learning. A presumed primary criterion of the effectiveness of that curriculum is the extent to which it accomplishes its stated aims (Bergquist, Gould, and Greenberg, 1981; Ratcliff, 1990).

Diversity by institutional type. Institutions of higher education are often grouped, coordinated, or controlled according to their curriculum. The institutions that make up the California State College and University System have curricula that reflect the admissions policies prescribed in the California State Master Plan. Two-year and community college systems consist of institutions offering a similar array of general and liberal, vocational and career, and adult and continuing education programs (Cohen and Brawer, 1989). Systems of higher education are organized and managed according to these curricular similarities.

Community colleges, historically black colleges and universities, and predominantly white colleges and universities attract different groups of students with different backgrounds, prior learning, and motivation. Students in their first year at community colleges and historically black colleges and universities showed gains in selected areas of undergraduate learning (writing, critical thinking, science and social science reasoning) equal to or greater than those of students attending four-year colleges and universities and predominantly white institutions. While their gains in learning were similar at each of these institutions, both the entering and exiting knowledge, skills, and abilities of students at these institutions varied significantly (Pascarella and others, 1994). These conclusions do not suggest that all African American students should attend historically black colleges and universities. Instead, it suggests that the curriculum of these institutions is appropriate to some African American students, while others may profit more from attending a predominantly white institution; the key is in the match among prior learning, experience, and abilities and the host institution's curriculum and extracurriculum. Similarly, these findings do not suggest that all students might as well attend community colleges because the first-year learning gains are comparable and the cost is lower. Each institution contains a self-selected population of students, and the key to success is finding the challenging and empowering curriculum appropriate to a given student's prior learning, skills, interests, and abilities.

Different institutions provide different curricula, which produce different types and degrees of learning. While there is variation in curriculum and learning *between* institutions, the variation in student learning is greater *within* institutions than between them (Pascarella and Terenzini, 1991; Ratcliff, 1993a; Pascarella and others, 1994). Thus, the effects of curricula on student learning vary profoundly among students, courses, and programs within individual institutions of higher education. While differences in undergraduate learning clearly do exist from institution to institution, these tend not to be as great as the differential effect of curricula within them, and those institutional differences often are largely attributable to the differences in prior learning of the self-selected population of students who choose them.

Curricular complexity. A curriculum can be seen as a plan for learning, an instructional system, a major subsystem of the university, a medium of student development, an analog to the structure of knowledge, and a representation of job skills (Toombs and Tierney, 1991). Also, a curriculum can be viewed from a variety of contexts, including college or university—or program—mission, purpose, or collective expression of what is important for students to learn; a set of experiences that some authorities believe all students should have; the catalogue or schedule of courses offered to students; the set of courses students actually elect from those available to them; the content of a specific discipline; and the time and credit frame in which the college provides education (Stark and Lowther, 1986). The very ambiguity and multiple uses of the term curriculum commend a curriculum committee to begin its work by selecting an operational definition and context for their work. Tyler (1950) has provided a fundamental conception of the basic elements of a curriculum organized around four questions that a committee engaged in design, development, or review activities can use as a guideline:

- What is to be accomplished?
- What learning experiences will help accomplish the purposes?
- How can these learning experiences be effectively organized?
- How can the effectiveness of the learning be evaluated?

These four questions lead the committee not only to consider major attributes of the curriculum, but also to do so in a sequence that reflects a widely adopted curriculum development process (Taba, 1962). *Curriculum development,* in turn, can be viewed as the development of plans for an educational program, including the identification and selection of educational objectives, the selection of learning experiences, the organization of learning experiences, and the evaluation of the educational program (Tyler, 1975).

Curricular theory or curricular model? Discussions of the curriculum may seem loftier if they are guided by theory or advance some model. However, these concepts are often confused as well. Scattered throughout the literature on the undergraduate curriculum are the terms *curricular theory* and *curricular model* (for example, see Brigham, 1982; Weiland, 1989). A *theory* is an explanation of something. A theory of the undergraduate curriculum would describe the relevant theoretical constructs. These constructs might include the major, minor, electives, or some idea of general or liberal learning. Such a theory also would explain how the constructs are related to each other (Borg and Gall, 1983). An interdisciplinary curriculum is defined through the amalgam of two or more disciplines, either concretely or abstractly. *Models* represent theoretical relationships. Curricular models describe observable behaviors. Thus, a curriculum based on demonstrable competencies includes activities to evaluate student attainment of desired skills.

Curricular models take at least two major forms. Dressel and DeLisle (1969); Biglan (1973a); Conrad (1978); Levine (1978); and Bergquist, Gould, and Greenberg (1981) are primarily concerned with describing the formal and informal organizational structures of institutions and their components. These are largely *descriptive* or *prescriptive models* of the way curriculum is or should be. Implicit in these models is the premise that undergraduate curriculum is purposeful beyond the level of the single course. Astin (1970), Pascarella (1985), Ratcliff (1990), the National Center for Research to Improve Postsecondary Teaching and Learning (McKeachie, Pintrich, Lin, and Smith, 1986), and the National Center on Postsecondary Teaching, Learning, and Assessment (Ratcliff and Associates, 1995) have constructed *analytic models* to discover the variables that affect student development and describe the nature of those variable interactions. These analytic models are derived from a differential hypothesis: that students with different educational and social backgrounds undergoing different undergraduate experiences show different rates of learning in different subject areas. Such a hypothesis includes variation in student characteristics, institutional characteristics, and the types of learning outcomes. Thus, two basic types of conceptual curricular models are those concerned with the structure, purpose, and process of undergraduate education and those concerned with assessing its differential effects.

The descriptive and prescriptive curricular models represent the nature and organization of the substantive elements of the curriculum. That is, they present ways to conceptualize and analyze the organizational structure of institutions, colleges, departments, and so on. The institutional-structural models focus on what the university or college prescribes for student study. In contrast, analytic curricular models do not examine curricular structure, organization, and purpose directly. Instead, they describe the relationship and interaction between institutional characteristics (of which the formal curriculum is but one factor) and student social, economic, and educational characteristics as they affect student learning, personal development, and maturation. In short, models for explaining the undergraduate curriculum can also be viewed as describing either the institution's intent or the interaction between student and college environment.

Curriculum designers, reformers, and scholars should not view these two types of models as dichotomous or contradictory; they serve as alternate constructions for framing the knowledge structures that make up the heart of the academic enterprise. A differentiated system of higher education—one that presumes that it is best to have different institutions, programs, and courses of study with different purposes, methods, and measures of attainment—presumes differential effects on student learning. The American undergraduate curriculum is based on a differential structure at the system, institution, and program levels that calls for the examination of those differential effects on students' intellectual, personal, and social growth (Ratcliff, 1996).

Bloom's definition of the curriculum (1981) illustrates both descriptive and analytic qualities of curriculum development. He defines the *manifest curriculum* (or formal curriculum) as the specified subject matter to be studied (such as science, mathematics, social studies, foreign languages, literature, or language arts), plus the behaviors needed for learning the subject matter. The manifest curriculum includes the written goals, objectives, rules, and regulations of an institution. By contrast, Bloom also suggested that there is a *latent curriculum* consisting of the way people value time, order, neatness, promptness, interpersonal relations, and so on. These values are not usually written down and specified, but are evidenced in daily living and interacting in learning environments. Finally, Bloom made a distinction between the terms instruction and curriculum. *Instruction,* according to Bloom, is the carrying out of the curricular goals and objectives, while *curriculum* is the stating, structuring, and ordering of them.

The strength of a curricular model like Bloom's rests on its ability to describe and reach meaningful conclusions. Yet models, being simplified or schematic representations, map just part of reality. An effective curricular model is one where the analyst can say with confidence, "Nothing that matters in the real world was left out" (Cronbach, 1983). For Bloom, curriculum is both process and outcome, latent and manifest, substantive and behavioral.

A working definition:

Curriculum refers to both the process and substance of an educational program. It comprises the purpose, design, conduct, and evaluation of educational experiences. Curricula exist at different levels, ranging from the single course to the educational program to the department or discipline to the college or university. The organization of curricula is defined by educational philosophy, the structure and content of the knowledge imparted, and the institutional context and climate. Effective curricula have coherence and explicit definitions of aims and standards of attainment. They accomplish their aims through sequence and structure of learning experiences to facilitate student learning and development. They provide sufficient content and coverage to exhibit but not exhaust the limits of the subject of study. They include mastery of basic terms, concepts, models, and theories as well as some application of them to situations appropriate to the student, the learning aims, and the institutional context. Good curricula have the hallmarks of effective instruction and the evidence of the enhancement of student learning.

This working definition allows us to identify the curriculum, taking into account the complexity, diversity, and dynamism implicit in it. To determine what a curriculum should be requires us to determine what it is and contrast it with some desired form of purpose, design, conduct, and evaluation (Lindquist, 1978).

It is easy to change the curriculum at the single course level, perhaps because underlying issues of philosophy and purpose, coherence and integration, development and outcomes are not immediately challenged. The inherent complexity and diversity of the curriculum are only marginally addressed. Curriculum change at the program level often begins and ends with discussions about degree requirements, prerequisites, and sequencing—with little careful examination of how the curriculum is defined or what philosophical underpinnings and assumptions have been made relative to the development and attainments of students. Large-scale curriculum reform may be facilitated by careful attention to the different contexts, levels, and meanings associated with the word *curriculum*.

Curricular Influences and Curricular Purposes

The curriculum is purposeful, reflecting the needs of society, the ways of knowing shared within a field, and the students' interests, abilities, and prior learning. Its aims are guided by its educational philosophy—but that philosophy is far from universal. In a single institution and on a single curriculum committee, it is common to find several competing philosophies (Chapter Four). Conflicting and alternate visions of the purposes of undergraduate education frequently also are encountered because curricula exist at multiple levels and across a variety of disciplines and fields. In planning, revising, or reforming curricula, it is important to be aware of each of these attributes.

Disciplinary influence. The role of individual disciplines as organizers of the undergraduate curriculum is largely a late nineteenth- and twentieth-century phenomenon. Prior to the rise of research universities, undergraduate education stressed the coherence and unity of knowledge in providing appropriate preparation for the professions (theology, law, medicine) and enlightenment for social, political, and economic leaders of the society (for example, see "The Yale Report of 1828," reprinted in 1961). With the development of new research universities such as Chicago, Stanford, Johns Hopkins, and Cornell, the teaching of research skills and the establishment of academic departments of disciplinary specialization were emphasized. Learned societies and disciplinary associations were established in the late nineteenth century and grew significantly in the twentieth century; through journals and conferences, these organizations provided a common language, discourse, and means of evaluating the merit of scholarship bounded by the discipline. Disciplines defined the means of communication, common methods and modes of inquiry, the exchange of research findings, and the creation of norms and values relative to the conduct of research (Beecher, 1989; Jencks and Riesman, 1968). Disciplinary inquiry often superseded institutional goals in defining the direction and purpose of undergraduate study. Today, colleges and universities often support a hundred or more undergraduate majors, most housed in discipline-defined departments, and all vying for influence over the direction, content, conduct, and evaluation of the undergraduate curriculum.

A *discipline* is literally what the term implies. That is, when one studies a discipline, one subjugates the ways one learns about phenomena to a set of rules, rituals, and routines established by the field of study. One conducts investigations according to these rules, classifying phenomena according to commonly adopted terms, definitions, and concepts. Relationships among phenomena are revealed through the frames provided by the discipline, and the researcher or student arrives at conclusions based on criteria for truth or validity derived from the field.

Disciplines can provide a conceptual framework for understanding what knowledge is and how it is acquired. Disciplinary learning provides a logical structure to relationships between concepts, propositions, common paradigms, and organizing principles. Disciplines develop themes, canons, and grand narratives to join different streams of research in the field and to provide meaningful conceptualizations and frameworks for further analysis (Shulman, 1987). Disciplines impart truth criteria used globally to define differences in the way knowledge is acquired and valued. Disciplines also set parameters on the methods employed in discovering and analyzing knowledge and in the ways they affect the development of students' intellectual skills (Donald, 1986).

Not only are paradigms for inquiry imparted by disciplines (Beecher, 1989; Biglan, 1973a, 1973b; Kuhn, 1962), but so too are values and norms regarding membership and scholarly conduct in the field (Holland, 1963) and preferred modes of learning (Kolb, 1981). Disciplines provide much structure and coherence to learning. It is easy to underestimate their power and importance in the advancement of knowledge and understanding at the undergraduate level. It is not clear whether a student or faculty member can be truly interdisciplinary without first mastering one or more disciplines.

The ascendancy of the disciplines in the late nineteenth century and their continuing dominance throughout the twentieth century have left an indelible imprint on the shape and direction of the academic major, often overwhelming the aims of general and liberal studies. In the late 1980s and 1990s, interdisciplinary studies, multiculturalism, feminist pedagogy, and a renewed concern for the coherence of the undergraduate program have challenged the dominance of academic major and called for cross-disciplinary collaboration.

Discipline-based curricula are a social construction developed by academics. Over time, knowledge has been organized into key terms, concepts, models, and modes of inquiry. Academics add to and test these knowledge constructs using their disciplinary associations as means of verbal and written communication. Curricular change is conditioned by the role of the disciplines in conserving and transmitting their organization and representation of what is worth knowing, why, and how. Such a conception of disciplinary knowledge emphasizes the transmission of knowledge from generation to generation, and from academic to novice.

Student influence. Several subjects of study—for example, English literature, the physical sciences, women's studies, and environmental studies—began outside the college curriculum (Brubacher and Rudy, 1976; Rudolph, 1977). There is an inexorable relationship between the curriculum and the extracurriculum. Subjects and topics become areas of student interest and find their way into the curriculum.

Contemporary research suggests that the line between curricular and extracurricular effects on students is blurred and overstated; students' out-of-class experiences are powerful determinants of what, how, and how well they learn (Pascarella and others, 1994). For example, Briar Cliff College (Iowa), a small liberal arts college affiliated with the Catholic Church, underwent significant extracurricular and then curricular change as a result of student unrest, concern, and activism during the 1960s and the early 1970s (Johnson, 1986). Briar Cliff never experienced mass protests on the issues of racism and the Vietnam War like those that occurred at many large American universities. Briar Cliff students and faculty drew their liberal sentiments from the national news depiction of ghetto violence and campus unrest, resistance to the draft, and the protest music of the time. Briar Cliff had a primarily young faculty during the 1970s. This faculty's idealism was further influenced by the college's Franciscan heritage, which emphasized values such as concern for the whole person. More recently there has been a focus on academic activism, which has resulted in the development of a peace curriculum as part of the undergraduate experience. Briar Cliff's experience illustrates how student initiative and interest can migrate from out-of-class activities to take an increasing role in shaping the formal curriculum.

Social criticism, particularly as voiced through historically underrepresented groups such as women, minorities, and gays, provides critical perspectives on the curriculum. These perspectives provide alternate frames for describing the structure of knowledge and the ways of knowing. For example, the ways that women students approach learning have direct implications for the way curriculum is organized and orchestrated, and for the choice of instructional strategy: "It can be argued . . . that students need models of impeccable reasoning, that it is through imitating such models that students learn to reason. But none of the women we interviewed named this sort of learning as a powerful experience in their own lives. . . . Women students need opportunities to watch women professors solve (and fail to solve) problems and male professors fail to solve (and succeed in solving) problems. They need models of thinking as a human, imperfect, and attainable activity" (Belenky and others, 1986).

Critical theorists argue that the conventional canons of inquiry associated with the Western intellectual tradition stress rationalism as the cure for human irrationality (Toombs and Tierney, 1991). Through reason events are planned, societies are organized, and lives are shaped. A logical but extreme end to this process is the so-called iron cage of reason, wherein an individual's freedom and freedom of inquiry are enchained by previously defined reason and rationality dictating every appropriate action. Today, the diversity of students and their attendant diverse approaches to learning influence what is taught, how it is taught, and how learning is judged.

Shulman (1987) has argued that the task of teaching is one of reframing disciplinary knowledge in forms that can be understood better by students. Teachers struggle to represent what they know in mental constructs that will render meaning and understanding to their students. The ways of knowing of women and other underrepresented groups challenge academics to represent knowledge, skills, and abilities through new epistemologies and pedagogies that allow for meaningful representations of what is to be learned, how best to learn it, and how to ascertain the extent of learning attained (see Chapters Six and Nine for further discussion of this point). Attendant to the diversification of the student population is the recognition that individuals may possess multiple intelligences, individually or collectively, to which a single pedagogy may be poorly addressed (Gardner, 1985). These, in turn, translate into multiple ways of knowing and learning with profound and practical implications for the undergraduate curriculum (Baxter-Magolda, 1992).

Curriculum reformers, designers, and researchers need to recognize that most colleges and universities are unlikely to find one form of undergraduate curriculum that best serves the learning of all students. This has profound import for general education curricula and some salience for majors and minors as well. Only in the most homogeneous of student groupings may a single curricular approach prove productive for all learners. However, unstructured and incoherent collections of courses are not likely to produce sustained long-term learning, either. Clusters, patterns, and sequences of courses aimed at the needs, interests, and abilities of salient subgroups of students may produce the most resilient reforms (Ratcliff and Associates, 1995).

Social, political, and economic influence. Social conditions exert significant influence on the purpose, organization, and structure of the curriculum. For example, during the nineteenth-century Industrial Revolution, demand for specialization increased and new scientific knowledge and new occupations emerged; in turn, these social trends supported the development and fragmentation of disciplinary knowledge. The Cold War and post-*Sputnik* era saw the rapid expansion of the sciences and technology in many Western and Eastern Bloc countries. The increased subsidization of research, science, and technology fostered disciplinary specialization and the rise of whole new specialties within disciplines. The undergraduate curriculum tilted toward scientific rationalism, specialization, and vocationalism.

While countless other social factors influence the undergraduate curriculum (as discussed in Chapter Six), an important emerging social goal for undergraduate education is the transfer of technological knowledge and skill in an effort to further economic development. The agricultural and mechanical university, pioneered through the Morrill Act of 1862 in the United States, is increasingly sought out to guide the process of technology transfer (Bergsma, 1986). Colleges and universities increasingly are urged to make their undergraduate curriculum more responsive to the needs of business and industry. Rapid growth in higher education enrollment in developed countries has paralleled the demand for college-educated knowledge workers, trained technicians, and specialists in those countries (Ratcliff, 1995). The social, economic, and technological demands for higher education have transformed the forms of knowledge, which in turn have created new stakeholders for the undergraduate curriculum (Walshok, 1995). This jumble of social, economic, and technological factors presents special challenges to curriculum reformers, designers, and scholars, for no one curriculum and no one institution can be entirely responsive to the vast array of new constituents.

Walshok (1995) has proposed a framework for revamping curricula based on this widening array of social demands. She suggests that the curriculum committee begin by sorting the types and dimensions of knowledge needs within a particular area of activity. Some efforts have been made along these lines. For example, Jones (1994) reviewed the literature on critical thinking, then contacted faculty, local employers of graduates, and relevant policy makers for specific institutions of higher education; these stakeholders were asked to rank and sort those aspects of critical thinking found in the literature that were particularly important or salient to them and their needs. Thus what constituted critical thinking was reshaped in terms meaningful to external constituencies.

After the key areas of knowledge are grouped, sorted, or clustered, the stake-holders advocating curricular reform can be profiled for their level of knowledge and experience relative to the areas of the curriculum to be changed. This process produces a matrix of needs to which curriculum designers, reformers, and analysts can respond (Walshok, 1995). Since no one institution is likely to be able to respond to all the needs identified through this process, such a matrix provides a heuristic for identifying desired changes in the curriculum.

When such an approach is taken to identify needed areas of curricular enhancement or reform, researchers have found that employers, policy makers, and faculty often agree on broad areas of nontechnical knowledge, skills, and abilities to be imparted in undergraduate education (Jones, 1994). Recent surveys and focus groups have suggested that employers and policy makers seek further development of these nontechnical skills among undergraduates. This research is not clear as to whether employers take for granted or value less the specialized education students receive at colleges and universities. However, it is clear that certain knowledge, skills, and abilities associated with general and liberal learning are highly desired among these external constituents (Romer, 1995; Jones, 1994; Walshok, 1995). These include:

- Higher-order applied problem-solving abilities
- Enthusiasm for learning on a continuous basis
- Interpersonal skills, including teamwork and collaboration, and oral and written communication skills
- Sense of responsibility for action (both personal and collective)
- Ability to bridge cultural and linguistic barriers
- Sense of professionalism

What is striking about this list (from Romer, 1995) is how closely it corresponds to many goals set for general education, and how divorced it is from the usual general education course requirements or any particular discipline. External stakeholders and social forces implore curriculum designers, reformers, and analysts to reframe knowledge and pedagogy according to emerging social trends and needs for an educated workforce, but it is remarkable how similar their requests are to the goals of general education and liberal learning (Jones, 1994).

In summary, then, curricular purposes are directed, influenced, and shaped by the academic disciplines and applied fields of study, by student expectations, prior learning, and abilities, and by social, political, and economic pressures from the society at large. These forces, internal and external, interact dynamically to define what the curriculum is as well as to create the expectations as to what it should be. Disciplines provide a strong paradigm for coherence and quality in a curriculum; however, those knowledge structures may not be the best representations of how students learn or of what society expects of higher education. Curriculum designers need to provide multiple forms of the curriculum for the diverse needs, interests, and abilities of students. Similarly, the expectations of employers and policy makers need to be carefully, closely, and systematically examined. Faculty, working in committees, must contend with and reconcile these often conflicting forces in formulating, renewing, or transforming the undergraduate curriculum.

Curriculum, Pedagogy, and the Culture At Large

Because curriculum is imported across disciplinary, institutional, and national boundaries, it needs to be adapted to the context and the culture from which the students originate. Curriculum innovations invariably undergo such adaptation—either willfully through the curriculum planners, or as a consequence of disjunctures with learners, disciplines, or social expectations within the home institution (see Chapter Thirty-One). Such adaptation contributes to variety and uniqueness in the curriculum.

College life, for faculties and students, has traditionally been separate from the values, norms, and behaviors of the larger society. The medieval university strove for independence from church and state. Academic leaders in nineteenth-century America borrowed the German distinction of *akademische Freiheit*, freedom inside and outside the university, to advance the notion of academic freedom (Brubacher and Rudy, 1976). Today, it is part of academic culture to refer to the "real world" outside the college or university to reinforce the notion that values, norms, and behaviors are different in academia. This interaction between the larger society and the academic culture of students and faculty is manifest in the undergraduate curriculum.

In the United States, an uneasy relationship exists between the academic community and the larger society. Since the Bush and Reagan presidencies, a declared cultural war has raged between the intelligentsia (largely housed in colleges and universities) and the social and political conservatives gaining ascendancy to political and public life. The latter accuse universities of harboring ideologically bounded and "politically correct" curricula wherein undergraduates are indoctrinated with radical values, norms, and beliefs.

During this cultural war, Katz (1994, p. 11) argued, the intellectual left sought to distance itself from the status of professional intellectual class, while those on the right sought to separate themselves from any affiliation with the so-called cultural elites. One outcome of these responses was to help redefine the tenuous role of intellectuals in the broader society. Katz writes, "Anti-intellectualism thus creates an environment in which professional intellectuals are apparently pitted against the public." As Hofstadter (1963) put it, "Once the intellectual was gently ridiculed because he was not needed; now he is fiercely resented because he is needed too much" (p. 12). The climate of anti-intellectualism in the United States constrains the potential for debate over so-called political correctness by delimiting the role of the people involved in the debate. The predominant or host culture mediates the undergraduate curriculum. If the larger society does not value a particular line of inquiry, discipline, or field of study, students will come to the college or university with little motivation to include it in their studies. Conversely, if a topic is unresolved in the larger society, it may find a transitory place in the curriculum.

The role of themes and troublesome topics. Themes may represent content knowledge to students in a familiar cultural context. Content knowledge in undergraduate classes is often structured so as to illustrate the existence of multiple themes in a written work. As the class reads and reviews several books on a given topic, these themes are intertwined to derive a parallel comprehension of the particular body of literature from which the books were drawn, as well as the history, society, and psychology represented in the works. These themes excite and involve the students in ways that speak directly to them. The coherent quality of a theme holds the potential to help them better understand literature in general, history, the world in which they live, and themselves. Such themes are the basis of courses often regarded as fads by some faculty. Yet themes and troublesome topics illustrate an important function of the undergraduate curriculum: it provides a safe haven away from political strife, social conflict, and the pressures of everyday life to examine unresolved social issues. In order to understand the role and life-cycle of a troublesome topic in the curriculum, we turn to the example of courses concerning Vietnam.

The Vietnam War has proven to be a difficult topic in the American college classroom. Society at large may very well be unreconciled about the correct interpretation of events leading to, during, and concluding American involvement in the Vietnamese civil war. In the 1980s, there was a dramatic increase in American college course offerings about the decade of the 1960s, particularly the period of the American involvement in Vietnam. Collison (1988) found the popularity of the courses to be a result of the demographics and background of the faculty teaching the courses and of the students' curiosity about protest movements. There was a meeting between two generations: younger faculty who had lived through and were unreconciled toward American involvement in Vietnam, and interested students who had grown up with the war on the evening news every night on TV. Some faculty felt the courses were essential to student understanding of modern life, whereas others believed that more research on the topic was needed. Israel (1985) lamented that the coming generation had little historical memory of the events of the Vietnam War and virtually no emotional investment in the issues discussed. He too felt a special obligation to engage students in an examination of this troublesome topic. The more recent waning of student interest in the topic may modify the instructors' approach to it and may ultimately contribute to its discontinuance from the curriculum.

The field of study imposes discipline and constraint on the passions fueling the interest in troublesome topics like the Vietnam War. Here the discipline renders an order to the examination of an issue otherwise charged with emotion. Pike (1985), for example, urged the use of objectivity in social science inquiry to weigh the conflicting interpretations of the war. He found that there has been a flood of new historical information vastly revising much of what anyone—left, right, or center—knew. Wilcox (1988) advocated the use of primary sources in teaching about the Vietnam War. The approach encouraged student questioning and discussion of issues surrounding the war. He urged the faculty to be certain that students know and understand the reasons for the war and not just repeat rhetoric. The emphasis, again, was on ways of knowing and understanding a troubling period in the collective consciousness of American society. For Wilcox, there appeared to be a belief that there is a correct interpretation of the events to be discovered.

As Kuhn (1962) has pointed out, it is the function of "normal science" to resolve and incorporate new information into the prevailing paradigmatic interpretation of events. It is the role of the political scientist to examine all major competing perceptions of the Vietnam War objectively. Yet it is the intersection between the troublesome topic, the culture at large, and the process and content of the discipline that produces the interest and shapes the inquiry.

Troublesome topics bring excitement, imagination, and motivation to the students who study them and the faculty who teach them. They illustrate the transitional nature of the undergraduate curriculum, as well. Subjects or topics of gripping interest to one generation of students may seem dull to the next. The coursework embodying troublesome topics may enter the curriculum from the extracurriculum, reside in the undergraduate program of study up to a decade or more, and wane or disappear as its salience to society subsides. Ultimately it may be discontinued for lack of student demand or may migrate to the secondary school curriculum as knowledge in the field of study becomes more advanced.

Culture and society affect the undergraduate curriculum. The effect may be indirect and may influence both the content and processes employed with undergraduates. So-called fad courses and new curricular themes should be regarded carefully by those reviewing and revising the curriculum. They may play an important role of mediating between the academy and the society at large. The curriculum becomes not only the way to infuse new knowledge into the college-educated populace, but also the medium to accomplish it. Teaching strategies are modified and new courses are adopted to motivate students, to introduce new subjects, to provide prerequisite concepts or language skills. Thus not only does the new knowledge enter the curriculum as new or adapted courses, but supplemental programs and coursework emerge to prepare and motivate students for the new subjects and fields of study. This tension between society and the academy, and the multiple forms and ways it manifests itself, creates a dynamic that propels curricular change. To miss this dynamic is to understate the role of the curriculum.

Building an Engaging Curriculum: Curricular Evaluation and Assessment

Assessment is the process of defining, selecting, designing, collecting, analyzing, interpreting, and using information to increase students' learning and development. It includes discussions about what should be assessed and how information will be used, not just the hands-on testing of students (Marchese, 1987). The terms *assessment, evaluation,* and *measurement* are used in confusing and contradictory ways. In order to be clear in our description, we use Lenning's (1980) differentiation of the terms. *Measurement* is the simple process of gathering and quantifying information. It serves as the basis for assessment and evaluation. *Assessment* occurs when measurements are analyzed. *Evaluation* occurs when judgments are applied to assessment efforts.

Assessment is commonly used in three principal contexts: the assessment of prior learning in preparation for college-level coursework; the assessment of college-level learning (of what students learned after one, two, or three years of college); and the assessment of college outcomes relative to college inputs (Sims, 1992, p. 5). Assessment is judged to be most beneficial when it leads to improvement of educational programs and student learning. To be beneficial, it must serve a formative role (Hawthorne, 1989, p. 55). To serve as constructive yardsticks for the success of the curriculum, assessment and evaluation activities need to provide timely feedback to guide improvement. That is, whether feedback goes to students so they can alter their learning strategies, or to the faculty so they can redirect or retarget the curriculum, it must arrive in time to make the necessary adjustments. It must be informative and timely, and must differentiate among those who are benefiting from the curriculum and those who are not.

As noted earlier, there are usually greater differences among students in a single institution than there are differences in students across institutions (Pascarella and Terenzini, 1991). Therefore, colleges and universities need to examine the relationship between coursework chosen by students in various subpopulations and the learning outcomes evidenced in the assessment of general education and general learned abilities. Information about these relationships can be useful in the planning of student advising, course scheduling, curricular change, and faculty instructional development activities, and in the selection of assessment methods and measures (Ratcliff, 1992). In particular, advising can be more effective when tailored to the needs of individual students.

The undergraduate curriculum is typically described in one of two ways. It is profiled either in terms of what is prescribed for students or in terms of what they acquire from their academic experiences. This distinction is represented in the difference between the questions, What does the curriculum intend for students to learn? and What in the curriculum affects student learning? Despite the widespread use of assessment in recent years, the prevalent way to view the college curriculum is still according to its intentions rather than according to its results (Ratcliff, 1990; Warren, 1975; Weiland, 1989). Determining the effect of the undergraduate curriculum on students can be difficult. Most research on undergraduate curricula presumes rather than tests the effect of different patterns of coursework and programs of study on student learning. Therefore, it is important to distinguish at the outset between those patterns of coursework intended to fulfill undergraduate program and degree requirements and those patterns of formal study that students actually choose (Boyer and Ahlgren, 1987; Ratcliff, 1990; Warren, 1975; Weiland, 1989). In fact, it is the gap between what was intended and what learning resulted from the curriculum that allows the identification of the discrepancy between curricular aims and educational attainment.

A Few Good Practices in Curricular Design

Coherence in content. A curriculum provides a sequence of learning experiences inside and outside the classroom, resulting in formal coursework to attain specific educational aims. There should be a clear connection between what is to be taught, how it is to be taught, and how learning is evaluated—a topic explored in more depth in Chapter Seven. The coherence between aims, design, and evaluation is premised upon the educational philosophy employed. A heritage-based curriculum refers to the value placed on the reflection and transmission of knowledge and cultural legacies. Its design calls for the identification of essential readings and works to be read, analyzed, and deliberated by students. The Great Books curriculum not only has goals of understanding, comprehension, and analysis of key thinkers and writers, but also bears an implicit design and sequence derived from the rationalist tradition of the Enlightenment. The foundations of inquiry, such as mathematics, language, and logic should precede advanced studies in the arts, humanities, social sciences, and natural sciences.

The curriculum of the medieval university had a design that included sequencing and prerequisites to achieve coherence as well as aims. The subjects of the *quadrivium* (arithmetic, geometry, astronomy, and music) were to follow and build upon study in the *trivium* (logic, grammar, and rhetoric). In America, structure and coherence in higher education curricula were reinforced by the ideals of liberal learning as embodied in the writings of John Henry Cardinal Newman. American philosophers and psychologists, principally John Dewey and Henry James, advocated an educational system that could help make social change and socialize individuals to laissez-faire social democracy. Humboldtian ideals fostered the pursuit and advancement of knowledge (associated with German traditions of the research university), but they have helped to break down coherence as scholars seek to teach to their disparate research interests (Ratcliff, 1993b).

Notions of the functional benefits of prescribed development and sequence in coursework now have been largely replaced by the more oblique notion of breadth and depth of study in undergraduate education. Most U.S. institutions of higher education seek coherence and purpose by requiring students to select from lists of courses a certain number of credits to meet degree requirements; these distributional general education requirements are the norm in more than 90 percent of colleges and universities (Toombs, Fairweather, Amey, and Chen, 1989). The evidence has shown that students at the same institution do not share a common curricular experience in their pursuit of the bachelor's degree (Boyer and Ahlgren, 1987; Ratcliff, 1990). Curricular coherence never was an expectation of an academic culture in which individual faculty members decide what they wish to teach and individual students decide what lectures and seminars to attend and what they wish to learn. *Lehrfreiheit* (the freedom to teach whatever the individual faculty member thinks is important) and *lernfreiheit* (the freedom of the student to study whatever interests him or her), in an absolute sense, may mitigate against effective and efficient programs and curriculum for mass higher education. A high-stakes environment is needed in which both student and institution share in the responsibility of demonstrating educational results.

Cognitive skill development. Curriculum planners are realizing that speaking, reading, writing, and related linguistic processes are instrumental in all areas of learning. In university departments, teachers of content subjects and language specialists are tending to look at the curriculum as a whole. Faculties in the various disciplines need to be aware of the linguistic process by which students acquire subject-specific information and understanding. English language development is coming to be regarded as the responsibility of all academic staff within and across departments, not just of the individuals charged with teaching English to students. Although the across-the-curriculum approach to reading and writing is often more difficult and complex to implement, it holds promise to assure the successful development of language proficiency (Cheong, 1985). English specialists in non–English-speaking countries are also instituting a policy of English language across the curriculum. In the United States, similar curricular reforms have been implemented to encourage and strengthen the development of writing and conceptual skills across the curriculum (Toombs, Fairweather, Amey, and Chen, 1989). Chapters Eighteen and Nineteen discuss this in more detail.

Summary

The undergraduate curriculum at most colleges and universities consists of a wide array of course offerings from which students select a limited number of courses to complete their undergraduate degree program. Student choice of coursework is constrained by institutionally defined degree requirements for general and liberal education, major and minor specializations, and elective studies. Students at a single institution rarely experience a common intellectual experience in the curriculum—no more than 20 percent of coursework—unless the institution specifically prescribes a common core of courses that all students must take. Such prescription is not the norm. Instead, the curriculum expands with the knowledge base, the needs of society, and the interests of the students and faculty. The practice of offering an increasing catalogue of courses developed and taught largely by individual faculty members reflects the implicit assumption that taking different courses produces different types of learning and that such differential learning is a positive attribute of the undergraduate curriculum.

The need for a wider assortment of coursework is a result of differential preparation for college. To the extent that secondary education programs uniformly prepare students for collegiate studies, the need for programs targeted at students with different educational backgrounds is minimized. Similarly, the extent to which higher education is open and accessible to a large proportion of high school graduates will affect the extent to which coursework will need to be crafted to students of differing abilities and interests. Gaps between the prior achievement of entering students and the knowledge, skills, and abilities needed to succeed in college coursework are endemic. Then too, changes are occurring continuously within courses and between courses to reflect shifts in the paradigms of inquiry within the field of study, in the nature of social need and cultural value for the subject of study, in the role a particular course or program may take in the overall curriculum of the college or university, or in the interests and inclinations of the students who enroll or the faculty who design the instruction.

The curriculum is described in two ways: by what its intended outcomes are to be or by what its effects are on student learning. Clearly, the prevalent way of portraying curriculum is by its purposes and intentions. Yet, to understand better the role the curriculum plays in higher education, it is incumbent on researchers to uncover its effects. The undergraduate curriculum is the primary educational policy of a college or university. To the extent that an institution develops its own policy, its effectiveness rests with the educational attainment of its students.

Curricular theory is largely descriptive or prescriptive rather than transformational. Curricular models seek to describe and explain how the curriculum functions rather than to direct or guide its effects on students. A prescriptive curriculum explains what students take, what faculty should teach, or what students should learn. A descriptive curriculum portrays how the academic program is organized so that it might be better understood in its entirety by faculty, advisers, and students.

Curricular content, sequence, and process are further constrained by the standards and expectations of associations and organizations representing the fields of study. These groups may accredit academic programs; impose licensure examinations upon graduates; transmit the values, norms, and behavior appropriate to the discipline's faculty; or simply influence the curriculum through the introduction of new knowledge, processes, conceptual frameworks, and modes of inquiry among its members.

The curriculum is strongly mediated by the students and the society that it serves. Faculty members educated and socialized in another culture or country may bring expectations of instructional practices, educational philosophy and purpose, and standards of achievement that may not match student or social interest in the subject area. Disciplinary associations may promote standards of practice not entirely appropriate to the students to be educated.

The curriculum is a powerful tool of academic and social policy in higher education. The prevalent practice has been to assume that the effects of the undergraduate curriculum were what they were intended to be. There is a growing realization that the gap between what is intended in the curriculum and what its effects are must be bridged. We are just beginning to understand the role of coherent curricular design and effective, informative evaluation in narrowing the gap.

References

Astin, A. W. "The Methodology of Research on College Impact. Part I." *Sociology of Education*, 1970, *43*, 437–450.

Baxter-Magolda, M. B. *Knowing and Reasoning in College: Gender-Related Patterns in Students' Intellectual Development.* San Francisco: Jossey-Bass, 1992.

Beecher, T. *Academic Tribes and Territories: Intellectual Enquiry and the Cultures of Disciplines.* Bristol, Pa.: Open University Press, 1989.

Belenky, M. F., Clinchy, B. M., Goldberger, N. R., and Tarule, J. M. *Women's Ways of Knowing: The Development of Self, Voice, and Mind.* New York: Basic Books, 1986.

Bergquist, W. H., Gould, R. A., and Greenberg, E. M. *Designing Undergraduate Education.* San Francisco: Jossey-Bass, 1981.

Bergsma, H. M. *Technology Transfer through Training: Emerging Roles for the University.* Paper presented at the second annual Regional Conference on University Teaching, Las Cruces, N.M., Jan. 8–10, 1986. (ED 280 336)

Biglan, A. "The Characteristics of Subject Matter in Different Academic Areas." *Journal of Applied Psychology,* 1973a, *57*(3), 195–203.

Biglan, A. "Relationships Between Subject Matter Characteristics and the Structure and Output of University Departments." *Journal of Applied Psychology,* 1973b, *57*(3), 204–213.

Bloom, B. S. *All Our Children: A Primer for Parents, Teachers, and Other Educators.* New York: McGraw-Hill, 1981.

Borg, W. R., and Gall, M. D. *Educational Research: An Introduction.* (4th ed.) New York: Longman, 1983.

Boyer, C. M., and Ahlgren, A. "Assessing Undergraduates' Patterns of Credit Distribution: Amount and Specialization." *Journal of Higher Education,* 1987, *58,* 430–442.

Brigham, T. M. "Social Work Education Patterns in Five Developing Countries: Relevance of U.S. Microsystems." *Journal of Education for Social Work,* 1982, *18*(2), 68–75.

Brubacher, J. S., and Rudy, W. *Higher Education in Transition: A History of American Colleges and Universities, 1636–1976.* (2nd ed.) New York: HarperCollins, 1976.

Cheong, L. K. "English Across the University Curriculum." Paper presented at a regional seminar of the SEAMEO Regional Language Centre, Singapore, April 26, 1985. (ED 262 613)

Cohen, A. M., and Brawer, F. B. *The American Community College.* (2nd ed.) San Francisco: Jossey-Bass, 1989.

Collison, M.N.K. "Age of Aquarius and Vietnam: Today's Students Flock to Courses about, 1960's." *Chronicle of Higher Education,* 1988, *34*(37), A33, 34.

Conrad, C. F. *The Undergraduate Curriculum: A Guide to Innovation and Reform.* Boulder, Colo.: Westview Press, 1978.

Cronbach, L. J. *Designing Evaluations of Educational and Social Programs.* San Francisco: Jossey-Bass, 1983.

Donald, J. G. "Knowledge and the University Curriculum." *Higher Education,* 1986, *15,* 267–282.

Dressel, P. L., and DeLisle, F. H. *Undergraduate Curriculum Trends.* Washington, D.C.: American Council on Education, 1969.

Gardner, H. *Frames of Mind: The Theory of Multiple Intelligences.* New York: Basic Books, 1985.

Hawthorne, E. M. *Evaluating Employee Training Programs: A Research-Based Guide for Human Resource Managers.* New York: Quorum Books, 1989.

Hofstadter, R. *Anti-Intellectualism in American Life.* New York: Vintage Books, 1963.

Holland, J. "Explorations of a Theory of Vocational Choice and Achievement II: A Four Year Predictive Study." *Psychological Reports,* 1963, *12,* 547–594.

Israel, J. "Vietnam in the Curriculum." *Teaching Political Science,* 1985, *12*(4), 181–186.

Jencks, C., and Riesman, D. *The Academic Revolution.* New York: Doubleday, 1968.

Johnson, P. *The Activist Decade: Its Influence on Briar Cliff College.* Sioux City, Iowa: Briar Cliff College, 1986. (ED 284 465)

Jones, E. A. *Essential Skills in Writing, Speech and Listening, and Critical Thinking for College Graduates: Perspectives of Faculty, Employers, and Policy makers.* University Park, Pa.: National Center on Postsecondary Teaching, Learning, and Assessment, 1994.

Katz, S. N. "The Teacher-Scholar, the University and Society." Paper presented at the Rutgers Conference on the Politics of Research, New Brunswick, N.J., Oct. 21, 1994.

Kolb, D. A. "Learning Styles and Disciplinary Differences." In A. W. Chickering and Associates, *The Modern American College: Responding to the New Realities of Diverse Students and a Changing Society.* San Francisco: Jossey-Bass, 1981.

Kuhn, T. S. *The Structure of Scientific Revolutions.* Chicago: University of Chicago Press, 1962.

Lenning, O. T. "Assessment and Evaluation." In U. Delworth, G. R. Hanson, and Associates, *Student Services: A Handbook for the Profession.* San Francisco: Jossey-Bass, 1980.

Levine, A. *Handbook on Undergraduate Curriculum.* San Francisco: Jossey-Bass, 1978.

Lindquist, J. *Strategies for Change.* Berkeley, Calif.: Pacific Soundings Press, 1978.

Marchese, T. J. "Third Down, Ten Years to Go: An Assessment Update." *AAHE Bulletin,* 1987, *40*(4), 3–8.

McClelland, J. C. *State, Society and University in Germany, 1700–1914.* Cambridge, England: Cambridge University Press, 1980.

McKeachie, W. J., Pintrich, P. R., Lin, Y. G., and Smith, D.A.F. *Teaching and Learning in the College Classroom: A Review of the Research Literature.* Ann Arbor: National Center for Research and Improvement on Teaching and Learning, University of Michigan, 1986. (ED 314 999)

Pascarella, E. T. "College Environmental Influences on Learning and Cognitive Development: A Critical Review and Synthesis." In J. Smart (ed.), *Higher Education: Handbook of Theory and Research,* Vol. 1. New York: Agathon Press, 1985.

Pascarella, E. T., and Terenzini, P. T. *How College Affects Students: Findings and Insights from Twenty Years of Research.* San Francisco: Jossey-Bass, 1991.

Pascarella, E. T., and others. *What Have We Learned from the First Year of the National Study of Student Learning?* Chicago: National Center on Postsecondary Teaching, Learning, and Assessment, University of Illinois, 1994.

Pike, D. "Teaching the Vietnam Experience as a Whole Course." *Teaching Political Science,* 1985, *12*(4), pp. 144–151.

Ratcliff, J. L. *Development and Testing of a Cluster-Analytic Model for Identifying Coursework Patterns Associated with General Learned Abilities of College Students: Final Report, May, 1990.* U.S. Department of Education, Office of Educational Research and Improvement, Research Division. Contract No. OERI–R–86–0016. University Park: Center for the Study of Higher Education, Pennsylvania State University, 1990.

Ratcliff, J. L. "Reconceptualizing the College Curriculum." *Perspectives: The Journal of the Association for General and Liberal Studies,* 1992, pp. 122–137.

Ratcliff, J. L. *What We Can Learn from Coursework Patterns About Improving the Undergraduate Curriculum.* University Park, Pa.: National Center on Postsecondary Teaching, Learning, and Assessment, 1993a.

Ratcliff, J. L. "Implementing a Quality Assurance Program based on Assessments of Student Learning in a Differentiated System of Higher Education." Paper presented at the first preconference of the International Committee, Association for the Study of Higher Education, State College, Pa., Nov. 1–2, 1993b.

Ratcliff, J. L. "A Rationale for a Differentiated System of Higher Education." *Tertiary Education and Management,* 1996, *2*(2), 127–137.

Ratcliff, J. L., and Associates. *Realizing the Potential: Improving Postsecondary Teaching, Learning, and Assessment.* University Park, Pa.: National Center on Postsecondary Teaching, Learning, and Assessment, 1995.

Romer, R. *Making Quality Count in Undergraduate Education. A Report for the ECS Chairman's "Quality Counts" Agenda in Higher Education.* Denver: Education Commission of the States, 1995.

Rudolph, F. *Curriculum: A History of the American Undergraduate Course of Study Since 1636.* San Francisco: Jossey-Bass, 1977.

Shulman, L. S. "Knowledge and Teaching: Foundations of the New Reform." *Harvard Educational Review,* 1987, *57*(1), 1–22.

Sims, S. J. *Student Outcomes Assessment: A Historical Review and Guide to Program Development.* Westport, Conn.: Greenwood Press, 1992.

Stark, J. S., and Lowther, M. A. *Designing the Learning Plan: A Review of Research and Theory Related to College Curricula.* Ann Arbor: National Center for Research on Postsecondary Teaching and Learning, University of Michigan, 1986. (ED 287 439)

Taba, H. *Curriculum Development: Theory and Practice.* Orlando, Fla.: Harcourt Brace Jovanovich, 1962.

Toombs, W., Fairweather, J. S., Amey, M., and Chen, A. *Open to View: Practice and Purpose in General Education.* University Park, Pa.: Center for the Study of Higher Education, 1989.

Toombs, W., and Tierney, W. *Meeting the Mandate: Renewing the College and Departmental Curriculum.* ASHE-ERIC Higher Education Report No. 6. Washington, D.C.: School of Education and Human Development, George Washington University, 1991.

Tyler, R. W. *Basic Principles of Curriculum and Instruction.* Chicago: University of Chicago Press, 1950.

Tyler, R. "Specific Approaches to Curriculum Development." In J. Schaffarzick and D. Hampton (eds.), *Strategies for Curriculum Development.* Berkeley, Calif.: McCutchan, 1975.

Veysey, L. *The Emergence of the American University.* Chicago: University of Chicago Press, 1965.

Walshok, M. L. *Knowledge Without Boundaries: What America's Research Universities Can Do for the Economy, the Workplace, and the Community.* San Francisco: Jossey-Bass, 1995.

Warren, J. B. "Alternatives to Degrees." In D. W. Vermilye (ed.), *Learner-Centered Reform: Current Issues in Higher Education.* San Francisco: Jossey-Bass, 1975.

Weiland, J. S. "General Education in the Universities after 1992." *European Journal of Education,* 1989, *24*(4), 371–377.

Wilcox, F. A. "Pedagogical Implications of Teaching 'Literature of the Vietnam War.'" *Social Education,* 1988, *52*(1), 39–40.

"The Yale Report of 1828." In R. Hofstadter and W. Smith (eds.), *American Higher Education: A Documentary History.* Vol. 1. Chicago: University of Chicago Press, 1961.

CHAPTER TWO

INSTITUTIONAL CONTEXTS

Elizabeth M. Hawthorne

The elaboration of the initial curriculum of higher education in the United States is a story of a dynamic society, what it wants to know about, and how it wants to learn it. From Harvard College of 1636, "founded . . . as a college of English university standards for the liberal education of the young men of New England, under strict religious discipline" (Morison, 1937, p. 22), to today's panoply of colleges and universities, the curriculum evolved through expansion, contraction, and modification.

Curriculum is how we organize what we teach, how we teach, and to whom we teach. The way in which curriculum is organized has defined the way in which it is taught. For example, the institutionalization of the disciplinary departments in the late nineteenth century allowed for in-depth coverage of fields, but imposed constraints on the integration of knowledge. Similarly, the development of the elective system, majors and minors, and the idea of general education to anchor the elective approach changed the face of undergraduate education. The ongoing debate about multidisciplinary and problem-centered rather than discipline-centered approaches to social problems and the interest in interdisciplinary approaches to teaching and learning have resulted in new curricula organized around problems such as environmental studies, world hunger, and poverty (Mayhew and Ford, 1971; Bergquist, Gould, and Greenberg, 1981). Still unresolved for many is whether women's studies or African American studies should be separate fields or integrated in the disciplines. These debates illustrate the continuing evolution of the curriculum as a reflection of social change and tensions.

Underlying Currents

Five significant underlying currents have influenced different groups to create the diversity of curriculum in American higher education. First, there has been a sustained tension between two opposing views of human nature. The view exemplified by Rousseau and Mill that people are good and that education uplifts the individual and the state to a higher good is in sharp contrast to a belief that individuals are predisposed to evil and need to be governed and controlled. The debates about curriculum in higher education have rarely moved far from this central philosophical dispute. As the liberal arts colleges evolved from their colonial college roots, they were at first dominated by the latter perspective. At the newly founded University of Virginia, Thomas Jefferson's attempt to give students choices of curriculum to suit their needs simply did not fit the prevailing view of the need to control youth to save them from their disposition toward evil; as a consequence, his vision of a curriculum for the University of Virginia was not realized until long after his death. Not until the latter part of the nineteenth century did the value of education to uplift and the essential goodness of people begin to dominate the discussion and practice of higher education.

Intertwined in this philosophical conflict are religion and religious values. A learned clergy was certainly important to the Pilgrims; the early debate about the role of Harvard in a deeply religious community was whether or not one reached God through inspiration or through education. This battle was fought throughout our history as different churches formed and made judgments about the importance of education to serve the needs of godliness. Religious disputes thus directly affected the founding of colleges. For example, conservatives who were distressed with Harvard's liberalism regarding church teachings founded Yale in 1701, and Catholic colleges were established to serve the needs of the Catholic church and its followers.

Contemporary undergraduate curricula reflect a recursive struggle between the desire to conserve and to apply knowledge, culture, and values and the aspiration to generate knowledge through disciplined study. The current debate over research versus teaching exemplifies this tension. Most certainly these differences affected the development of the American research university, where the creation of knowledge was a guiding principle. The research university influenced the organization and content of undergraduate curriculum and, among other things, provided a rationale for the junior college.

An additional current affecting the college curriculum is the pragmatic and diverse nature of Americans. We approach our needs with entrepreneurial vigor (see Boorstin, 1958). Rather than fix something that is broken, Americans often just start something new. For example, new colleges and curricula have been developed to address diverse special interests—farmers (the Pennsylvania Agricultural College), engineering (Massachusetts Institute of Technology), women (Mt. Holyoke), and African Americans (Fisk).

Local interests have also played a significant role in the development of curriculum and institutions. For example, Western pioneers were isolated and unable to turn to friends and family back East when their security was threatened. Colleges were needed to help the people learn to think critically for their survival and development. A college uniquely suited to its locale, Berea College in Appalachian Kentucky, serves local students' needs by incorporating a work component into the curriculum. Thus, economically poor students can avail themselves of a college education while learning valuable skills and earning their income. Even the land-grant institutions, although prompted by federal legislation, took on peculiarly local flavors; few confuse Wisconsin with Michigan State despite many similarities.

These underlying social and historical currents are expressed through the many individuals and groups, both external and internal to institutions, who have transformed college curriculum in profound ways, including philanthropists, government policy makers, trustees, and institutional leaders. Faculty and students, too, bring significant voices to the design and implementation of college curricula in existing institutions and in the beginning of new colleges with new curricula.

External agents, often through philanthropy, shape programs by offering incentives for their development. For example, the expanded electrical engineering program in the late nineteenth century at Union College in Schenectady, New York, was supported and encouraged by a gift from General Electric (Rudolph, 1977). More recently, philanthropists have supported women's studies, environmental studies, and free enterprise programs (for example, see Fosdick, 1962).

One can consider, too, the range of government policies that have affected curriculum, including Title IV (Student Assistance) and Title IX (Equal Opportunity) of the Higher Education Act, which influence who goes to college—and thus whose voices are expressed and heard. Similarly, the sponsorship of an institution can affect the direction of its curriculum. State sponsorship has tended to foster more utilitarian, more liberal, and more democratic (Steffens, 1971)—and certainly more secular—curriculum than many private institutions.

Curriculum is deliberately shaped by the interests of institutional leaders. During the nineteenth century, when individual college presidents played a dominant role in curriculum development, many promoted their views of the curriculum with varying degrees of success. Such notables as Eliphalet Nott at Union, Francis Wayland at Brown, and Henry Philip Tappan at Michigan come to mind (see Brubacher and Rudy, 1976; Rudolph, 1990). Further, curriculum has been modified by the design of institutional leaders (trustees, presidents) seeking to address the needs and interests of special groups, for example, women, African Americans, the well-to-do, or local student bodies. Members of agricultural societies, who frequently served on boards of land-grant institutions, were able to influence the inclusion or exclusion of other programs (such as engineering) in their institutions (Bezilla, 1981). Certainly, institutional leaders seeking to preserve the existence of their fiscally vulnerable institutions have changed curriculum to attract newcomers. "When a college is on the verge of oblivion, there is no problem in its achieving instant curricular revision" (President Millar Upton of Beloit, cited in Rudolph, 1977, p. 19).

The intellectual interests of faculty also determine what is taught. For example, Jacob Abbott and his colleagues at Amherst introduced English literature and political economy early in the nineteenth century (Schmidt, 1957). Whatever the catalogue may say, two individuals teaching the same course and the same material can teach very different ideas. Surely, the Baptist president of Bucknell was unlikely to teach the senior classes in the same way as the Presbyterian president of Princeton. As new fields emerged through disciplined inquiry here and abroad, for example, history, psychology, and scientific fields, they, too, became part of the undergraduate curriculum.

The interests and creativity of faculty also shape the way in which instruction is delivered. Under the leadership of scientist Josiah Meigs at the new University of Georgia as the nineteenth century began, "science was to be taught 'in all possible cases by experiment'" (Dyer, 1985, p. 13). This was a departure from the methods (predominantly recitation) and content (Latin, Greek, Hebrew, logic; natural, mental, and moral philosophy; mathematics, divinity with some history and botany) (see Rudolph, 1977, p. 31) at Meigs's alma mater, Yale, and other colonial colleges. With the advent of science, especially in the newer nineteenth century institutions, "The old-fashioned curriculum disappeared, of necessity, and many combinations of studies are permitted in the most conservative institutions" (Gilman, 1971, p. 14).

The availability of new materials similarly altered the content of what was taught, if not the course titles, resulting in changes in the nature of the academic experience for the students. The change from 1724 to 1769 was dramatic, with the content of the latter curriculum—at least at Harvard—not resembling that of the former (Morison, 1937). For example, the old Aristotelian readings in ethics and metaphysics changed to include Locke's "Essay on the Human Understanding." Students in this newer curriculum included Samuel and John Adams, who probably also benefitted from the addition of exhibitions for the purposes of improving students' oratorical skills (Morison, 1937).

The students who come to an institution shape its curriculum in three ways. One way has been through student demands. Student demands for relevance in the curriculum instigated the addition of new courses and programs in the 1960s and 1970s. More than a few colleges added career curricula to attract the practical-minded students of the 1970s. Students have further affected curriculum by developing their interests outside the curriculum, legitimizing new areas of inquiry (such as American history and literature in the eighteenth and nineteenth centuries) that were later incorporated into the curriculum (Brubacher and Rudy, 1976). Finally, institutions have developed special curricula to serve selected student groups, for example, honors programs and developmental education programs that dominate some community colleges and speckle the landscape of American higher education in an era of access.

Thus different philosophical and religious perspectives, conflicting positions on the creation versus the conservation of knowledge, American pragmatism and diversity, and local interests affected a variety of groups whose energy and purposefulness singularly and collectively created the undergraduate curricula of American colleges as we know them today.

Undergraduate curriculum has certainly changed since 1636 within institutions, but it also changed, often profoundly, because new institutions were begun. New institutions and new institutional types have altered the undergraduate curriculum first by their presence and second by their influence on traditional, albeit evolving, institutions.

Before the curricular evolution of originally undergraduate institutions is elaborated on, however, the influence of the American research university on undergraduate curriculum must be acknowledged. The openness to new fields of study embraced by research institutions such as Cornell University (Rudolph, 1977) positioned undergraduate education to offer preparation for diverse fields of endeavor. The effects of the American research university were evident in new content, even new fields of study; new modes of organization, such as academic departments, the elective system, and the introduction of majors and minors; new pedagogy, including seminars and laboratories (Hawkins, 1971); increasing professionalization of faculty (Gruber, 1975); the academic climate, emphasizing free inquiry (Veysey, 1965); and the secularization of undergraduate curriculum (Hofstadter and Hardy, 1952). These developments reflected the idea that knowledge had a social function; their historical impact was to open higher education to more and different populations of students, thus altering the very nature of the collegiate experience.

One Illustration of Change: The Liberal Arts College

The classical colonial colleges, starting with Harvard College in 1636, were the foundation of American higher education curriculum. The liberal arts colleges have had in common a commitment to learning, intellectual discipline, and the education of the individual for citizenship. However, the liberal arts colleges are and were not a monolith (see Robson, 1983).

Competition among the different nationalities and their religious denominations contributed to the expansion of the liberal arts colleges, for example, the Scotch-Irish and Germans in Pennsylvania in the early nineteenth century (Hefelbower, 1932, p. 9). The role of science in the liberal arts colleges also varied, in large measure due to the cost of equipment, the enlightenment of the faculty and trustees, and the availability of properly trained professors. For example, while science was deemed integral to the curriculum of the new Methodist university, Northwestern, the "prevailing view at the time was that 'science was a useful tool in demonstrating the wondrous ways of God'" (Williamson and Wild, 1976, p. 17). At Harvard, science was tangential and tolerated, certainly not celebrated. However, the University of Pennsylvania was strong on science from the beginning (see Brubacher and Rudy, 1976). Social issues such as slavery in the nineteenth century and civil rights in the twentieth century were often likely to be indicators of differences among the colleges. *A curriculum designed for the intellectual elite is not likely to be the same as that intended for a more varied student population.* Thus catalogues may have had similarities, but the needs of the founding churches were to promulgate faith as they knew it—otherwise, they would have been content to send their children to the colleges founded by other denominations.

Within the early liberal arts colleges, the curriculum was also far less static than is sometimes assumed. Throughout the colonial period and into the nineteenth century, many of the liberal arts colleges introduced changes in their curriculum. In the mid-eighteenth century, Benjamin Franklin was concerned with practicality and instituted applied scientific study at the College of Philadelphia. Eliphalet Nott at Union set up a course of study in modern languages alongside the traditional classical curriculum (Schmidt, 1957). Bold experiments in the traditional colleges often faltered and failed, however, because of the students' reluctance to participate (Klein, 1930; Burke, 1982). Still, departures from the classical curriculum were sufficiently commonplace to prompt a vigorous defense of the old-time curriculum ("The Yale Report of 1828," 1961).

The Yale Report failed to halt the tides of change; however, it left nagging doubts about changing the curriculum because to be different in many ways was to be inferior. The understandable conservatism of the old colleges, born to foster tradition by teaching it to the young, argued for new kinds of institutions to be born because the keepers of the light resisted bringing the novel into their sanctuaries.

Manifold Needs for New Colleges

As knowledge expanded through research abroad and in the growing country, other needs became apparent. There was more to learn—and different ways to learn—than the classical curriculum provided. Normal schools were developed to train teachers for the expanding public education systems throughout the country and new curricula were developed for this purpose. Similarly, under the aegis of the Morrill Acts of 1862 and 1890, the land-grant universities were launched. Political, social, and economic factors coalesced in the nineteenth century to drive the founding of colleges for women and what would become historically black colleges. Finally, the two-year, junior, or (later) community colleges emerged to expand access to higher education to location-bound, sometimes economically disadvantaged students.

The benefit of a new institution is that it is freed of the constraints of tradition. Daniel Coit Gilman, the first president of Johns Hopkins University, noted at the beginning of the twentieth century: "The gifts of Johns Hopkins, of Rockefeller, of Stanford, of Tulane, promoted the establishment of new institutions, in sympathy with the older colleges, yet freer to introduce new subjects and new methods" (Gilman, 1971, p. 14).

Still, it was difficult for the new institutions to depart dramatically from the archetype of the colonial colleges because these old colleges represented the best in higher education—the education of the human mind founded on ageless values (see Levine, 1986). Who was there who would think to improve upon what was done in the East?

Thus, in the new republic, new institutions were started to provide specified kinds of instruction required by a dynamic industrializing country during a period of intellectual enlightenment and burgeoning scientific research. Still, the development of new kinds of institutions did not leave the old colleges unchanged and insulated. Indeed, they adapted their curriculum, changed in multiple ways because of communication, collaboration, and competition without necessarily losing individual institutional identity.

New Institutional Types

One category of these new institutions includes those determined to introduce new content, for example, land-grant colleges and universities, trade and business schools, and normal schools. Another category of new institutions is made up of colleges prompted by an interest in bringing new student populations into higher education—separate from the mainstream of the white, Christian, middle- to upper-class, male student population—for example, colleges for women and colleges for African Americans. Finally, we turn to the community colleges for location-bound students with varying degrees of academic talent and financial resources. Each institution type continues to this day, although rarely in its pure, original form because of the mobility of ideas and people.

New Material to Teach

While the liberal arts colleges were introducing new curriculum content and methods, so too were the new institutions designed to focus on curriculum not readily available in the old colleges. The development of new curriculum was largely driven by new ideas requiring dissemination, expansion of public schools, and the expansion of the country to the West, where new opportunities abounded. For example, farming was important to the economy and lifestyle in the West; propelled by awareness of new techniques for farming and the appetite for improvement, the agricultural colleges were conceived. The engineering curricula pioneered by West Point, MIT, and Rensselaer Polytechnic were in demand because of the expansion of the country to areas with rich natural resources and the need for an infrastructure for communication, transportation, and commerce. These were soon combined by federal incentive to become the land-grant colleges and universities, a title more descriptive of the source of initial funds than their purpose.

Finally, industrial growth, the invention of the typewriter, and the concentration of population in the cities created new jobs in increasingly larger companies, making a market for business education and technical workers and leading to the creation of trade and business schools. This same trend later, in part, led to the establishment of the junior colleges. These new postsecondary education institutions not only taught new material but experimented with new instructional approaches.

Normal Schools. The public normal school was an idea borrowed from the Prussian system of education ("Henry Barnard on German Teachers . . . ," [1835] 1974). The normal schools prepared primary school teachers while teachers' colleges and, to a lesser extent, liberal arts colleges prepared secondary school teachers. For example, Phillips Academy in Andover, Massachusetts, added a three-and-a-half-year teacher training program (for males only) to its secondary curriculum around 1834. Entrance examination covered the "sounds of English letters, rules of spelling, reading, geography, first principles of etymology and syntax, intellectual arithmetic, history of the U.S., ground rules of written arithmetic, and fractions" ("Samuel Read Hall's . . . ," [1837]). The first state-supported normal school was in Massachusetts in 1839.

The idea of separate institutions for teacher training, while modeled elsewhere, was necessitated in the United States by the disinterest of existing colleges in playing the role determined for the normal schools. Harper's observation sums up the likely conditions: "Because the academies and colleges looked down with contempt on the normal schools from the aloofness of their classical curriculums, the normal schools took a fierce joy in glorifying the branches of common everyday learning" (1939, pp. 30–31).

Individual institutions established to train primary school teachers for the burgeoning system of common or public schools were early examples of single-purpose colleges. Their relationship to traditional colleges, the standard of higher education, varied. For example, in Michigan, the normal schools consistently looked over their shoulders at the universities. In Illinois, the normal schools preceded universities and stood in for them (see Harper, 1939, pp. 776–781). That they were often more secondary than collegiate in nature stigmatized them (Wasserman, 1978). Nonetheless, they contributed to development of the undergraduate curriculum. First, through normal schools, public sponsorship linked higher education directly to the needs of the state, recognizing that preparing teachers for children was in the best interests of a democratic state (Harper, 1939). John Quincy Adams observed: "We see monarchs expending vast sums, establishing normal schools thruout [sic] their realms, and sparing no pains to convey knowledge and efficiency to all the children of their poorest subjects. Shall we be outdone by kings?" (quoted in Harper, 1939, pp. 23–24).

The normal schools also offered practice of the profession through the presence of the model school attached to the normal school for student teaching and observation. The success of the normal schools, especially the state schools, might well be attributed to their ability to train individuals who became better teachers than those without benefit of the normal school experience. The public responded to the message of a utilitarian value for higher education. The normal schools legitimized the value of the single-purpose institution for that era so that studies not favored in the liberal arts colleges might be pursued without the stigma likely when they coexist in one institution. "It will give to teachers that sense of responsibility and dignity that will gain the respect of the world" (David Felmley, president of Illinois State Normal, in Harper, 1939, pp. 114–115). This argument was also used for separate institutions for African Americans and for women. It was an argument that marginalized both groups.

Using a summer school format (see Harper, 1939) and continuing education, the normal schools closely linked practitioners with the normal school faculty, fostering a useful flow of ideas (Altenbaugh and Underwood, 1990, p. 165; "First

Annual Circular . . . ," [1851] 1929, pp. 57–59). The normal schools began as student-centered institutions. Students could enroll for all or part of the program, which was constructed in modules to accommodate past experience and the inability of students to afford longer periods without an income. Textbooks, libraries, apparatus, model schools linked with the normal schools for practice and observation of the aspiring teachers, visitations of exemplary schools, guest lecturers, and a public examination "followed by an exhibition" (Barnard, [1851] 1929, p. 60) were all features of these new institutions, which concerned themselves with personal interest in students and a spirit of professionalism (Harper, cited in Harcleroad, Sagen, and Molen, 1969).

Agriculture and Engineering—the Land-Grant Idea. Agricultural education and engineering education married in the land-grant institutions—a marriage of convenience that represented a shared commitment to practical, useful education in the nation's service (a concept later developed at Wisconsin under Bascom and then Van Hise) (Hoeveler, 1989). The establishment of land-grant institutions under the two Morrill Acts was undertaken for multiple reasons, but clearly the failure of existing colleges to embrace the applied arts, especially agriculture and engineering, created an opportunity for new institutions with new curricula to develop.

Although slow to develop, these institutions were important because a change in the country called for new kinds of education. Indeed, the transition from the more traditional curriculum (allowing for the creeping entrance of science into the classical curriculum or grafted alongside in the old-time colleges) was gradual even with new institutions and apparently intended to be so. Morrill reportedly "did not intend them to be agricultural schools . . . He expected [them] to be schools of science rather than classical colleges; that the schools be, in fact, colleges and not institutions of lower grade. . . . But in all he wished as a prominent feature the 'useful sciences' be taught" (from a talk cited in Klein, 1930, p. 20).

The land-grant colleges and universities that eventually flourished under the Morrill Acts of 1862 and 1890 were built on the foundations of earlier efforts to train the farmer and the engineer, both of whom were needed for a vigorous, growing country experiencing the benefits of rich natural resources, extensive lands, and the fruits of scientific research (the latter still largely conducted in Europe).

One of the earliest initiatives for collegiate-level agricultural education came from the Norfolk Agricultural Society in Massachusetts under the leadership of Marshall P. Wilder, who called for "the encouragement of agricultural education and the improvement of agriculture in all its departments" (True, 1929, p. 27). By 1853, there were calls for "farmers' institutes" modeled after teachers' institutions. The *lyceum movement,* begun in Connecticut by Josiah Holbrook (see

"Josiah Holbrook's Proposal . . . ," [1828] 1974) after his agricultural school failed, offered the platform for lecturers to disseminate information about agriculture and other subjects; extensive publications about agriculture fostered discussion of the relationship between science and agriculture and set the stage for more formal tuition. According to True (1929), various initiatives at existing colleges in the eighteenth and early nineteenth centuries to incorporate science in the curriculum were important sources of texts and ideas for the future agricultural colleges. Agriculture was even listed in the 1842 Amherst College catalogue.

Many of the efforts to add professorships of agricultural education in existing institutions were not successful (see True, 1929). A notable exception was Yale College, where John Pitkin Norton offered a series of lectures on the connections of science with agriculture beginning in 1847 (True, 1929), leading eventually to the establishment of the Yale—later Sheffield—Scientific School. What cemented this experiment was less the interests of the state legislature, generous private gifts, and instructor interest, but the skill of Norton in attracting more and more students each year. The market spoke. According to True, these and other efforts to graft agricultural education onto existing colleges were not eminently successful or widespread and even Jefferson's desire to offer the study of agriculture at the new University of Virginia "met with very little response" (1929, p. 57). Clearly, existing institutions experimented with new curricula, but the promotion of new curricula was more successful in new institutions once a benefit had been demonstrated.

The path to collegiate agricultural education was indeed rocky despite the dominance of the agricultural societies in the schools' formation and governance (see Blair and Kuhn, 1965, on Michigan State; Bezilla, 1981, on Penn State; and Lang, 1989, on Cornell). At Michigan Agricultural College, for example, the curriculum was the traditional academic coursework plus the sciences and English—except that there was no Latin or Greek. The college was initially run by the State Board of Education, who in 1860 "replaced the four year program with its broad emphasis on liberal and scientific studies, with what may be called a two year trade-school course" (Blair and Kuhn, 1955, p. 10).

Realizing that enrollment in agriculture was dismally low in the 1880s because the first two years of the curriculum were general education and the farmers saw no useful value for their sons in that, Wisconsin (under the leadership of Dean Henry) initiated a "short course" on agriculture that did not lead to a degree, but did teach scientific farming and ideas that the farmers needed. Beginning in 1885 with 19 students, who received manual and scientific training and later cultural training through debating, the program grew to 393 by 1907 (Steffens, 1971, p. 122). Wisconsin's willingness to adjust the delivery of the education to suit student interest was a major contribution to higher education. Most important, not unlike the normal schools, the demonstrated benefits in the improvement of agricultural production in the state linked the university with its people more intimately perhaps than any other higher education institution had done.

Few texts and even fewer faculty were available to teach the new curriculum at first. Klein noted that there was not sufficient research in agriculture and engineering to provide a satisfactory postsecondary education (1930, p. 2), although the years of Norton, then Porter, then Johnson at Yale belie that to some extent. The talent and dedication of the few laid a solid basis for growth, however. Professor Isaac P. Roberts, agriculture teacher in the Iowa State Agricultural College in 1869, recorded:

> I began to tell the students what I knew about farming. It did not take me long to run short of material and then I began to consult the library. I might as well have looked for cranberries on the Rocky Mountains as for materials for teaching agriculture in that library. Thus, fortunately I was driven to take the class to the field and farm, there to study plants, animals and tillage at first hand. . . .
> I suppose I was the first teacher of agriculture to make use, in a large way, of the fields and stables of the countryside as laboratories. . . . [quoted in Klein, 1930, p. 21]

The merger of ideas from many sources to create an agricultural curriculum represents a creative initiative in postsecondary education and a standard of eclecticism that characterize higher education in the United States today.

Engineering education. Engineering education began in the fields surveying with George Washington and others. Formal engineering education can be traced to RPI. The new Rensselaer Institute in 1824 was "to instruct persons 'in the application of science to the common purposes of life'" (True, 1929, p. 40)—a trendsetting policy. (West Point in 1802 earlier offered engineering education.) The MIT curriculum in 1865 included a unique combination of basic education courses, scientific courses in applied fields, and evening lectures for the general public, serving as a model for many later schools (Brubacher and Rudy, 1976, p. 62). By 1866, Lehigh had been established, offering baccalaureate programs in civil, mechanical, mining, and metallurgical engineering (Bezilla, 1981, p. 10). These are enduring institutions (although there were others that did not endure; see Bezilla, 1981) that speak today to the need for the service they provide to both civilian and military life.

Instructional innovation was a hallmark of the new agricultural and engineering institutions. Scientific instruction had been primarily lectures enhanced by the introduction over time of experiments in labs and in the field (Klein, 1930, p. 23). Instruction in agriculture and engineering in the land-grant and other specialized schools included lectures, but also emphasized active learning experiences like inspection trips, summer internships, and survey camps for civil engineering students (Klein, 1930, p. 806). Under Amos Eaton, instruction at Rensselaer adumbrated the active learning ideas of today: "The students are to be divided into sections, not exceeding five in each section. These are not to be taught by seeing experiments and hearing lectures, according to the usual method. But they are to lecture and experiment by turns, under the immediate direction of a professor or a competent assistant. Thus, by a term of labor, like apprentices to a trade, they are to become operative chemists" (True, 1929, p. 42). These approaches were not readily available elsewhere in higher education at that time. Only a new institution was prepared to venture forth so boldly.

Marginalized Students

The development of different kinds of new institutions contributed to secularizing, liberalizing, and vocationalizing higher education. New institutions expanded access for different social classes, for women in some cases, and for specifically rural and urban populations. Other colleges emerged on the scene to address the postsecondary education needs of other excepted groups, specifically women and African Americans, contributing to the discourse on curriculum in higher education, the nexus between higher education and the American society, and thus the purposes of higher education in the United States.

Women's Colleges. Not until 1834, when Oberlin admitted women, was there attention to a significantly different student population with unique needs. The founding of colleges for women is a study in contrasting views of women's capabilities and their role in society; those views, of course, changed over time and directly affected college curriculum. Contemporary beliefs regarding the health and mental ability of women affected higher education for women (Solomon, 1985; Palmieri, 1983). These included the belief that active study would impair the health of women and interfere with their responsibility to bear children (see Mrozek, 1983). In the new nation, women assumed responsibility to nurture the young in a democracy craving educated citizens (see Horowitz, 1984) so the idea of their education, at least up to a point, was viable (see Townsend, 1990).

Coeducation was provided at Oberlin in 1837 and at Antioch in 1852. Antioch even employed a female faculty member, Miss R. M. Pennell, Professor of Physical Geography, Drawing, Natural History, Civil History and Didactics. "It [Antioch] recognizes the claims of the female sex to equal opportunities of education with the male, and these opportunities it desires to confer" (Cohen, 1974, p. 1501). The coeducational public University of Iowa opened its doors in 1855. Debates about the fitness of coeducation raged throughout the nineteenth century and into the twentieth (see Barnard, 1882; "Charles W. Eliot . . . ," [1869] 1974; Cutler, 1884).

One prevailing view of women's role was as mothers and teachers and the keepers of the culture as expounded by Emma Willard, Mary Lyon, and Catherine Beecher in the early nineteenth century. Protection was needed for delicate females and the female seminary exemplified by Mary Lyon's Mt. Holyoke in 1837 dominated the higher education of women for several decades (a slight level above the normal schools). The feminine curriculum included domestic instruction and the ornamental arts, for example, "drawing and painting, elegant penmanship, music, and the grace of motion" ("Emma Willard . . . ," [1819] 1974). Also offered were introductory academic subjects such as English literature, math, and science. Even colleges that presumed comparability to the curriculum at men's colleges often omitted Greek and Latin (see Horowitz, 1984; Solomon, 1985).

In contrast, the curriculum at Vassar (Horowitz, 1984, p. 3) was designed to be comparable to that at Yale and, thus, a new population of college students was introduced into the traditional curricular mode of American higher education. However, Horowitz points out that outside the college curriculum, the experience of women students at Vassar was very different from that of men at the traditional institutions.

Henry Durant at Wellesley went beyond the Vassar model by employing female faculty throughout the college (Horowitz, 1984) and offering modern scientific labs and a library collection rivaling Harvard's. Its curriculum was at once classical and contemporary (Palmieri, 1983). Bryn Mawr under M. Carey Thomas moved the college from "moral discipline to academic rigor" (Solomon, 1985, p. 49) thus setting a standard for the education of women—and men, too—that was secular and intellectually challenging. The curricula provided for women varied but the provision of vocational training in early colleges for women (see Rudolph, 1990) spoke to the limited availability of sufficient numbers of women students with the preparation for full collegiate instruction—and the means to afford the full four years of a college education (see Solomon, 1985). Thus the development of colleges for women spoke, as did development of each of the other new institutional types in American higher education, to the colleges' sensitivity to potential enrollment and the need to modify a curriculum to maintain the viability of the institution for the students.

According to Schmidt, the main contribution to the collegiate curriculum by women's colleges was in the area of the fine arts, where such study was made "intellectually respectable" (p. 142). Women's colleges were more likely to offer modern languages than their male counterparts (for example, see Palmieri, 1983; Townsend, 1990). Sarah Lawrence (1925) and Bennington (1932) departed from tradition in curriculum by allowing for individual courses of study for students (Schmidt, 1957, p. 144).

Still, there is no evidence that innovations in the curriculum for women (like those in the curriculum for African Americans in the nineteenth century, discussed in the next section) substantively influenced the discourse concerning the education of men—except perhaps at the coeducational institutions, probably because of the marginality of women and African Americans as students. The inclusion of women in higher education, however, did raise new questions about the purpose of higher education and how curricula were to be altered to accommodate new voices. The curriculum debates about education for women—women as keepers of the family or women as professionals in a worldly environment—reflected societal debates about the role of women in society. Educators sought to relate the collegiate experience for women with the life experiences they were expected to have. Thus, social conditions and values strongly drove the curriculum at women's colleges and starkly demonstrated the tight linkages between the two.

Colleges for African Americans. The establishment of colleges for African American students contributed to the continuing dialogue about the purposes of higher education. The debate between those who advocated pragmatic education for vocational pursuits and those advocating a liberal education to develop youth for leadership was exemplified in the construction of curriculum of the historically African American institutions. The social context of curriculum development is particularly represented by these institutions. What they taught, for what purposes, and for whom raised significant questions about higher education that continue to be asked today.

The primary move toward the establishment of colleges for African American students followed the Civil War. The most marginalized students in higher education evidently required a special kind of education—one that would equip them with tools for self-maintenance. Starting with a population of students who could not read, the education early on was decidedly precollegiate. These colleges labored under difficult circumstances.

There were several kinds of champions of education for African Americans. There were some whites, often with deeply religious motivation, who were supportive of full educational opportunities for African Americans. Other whites were "paternalistic and dictatorial" (Smith, 1984, p. 137). This stance in many cases led to a struggle for control by African Americans, for example at Howard University where in 1926 Mordecai Johnson became its first African American president (Smith, 1984). Some African Americans advocated vocational training so that the recently freed illiterate slaves could learn a trade and become independent and self-supporting. The Hampton Institute and Tuskegee Institute exemplified this perspective; the major spokesman for this point of view was

Booker T. Washington (see Brubacher and Rudy, 1976, p. 76). Southern whites often preferred this lest the former slaves get too much education. On the other hand, many African Americans were advocating liberal education for their people, a position eloquently defended by W.E.B. Du Bois ([1903] 1974). Private colleges for African Americans that promoted the liberal arts education included Fisk, Atlanta, and Spelman.

The politics of the period—Reconstruction and the hostile feelings it engendered—greatly influenced the development of curriculum as Southern whites hardened in their views and Northern whites lost interest in the issues. The provision of industrial education served as a means of social control during the repressive racial milieu of the South following Reconstruction—an approach resembling the path later taken by junior and community colleges designed for those poorly served by higher education, who were often not seen as worthy of a college education (Karabel, 1972).

The general poverty in the South and the incredible destruction during the Civil War left the South with an impoverished educational system for whites and African Americans both. Moreover, racism was a continuing factor in how decisions were made to educate African Americans in the South and in the North. African American institutions were constantly hindered in their expansion by the limited precollegiate experiences of their students and limited resources in some cases caused by racism and low expectations for African American students. Curriculum was directly affected by these conditions because the expressed purpose of colleges established for African Americans was for service in light of the prevailing social and economic conditions. Missionaries wanted "social equity and experimentation" (Browning and Williams, 1978, p. 74), education and religious leadership, and the freedom to pursue agricultural and industrial studies (Hedgepath, Edmonds, and Craig, 1978, p. 17). Additionally, the establishment of separate public schools for African Americans and whites necessitated the preparation of African Americans to teach in these schools and thus several institutions for African Americans focused on teacher education.

Still, the lure of an academic education was central and each college sought to move in that direction as soon as possible. Creative efforts to excel despite pressure from white Southerners seeking to continue the public colleges as trade schools led to designations such as "Agricultural Latin" to accommodate vocationally intended courses that were liberal in content. Opening in 1866, Fisk graduated its first class (of four) in 1875, although the normal school had been functioning since its founding (Richardson, 1980). The understanding at Fisk was that leadership for freed slaves was necessary and education was the path to follow. Traditional African American institutions did prepare doctors, lawyers, dentists, and ministers in addition to teachers. "In general the private colleges emphasized an academic curriculum, while the public colleges emphasized more vocational training" (National Center for Education Statistics, 1985, p. 2).

While most of the land-grant colleges for African Americans, according to Smith (1984, p 136), were more college preparatory than collegiate, they moved as swiftly as they could toward full collegiate status. A U.S. Bureau of Education study conducted in 1916 found that collegiate-level work was widespread at the 1890 land-grants (Holmes, 1934, p. 52), although technical instruction focused on manual trades more than engineering fields. While funding and personnel limitations can account for this, according to Klein (1930, pp. 876–879), job opportunities and the views of institutional leaders and funding sources about the role of the Negro in American society likely drove the curriculum choices.

Thus, even after World War II, most historically black colleges and universities did not offer much in the way of scientific farming, research science, or engineering and related technical areas because of limited resources (Humphries, 1992, p. 5). The legacy of the establishment of these institutions under stressful and controversial conditions has helped, however, to make them flexible as they developed into the twentieth century. "Black colleges believe in a liberal arts education, but they also insist on the utility of the liberal arts and do not fear to combine them with career education" (Kannerstein, 1978, p. 47). The debate about the right kind of education for African Americans was not unlike that about educating women—were they to remain in their traditional roles or break from them?

While both colleges for women and those for blacks debated curricular issues long before traditional institutions addressed similar ideas, it appears that social, economic, and political conditions drove the changes in older institutions rather than any desire to imitate the marginalized institutions.

Community Colleges—Crossing Categorical Boundaries

For what purpose did community colleges begin? From Harper's University of Chicago perspective (1939), these new institutions were intended for students who might or might not continue to the university. Their purposes were in fact many: to relieve the enrollment of freshmen and sophomores on colleges seeking to become universities, to serve as the bridge between high school and college (the "isthmian" view offered by Koos, 1925), to keep children closer to home (Pedersen, 1994), to support the local economy (Pedersen, 1995), or to provide paths to semiprofessional careers (see Eells, 1941, and Engleman and Eells, 1941).

The new institutions early relinquished their control over curriculum, leaving it to the will of the universities. Koos's 1925 data indicated that, particularly for the public, mostly high-school–linked junior colleges, the goal was to provide for the first two years of college en route to a university degree. By 1965, Blocker, Plummer, and Richardson confirmed that "the college-parallel division offers the least opportunity . . . for experimentation by the junior college" (p. 213). The advocates of junior colleges to serve this function, for example, William Rainey Harper (at the University of Chicago) and William Starr Jordan (at Stanford), were interested in protecting the integrity of the university idea—upper division, specialized work akin to the German universities (see Newman, 1955). As a terminal educational experience, the curriculum tended to mirror the curriculum of baccalaureate colleges for the freshman and sophomore years, building on the work completed in the high schools. Curricular offerings were often determined by local notions of general education and by faculty interests.

Opportunities for innovation, however, were afforded through the expansion of technical and vocational education, community service, and student affairs (Blocker, Plummer, and Richardson, 1965). In fact, from the beginning, the junior colleges responded to the "need of certain vocational and completing courses for the large number of students who can not or should not go to the university" (McDowell, [1919] 1986, p. 77). Occupational areas including education, agriculture, and commerce constituted 25 percent of the courses offered by the fifty colleges included in Koos's 1925 study (pp. 32–33). Thus, unlike any other postsecondary education, the emerging junior colleges combined preprofessional and occupational coursework in the same institution.

Like baccalaureate institutions before them, the junior colleges viewed postsecondary education curriculum as a vehicle for the preparation of citizens. But they also introduced the economic value of postsecondary education—that junior colleges were to assist students in finding and preparing for meaningful employment (see Snyder, 1941, p. 22).

In some community colleges, students were from upper- and upper-middle-class families (Pedersen, 1995). Not until the post–World War II era were the doors fully open, resulting in an exponential increase in the number of colleges (Dougherty, 1994) determined to provide access through proximity and price. Open doors invited a cross-section of students unlike any other colleges in the United States and, likely, the world. The attraction to the community or junior college of different student populations with different expectations for their education provided the opportunity for these colleges to extend the range of curricular offerings. According to Medsker's comprehensive study of community colleges in 1960, "Community colleges of today serve in most cases marginalized students who are too poor, too under-prepared, too unmotivated, or too unsophisticated to attend a baccalaureate institution" (p. 134). Accordingly, the two-year colleges expanded their offerings in developmental (remedial) education, and expanded student services (Engleman and Eells, 1941).

Indeed, one could speculate that the provision of occupational or technical education of the kind offered in the earlier junior colleges—more so than that provided in the early women's and African Americans' colleges—helped make legitimate the provision of occupational, vocational, or semiprofessional programs (see Engleman and Eells, 1941) in four-year colleges. Many programs originating in two-year colleges as terminal programs conferring associate degrees, such as those in business, engineering technology, hotel and restaurant management, and physical therapy (see Eells, 1941), were later expanded to baccalaureate degrees offered by older colleges and universities. Other change influences were operating, too. Consider, for example, the impact of career opportunities in a technologically sophisticated period, and the practical orientation of types of students new to higher education in the United States—minorities and the poor (with the advent of expanded financial aid opportunities through Title IV of the Higher Education Act of 1965 and later amendments).

More than any other institution, the junior college brought to the table the questions raised by institutions seeking to expand the benefits of postsecondary education to more individuals and attempting to find answers to the content, the methods, and the controls for such curriculum. Numbering over 1,300 and serving more than half of college freshmen and sophomores in the United States, the community colleges share a common mission throughout the nation, one that is flexible enough to accommodate locally driven curricula.

Conclusions

The dominant question in the study of curriculum in higher education should be: For what purpose? As has been seen in this chapter, the way in which American higher education chose to respond has been by developing new institutions with different responses to the same question and offering an array of curricula responsive to the choice made. Once the course was charted, once the institution began, each institution and institution type changed; each changed for many reasons, but most importantly because outside pressures—new students, new faculty, new knowledge, and new community (writ large and small) needs for citizens and employees—made their concerns known and the institutions responded. Each new type of institution developed its own curriculum to address unmet needs in society. The pattern is one of increasing practicality, application, relevance, and vocationalism interspersed with frequent calls for serious intellectual inquiry (for example, "The Yale Report of 1828," 1961; Hutchins, 1936; *General Education in a Free Society,* 1945). Further, the desire for academic credibility and higher status (see Altenbaugh and Underwood, 1990, p. 151) moved most single-purpose institutions like the normal schools into the mainstream of higher education, within universities—often by becoming universities—and stressing academic courses over applied courses. Such a synergy between and among higher education institutions is the map on which postsecondary education is drawn in the United States.

While each type remains identifiable, their missions and curricula are less distinct than they were when they were created. The hallmark of American higher education is the diffusion of innovation from institution to institution, from region of the country to region of the country, from institution type to institution type. The competitive spirit is reflected in the search for and adoption of ideas that work to maintain the viability of the institution, to respond to constituents including students, faculty, policy makers, and donors. Although a small number of prestigious liberal arts colleges adhere to a liberal arts curriculum, the vast majority of these colleges have added a variety of career-related curricula such as business, education, or allied health fields that often eclipse the liberal arts. Similarly, the land-grant institutions frequently have extensive liberal arts curricula on their campuses, competing for prestige and students with their traditional applied engineering, mining, and agricultural programs.

What then is the purpose of a higher education and how should we provide that education? The purpose of higher education in the United States has from its very beginning been to prepare learned and mature, resourceful citizens (McGrath, cited in Miller, 1950, p. 12). We have approached the task with incredible creativity and have before us a remarkable array of options for students of all backgrounds and interests.

References

Altenbaugh, R. J., and Underwood, K. "The Evolution of Normal Schools." In J. I. Goodlad, R. Soder, and K. A. Sirotnik (eds.), *Places Where Teachers Are Taught*. San Francisco: Jossey-Bass, 1990.

Barnard, H. *Normal Schools, and Other Institutions, Agencies, and Means Designed for the Professional Education of Teachers. Part 1, United States and British Provinces*. Greeley: Colorado State Teachers College, 1929. (Originally published 1851.)

Barnard, H. "Education." In L. P. Brockett (ed.), *Our Country's Wealth and Influence*. Hartford, Conn.: L. Stebbins, 1882.

Bergquist, W. H., Gould, R. A., and Greenberg, E. M. *Designing Undergraduate Education*. San Francisco: Jossey-Bass, 1981.

Bezilla, M. *Engineering Education at Penn State: A Century in the Land-Grant Tradition*. University Park: Pennsylvania State University Press, 1981.

Blair, L., and Kuhn, M. *A Short History of Michigan State*. East Lansing: Michigan State College Press, 1955.

Blocker, C. E., Plummer, R. H., and Richardson, R. C., Jr. *The Two-Year College: A Social Synthesis*. Englewood Cliffs, N.J.: Prentice Hall, 1965.

Boorstin, D. J. *Americans: The Colonial Experience*. New York: Random House, 1958.

Browning, J.E.S., and Williams, J. B. "History and Goals of Black Institutions of Higher Learning." In C. V. Willie and R. R. Edmonds (eds.), *Black Colleges in America: Challenge, Development, Survival*. New York: Teachers College Press, 1978.

Brubacher, J. S., and Rudy, W. *Higher Education in Transition: A History of American Colleges and Universities, 1636–1976.* (3rd ed.) New York: HarperCollins, 1976.

Burke, C. B. *American Collegiate Populations: A Test of the Traditional View.* New York: New York University Press, 1982.

Cohen, S. "Charles W. Eliot on the Education of Women (1869)." In S. Cohen (ed.), *Education in the United States: A Documentary History.* Vol. 3. New York: Random House, 1974.

Cutler, C. "Shall women now be excluded from Adelbert College of Western Reserve University?" An argument presented to the Board of Trustees, Nov. 7, 1884.

Dougherty, K. *The Contradictory College: The Conflicting Origins, Impacts, and Futures of the Community College.* Albany: State University of New York Press, 1994.

Du Bois, W.E.B. "The Talented Tenth (1903)." In S. Cohen (ed.), *Education in the United States: A Documentary History.* Vol. 4. New York: Random House, 1974.

Dyer, T. G. *The University of Georgia: A Centennial History.* Athens: University of Georgia Press, 1985.

Eells, W. C. *Present Status of Junior College Terminal Education.* Terminal Education Monograph No. 2. Washington, D.C.: American Association of Junior Colleges, 1941.

"Emma Willard on the Education of Women (1819)." In S. Cohen (ed.), *Education in the United States: A Documentary History.* Vol. 3. New York: Random House, 1974.

Engleman, L., and Eells, W. C. *The Literature of Junior College Terminal Education.* Terminal Education Monograph #1. Washington, D.C.: American Association of Junior Colleges, 1941.

"First Annual Circular of the State Normal School at New Britain." In H. Barnard, *Normal Schools, and Other Institutions, Agencies, and Means Designed for the Professional Education of Teachers. Part 1, United States and British Provinces.* Greeley: Colorado State Teachers College, 1929. (Originally published 1851.)

Fosdick, R. B. *Adventure in Giving: The Story of the General Education Board.* New York: Harper-Collins, 1962.

General Education in a Free Society. Report of the Harvard Committee. Cambridge, Mass.: Harvard University Press, 1945.

Gilman, D. C. "The Launching of a University." In J. C. Stone and D. P. DeNevi (eds.), *Portrait of the American University, 1890–1910.* San Francisco: Jossey-Bass, 1971.

Gruber, C. S. *Mars and Minerva.* Baton Rouge: Louisiana State University Press, 1975.

Harcleroad, F. F., Sagen, H. B., and Molen, C. T., Jr. *The Developing State Colleges and Universities: Historical Background, Current Status, and Future Plans.* Iowa City, Iowa: American College Testing Program, 1969.

Harper, C. A. *A Century of Public Teacher Education.* Washington, D.C.: National Education Association, 1939.

Hawkins, H. "The University-Builders Observe the College." *The History of Education Quarterly,* 1971, *11,* 353–362.

Hedgepath, C. M., Jr., Edmonds, R. R., and Craig, A. "Overview." In C. V. Willie and R. R. Edmonds (eds.), *Black Colleges in America: Challenge, Development, Survival.* New York: Teachers College Press, 1978.

Hefelbower, S. G. *The History of Gettysburg College: 1832–1932.* Gettysburg, Pa.: Gettysburg College, 1932.

"Henry Barnard on German Teachers (1835)." In S. Cohen (ed.), *Education in the United States: A Documentary History.* Vol. 2. New York: Random House, 1974.

Hoeveler, D. J., Jr. "The University and the Social Gospel: The Intellectual Origins of the

'Wisconsin Idea.'" In L. F. Goodchild and H. S. Wechsler. *ASHE Reader on the History of Higher Education*. New York: Ginn Press, 1989.

Hofstadter, R., and Hardy, C. D. *Development and Scope of Higher Education in the United States*. New York: Columbia University Press, 1952.

Holmes, D.O.W. *The Evolution of the Negro College. Contributions to Education, No. 609*. New York: Bureau of Publications, Teachers College, Columbia University, 1934.

Horowitz, H. L. *Alma Mater*. Boston: Beach Press, 1984.

Humphries, F. "Land-Grant Institutions: Their Struggle for Survival and Equality." In R. D. Christy and L. Williamson (eds.), *A Century of Service. Land-Grant Colleges and Universities, 1890–1990*. New Brunswick, N.J.: Transaction Press, 1992.

Hutchins, R. M. *The Higher Learning in America*. New Haven, Conn.: Yale University Press, 1936.

"Josiah Holbrook's Proposal for a Constitution for the American Lyceum (1828)." In S. Cohen (ed.), *Education in the United States: A Documentary History*. Vol. 2. New York: Random House, 1974.

Kannerstein, G. "Black Colleges: Self-Concept." In C. V. Willie and R. R. Edmonds (eds.), *Black Colleges in America: Challenge, Development, Survival*. New York: Teachers College Press, 1978.

Karabel, J. "Community Colleges and Social Stratification." *Harvard Educational Review*, 1972, *42*(4), 521–562.

Klein, A. J. *Survey of Land-Grant Colleges and Universities*. Bulletin No. 9, Vol. 1. Washington, D.C.: U.S. Government Printing Office, 1930.

Koos, L. V. *The Junior-College Movement*. New York: Ginn Press, 1925.

Lang, D. W. "The People's College, the Mechanics of Mutual Protection and the Agricultural College Act." In L. F. Goodchild and H. S. Wechsler, *ASHE Reader on the History of Higher Education*. New York: Ginn Press, 1989.

Levine, D. O. *The American College and the Culture of Aspiration, 1915–1940*. Ithaca: Cornell University Press, 1986.

Mayhew, L. B., and Ford, P. J. *Changing the Curriculum*. San Francisco: Jossey-Bass, 1971.

McDowell, F. M. *The Junior College*. U.S. Department of the Interior, Bureau of Education Bulletin 1919, No. 35. Washington, D.C.: U.S. Government Printing Office, 1919. In T. Diener, *Growth of an American Invention: A Documentary History of the Junior and Community College Movement*. New York: Greenwood Press, 1986.

Medsker, L. *The Junior College*. New York: McGraw-Hill, 1960.

Mill, J. S. "Inaugural Address, University of St. Andrews (Scotland), February 1, 1867." Cited in R. Thomas, *The Search for a Common Learning: General Education, 1800–1960*. New York: McGraw-Hill, 1962.

Miller, R. D. (ed.). *General Education at Mid-Century: A Critical Analysis*. Proceedings of the Conference on General Education, sponsored by the Florida State University and Department of Higher Education, National Education Association of the United States. Tallahassee, Florida, Nov. 21–23, 1950.

Morison, S. E. *Three Centuries of Harvard: 1636–1936*. Cambridge, Mass.: Harvard University Press, 1937.

Mrozek, D. J. *Sport and American Mentality, 1880–1910*. Knoxville: University of Tennessee Press, 1983.

National Center for Education Statistics. *The Traditionally Black Institutions of Higher Education: Their Development and Status, 1860 to 1982*. Historical Report NCES–302–85. Washington, D.C.: National Center for Education Statistics, 1985. (ED 258 506)

Newman, J. H. Select Discourses from *The Idea of a University.* London: Syndics of the Cambridge University Press, 1955.

Palmieri, P. *"Incipit Vita Nuova:* Founding Ideals of the Wellesley College Community." *History of Higher Education,* 1983, *3,* 59–78.

Pedersen, R. T. "Value Conflict on the Community College Campus: An Examination of Its Historical Roots." In A. M. Hoffman and D. J. Julius (eds.), *Managing Community and Junior Colleges: Perspectives for the Next Century.* Washington, D.C.: College and University Personnel Association, 1994.

Pedersen, R. T. Unpublished manuscript, 1995.

"President Francis Wayland of Brown University Calls for Reform of American Colleges (1842)." In S. Cohen, ed., *Education in the United States. A Documentary History.* Vol. 2. New York: Random House, 1974.

Richardson, J. M. *A History of Fisk University, 1865–1946.* University: University of Alabama Press, 1980.

Robson, D. W. "College Founding in the New Republic, 1776–1800." *History of Education Quarterly,* 1983, *23*(3), 323–341.

Rudolph, F. *Curriculum: A History of the American Undergraduate Course of Study Since 1636.* San Francisco: Jossey-Bass, 1977.

Rudolph, F. *The American College and University: A History.* Athens: University of Georgia Press, 1990.

"Samuel Read Hall's Teacher-Training Course at Phillips Andover Academy." From *American Journal of Education,* 1837, *V,* p. 379.

Schmidt, G. P. *The Liberal Arts College: A Chapter in American Cultural History.* New Brunswick, N.J.: Rutgers University Press, 1957.

Smith, E. "Before and After Brown: Education Context of Change." In *Brown v. Board of Education of Topeka: An Assessment Thirty Years Later.* Speech presented at Institute, West Virginia, Feb. 10–11 and Apr. 11–13, 1984. (ED 264 348)

Snyder, W. H. "Curriculum Development." In L. Engleman and W. C. Eells (eds.), *The Literature of Junior College Terminal Education.* Terminal Education Monograph #1. Washington, D.C.: American Association of Junior Colleges, 1941.

Solomon, B. M. *In the Company of Educated Women.* New Haven, Conn.: Yale University Press, 1985.

Steffens, L. "Sending a State to College: What the University of Wisconsin Is Doing for Its People." In J. C. Stone and D. P. DeNevi (eds.), *Portrait of the American University, 1890–1910.* San Francisco: Jossey-Bass, 1971.

Townsend, L. "The Gender Effect: The Early Curricula of Beloit College and Rockford Female Seminary." *History of Higher Education Annual,* 1990, *10,* 69–90.

True, A. C. *A History of Agricultural Education in the United States: 1785–1925.* U.S. Department of Agriculture, Misc. Pub. No. 36. Washington, D.C.: U.S. Government Printing Office, 1929.

Veysey, L. *The Emergence of the American University.* Chicago: University of Chicago Press, 1965.

Wasserman, J. "Wisconsin Normal Schools and the Educational Hierarchy, 1860–1890." In E. Rutkowski (ed.), *The Papers and Proceedings of the Combined Annual Meetings of the Midwest History of Education Society and the History of Education Society,* Chicago, Oct. 27–29, 1978, pp. 3–10.

Williamson, H. F., and Wild, P. S. *Northwestern University: A History. 1850–1975.* Evanston, Ill.: Northwestern University, 1976.

"The Yale Report of 1828." In R. Hofstadter and W. Smith (eds.), *American Higher Education: A Documentary History.* Vol. 1. Chicago: University of Chicago Press, 1961.

CHAPTER THREE

KEY TURNING POINTS IN
THE EVOLVING CURRICULUM

Arthur Levine, Jana Nidiffer

The current pattern of American undergraduate education is a result of almost 2,500 years of historical evolution. The roots of our higher education, however, stem mostly from ancient Greece and Rome, the Middle East, and what is currently defined as Western Europe. In general, developments in Asia have had little impact on this country because the Eastern and Western traditions have not intermingled. If they had, our system of higher education might look quite different.

The first formal schools of higher learning or advanced education existed in fifth-century-B.C. Athens. Education flourished in Greece to such an extent that Rome imported the Greek system of higher learning, including Greek language instruction. Throughout its history, Rome followed closely the model of higher education in the earlier Hellenic culture. The primary difference was that Roman higher education was more closely tied to the state than Greek higher education, which was generally a private enterprise.

With the decline of the Roman Empire in the fifth century A.D., scholarship in Western Europe was eclipsed until the end of the ninth century. Much of the literature of antiquity was lost to the West either through neglect or barbarian destruction. The center of intellectual activity shifted to Constantinople and the Arab world. It was not until the twelfth century that the scholarship of the Byzantines and Muslims—and many of the lost classics that had been preserved in the universities of Constantinople and the Arab world—made their way to western Europe through Spain and southern Italy.

During this period of decline, the principal institutions for higher learning in Western Europe were the monasteries and the schools associated with cathedrals. In A.D. 789, Charlemagne decreed that every Frankish cathedral and monastery should establish a school for the education of both clergy and laymen. In northern Europe, cathedral schools became the intellectual centers, and in southern Europe private schools served this function. Students gathered around cathedral schools and great teachers, attracting additional teachers and more students. Out of these groupings, called *studium generale,* the first universities developed during the renaissance of the twelfth century.

Bologna and Paris were the most famous of the early medieval universities. Both emphasized advanced degree preparation, notably in law and theology, respectively. In England, Oxford University was modeled on Paris (established seven decades earlier), but it placed greater emphasis on the arts and bachelor's curriculum than either Paris or Bologna. A second English university, founded at Cambridge by Oxford faculty and students, continued this undergraduate emphasis. By the thirteenth century, many of the major features of contemporary higher education had emerged, including degrees, faculties, colleges, courses, examinations, and commencement, although there were no endowments in the current sense, no laboratories, and (with rare exceptions) no university libraries or university-owned buildings. By the seventeenth century, at the time of the colonization of North America, most of the countries of Europe had established universities on this medieval model.

The first American college was founded in 1636 by the General Court of Massachusetts. It was modeled after Emmanuel College, one of the many collegiate units at Cambridge University, but was by no means a replica of that institution. By the time of the Revolutionary War, more than fifteen colleges had been founded, nine of which survive.

The colonial college was a teaching institution whose mission was narrow in scope and relatively unambiguous. It sought to impart to students a basic body of classical knowledge and useful intellectual skills. The students were by and large the elite of colonial society. When they finished college, they had learned the culture of their class, had been taught the morality of the Christian world, were prepared to assume socially prestigious vocations (often as clergymen), and would as a result enjoy the fruits of colonial life. Many elements of undergraduate education of that period can be found in present-day colleges, including the bachelor of arts and master's degrees, a four-year course of study, general education, prescribed programs of study, dormitory living and residential education, a concern for character, and a commitment to the principle of *in loco parentis,* the last of which is now virtually relegated to history.

Countries other than England also had major influences on American higher education. The Scottish impact was first felt early in the eighteenth century, as Scottish doctors and scientists emigrated to the colonies and as Americans studied medicine at the University of Edinburgh. Scottish contacts encouraged American colleges to offer instruction in more practical subjects such as medicine, to expand existing courses and programs of study in the natural sciences, and to experiment further with laboratory research and inductive logic.

From France came the Enlightenment in all its glory. France touched a sympathetic chord in the United States not only for being an ally in the American Revolution but also with its own revolutionary war thirteen years later. The French added to the Scottish contribution in science, research, and professional education. They pioneered the study of modern language and teacher education. France also influenced America with its literature on political theory and its revolutionary, antireligious spirit, which was at least briefly popular among college students in the United States. The concepts of the French philosophers influenced Thomas Jefferson's proposal for the radical experiment in university education introduced at the University of Virginia.

A fourth country influencing higher education in America was Germany. By the early nineteenth century, the intellectual movement known as modernism was taking root in the universities in Germany and elsewhere in Europe. Modernism represented a profound change in how intellectuals perceived the nature of knowledge: from something that was divinely revealed with perhaps magical qualities to something that could be discovered based on empiricism. As a result, new fields of knowledge were more rapidly introduced into the university curriculum, the role of the professor began its shift from teacher to researcher, and the belief that there was one single core of knowledge that every educated person should know began to wane. The introduction of new disciplines and the changing role of the faculty produced confusion in American higher education in the first part of the nineteenth century. The classical curriculum came under attack and was staunchly defended by the faculty of Yale in 1828. Nevertheless, new types of institutions teaching new types of students, and emphasizing studies other than classical, gradually appeared on the American landscape.

Nineteenth-century Americans, intrigued by the changes in Europe, began to go to Germany for advanced study. Upon completion of their studies, they usually returned to the United States to seek college faculty positions. The major German contribution to American higher education thus involved accelerating the development of graduate education and cementing the role of research in the university. Other features of contemporary American higher education that originated in Germany are the organization of the faculty and the curriculum according to

academic disciplines, the major or concentration, academic freedom, wide latitude for students in choosing courses, scholarly library collections, theses, laboratory courses, and seminar instruction.

Once fully integrated into the American college—by the late nineteenth
century—the blend of British, Scottish, French, and German influences combined
with America's own Jeffersonian democratic ideals to produce in the twentieth century a new conception of college education based upon meritocratic standards.
Students were less frequently admitted to college simply because they were the
socially elite but more often because they represented the intellectually most capable of society. The students at a particular institution learned a basic body of
knowledge, but it was no longer the classical colonial curriculum, nor was it thought
to be an all-inclusive body of knowledge. Ironically, by the early twentieth century,
there was less furor about the nature and mission of higher education than in the
early nineteenth century. Although there was a panoply of new institutional models by the early part of this century—including community colleges, normal schools,
liberal arts colleges, technical institutes, and major research universities—a growing acceptance (albeit a reluctant one by many) that a college education would mean
different things to different students began to emerge. More emphasis was placed
on the development of intellectual skills so that college graduates would be able to
keep up with an expanding body of information and facts. Moral training and education for personal growth became less prominent in the college. After graduation,
the student was still able to obtain a good job, usually outside the clergy, that would
enable him or her to enjoy the good life of the society.

Another important element in the development of the American college was
a commitment to serve the needs of the public. Historians disagree about how
well the earliest American college fulfilled this need and even about whether the
college was a popular institution, but it is known that when Andrew Jackson assumed the presidency in 1828, popular feeling about higher education and the
value of its program was declining. By the 1850s, enrollments were decreasing not
only in proportion to the population but in absolute numbers. The rationale generally offered for these declines, which lasted until the end of the Civil War, is that
the colleges were failing to meet the public need for utilitarian instruction. Since
that time, a number of events, including the 1862 Morrill Land-Grant Act, the
birth of the Wisconsin Idea in 1904, and the 1947 Report of the President's Commission on Higher Education, as well as the Higher Education Act of 1965, have
made public service a central mission of American higher education. As a result
of that mission, contemporary colleges and universities engage in field study
and experimentation; offer extension, correspondence, and off-campus study; provide technical, vocational, and recreational courses; maintain a close relationship
with business and government; and undertake research on social problems.

One outcome of this collegiate commitment to serve public needs, in combination with free secondary education and compulsory high school attendance laws, has been a growth in the proportion of the population attending college. With this development has come an acceptance of mass access to higher education and a movement toward universal access, making admission to colleges and universities now potentially available to all in the society who desire it. As a result, the notion that there is a single body of knowledge that all educated people must possess moved from grudging acceptance to complete untenability in the face of the large number of services higher education now offers and the diversity of learner needs and interests. Moreover, the kinds of skills taught vary from student to student, and from the three Rs (reading, writing, and arithmetic), to practical technical and vocational skills, to more abstract research skills.

Interest in personal development has increased in importance. However, the growth in the proportion of college graduates in society throughout the twentieth century has meant that the graduates must compete harder for a relatively smaller pool of good jobs and are consequently not assured of the good life merely by a college degree. Although college graduation still has a positive effect on a student's lifetime earnings and the real wages of individuals with only a high school diploma are declining, college is no longer the guarantee it was once perceived to be.

But higher education is changing yet again in the last part of this century and the sources of tension and stress on institutions are many and growing. Spiraling costs are making higher education less accessible to the poor and causing middle-class students to forfeit college choice. To cut costs, many colleges and universities are downsizing, reducing their faculty, cutting services, and paring academic programs. The once-accepted notion that each institution can render the full range of curriculum offerings seems less realistic.

In the past decade, there has been many a criticism of higher education in the national conversation. High costs, low levels of productivity, and neglect of teaching are chief among the reproaches. The curriculum is also under attack from many quarters, both intellectual and political. Some critics argue that the curriculum has lost coherence and charge that higher education should again define a core body of knowledge based on a traditional canon. This core should be the centerpiece of undergraduate education. Others argue for a more inclusive curriculum reflecting the multicultural nature of contemporary American society. The scholarship of the last quarter century in women's studies, black studies, Asian studies, Third World studies, and other perspectives is seeking more inclusion in the curriculum. The intellectual movement of postmodernism, coming approximately a century and a half after modernism held sway, is again challenging the very nature of knowledge creation. The postmodernists are seeking to change some fundamental assumptions in the disciplines—even in the sciences, which are often viewed as exempt from philosophical and political critique. As a result of these pressures, the curriculum has become a battleground.

In sum, over the past almost 360 years, higher education in the United States has developed through a process of addition or accretion. The Scottish, French, and German influences and the American commitment to service and utilitarianism have supplemented the functions of the colonial English college rather than replacing them. New functions, new subjects, new intellectual currents, new modes of instruction, new courses and settings, and new clienteles have been added to the old, resulting in the most comprehensive and diverse educational institutions yet developed: multiversities and multiple-purpose colleges rather than the unitary institutions of old. But the era of unchecked growth has come to an end. Higher education, now a mature rather than expanding industry, is seeking to find the best model for meeting the student needs of the early twenty-first century.

Antecedents of American Higher Education

This chronology traces the development of Western higher education into the seventeenth century, ending with the founding of Harvard.

532–500 B.C.   Pythagoras teaches philosophy to a group of disciples organized as a quasi-religious community. The disciples are admitted on a probationary status and are required to observe a silence varying from two to five years. Diet and clothing are also restricted. The Pythagoreans become active in public affairs in what is now southern Italy. The Pythagorean philosophy is not particularly popular in Athens, and the Pythagorean school dies out in the fourth century B.C.

460 B.C.   Hippocrates is born on the Greek island of Cos. During his lifetime, he writes more than seventy books on medicine, and Cos becomes one of the earliest centers for medical training, which is carried on in an apprenticeship fashion.

445 B.C.   Protagoras becomes one of the first Sophists. The Sophists are commercial Athenian philosophers who train students in the two practical skills needed for politics—dialectic (persuasion) and rhetoric (oratory). They are credited with originating the public lecture. The Sophists are criticized by Plato, Isocrates, and Socrates for their cynical, pragmatic approach to life. Other well-known Sophists include Gorgias and Prodicus.

425 B.C.   Socrates (470–399 B.C.), considered a gadfly about Athens, preaches a philosophy that virtue is knowledge, utilizing a question-and-answer pedagogy that has since come to be called the *Socratic method*. Socrates has no school, accepts no student fees, and offers no classes. Instead, he engages in daily public discussions with any who will respond to his questioning. In 399 B.C., he is condemned by an Athenian jury and executed for impiety and corrupting the young.

390 B.C.   Isocrates establishes a school of higher learning. The curriculum is five to six years in length and includes gymnastics, music, literature, history, philosophy, and, in a student's final years of study, rhetoric. The program is more academic than that of the Sophists and more practical than that of Plato, whose teaching is described in the next section. Isocrates accepts any student who can pay the tuition. His students come from Athens as well as abroad.

387 B.C.   Plato, a student of Socrates, establishes the Academy near Athens. The Academy, a religious association dedicated to the Muses, consists of a small piece of land containing a garden, a home for Plato, and small huts constructed by students. The Academy offers instruction in gymnastics, music, poetry, literature, mathematics, and philosophy. The curriculum is based on Plato's philosophy of society as described in *The Republic,* in which Plato identified three primary classes in Athenian society—artisans, soldiers, and philosophers. Higher education—that is, education for those seventeen years of age and older—is concerned with the training of both soldiers and men of public affairs. Ages seventeen to twenty are spent on military instruction. Mathematics is studied from ages twenty to thirty. Ages thirty to thirty-five are spent in the study of philosophy. Each more advanced subject is used to screen out those unfit for further study. It is expected that the individuals ultimately studying philosophy will be few in number, and those performing best would ideally be the rulers of the society. The Academy ceases operation in A.D. 529.

335 B.C.   Aristotle, the teacher of Alexander the Great, establishes the Lyceum near Athens. The Lyceum is more empirical than Plato's Academy. Aristotle divides education into three life stages. From birth through pubescence, education focuses on physical development. From puberty to seventeen, the student studies music, mathematics, grammar, literature, and geography. This combination of mathematics and literature is referred to as *enkuklios paideia,* a general education preparatory for the study of philosophy. Education from seventeen on includes military training and study of the biological and physical sciences, ethics, rhetoric, and philosophy. In the mornings Aristotle lectures to a small, select group in advanced problems of philosophy. In the afternoons he instructs larger groups on more popular topics in the subject of rhetoric. Aristotle popularizes a technique used earlier by Protagoras—presenting a thesis and arguing each side in turn. Under Aristotle's leadership, the Lyceum also engages in scientific and historical research. The school continues operation until approximately A.D. 200.

330–314 B.C.   Xenocrates, the director of Plato's Academy, requires that students complete the *enkuklios paideia* prior to entrance.

308 B.C.   Zeno develops the stoic philosophy. The name is taken from the place where he customarily lectures—the *stoa pokile* or painted colonnade. The stoic philosophy emphasizes peace of mind and moral worth, both of which, according to Zeno, require avoidance of excesses.

306 B.C.   Epicurus establishes a small school called the Kepos, or garden. The school is based upon a philosophy called epicureanism, which emphasizes simple pleasures, relaxation, and friendship.

c. 280 B.C.   The Museum, an institute for advanced studies, is founded in Alexandria, Egypt, by Ptolemy I or Ptolemy II. Though not intended as a school, the Museum's scholars in philosophy, rhetoric, medicine, and literature attract disciples. The scholars are free from taxes and receive free meals at a common table. Associated with the Museum is the largest library in the world, which at its peak contains at least 200,000 volumes. The Museum endures for over five centuries, failing sometime before A.D. 300.

200–100 B.C.   The Ephebia, Athenian institutions for compulsory military training for men between the ages of eighteen and twenty, are transformed into finishing schools for the wealthy. Literary and scientific studies enter the curriculum. Foreigners are admitted.

First century B.C.   Dionysius of Halicarnassus complains that Greek higher education fosters premature specialization. Some students begin to specialize in rhetoric even before completing the *enkuklios paideia* or general education.

92 B.C.   Platus Gallus establishes a Latin school of rhetoric in Rome. Until this time, rhetoric, considered the most prestigious of subjects, was generally taught in the Greek language by Greeks. When expansion brought Rome into contact with Greece, Rome imported the teachers, pedagogies, and forms of education of the richer Hellenic culture. Rhetoric continued to be taught in Greek because much of the literature had not been translated into Latin, because Greek was considered an international language, and because knowledge of Greek was a sign of culture in Rome. In fact, few Roman Latin-language schools were even established in less popular subjects such as medicine, science, and philosophy.

55–46 B.C.   Cicero is active in shaping Roman higher education. Among his accomplishments are three classic works on oratory—*De Oratore, Brutus,* and *Orator*—in which he surveys oratorical principles and practices. Cicero, who studied academic, epicurean, and stoic philosophy, also serves as a conduit in transmitting

Greek philosophy to Rome. As a result, he is credited with bringing to Rome the rudimentary vocabulary of philosophy.

50–25 B.C. Varro, a Roman scholar, describes the *disciplinae liberae* (liberal arts) as grammar, rhetoric, and dialectic (the *trivium*); arithmetic, music, geometry, and astronomy (the *quadrivium*); and medicine and architecture. The *disciplinae liberae* is the Roman formulation of the *enkuklios paideia* adopted from Greece.

A.D. *51* Paul, the apostle of Jesus, lectures throughout the Mediterranean on the philosophy of Christianity.

69–79 Roman Emperor Vespasian establishes the equivalent of endowed chairs in rhetoric in both Greek and Latin at the University of Athens. Throughout this century, numerous schools of rhetoric are founded in Rome. Perhaps the most famous is Quintilian's school, which teaches geometry, arithmetic, astronomy, and music. The last three to four years at the school are spent in the study of rhetoric.

100 Two law schools are established in Rome. The schools of law, which had no Greek precursor, grow out of apprenticeships to which Cicero is credited with adding theoretical expositions.

177–178 Emperor Hadrian establishes the University of Rome.

179 Pantaenus becomes head of the Catechetical School of Alexandria. Catechetical schools offer instruction culminating in baptism, which is necessary for admission into the church. The catechetical schools resemble the Pythagorean school. For example, the Alexandria School offers a program based on the Greek curriculum that includes philosophy and the *enkuklios paideia*.

224–651 The Academy of Gondeshapur is established in Persia. The Academy's curriculum includes philosophy, astronomy, ethics, theology, law, finance, religion, medicine, and government. It is through this institution that a number of the Greek classics in science and mathematics reach the Arab world and subsequently are transmitted to Western scholars. Byzantine scholars are credited with preserving the majority of the classics.

300–400 Medical education is first available in Latin.

328–373 Athanasius brings monasticism to Rome. Monasteries permit groups of people to follow the ascetic life by isolating themselves from temporal concerns and devoting themselves to religion. Christian monasteries have some of the same characteristics as the philosophical schools of Greece. In fact, early Christians refer to their beliefs as philosophy, and words like *secta*, *haeresis*, and *cathedra* or *thronos* are adopted from the vocabulary of the Greek philosophical schools.

334   Emperor Constantine requires that students of architecture be at least eighteen years old and have completed the study of the liberal arts.

354   The catechetical schools are first governed by common rules or canons.

361   Emperor Julian forbids Christians to teach in schools of rhetoric and grammar because they do not honor the gods of the men whose writings are being taught.

410–427   Martianus Capella writes *The Marriage of Philosophy and Mercury,* in which he summarizes the state of knowledge of his age. Capella offers what is considered an all-inclusive treatment of the seven liberal arts, which consist of the *trivium* and *quadrivium.* His book is a popular medieval text. At the time Capella writes, Western European scholarship has already entered a four-century eclipse. During this period, much of the literature of antiquity is lost. Centers of advanced intellectual activity are found in Constantinople, Persia, and the Arab world.

425   Theodosius II creates the University of Constantinople. The university has thirty-one faculty members in grammar, rhetoric, philosophy, and law. Grammar and rhetoric are taught in both Latin and Greek. The university operates with lapses until 1453.

460   Lawyers must pass an examination in law before they can practice in Roman courts.

493–526   Theodoric encourages a brief revival of education in Italy. There are law schools in Rome and schools of grammar and rhetoric in Milan. Boethius becomes famous as a teacher of logic, metaphysics, and ethics.

500–599   Children bound for the priesthood are required by the church to go to schools under the control of a bishop. As a result, the catechetical schools are replaced by schools with larger teaching staffs, greater physical plants, and direct bishop's control. They are called cathedral schools, and are one of two primary sources of education during the period of scholarly decline following the fall of Rome. The other is the monastery.

529   Benedict, a senator, leaves Rome in the wake of a scandal to seek a solitary, penitent life. His spiritual example attracts others and leads to the creation of the Benedictine order. Benedictines devote seven hours each day to labor—generally manual labor, though literary work is possible. Another two to five hours each day are spent in reading. As a result, monasteries founded by the Benedictine order and other monasteries like them become the principal agencies for the training of scholars, for copying and preserving literature, for disseminating new manuscripts, and for collecting libraries. Most monasteries, however, emphasize study as a means of discipline, not as an end in itself; the scholarship of monks is concerned almost entirely with the scriptures and theological writing; many monks are uneducated; and many monasteries pay little or no attention to learning.

750–1100 For approximately 350 years, Muslims build universities that are outstanding institutions for advanced studies of their day. They include Nizamiyah and Mustansiriyah in Baghdad and Cordoba, Toledo, and Granada universities in Spain. The schools offer both vocational and professional programs.

789 Charlemagne decrees that all Frankish monasteries and cathedrals should have schools for the education of clergy and orders that education also be provided for laymen. This results in the expansion of the number of educational institutions and improvement in the quality of the existing schools. The cathedral schools—which are more often located in urban areas, more willing to admit nonclerics, and more inclined to expand the curriculum beyond the narrowly ascetic subjects—become the centers of scholarly ferment leading to the formation of universities.

980 Gerbert of Aurillac (c. 945–1003), an instructor at the cathedral school at Rheims, is credited with reviving the study of mathematics. The curriculum at Rheims consists of grammar, followed by dialectic and rhetoric, and then the *quadrivium.* Cathedral schools like Rheims are built around great scholars who teach with the approval of (or, more correctly, a license from) the local bishop. There are few cathedral schools in southern Europe, and as a result nonchurch schools develop in the south.

c. 1000 Bishop Fulbert (c. 960–1028) establishes the cathedral school at Chartres. He is appointed by Gerbert, now Pope Sylvester II. Fulbert's field of study is medicine, an area in which Chartres already has a considerable reputation. With the possible exception of the cathedral school in Orleans, Chartres is credited with offering the most complete and thorough program of classical studies of all the cathedral schools during the early twelfth century. The curriculum at Chartres expands upon the classical *trivium* and *quadrivium,* utilizes previously proscribed works of the pagan Greeks and Romans, and provides no instruction in theology as a field of study. Bernard and Therry are among the best known of the Chartres teachers of this era.

1053–1080 Guibert of Nogents, an unhappy student, complains of the paucity of grammar instructors in the larger cities. The number of teachers is few and their quality is poor. By the early 1100s, the subject flourishes and schools are so numerous that anyone with money can study grammar if he chooses.

1099   Abélard starts a school near Paris. His reputation as a teacher and his great differences in philosophy from William of Champeaux of the Paris cathedral school make Paris an intellectual center for students. Abélard attracts thousands of students. In fact, estimates (which are probably exaggerated) indicate that he draws as many as thirty thousand students. The presence of large numbers of students draws additional teachers to Paris as well. The combination results in the creation of the University of Paris in the mid-twelfth century. The cathedral school of Chartres, only fifty miles away, pales as an intellectual center as Paris grows in stature.

1100   The University of Salerno is well known across Europe. Its fame is spread by knights returning from the crusades. Salerno has been a medical center for at least three hundred years, but it is credited with becoming the first Western European university when a school for the teaching of medicine is specifically created. The staff is composed of monks, and the curriculum consists of the surviving classic works in medicine, including those of Galen, Hippocrates, and Isaac Judeus.

c. 1100   The University of Bologna is the first formally organized university in non-Muslim Europe. Its prior history is much like that of Paris. The great educational repute of Bologna as a city attracted large numbers of students, causing an influx of instructors to teach them. The University of Bologna emphasizes the study of civil and canon law. Irnerius (1067–1138) is credited with establishing the law school. Bologna also has a lesser arts curriculum concentrating upon the *trivium*. Grammar and rhetoric are cognate subjects that must be mastered before a student can study the law. Forty-eight months of study are required to earn the bachelor's or first arts degree. Late in the thirteenth century, Bologna adds a faculty in medicine. Theology, the other common faculty in medieval universities, is never established. Unlike other universities of this period, Bologna is largely controlled by its adult students, not its faculty. Students determine even matters of lecture organization. Faculty are charged fines for violating student-centered rules of classroom discipline, including being absent and giving a lecture attended by five or fewer students. Control of graduation and admission standards is left to faculty, however. Beginning in the early thirteenth century, successive popes wrest control of the university governance from both faculty and students.

1150   The great University of Paris, built from three cathedral schools, is formally organized. Paris develops faculties in canon law, theology, and arts. The pope prohibits the study of civil law, common at other schools, viewing Paris as a religious institution. In fact, Paris is best known for its school of theology. An arts curriculum is a prerequisite for study in theology, canon law, and medicine. A student can enter the arts faculty at age twelve as long as he is able to read, write, and speak

Latin. The average age of entrance is fifteen or sixteen, however. Six years of study are required to earn the first arts degree—master of arts. During these six years a student studies under several scholars, defends a thesis, becomes a bachelor or apprentice teacher, continues his studies under a master, and passes a public examination. The basic arts curriculum emphasizes Latin, logic, and grammar. There is no science or laboratory study, nor is the whole of the classical *trivium* and *quadrivium* found at Paris. Few books are available for study. There are three primary forms of instruction—lectures by licensed teachers or masters, informal lectures by bachelors and other nonlicensed teachers, and reviews in student lodgings.

1167   English scholars forced to leave France for political reasons congregate in Oxford, a small school town near London. The original Oxford program is a copy of the Paris program. In time, the *quadrivium* and modern French are adopted. The undergraduate or arts faculty is preeminent rather than the graduate faculty.

1180   The first recorded residence officially associated with a university is established by Josse de Lordes of Paris to serve as lodging for eighteen poor scholars. The creation of this *"College de Dix-Huit"* marks the beginning of collegiate education that links the living situation with learning. By 1500 there are sixty-eight colleges.

1209   Three thousand students are in attendance at Oxford, but following the hanging of three students by local townspeople, there is a mass exodus to Cambridge. As the early medieval university has no buildings of its own, such moves or threats thereof are frequent. Classrooms are usually located in a teacher's home or in rented halls.

1214   At the demand of the pope, who views universities as church colonies, King John decrees that the town of Oxford atone financially and physically for the Oxford hangings. The itinerant scholars, no longer fearing local headhunters, return.

1215   The first fully prescribed arts curriculum is required at Paris.

1231   Frederick II forbids the practice or teaching of medicine anywhere within his empire by anyone without a license from the University of Salerno. He specifies a minimum period of study and an arts course prior to medical study.

1260   Sir John de Balliol, as a penance required by the church, establishes the first Oxford residential college.

1264   Walter de Merton establishes the first college at Oxford not intended solely as housing for indigent students. He grants it large landholdings, scholarship aid, and an administrative staff.

1266   Roger Bacon, a Franciscan monk and one of the best-known teachers of the Middle Ages, lectures at Oxford. He rejects the methodology of scholasticism, the principal way of discovering the truth during the Middle Ages. *Scholasticism* is characterized by employment of the dialectic, a form of logic that involves disputation or discrimination of truth from error in matters of opinion. Bacon favors a precursor of modern scientific method, emphasizing experimentation and observation. He also applauds the study of modern language. For these departures from tradition, Bacon is subsequently jailed for twelve years despite his devotion to Christian principles.

1300   European traffic in scholarly Muslim works ceases as political conditions bring a decline in Islamic scholarship. For more than a hundred years prior to this time, Muslim scholarship has been an important source of new books and knowledge for Western European scholars.

1353   King Charles IV establishes the University of Prague, the first university in central Europe.

1413   The Scottish University of Saint Andrews is founded. Its curriculum is a mix of Bologna and Paris programs.

1538   The University of St. Thomas Aquinas, the first in the New World, is founded in Santo Domingo.

1560   The first scientific academy, the Academia Secretorum Naturae, is founded in Naples. Scientific academies are a response to the absence of—and even opposition to—scientific study in the universities.

1575   Calvinists establish the University of Leiden.

1582   Calvinists establish the University of Edinburgh.

Education in America

This chronicle traces the history of higher education in this country, noting important developments elsewhere only to the extent that they contributed to the development of the American model.

1636   Harvard College, a Puritan institution and the first American college, is founded by the General Court of Massachusetts. The new college is patterned after Emmanuel College at Cambridge University in England. Students are required to pass an oral examination and write an essay in Latin to be admitted to the college. The students are in their midteens. The original fully prescribed curriculum is based on the classical *trivium* and *quadrivium* and consists of logic, Greek, rhetoric, astronomy, Aramaic, Hebrew, Syriac, ethics and politics, mathematics, history, botany, and catechism. All of the later colonial colleges will have similar academic programs and be controlled by Protestant religious sects.

1636 The first college preparatory school is started in Charlestown, Massachusetts, to prepare students for the first year of college.

1642 Harvard awards the first nine bachelor's degrees in America. A master of arts degree is awarded after a student completes three years of further study beyond the bachelor's degree.

1647 The Massachusetts legislature directs towns of over one hundred households to establish a school to prepare students for college. Towns half that size are required only to teach reading and writing.

1692 A second American college, William and Mary, is established. It is influenced by the Scottish conception of higher education. Greater emphasis is placed on mathematics, history, and science than at Harvard. By the time of the Revolutionary War, William and Mary is experimenting with curricular election and an honors code.

1694 The University of Halle is established in Germany. Lectures are given in the vernacular rather than Latin, and scholasticism is attacked. Sometimes labeled the "first modern university," the University of Halle and the University of Göttingen (founded in 1737), which followed its lead, influenced the development of the German research university that served as inspiration to the American research model over a century later.

1728 Harvard establishes a professorship in mathematics and natural science.

1745 Knowledge of arithmetic is made an entrance requirement at Yale College.

1756 The College of Philadelphia introduces a more utilitarian curriculum than the other colonial colleges. Three years are required to earn a degree. Equal portions of the curriculum are devoted to classical languages; mathematics and science; and logic, metaphysics, and ethics. New subjects, such as political science, history, chemistry, navigation, trade and commerce, zoology, mechanics, and agriculture are added to the curriculum.

1765 The College of Philadelphia establishes the first chair in medicine in the colonies.

1770 Two literary societies are created at Princeton. The extracurricular literary societies quickly become popular at other colleges as well. They are essentially debating clubs designed to provide the intellectual stimulation lacking in the formal college curriculum, which is dominated by recitation. The literary societies are controlled and financed by students. Until the Civil War, they remain a center of student interest, rivaling and occasionally undermining a college's undergraduate program.

1776   Phi Beta Kappa is started at William and Mary College.

1779   William and Mary College establishes the first chair in law in the United States and allows a small amount of curricular election.

1783   Yale rejects an otherwise fully qualified woman applicant for admission because of her gender.

1785   President Ezra Stiles of Yale adopts one of the first grading systems in the colonies. It is a four-point grading system that contains the following categories: *optimi,* second *optimi, inferiores (boni),* and *pejores.*

1785   The first state college, the University of Georgia, is chartered.

1789   The first Catholic college, Georgetown, is established.

1802   The U.S. Military Academy, which emphasizes technical education, is founded. It is the first college to offer formal instruction in engineering.

1815   Three American students—Edward Everett, Edward Cogswell, and George Ticknor—seek further education in Germany—the first of some ten thousand over the next century.

1819   Based upon his German experiences, George Ticknor, now a Harvard professor, criticizes Harvard for the poor quality of its libraries, the exclusion of modern languages from the curriculum, and the lack of specialized departments.

1821   Emma Willard starts an institution of higher learning for women in Troy, New York.

c. 1823   A blackboard is used by an instructor at Bowdoin College for the first time.

1824   The University of Virginia opens. Students are offered eight possible fields of study ranging from anatomy and medicine to ancient languages. Degree programs within each field are completely prescribed. However, nondegree programs that allow students to choose whatever courses they please are also offered. Award of degrees is based entirely upon the passage of general examinations within each field of study. There is no university-wide degree.

1824   Rensselaer Polytechnic Institute, the first entirely technical school, is founded to instruct children of farmers and mechanics in theoretical and mechanical sciences. Rensselaer becomes the first college to offer extension courses and laboratory instruction.

1825   Miami University in Ohio permits the substitution of modern languages, practical mathematics, and political economy for certain subjects in the traditional or classical curriculum.

1825   President Philip Lindsley of the University of Nashville adopts a curriculum accenting utilitarian, vocational, and research concerns.

1825   Major changes are made in the Harvard curriculum as a result of the first institutional self-study. The changes include departmentalization of faculty and curriculum; permitting juniors and seniors a small number of elective courses, establishment of partial courses, which allow nondegree students to study only selected parts of the curriculum, particularly modern languages, and introduction of some self-pacing of the curriculum.

1825   The first Greek letter social fraternity, Kappa Alpha, is created at Union College.

1826   Union College introduces a scientific curriculum, which includes modern languages, mathematics, and sciences, as an alternative to the classical program. The *parallel* course, as it is called, is a nondegree program.

1828   The faculty at Yale responds to the growing criticism of the American college. The purpose of college, according to the Yale Report, is to provide "the discipline and furniture of the mind." *Discipline* refers to the need to expand the powers of the mental faculties; and *furniture* speaks to the need to fill the mind with knowledge. The Yale faculty indicates that each of the subjects in its classical curriculum has a special role in providing discipline and knowledge. Their report is a rebuff to critics and institutions offering technical or partial courses of study. The most important subject in the Yale curriculum is said to be the classical languages, which provide "the most effectual discipline of mental faculties." Modern languages are dismissed as being of lesser educational value. The report affirms the use of lecture and recitation modes of instruction while rejecting the study of professional subjects in college. Breadth of learning gained in classical study is seen as the best preparation for any profession. The mission of the college is sharply defined. The faculty feel that institutions other than colleges should provide the popular studies that are being demanded of institutions such as Yale.

c. 1828   Kenyon College introduces faculty advising. Each student is teamed with one member of the Kenyon faculty.

1830   Columbia University adopts a program that includes both science and modern languages.

1831   Ohio University establishes a program to prepare public school teachers.

1833   Oberlin College is the first college to admit women to a formerly all-male institution.

1835   Rensselaer Institute awards the first engineering degree.

1836   The first degree-granting women's college, Wesleyan Female College (Macon, Georgia), is founded.

1837   The People's College is established in New York state to provide science and technical education to craftsmen.

1839   The first normal school for the preparation of teachers is established in Lexington, Massachusetts. It later relocates to Framingham, Massachusetts.

1845   Union College becomes the first liberal arts college to inaugurate an engineering program.

1846   Yale makes two faculty appointments in agriculture.

1847   The tuition-free Academy of New York City, later City College of New York, is chartered by the New York state legislature.

1847   Yale takes the first tentative steps toward the creation of a graduate school.

1847   Harvard creates the Lawrence Scientific School, which emphasizes the study of geology and zoology. Instruction does not initially lead to a bachelor's degree. The educational requirements for admission are considerably less than those of Harvard College. Students are required only to have had a good common school or elementary school education.

1849   Avery College for blacks begins in Pennsylvania.

1850   Under the leadership of President Francis Wayland, Brown University adopts a curriculum including a nondegree partial course, variable student loads, an increased number of science courses, a modified extension program, a greater number of free electives, and a new degree to be awarded for nonclassical study—the Bachelor of Philosophy (Ph.B.). Insufficient funding, declining quality in students, and a lack of public support end the program four years later.

1851   A business school is established at the University of Louisiana.

1851   Harvard awards the first bachelor of science degrees to students who complete programs in the sciences. The standards for admission in B.S. programs are lower than B.A. courses.

1852   In his inaugural address as president of the University of Michigan, Henry Tappan proposes that the university develop extensive programs in the fine arts, natural sciences, and utilitarian subjects; that students be permitted elective courses; that the degree of bachelor of science be awarded in science programs; and that graduate work be added to the activities of the university. Tappan's eleven-year tenure also includes experimentation with an experimental recognition of lower division coursework offered in area high schools.

1852   Yale and Harvard engage in the first intercollegiate sports contest, a boat race.

1853   The University of Michigan offers the first earned master's degree—that is, a degree based upon completing a particular program rather than simply putting in a specified number of years beyond the bachelor's degree.

1854   Yale establishes a unit separate from the rest of the college, like the Lawrence Scientific School at Harvard. It offers a two-year course of study that emphasizes applied chemistry. (In 1861, this unit is named the Sheffield Scientific School.)

1854   The American Missionary Society is formed to bring higher education to blacks. Within six years it establishes six black colleges.

1855   The first state agricultural college was Michigan State University.

1861   Yale University awards the first Ph.D. degree.

1862   Congress passes the Morrill Land-Grant Act, which authorizes the sale of federal lands to provide funds for the support of colleges offering instruction in "agriculture and mechanic arts without excluding other scientific and classical studies and including military tactics."

1868   Cornell University opens its doors. The motto of the new college is "any person—any study." Science is made an integral part of the curriculum. Students are given a wide choice in subjects for study as well as manual labor experiences. The group system, which offers students a choice of internally coherent course of study, is adopted.

1868   The University of Missouri creates a school of education.

1869   Harvard President Charles W. Eliot, in his inaugural address, proclaims his belief in the elective system. Within six years, most of the required courses in the Harvard curriculum are relegated to the freshman year.

1869   Charles Kendall Adams emphasizes seminar instruction in an experimental program at the University of Michigan.

1870   The variable quality of candidates for admission causes the University of Michigan to begin periodically to visit and inspect local high schools.

1870   The Harvard catalogue begins to list courses by subject rather than by the student class for which they are intended.

1870   College enrollments equal 1.7 percent of the eighteen- to twenty-one-year-old population.

1876   The Johns Hopkins University, the first American research university, is established in Baltimore. The new school, emphasizing graduate education, is modeled after the German research university. At Johns Hopkins, an undergraduate education is three years long. Laboratories and seminars are popular modes of instruction.

1878   The Johns Hopkins catalogue of 1877–78 makes the first known reference to the terms *major* and *minor.*

1878   New York state establishes a system of uniform high school examinations, called Regents Examinations.

1881   Harvard begins to offer term-length courses, called *half courses.*

1885   The first regional accrediting association, the New England Association of Colleges and Secondary Schools, is established.

1886   Chapel attendance is made voluntary at Harvard.

1888   Clark University, an institution specializing in graduate education, is established. Its first president is G. Stanley Hall, a Johns Hopkins–trained psychologist and one of the founders of modern psychology. Hall is especially noted for his pioneering research in the field of child and adolescent psychology and as the founder of the *American Journal of Psychology* (1887).

1890   A second Morrill Land-Grant Act is passed by Congress. The legislation provides for an annual federal appropriation to land-grant colleges and encouragement for similar state support. The act also stipulates that no state will receive appropriations if they deny admission to the land-grant college on the basis of race unless they provide separate but equal facilities. Seventeen states choose this option.

1890   President Eliot merges the graduate and undergraduate faculties at Harvard.

1890   Harvard establishes the Board of Freshman Advisers, a body specifically concerned with counseling new students.

1891   The Educational Exchange of Greater Boston, a free-standing broker-age organization, is created to advise and counsel adult students.

1892   The National Education Association appoints a Committee of Ten on col-lege and school relations to help standardize the high school curriculum.

1892   With money from John D. Rockefeller and leadership from William Rainey Harper, the University of Chicago is created. Many of the curricular innovations of the waning century find a home at Chicago. The university develops high-quality graduate and research programs, a residential undergraduate college like those of Oxford and Cambridge, and programs of service to society.

1896   The lower division program at the University of Chicago is designated the Junior College. After two years of experience with this program, the university awards associate's degrees.

1898   The first professional school of forestry is created at Cornell University.

1899   Yale permits undergraduates to include law and medical courses in their programs.

1900   College enrollments equal 4 percent of the eighteen- to twenty-one-year-old population.

1901   The first College Entrance Examination Board tests are administered.

1901   The first public junior college is established in Joliet, Illinois.

1902   Charles W. Eliot persuades the Harvard faculty to abandon the four-year requirement for the B.A. By 1906, 41 percent of Harvard students graduate in three to three and one-half years.

1903   W.E.B. Du Bois advocates general and vocational education for the "tal-ented tenth" of African Americans.

1904   Charles Van Hise, president of the University of Wisconsin, proposes the Wisconsin Idea. The state of Wisconsin is to be regarded as the campus of the university. Faculty expertise is applied to state problems. The university becomes involved with the state legislature, local government, civic groups, and the office of the governor. Higher education is expanded throughout the state as the uni-versity offers extension and correspondence courses on popular topics and tech-nical subjects.

1904   City College of New York requires all new faculty to hold a Ph.D.

1905   The Columbia University faculty, under the leadership of Nicholas Murray Butler, adopts the "professional option" plan, which allows students to enroll jointly in professional school programs and the undergraduate college with a time savings in earning both degrees.

1906   The University of Cincinnati establishes the first cooperative work-study program in its school of engineering.

1906   The Carnegie Foundation for the Advancement of Teaching establishes minimum institutional criteria to qualify institutions for a faculty pension program. These include having six full-time faculty, department chairmen with Ph.D.'s, a four-year liberal arts program, a secondary school completion requirement for admission, and a nondenominational orientation.

1908   The Carnegie Foundation for the Advancement of Teaching develops the Carnegie unit as a standard measure of time in which students are exposed to high school subjects.

1909   City College of New York inaugurates the first night-school program leading to a bachelor's degree.

1909   Harvard President A. Lawrence Lowell introduces a system of concentration or majors and general education distribution requirements. Students are required to take six year-long courses in three fields outside the major area.

1910   Reed College, stressing independent study and scholarship, is founded. Students are required to pass a comprehensive examination and write a senior thesis before graduating.

1910   President Lowell of Harvard introduces a comprehensive examination in the major. Students who do well on the examination graduate with honors. The Harvard tutorial system is instituted to help students prepare for the examination.

1913   A committee of the National Education Association recommends reducing the common breadth component of undergraduate education by at least two years.

1914   During the presidency of Alexander Meiklejohn, the first survey course, "Social and Economic Institutions," is created at Amherst College.

1919   A general education core course, "Contemporary Civilization," is adopted at Columbia.

1920   Reserve Officer Training Corps (ROTC) is established by the National Defense Act.

1920   College enrollments equal 8 percent of the eighteen- to twenty-one-year-old population.

1921   Arthur E. Morgan introduces work-study or cooperative education at a liberal arts college, Antioch College.

1921   Swarthmore College President Frank Aydelotte develops an honors program.

1925   The Oxbridge cluster college concept is put into operation in the establishment of the Claremont Colleges.

1927   Alexander Meiklejohn establishes an experimental college at the University of Wisconsin.

1928   The Harvard Houses, residential academic units, are created.

1928   Many years of undergraduate reform begin at the University of Chicago.

1928   Pasadena High School and Pasadena Junior College merge to form a four-year institution containing grades 11 to 14.

1929   Sarah Lawrence College, one of the earliest progressive schools, is founded.

1930   College enrollments equal 12 percent of the eighteen- to twenty-one-year-old population.

1932   Bennington College begins operation with a curriculum emphasizing the progressive philosophy of education.

1932   The General College, a two-year general education division, is established at the University of Minnesota.

1933   Black Mountain College, an experimental college, is founded.

1935   Framingham Teachers College, the first normal school, offers the bachelor of science degree in education.

1937   Stringfellow Barr and Scott Buchanan introduce the Great Books curriculum at St. John's College in Annapolis, Maryland.

1941   College enrollments equal 18 percent of the eighteen- to twenty-one-year-old population.

1944   The G.I. Bill, Serviceman's Readjustment Act, is passed by Congress. This legislation, providing direct financial assistance for returning soldiers to attend college, enables 2.25 million veterans to enroll at the two thousand American colleges and universities of the day.

1945   The Committee on the Objectives of a General Education in a Free Society produces the "Redbook" at Harvard. The Redbook offers a history of education in America, a theory of general education, and a prescription for the teaching of general education in secondary schools, at Harvard College, and in the community. It specifies that general education is distinct from specialization and should embrace the humanities, social sciences, and natural sciences, and recommends that six of the sixteen year-long courses required for graduation be reserved for general education. The report states that general education helps people "to think effectively, to communicate thoughts, to make relevant judgments, [and] to discriminate among values." The recommendations of the Redbook are adopted all over America, but not in Cambridge.

1947   The President's Commission on Higher Education for Democracy issues its report. The report calls for tuition-free education for all youth through the first two years of college; financial assistance for needy but competent students in tenth through fourteenth grades; lower tuition charges in upper division, graduate, and professional schools; expansion of adult education; elimination of barriers to equal access in higher education; development of community colleges; and rededication of the curriculum to general education.

1951   Advanced placement or advanced study programs begin at twelve colleges and secondary schools under Ford Foundation auspices.

1951   Early admission programs that admit students to college after the junior year of secondary school are initiated by twelve colleges with Ford Foundation support.

1957   The Soviet Union launches *Sputnik,* the first artificial satellite. This Russian space achievement spurs the development of accelerated science and language instruction in the United States.

1958   The National Defense Education Act provides for undergraduate loans, graduate fellowships, institutional aid for teacher education, and broad support for education in the sciences, mathematics, and foreign languages.

1958   The 4–1–4 calendar, with its credit-bearing winter mini-term for intensive study or field study, is proposed in the 1958 Hampshire College Plan. In 1960, it is adopted at Eckerd College.

1959–60   In the aftermath of *Sputnik,* two colleges offering rigorous honors programs—Oakland University (Michigan) and New College (Florida)—are established.

1960   Almost 500 of the nation's more than 2,000 colleges are single-sex (236 for men and 259 for women).

1960 Framingham Teachers College, the first normal school, becomes Framingham State College. It is authorized to offer a range of B.A. and B.S. degrees and within a year is permitted to award master's degrees.

1963 College Board scores begin to decline nationally.

1963 Clark Kerr publishes *The Uses of the University*, defining the modern university as a "multiversity."

1964 College enrollments equal 40 percent of the eighteen- to twenty-one-year-old population.

1964 Massive student disorder at the University of California, Berkeley, brings campus unrest of the 1960s to national attention.

1965 The Experimental College (Tussman College), modeled on the Meiklejohn College at Wisconsin, begins four years of operation at the University of California, Berkeley.

1965 The first free university, a student-organized and student-run experimental college, is created at Berkeley.

1965 The Higher Education Act of 1965 provides institutional aid to private and public colleges as well as individual students. Included in the bill is money for research, libraries, recruitment of disadvantaged students, educational facilities, developing colleges, community colleges, occupational education, and improvement of undergraduate education. Student aid programs include educational opportunity grants for those with low income, guaranteed student loans, work-study assistance, and fellowship grants.

1965 Upward Bound, a program to prepare students with academic potential but lacking in motivation or academic skills for college, is developed by the Carnegie Corporation and the Office of Economic Opportunity.

1966 New York state approves the SEEK (Search for Education, Elevation, and Knowledge) program, providing for academic, psychological, and financial assistance at senior colleges at the City University of New York to students from designated poverty areas who have high school diplomas but lack qualifications for university entrance.

1966 The Keller Plan for self-paced learning is developed.

1967 The Carnegie Commission on Higher Education is formed to study the structure, functions, financing, and future of higher education.

1967   The College Level Examination Program, which tests subject proficiency at college standards, is established.

1968   A program of "Special Services for Disadvantaged Students," including remedial instruction, counseling, and support services, is created by the Higher Education Amendments of 1968.

1968   An "early college," Simon's Rock, in Great Barrington, Massachusetts, offers a college education to sixteen- to twenty-year-olds.

1968   Executive Order 11375 requires that organizations with federal contracts agree not to discriminate against employees or applicants for employment on the basis of sex, race, color, religion, or place of national origin. The Department of Labor is charged with issuing rules and regulations and ensuring compliance, which leads to the establishment of affirmative action regulations.

1968   San Francisco State College becomes the first predominately white institution to establish a black studies program.

1969   At the urging of students, Brown University radically alters its undergraduate program.

1969   San Francisco State College becomes the first predominately white institution to establish an Asian American studies program.

1970   City University of New York abandons selective admissions in favor of open admissions. All high school graduates are guaranteed admission to some branch of the university no matter what their previous academic performance may have been.

1970   College enrollments equal 48 percent of the eighteen- to twenty-one-year-old population.

1970   Hampshire College, a cooperative endeavor on the part of four neighboring colleges in the Connecticut River Valley, admits its first class. Graduation is based exclusively upon passing six comprehensive examinations.

1970   San Diego State University and Cornell University adopt the first women's studies programs.

1970   Slightly more than 6 percent of all first-time freshman are older than twenty-one.

1970   The Legal Defense and Education Fund of the NAACP files suit against the U.S. Department of Health, Education, and Welfare (HEW) charging that the Office of Civil Rights has failed to enforce Title VI of the 1964 Civil Rights Act by not withholding federal funds to ten states found to be operating racially segregated systems of higher education. The states are: Arkansas, Florida, Georgia, Louisiana, Maryland, Mississippi, North Carolina, Oklahoma, Pennsylvania, and Virginia. The so-called "Adams Case" is named after Kenneth Adams, a Mississippi high school student seeking admission to a predominately white university.

1970   The number of single-sex institutions falls to 347 (154 for men and 193 for women). Most of those are private, religiously oriented colleges. Among the most recent conversions to coeducation are Yale University and the University of Virginia.

1970   The Regents External degree, awarded entirely on the basis of examinations and college-equivalent credit, is created by New York State.

1971   A task force of the U.S. Department of Health, Education, and Welfare directed by Frank Newman urges an expansion of noncollege educational opportunities, a break with the four-year lockstep pattern of college education, off-campus programs, diversification of college faculty, commitment to minority education, equality for women, new educational enterprises, greater college autonomy, and revival of college missions.

1971   Empire State College (part of the State University of New York system) is founded with a contract-based, individualized curriculum. In the same year, New College of Sarasota, Florida (later named New College of the University of South Florida) also adopts an individualized curriculum.

1972   The Fund for the Improvement of Postsecondary Education and the National Institute of Education are established by the Education Amendments of 1972.

1973   Students at Alverno College in Milwaukee, Wisconsin, must demonstrate competence in eight "abilities" in order to graduate. The eight areas are: communication, analysis, problem solving, valuing, social interaction, taking responsibility for the global environment, effective citizenship, and aesthetic response. There are no grades for students. Faculty live under a "teach well or perish" rather than "publish or perish" dictum.

1973   The Capital Higher Education Service, Inc., a free-standing educational brokerage organization, is created in Hartford, Connecticut.

1974   The U.S. Department of Health, Education, and Welfare accepts desegregation plans from eight of ten states charged with operating segregated higher education systems in the Adams Case. The department turns Louisiana and Mississippi over to the Justice Department for investigation.

1974   The U.S. Supreme Court declares moot—that is, of no practical significance—the case of *De Funis* v. *Odegaard,* which challenges the right of institutions of higher education to apply different standards for affirmative action minority admissions.

1975   California administers a statewide proficiency examination to allow students to leave high school early.

1975   National Council for Black Studies is founded.

1976   In *Bakke* v. *The Regents of the University of California,* the California Supreme Court rules that affirmative action admissions at the University of California, Davis, medical school violate the equal protection clause of the Fourteenth Amendment of the United States Constitution. The Regents appeal the decision to the U.S. Supreme Court.

1976   The Virginia Board of Education votes that, beginning in 1978, high school students be required to achieve minimum proficiency levels in reading, writing, speaking, computational skills, and U.S. history and culture in order to graduate.

1977   National Women's Studies Association is founded.

1978   Harvard University launches the Harvard Plan of General Education. The Plan is not a core curriculum, a great books program, or a set of loose distribution requirements. Rather, students take ten courses from among one hundred offered in five substantive areas: literature and the arts, history, social and philosophical analysis, science and mathematics, and foreign languages and cultures. The program is widely criticized, especially off campus, yet deemed relatively successful for students.

1979   The Department of Education is created. It takes over jurisdiction in the Adams Case.

1979   Women outnumber men in first-time student enrollment figures.

1982   Freshmen students in most degree programs at Stevens Institute of Technology are required to buy a personal computer.

1983   Association for Asian American Studies is founded.

1984   Secretary of Education William Bennett issues "To Reclaim a Legacy: A Report on the Humanities in Higher Education." The report states that the undergraduate curriculum in the humanities has eroded and the overall coherence of most humanities programs has declined. Among other things, the report calls for a common core curriculum in the humanities and Western civilization that should be required of all students.

1985   Formal women's studies programs exist in over 450 colleges and universities.

1986   There are only 102 women's colleges in the U.S.

1986   *Tomorrow's Teachers: A Report of the Holmes Group* is published, including a list of proposals for reforming teaching and undergraduate teacher education. Dealing with similar matters, *A Nation Prepared: Teachers for the Twenty-First Century* was issued by the Carnegie Forum on Education and the Economy's Task Force on Teaching as a Profession. Among other things, *A Nation Prepared* calls for undergraduates who aspire to teaching careers to earn a liberal arts degree rather than a bachelor of education degree.

1987   A U.S. District Court judge dismisses the Adams Case.

1987   Allan Bloom publishes *The Closing of the American Mind: How Higher Education Has Failed Democracy and Impoverished the Souls of Today's Students.* It becomes a virtual clarion call for curricular reform.

1987   Women constitute a majority of all college students at 53 percent.

1988   Stanford abolishes its long-standing, one-year course requirement in Western civilization and replaces it with a new course, "Cultures, Ideas, and Values." Most sections of the new course require books that deal with issues of race and gender or are authored by American minority members, women, or Third World writers.

1988   The first gay and lesbian studies department is founded, at City College of San Francisco.

1988   The Madison Plan, conceived by University of Wisconsin president Donna Shalala, is adopted to address the university's need for greater diversity. The Plan calls for increasing minority student financial aid, recruitment, and retention. In addition, the Plan outlines a new ethnic studies requirement for all undergraduates and proposes creating a Multicultural Center on campus.

1988   The U.S. Department of Education investigates Harvard and the University of California, Los Angeles, among other prominent institutions, on allegations of illegally limiting the number of Asian American students accepted for admission.

1989   The U.S. Court of Appeals reverses the decision of the lower court in the Adams Case.

1989   There are formal women's studies programs in 615 colleges and universities.

1990   Adults between the ages of twenty-two and sixty-four comprise 47 percent of all undergraduates.

1990   Undergraduate college enrollments equal more than 32 percent of the nation's eighteen- to twenty-one-year-old population.

1990   *Scholarship Reconsidered: Priorities of the Professoriate,* by Ernest Boyer of The Carnegie Foundation for the Advancement of Teaching, urges colleges and universities to expand their definitions of scholarship beyond disciplinary research to include the integration and application of knowledge and the scholarship of teaching when making promotion and tenure decisions.

1990   The Carl D. Perkins Vocational and Applied Technology Act establishes technical preparation programs linking curriculum at community colleges, vocational institutes, and high schools, as well as encouraging the development of college-to-work programs.

1990   The U.S. Court of Appeals dismisses the Adams Case, stating that civil rights groups cannot sue the federal government, but must instead sue the colleges or the states involved.

1990   The U.S. Justice Department sues the Virginia Military Institute (a public institution) on behalf of an unnamed female applicant over its men-only admission policy.

1990   The U.S. Department of Education clears Harvard of charges that it imposed quotas on the admission of Asian American students; however, it finds that the UCLA math department did use quotas.

1991   The U.S. Department of Education clears UCLA's math department (which appealed the 1990 findings) of charges that they limited the number of Asian American students admitted.

1991   U.S. District Court rules that City College of City University of New York had violated the constitutional rights of philosophy professor Michael Levin by punishing him for espousing his views on the intellectual inferiority of African Americans.

1992   The U.S. Court of Appeals rules against the Virginia Military Institute (VMI) saying it did not adequately justify discriminating against women and instructs the VMI to admit women or provide equivalent training elsewhere.

1993   Leonard Jeffries, professor of black studies at City College of City University of New York, is awarded $360,000 in damages and reinstated as chair of the black studies department when a U.S. Court of Appeals states that the college violated his first amendment rights. He was removed from his post in 1992 after creating a controversy on campus by espousing Afro-centric views, including his belief that Jews had a disproportionately large role in the African slave trade.

1993   Louisiana District Court rules that the current practice of one coordinating board overseeing three separate governing boards (one of which manages the Southern University System, the nation's only historically black university system) amounted to segregation. The ruling obligates Louisiana to eliminate duplicative programs in historically white and black institutions located in the same community so that students might select an institution "without regard" to its historical racial identity.

1993   Shannon Faulkner is admitted to the Citadel (a public military institution in South Carolina) after leaving all references to her gender off her application. The Citadel refuses to admit her after learning she is female. In the same year, the U.S. Supreme Court refuses to hear an appeal by VMI to remain all-male.

1994   A Federal Appeals Court overturns the ruling of the Louisiana District Court on the issue of desegregation in higher education.

1994   A Federal District Court judge orders the Citadel to admit Faulkner. The Citadel appeals the decision.

1994   An interactive video network involving two-way communication links North Dakota's eleven geographically scattered state colleges and universities. Professors teaching at one location now have students sitting in different cities and towns across the state participating in class discussion. Three institutions—University of North Dakota, North Dakota State University, and North Dakota State College of Science—offer complete undergraduate and graduate degree programs in business, nursing, and education via the video network.

1994   Due to shrinking enrollments and a $1 million deficit, the president of Bennington College, Elizabeth Coleman, downsizes the college. She fires several faculty members, eliminates academic divisions, abolishes tenure by putting all faculty on renewable contracts, and changes the academic program. For example, among the literature faculty, she retains only those who are active writers and fires those whose specialties are criticism or analysis.

1994   Oklahoma City Community College initiates a twenty-four-hour class schedule.

1994   The U.S. Supreme Court orders the U.S. Court of Appeals to reconsider its decision in the Leonard Jeffries case.

1995   U.S. Court of Appeals approves a VMI plan to begin a military-type train-ing course for women at nearby Mary Baldwin College. In a related case, a three-judge panel from the U.S. Court of Appeals agrees to hear the Citadel case to determine if "separate but equal" applies to single-sex higher education. The court then orders the Citadel to admit Shannon Faulkner, who subsequently resigns after less than a week, citing both emotional and medical reasons.

1995   The Board of Regents of the University of California decides to end racial preferences as criteria in admissions decisions, effectively ending affirmative ac-tion policies based on race for the state system.

1995   The Board of Trustees for the City University of New York (CUNY) votes to eliminate all remedial programs at its four-year institutions.

References

Andelman, H. *The Holiversity: A Perspective on the Wright Report.* Toronto: New Press, 1973.

Aries, P. *Centuries of Childhood: A Social History of Family Life.* New York: Random House, 1962.

Baldridge, J. V., Roberts, J. W., and Weiner, T. A. *The Campus and the Microcomputer Revolution: Practical Advice for Nontechnical Decision Makers.* New York: Macmillan, 1984.

Brubacher, J. S., and Rudy, W. *Higher Education in Transition: A History of American Colleges and Universities, 1636–1976.* (3rd ed.) New York: HarperCollins, 1976.

Butts, R. F. *Education of the West: A Formative Chapter in the History of Civilization.* (Rev. ed.) New York: McGraw-Hill, 1973.

Carnegie Foundation for the Advancement of Teaching. *Missions of the College Curriculum: A Contemporary Review with Suggestions.* San Francisco: Jossey-Bass, 1977.

Cheit, E. F. *The Useful Arts and the Liberal Tradition.* New York: McGraw-Hill, 1975.

Clarke, M. L. *Higher Education in the Ancient World.* New York: Routledge & Kegan Paul, 1971.

Dressel, P. *The Undergraduate Curriculum in Higher Education.* New York: Center for Applied Re-search in Education, 1966.

Ford, N. A. *Black Studies: Threat or Challenge.* Port Washington, N.Y.: National University Pub-lications, 1973.

Gaff, J. G. *General Education Today: A Critical Analysis of Controversies, Practices, and Reforms.* San Francisco: Jossey-Bass, 1983.

Haskins, C. H. *The Rise of Universities.* Ithaca, N.Y.: Cornell University Press, 1967.

Hofstadter, R., and Smith, W. (eds.). *American Higher Education: A Documentary History.* (2 vols.) Chicago: University of Chicago Press, 1961. These volumes contain most of the critical documents in the history of U.S. higher education, or excerpts thereof, accompanied with background glosses.

Lucas, C. J. *American Higher Education: A History.* New York: St. Martin's Press, 1994.

Minton, H. L. (ed.). *Gay and Lesbian Studies.* New York: Haworth Press, 1992.

Pearson, C. S., Shavilik, D., and Touchton, J. G. *Educating the Majority: Women Challenge Tradi-tion in Higher Education.* New York: ACE/Macmillan, 1989.

Rashdall, H. *The Universities of Europe in the Middle Ages.* (3 vols.) Oxford, England: Clarendon Press, 1936.

Rudolph, F. *Curriculum: A History of the American Undergraduate Course of Study Since 1636*. San Francisco: Jossey-Bass, 1977.

Rudy, W. *The Evolving Liberal Arts Curriculum*. New York: Teachers College Press, 1960.

Schachner, N. *The Medieval Universities* (Perpetua ed.). New York: Barnes, 1962.

Sloan, D. *The Scottish Enlightenment and the American College Idea*. New York: Teachers College Press, 1971.

Thwing, C. F. *A History of Higher Education in America*. Englewood Cliffs, N.J.: Prentice Hall, 1906.

Touchton, J. G., and Davis, L. *Fact Book on Women in Higher Education*. New York: ACE/Macmillan, 1991.

Veysey, L. *The Emergence of the American University*. Chicago: University of Chicago Press, 1965.

Wieruszowski, H. *The Medieval University: Masters, Students, Learning*. Princeton, N.J.: Nos Reinhold, 1966.

"The Yale Report of 1828." In R. Hofstadter and W. Smith (eds.), *American Higher Education: A Documentary History*. Vol. 1. Chicago: University of Chicago Press, 1961.

CHAPTER FOUR

PHILOSOPHIES AND AIMS

Barbara S. Fuhrmann

As discussed in Chapters Two and Three, the curriculum, even the very purpose of higher education, has been and continues to be dependent upon the historical context in which the curriculum is designed, the location in which questions concerning higher education are asked, and the nature of the students involved in that time and at that place. In the words of Rudolph, "The curriculum has been an arena in which the dimensions of American culture have been measured, an environment for certifying an elite at one time and for facilitating the mobility of an emerging middle class at another. It has been one of those places where we have told ourselves who we are" (1977, p. 1). The notion of what a curriculum should be and what it should accomplish has undergone a remarkable four-hundred-year development guided by differing educational philosophies.

In the U.S. colonial period (approximately 1600–1800), the guiding philosophy was one in which the sons of the elite were subjected to a rigidly prescribed curriculum of Greek, Latin, mathematics, and moral truths, a curriculum designed for the express purposes of infusing moral standards into vulnerable young minds, for training future ministers, and for ensuring the continuation of a stratified society under the control of the economic and social elite. Higher education was the province of only a few, and was thus impractical, expensive, and of little importance to the vast majority of society.

By the nineteenth century, such elitism and impracticality had become untenable, and the philosophy of the curriculum gradually evolved into one that emphasized democratic values, access, and the potential for advancing individuals socially and economically through education. Simultaneous with this broader purpose of higher education in the United States, German universities began to emphasize the role of the scholar, the importance of scholarly endeavor, and the contributions of research. Curricular philosophy began to acknowledge the development of intellectual skill rather than rote memorization, and the rise of science led to specialization, experimentation, various forms of inductive and collaborative learning, and the birth of the concept of the *ivory tower*, in which a community of scholars could immerse itself in the life of the mind, isolated from the trivia and distractions of everyday life. But by the close of the century, higher education began to see itself as meeting the needs of a broader population, including women and first-generation college students, and began to emphasize the process as well as the content of learning.

In the first half of the twentieth century, the social interests of an ever-increasing and less intellectually elite student body further outweighed the more traditional academic values of the previous century, and colleges experimented with a variety of techniques designed to stimulate students, personalize the curriculum, and provide for the more practical needs of the society. In an effort to respond to societal needs, three important philosophical viewpoints developed. First was the utilitarian or vocational view that stresses job preparation skills; second was the scientific view that stresses the centrality of research and the dissemination of new knowledge; and third was the liberal learning view that stresses the importance of human development and the intellectual habits of mind that lead to lifelong learning. These often conflicting philosophies of the curriculum have coexisted in our colleges and universities throughout the twentieth century and continue to be the source of challenges from all fronts.

As we approach the twenty-first century, new questions and challenges confront us, particularly in integrating the vast changes discussed in Chapter Six of this book: sometimes frightening demographic, social, and economic trends, cultural pluralism, increased global interdependence, and the implications of the development of new technologies. Higher education is challenged to provide more, to more people, in more settings, using more techniques, with greater accountability—in less time and at less cost than ever before. The overriding philosophy of the future often seems to be a simple "Do it all, and do it cheap."

Table 4.1 compares some of the major philosophical premises from each of these historical periods. Note that while beliefs about the goals of higher education have changed considerably over the approximately four hundred years represented, none from an earlier period is necessarily replaced by the thinking of the subsequent period, and all can be found in some form in contemporary educational philosophy. Change has been more additive than revolutionary, and

TABLE 4.1. THE EVOLUTION OF EDUCATIONAL GOALS AND VALUES: PREDOMINATE THEMES.

Colonial Period	Nineteenth Century	Twentieth Century	Twenty-First Century?
Higher education is for the elite.	Higher education should be widely accessible.	Students should alternate course work and on-the-job experience related to their course of study.	Students must learn how to manage change.
Higher education is for men.	Rote memory should not be emphasized in college.		Students must be technologically proficient.
The curriculum is predetermined.	College should prepare students for jobs.	Education is a lifelong process.	Students should learn to interact in a variety of cultural environments.
The curriculum should discipline young minds.	College should teach practical and popular subjects.	Independent learning should be fostered.	Higher education does not precede productive work.
Diligence and responsibility are the hallmarks of an educated man.	Students benefit from hands-on learning in laboratories and other real-world settings.	The curriculum must be practical and relevant.	The values of a liberal education must again become the foundation of higher education.
Social needs will be met by an elite, homogeneous-thinking, closed group.	Students know what they need to learn.	Career preparation is an expected outcome of a college education.	Colleges must be held accountable for the knowledge and skills of their graduates.
Men learn through rote memorization.	Student interests should dictate what they learn.	Universities must create and discover new knowledge.	Colleges should prepare all students for productive employment.
Greek, Latin, mathematics, and moral truths form the content of the curriculum.	Specialization within a field is an important goal of education.	Interdisciplinary coursework is essential to student learning.	Interdisciplinary work and understanding must be fostered along with specialized knowledge and skills.
Idle minds are the devil's playground—there is no room for humor or fun in the college life.	Colleges should meet the social and physical needs of students as well as their intellectual needs.	College must prepare broadly educated citizens to assume civic responsibilities.	Colleges should provide both a common core of learning and a wide variety of professional preparation.
Learning occurs best in an adversarial environment that pits teacher against student.	Colleges should help students become independent learners.	Student self-awareness should be developed in college.	Students learn in a variety of ways; all must be understood and fostered.
Learning is hard work and demands personal sacrifice and discipline.	Students should learn to think inductively as well as deductively.	Teachers should facilitate rather than direct student learning.	
Teachers know what students should learn.	Recreation is an important part of college life.	College should develop students' problem-solving and decision-making skills.	
		Theories of human learning should provide the foundation for teaching strategies.	

although current thinking emphasizes access, excellence, community, and diversity, we nevertheless don't have to look too far within many institutions to find vestiges of even the most conservative thinking that prevailed in the colonial period.

Origins of Curricular Philosophies

While we have evolved from higher education's infancy, which featured widespread agreement about the purposes of a college education, we nevertheless can identify the indispensable components of education that pervade various philosophies of the curriculum. These can be expressed as a number of foci or questions, the answers to which constitute a particular philosophy of the curriculum. The *knowledge focus* asks the question: What should people in an educated society know? The *skill focus* asks: What should people in an educated society be able to do? And the *character focus* asks: What should people in an educated society value, and how then should they behave? In addition, various thinkers differ in terms of the population for whom a higher education should be provided, the appropriate functions in society of institutions of higher education, and the proper roles and responsibilities of faculty.

The Ideals of Liberal Learning

Although the specifics of the educational philosophies of Newman, Dewey, Whitehead, and Hutchins, discussed in this section, are quite different from one another, all four reach somewhat similar conclusions concerning the ultimate aims of education. All contributed significantly to current conceptions of the centrality of liberal learning in developing intellectual habits of mind that can be applied to all areas of human endeavor and that form the basis of lifelong intellectual pursuit.

John Henry Cardinal Newman ([1873] 1982) idealized an educational environment composed of a community of learners: teachers and students interacting through intellectual discourse in all branches of universal knowledge. His ideal emphasized the great human principles, philosophy, truth, and the relationships among branches of knowledge. Although he acknowledged the sciences and mathematics, in his view the major vehicles for intellectual discourse were literature and religion. Study of these subjects and their relationships would lead to skills that are best described as habits of the mind, primarily reason and dispassionate balance of thought. Students with such skills would develop the character traits of gentlemanly thought and behavior, a cultivated intellect, refinement, and basic wisdom. In Newman's view, professional training, research, and service to the community all lay outside the university. The university should focus entirely on intellectual development, which itself would be fostered through an intellectual tradition in which students learn primarily through close contact with both teachers and fellow students.

John Dewey ([1916] 1967) did not write a great deal about higher education, but his views concerning education in general were so powerful as to have impact from nursery school through postgraduate training. Dewey responded to the development of industrialization by proposing a theory of education that emphasizes the human capacity to constantly reconstruct experience and thereby make personal meaning from that experience. Dewey contributed to educational philosophy the understanding that we are not merely passive receptacles of fixed knowledge, but that we must interact with both things and ideas if we are to understand them, own them, and eventually transform them.

Like the cognitive psychologist Jean Piaget, Dewey believed that each of us must create our own knowledge through interacting with elements in our environment. He also believed that education should develop the intellectual capacities of all individuals, regardless of race, gender, or socioeconomic standing.

The subject of higher education, to Dewey, was all of societal life, fundamental human needs, and common human concerns. He was not interested in having all people learn certain common knowledge, but rather believed that all of us should gain from our education the freedom to develop our capacities. His curriculum includes the social and natural sciences, but rather than moving from the general to the specific, proceeds instead in the inductive mode from the concrete to the more abstract. In Dewey's thinking, as in the thinking of many modern educators, the ultimate capacity, and the goal of all education, is to develop our competence as problem solvers. To achieve such universal problem solving, students should be directly involved in their own learning. Dewey contributed to our thinking the concepts of active, experiential, and problem-based learning. He strongly opposed all forms of specialization and compartmentalization, emphasizing the wholeness of experience and the necessity to integrate all imposed dichotomies. Thus Dewey, were he commenting today, would likely oppose the current organization of higher education into departments, the separation of general education and the specialization inherent in majors, differentiation between the sciences and the humanities, and the tendency to separate theory from practice.

Alfred North Whitehead ([1929] 1968) also proposed a holistic approach to education, which focused on the present and was appropriate for the developmental stage of the individual student. His approach stemmed from his awareness that learning is cyclical, proceeding from an interested and wide-ranging exploration of a topic (romance), through a more systematic investigation and analysis of the specifics of the subject (technical proficiency), to an eventual generalizing and application of the principles that the individual has developed through the more systematic study of the subject (generalization). This cyclical process occurs in each of us, in every area of our lives. While it is true that the earlier stages are more generally characteristic of younger people, it is also true that each of us engages in all three simultaneously in different areas of our learning. Thus we become more competent in some areas than in others, based on both personal preference and exposure.

Whitehead proposed no common curriculum, but rather emphasized the need for each college to develop its own limited curriculum based on its analysis of its own needs. For Whitehead, depth was more important than breadth. He wanted every graduate to have something he knew and could do very well (specialization) within a broad understanding of the whole of learning (generalization). Like Newman and Dewey, he emphasized habits of mind: engagement, activity, and reverence for learning, but unlike them, he thought that although faculty should be focused primarily on their teaching and their students' learning, some engagement in research and other scholarly pursuits complemented rather than detracted from their ability to develop their students' learning. Whitehead introduced the concept of the disciplinary specialty (the contemporary major) as a focus of study to be pursued following more general, universal study designed to instill appropriate habits of mind. In Whitehead's words ([1929] 1968, p. 11): "The general culture is designed to foster an activity of mind; the specialist course utilises this activity." Whitehead's impact on the modern college and university is clearly seen in the expectation that students first study broadly (general education), then specialize (major).

Robert Maynard Hutchins ([1936] 1968) also saw higher education as needing to focus on intellectual development and the great truths of all humanity. He differed from the student-centered approaches of Dewey and Whitehead and proposed that there are certain universal studies that should form the basis of a liberal education. For him, these are represented in the "Great Books," the classics that have borne the test of time, become relevant for every generation, and represent the best in human thinking. In his view, these should become the common text for a liberal education, and would provide sufficient intellectual capacity and knowledge for a productive life. (Several liberal arts colleges in the United States today maintain Hutchins's Great Books approach to the curriculum.) In Hutchins's view, a few highly selected students would go beyond the great books to study in research universities, which would be reserved for specialization in the fundamental disciplines of metaphysics, social science, and science, and to technical institutes, which would provide training for the professions.

Research as the Primary Responsibility of the University

The German universities promoted the centrality of science and the responsibility to stimulate the development of new knowledge as the primary responsibility of university faculty. In this country, Thorstein Veblen (*The Higher Learning in*

America, [1918] 1968) and Abraham Flexner (*Universities: American, English, and German,* [1930] 1968) advocated scientific and scholarly inquiry as the primary focus of higher education, with the teaching of students being necessary only to support further scholarship. Both were severely critical of higher education as they saw it evolving; they blamed elementary and secondary schools for not preparing students either for higher education or for careers, and they both reserved the ideals of higher education for the intellectually capable. They opposed wide access to higher education and believed that liberal education as well as professional education and training for jobs (both considered "practical") should not be allowed to distort the purpose of the university. Like Hutchins, they believed that liberal education belongs in the undergraduate college, which also should not be distorted by utilitarian purposes but should exist to introduce selected students to the life of scholarly inquiry in preparation for the true scholarship of the university. All utilitarian functions, including professional training, belong outside higher education. Additionally, what is now considered the service mission of higher education is not appropriate for the university. In their view, the job of higher education is to investigate, study, and understand, and to prepare students to carry on in the same activities—not to prepare people for jobs or to influence society; these responsibilities ought to be the province of other institutions. In the ideal universities envisioned by Veblen and Flexner, researchers would be free from the demands of teaching undergraduates and supported entirely in their pursuit of scientific knowledge. In Veblen's words, the university "should come into action as a shelter where the surviving remnant of scholars and scientists might pursue their several lines of adventure . . . without disturbance to or from the worldly-wise" ([1918] 1968, p. 209).

Flexner would certainly have agreed, as he proposed removing both undergraduate education as a whole and professional education from the realm of university life, which would be reserved for "a free society of scholars . . . left to pursue their own ends in their own way" ([1930] 1968, p. 216). Even today, many university scholars adhere to this view of the purpose of the university, and modern reward systems in higher education continue to promote the preeminence of pure research, especially in universities designated as research institutions.

Synthesis of the Modern University

Clark Kerr, a self-proclaimed optimist, coined the term "multiversity" in *The Uses of the University* (1963) to describe modern higher education, particularly the very large universities that promote teaching, research and scholarship, and service to the community as a whole as their proper province. These are the research and comprehensive universities attended by the majority of modern college students.

Kerr describes a highly pluralistic institution that is capable of meeting all these needs, and that is necessarily confusing. He recognizes that both students and faculty can get lost in the maze of offerings and conflicting agendas, but he believes that the benefits far outweigh the problems. To Kerr, the very complexity of providing a liberal education, disciplinary and professional specialties, a plethora of opportunities for scholarly inquiry and the dissemination of new knowledge, and the challenge to use the expertise of its faculty to solve the problems of society makes the modern university the exciting, innovative, and important institution that it has become.

The ideas first presented by these classic philosophers of higher education remain at the heart of curriculum conversations today. Table 4.2 identifies these thoughts and their originators, as well as the contributions of the developmentalists and radical reformers of the mid–twentieth century.

Modern Additions to Curricular Philosophy

The underpinnings of virtually all current ideas concerning the higher education curriculum were introduced by the important educational philosophers of the late nineteenth century and the first two-thirds of the twentieth century. The only exception is that of the role of preparation for a career, which arose not out of philosophical reflection, but rather out of societal demands. Since then, educational writers have responded to both the earlier philosophers and to the incremental growth of demands on higher education resulting from an increasingly technological society. While space does not permit an exhaustive summary of these

TABLE 4.2. THE ORIGINS OF COMMON CURRICULAR IDEAS.

Source	Concept
Henry Cardinal Newman:	The community of scholars
John Dewey:	Active learning, experiential learning, problem solving
Alfred North Whitehead:	General education and specialization
Robert Maynard Hutchins:	Great Books curriculum
Thorstein Veblen and Abraham Flexner:	Focus on research and scholarship
Clark Kerr:	The multiversity
The developmentalists:	Curricula and pedagogy geared to stages of student development
The radicals:	Student-centered curricula and pedagogy

writers' many contributions, a few of the more influential warrant at least a brief mention in this broad survey of curricular philosophy.

Developmental Psychologists

Twentieth-century developmental psychologists base their work on an understanding of human development. Each posits a common sequence of development in every individual, with educational philosophy based on the needs of individuals at the appropriate stage of development. But these were not the first thinkers to focus on student needs. Remember that prior to the psychologists' specific identification of developmental stages, development also served as the basis for the student-centered educational philosophies of John Dewey and Alfred North Whitehead introduced earlier in this chapter.

Jean Piaget (*Science of Education and the Psychology of the Child*, 1970) studied *cognitive development* in children, noting that all people, regardless of circumstance, develop through identifiable stages of intellectual ability, but that not all people reach the highest stage, in which abstract thinking and hypothesizing are possible. The implication of this finding is that a significant portion of the college population may be unlikely to be able to participate in an education that demands sophisticated thinking skills. As higher education becomes increasingly accessible to ever-widening student populations, differences in cognitive development become even more salient in the development of appropriate higher education curricula and outcomes.

Erik Erikson (*Identity, Youth and Crisis*, 1968) examined personal psychological and social development rather than intellectual or cognitive development, with his theory demonstrating that individuals at each of eight identifiable stages of life fulfill their needs through a complex balancing of tensions. According to Erikson, late adolescents and young adults are motivated by their needs for establishing identity, for developing psychological intimacy with others, and for beginning to contribute to society. An appropriate college curriculum would serve these needs by providing students with experiences by which they could attain a consistent view of themselves as productive members of society.

Lawrence Kohlberg ("Stages of Moral Development as the Basis for Moral Education," 1971) focused on moral development, noting in particular that the highest levels of moral thinking and behavior are dependent on attaining sophisticated cognitive skills. A college curriculum built around moral development theory would require students to deal with moral dilemmas in an attempt to solve perennial ethical problems.

William Perry (*Forms of Intellectual Development in the College Years*, 1970) added to the theories of Erikson and Kohlberg by examining the specific stages of cognitive and moral development that college students attain as they progress through the college years.

Arthur Chickering ("Developmental Change as a Major Outcome," 1976) combines all the developmental theories into a comprehensive theory of higher education based on the belief that development in the various areas is not only linked, but mutually interdependent. In his view, colleges and college faculty need to be far more aware of how students progress through the stages, and to base the curriculum and their teaching and interactions with students on this awareness. A college basing its curriculum and teaching in developmental theory would aid students in developing through four comprehensive stages, moving dynamically through ever more complex levels of psychological, cognitive, social, and moral development.

Midcentury Radicals

Those of us who were in graduate schools of education in the late 1960s and early 1970s were often caught up in the reform agendas emanating from the early and mid-1960s, and we were introduced to the more radical educational ideas of Freire, Goodman, Illich, and Rogers, who believed that modern higher education was so far off the mark that nothing short of dismantling the curriculum was acceptable. All also believed in the inherent capability of students to be self-directed, and each therefore posited a highly student-centered philosophy of education. (No wonder we who were students at the time resonated to their reform agendas!)

Paul Goodman (*The Community of Scholars*, 1962) proposed decentralizing, doing away with trappings like grades, credits, and degrees, and building instead small communities of teachers, students, and community resource persons engaged in small-group discussion of important issues.

Carl Rogers (*Freedom to Learn*, 1969), a therapist of the humanistic school, proposed small, intensive group experiences in which individuals would come to experience themselves and others in the world and to free themselves from external demands. They would learn to trust themselves and others and to rely on their basic instinct for developing a meaningful life through healthy relationships and joy in learning.

Ivan Illich (*Deschooling Society*, 1971) proposed doing away with schools altogether, and creating instead *learning webs* that would provide learners with access to learning resources. Learning would be at the discretion of learners, with the networks providing access to formal educational programs in a variety of settings, skill exchanges that would facilitate matching learners with people who have something to teach them, peer matching for collaborative learning endeavors, and reference services for additional matching of people with services to offer.

Paulo Freire (*Pedagogy of the Oppressed*, 1970) considered students oppressed by the system and proposed radical reform based on student freedom to tackle challenges posed by teachers. Teachers and students would interact as equals, each reevaluating their positions based on feedback from the other. Curricular content should represent the nature of the oppression, as a means to engage students in critical analysis.

Late Twentieth-Century Challenges

First emerging late in the 1980s and early 1990s, a spate of criticisms of higher education began to shake the very foundation of the curriculum as it had developed over the previous century or so. The titles alone of some of the most vocal tell the story as it has escalated through the past two decades: *Common Learning* (Carnegie Foundation, 1981); *The Modern American College: Responding to the New Realities of Diverse Students and a Changing Society* (Chickering and Associates, 1981); *Liberating Education* (Gamson, 1984); *Experiential Learning: Experience as the Source of Learning and Development* (Kolb, 1984); *Involvement in Learning: Realizing the Potential of American Higher Education* (National Institute of Education, 1984); *Preparation for Life? The Paradox of Education in the Late Twentieth Century* (Burstyn, 1986); *Practical Intelligence: Nature and Origins of Competence in the Everyday World* (Sternberg and Wagner, 1986); *The Closing of the American Mind: How Higher Education Has Failed Democracy and Impoverished the Souls of Today's Students* (Bloom, 1987); *Cultural Literacy: What Every American Needs to Know* (Hirsch, 1987); *New Priorities for the University: Meeting Society's Needs for Applied Knowledge and Competent Individuals* (Lynton and Elman, 1987); *Education and Learning to Think* (Resnick, 1987); *Contesting the Boundaries of Liberal and Professional Education: The Syracuse Experiment* (Marsh, 1988); *In the Age of the Smart Machine: The Future of Work and Power* (Zuboff, 1988); *Information Anxiety* (Wurman, 1989); *Transforming Knowledge* (Minnich, 1990); *New Life for the College Curriculum* (Gaff, 1991); *An American Imperative: Higher Expectations for Higher Education* (Johnson Foundation, 1993); and *Troubled Times for American Higher Education: The 1990s and Beyond* (Kerr, 1994), to name just a few. As these titles reveal, criticisms of higher education in America include the following:

- Higher education has lost sight of its purpose to stimulate intellectual development.
- Higher education has become little more than a certification mill.
- Higher education doesn't prepare students adequately for the world of work.
- Students leave college with a degree that fails them in a complex and changing world.
- Colleges serve the purposes of elite faculty rather than the needs of society.

- Colleges sacrifice students on the altar of unimportant faculty research.
- Faculty don't work effectively or efficiently (or hard enough).
- The costs of higher education have expanded beyond reason.
- The curriculum fails to help students integrate their learning.
- Teachers rely on outmoded methods of instruction (especially lecture and discussion focused on the instructor).
- Higher education is responsible for the moral decline of the nation.
- Higher education is responsible for our economic decline.
- Colleges fail to address the needs of women and underserved minorities.
- Higher education has failed to teach students competence in a global economy.

While those of us in colleges and universities often feel besieged with unwarranted criticism and held responsible for situations clearly beyond our control, we nevertheless must appreciate that higher education in the United States has entered a new era. Except for the most elite colleges (those prestigious places in which bright and often wealthy undergraduate students still spend four uninterrupted years in the company of some of the best minds in the country), the ivory tower has crumbled, and colleges and universities are being required to be accountable in ways that were previously unimagined. Our responses to these pressures will determine our success not only in maintaining the excellence of a system that has been the envy of other nations, but in meeting the demands of society in the twenty-first century.

In response to criticism, current trends in higher education are focused on change. As the remainder of this book details, demographic changes, especially a vast increase in the number and proportion of previously underserved minorities, are forcing us to reexamine our curricula in light of their needs. Greater emphasis on the skills of oral and written communication and the ability to function effectively in a multicultural society will continue, but additional emphasis is also being placed on developing an ideological foundation. In the first part of the twentieth century, a college education was often designed to challenge traditional thought and values, to open young minds to a diversity of ideas. In the 1990s, demographic and social change has resulted in young people being exposed to great diversity (too much, too soon?) and we are being challenged to provide an anchor for students adrift in the sea of change.

General or liberal education has been challenged on the basis of its failure to provide an integrating learning experience, with a national movement away from distribution requirements and toward more coherent core curricula. It will require close examination of curricular aims and the measurement of student outcomes, as well as closer articulation between liberal and professional education, to improve coherence and specificity of outcomes in both general education and the major. Every area of the curriculum is being examined for its contribution to both a broadly educated society and to disciplinary competence in the new technological world.

References

Bloom, A. *The Closing of the American Mind: How Higher Education Has Failed Democracy and Impoverished the Souls of Today's Students.* New York: Simon & Schuster, 1987.

Burstyn, J. N. (ed.). *Preparation for Life? The Paradox of Education in the Late Twentieth Century.* Philadelphia, Pa.: Falmer, 1986.

Carnegie Foundation for the Advancement of Teaching. *Common Learning.* Washington, D.C.: Carnegie Foundation for the Advancement of Teaching, 1981.

Chickering, A. W. "Developmental Change as a Major Outcome." In M. T. Keeton and Associates, *Experiential Learning: Rationale, Characteristics, and Assessment.* San Francisco: Jossey-Bass, 1976.

Chickering, A. W., and Associates. *The Modern American College: Responding to the New Realities of Diverse Students and a Changing Society.* San Francisco: Jossey-Bass, 1981.

Dewey, J. *Democracy and Education.* New York: Free Press, 1967. (Originally published 1916.)

Erikson, E. *Identity, Youth and Crisis.* New York: Norton, 1968.

Flexner, A. *Universities: American, English, and German.* London: Oxford University Press, 1968. (Originally published 1930.)

Freire, P. *Pedagogy of the Oppressed.* (M. B. Ramons, trans.). New York: Continuum, 1970.

Gaff, J. G. *New Life for the College Curriculum: Assessing Achievements and Furthering Progress in the Reform of General Education.* San Francisco: Jossey-Bass, 1991.

Gamson, Z. F. *Liberating Education.* San Francisco: Jossey-Bass, 1984.

Goodman, P. *The Community of Scholars.* New York: Vintage Books, 1962.

Hirsch, E. D. *Cultural Literacy: What Every American Needs to Know.* Boston: Houghton Mifflin, 1987.

Hutchins, R. M. *The Learning Society.* New York: Mentor, 1968. (Originally published 1936.)

Illich, I. *Deschooling Society.* New York: HarperCollins, 1971.

Jencks, C., and Riesman, D. *The Academic Revolution.* New York: Doubleday, 1968.

Johnson Foundation. *An American Imperative: Higher Expectations for Higher Education.* Racine, Wisc.: Johnson Foundation, 1993.

Kerr, C. *The Uses of the University.* Cambridge, Mass.: Harvard University Press, 1963.

Kerr, C. *Troubled Times for American Higher Education: The 1990s and Beyond.* Albany, N.Y.: State University of New York, 1994.

Kohlberg, L. "Stages of Moral Development as the Basis for Moral Education." In C. M. Beck and others (eds.), *Moral Education: Interdisciplinary Approaches.* Toronto: University of Toronto Press, 1971.

Kolb, D. A. *Experiential Learning: Experience as the Source of Learning and Development.* Englewood Cliffs, N.J.: Prentice Hall, 1984.

Lynton, E. A., and Elman, S. E. *New Priorities for the University: Meeting Society's Needs for Applied Knowledge and Competent Individuals.* San Francisco: Jossey-Bass, 1987.

Marsh, P. T. (ed.). *Contesting the Boundaries of Liberal and Professional Education: The Syracuse Experiment.* Syracuse, N.Y.: Syracuse University Press, 1988.

Minnich, E. K. *Transforming Knowledge.* Philadelphia: Temple University Press, 1990.

National Institute of Education. *Involvement in Learning: Realizing the Potential of American Higher Education.* Report of the Study Group on the Conditions of Excellence in American Higher Education. Washington, D.C.: U.S. Government Printing Office, 1984.

Newman, J. H. *The Idea of a University.* Notre Dame, Ind.: University of Notre Dame Press, 1982. (Originally published 1873.)

Perry, W. G. *Forms of Intellectual Development in the College Years.* Troy, Mo.: Holt, Rinehart & Winston, 1970.

Piaget, J. *Science of Education and the Psychology of the Child.* New York: Orion, 1970.

Resnick, L. *Education and Learning to Think.* Washington, D.C.: National Academy Press, 1987.

Rogers, C. R. *Freedom to Learn.* Columbus, Ohio: Merrill, 1969.

Rudolph, F. *Curriculum: A History of the American Undergraduate Course of Study Since 1636.* San Francisco: Jossey-Bass, 1977.

Sternberg, R. J., and Wagner R. K. (eds.). *Practical Intelligence: Nature and Origins of Competence in the Everyday World.* New York: Cambridge University Press, 1986.

Veblen, T. *The Higher Learning in America.* New York: Hill & Wang, 1968. (Originally published 1918.)

Whitehead, A. N. *The Aims of Education and Other Essays.* New York: Free Press, 1968. (Originally published 1929.)

Wurman, R. S. *Information Anxiety.* New York: Doubleday, 1989.

Zuboff, S. *In the Age of the Smart Machine: The Future of Work and Power.* New York: Basic Books, 1988.

CHAPTER FIVE

STRUCTURES AND PRACTICES

Philo A. Hutcheson

Unlike many nations of the world, the United States does not have a national system of higher education or a national curriculum. The result is, in many respects, unique and tremendous variation among colleges and universities. Yet there are also common curricular structures and practices that most institutions follow, including general characteristics of degrees, credits, and structures of curriculum, which are worth exploring in some depth.

Degrees and Credits in U.S. Higher Education Today

Higher education institutions in this country tend to offer degrees at one of four levels: the associate, the bachelor's, the master's, and the doctorate. Each of these degrees is typically structured by courses and credits, although there is a decided tendency to define each in terms of the presumed number of years necessary to complete the degree as a full-time student. When it comes to the underlying educational content, however, the structure of courses and credits varies both over time and among institutions.

Although faculties and institutions initially developed degrees to certify that students had completed a specified course of study, the degree sometimes becomes reified and takes on a reality of its own. For example, as employers come to rely upon a degree as a credential, some students concentrate on the process of getting a degree rather than on the process of learning that it represents (Rudolph, 1977).

There are two levels of undergraduate degrees, the associate degree and the bachelor's degree. The associate degree is the characteristic degree of community colleges (an institutional type of U.S. origin). Students pursue postsecondary studies for two years and earn one of three degrees: the associate of arts degree, the associate of science degree, or the associate degree of applied science (Cohen and Brawer, 1989). Generally, the associate of arts or science degree is intended for students who plan to transfer to baccalaureate programs at four-year institutions, while students pursuing the associate of applied arts or science degree typically plan to enter directly into the workforce (Levine, 1978, p. 164). There are also diplomas and certificates offered for anywhere from a few months to two years of study. These certificates are usually offered at postsecondary technical institutes, and only occasionally do four-year institutions accept any of the coursework in those programs for baccalaureate credit (Cohen and Brawer, 1989).

The bachelor's degree easily represents the greatest diversity of degrees in the United States. Students spend four years in postsecondary education in any of a tremendous variety of program areas—literally ranging from art history to poultry to zoology (Rudolph, 1977, p. 9). These program areas represent several hundred majors, and although there are not as many specific bachelor's degrees as there are majors, nevertheless there are hundreds of bachelor's degrees. The two most typical are the bachelor of arts and the bachelor of science (Cass and Cass-Liepman, 1994). By the time of the Revolutionary War, all colleges offered the bachelor's degree as a four-year program of study, with three terms in each academic year. Throughout the nineteenth and twentieth centuries, colleges and universities have experimented with three-year baccalaureates, and some institutions have attempted two-year programs or credit by examination (Levine, 1978).

There are two levels of advanced, or postbaccalaureate, degrees (other than law, medical, and other professional degrees), the master's degree and the doctorate. The master's degree has exhibited considerable change during its 350-year history in the United States, as will become evident in the extended discussion of the degree later in this chapter. Typically, students study for one to three years of postbaccalaureate education to earn the master's degree (Conrad, Haworth, and Millar, 1993). The doctorate is the highest earned degree offered by U.S. colleges and universities. For several decades, doctoral degree requirements have been relatively uniform; students spend approximately three years in coursework and write a thesis reviewed and approved by a faculty committee (Spurr, 1970, pp. 117–119).

For the most part, higher education measures specific progress toward degrees through a credit system, despite the general tendency to describe degrees in terms of the number of years expected for completion. Individual institutions implemented the credit system in the late 1800s, as they added more courses and programs to the earlier classical curriculum, and it became increasingly difficult for them to assure comparable quality across diverse courses of study. To provide a way to compare academic programs and to measure quality in one form, the Carnegie unit was developed in 1908. Originally devised to measure secondary school students' achievement, one credit referred to a course meeting five days each week for a year of secondary school. Various academic groups recommended a certain number of Carnegie credits be required for admission to colleges and universities. Prodded by the Carnegie Foundation for the Advancement of Teaching, institutions moved to adopt the requirements for college admission. (The Carnegie Foundation offered college faculties a pension for adhering to certain standards, including students' completion of a specified number of course credits.) Colleges and universities adopted this quantitative course accounting by listing each course with a number that reflected the number of hours students were expected to spend in class (Levine, 1978, pp. 158–161). This standardization allowed colleges and universities to build specialized programs without identifying specific curricular values; all courses became equal in the eyes of the institution (Veysey, 1965, pp. 311–312).

A year of coursework is typically and approximately nine months in length, composed of terms designated either as semesters or quarters. These are typically measured in the context of two academic calendars, the quarter and the semester systems. The quarter system is composed of three ten-week terms (with the fourth quarter being the optional summer term), and the semester system is composed of two fifteen-week terms. There are other academic calendars, such as the 4–1–4 calendar, in which students have a one-month course between two semesters, and the trimester system (a variant on the semester calendar). A few institutions have other calendars, including the block system wherein students spend approximately one month at a time on a course, the open-entrance term system, and the variable-length term system (Levine, 1978).

Generally, the associate degree requires approximately 60 semester hours or 90 quarter hours (Spurr, 1970, p. 45), and the bachelor's degree is composed of approximately either 120 semester hours or 180 quarter hours (Levine, 1978, p. 162). Although the credit system is primarily constructed on the basis of the number of hours of classroom experience, there are several ways in which students, especially at the undergraduate level, may earn credits by examination. Many institutions allow students to take institution-specific examinations, and there are also several national standardized examinations, such as the College Level Examination Program, which students may take to earn undergraduate credits (Levine, 1978). Some institutions also use evaluation of students' life or career experiences as substitutes for academic credits (Gamson, 1989).

The credit system allows for not only the standardization of courses within institutions but also, to some degree, for standardization among institutions. For example, students completing an associate degree may supposedly transfer their credits to a four-year institution, just as students at a four-year institution could supposedly transfer credits to another four-year institution. This model of standardization, as envisioned by the educational leaders of the late 1800s, often is not fully effected. Institutions may choose to refuse credits, frequently on the basis of the judgment that the other institution's courses are not sufficiently similar to justify transfer of credit. The complexity of this contrast between model and practice is evidenced in research by Prager (1954), in which she found that within institutions offering both associate and baccalaureate degrees, students were often unable to transfer credits. Nor do most four-year institutions accept credits from vocational postsecondary institutions, although that policy may be changing. In Georgia, for example, the agencies responsible for vocational postsecondary institutions and the public university system have formally agreed to establish means of transferring credits from the vocational institutes to the public colleges and universities ("A Student-Centered Collaboration for Public Post-Secondary Education in Georgia," Dec. 8, 1994).

The credit system is so extensive that as of the late 1960s, institutions began to standardize continuing education, an area with programs as diverse as substance abuse counseling and small business development. Institutions offer one continuing education unit for every ten contact hours (National Task Force on the Continuing Education Unit, 1974). Generally colleges and universities do not accept these credits toward the fulfillment of degrees.

Nor do higher education institutions typically accept credits in remedial or developmental education programs for degree credits. Colleges and universities use developmental education to prepare students for postsecondary studies, with specific focus on English, reading, and mathematics. The area of developmental studies has moved from simply offering students basic study skills to include not only the areas noted above but also preparation in the academic disciplines and personal support through general counseling (Tomlinson, 1989). Although the term *developmental education* is a fairly recent one, the concept has long been a part of U.S. higher education. The nation's secondary schools have been no more systematic than the colleges and universities, and many institutions had preparatory programs in the 1800s (Veysey, 1965).

The means of establishing degree and institutional standards primarily occurs through regional accrediting associations. These organizations establish standards in such areas as the curriculum, faculty credentials, and institutional resources, and the accrediting process tends to occur every three to ten years, depending on the overall strength of the institution. There is an important set of additional accrediting associations for professions and occupations. These specialized accrediting organizations, often created by members of the profession or occupation seeking accreditation, also establish standards in the areas reviewed by regional associations, although they focus on the parts of the institutions that offer specific preparation for the occupation. In both cases, institutional participation is voluntary, although a college or university would be ill-advised (and probably short-lived) if it were to ignore regional accreditation or accreditation in such areas as medicine or law (Young and others, 1983). In recent years, federal student financial aid has been tied to attendance at an accredited institution.

Since the mid-1960s, state associations authorized by the Higher Education Act of 1964 have increasingly become the means for the legal authorization of degrees, especially for institutions seeking to offer new degrees. These state governing or coordinating boards have responsibility for both private and public institutions. Within institutions, although the governing boards are typically vested by state charter with the authority to grant degrees, these boards have delegated that power to presidents and, from them, to faculties. Hence much of the decision making for curriculum occurs within faculties, with nearly pro forma approval by administrations and governing boards (Rudolph, 1977). This is especially true in the case of the atomistic levels of curriculum, such as courses and even departmental requirements for majors and minors. Only in the case of major revisions is the board likely to be involved, even simply in terms of discussion, and only in the case of degree program changes is the state governing or coordinating board likely to be involved. In that case, the involvement is likely to be extensive, with the college or university providing detailed documentation regarding faculty and staff resources, institutional financing of the new program or degree, and potential for student enrollment in view of current programs or degrees already offered by the institution and in the state. State university systems also have the same method of evaluating proposals for new programs at public colleges and universities (Berdahl, 1971; Hines, 1988).

Curriculum Structures in the United States

Now, if the professor of American history gets sick, the professor of English history cannot take his work. And in a university, if the professor of American history from 1860 to 1864 gets sick, the professor of American history from 1865 to 1870 cannot take his work. [Hutchins, 1953, p. 35]

Although that caustic commentary dates from more than forty years ago, it is no less true today. Academic specialization, which began to develop its institutional form in the 1860s in the United States, continues. Yet, there are important and substantial exceptions to the specialized university, and it is useful to examine not only academic specialization but also how the exceptions have arisen and how they sustain themselves.

Curriculum in the United States at the institutional level easily represents a series of innovations; different institutions have tried different curricular patterns over time (Wegener, 1978). For example, the journal of the Association of American Colleges and Universities, *Liberal Education,* has from its outset documented the variety of curricular innovations in this country. Nationally, however, there are strong currents of conformity, one from 1636 to the late 1800s, the other from the late 1800s to the present. For the first 250 years, U.S. higher education tended to emphasize unitary knowledge in curriculum, a knowledge centered on ancient Greek and Roman literature and Christianity. Generally colleges and universities required students to take specific courses in a specific sequence; this prescribed curriculum provided a structural complement to unitary knowledge. Since the late 1800s, the nation's colleges and universities have offered a curriculum based on electives; knowledge, in curricular terms, is specialized and segmented.

Specialization, unitary knowledge, and prescription have long histories in Western higher education. Arthur Levine argues that as early as the first century B.C., Greek scholars were complaining about specialization in higher education. He also notes that by 1215, the faculties at the University of Paris had begun to require a "fully prescribed curriculum" (Levine, 1978, pp. 491, 498). In the United States, the Yale Report of 1828 continued that tradition ("The Yale Report . . . ," 1961). John Henry Cardinal Newman's *The Idea of a University* evoked centuries of tradition in regard to the concept of the unity of knowledge. Newman argued that theology stood at the center of all knowledge (Newman, [1873] 1982, pp. 32–53). It is the specialization of the U.S. professoriate, however, that has had substantial and enduring consequences for curricular issues in this country, particularly at the levels of bachelor's and doctoral degrees.

From Unitary Knowledge to Academic Specialization

The bachelor's and doctoral degrees most reflect the influence of academic specialization, an influence that began in the United States in the early 1800s. Initially, however, the baccalaureate represented a unitary, prescribed curriculum, and no institution in this country awarded the doctorate until the middle of the nineteenth century. Harvard College awarded the first bachelor of arts degrees in 1642, and the other colonial colleges followed suit (Brubacher and Rudy, 1958, p. 23). The curriculum of the colonial colleges was a prescribed one that emphasized the importance of classical studies. As the faculty of Yale College wrote in 1828, "To establish this truth, let a page of Voltaire be compared with a page of Tacitus. . . " ("The Yale Report. . . ," 1961, p. 290). In the prescribed curriculum, students took classes in Latin, Greek, Hebrew, rhetoric, and logic, as well as natural, mental, and moral philosophy; they did not have electives (Rudolph, 1977, pp. 29–30).

By the early 1800s, scientific investigation—as a practical matter and as a theoretical construct—began to influence curricula and degrees in the United States. Rensselaer Polytechnic Institute awarded a bachelor of natural science in 1835, and in 1851 Harvard's Lawrence Scientific School awarded the nation's first bachelor of science degree (Levine, 1978, p. 157). These degrees represented shifts in the curriculum, as colleges approved the selection of courses in such areas as the modern languages—including at some institutions the study of English—and the sciences (Rudolph, 1977, pp. 61–65). The primary source of the influence of scientific investigation was Germany; professors at universities at Halle and Göttengen, and eventually in formal organizational terms at the University of Berlin, pursued new methods and fields of inquiry. In the early 1800s, U.S. scholars began to study in Germany, returning to colleges and universities enthusiastic about the new forms of understanding. The sciences had been the purview of natural philosophy, the social sciences and humanities of mental and moral philosophy. These areas became increasingly diverse and eventually fragmented as the "rigorous and precise examination of phenomena, whether natural or historical," engaged increasing numbers of professors, excited about the discovery of new truths (Veysey, 1965, p. 127). The disciplines provided structures of knowledge, and as discussed later in this chapter, their organizational form became the department (Veysey, 1965, p. 142).

Yale awarded the first Ph.D. in 1862, but the degree did not take hold until much later in the century; ironically, Yale was among the last of the large Eastern schools to embrace disciplinary scholarship and graduate education (Levine, 1978, p. 158; Veysey, 1965, p. 235). The three students receiving that first doctorate had studied for two years after earning their bachelor's degrees and also submitted theses, typical of requirements for the doctorate at U.S. colleges and universities for the remainder of the century. The Johns Hopkins University was the first to implement more rigorous requirements—including three years of study, a thesis format, and language examinations. The earliest national effort to effect standards came from graduate student recommendations, and eventually the Association of American Universities and the National Association of State Universities proved instrumental in the development of standards (Spurr, 1970, pp. 117–119).

Veysey (1965) argues in *The Emergence of the American University* that by the end of the 1800s both professors and administrators had become eager to assume the role of scientific investigation—including the accompanying levels of specialization—found in the German university. Furthermore, U.S. colleges and universities, in eventual response to the Morrill Land-Grant Act of 1862, began offering a variety of vocational and professional programs that encouraged specialization. The opening of Cornell University in 1868 marks the advent of the institutionalization of electives resulting from utilitarian education and specialization in the developing disciplines (Veysey, 1965; Johnson, 1981).

The institutionalization of the utilitarian, or vocational, subjects created a multiplicity of fields of study, with accompanying developments of degrees and schools. These include a variety of preprofessional and vocational programs—education and business in the early 1900s, for example, or social work and criminal justice now—as well as professional programs, such as the rise of the master's of business administration in the 1920s (Levine, 1986, pp. 54–67). From the mid-1800s to the early 1900s, education (particularly teacher education) had its own institutions. Several states had normal schools for the education of teachers—during the first few decades of the twentieth century these institutions typically grew into state colleges and then eventually state universities offering the master's or the doctorate degree (Herbst, 1989). All the preprofessional and vocational developments are loosely styled, and perhaps caricatured, as market driven (Riesman, 1980), given the long history of student interest in the career outcomes of higher education, as Brubacher and Rudy argue (1958, p. 196).

One consequence of these roles of scientific investigation and utilitarian education was a shift in the structure of the curriculum. While the 1980s and 1990s have seen a surfeit of critics suggesting that the events of the 1960s caused a dramatic loosening of college graduation requirements, these changes have been occurring throughout the twentieth century. Frederick Rudolph notes that over a fifty-year period, electives rapidly replaced required courses; from 1890 to 1940 colleges shifted from requiring most courses to requiring fewer than half (Rudolph, 1977, p. 246). As Eliot, president of Harvard and one of the most influential of all nineteenth-century educators argued, "It is obvious that a university that undertakes thus to deal with all subjects of knowledge must offer a very large total of courses, and that in a certain sense, therefore, the choice of the individual student has a large range" (1908, p. 133). Although Rudolph does not attend to the consequences of utilitarian education as much as other scholars—suggesting rather that the curriculum histories of Harvard and Yale define the U.S. experience—he captures its consequence. By 1960, he notes, U.S. colleges and universities had awarded 2,452 different kinds of degrees; 532 of those were different kinds of bachelor's degrees awarded in 1960 (Rudolph, 1977, pp. 1, 9).

As early as 1877, the Johns Hopkins University catalogue referred to the major and the minor, with their reliance upon electives and their representation of the importance of the disciplines (Levine, 1978, p. 506). Initially the elective system was without restraint; students could take whatever courses interested them, without regard to sequence or relationships among the courses. In the words of an early historian of college curriculum, "The *liberalizing and equalizing* of studies in the curriculum since 1870 is too well known to require extended comment" (Snow, 1907, p. 173). In order to overcome the problem of students' choosing a smattering of introductory courses and compiling those courses into the number necessary for graduation without regard to substantive examination of any discipline or field, faculties developed the major. The major and the minor organized the knowledge of an area for students, so that they would learn at increasingly advanced levels as they took more courses (Rudolph, 1977, pp. 227–229).

Often the major requires more credit hours in the bachelor of science degree programs than in bachelor of arts programs. In the case of the former, students are likely to spend anywhere from 21 percent to 70 percent of their coursework in the major, while in the latter they are likely to spend from 21 percent to 50 percent of their time in the major (Levine, 1978, p. 31). The relationship between electives and the multiple fields resulting from science and utility proved very strong; a survey of curriculum changes in the late 1960s and early 1970s revealed that the number of electives available to students was increasing, even in majors (Rudolph, 1977, p. 248), although the curriculum changes of the 1980s and 1990s added more structure and requirements (Gaff, 1991).

One innovation that draws upon the disciplines is that of interdisciplinary studies. These fields arose in the 1930s when American studies became popular, allowing the concept of culture to serve as one of its organizing principles. Rudolph suggests that other area studies—Russian studies, Latin American studies—developed not so much as cultural areas but rather as the result of government and foundation interests in foreign policies (Rudolph, 1977, pp. 249–250). This impulse apparently reversed in the early 1970s with the advent of such interdisciplinary studies as women's studies and black studies, areas much more reliant on cultural issues for content and analysis. Nevertheless, these fields typically rely on the disciplines at the graduate level for their faculties, and the interdisciplinary majors often use electives (Carnochan, 1993; Conrad, 1978; Rudolph, 1977).

The development of academic specialization has deeply structured not only the curriculum in this country but also the organization of higher education institutions. Organizationally, almost all colleges and universities have academic departments that reflect the disciplines and utilitarian fields of study—such as biology, education, and sociology. The department represents the discipline or field of study, including at the level of doctoral study where research, or the production of knowledge, receives the most attention from professors (Trow, 1977, p. 15). Arguments on behalf of departments suggest that they provide the academic community for "the development, preservation, and transmission of knowledge" (Andersen, 1977, p. 8). Those less favorably disposed toward departments have argued that they foster specialization to the exclusion of other epistemologies and to the exclusion of campus unity while inhibiting innovation because of resistance to new subspecialties and research methods (Harrington, 1977, p. 57).

Thus the elective system has characterized the curricular pattern in U.S. higher education since the late 1800s. This pattern has variations, such as the distribution requirements common at so many colleges and universities, in which students may select courses from among many in designated areas to meet graduation requirements and the patterns of requirements for majors and minors (Conrad, 1978, pp. 51–52; Rudolph, 1977, p. 254). Meiklejohn (1916) argued for this sort of distribution of requirements in his inaugural address at Amherst College in 1912. This form of graduation requirements assures that students investigate many different fields. It has characterized undergraduate education for much of the twentieth century (Conrad, 1978).

Regardless of adaptations, however, the elective and discipline pattern is the dominant theme in U.S. higher education. For students, perhaps the most pernicious of the results of the elective and discipline pattern has been scientific illiteracy, as professors of science were least likely to develop courses for students not majoring in their disciplines (Rudolph, 1977, p. 255). Perhaps the strongest argument against the use of electives—and their organizing structure, the disciplines—is that in view of the number of disciplines, it is difficult for students to have a coherent education; the whole may not be more than the sum of the parts. Regardless of the obstacles to providing a coherent undergraduate curriculum, there have been repeated attempts to do so. These debates have occurred within institutions and at the national level; the next section offers some important examples of those debates.

General Education Structures

There are curricular exceptions to the elective system, and even to the disciplines, at some colleges and universities in this country. Some of the exceptions reflect age-old traditions while others reveal more contemporary conceptions of higher education. Given that the arguments for general education call upon a historical understanding of the curriculum, this section addresses general education as a reform effort devoted to building upon what higher education once did rather than restructuring the delivery of curriculum itself.

Although the prescribed curriculum faded away, it did not die. Aspects of its nature—including in some instances the conception of unitary knowledge argued by Newman and Hutchins—persist. Its most enduring conception takes the form of general education, although there is a curious characteristic to general education debates. Educators such as Newman and Hutchins assumed that general education represents shared knowledge in one form or another; they argued that because knowledge exhibits unitary characteristics, all students must have prescribed coursework, shared knowledge, in that specific area of knowledge (Newman, [1873] 1982, pp. 38, 52–53; Hutchins, 1936, p. 85). The debates about general education—particularly widespread in the 1970s and 1980s—often receive the most attention, yet most colleges and universities, including those that list general education requirements in their catalogues, do not require shared knowledge. A 1990 study of graduation requirements concluded that over 90 percent of the nation's colleges and universities require students to select from lists of courses rather than to take prescribed courses (Toombs, Fairweather, Amey, and Chen, 1989). Hence general education has assumed institutional meanings that differ from the arguments of its major proponents. This examination of general education illuminates a fundamental tension in the discussions of undergraduate curriculum in the United States: the importance of general education while electives hold sway.

One of the more renowned general education programs was at the University of Chicago. Its faculty began development of a general education program in the 1920s, but it was President Robert Hutchins and his confederates at the University who developed the arguments for a Great Books curriculum in the 1930s (Dzuback, 1991, pp. 186–189; Hutchins, 1936). St. John's College began a similar program in 1937, primarily at the urging of professors who had left the University of Chicago—particularly Stringfellow Barr and Scott Buchanan (Rudolph, 1977). Students at St. John's study about a hundred classic books selected on the basis of the texts' emphasis on metaphysics, "the perennial rational principles that undergird the universe" (Brubacher and Rudy, 1958, p. 268).

Columbia University, in contrast, began a shift in the early 1900s from traditional unitary knowledge to shared interdisciplinary knowledge as evidenced by its well-known course "Introduction to Contemporary Civilization" (Belknap and Kuhns, 1977). Rather than the usual focus on what is known, this form of general education focuses on the process of knowing. It particularly emphasizes understanding through the examination of contemporary problems (Conrad, 1978, p. 13).

One often-cited example of curricular reform focusing on general education is the Experimental College at the University of Wisconsin, established by Alexander Meiklejohn (Meiklejohn, [1932] 1981; Veysey, 1973; Rudolph, 1977; Grant and Riesman, 1978; Levine, 1978). The college began in 1927 without classes or credits, with the all-male faculty and students living in a dormitory together, examining in the first year ancient Greece and in the second year the contemporary United States. Yet despite Wisconsin's history of experimenting with its university, as in the case of the Wisconsin Idea, with its purposeful link between state needs and university programs, the Experimental College closed after five years. Initial problems included professors' ambiguity given their "joint faculty appointments between the colleges and the disciplines" (Levine, 1978, p. 346). Finally, however, pressures from "fraternities, local politicians, and unfriendly professors" as well as anti-Semitic and anti-Communist attacks on the program and its largely out-of-state enrollment provided the impetus for closing the program (Veysey, 1973, p. 56).

More recently, many colleges and universities reexamined their approaches to the core curriculum in the 1970s and 1980s, analyzing the courses that ostensibly provided a certain commonality in the education of all students at each institution. In most cases, the course requirements were neither unitary nor prescriptive, offering instead sets of requirements evidencing agreements among faculty members about what all students should learn. As a result of these reexaminations, many colleges and universities developed innovative practices in attempts to revitalize their curricular offerings (Gaff, 1983). For example, in the mid-1980s, Hamline University in St. Paul, Minnesota, developed a core curriculum that emphasized writing and oral communication across the curriculum, from a seminar for all first-year students to the requirement that all majors offer a required writing-intensive course (Gaff, 1991, p. 131). Some of the core curriculum examinations attracted a great deal of national attention, as was the case at Stanford University. Critics and disciples of the Western canon—at the university and external to it—debated the nature of and changes to the core curriculum (Carnochan, 1993).

Most institutions that have revised general education programs, whether the programs rely upon what is known or the process of knowing, have struggled with substantial constraints. Faculty members are products of their specialized graduate educations, and they think in terms of the disciplines for their courses. Furthermore, they tend to have little education in the broad areas of knowledge typically required in general education. Nor do their interpretations of knowledge necessarily include newer specialized interpretations such as feminism or minority literature (Aiken and others, 1987; Anderson, 1987; Gates, 1992). Increasingly, students are coming from disparate backgrounds, and traditional general education approaches, calling upon texts of Western Europe, have problematic meaning for many students. Finally, the programs often have unclear goals and ambiguous ideals (Cross, 1976; Gaff, 1983, pp. 13–22). Thus reform attempts in undergraduate curriculum that address general education face a variety of important, even contradictory, issues.

Institutional Innovations in Curriculum

There are other substantial issues in innovations in the curriculum. Conrad (1978, p. 13) argues that there is an additional approach to curriculum, one that centers on the development of student competencies. Alverno College is undoubtedly the best known of the institutions that have developed a curriculum focusing on student outcomes. Students must demonstrate competencies in eight areas at Alverno, and they must achieve certain developmental levels in each of the competencies. The Alverno faculty has periodically redefined the list, but in 1996 the eight areas were communication, analysis, problem solving, valuing, social interaction, global perspectives, effective citizenship, and aesthetic response. Another institution with a competency-based curriculum is Metropolitan State University in Minneapolis–St. Paul, Minnesota. Metropolitan State differs from Alverno in that its students are primarily working adults who are responsible for developing their programs (Conrad, 1978, pp. 40–42; Levine, 1978, pp. 405–409).

Not all innovations sustain themselves. For example, Conrad (1978), Levine (1978), and McHenry and others (1977) all note several institutions that in the 1970s experimented with different curricular patterns; some of those institutions returned to some variation of the elective and discipline pattern, while others have continued their innovations. The University of California, Santa Cruz, and to a lesser degree, the University of Wisconsin, Green Bay, now offer curricula more reflective of the disciplines. Sterling and Mars Hill Colleges now offer a curriculum completely grounded in the disciplines, in contrast to their efforts in competency education in the 1970s. Goddard College, however, continues to emphasize a nearly radical egalitarian student-development curriculum. Evergreen State College maintains an interdisciplinary program with no required courses. Hampshire College continues to offer a highly individualistic program with considerable emphasis on student effort (Cass and Cass-Liepman, 1994). Thus, institutions can and do develop curricular innovations despite the strength of electives and disciplines and their organizational components, academic departments.

The University of California, Berkeley (UCB) provides an example of the strength of the elective and discipline pattern in a mid-1960s attempt to restructure the curriculum for selected students and in a 1966 report by a Berkeley faculty committee. Modeling the college founded by Meiklejohn at the University of Wisconsin, in 1965 Joseph Tussman developed a two-year curriculum at UCB, emphasizing such themes as "war and peace, freedom and authority, the individual and society, acceptance and rebellion, and law and conscience." The program used seminars and lectures rather than courses (Levine, 1978, p. 374). It lasted until 1969, failing largely because students had little voice in its development just when they had begun to demand such a voice and faculty members could not dedicate the substantial time necessary for intensive teaching. The latter problem echoed an extensive report by a committee of UCB professors, a report that highlighted the problems of large undergraduate classes and a research-oriented faculty (Select Committee on Education, 1966).

The tally of institutions where innovation failed hardly suggests that innovations will necessarily fail. Rather, it serves to illustrate the institutional nature of innovation and the strength of the elective and discipline pattern, suggesting the following characteristics of successful curriculum innovation or reform. Institutions, either nationally or individually, must have relative autonomy from a variety of agencies, including the federal and state governments. This autonomy may be de facto or the result of inattention. Equally important is the absence of controlling traditional scholarly views, which may, as in the case of several institutions ranging from St. John's College and its general education reform to Metropolitan State University and its student-development innovation, result from conscious faculty decisions to transcend the disciplines. This odd combination leading to autonomy must be complemented by economic conditions—those curricula that are economically safe or rigorous are unlikely to undergo much in the way of substantial revisions. An oft-cited example of curriculum reform, the Harvard General Education Report of 1945, presents in fact a curious example, since very little curricular change actually occurred at Harvard following the issuance of the report (Levine, 1978; Rudolph, 1977). While neither Levine nor Rudolph offer a conclusion based on Harvard's secure position, a well-rewarded, productive faculty and a student body assured of a Harvard degree might find little reason to implement change.

It appears that large universities are marked more by repeated but failed attempts at innovation than are smaller colleges and universities. Several large universities attempted curricular innovations during the twentieth century; few of those innovations survived (Grant and Riesman, 1978, p. 369). While a number of curricular innovations failed among small colleges, too, there are also many instances of those innovations continuing today. Large universities and their faculties are most committed to research, an activity fundamentally intertwined with doctoral education and academic specialization (Trow, 1977, pp. 32–33). Small institutions often emphasize teaching rather than research, seeking to find ways for students to connect diverse areas of knowledge; thus small institutions have a certain flexibility in curriculum reform that large universities do not share (McHenry, 1977, pp. 223–224).

Academic Specialization and the Persistent Structure of Curriculum

In conclusion, there may be as many recommendations about the reform or innovation in curriculum as there are types of degrees and curricula. Professors, administrators, and representatives from national and federal agencies are prolific in this regard, with commentaries ranging from essays to book-length treatments (Carnegie Foundation for the Advancement of Teaching, 1977; Cheney, 1989; Project on Redefining the Meaning and Purpose of Baccalaureate Degrees, 1985), continuing a tradition evidenced in the 1828 Yale Report. This diversity of opinion on the part of people skilled in argument represents one of the major obstacles to widespread reform in higher education curriculum.

While curriculum reform is often cast as a set of political or economic issues—trading enrollments for enrollments, for example, as Cohen and March (1986, pp. 106–107) argue—a more accurate representation seems to be that professors and administrators are vested in curricular decisions, that curriculum is how they understand knowledge in its important forms. The enduring nature of philosophy in the form of one-person departments of some small colleges suggests that professors and administrators are unwilling to sacrifice too much on the altar of enrollment management, and that despite the few students that philosophy draws, it is a significant area of study. There is a fundamental commitment to some vague form of higher education. The vagueness, however, is problematic, since proponents of one form of curriculum or another lay claim to any number of issues. Arguments for civic and global responsibility, teaching and research issues, student demand, faculty interest and preparation, financial resources, and moral and ethical development all vie for prominence (Levine, 1978, pp. 250–417). One possible obstacle to curriculum innovation or reform is that administrative visions and financial restrictions may break down or create boundaries for faculty discussion of curricular changes.

The diversity of opinion, however, is balanced against another deeply rooted characteristic, the doctoral education of professors and administrators. The curriculum is based on disciplines, and the university is based on departments organized according to disciplines. While there are exceptions, they are indeed exceptions. For more than a century, graduate education programs have primarily conceived of the doctorate as disciplinary and content driven, a research degree. Research in specialized fields, as Hutchins so harshly noted in the early 1950s, characterizes U.S. higher education at all levels. The introduction and subsequent lack of attention to the doctorate of arts, a degree expressly designed for the college teacher, speaks clearly to the power of the research ethos. The graduate schools have staffed U.S. colleges and universities, and even professional schools with substantial commitments to clinical approaches—such as business schools—have adopted forms of disciplinary education. Vocational emphases also further the use of electives, as Cornell University exemplified in its foundation. In the words of Ezra Cornell, "I trust we have laid the foundation of a University—'an institution where any person can find instruction in any study'" (quoted in A. B. Cornell, 1884, p. 201).

Innovations and reforms survive for a variety of reasons. Faculty interests are broad ranging, albeit often constrained by academic specialization, and professors find expressions of knowledge in different curricula. Experiments at large universities such as Berkeley and at small colleges such as Alverno indicate the range of faculty interests. The variety of higher education institutions, public acceptance of that variety, and the value of choice in U.S. higher education all play major roles in the maintenance of various curricula. Curiously, and despite the urging of politicians interested in assessment, it remains difficult to assess the actual (as opposed to perceived) effects of these various curricular designs. The most comprehensive summary of college effects, by Pascarella and Terenzini (1991, pp. 62–161), indicates that differences among colleges are minimal, especially when students' socioeconomic status and academic preparation are held constant. Nevertheless, we have accepted the idea that different curricula provide different learning experiences for different students; the prevailing concept is that the Alverno student does not belong at St. John's (Rudolph, 1977, p. 153).

Finally, it is worth closing with a return to the opening point: there is no commitment to a particular national curriculum in this country, despite the consistent reports from federal and national agencies. Institutions—shaped by faculty, students, history, and environmental pressures—must continuously seek new ways to answer the age-old curriculum question: How do we best educate?—a question that spurs debate and fosters growth and improvement.

References

Aiken, S. H., and others. "Trying Transformations: Curriculum Integration and the Problem of Resistance." *Signs*, 1987, *12*(2), 255–275.

Andersen, K. J. "In Defense of Departments." In D. E. McHenry and others (eds.), *Academic Departments: Problems, Variations, and Alternatives*. San Francisco: Jossey-Bass, 1977.

Anderson, M. "Changing the Curriculum in Higher Education." *Signs*, 1987, *12*(2), 222–254.

Belknap, R. L., and Kuhns, R. *Tradition and Innovation: General Education and the Reintegration of the University, a Columbia Report*. New York: Columbia University Press, 1977.

Berdahl, R. O. *Statewide Coordination of Higher Education*. New York: American Council on Education, 1971.

Brubacher, J. S., and Rudy, W. *Higher Education in Transition: An American History, 1636–1956* (1st ed.) New York: HarperCollins, 1958.

Carnegie Foundation for the Advancement of Teaching. *Missions of the College Curriculum: A Contemporary Review with Suggestions*. San Francisco: Jossey-Bass, 1977.

Carnochan, W. B. *The Battleground of the Curriculum: Liberal Education and American Experience*. Stanford, Calif.: Stanford University Press, 1993.

Cass, M., and Cass-Liepman, J. (eds.). *Cass and Birnbaum's Guide to American Colleges*. New York: HarperCollins, 1994.

Cheney, L. V. *50 Hours: A Core Curriculum for College Students.* Washington, D.C.: National Endowment for the Humanities, 1989.

Cohen, A. M., and Brawer, F. B. *The American Community College.* (2nd ed.) San Francisco: Jossey-Bass, 1989.

Cohen, M. D., and March, J. G. *Leadership and Ambiguity: The American College President.* Boston: Harvard Business School, 1986.

Conrad, C. F. *The Undergraduate Curriculum: A Guide to Innovation and Reform.* Boulder, Colo.: Westview Press, 1978.

Conrad, C. F., Haworth, J. G., and Millar, S. B. *A Silent Success: Master's Education in the United States.* Baltimore, Md.: Johns Hopkins University Press, 1993.

Cornell, A. B. *"True and Firm": Biography of Ezra Cornell, Founder of the Cornell University.* New York: Barnes, 1884.

Cross, K. P. *Accent on Learning: Improving Instruction and Reshaping the Curriculum.* San Francisco: Jossey-Bass, 1976.

Dzuback, M. A. *Robert M. Hutchins: Portrait of an Educator.* Chicago: University of Chicago Press, 1991.

Eliot, C. W. *University Administration.* Boston: Houghton Mifflin, 1908.

Gaff, J. G. *General Education Today: A Critical Analysis of Controversies, Practices, and Reforms.* San Francisco: Jossey-Bass, 1983.

Gaff, J. G. *New Life for the College Curriculum: Assessing Achievements and Furthering Progress in the Reform of General Education.* San Francisco: Jossey-Bass, 1991.

Gamson, Z. F. *Higher Education and the Real World: The Story of CAEL.* Wolfeboro, N.H.: Longwood Academic, 1989.

Gates, H. L., Jr. *Loose Canons: Notes on the Culture Wars.* New York: Oxford University Press, 1992.

Grant, G., and Riesman, D. *The Perpetual Dream: Reform and Experiment in the American College.* Chicago: University of Chicago Press, 1978.

Harrington, F. H. "Shortcomings of Conventional Departments." In D. E. McHenry and others (eds.), *Academic Departments: Problems, Variations, and Alternatives.* San Francisco: Jossey-Bass, 1977.

Herbst, J. *And Sadly Teach: Teacher Education and Professionalization in American Culture.* Madison: University of Wisconsin Press, 1989.

Hines, E. R. *Higher Education and State Governments: Renewed Partnership, Cooperation, or Competition?* ASHE-ERIC Higher Education Report No. 5. Washington, D.C.: School of Education and Human Development, George Washington University, 1988.

Hutchins, R. M. *The Higher Learning in America.* New Haven, Conn.: Yale University Press, 1936.

Hutchins, R. M. *University of Utopia.* Chicago: University of Chicago Press, 1953.

Johnson, E. L. "Misconceptions About the Early Land-Grant Colleges." *Journal of Higher Education,* 1981, *52*(4), 333–351.

Levine, A. *Handbook on Undergraduate Curriculum.* San Francisco: Jossey-Bass, 1978.

Levine, D. O. *The American College and the Culture of Aspiration, 1915–1940.* Ithaca: Cornell University Press, 1986.

McHenry, D. E. "Toward Departmental Reform." In D. E. McHenry and others (eds.), *Academic Departments: Problems, Variations, and Alternatives.* San Francisco: Jossey-Bass, 1977.

McHenry, D. E., and others, eds. *Academic Departments: Problems, Variations, and Alternatives.* San Francisco: Jossey-Bass, 1977.

Meiklejohn, A. "The Aim of the Liberal College." In M. G. Fulton (ed.), *College Life: Its Conditions and Problems.* New York: Macmillan, 1916.

Meiklejohn, A. *The Experimental College* (edited and abridged by J. W. Powell). Cabin John, Md.: Seven Locks Press, 1981. (Originally published 1932.)

National Task Force on the Continuing Education Unit. *The Continuing Education Unit: A Unit of Measurement for Non-Credit Continuing Education Programs.* Washington, D.C.: National University Extension Association, 1974.

Newman, J. H. *The Idea of a University.* Notre Dame, Ind.: University of Notre Dame Press, 1982. (Originally published 1852.)

Pascarella, E. T., and Terenzini, P. T. *How College Affects Students: Findings and Insights from Twenty Years of Research.* San Francisco: Jossey-Bass, 1991.

Prager, C. "Transfer and Articulation Within Colleges and Universities." *Journal of Higher Education,* 1954, *64*(5), 539–554.

Project on Redefining the Meaning and Purpose of Baccalaureate Degrees. *Integrity in the College Curriculum: A Report to the Academic Community.* Washington, D.C.: Association of American Colleges, 1985.

Riesman, D. *On Higher Education: The Academic Enterprise in an Era of Rising Student Consumerism.* San Francisco: Jossey-Bass, 1980.

Rudolph, F. *Curriculum: A History of the American Undergraduate Course of Study Since 1636.* San Francisco: Jossey-Bass, 1977.

Select Committee on Education. *Education at Berkeley: Report of the Select Committee on Education.* Berkeley: University of California Press, 1966.

Snow, L. F. *The College Curriculum in the United States.* New York: Teachers College Press, 1907.

Spurr, S. H. *Academic Degree Structures: Innovative Approaches.* New York: McGraw-Hill, 1970.

"A Student-Centered Collaboration for Public Post-Secondary Education in Georgia." Atlanta: Georgia Department of Technical and Adult Education, Dec. 8, 1994.

Tomlinson, L. M. *Postsecondary Developmental Programs: A Traditional Agenda with New Imperatives.* ASHE-ERIC Higher Education Report No. 3. Washington, D.C.: School of Education and Human Development, George Washington University, 1989.

Toombs, W., Fairweather, J. S., Amey, M., and Chen, A. *Open to View: Practice and Purpose in General Education.* University Park, Pa.: Center for the Study of Higher Education, 1989.

Trow, M. "Departments as Contexts for Teaching and Learning." In D. E. McHenry and others (eds.), *Academic Departments: Problems, Variations, and Alternatives.* San Francisco: Jossey-Bass, 1977.

Veysey, L. *The Emergence of the American University.* Chicago: University of Chicago Press, 1965.

Veysey, L. "Stability and Experiment in the American Undergraduate Curriculum." In C. Kaysen (ed.), *Content and Context: Essays on College Education.* New York: McGraw-Hill, 1973.

Wegener, C. *Liberal Education and the Modern University.* Chicago: University of Chicago Press, 1978.

"The Yale Report of 1828." In R. Hofstadter and W. Smith (eds.), *American Higher Education: A Documentary History.* Vol. 1. Chicago: University of Chicago Press, 1961.

Young, K. E., and others. *Understanding Accreditation: Contemporary Perspectives on Issues and Practices in Evaluating Educational Quality.* San Francisco: Jossey-Bass, 1983.

CHAPTER SIX

SOCIAL FORCES SHAPING THE CURRICULUM

Mildred García and James L. Ratcliff

Colleges and universities, though basically conservative institutions, are evolving in relation to the broader social context, and that evolution has an impact on the curriculum. Often curriculum committees and academic administrators try to make broad changes in the curriculum, and often these efforts result in minor modification or outright failure rather than broad transformation. To plan a more targeted, purposeful, and inclusive curriculum, one must consciously examine and assess the external forces and broader social context that give impetus, direction, and constraints for curricular changes.

We are at the threshold of the twenty-first century and grappling with what it means to be an educated person in the new millennium. As we approach our curriculum, we are forever cognizant that our institutions are creating new leaders and educating citizens who are building a nation that strives to be a just, democratic society. Preparing our leaders for this new era will entail not only deliberately shaping a curriculum within our institutions but understanding that it is also shaped by the world in which we live. What will students need to know in order to navigate our new global reality and be successful?

A *curriculum* has been defined as a body of courses presenting the knowledge, principles, values, and skills that are the intended consequences of an undergraduate education. The institution's definition of the undergraduate program of study communicates the faculty's view of what constitutes an educated person. The curriculum is a social construct undergoing continuous revision and modification.

Curriculum leaders need to analyze those influences that impinge on the curriculum. We need to reevaluate what it is that students need to know in our global society. Prior to any major curriculum change, department chairs, program directors, curriculum committees, deans, and chief academic officers should systematically examine the specific demographic, social, political, economic, and technological forces that will influence undergraduate education at their institution.

Demographic Influences

As the United States experiences an explosion in the diversity of peoples and cultures among its population, so do its colleges and universities. In ten years, from 1982 to 1992, there was a 51.5 percent increase in students of color among U.S. undergraduate enrollments; in 1992 alone, 23 percent of undergraduate enrollments nationwide were students of color (Carter and Wilson, 1994). In addition to ethnic and racial diversity, women of all ages, colors, and classes have entered higher education in large numbers and represent 55.2 percent of the undergraduates enrolled on our campuses. Although women undergraduate students are still thought of as a minority or special-interest population, they have been in the majority on most campuses since the 1980s.

The students in our classrooms are vastly different from those of fifty years ago. Excluded for years from higher education, this new and heretofore ignored student population has triggered a revolution within the academic disciplines. Their new insights, knowledge, and experience have challenged our knowledge base. Academics have been confronted with demands to include knowledge that had been excluded, to rethink their understandings and theoretical underpinnings, and to transform what they teach, how they teach, and why they teach it.

Women's studies programs exemplify this dynamic change within the curriculum. As they gained impetus in the 1970s, they served to break down barriers between academic disciplines and encourage students and faculty to find unifying themes, concepts, and forces across bodies of knowledge. Introductory courses to women's studies examine multiple academic disciplines by including such topics as the history of women, the philosophy of gender and how knowledge is constructed, the economic reality of women, and the biology of the sexes. Such crosscutting themes, forces, and factors provide the grounds for liberating dialogue and impart new social and personal relevance to undergraduate education.

In the 1970s, women's studies programs began to proliferate and they attracted women into the academy. Unfortunately, they were often marginalized and had little impact on the broader undergraduate curriculum. Because of this marginality, women felt alienated in academic settings and communicated that their formal education was either irrelevant or peripheral (Belenky, Clinchy, Goldberger, and Tarule, 1986). By the 1980s, however, research done by feminists in the field documented how developmental theory had been established to validate men's experience and competence as the baseline for everyone at the expense of women's development (Gilligan, 1982). Feminist writers convincingly argued that there is a masculine bias at the very heart of most academic disciplines and that very little thought had been given to modes of learning, knowing, and valuing common to women. Important research on women's interests, needs, and ways of knowing emerged (Belenky, Clinchy, Goldberger, and Tarule, 1986).

Currently, feminists on our campuses are challenging the root of the established system that shapes undergraduate curricula (Minnich, 1990). Dialogues in institutions across the country question the normative standards upon which curricula are based. Spurred by the feminists, much of the curriculum discussion examines what it means to establish educational standards and quality in different contexts and cultures.

Racial and ethnic *pluralism*, the study of diverse groups, has also been incorporated into many undergraduate curricula as a way of understanding difference and sameness. Ethnic studies curricula originated in the campus protests during the U.S. Civil Rights movement of the 1960s, and there has been at least two decades of work in developing a better understanding of our diverse society. Yet, as Gates (1992) writes so eloquently, no one would have predicted that pluralism and multiculturalism would be topics so nationally debated in the late twentieth century and found as front-page stories of national newspapers and popular magazines, television shows, and radio commentaries. He reminds us that W.E.B Du Bois predicted that the color line would be the problem of the twentieth century, and Gates predicts that ethnic differences that encompass color, gender, and class will be the problem to confront in the twenty-first century. Add sexual preference to this mix and we see emerging front-line issues for our society as a whole and for our colleges and universities in particular.

Those involved in the development of multiculturalism and curriculum transformation argue that multiculturalism and diversity are central to preparing persons for the next century. The increased globalization of our society and interdependence among countries has renewed interest in the study of non-Western cultures and foreign languages. The rapid socioeconomic, political, and environmental transformations both within and beyond the United States have heightened the need of preparing students for an interdependent world of great cultural multiplicity (Schmitz, 1993). In addition, multiculturalism enhances the creation of new knowledge. Often, the knowledge base of the various disciplines and fields of study has grown within the context of the dominant U.S. society; examination of the predominate concepts, ideas, models and theories in light of gender, ethnic, racial, and cultural differences in countries throughout the world tests and challenges prevailing interpretations and understandings. Different perspectives push disciplines to rethink the questions they ask, the methods they use, and the standards by which excellence is judged. The presence of diversity on campus also challenges assumptions about content and raises important questions about how effective the teaching and learning process will be if a growing proportion of students perceive themselves to be left out or alienated by what is taught (García and Smith, 1996).

Today, new questions are emerging about the role of such discrete programs as women's studies and ethnic studies. The call is to compare and contrast throughout academic programs and to infuse the undergraduate curriculum broadly with multiculturalism (Magner, 1991). As Minnich (1990) so clearly points out, unless our conversations about the curriculum are accompanied by ongoing work on how the dominant curriculum can be reconceptualized to be receptive to the study of the majority of humankind and how to deliver this body of knowledge to our pluralistic student body, we are at risk of creating curricula that continue to grow exactly as in the past—atomistically and increasingly distant from the students and society they serve.

Political Influences

The dynamic change fostered by efforts to study diversity in the disciplines, in general education, and in college pedagogy on our campuses has reignited conservative voices that yearn for a simpler time when cultural diversity was not such a central concern, Western civilization was celebrated, and truth seemed clear. These voices seek to return higher education to times when those who were different were silenced and excluded from our classrooms, when single canons and grand narratives were heralded in the disciplines, and when content was based on majority norms and unitary concepts of IQ. The 1990s have seen voters in California pass Proposition 187—a law designed to bar access to public schooling, welfare, and medical services for individuals who are not U.S. citizens, even if they can prove legal immigration status. The University of California Board of Regents voted to eliminate the use of affirmative action in admissions and hiring procedures on their campuses. These are examples of political actions that can have chilling impacts on higher education in general and on the curriculum in particular.

Culture Wars

Fueled by the politics of the Reagan era and by the Republican revolution, public discourse called for the return to the traditional curriculum. Stiff and significant resistance to changes in the canons was evident on campuses, and the society at large joined the debate turning to those with political beliefs to lead the battle. Beginning in the mid-1980s, it became commonplace to refer to the discourse, dialogue, and disagreement regarding the canons of the undergraduate curriculum as *culture wars,* due to the focus given to issues of diversity and multiculturalism on campus and in society. Some argue that the new curriculum politicizes higher education and balkanizes our society (Bloom, 1987; D'Souza, 1991).

Bloom's best-seller *The Closing of the American Mind* illustrated the interface between the academy and the public at large regarding the undergraduate curriculum. Philosopher and novelist Walker Percy writes of the public fascination with the book: "I think the title has a lot to do with it. You go to a bookstore in a small town in Louisiana and see the damned thing piled up. It turns out that a lot of parents are buying it for their kids in college. It struck a nerve with parents who think that those damned professors are screwing up their kids" (Walter, 1989, p. 16). Bloom's book and its public popularity struck a raw nerve in the academy. The former chancellor of the State University of New York (SUNY), Clifton Wharton, labeled the book "racist and elitist" (Heller, 1988). The Vermont Humanities Council made it the focus of its annual conference and sponsored a series of public town meetings to discuss the book and its implications for the undergraduate curriculum (Hirschorn, 1987). Most academics derided it.

The book stimulated discussion and dialogue in disciplines such as art (Schensul, 1990), anthropology (Carroll, 1990; Morgen, 1990; Schensul and Carroll, 1990), English (Smith, Rose, and Goodman, 1993), economics (Gift and Krislov, 1991), history (Lawler, 1989), and philosophy (Douglas, 1991; Mathie, 1991; Silliman, 1990). It also promoted research on whether undergraduate students were open to the enrichment, analysis, and illumination great literature offers (Caverzasi, 1992) and on what curriculum might better involve students in broad inquiry in the humanities, social sciences, and natural sciences (Morgan, 1991). Furthermore, the debate on the viability and validity of cultural relativism as a premise for the structure of knowledge within the academy was ignited (Moses, 1990, Nathan, 1991; Wake, 1991). It gave new focus and forum to the role of feminist studies and cultural studies in the transformation of the curriculum. It called into question the role of different types of institutions of higher education in providing liberal education (Edington, 1990; Sasseen, 1990; Standley, 1988).

Most significantly, Bloom's book served as a catalyst to the debate over disciplinary and interdisciplinary studies and over core requirements and student choice of topics of study. Bloom charged that the contemporary university does not have a vision of what a human being must know to be considered educated, and that such a vision was a fundamental responsibility of higher education. The demand in the popular press to find the essentials of undergraduate studies resulted in renewed calls for a core curriculum (Clavner, 1990). Bloom's call for a reinstitution of Great Books study raised questions as to what are or are not great works that stimulate students' imaginations. Equally important was the pedagogical issue of how certain course materials were superior to others in engendering independent thinking and analysis among students. Chapman (1992), for example, argued that instead of placing faith in a particular reading list, the faculty should focus on the development of the rhetorical powers of students.

D'Souza (1991) alleged that American academics were seeking to promote the goals of liberal education while acceding to the partisan polemics of the advocates of feminism, sexual orientation, and racial and ethnic diversity. He argued that activist faculty and students had split institutions of higher education on moral grounds, charging that universities were structurally racist, sexist, homophobic, and class biased. These charges formed the foundation for a double standard for the hiring and promotion of minority faculty and the admission and grading of minority students. Such practices, D'Souza argued, were not an exploration of new ideas and paradigms, but rather the creation of an environment where free speech rights of students and faculty are suppressed. Kelebray (1992) associated the current multicultural concerns with socialism and advocated defending traditional forms of the study of Western civilization.

Other scholars advocated education for cultural pluralism, however, and retorted that education has in fact always been political and never neutral. If we are to respond to the changing population on our campuses and prepare students for a culturally pluralistic society, they add, students must learn about various peoples and develop skills to negotiate difference. Who decides what is to be included and excluded, how questions are framed, and how content is taught shapes our consciousness and shapes our collective identity.

The culture wars tend to assume a false dichotomy, a dichotomy that views knowledge as either uncritically inclusive of diverse perspectives or limited to the perspective of male, majority Western thought. In essence, de-centering the curriculum is not an either-or dichotomy but is founded on the rational appreciation of all voices, perspectives, and paradigms relevant to the matter at hand. Including the newfound information adds intellectual vitality and invigorates knowledge. The dynamic tension created by those who advocate a more diverse, inclusive curriculum and those who would maintain the traditional canon of inquiry can breathe new life into the curriculum and make it a forum for social renewal. Through the study of difference, we can create a society that is interactive, dynamic, and able to prepare us for a world that is already multicultural (Abalos, 1996; Gaff, 1992; García and Smith, 1996; Gates, 1992; Moses, 1990; Schmitz, 1993).

Government Action

Political influences on the undergraduate curriculum also tend to divide among national, state, local, or regional forces as well as along ideological lines. While the

United States has no national higher education curriculum, Cuban (1990) has argued that the current impetus to improve critical thinking and problem solving, oral and written communication, and mathematics and science learning among undergraduates is prompted by mixed motives. He argues that national goals are advocated in these areas of learning to reduce bureaucracy in the curriculum by focusing on outcomes rather than requirements, to give more direction, control and coherence to a curriculum through more rigorous oversight of its accomplishments, to raise educational standards as a means to preparing a more competitive cadre of knowledge workers in the global marketplace, and to improve student teaching and learning.

The dynamics of political influence can also been seen in other countries. Antikainen (1990), for example, found that national policies toward undergraduate (first degree) education in Finland divided between those who argue that government lacks a clear comprehensive view of what the curriculum should achieve, those who defend social and democratic aims of educating citizenry, and those who argue for a curriculum aimed at international competitiveness and economic development. These political goals for a postsecondary curriculum may be complementary, contradictory, or competing.

In the 1960s, the Indian Community Action Programs sponsored by the U.S. Office of Economic Opportunity (OEO) encouraged Native Americans living on reservations to reform their tribal government away from the uniform model set by the Bureau of Indian Affairs. Tribal governments assumed more structure and responsibility. The OEO also provided grants for tribal leaders to gain an education in administration and leadership; these grants were made through consortia established with several major universities (Jojola and Agoyo, 1992). While the direct impact of such programs on universities was to modify business and public administration curricula, the new tribal leaders set courses for the economic development of the tribes. These new directions included recreation and mineral extraction programs that in turn created demand for Native Americans educated in fields critical to the economic development initiatives. In this way, federal sponsorship enhanced the participation of an underrepresented group in higher education; this participation was accompanied by significant revision and redirection of specific curricular programs toward the needs of tribal governments and native peoples.

Government policies on financial aid for students have also had a penetrating effect on university curricula. Increasingly, states are demanding results and are applying academic performance and pursuit as criteria. Furthermore, policy makers are increasingly intolerant of the use of financial aid to support remedial or developmental education. State-supported assistance programs for part-time students are being eliminated, and Congress is considering tying financial aid eligibility to citizenship, so that even legal residents would be denied aid. Furthermore, the federal aid has shifted from grants to loans—and student loans are expected to be cut by $10 billion over the next seven years (Rodriguez, 1995).

A profound influence on community college curricula has been federal legislation, particularly the Carl D. Perkins Vocational Education Act (Perry and others, 1992). This act has stimulated enrollment in vocational programs, employer needs assessments and workforce development analyses; it has promoted the creation and growth of programs in agriculture, health occupations, natural resources, public safety, business education and consumer economics. It has paid for the creation of college career counseling, job placement, and cooperative work experience programs, supported programs and services for disadvantaged students, promoted greater gender equity in career programs, and provided specific services to single parents, displaced homemakers, and prison inmates. Thus, this act has significantly altered the programs and services offered by community colleges accepting grants under its articles; it has also supported new and nontraditional groups of students being served by these colleges.

Vocationalism

The increase in vocational and technical education students and the growth and development of career programs have brought criticism to community colleges and calls to restore their collegiate function (Clowes and Levin, 1989; Eaton, 1994). Orfield and Paul (1992) found that those states with a greater commitment to community colleges have lower rates of baccalaureate completion. Community college leaders and federal officials have stressed the vocational role of two-year colleges, while studies of community needs and student interests suggest demand for low-cost local equivalents of the first two years of a bachelor's degree (Frye, 1992).

The vocationalization of curricula is not limited to the community college sector. A British university project developed courses for union members. The new curriculum included an examination of changes affecting industry, the workforce, and social, political, and economic systems. The purpose was to provide unions with a cadre of leaders who better understood the immediate forces acting on the businesses and industries in which their members worked, as well as to know of general social and political trends on the role and functioning of unions (McIlroy, 1989). The results of the union-supported project were to expand the diversity of students served by the university, adding individuals with new, work-related interests and concerns.

Students, particularly those drawn to higher education for pragmatic and vocational reasons, tend to enroll in curricular subjects they perceive to be growth areas of the economy (for example, health, business, computers). The subjects they choose may not turn out to be the growth areas of the economy far into the future. Nonetheless, this is unlikely to deter students from such enrollment choices. Thus, planners of undergraduate curricula would be well advised to develop broad social understanding of markets, peoples, and occupational mobility. The intense vocationalization of student choices regarding which college to attend and which course of study to select suggests the need to cultivate and change vocational programs according to economic realities, by making coursework stimulating and amenable to workplace trends, including flexibility, problem solving, and teamwork. Partnerships with secondary schools also promise to build a better-articulated system of education by ensuring that precollege preparation also becomes a major goal of institutions, especially community colleges.

Economic Influences

The economic recession that plagued the United States in the late 1980s and early 1990s influenced the curricula of colleges and universities in direct and indirect ways. During this period, the economy increased by 20 percent but the service industries grew by 29 percent. According to projections by the American Council on Education and contrary to conventional wisdom, the continued growth of the service sector will require individuals with high-level skills, not low-level as is commonly believed (Ottinger, 1992). Thus, colleges and universities may play a key role in the educational quality of the workforce as the demand for labor continues to shift with economic and technological changes. The economic downturn of the late 1980s and early 1990s differed from previous ones by its large impact on some service sectors like retail trade, real estate, and air transport. Of the new jobs created, most may be centered in the service sector, not manufacturing.

This structural shift in the economy may call for increased technical, communications, management, and problem-solving skills developed in postsecondary education. To highlight this point, between 1980 and 1990 jobs in industries such as social service, engineering management, health, and business increased 59 percent. This percentage is significantly greater than either the overall growth in the economy or the growth in the service sector generally. Growth in the service sector is expected to continue through the 1990s, mainly in business, health, legal, social, educational, and financial services. By 2005, jobs in health services will increase 47 percent, encompassing a broad range of occupations, including nurses, doctors, and technicians. Such growth signals a demand for teachers, social workers, business managers, lawyers, health technicians, and physicians (Ottinger, 1992). The shift in the nature and quality of the workforce, and the increased reliance of the economy on college-educated service workers, are fundamental realities. Colleges and universities should systematically review local, regional, national, and global economic trends to assure that the undergraduate curriculum is relevant to these new realities.

Finances and Workforce Changes

Both the quality and character of the curriculum are determined by the investment of financial resources that society is willing to make (Carnegie Foundation, 1977). For example, slow growth in the workforce led J. Sargent Reynolds Community College to shift the aims of selected career programs from new worker preparation to worker retraining and to increasing worker productivity (Pederson, 1989). Indeed, the nation and many states have established programs for dislocated workers to retrain and reeducate for a new career; government programs provide powerful incentives for nontraditional students to swell the ranks of undergraduates as well as encourage institutions to adjust or adopt programs and services to meet this clientele (Blong and Shultz, 1990). Often such programs are more successful when they are created de novo for the new student clientele rather than when they represent modifications to the existing curriculum (Katsinas and Lacey, 1990).

The institution's capacity to respond to increased enrollment, particularly from nontraditional student groups, may, however, appear especially limited during times of economic recession and financial constraint. During the 1980s, the California State University system was forced to make significant budget cuts that affected the undergraduate curriculum directly and indirectly (Zemsky and Massy, 1990); declining state support for higher education may inhibit the capacity of institutions to adapt curricular programs needed to meet the needs of students new to higher education (Gold, 1990).

In recent years, college tuition has outpaced inflation. Higher education is both labor and technology intensive, making it highly sensitive to cost increases in either sector. These cost increases are then transferred to students, increasing their out-of-pocket costs for tuition. The result of these increases threatens to affect access to higher education as federal and state support continues to erode as well. With increasing costs and declining federal and state resources (either in direct aid or through student grants and loans), colleges and universities will need to reduce the costs of education, which are highly labor intensive, in order to economize. Several institutions are offering fewer courses in required areas and increasing student time to degree completion. Successive cuts in the operating budget need not necessarily result in deteriorating, diminished, or devastated educational programs, however. Chapter Twenty-Five discusses ways curricular reform can lead to substantial savings *and* an improved design for undergraduate education. Colleges and universities facing serious economic constraints must undergo comprehensive institutional analyses to maximize efficiency and still maintain or improve the quality of the educational program. Also, alliances with the private sector may be critical if the capital and resources necessary for curricular expansion are to be obtained.

Industry Participation

The BMW company gave a great boost to the South Carolina technical colleges, as well as the state's business environment and transportation services, in selecting that state as the location for its first U.S.-based assembly plant (Baldwin, 1992). Critical to BMW's decision was the perceived flexibility of the curriculum of the technical colleges' programs in meeting the workforce development needs of the company. In a study of Norwegian higher education, Eide (1991) found that major shifts in the economy and changes in industrial production have their impact on the curriculum. He discovered that the increasingly complex skill needs in the economy bring about the introduction of elements of humanistic studies and the social sciences into specialized fields such as engineering and medicine.

As the economic shifts cause restructuring of major industries and growth in new fields requiring knowledge and service workers, the need for colleges and universities to develop undergraduate curricula responsive to the older worker who is retraining or seeking further education will become even more important. Under rapidly changing economic conditions, it may well be the nontechnical skills and the products of a liberal education that are most valuable, rather than specific job training. Two- and four-year institutions faced with the need to strengthen employment skills of mature adults may develop new comprehensive educational programs that employ a curriculum beyond the traditional divisions of general education, major, minor, and elective. Given the accelerating technological changes in the workplace and an increased willingness of corporations to terminate long-term employees in midlife, higher education must take up the slack to help this experienced cadre to acquire new skills to prepare for new jobs. The capacity of healthy people to live and work longer is well established.

Local corporations are assisting in the development of programs that meet their needs. Programs like Westchester Community College's customer service program, which is subsidized by local businesses, provide older workers with computer and office skills. At the same time, these retraining programs are developing generic skills in communications, math and science, problem solving, and critical thinking.

Technology

There has been an explosion in communications technology. Terms such as information superhighway, virtual reality, World Wide Web, e-mail, and Internet communications have become common in the everyday language. Connecting our nation internationally through this technology has changed how we communicate and conduct business. For our students to be prepared to enter the global market, our campuses need to be at the cutting edge of this new technology.

This technological revolution has also brought about change regarding how we are instructing, interacting, discovering, and learning on our campuses. (Chapter Twenty-Three discusses this point in more detail.) We are grappling with acquiring the necessary equipment and learning the new technology while at the same time trying to keep up-to-date with the latest innovations. Placing a stand-alone powerful computer on each faculty desk has become a first step for many campuses, such as Montclair State University in New Jersey, but the impact on curriculum does not stop there.

The full range of technology available offers the potential to change how and where learning takes place. While most faculty have these resources available to them, only a few have yet taken the opportunity to incorporate these resources in their courses. Some faculty are using technology as a way to supplement classroom instruction and note that it allows for enormous latitude in the ways teaching and learning occur. The World Wide Web is also being used as an information delivery tool and used to distribute course materials. Lecture notes, assignments, calendars, course syllabi, and other related materials are made available to students via the Web. Much of the instruction using this technology, however, continues to convey the same kinds of information as before, and to center on classes held at a specified time and place. By contrast, the *virtual classroom* model offers courses or entire degree programs delivered in whole or in part over the Web in combination with Internet newsgroups, e-mail, Telnet, and video conferencing. Offering an interactive learning environment opens the possibility of students' taking courses with a particular instructor or being enrolled in a college program that is not in the same geographical area. It also opens the possibility of delivering programs to students who live in remote or inaccessible places, to students whose physical movement is impaired or otherwise restricted, and to students who simply prefer to learn from home, office, or hotel room.

An institution, for example, now has the potential to offer courses to other institutions who lack faculty in the required discipline. Oklahoma State University offers German to high schools around the state (Noon, 1995). Two days a week of broadcast stresses student-teacher interaction, speaking and listening practice, and cultural vignettes. The broadcast even has commercials using cultural material in German. The three nonbroadcast days, students work with computer programs, textbooks, and vocabulary quizzes. A toll-free number is available for the student to reach a native German-speaking instructor. Master teachers in the arts are also using video conferencing to conduct master classes in varying locations throughout the world. World-renowned violinist, violist and conductor Pincus

Zuckerman is able to give his private lessons and master classes using video conferencing. Southwestern Oklahoma State University has implemented a distance learning network between its two campuses (sixty miles apart) and also links with two high schools, a junior college, and a vocational technical center (Grush, 1996).

But flexibility in the way we offer a curriculum is not the only advantage brought about by this new technology. Campuses are also creating and discovering new skills. Fashion Institute of Technology creates fabrics, defining colors and textures via a computer package before the fabric is actually produced in the new designs. Breakthroughs in ecology, conservation biology, and wildlife management are also being discovered at SUNY Stony Brook.

Yet, this new technological era does bring with it new issues. How will we offer knowledge? What will constitute a learning environment? How will student-faculty ratios be analyzed and how will faculty loads be affected? Furthermore, there are those who feel that technology brings about the loss of intellectual reading (Birkerts, 1994) and that with technology we will lose connection and relations with each other. The fear is that our interaction will be shallow and will minimize the human relations and communication skills of learners. And what will happen to students who do not have access to this new technology in their K–12 years? Are we in higher education falsely assuming that every student entering our doors is technologically literate? Will those students who attend the schools described in Kozol's *Savage Inequalities* be prepared for this new era? If not, how will we in higher education deal with this population?

The technological revolution has brought about alternatives to our traditional approaches to the curriculum. Although no one really knows or is able to forecast the institution of the future and the effects on our campuses, most agree that this new tool will radically revise how we construct, structure, archive, and teach knowledge.

Conclusions

Demographic, political, economic, and technological forces have direct and indirect impacts on the curriculum. College and university curricula are swayed by changing student interests and by demands for specific courses and programs of study. More vocationally oriented institutions are engaged in systematic planning processes to adjust and change their program mixes to job market and student demands. These curricular changes are often accomplished through traditional and rational planning strategies: needs assessments, goal-setting discussions, task and work analyses, employer and graduate evaluations, and program completion and job placement records.

Students select courses and shape curricula through their enrollment and attendance patterns. Faculty give coherence, purpose, and integrity to the curriculum they design by providing logical sequences and combinations of coursework designed to produce specific student learning outcomes. In doing so, they must balance student diversity of interests, backgrounds, and motives for enrollment with the knowledge, skills, and abilities to be imparted and the societal demand for such education.

Governments play a large role in reshaping the curriculum. The U.S. federal government provides financial aid to large numbers of students and stimulates specific groups of new students, including disabled persons, displaced homemakers, prison inmates, and the unemployed to be served by higher education. It provides funds through such mechanisms as the Job Partnership Training Act and the Carl D. Perkins Vocational Education Act to prompt institutions with comprehensive curricula to develop new programs and services attuned to vocational aims and the needs of specific student groups. Similarly, college and university commitments to the locale or region may bring a curriculum in education or social work in contact with social service agencies, halfway houses, and unemployment and rehabilitation services agencies. However, the broad social and economic changes may have more profound and longer-lasting effects on the curriculum than major government policy shifts or initiatives. Increased flows of students across national borders in exchange programs, together with the new global economic and political settings, set the stage for profound internationalization and integration of an undergraduate curriculum in the coming decade (Wagner and Schnitzer, 1991).

What do these external forces mean for the academic dean, the curriculum committee, or the department chair? Using the mission statement of the institution as the point of departure, academic leaders need to engage the faculty in determining how the external influences are affecting their institution and thus their academic disciplines. They also need to make sure their academic programs are preparing their students for the social, political, economic, and global realities they will face. Faculty are socialized to focus on their disciplines when designing curricula and courses, and they may need assistance in understanding market perspectives.

One paradigm used by colleges and universities is the use of an environmental scan. Often performed by a community or professional advisory committee, such efforts may highlight the changing nature of work technology and culture likely to inform the education of future citizens and workers. Using all the stakeholders of the college community, the next phase would entail campuswide discussions on each of the external influences to examine how the institution is addressing each.

Forums could be held that would, for example, review the student population being served by the institution and consider how its alumni are faring. Questions that could be asked include, Who is in the student population? What are the projections for the future? How is the institution responding to the changing population? Is the curriculum responding to the needs of the population it serves? If not, where is it not meeting its stated mission?

Furthermore, campus forums could be held for each of the broad classes of external factors—the political, economic, and technological influences—affecting that particular institution. Addressing the political influences that are most pressing to the college would reveal to all campus constituencies the realities of local, federal, and state influences. Discussing the public's loss of confidence in higher education, understanding the reasons for the backlash against recent initiatives to teach multicultural perspectives, and addressing the external calls for accountability can promote invigorating dialogue regarding the position an institution will take.

Connecting with the economic realities of the population one serves will bring common understanding regarding the relationship between education and employability. Is it the role of the campus to work with those who have been retrenched from their place of employment? What will happen, for example, to the forty thousand employees scheduled to leave AT&T over the next three years (1996–1999)? What types of educational retraining will they need to be productive citizens? And as many institutions recognize that the traditional eighteen- to twenty-two-year-old student is only one portion of the campus population, what academic offerings will be required for senior citizens, aging baby boomers, new immigrants, and those from urban areas who have not attended our best schools? Not only will questions regarding the needs of constituencies arise, but how will the institution serve an ever-increasing and increasingly diverse student population with declining resources? What programs are essential to continue, which ones can be shared with other institutions, which ones duplicate offerings of other area campuses and need to be eliminated, and what new programs need to be implemented?

Before an institution charges into technology, it is best to develop a clarity of purpose and to pose some fundamental questions regarding curriculum integration. At what stage is the institution regarding technological knowledge? What types of technology will the institution become involved in? Who will lead the institution through a thoughtful and cost-effective comprehensive plan for implementation? What types of technology are appropriate for the institution based on its mission, culture, and use?

At the end of these forums, each group would prepare a report to the advisory committee that could then be shared with the entire campus. The advantages of these forums would be the actual process of discussing, debating, and reaching common understandings of the external forces that continually affect higher education curricula. Since no single institution can address all the external forces at the same time, collectively the campus community can determine which ones are most pressing at this point in the institution's history. The challenge is to take advantage of these external influences as opportunities while maintaining or enhancing curricular quality.

The priorities of the federal government in worker retraining may or may not correspond to institutional and programmatic goals. Incentives provided to attract new students to higher education invariably create the need for rethinking the undergraduate curriculum. When new student populations are served, the institution, the program, and the curriculum leader have a responsibility to oversee the adaptation or transformation of the curriculum to meet the new learners' needs and to stimulate, challenge, and engage their interest. This can best be accomplished when the undergraduate curriculum is viewed as a malleable, dynamic entity undergoing ongoing transmutation in response to external forces and factors. Curriculum committees review and revise undergraduate programs not because previous committees failed, but because the curriculum is constantly changing in response to the external forces, factors, trends, and issues that give it life, meaning, and vitality.

References

Abalos, D. *Strategies of Transformation Toward a Multicultural Society.* Westport, Conn.: Greenwood Press, 1996.

Antikainen, A. "The Rise and Change of Comparative Planning: The Finnish Experience." *European Journal of Education,* 1990, *25*(1), 75–82.

Baldwin, F. "South Carolina Wins the Prize." *Appalachia,* 1992, *25*(4), 3–10.

Belenky, M. F., Clinchy, B. M., Goldberger, N. R., and Tarule, J. M. *Women's Ways of Knowing: The Development of Self, Voice, and Mind.* New York: Basic Books, 1986.

Birkerts, S. *The Gutenberg Elegies: The Fate of Reading in an Electronic Age.* Boston: Faber & Faber, 1994.

Blong, J. T., and Shultz, R. M. "The Dislocated Worker: When Training Is Not Enough." *Community, Technical and Junior College Journal,* 1990, *60*(4), 28–32.

Bloom, A. *The Closing of the American Mind: How Higher Education Has Failed Democracy and Impoverished the Souls of Today's Students.* New York: Simon & Schuster, 1987.

Carnegie Foundation for the Advancement of Teaching. *Missions of the College Curriculum: A Contemporary Review with Suggestions.* San Francisco: Jossey-Bass, 1977.

Carroll, T. G. "Who Owns Culture?" *Education and Urban Society,* 1990, *22*(4), 346–355.

Carter, D. J., and Wilson, R. *Twelfth Annual Status Report on Minorities in Higher Education.* Washington, D.C.: American Council on Education, 1994.

Caverzasi, P. L. "On Teaching Literary Classics." Paper presented at the annual meeting of the National Council of Teachers of English, Louisville, Ky., Nov. 18–23, 1992. (ED 359 544)

Chapman, D. W. "Writing a Core Curriculum: Classic Books and Student Compositions." Paper presented at the annual meeting of the Conference on College Composition and Communication, Cincinnati, Ohio, Mar. 19–21, 1992. (ED 346 480)

Clavner, J. "Putting Bloom and Hirsch to Work: Core Concepts in the Social Sciences." Paper presented at the spring conference of the General Educators of Ohio, Dayton, May 4, 1990. (ED 326 482)

Clowes, D. A., and Levin, B. H. "Community, Technical, and Junior Colleges: Are They Leaving Higher Education?" *Journal of Higher Education*, 1989, *60*(3), 350–355.

Cuban, L. M. "Four Stories About National Goals for American Education." *Phi Delta Kappan*, 1990, *72*(4), 264–271.

Douglas, N. "After Bloom After Philosophy or How Philosophy Sold Its Birthright for a Free Lunch." *Interchange*, 1991, *22*(1–2), 79–88.

D'Souza, D. *Illiberal Education: The Politics of Race and Sex on Campus*. New York: Free Press, 1991.

Eaton, J. S. *Strengthening Collegiate Education in the Community College*. San Francisco: Jossey-Bass, 1994.

Edington, R. V. "Allan Bloom's Message to the State Universities." *Perspectives on Political Science*, 1990, *19*(3), 136–145.

Eide, K. *Higher Education and Employment: The Changing Relationship. The Case of the Humanities and Social Sciences*. Paris: Organisation for Economic Cooperation and Development, 1991. (ED 353 936)

Frye, J. *The Vision of the Public Junior College, 1900–1940: Professional Goals and Popular Aspirations*. New York: Greenwood Press, 1992.

Gaff, J. G. "Beyond Politics: The Educational Issues Inherent in Multicultural Education." *Change*, Jan./Feb. 1992, pp. 31–35.

García, M., and Smith, D. "Reflecting Inclusiveness in the College Curriculum." In L. Rendón and R. Hope (eds.), *Educating a New Majority: Transforming America's Educational System for Diversity*. San Francisco: Jossey-Bass, 1996.

Gates, H. L., Jr. *Loose Canons: Notes on the Culture Wars*. New York: Oxford University Press, 1992.

Gift, R. E., and Krislov, J. "Are There Classics in Economics?" *Journal of Economic Education*, 1991, *22*(1), 27–32.

Gilligan, C. *In a Different Voice: Psychological Theory and Women's Development*. Cambridge, Mass.: Harvard University Press, 1982.

Gold, S. D. "State Support of Higher Education: A National Perspective." *Planning for Higher Education*, 1990, *18*(3), 21–33.

Grush, M. "Breaking Down Barriers with Video Conferencing—Pinchas Zukerman Master Classes." *Syllabus*, Jan. 1996, pp. 14, 52.

Heller, S. "Bloom's Best Seller Called 'Racist' and 'Elitist' by Former SUNY Chief." *Chronicle of Higher Education*, 1988, *34*(19), A1, A12.

Hirschorn, M. W. "Vermonters Ask: 'Can Virtue be Taught?'" *Chronicle of Higher Education*, 1987, *34*(13), p. A3.

Jojola, T. S., and Agoyo, H. "One Generation of Self-Determination: Native American Economic Self-Reliance in New Mexico." Paper presented at the annual meeting of the National Rural Studies Committee, Las Vegas, N.M., May 14–16, 1992. (ED 354 130)

Katsinas, S. G., and Lacey, V. A. "Common Factors that Appear to Lead to Success in Nontraditional Economic Development: Implications for Policy and Practice." *Community Services Catalyst*, 1990, *20*(3), 17–26.

Kelebray, Y. G. "Multiculturalism on the Mind." *Canadian Social Studies*, 1992, *26*(3), 98–99.

Kozol, J. *Savage Inequalities*. New York: Crown, 1991.

Lawler, P. A. "Bloom's Idiosyncratic History of the University." *Teaching Political Science*, 1989, *16*(4), 174–179.

Lawler, P. A. "Reflections on Bloom and His Critics." *Journal of General Education*, 1992, *41*, 273–285.

Magner, A. "Black Intellectuals Broaden Debate on Effects of Affirmative Action." *Chronicle of Higher Education*, 1991, *38*(8), A17, A22–23.

Mathie, W. "Philosophers, Gentlemen, and Saints: The Dilemma of Liberal Education." *Interchange*, 1991, *22*(1–2), 39–56.

McIlroy, J. "Back to the Future." *Adults Learning*, 1989, *1*(3), 73–75.

Minnich, E. K. *Transforming Knowledge*. Philadelphia: Temple University Press, 1990.

Morgan, P. "Bloom, Frye, and the Academic Aspiration After the Unity of Knowledge." *Interchange*, 1991, *22*(1–2), 29–38.

Morgen, S. "Challenging the Politics of Exclusion: The Perspective of Feminist Anthropology." *Education and Urban Society*, 1990, *22*(4), 393–401.

Moses, Y. T. "The Challenge of Diversity: Anthropological Perspectives on University Culture." *Education and Urban Society*, 1990, *22*(4), 402–412.

Nathan, G. J. "Rethinking Relativism." *Interchange*, 1991, *22*(1–2), 89–96.

Noon, J. P. "Technology Across the Curriculum." *Syllabus*, Sept. 1995, pp. 26, 28, 30, 34–35.

Orfield, G., and Paul, F. G. *State Higher Education System and College Completion: Final Report to the Ford Foundation*. New York: Ford Foundation, 1992.

Ottinger, C. "What Is the Service Sector?" *ACE Research Briefs*, 1992, *3*(4), pp. 1–12. (ED 351 971)

Pederson, N. C., Jr. "Conditions Favorable to Community College/Business Partnerships." *Community Services Catalyst*, 1989, *19*(1), 13–15.

Perry, K., and others. *Examining the Impact: A Summary of the Carl D. Perkins Vocational Education Act, 1983–84 through 1990–91*. Sacramento: California Community Colleges, 1992. (ED 354 056)

Rodriguez, R. "National Latino Leaders Lash Out at Republican Legislative Attacks." *Black Issues in Higher Education*, Aug. 24, 1995, pp. 36, 38.

Sasseen, R. F. "Liberal Education and the Study of Politics in a Catholic University." *Perspectives on Political Science*, 1990, *19*(3), 146–152.

Schensul, J. J. "Organizing Cultural Diversity Through the Arts." *Education and Urban Society*, 1990, *22*(4), 377–392.

Schensul, J. J., and Carroll, T. G. "Introduction: Visions of America in the 1990s and Beyond: Negotiating Cultural Diversity and Educational Change." *Education and Urban Society*, 1990, *22*(4), 339–345.

Schmitz, B. "Cultural Pluralism in the Academy." *Washington Center News*, 1993, *7*(1), 1–13.

Silliman, M. "The Closing of the Professorial Mind: A Meditation on Plato and Allan Bloom." *Educational Theory*, 1990, *40*(1), 147–151.

Smith, J., Rose, M., and Goodman, P. "In Search of a Lost Pedagogical Synthesis." *College English*, 1993, *55*(7), 721–744.

Snyder, T. D., and Hoffman, C. M. *Digest of Education Statistics 1993*. Washington, D.C.: National Center for Education Statistics, 1993.

Standley, F. "William Bennett, Allan Bloom, E. D. Hirsch, Jr: 'Great Nature Has Another Thing to Do to You and Me. . . . '" *Teaching English in the Two-Year College*, 1988, *51*(4), 266–277.

Wagner, A., and Schnitzer, K. "Programmes and Policies for Foreign Students and Study Abroad: The Search for Effective Approaches in a New Global Setting." *Higher Education*, 1991, *21*(3), 275–288.

Wake, S. D. "The University and Democratic Life: Allan Bloom's Attack." *Interchange,* 1991, *22*(1–2), 66–78.

Walter, S. "Nuns, Nazis, and the Poor Old Pope: An Interview with Walker Percy." *Crisis,* 1989, *7,* 16–19.

Zemsky, R., and Massy, W. F. "Cost Containment: Committing to a New Economic Reality." *Change,* 1990, *22*(6), 16–22.

PART TWO

CENTRAL AIMS OF UNDERGRADUATE EDUCATION

At the turn of the twentieth century, the unity of knowledge was beginning to fracture. The inherent tidiness of the liberal arts as the core of a baccalaureate education was threatened by the creation of disciplines, disciplinary societies, and whole new fields of applied knowledge. As Boorstin has written (1994, p. 161), "printed books created literacy. Books created the demand for books." Print and now computer technology know no bounds of expansion save the interests and needs of individuals. Colleges and universities are in the knowledge generation business, and that business is being fundamentally and exponentially accelerated in fields as disparate as music, medicine, and meteorology by the new technologies of discovery and communication. The expansion of knowledge through these media promises to make it increasingly difficult for university faculties to chart common ground in the undergraduate curriculum.

Our current catalogues of undergraduate curricula create the environment of election and choice among multiplying arrays of courses, seminars, laboratories, lectures, performances, studios, and clinical practice sessions. We have created what Boorstin calls "the grand new power of exclusion" (1994, p. 164). Like the expanding array of cable television channels, the undergraduate curriculum has permitted the exclusion of whole fields of knowledge from the undergraduate experience simply through the students' power to elect and avoid that which is unpalatable, unimaginable, or not of immediate interest (Adelman, 1994; Boyer and Ahlgren,

1987; Ratcliff, 1992, 1993). Students take what appeals to them, what is less threatening to them, or what is familiar to them. As custodians of the curriculum, faculties have the ongoing responsibility to cull the incidental from the fundamental in facilitating the intellectual and personal development of students.

Central to the task of deciding what should constitute the common learning associated with an undergraduate degree is the concept of *development*. Students come to college with certain knowledge, skills, and abilities. Certain of these talents—such as communication and mathematical skills—will be enhanced through collegiate learning, while others—intellectual skills such as critical thinking, analytic reasoning, and problem solving—may be encountered directly for the first time. The challenge of designing undergraduate curricula is to engage an increasingly diverse student population at their various levels of knowledge, skill, and ability, and sequentially to provide involving, empowering, and enlightening learning experiences. In envisioning the developmental task of the curriculum, we need to avoid the tempting trap of determinism. If what is to be developed is fully manifest to us, then the curriculum and the work of the faculty lose life and become mechanical. The next stages in an individual's personal and intellectual development are never fully known, linear, and predictable. The very unpredictability of the unveiling of knowledge and new understandings about our world causes us to revisit the curriculum, rethink the common ground,

and recast the means and methods of engendering it in the next class of students.

What constitutes the common ground—the common learning—associated with the American associate and baccalaureate degrees will remain a regenerative task of social construction. Certainly not all knowledge, skills, and abilities available in the undergraduate curriculum can be had by all students; thus, that which faculties offer as the common learning must reflect the best wisdom of the time as to what a college graduate ought to know and be able to do. This section is devoted to the characteristics of that common learning—quality, coherence, development of intellectual skills, appreciation of difference and diversity—as well as to the provision for students less prepared to succeed in college.

In Chapter Seven, Ratcliff examines the events leading to calls for greater quality and coherence in general education during the 1980s, indicating specific problems associated with the disintegration of the curriculum and the disengagement of students. He illustrates how consistency can be mistaken for coherence in curricular design, and how general education programs can be most effectively designed for salient subgroups of students on increasingly heterogeneous campuses, rather than rewriting requirements as if one curricular shoe fit all students. He analyzes the call for increased educational standards and juxtaposes it to the call for greater entrepreneurial spirit and empowerment among students, and closes with an examination of the role of assessment in relating curricular offerings to curricular goals and actual results.

In Chapter Eight, Doherty, Chenevert, Miller, Roth, and Truchan discuss the development of intellectual skills—what these skills are, what we know about how they are effectively developed, and how they are understood by students through their course of study. They urge faculties to cluster intellectual skills that seem to be similar or that seem to draw upon related talents, such as the communication skills of writing, speaking, listening, and reading, so that general education curricular goals can be stated, instructional programs directed, and assessment techniques devised in a concise, clear, and purposeful manner.

Their experience suggests that faculty from disparate disciplines can come to some common sense of what skills are to be developed, what constitutes a coherent, sustained program to facilitate their development, and how best to tell when such development has been attained by students. Such clustering of skills provides for integration of knowledge across disciplines—horizontal integration—but also can provide the basis for vertical integration of general education, major, and minor through the recognition of a progressive scheme from general to specialized and discipline-specific forms of such skills as critical thinking, analytic reasoning, and problem solving. The vertical and horizontal integration of the curriculum around clusters of skills also suggests new focal

points (on skills as well as content), on instructional strategies (emphasizing performance of skills), and on assessment of these skills. Such attention to intellectual skill development promises to provide greater forms of coherence and attainment of purpose in imparting the common learning.

What should be done with regard to diversity in the curriculum? In Chapter Nine, McTighe Musil provides the basic alternatives: suppress it, segregate it, celebrate it, engage with it. By engaging, she suggests that the faculty and students allow themselves to uncover the often uncomfortable differences in themselves and in their learning. In doing so, they must confront, contend, and cogitate upon the uncertain and the unexpected that expanding and diverse environments bring. Musil examines the task of creating an inclusive intellectual community as fundamental in charting a common course. The faculty committee charged with creation of a renewed general education curriculum can cast its instructional designs to capture, embody, consider, and reflect upon this larger social debate. Certain myths about the curriculum—its completeness, its eternal salience, its universality, its inherent quality, its presumed distance from politics—need careful scrutiny in the course of analysis.

One of the persistent problems in American higher education has been that students who enter the system do not always have the prerequisite basic knowledge, skills, and abilities to succeed in the common learning provided. In Chapter

Ten, McGrath and Townsend trace the ways that colleges and universities contend with the educational deficits of their students. They contrast the concept of *remediation,* in which educational deficits are defined relative to institutional goals rather than student needs, to *developmental education,* in which specific weaknesses are diagnosed, appropriate curricular remedies are prescribed, and the aim is the fitness of the individual to the environment, and not the other way around.

Remediation has a deterministic quality to it: the knowledge and skills lacking or needed can be clearly identified, the means to impart those skills can be marshaled, and the readiness of the remedial student to enter college-level studies can be calculated. In contrast, developmental education advocates improvement of personal as well as intellectual skills. Hybrid developmental-remedial programs have lacked clarity of purpose. As McGrath and Townsend point out, the disparity in outcomes defined for each type of program makes mixed programs notoriously difficult to evaluate, which has reduced faculty interest in monitoring their efforts. Developmental-remedial programs have become enclaves within the curricular organization, yet they remain fundamental to defining admissions and placement criteria: Who possesses the ability to succeed in the college classroom and who does not? The availability and effectiveness of such efforts determine the character and qualities of students as they enter the regular collegiate program.

Diversity in the knowledge base, diversity in the social and demographic qualities of students, and diversity in the knowledge, skills, and abilities students bring with them as they enter college all point profoundly to the challenges presented in finding a curriculum of common learning. What does it mean to possess an associate's or a bachelor's degree? What should a college-educated individual possess in personal and intellectual skills, regardless of field of study or discipline selected? In this section of the *Handbook,* we examine these questions, offer alternative ways to conceptualize the issues, and provide examples of how some colleges and universities are grappling with the problems resulting from these issues.

References

Adelman, C. *Lessons of a Generation: Education and Work in the Lives of the High School Class of 1972.* San Francisco: Jossey-Bass, 1994.

Boorstin, D. J. *Cleopatra's Nose: Essays on the Unexpected.* New York: Vintage Books, 1994.

Boyer, C. M., and Ahlgren, A. "Assessing Undergraduates' Patterns of Credit Distribution: Amount and Specialization." *Journal of Higher Education,* 1987, *58,* 430–442.

Ratcliff, J. L. "Reconceptualizing the College Curriculum." *Perspectives: The Journal of the Association for General and Liberal Studies,* 1992, pp. 122–137.

Ratcliff, J. L. *What We Can Learn from Coursework Patterns About Improving the Undergraduate Curriculum.* University Park, Pa.: National Center on Postsecondary Teaching, Learning, and Assessment, 1993.

CHAPTER SEVEN

QUALITY AND COHERENCE IN GENERAL EDUCATION

James L. Ratcliff

During the 1980s, American higher education struggled with the twin issues of bringing coherence and quality to higher education. Nonetheless, we can still ask, "What is quality in a curriculum?" and "What is curricular coherence?" It is useful to examine how the two concepts are related and what they mean for curriculum development, reform, and assessment in general education.

While the aim of general education can be traced back to the founding of the Junior College by Harper at the University of Chicago and the founding of the General College at the University of Minnesota, its great impetus came as a result of World War II. Concerned and perplexed about how the higher education population in Germany and Italy, particularly the intelligensia, could fall victim to charismatic and totalitarian leaders, the Harvard Committee on General Education provided rationale and structure to fifty years of curriculum development:

> It is important to realize that the ideal of a free society involves a twofold value, the value of freedom and that of society. *Democracy is community.* . . . We are apt sometimes to stress freedom—the power of individual choice and the right to think for oneself—without taking sufficient account of the obligation to cooperate. . . ; democracy must represent an adjustment between the values of freedom and social living. . . . This logic must further embody certain intangibles of the American spirit, in particular, perhaps, the ideal of cooperation

on the level of action irrespective of agreement on ultimates—which is to say, belief in the worth and meaning of the human spirit." [1945, pp. 41, 76]

Today, those who teach about community and cooperation have faced new challenges—fractious faculty, fragmented curricula, and diversifying student populations.

In a review of the literature, Gaff (1983, pp. 7–8) summarized the purposes of general education. He found that it

- Is rooted in the liberal arts and sciences
- Stresses breadth of knowledge, languages, and methodologies
- Strives for integration, synthesis, and cohesion of learning
- Encourages appreciation of one's heritage and of other cultures
- Examines values and controversial issues
- Prizes a common educational experience for all students
- Expects mastery of linguistic, analytic, and computational skills
- Fosters personal development and an expanded view of self

This chapter examines how the initiatives, reforms, and transformation of general education have been driven by the quest for quality and coherence.

During the past decade, more than 90 percent of colleges and universities engaged in some kind of revision or reform of their undergraduate curriculum (Gaff, 1989). Over the same period, nearly 80 percent of colleges and universities implemented some kind of assessment of student learning. The American Council on Education's *Campus Trends* repeatedly reported that most colleges and universities were engaged in curriculum reform (El-Khawas, 1990, 1995). This has led Eaton (1991) to raise some rather uncomfortable questions about this flurry of activity: "From a negative point of view, one can point to little in the way of completed curricular modifications or, more important, changes in student performance . . . as the 1980s ended. Worse, one might view the decade . . . as an essentially unimportant ten-year saga during which the higher-education community continued an apparently endless and unproductive dialogue with itself on academic issues as opposed to engaging in constructive action. . . . Did institutional descriptions of academic reform fail to focus on those intended to benefit but, instead, confuse expectations of student performance with descriptions of faculty involvement?" (pp. 61–63).

Others have been skeptical as to the impact of curricular reform in general education on improved coherence and quality in the undergraduate program. In his study of the outcomes of general education, Astin (1992) concluded, "The particular manner in which the general education curriculum is structured makes very little difference. . . . Since over 90 percent of all general education programs use a 'distributional' system, basically these findings mean that the major varieties of implementation for distributional systems do not appear to make much difference" (p. 425).

Without a new wave of curricular rethinking and reform based on coherence, development of cognitive abilities, and program options geared to student interests, abilities, and prior achievement, general education is unlikely to produce meaningful and ascertainable results. Throughout the literature, coherence has been a fundamental characteristic of an effective general education curriculum (Association of American Colleges, 1985; Boyer, 1987; Gaff, 1989; Ratcliff, 1993; Ratcliff and Associates, 1995; Zemsky, 1989). *Coherence,* as I use it here, is different from simple consistency, and is too complex to define in a few words. I'll return to the concept later, but for now it is enough to say that it refers to the probability that most students will encounter logical sequences of coursework leading to useful and long-lasting skills and insights about the world.

Coherence—Support and Opposition

In the 1980s, two reports called for greater attention to the quality and coherence of general education. *Involvement in Learning* (National Institute of Education, 1984) suggested that the quality of undergraduate education was indicated by its impact on students and urged faculty and institutions to assess learning in order to determine quality. *Integrity in the College Curriculum* (Association of American Colleges, 1985) called for institutions to reexamine general education to bring greater coherence to the curriculum and learning experiences that students encounter. Thus there has been an explicit link between quality and coherence. Coherence can enhance program quality. However, quality is traditionally judged by reputation, rankings, and resources, or more recently by the assessment of student learning (Astin, 1991). While great strides have been made in the improvement of general education and assessment of the quality of programs (Gaff, 1989; Banta and Associates, 1993), the tasks of increasing quality and coherence still remain serious challenges to strengthening the education of undergraduate students.

The impetus to reform general education during the 1980s was the development of the personal, intellectual, and social capacities of individual students. The common laments were that students knew too little about science, mathematics, history, and culture, and that they lacked the abilities to think and communicate effectively. Further, critics presumed that quality could be enhanced if a desired coherence of purpose were found in the general education curriculum. These assumptions ran counter to the Humboldtian (German research university) concepts of freedom of learning, the unity of teaching and research, and the primacy of the advancement of knowledge as the mode and aim of higher education (Veysey, 1965; Ratcliff, 1996).

It remains true that faculty from all forms of baccalaureate-granting institutions are rewarded more today for research than for teaching; research shows that faculty who publish more receive higher salaries (Fairweather, 1992). The research university leads the academic procession, and with it we have the celebration of research.

The reform efforts of the 1980s and the reports that spawned them sounded the end to the "academic revolution" and its reliance on Humboldtian ideas. Since the end of the decade and continuing into the 1990s, there have been new calls for reform based on assessment as well as on knowledge of effective practice (Gaff, 1989; Ratcliff and Associates, 1995; Zemsky, 1989). The academic revolution, as Jencks and Riesman (1968) presented it, represented the ascendancy of the disciplines, the explosion of knowledge, and the empowerment of academic departments and specializations within the university (Jencks and Riesman, 1968). The other forms of higher education—the community colleges, liberal arts colleges, comprehensive institutions, and doctoral granting universities—have drifted toward the ideals of the research university (Trow, 1974, 1988) or followed innovations produced by them like the tail of a snake following its head (Riesman, 1958).

The effect of the primacy of research in twentieth-century higher education has been both positive and negative. On one hand, as fields of knowledge expanded, new subdisciplines and specialties emerged; many new fields crossed disciplinary boundaries to erect their own knowledge bases, concepts, terms, models, genres, theories, and modes of inquiry. Fields as diverse as computer science, women's studies, and ecology became part of the undergraduate curriculum. On the other hand, while research and the expansion of knowledge had a dynamic and generative effect, it also fragmented notions of common learning and constantly challenged the content and pedagogy of general education.

The ascendancy of the professoriate to power had profound effects on the curriculum:

> From the very start, the professionalization of university professors brought conflict on many fronts. Late-nineteenth- and early-twentieth-century academic histories report many battles in which the basic question was whether the president and trustees or the faculty would determine the shape of the curriculum, the content of particular courses, or the use of particular books. The professors . . . lost most of the publicized battles, but they won the war. [Jencks and Riesman, 1968, p. 15]

From the late nineteenth century to the middle of the twentieth century, the revolution in the American undergraduate curriculum was profound and produced the educational programs we take for granted today. The adoption and use of these programs was strikingly uniform. The numbered course; the unit system of credits; the lecture, lecture discussion, and seminar methods of instruction; the departmental organization of courses and programs; and the elective system of course selection all were widely adopted within this time frame and with little variation. More than 90 percent of colleges and universities adopted a distributional plan of course selection for the general education curriculum (Toombs and others, 1991; Veysey, 1973). The result was a bureaucratic and impersonal higher education system catering to rapidly increasing numbers of students. The consequences of these changes included an abandonment or reduction of curricular coherence.

Indeed, curricular coherence never was an expectation of an academic culture in which individual faculty decide what they wish to teach and individual students decide what lectures and seminars to attend and what they wish to learn. Course proliferation was a common characteristic of curricular growth in the 1960s and 1970s (Veysey, 1973). *Lehrfreiheit* and *lernfreiheit*, in an absolute sense, may militate against effective and efficient programs and curricula for mass higher education. Thus it is not surprising to find that students even in the same graduating class at the same institution do not share a common curricular experience in their pursuit of the bachelor's degree (Boyer and Ahlgren, 1987; Ratcliff, 1990, 1993).

Not only is there significant variation in learning within any single class of students, but there is also significant year-to-year variation. Due to the expansiveness of the curriculum and the course availability in any given term of enrollment, students in one graduating class may select from a schedule of classes that is as much as 25 percent different in coursework from the schedule that first-year students will encounter (Ratcliff, 1990, 1993). This is true in all but the smallest of colleges. This variation in learning experiences alters the extent and type of knowledge, skills, and abilities students acquire and their performance on test batteries. It does not necessarily portray year-to-year dips and rises in graduating students' abilities. Rather, it may simply be a function of the courses and subjects they choose to study. When a university offers an undergraduate the opportunity to pick thirty-five to forty-five courses—from a curriculum of three to five thousand courses—to complete the baccalaureate degree, it is little surprise that different college graduates evidence different levels and types of knowledge, skills, and abilities. While it is the individual student, not the collective student body, who needs to experience coherence in the curriculum, current curricular configurations largely do little to promote such connected learning.

Currently, all institutions of higher education (except those with very selective admissions policies) serve both students with high levels of academic preparation and students with significant educational deficits. Colleges and universities collectively provide a variety of curriculum and extracurriculum that is responsive to the diverse educational needs of the population. Yet individually, these institutions need a general education program that is targeted to the needs and interests of significant subgroups within the campus environment rather than presuming that one general education program will best develop the talents of all students regardless of interest, prior achievement, or ability (Ratcliff and Associates, 1995). A high-stakes environment is needed where both student and institution share in the responsibility of demonstrating educational results.

In the 1980s, the leadership of research universities began to falter. Institutions such as Alverno College, Northeast Missouri State University (as of 1996, Truman State University), King's College, and Miami Dade Community College were hailed as leaders in innovation in quality and coherence. The Humboldtian ideals of the research university started to give way to a reexamination of the commitment of higher education to the preparation and development of individual students. In this shift, educational philosophy came to be of paramount importance. The preponderance of colleges and universities seeking to improve, reform, or transform the undergraduate curriculum (El-Khawas, 1990) did so by seeking ways to foster greater intellectual growth and development, greater connections between learning situations and environments, and greater dialogue and discussion among students and faculty about enhancing the curriculum and targeting it to the aims of general education and liberal learning.

What Is Coherence?

It is a frequent and increasingly documented claim that a fragmented curriculum is less effective than a coherent one (Barnes, 1987; Veysey, 1973; Ratcliff and Associates, 1995). Buchmann and Floden (1992) contrast coherence to consistency, noting that "while *consistency* implies logical relations and the absence of contradictions, *coherence* allows for many kinds of connectedness, encompassing logic but also associations of ideas and feelings, intimations of resemblance, conflicts and tensions, previsagements and imaginative leaps. . . . Implicit adherence to consistency brings in a lot more regimentation than we need to rise above randomness. A program that is too consistent fits students with blinders, deceives them, and encourages complacency" (p. 4).

Describing coherence as a "rebel angel"—advancing learning but escaping control—they urge curriculum designs that provide students with more opportunities to figure out how different elements, themes, or ideas can be connected and applied to social situations and human reflection. Coherence is an evolving social construct, not a linear framework into which all rational action and thinking must fit. In the search for a coherent curriculum, we must be wary of mechanistic attempts to impose consistency in the name of "cumulative learning experiences" and "maximizing educational impact." The goal of coherence can be defeated by the slavish adoption of consistency across curricula.

Of course, there are educational benefits to having access to a wide array of course offerings and specialized studies (Ratcliff, 1992b). One less obvious benefit of an unintegrated curriculum is mentioned by Scheffler ([1956] 1973): "A student who gets all his education screened through some neat integrative framework imposed in advance by others, without being forced to make his own sense of the discordances and discrepancies patent in experience, has been effectively protected from thinking altogether" (p. 106).

A key unanswered question in the debate over coherence in general education is, Who provides or creates that coherence—the student, or the faculty in designing the curriculum? Rather than a dichotomy, the answer may represent an inherent tension within general education curriculum.

Unfortunately, the current prevailing practice of packaged bodies of knowledge developed and taught by individual instructors does not lead students to learn that the precisely defined methods, modes of inquiry, models, and theories presented in the curriculum are in practice fraught with discord, debate, and disagreement. The general education many students encounter may produce a false sense of hegemony or harmony in the world of scholarship, and may not adequately represent the intellectual fervor that is the hallmark of advanced knowledge (Ratcliff, 1992b).

Is a call to coherence that allows for contention and creativity within the curriculum at odds with the quest for quality and standards? Behavioral approaches to quality assessment, for example, involve measuring actual performance against established standards. Such approaches disaggregate larger curricular goals into smaller steps, termed behavioral objectives, in an instructional-systems approach to generating coherence among that which is to be learned (House, 1982). Buchmann and Floden (1992) see a natural gravitation toward slavish consistency and the elimination of conflict in models of curricular choice based on hierarchies of goals and objectives. They warn of subordinating thought and imagination to intellectual frameworks. They are in concert with John Keats, who suggested, "We hate poetry that has a palpable design upon us" (Forman, 1952, p. 95). Art indeed may be an appropriate metaphor for curricular coherence. Artists are notoriously not like-minded, and their creations and expressions need not be homogenous. The university, to fulfill its commitment to *universitas,* needs to encompass the breadth of knowledge as well as make a home for that messy discourse labeled as the advancement of knowledge in the fields of study and disciplines it harbors. Citing Wollheim (1968), Buchmann and Floden suggest that coherence is a social construction "midway between the artist and audience, both of whom must create unity—in composing and interpreting—but neither of whom should impose a unifying structure upon the other" (1992, p. 6.). The coherent curriculum is neither totally prescriptive nor an abrogation of design for learning.

Multiculturalism as an Example of Coherence

In reflecting on ways to represent divergence and difference among peoples, perspectives, and paradigms, consider the effort to incorporate multiculturalism into the general education curriculum. The concept of culture has provided a powerful, natural frame for understanding the arts, economy, society, politics, humanities, language, and history of groups of people. Nevertheless, current curriculum and course content fail to realize the potential of this concept to provide coherence. At a faculty senate meeting, an African American student spoke out in frustration: "The word 'multiculturalism' is just a word [here]. I am looking at you and I am listening to what you are saying, and thinking how closed-minded you are. No one here practices multiculturalism. Multiculturalism is not something you say; you have to *do* it. *You have to like it!* The policies of this college do not reflect a concern with multiculturalism. Our courses do not reflect the history and literary traditions of our community. To you, 'multiculturalism' is a word you twist and turn" (quoted in Bensimon, 1994).

Many faculty and department chairs interviewed confessed that they did not know what multiculturalism is. When a college sets a general education goal, such as "the students should understand and appreciate other peoples and cultures," it takes on a task in curricular coherence that cannot be easily satisfied by adding to the list of distributional choices in general education. Enormous differences do exist among students, faculty, and peoples in the United States. Single institutions cannot readily be all things to all people (Cohen and Brawer, 1989; Ratcliff, 1995), and few institutions have found a serious and significant way to incorporate multiculturalism fully into the curriculum. Diversity courses are often add-ons rather than integral to the reform and redesign of the curriculum toward the aims of greater coherence and quality (Bensimon, 1994).

Multiculturalism, as a task in integration and coherence, is not achieved by holding the art and literature of one culture to the standards of a prevailing one. Saul Bellow once said, "When the Zulus produce a Tolstoy, we will read him" (quoted in Taylor, 1992). By contrast, it can be argued that the whole value of studying about the Zulus is precisely that their work *will not* reproduce the standards, values, and judgments of Western culture; it will represent an art and an aesthetic all its own. Studying ideas, cultures, and perspectives other than one's own was linked to the development of intellectual inquisitiveness and critical thinking in the National Center research. Early exposure to a variety of peoples, perspectives, cultures, and ideas fosters intellectual development and inquisitiveness. Students are normally not disposed to such exposure or reflection, but they can develop it through a coordinated and coherent course of study. Such exposure can be enhanced through racial and cultural workshops, cultural studies centers, student clubs and organizations that give focus to diversity, and collaborative learning environments. Each can complement and supplement a coherent general education curriculum in achieving broad ends involving complex knowledge, skills, and abilities (Terenzini, Springer, Pascarella, and Nora, 1995; Ratcliff and Associates, 1995).

Student learning of broad cognitive abilities, such as analytic reasoning, quantitative comparison, or reading with comprehension does not relate to specific disciplinary learning. Students showing large growth and improvement in analytic abilities, for example, enrolled in a variety of social science and applied science coursework (Ratcliff and Associates, 1995; Astin, 1992). Students enrolled in an integrated curriculum organized around decision making showed significantly greater gains in learning toward a general education goal in moral reasoning than those enrolled in a conventional distributional plan (Mustapha and Seybert, 1991). When complex concepts such as multiculturalism or complex abilities like critical thinking are set into the general education curriculum, coherence among courses becomes extremely important.

Implementing Coherence

Through research conducted at the National Center on Postsecondary Teaching, Learning, and Assessment, we found that students learn more from logical sequences of courses that build on one another than from independent and unrelated courses. For instance, we find that a student enrolling in one five-credit course in physics, one five-credit course in chemistry, and one five-credit course in biology does not show much achievement in scientific knowledge and reasoning, or in analytic or quantitative skills, even though he or she may have completed the general education requirements of the degree (that is, fifteen credits in science). The same student taking a planned sequence of coursework in one of those scientific fields (for example, organic, inorganic, and molecular chemistry) acquires more general knowledge and is more familiar with key terms, concepts, models, theories, methods, and modes of inquiry associated with the discipline.

General coursework and work in the major are more effective when they require students to engage in planned sequences of learning and offer a modest diversity of such sequences responsive to variation in student interests, abilities, and prior achievement (Ratcliff, 1993; Ratcliff and Associates, 1995). This topic is developed in more detail later in the *Handbook*. Chapter Eight advocates using clusters of intellectual skills as a unifying framework for general education goals, curriculum, and assessment, and Chapter Fifteen illustrates the value of integrated sequences of courses. Noting that in art and music, history and practice have been separate in the curriculum, the author of Chapter Fifteen points to curriculum that integrates the study of the arts, provides sequences of courses that lead to the development of depth of learning in them, and ties the study of the arts to a broader understanding of culture.

In providing curricula to meet general education goals, institutions have not yet recognized the true extent of variation in student learning (Pascarella and Terenzini, 1991; Ratcliff and Associates, 1995). Open election of courses gives lip service to individual differences, but that presumes that all differences are ones of preference, interest, and taste, rather than of types and extent of prior learning. Provision for differences in student learning cannot be effectively addressed by providing endless choices among single courses, as in distributional general education schemes, nor can it be addressed through a rigid core curriculum that is blind to such differences. In an institution with a wide array of general education coursework and great diversity in student interests, abilities, and prior learning, neither highly structured core curricula nor distributional general education requirements may be most effective in enhancing cognitive abilities. Coursework clustered in sequences to promote the growth and development of student understanding of terms, concepts, ideas, themes and theories leads to greater gains in learning in general education (Jones and Ratcliff, 1991; Ratcliff and Associates, 1995).

Portland State University has developed an integrated general education curriculum that relies on clusters of courses to provide multiple pathways for students to achieve the program aims. Students choose among clusters built to work together to impart and reinforce themes, concepts, and theories. Prior to choosing particular clusters, first-year students enroll in a year-long course called "Inquiry," which is designed to cultivate students' abilities to examine new areas of learning holistically, critically, and reflectively and to develop a commitment to lifelong learning. Each section of the course is organized by different teams of five faculty and different themes involving the sciences, social sciences, humanities, and arts. Each general education goal is to be assessed over time to track growth and development—first as students enter the University, then as they progress through midpoints, as they graduate, and as alumni (White, 1994). At California State University, Northridge, faculty created an interdisciplinary program of linked upper division courses (Fieweger, 1994). Madonna University (Michigan) has constructed an interdisciplinary program linking key humanities courses in the general education program with corresponding teacher education sequences (Nolan, 1994). San Jose City College created alternative time frames for its general education program to create an Afternoon College to better respond to the needs of working adult students. Each time frame represents an alternate pathway to accomplishing the aims and requirements of its general education program. Chapters Twenty-Four through Thirty describe several other approaches and program examples for achieving better coherence in the curriculum.

Assessment and Coherence

Efforts at curricular reform and those devoted to establishing systems of assessment in the 1980s proceeded somewhat independently from one another. The decade did produce exemplars in the field—institutions and programs that attempted to use assessment to improve quality (Banta, 1993). However, there is little evidence to suggest that assessment information generally was used in concrete and specific ways to improve either the coherence or the quality of undergraduate teaching and learning (Steele and Lutz, 1995).

Nonetheless, once a college or university recognizes the variation in student interests, abilities, and prior educational achievement and provides multiple pathways to achieving the general education goals, the task remains to develop assessments that monitor student learning and take into account diversity in curriculum and clientele.

As a way to be fair and equitable, institutions have tended to assume that all students are the same. While most colleges and universities have recognized the growing diversity of students within their halls, they have not incorporated this knowledge in effective and concrete ways into planning their educational program and services (Ratcliff and Associates, 1995). Activities and efforts at the institutional level treat diversity as a human relations problem rather than a means to enrich the educational experiences of faculty and students. Too often, educational programs and services remain atomistic, lacking coherence and cogency for the variety of students enrolling.

The general education curricula of our institutions provide wide arrays of subjects and modes of inquiry reflecting the complexity and diversity of our knowledge, peoples, technology, economy, and geography. What remains lacking are clear standards for educational attainment in general education. Most institutions have relied on credits accumulated and grades earned as proxies for accomplishment. They have paid little attention to cumulative effects or integration of learning to attain general education goals. Across institutions, there is little common understanding regarding the levels of attainment associated with general education today. This situation prevails in spite of a decade of curricular reform and assessment. To improve teaching and student learning, we need a system (and institutions) with clear learning standards for general education, not merely for credits earned and grades received (Ratcliff and Associates, 1995).

Coherence in general education curricula can be assessed according to the students' gains and levels of attainment relative to:

- Competence in key intellectual skills, such as oral and written communication, critical thinking, and problem solving
- Integration of knowledge, languages, and methodologies across the liberal arts and sciences
- Understanding of one's heritage and its relation to other peoples and cultures
- Reflective and analytic ability to examine underlying values and controversial issues

Assessment of coherence begs the question of what constitutes quality in general education curricula.

What Is Quality?

What is and is not a quality curriculum is largely the result of our educational philosophies, beliefs, values, and normative positions (Fuhrmann and Grasha, 1983; van Vught, 1994). Barnett (1992) writes, "What we mean by, and intend by, 'quality' in the context of higher education is bound up with our values and fundamental aims *in* higher education. We cannot adopt a definite approach to quality in this sphere of human interaction without taking a normative position, connected with what we take higher education ultimately to be. In turn, what we take higher education to be will have implications for how we conceive of quality, how we attain it, how we evaluate our success in achieving it, and how we improve it" (p. 16).

Like the undergraduate curriculum, quality is a social construct. Just as an outstanding film is not merely a replication of a life story, general education is more than the transmission of a fixed body of knowledge to passive minds. The cinematographer seeks to bring the audience vicariously to new perspectives, imagination, and reflections through the art itself. Likewise, the faculty develop general education curricula to create representations of knowledge, culture, scholarship, and perspective that allow students to engage in and experience various backgrounds, interests, and abilities through discovery and inquiry. Such social representation of curriculum is at the heart of general and liberal learning. However, to the extent that individual faculty members create the general education curriculum in an atomistic assemblage of single courses, quality is limited to the values and expectations of the academic staff, one by one. Inasmuch as individual faculty members may all hold quite different philosophies of education shaped and mediated by their disciplines and prior educational experiences, the general education curriculum formulated on a distributional requirement model may most kindly be termed eclectic. As Glazer notes, "Eclecticism assumes that the lack of consistency among the assumptions underlying different theories and the absence of coherence in resulting combinations are unproblematic. Eclecticism in theoretical understanding has an interesting parallel with American willingness to entertain diverse demands on the political system without concern for their contradictions and incompatibilities. . . . The liberal philosophical epistemology views truth as pluralistic" (1988, p. 297). The eclectic is clearly the implicit philosophy guiding general education organized around free election across broad bands of knowledge such as humanities, fine arts, social science, science, and mathematics. The eclectic curriculum may provide no clear representation and coherent sequence of experiences to engage and involve students.

A related issue in the definition of curricular quality is the setting of educational standards. Is quality defined by attainment of predetermined standards or is it the development of the personal and intellectual powers of imagination, creation, enterprise, and effective action? At which type of goal should the quality general education program aim? In reality, the question so often posed is a false dichotomy. A high-quality educational program must attend to the developmental needs of individual students if they are to fully benefit from the program. At the same time, there must be clear standards for the educational program to protect its integrity and effectiveness from dilution from above and below.

Without clear entrance criteria based on curricular goals and prior achievement relative to those goals (for student selection, diagnosis, and guidance), the curriculum will be watered down to meet the needs of students less prepared to benefit. Without clear exit criteria, the curriculum may be extended and expanded with additional specialized courses not germane to the educational goals. Clear definitions of who can benefit from the collegiate experience are needed (at a minimum) on admission, at transfer, and on graduation. But how can such clear definitions be reconciled with what we know about creative talents, analytic skills, entrepreneurialism, and empowerment?

I have found that the question can be best addressed through analogy. As we board a commercial airliner, we want pilots who are fully competent to operate the plane. We want individuals who will rigorously review the checklists of aircraft readiness for takeoff. Here the compliance with standards of practice may mean life or death. Similarly, once airborne, we want those same pilots to use their creative judgment in coping with bad weather, air turbulence, and other unexpected and unpredictable events that may imperil the flight. During a blinding snowstorm, we do not want those pilots to take out their manuals and go over their checklists! The quality educational program has criteria, methods, and measures for determining the attainment of the knowledge, skills, and abilities that all should acquire. It also has provision for students to develop, demonstrate, and evaluate their imaginative and creative talents—for which a known outcome would be a constraint on creativity, initiative, and industry. What constitutes quality is heavily determined by educational philosophy, and within the academy several philosophies operate simultaneously, confusing and confounding the task of finding a common learning.

Educational Philosophy and Curricular Quality and Coherence

Several educational philosophies have competed for predominance in American higher education. Each shapes the curriculum differently. As noted in Chapter Four, three important philosophical viewpoints developed in the nineteenth century. First was the utilitarian or vocational view that underscores job preparation skills; second was the scientific view that stresses research and the dissemination of new knowledge; and third was the liberal learning view that emphasizes the importance of human development and intellectual habits of mind. While these competed for primacy, higher education fostered eclecticism, allowing and assuming that all could reside within the same institution—Kerr's *multiversity* concept (1963)—or that different institutions could possess different philosophies and missions. Similar pragmatic, comprehensive, and utilitarian visions were given to community colleges as well during the 1960s and early 1970s (see, for example, Gleazer, 1968). The hallmark of the pragmatists is that the curriculum is likely not to be shaped by any one philosophy, value set, or normative perspective. A logical conclusion and criticism of the pragmatists, therefore, is that the curriculum is unlikely to achieve any cogent or coherent curricular aims. Implicit in such philosophical eclecticism was that different philosophies can coexist and offer a richer, deeper form of higher education than one in which all institutions of one sector are organized on a single philosophy. Philosophical eclecticism contrasts with the approach taken in much of northern Europe, for example, where the university sector is driven by Humboldtian philosophy and ideals, and the vocational higher education sector is organized around the philosophy of utilitarianism and careerism.

Each philosophy provides a framework for setting criteria to determine what high-quality teaching and learning are and for specifying the role and type of curricular coherence that will attain that quality. Philosophies tell us what to value in an education as well as how to obtain an education and how to recognize an educated individual; in short, they offer truth criteria for determining what constitutes high quality. For example, for *perennialists* or *essentialists,* the value of education is in preserving and transmitting language, knowledge, and values that provide the basis for culture. Certain issues and ideas have recurrent value and provide the core questions confronted by a civilized society. From their vantage point, there is a definable canon that should provide the foundation for any liberally educated person. While it is customary to associate perennialism with Robert Maynard Hutchins, Mortimer Adler, and more recently with William Bennett, Ernest Boyer, Lynn Cheney, and Arthur Levine (Bennett, 1984; Boyer and Kaplan, 1977; Boyer and Levine, 1981; Boyer, 1987; Cheney, 1989; Hutchins, [1936] 1968; Levine, 1978), there are perennialist intentions behind those in women's studies, black studies, or Latino studies who seek to recognize the knowledge, values, and traditions of underrepresented groups in the humanistic, social science, and scientific traditions. The intent is similar: to preserve, perpetuate, and transmit the views and values of important writers, artists, scientists, and social leaders who preserve and advance certain traditions and culture.

Perennialists find quality through the identification of key writers, ideas, and works. Curriculum coherence is derived from a series of choices as to what key ideas or writers all students should be exposed to. The emphasis is on prescription because the values of such key ideas, questions, and writers have timeless qualities of imparting or stimulating student reflection against the issues of the day. Curriculum can be organized into a concise, coherent core embodying such prescriptions. Perennialists presume the preparation of the students who come to such curriculum to be fairly uniform—those who are prepared can participate and learn, and those who cannot should not be there.

Such views rely on rational argument and persuasion to rally faculty to a common view of what the essential qualities of the program should be. These qualities are attained by identifying the central qualities of the culture, the hallmarks of an educated individual, or the fundamentals of an educated people. Trying to find such a common definition of essentials can be unfruitful, frustrating, and unproductive (Gaff, 1983; van Vught, 1994; Veysey, 1973). As Chapter Thirty-One notes, there are limitations to such rationalist views of curricular change. While some successful models do employ truly and fully prescribed core curriculum in general education, they are generally limited to the 5 percent of colleges with very homogeneous student populations or driven by a common and clear educational mission like that shared by many Catholic colleges and universities (Astin, 1992; Brubacher and Rudy, 1976; Jones and Ratcliff, 1991; Veysey, 1973).

Related to essentialist philosophies of education are the *objectivists.* Their underlying assumption is that it is possible to identify and measure certain aspects of higher learning across disciplines, departments, even institutions and systems.

Based on cognitive development psychology and information processing theories of education, objectivists range from the extreme argument that "if it's worth knowing, it's worth assessing," to more consensual views. The objectivist view of general education curriculum implies that by "using a common methodology across the system, and quantifying [learning] in the same way, an objective measure of quality results" (Barnett, 1992, p. 46). The objectivist is likely to use pragmatic means to identify consensually based criteria for quality and then to subject the faculty, the students, and the curriculum to these criteria as constraints in shaping teaching and learning to predetermined ends (Jones and others, 1994). Quality implicitly resides in those participating in the consensual process to identify criteria. The DACUM (literally, "Develop A Curriculum") process has been used successfully in community colleges to generate general education goals, methods, and assessment criteria based on consensus derived from community, business, and educational leaders (for example, see Pima Community College District, 1994). Dynamic or static definitions of criteria, methods, and measures for assessing curricular quality may be chosen.

While there are several other educational philosophies that are influential in establishing the goals, curriculum, and evaluation of general education—pragmatism, feminism, humanism, to name a few—it is not uncommon to find all present among the faculty. Confusion of philosophies contributes to confusion among definitions of quality and coherence. Add to this cacophony of philosophies the fact that in a modern urban area with several institutions of higher education, students may enroll serially and concurrently in one or more community colleges, liberal arts colleges, regional state colleges, and state universities to complete their general education. Transcript studies affirm the phenomenon of students enrolling in three, four, and five institutions to attain a bachelor's degree (Adelman, 1995; Ratcliff, 1990; Ratcliff and Associates, 1995). It may not even be possible to formulate a coherent general education program on an institution-by-institution basis as students transfer in increasing rates, a question explored further in Chapter Twenty-Seven. Given that each institution has its own goals, curricular requirements, and perhaps assessment techniques, there is even more need to examine what constitutes quality and coherence in general education.

Assessing Quality

The assessment of the quality of educational programs has been a traditional characteristic of higher education. Historically, the French gave responsibility to external authorities for determining quality of university programs, while the English gave such responsibility to a self-governing community of fellows (Cobban, 1988). Both traditions are exercised today in American higher education. The various states, which have constitutional responsibility for the establishment and provision of education, generally have not taken a very active role in overseeing higher education or in determining its quality. Defining the quality of specific curricular programs is often delegated by a state or a higher education institution to learned societies (such as the National Foreign Language Teachers Association, the American Psychological Association, or the American Chemical Society) and the professional licensure associations, such as the Accrediting Board for Engineering Education, or the American Association of Schools and Colleges of Business. The latter have specific and articulated expectations for general education (for example, see American Occupational Therapy Association, 1991). States have relied on regional accrediting associations to determine overall institutional quality, including the quality of general education curricula. Where states have insisted on institutions developing student assessment plans, greater levels of effort and direction have been achieved in determining the impact of college on student learning (Ewell, 1993). The French model of external reviewers can be regarded as the archetype of quality assurance for accountability, while the English model of peer review provides the archetype of quality assurance for the enhancement of programs and the improvement of teaching and learning. Today, most efforts and quality assurance engage both accountability and improvement models (van Vught, 1994). Chapter Twenty-Nine explores these concepts in more detail.

Most baccalaureate-granting institutions today have an expansive curriculum representing the explosion of knowledge and diversity of students and modes of inquiry that characterize higher education at the end of the twentieth century. The undergraduate curriculum is in disarray, out of control, a growing and moving target (Levine, 1985; Ratcliff and Associates, 1995). The lack of coherence in the baccalaureate program is in part a function of the development of higher education itself. Perhaps to a large degree the undergraduate curriculum should have an untidiness to it if we, particularly those of us at universities, are to have it project the full range of knowledge, skills, and abilities resulting from advanced learning in our complex society.

General education is an institutional attempt to make sense of this disarray—this moving target—we call the undergraduate curriculum. Using the full undergraduate curriculum as its foundation, general education articulates to students and faculty alike the academic purposes and policies of the institution. It proposes that by selecting certain courses from the aforementioned array, certain types of learning regarded as important by the institution will be achieved.

Unfortunately, the old guideposts often used in setting academic purpose and policy—breadth and depth in learning, notions of core curriculum, and the exclusive role of certain disciplines (such as math) in developing particular abilities (such as making quantitative comparisons and interpreting data)—have not kept pace with the expanding undergraduate curriculum, with the increasing diversity of students, and with the proliferating modes of inquiry. For example, low-achieving students at the institutions examined in the Differential Coursework Patterns Project (Ratcliff, 1993) did not complete the science sequences intended to be part of the general education sequence. Chemistry 101, 102, and 103 include organic and inorganic chemistry and are intended as a curricular package to introduce students to the principal concepts, terms, theories, and nature of inquiry characterizing the discipline. Thus, this chemistry sequence is designed to produce a depth of learning that theoretically contributes to the general education goals of the institution. Similar sequences may be chosen in biology, physics, and astronomy. High-achieving students usually select and complete one of these sequences, fulfilling part of their general education requirements. Low-achieving students, on the other hand, take Chemistry 101 and receive a low or failing grade. Next they enroll in Physics 101, repeat the experience, and move on to Biology 101. Depth as intended is not attained by these students, although they do amass the requisite number of science credits to meet the general education requirements. Instead, breadth takes on a new and sad definition of sequential exposure to negative educational experiences. General education committees and undergraduate deans need to identify and learn more about the science experiences of students who succeed and have positive learning encounters with scientific disciplines. The example illustrates how more must be done for those students who are in various ranges of abilities.

Astin (1992) found that true core curricula produce striking educational benefits in terms of cognitive and personal development. However, only 5 percent of colleges have true core curricula, and those are among the smallest of institutions; they attract discrete, self-selected student populations that tend to be quite homogeneous. Through assessment of general education, it is possible to gauge whether a distributional design, a core curriculum, or a modified system of prescribed courses, course clusters, and capstone experiences (Jones and Ratcliff, 1991; White, 1994) best serves the salient subgroups of students enrolling at one's institution. (For further discussion, see Chapters Twenty-Five and Twenty-Eight.)

What is needed is a new wave of general education reform wherein basic institutional requirements reflect the variation in student learning and the clear assessment of curricular goals upon admission, transfer, and graduation. In moving toward that reform goal, a better gauge is needed to guide general education deliberations regarding quality and coherence.

Assessment serves to describe and monitor student progress toward a specified set of criteria. If the assessment is to be of general education, then those criteria clearly should be established by the general education goals of the institution. While this should be patently clear, an amazing number of institutions in 1995 would willingly judge student learning on one set of measures (or no measures at all!) while formulating general education according to a different philosophy or model of student learning (Steele and Lutz, 1995). There are many users of the American College Testing's College Outcome Measures Program (ACT-COMP), Riverside Publishing's College Basic Academic Subjects Exam (C-Base), Educational Testing Service's Academic Profile, and ACT's Assessment of Student Skills for Entry Transfer (ASSET) who have not determined whether what is measured by these tests corresponds at all to their institutional goals for general education. Nearly one-quarter of all colleges and universities have no assessment criteria, plan, or practice, and have no intention of developing one (Steele and Lutz, 1995).

Criteria used in assessing general education should be broad, including content learning, cognitive development, attitudes and motivation toward learning, and basic persistence to degree completion. Given the diversity of learning that occurs in college, general education assessment criteria must be broad enough to include all the major types of learning imparted by the institution. To attain quality and coherence in the curriculum, a great deal is admittedly being asked of assessment here! Our expectations need to be tempered with the realities of the state of the art. Because assessment is a new and imperfect science, general education and assessment committees (hopefully working in unison) should not presume that any one set of measures of general learning will capture all content, all forms of cognitive development, or all values and frames of reference a student may gain from her or his collegiate experience. (Chapter Twenty-Eight goes into the subject of evaluation in more detail.)

General education has multiple purposes. To monitor attainment of multiple purposes requires multiple measures. Students enter college with different types and degrees of knowledge, skills, and abilities. To monitor the variation in entering student abilities, again multiple measures are required. Taking different coursework in college produces different learning. Multiple measures are once again called for. Cognitive development gained during the college years ranges from basic communications and computational skills to higher-order reasoning abilities such as creative thinking and problem solving. To describe student cognitive development, multiple measures are needed to paint the full spectrum of enhanced capacities. So long as we use a limited array of measures in assessing student learning, the connection between the general education curriculum and student learning will remain tangential. On the other hand, while an expansive array of measures is desirable, it need not be limitless. The number of criteria used can be determined by the number, breadth, and depth of the general education curricular goals.

Putting It All Together

Given that there is great variation in student preparation, knowledge structures, and learning encompassed by general education and liberal learning, the quest for quality and the search for coherence cannot be meaningfully addressed by the question, *Which general education program provides a better education?* General education programs provide more productive learning when targeted to students with specific abilities, interests, and aims. The search for a single, one-size-fits-all general education curriculum holds little meaning to anyone other than those who think there is but one standard for quality throughout higher education. Instead, the guiding question for those seeking greater curricular clarity and impact should be, *Which groups of students benefit most from which general education curricula?* Only by answering the second question can we hope to show substantial increases in such cognitive abilities as the students' capacity to reason critically, communicate clearly, or solve problems.

The curriculum has always been viewed as a developmental sequence of learning events in the United States, with courses building on the learning imparted by the preceding ones. Essentialist and constructionist theories of curriculum stress the importance of combinations of subjects (core curricula, Great Books, and so on) as influential on general learning. Behaviorists emphasize the process of learning and focus on skill development. Still, they too see the logical sequence of tasks, from the simple to the complex, as a necessary element in the learning process.

The point is that most models and theories of curriculum call for a developmental sequence of learning. In determining the quality of postsecondary educational programs, we are not interested in determining the sum of all types of learning experiences, nor the average performance of students in learning such abilities, but rather the effectiveness of the progression of learning in producing the desired results. General education curricula should articulate the quality criteria by which their graduates should be judged. Those with oversight of the general education curriculum should assume responsibility and leadership for the assessment of its graduates according to such criteria. And they should adopt methods of assessment commensurate with their philosophy, premises, and purposes.

Our task in constructing a meaningful general education program for various groups is to provide curricular sequences that emulate the experiences of the successful students and that inhibit the selection of coursework patterns associated with students who did not improve much in general learning in college. This conception of general education rejects the standard distribution design for general education employed by most colleges and universities. Simply providing students with a wide range of choices to fulfill breadth and depth requirements, attempting to ensure exposure to the arts and humanities, social sciences, mathematics, and the life and physical sciences, is not enough. It does not provide a match between students' abilities and learning experiences. It does not contribute a sequential program of intellectual development that will heighten higher-order reasoning skills in students. In short, distributional plans for general education fail us because they allow for the failure of the lower-ability students and do not give an ordered plan of intellectual development among those students who do succeed.

This criticism of distribution plans for general education should not be interpreted as an affirmation of Cheney's *50 Hours* of core curriculum (1989) or similar prescriptions. The finding that variation in student learning is greater within colleges than between them also means that one intellectual shoe does not fit all freshmen feet. The other end of their bodies does the thinking. The efficacy of a single set of courses, a core, to foster the intellectual development of college students can be easily examined using assessment results. In any large or complex institution, one can divide a group of graduating seniors into those who entered college at or above the mean of SAT scores and those below the mean. Sort (cluster analyze) the courses these students took by the gains they demonstrated on the assessment measures (Jones and Ratcliff, 1991). If a core curriculum would be a superior arrangement, then both the high-ability and low-ability students who showed large gains would have taken basically the same coursework. If these two groups would benefit from distinctively different curricular sequences, then those who showed large gains from the low-ability group would have taken different courses than those who showed large gains from the high-ability group. Assuming that the assessment criteria mirrored the intent of the curriculum, where overlap between the two groups occurred, a core curriculum would be justified, and where there was no overlap, separate curricular sequences for each group would be appropriate means to achieve the general education goals. The National Center on Postsecondary Teaching, Learning, and Assessment research on this problem does not support a single core curriculum in institutions with diverse student populations. In the institutions with a distributional general education plan we examined, our research indicated that the implementation of a unitary core curriculum might actually militate against student learning, particularly among lower-ability students.

For the 90 percent of colleges and universities that have distributional plans for general education, the reform that makes the most sense in light of the research I have sketched today is one based on a comprehensive assessment of gains in student learning. That assessment should include selected disciplinary content, cognitive development, motivation, and attitudes toward learning and student persistence to degree. The results of that assessment should then be used to differentiate those students who showed large gains in learning in these areas from those who showed less improvement. In short, the aim of the assessment should be to identify the variation among students in the institution so as to describe student learning environments (curricular and extracurricular) that were more and less productive for the students who enrolled and engaged in them. Gains in general student learning can serve as criteria for such sorting of curricular sequences. Once such sorting has taken place, questions about the efficacy of particular general education structures and the contribution of specific course sequences to the attainment of educational goals can be approached. Curriculum committees need to work closely with institutional researchers to better understand the effects of the general education courses on student attainment of general education goals. Such assessments are at the heart of efforts by the regional accreditation associations (the Southern Association of Colleges and Schools, the North Central Association of Schools and Colleges, and so on) to improve institutional effectiveness.

General learning is associated with both the upper division and the lower division. Many junior- and senior-level courses were found to be associated with improvement in general cognitive skills, particularly analytic reasoning and the ability to make quantitative comparisons. Today, several colleges and universities are including capstone projects, experiences, and seminars as ways to encourage students to synthesize their general and liberal learning, as discussed in Chapter Twenty-Eight. They are also using cornerstone courses to synthesize and assess learning across disciplines horizontally (breadth) and at the end of single-discipline course sequences (depth). If we are to be concerned with improvement in student learning, the major and general education must be treated together. We must examine how elective, major, and minor coursework work together to produce gains in general learning described in comprehensive assessments of student outcomes. Again, studies using assessment data and transcript information identify those upper division courses that foster attainment of general education goals (see Adelman, 1995; Jones and Ratcliff, 1991; Ratcliff, 1990, 1993; Ratcliff and Associates, 1995; Zemsky, 1989). The developmental relationship between lower division and upper division can be more clearly described and cast into multiple clusters of curricula based on effective student learning communities and subenvironments.

Courses with different intents, orientations, or ways of framing knowledge may be equally valuable in developing general cognitive abilities. At several of the institutions we examined, courses such as "Western Literature" were found in the same set of coursework as certain diversity courses such as "Feminist Literature," in that both were found to be associated with close reading of the text, learning how to ferret out authors' interpretations while reading passages, and learning how to identify themes within the narrative. Different frames and content may provide different pathways to comparable curricular purposes. The formation of multiple clusters of sequential, developmental curricula frees faculty and students from the search for the one best pathway to student learning and may actually diminish the role of the general education committee as an ideological battleground—though I am not so naive as to suggest that all controversy in the general education curriculum can be resolved by linking assessment and enrollment patterns. As the Association of American Colleges notes, "General education involves many tensions: between what to teach and how to teach it, between the great classics of the past and contemporary works, between the classroom and students' out-of-class life, between students' individual objectives and the needs of the community, between what students want and what their institution thinks they need" (Zemsky, 1989, p. 5).

First and foremost, the curriculum serves to educate students. It is also the crucible in which we examine and test ways to come to terms with important social issues. However, if we cannot see the results of our efforts, we should not go mucking about with curricular change. If a general education innovation holds promise to enhance student learning in some way, then there should be a means to ascertain whether that improvement has occurred or not. Linked analysis of assessment and enrollment data holds the promise of identifying when—and, more important, under what circumstances—improvements have been made to the general education curriculum.

The agenda involved in establishing meaningful standards for teaching and learning within general education is a sizeable one. Goals are difficult to clarify in general education due to the competing philosophies and pedagogies employed. The aspects of curricula best measured according to standards are often different from those best judged for their development of creativity, entrepreneurial spirit, intellectual insight, and empowerment. Effective educational programs need careful delineation between attending to standards and empowering the intellect, for quality involves both. We must devise general education assessments that provide early feedback to students so that they can adjust their learning to move readily toward the standards once established, and we must provide such feedback in a timely fashion so that they have a chance to use such information. Finally, we must not limit our sights merely to that which is easily measured, or we will surely reduce and trivialize general education.

Coherence and quality can be hallmarks of the twenty-first-century general education curriculum. Jones and Ewell (1993, pp. 9–13) have summarized the literature on what constitutes "good practice" in undergraduate education:

1. *Create high expectations for student learning.* Students appreciate general education's aims and goals; faculty need to be clear that they expect students to attain them.

2. *Provide coherent, progressive learning.* Students learn, grow, and develop when the first step is not too high, when each step is a reasonable and connected elevation from the preceding one, and when there are clear standards for attainment in sight.

3. *Create synthesizing experiences.* Students benefit from the challenge of synthesizing their learning through essays and journal keeping, capstone and cornerstone courses, and integrative experiences in cooperative and service learning.

4. *Integrate education and experience.* The relevance to students' lives, aspirations, and perceptions is brought home when education is bolstered by application and experience.

5. *Create active learning experiences.* Students who are engaged in their studies learn more. First-generation students may need validation that their involvement is a legitimate part of the learning process.

6. *Require ongoing practice of skills.* Skills, once learned, soon atrophy without practice. For example, second-language learning in college suffers from students' lack of practice.

7. *Assess learning and give prompt feedback.* Students cannot improve their learning unless they receive constructive suggestions for improvement in time to adjust their behavior to enhance their efforts.

8. *Plan collaborative learning experiences.* Students are affirmed in their learning by their peers' support, criticism, and collaboration. Collaborative learning promotes behavior expected after college.

9. *Provide considerable time on task.* The press to cover the material leaves much of general education cursory; key knowledge, skills, and abilities are fostered by thorough explanation, discussion, and application.

10. *Respect diverse talents and ways of knowing.* Not all students learn the same way. Making a student conform to the predominant curriculum may militate against success. Diversity challenges the curriculum to represent learning in multiple, coherent, purposeful forms.

11. *Increase informal contact with students.* A minority of students' time is spent in the classroom. Students value the mentoring and advice offered by faculty outside the classroom. Make the curriculum and extracurriculum work together to support student learning.

12. *Give special attention to the early years.* The transition to college (and between colleges) presents significant social and academic adjustments for students. Instilling a thirst for inquiry and reflection early on will set the stage for more rapid growth, development, and educational attainment.

All twelve of these good practices can apply to the major or minor as well as to general education. They have been affirmed by National Center research (Ratcliff and Associates, 1995), and by numerous other studies (Pascarella and Terenzini, 1991). Each provides a unifying principle to promote great unity, coherence, purpose, and engagement in the curriculum. None should be applied without careful regard to curricular diversity and the specific background and needs of salient subgroups of students.

We end our discussion as we began. There is substantial evidence that we can judge the quality of higher education by examining its impact on students. As higher education serves greater proportions of the population, students become more diverse in background and abilities. As society becomes more complex, knowledge structures and technologies expand, creating a knowledge explosion and curricular proliferation. Students do benefit from purposeful higher education devoted to their intellectual and personal development. They welcome and benefit from frequent assessment, feedback, and academic counseling. In short, there is merit to judging the quality and coherence of general education based on the results of student assessments of learning. Yet, such assessment becomes problematic when different institutions offer different curricula, and when different states in a federal system hold different implicit or explicit educational standards, policies, and expectations.

Instead of looking for the one best curriculum for all students, we need to begin to examine which coursework patterns and sequences advance which types of learning for which types of students. To do this, we need to enlarge our range of measures of general education and liberal learning. At minimum, we need measures of subject-matter learning that reflect our notions of breadth and depth in the curriculum, measures of cognitive development from basic communications and computational skills to critical thinking and problem solving, indicators of student attitudes and proclivities toward learning itself, and evidence of the students' progress, persistence, performance, and degree attainment.

We need to sort through the vast array of our undergraduate curriculum to identify the patterns of coursework taken by the students who make the largest progress toward our general education assessment criteria. We know that most students learn best in groups, and that students who show the greatest gains in college take specific sequences of courses. We can build multiple core curricula reflecting these naturally occurring student learning subenvironments or communities. We can shape the curricular experiences of these communities so as to maximize learning toward the stated institutional goals of general education. We know that what students take in college can make a difference in their lives. Our task now is to align the general education curriculum to what we have garnered about student learning, good instructional practices, and assessment of general education. New paradigms of general education reform await us. The guideposts to quality and coherence are there. Let us take up the challenge and begin the task.

References

Adelman, C. *The New College Course Map and Transcript Files: Changes in Course-Taking and Achievement, 1972–1993.* Washington, D.C.: Office of Educational Research and Improvement, U.S. Department of Education, 1995.

American Occupational Therapy Association. Committee on Allied Health and Accreditation. "Essentials and Guidelines for an Accredited Educational Program for the Occupational Therapist." *American Journal of Occupational Therapy,* 1991, *45*(12), 1077–1084.

Association of American Colleges. *Integrity in the College Curriculum: A Report to the Academic Community.* Washington, D.C.: Association of American Colleges, 1985.

Astin, A. W. *Assessment for Excellence: The Philosophy and Practice of Assessment and Evaluation in Higher Education.* New York: ACE/Macmillan, 1991.

Astin, A. W. *What Matters in College? Four Critical Years Revisited.* San Francisco: Jossey-Bass, 1992.

Banta, T. W., and Associates. *Making a Difference: Outcomes of a Decade of Assessment in Higher Education.* San Francisco: Jossey-Bass, 1993.

Barnes, H. L. "The Conceptual Basis for Thematic Teacher Education Programs." *Journal of Teacher Education,* 1987, *38*(4), 13–18.

Barnett, R. *Improving Higher Education: Total Quality Care.* London: Society for Research in Higher Education and the Open University Press, 1992.

Bennett, W. J. *To Reclaim a Legacy: A Report on the Humanities in Higher Education.* Washington, D.C.: National Endowment for the Humanities, 1984.

Bensimon, E. M. (ed.). *Multicultural Teaching and Learning: Strategies for Change in Higher Education.* University Park: National Center on Postsecondary Teaching, Learning, and Assessment, Center for the Study of Higher Education, Pennsylvania State University, 1994.

Boyer, C. M., and Ahlgren, A. "Assessing Undergraduates' Patterns of Credit Distribution: Amount and Specialization." *Journal of Higher Education,* 1987, *58,* 430–442.

Boyer, E. L. *College: The Undergraduate Experience in America.* New York: HarperCollins, 1987.

Boyer, E. L., and Kaplan, M. *Educating for Survival.* New Rochelle, N.Y.: Change Magazine Press, 1977.

Boyer, E. L., and Levine, A. *A Quest for Common Learning.* Washington, D.C.: Carnegie Foundation for the Advancement of Teaching, 1981.

Brubacher, J. S., and Rudy, W. *Higher Education in Transition: A History of American Colleges and Universities, 1636–1976.* (2nd ed.) New York: HarperCollins, 1976.

Buchmann, M., and Floden, R. E. "Coherence, the Rebel Angel." *Educational Researcher,* 1992, *21*(9), 4–9.

Cheney, L. V. *50 Hours: A Core Curriculum for College Students.* Washington, D.C.: National Endowment for the Humanities, 1989.

Cobban, A. B. *The Medieval English Universities: Oxford and Cambridge to 1500.* Berkeley: University of California Press, 1988.

Cohen, A. M., and Brawer, F. B. *The American Community College.* (2nd ed.) San Francisco: Jossey-Bass, 1989.

Eaton, J. S. *The Unfinished Agenda: Higher Education and the 1980s.* New York: Macmillan, 1991.

El-Khawas, E. *Campus Trends, 1990.* Higher Education Panel Report No. 80. Washington, D.C.: American Council on Education, 1990.

El-Khawas, E. *Campus Trends, 1995.* Higher Education Panel Report No. 85. Washington, D.C.: American Council on Education, 1995.

Ewell, P. T. "The Role of States and Accreditors in Shaping Assessment Practice." In T. W. Banta and Associates, *Making a Difference: Outcomes of a Decade of Assessment in Higher Education.* San Francisco: Jossey-Bass, 1993.

Fairweather, J. *Teaching, Research, and Faculty Rewards: A Summary of the Research Findings of the Faculty Profile Project.* University Park: National Center on Postsecondary Teaching, Learning, and Assessment, Center for the Study of Higher Education, Pennsylvania State University, 1992.

Fieweger, M. "Strategy for Curricular Change." *Liberal Education,* 1994, *80*(1), 34–35.

Forman, M. B. *The Letters of John Keats.* London: Oxford University Press, 1952.

Fuhrmann, B. S., and Grasha, A. F. *College Teaching: A Practical Handbook.* Boston: Little, Brown, 1983.

Gaff, J. G. *General Education Today: A Critical Analysis of Controversies, Practices, and Reforms.* San Francisco: Jossey-Bass, 1983.

Gaff, J. G. "General Education at the Decade's End: The Need for a Second Wave of Reform." *Change,* 1989, *21,* 11–19.

Glazer, N. Y. "Questioning Eclectic Practice in Curriculum Change." *Signs: A Journal of Women in Culture and Society,* 1988, *98,* 293–322.

Gleazer, E. J., Jr. *This is the Community College.* Boston: Houghton Mifflin, 1968.

Harvard Committee on General Education. *General Education in a Free Society.* Cambridge, Mass.: Harvard University Press, 1945.

House, E. "Alternative Evaluation Strategies in Higher Education." In R. Wilson (ed.), *Designing Academic Program Reviews.* New Directions for Higher Education, no. 37. San Francisco: Jossey-Bass, 1982.

Hutchins, R. M. *The Learning Society.* New York: Mentor, 1968. (Originally published 1936.)

Jencks, C., and Riesman, D. *The Academic Revolution.* New York: Doubleday, 1968.

Jones, D. P., and Ewell, P. T. *The Effect of State Policy on Undergraduate Education: State Policy and Collegiate Learning.* Denver, Colo.: Education Commission of the States, 1993.

Jones, E. A., and Ratcliff, J. L. "Which General Education Curriculum Is Better: Core Curriculum or the Distributional Requirement?" *Journal of General Education,* 1991, *40*(1), 69–101.

Jones, E. A., and others. *A Plan for Validating Criteria and Measures to Monitor Progress toward National Education Goal 5. 5: Identifying College Graduates' Essential Skills in Writing, Speech and Listening, and Critical Thinking.* University Park, Pa.: National Center on Postsecondary Teaching, Learning, and Assessment, Center for the Study of Higher Education, 1994.

Kerr, C. *The Uses of the University.* Cambridge, Mass.: Harvard University Press, 1963.

Levine, A. *Handbook on Undergraduate Curriculum.* San Francisco: Jossey-Bass, 1978.

Levine, A. E. "Program: A Focus on Purpose and Performance." In A. E. Levine and J. Green (eds.), *Opportunity in Adversity.* San Francisco: Jossey-Bass, 1985.

Mustapha, S. L., and Seybert, J. A. "Moral Reasoning in College Students: Effects of Two General Education Curricula." *Educational Research Quarterly,* 1991, *14*(4), 32–40.

National Institute of Education. *Involvement in Learning: Realizing the Potential of American Higher Education.* Report of the Study Group on the Conditions of Excellence in American Higher Education. Washington, D.C.: U.S. Government Printing Office, 1984.

Nolan, E. "Teacher Preparation: Integrating the Humanities." *Liberal Education,* 1994, *80*(1), 16–19.

Pascarella, E. T., and Terenzini, P. T. *How College Affects Students: Findings and Insights from Twenty Years of Research.* San Francisco: Jossey-Bass, 1991.

Pima Community College District. *Student Outcomes Assessment Plan.* Institutional Effectiveness Series, No. 5. Tucson, Ariz.: Pima Community College District, 1994. (ED 375 916)

Ratcliff, J. L. *Development and Testing of a Cluster-Analytic Model for Identifying Coursework Patterns Associated with General Learned Abilities of College Students: Final Report, May, 1990.* U.S. Department of Education, Office of Educational Research and Improvement, Research Division. Contract No. OERI–R-86–0016. University Park: Center for the Study of Higher Education, Pennsylvania State University, 1990.

Ratcliff, J. L. "Reconceptualizing the College Curriculum." *Perspectives: The Journal of the Association for General and Liberal Studies,* 1992a, pp. 122–137.

Ratcliff, J. L. "Undergraduate Education." In B. R. Clark and G. Neave (eds.), *The Encyclopedia of Higher Education.* Tarrytown, N.Y.: Pergamon Press, 1992b.

Ratcliff, J. L. *What We Can Learn from Coursework Patterns About Improving the Undergraduate Curriculum.* University Park, Pa.: National Center on Postsecondary Teaching, Learning, and Assessment, 1993.

Ratcliff, J. L. "A Rationale for a Differentiated System of Higher Education: The Person-Environment Fit Model of Student Learning." *Tertiary Education and Management,* 1996, *2*(2), 127–137.

Ratcliff, J. L., and Associates. *Realizing the Potential: Improving Postsecondary Teaching, Learning, and Assessment.* University Park, Pa.: National Center on Postsecondary Teaching, Learning, and Assessment, 1995.

Riesman, D. *Constraint and Variety in American Education.* (Rev. ed.) Lincoln: University of Nebraska Press, 1958.

Scheffler, I. "Science, Morals, and Educational Policy." In I. Scheffler (ed.), *Reason and Teaching.* New York: Routledge & Kegan Paul, 1973. (Originally published 1956.)

Steele, J. M., and Lutz, D. A. *Report of ACT's Research on Postsecondary Assessment Needs.* Iowa City, Iowa: College Level Assessment and Survey Services, American College Testing Program, 1995.

Taylor, C. *Multiculturalism and "The Politics of Recognition": An Essay by Charles Taylor with Commentary by Amy Gutmann, editor, Steven C. Rockfeller, Michael Walzer, Susan Wolf.* Princeton, N.J.: Princeton University Press, 1992.

Terenzini, P. T., Springer, L., Pascarella, E. T., and Nora, A. "Influences Affecting the Development of Students' Initial Thinking Skills." *Research in Higher Education,* 1995, *36*, 23–39.

Toombs, W., and others. "General Education: An Analysis of Contemporary Practice." *Journal of General Education,* 1991, *40*, 102–118.

Trow, M. A. "Problems in the Transition from Elite to Mass Higher Education." In *Policies for Higher Education.* Paris: Organisation for Economic Cooperation and Development, 1974.

Trow, M. A. "The Analysis of Statutes." In B. R. Clark (ed.), *Perspectives on Higher Education: Eight Disciplinary and Comparative Views*. Berkeley: University of California Press, 1988.

van Vught, F. "The New Context for Academic Quality." Paper presented at the symposium entitled University and Society: International Perspectives on Public Policies and Institutional Reform, Wirtschaftsuniversität Wien, Vienna, Austria, June 9–10, 1994.

Veysey, L. *The Emergence of the American University*. Chicago: University of Chicago Press, 1965.

Veysey, L. "Stability and Experiment in the American Undergraduate Curriculum." In C. Kaysen (ed.), *Content and Context: Essays on College Education*. New York: McGraw-Hill, 1973.

White, C. R. "A Model for Comprehensive Reform in General Education: Portland State University." *Journal of General Education*, 1994, *43*(3), 168–229.

Wollheim, R. *Art and Its Objects*. New York: Penguin, 1968.

Zemsky, R. *Structure and Coherence: Measuring the Undergraduate Curriculum*. Washington, D.C.: Association of American Colleges, 1989.

CHAPTER EIGHT

DEVELOPING INTELLECTUAL SKILLS

Austin Doherty, James Chenevert, Rhoda R. Miller,
James L. Roth, Leona C. Truchan

Since the mid-1980s, there have been numerous calls to focus the efforts of the American education community on the development of intellectual skills. For example, the 1985 report of the Project on Redefining the Meaning and Purpose of Baccalaureate Education sponsored by the Association of American Colleges (1985) directly addressed the "methods and processes, modes of access to understanding and judgment that should inform all study." While the report acknowledged the importance of careful study of the traditional disciplinary fields of undergraduate education, it also stated that "how that subject matter is *experienced* [italics added] is what concerns us here." The National Education Goals Panel (1992) identified "advanced ability to think critically, communicate effectively, and solve problems" as "skills necessary to compete in a global economy and exercise the rights and responsibilities of citizenship." "Time for Results," the Governors' 1991 Report on Education (1986), emphasized the acquisition of knowledge, but also "the development of increasing levels of ability to organize and use that knowledge."

These studies and reports represent a pragmatic concern with relevance and application that has been central to American higher education throughout most of its history. From the colonial colleges' emphasis on ethical character development to the land-grant emphasis on education for a modern agricultural and industrial society, education for the purpose of solving problems and conducting the affairs of the democracy has been highly valued.

As colleges and universities adopted a disciplinary organization with a focus on the knowledge bases appropriate to individual fields, educators seem to have assumed that students would continue to develop intellectual skills by studying the subject matter of those fields. Today we realize that this assumption may be unwarranted. An emphasis on transmitting the results of disciplinary scholarship to students has tended to overshadow our historic concern with how students develop their knowledge and how they apply it. The current concern over intellectual skills serves as a reminder that whom we teach is as important as what we teach. Skills cannot be transmitted from instructors to students; students have to develop them. This means that we must attend to the most effective ways in which our students learn.

As clear as these calls for an explicit emphasis on intellectual skills have been, they have not as yet had the broad transforming impact on the undergraduate curriculum that their authors desired. While there has been much debate over the definition of individual intellectual skills such as critical thinking, problem solving, and communication, little attention has been given to the way student development of multiple skills could provide a coherent focus for the entire curriculum. There is no common understanding or common language for conceptualizing an intellectual skill-centered education. Until we who teach undergraduates take this kind of education seriously in scholarly discussion, there will not be a common language.

Our purpose, then, is neither to review the existing scholarship nor to recommend a specific conceptual model for intellectual skills development. Instead, it is to raise questions that we hope will initiate a broad dialogue about intellectual skills among teaching colleagues across the spectrum of American education. What do we mean by intellectual skills as a focus for undergraduate education? What would some of the consequences and implications be if we emphasized intellectual skills? What would we have to do to transform our curricula? What are the implications for teaching and for assessing student performance? Our hope is that when we think together, some aspects of a common language and a common understanding will result.

What Do We Mean by Intellectual Skills?

The first step in promoting dialogue must be to establish some linguistic common ground. One approach to arriving at a common language is to agree provisionally to experiment with a common language. We can agree to talk about intellectual skills even though some of us have made a reasoned commitment to the term *abilities* or some other synonym in our own practice. We can try to group together clusters of skills rather than insist from the outset that one college's definition of "conceptual comprehension" is completely different from another's "analysis and appraisal."

This is not to propose a uniform approach that ignores the uniqueness of various existing efforts to address intellectual skills issues. In the long run, a rich and varied terminological palette may be the best resource for creative change in a variety of institutional settings. But for now and for the sake of this desired collaboration, we are suggesting that some distinctions are not significant enough to be allowed to get in the way of dialogue.

Knowledge Versus Skills

The terminological distinction most often responsible for sidetracking discussions of intellectual skills is the distinction between content and process. "If I teach skills to my students, how will I have enough time to teach them the essential knowledge in the field?" This dichotomy only makes sense if we use the word knowledge loosely and incorrectly as a synonym for data or information. We often say that professors transmit or impart knowledge to students, but knowledge is too complex a phenomenon to be characterized this simply. Knowledge is what an individual knows. What knowledge is to a professor—the interpretation of some experience—is mere data to a student, unless and until that student makes it into knowledge for herself or himself. Knowledge cannot be opposed to skills because knowledge does not exist apart from the mental operations that transform information into knowledge. Those mental operations are *intellectual skills*.

If we can agree that knowledge should not be separated from the knower, then perhaps neither should we think of intellectual skills as separate from the skilled person. Just as knowledge is not an object that can be delivered from one person to another, intellectual skills are not tools that one picks up to accomplish a given task. As educators, we almost always observe and evaluate students applying particular theorems or outlining the logic of a particular argument. In these circumscribed situations, intellectual skills can appear to be highly task specific. But if we think of those observations as contextualized examples of the overall performance of the skilled individual, we need not be limited by this image of skills as tools.

Thinking of the skilled individual rather than the individual's skills can also assist us in conceptualizing intellectual skills in a holistic way. It is extraordinarily difficult to isolate individual intellectual skills as they are manifested in behavior. Effective communication, for example, incorporates thinking, decision making, sensitivity to the values and beliefs of the audience, and many other skills. Separating this integrated performance into individual skills works as a teaching strategy to assist less experienced students to understand more clearly what steps they can take to become effective. The same caveat that we expressed earlier about subject matter applies to skills as well: we do not teach problem solving or decision making; we teach students to become problem solvers and decision makers in their lives.

Intellectual Skills Versus Abilities, Competencies, Attitudes, Dispositions

The general term we choose, as well as the connotations we give that term, can either promote or shut down discussion. We should, therefore, emphasize the broadest and most inclusive understanding of intellectual skill and its connections to, rather than distinctions from, other ways of describing students' educational achievements. Skill, ability, competency, attitude, habit, and disposition are not interchangeable terms. Those who write about education use them in specific ways. Fortunately, usage overlaps. The term skill used in one context may be virtually indistinguishable from ability in another context and competence in a third (Perkins, Jay, and Tishman, 1993).

Skill is a perfectly good word. Unadorned by adjectives, it is admirable. In the context of the work of an artist, for example, it conjures up thoughts of elegance and virtuosity. But until now, in educational circles we have tended to modify the word, to tailor it to very specific applications: basic skills, study skills, school-to-work skills. And the more we have limited it, the more we have stripped it of its complex and open-ended meanings. Recently, we have encountered various efforts to effect a different kind of modification that broadens the connotations—higher-order thinking skills, intellectual skills, problem-solving and critical-thinking skills—and strongly implies that skills are central to all aspects of higher education.

Rather than discard more limited constructions such as basic skills in favor of those more flattering to the higher levels of education, we have chosen to highlight the juxtaposition of basic skills and higher-order intellectual skills, suggesting that students become skillful in progressively more sophisticated ways as they move along the educational continuum. This notion of progressive development fits well with research arguing that significant aspects of intelligence are teachable rather than being relatively fixed traits (Covington, 1992). Whether these basic and higher-order skills are actually different skills or are developmentally distinct dimensions of the same intellectual skills is open to debate. Do the differences between basic reading comprehension and higher-order criticism outweigh the resemblances? Is there a point at which writing skills end and higher-order communication skills begin? We think it is reasonable to regard them as more or less complex dimensions of the same skills—especially at a time when we are educating ourselves about the meaning and development of intellectual skills.

What Intellectual Skills Should We Talk About?

Is there a specific set of commonly agreed-upon intellectual skills that should be central to undergraduate education? The colleges, universities, and postgraduate professional schools that have attempted to transform their curricula to emphasize the development of skills have identified and defined scores of different intellectual skills (Consortium for the Improvement of Teaching, Learning, and Assessment, 1992; Schulte and Loacker, 1994; Walker, 1994). Descriptions of intellectual skills vary greatly in levels of specificity. Some are very large and holistic: professionalism, understanding, research. Others are very narrowly defined: comparing, organizing, synthesizing. In effect, these designate as separate intellectual skills the processes involved in demonstrating the more complex skill of analytical reasoning. Other descriptions are very domain specific, as in the distinction between hermeneutic analysis in religious studies and historical consciousness in history.

The variety of descriptors and definitions is in some ways healthy. It suggests that faculty are grappling with the meaning of intellectual skills in the varied contexts of their teaching and of their understandings of their disciplines. They are not simply overlaying a set of externally generated skill-based expectations on their existing curricula. The variety also suggests a sensitivity to institutional missions and the unique needs of different student bodies. Those who would like to have a standardized national assessment of intellectual skills may find these local initiatives somewhat frustrating. The variety makes comparable judgments of institutional quality more difficult, but, on the whole, it seems to offer the best hope for transforming education.

Yet there are reasons we should be interested in some consensus over the way we define intellectual skills and some limits to the variety of intellectual skills in our programs. Our responsibility is not merely to discern whether our students possess intellectual skills; it is to teach them how to develop and use these skills. So when we define and describe intellectual skills, we are discoursing on the meaning of higher-order reasoning in our fields in ways that help students understand how they can be effective in learning and in applying their learning. They need descriptions that help them understand what an intellectual skill looks like as it is practiced, but not descriptions so subtle and full of nuances that students would already have to possess the skill to understand the description. As scholars in our disciplines, we may know what research skill or professionalism looks like when we see it, but this is not the point. Our students are the ones who need to learn how to go about doing research or being professional. We have to break open these complex abilities so that students can understand and develop them.

Students develop intellectual skills in many different contexts during their undergraduate years. Their learning of these skills would not be efficient if, in every different discipline's courses, they encountered a set of highly specific intellectual skills with no clearly recognizable connections to skills in other courses. Unless we faculty explore with each other the analogies between different higher-order intellectual skills that are domain specific, unless we incorporate a sense of those connections in our teaching, it is unlikely that many students will recognize the possibility and desirability of adapting a skill such as moral reasoning developed in the humanities for later use in developing a theory of professionalism in a senior seminar in psychology.

We propose, as a first step in encouraging dialogue and collaboration among faculty, the provisional reduction of the large numbers of intellectual skills to clusters of skills that seem to be more similar than they are different. Scholars may argue forever over whether critical thinking is primarily a proactive problem-solving skill or a reflective metacognitive skill. But the salient point for educational purposes should be what these different conceptions *together* can contribute to students' development of higher-order reasoning. To promote discussion of possible connections and commonalities, we recommend the grouping of intellectual skills into a few larger categories such as the following:

Operational Skills

- *Communication and Literacy* (reading, writing, speaking, listening, visual communication, kinesthetic communication, interpreting the meaning of artworks and artifacts)
- *Quantitative Literacy* (numeracy)
- *Reasoning* (thinking, problem solving, analysis, conceptual comprehension, integrative comprehension, critical thinking and decision making, analysis and appraisal)
- *Interpersonal Effectiveness* (social interaction, teamwork, collaborative learning, cooperative learning)

Value-Focused Skills

- *Aesthetic Responsiveness* (creative response, aesthetic values)
- *Citizenship* (civic, social, and personal responsibility, social awareness)
- *Responsible Participation in the Global Environment* (global perspectives, cultural awareness, cross-cultural awareness, multicultural sensitivity)
- *Ethics* (making value judgments, using ethical considerations in decision making, resolving ethical dilemmas, professional ethics, valuing in decision making)

We recognize, of course, that all skills are based on underlying values or assumptions. This distinction between broad categories of skills nonetheless seems useful. Our experience, and the experience of other colleges and universities working on an *intellectual skills approach,* has been that faculty from the different disciplines at an institution can come to agreement on general definitions of a common set of intellectual skills while preserving the domain-specific sense of those skills in their own courses. What they need are a few common starting points for that collaboration, such as the idea that logic, analysis, synthesis, and critical thinking are all part of the same complex skill.

Once we have begun to consider the possibility that there are general intellectual skills that have specific manifestations in different academic and professional fields—and the possibility that these skills are developmental across the entire spectrum of education, from elementary school through the continuing education of the professions—we are faced with an array of implications. An intellectual skills approach changes the way we think about the structure of the curriculum, the way we think about teaching and assessing our students, and the way we relate as educators across levels of education.

Implications for Curricular Planning and Design

If we were to think about intellectual skills in the way that seems to be emerging—the concept of these skills as arrayed along a continuum from basic to higher-order levels of skills, defined as attributes of the person rather than as tools for a given task, and related in a limited number of clusters—the implications for our understanding of the curriculum would be dramatic. First of all, we would need to place our students at the center of our thinking when we conceptualize and design our curricula. Instead of asking ourselves what subject matter we are going to teach to our students, we would need to ask instead how the unique aspects of our disciplines make them appropriate frameworks to help students develop the knowledge and intellectual skills they need.

The focus for the teaching of intellectual skills would not be restricted to pre-college or general education courses. Based on the assumption of an open-ended range of skills, every course, from freshman composition to the senior capstone seminar in biochemistry, would emphasize the development of intellectual skills. Theoretically, some intellectual skills may be of such high order that they would not be appropriate before advanced seminars in Ph.D. programs. Others would be accessible to younger children and would provide a clearly recognizable foundation for higher-order skills. In the same way that we would determine the appropriate complexity of subject matter for each course, we would also set expectations for the level of intellectual skills appropriate to each course.

In addition to expanding the teaching and learning of intellectual skills to all courses in the educational spectrum, a skills emphasis would allow us to conceptualize integration and coherence in the curriculum in new ways. There would be the potential for better vertical integration of beginning-, intermediate-, and advanced-level courses within a discipline. A junior-level course in poetry, for example, could be planned to take advantage of students' previously demonstrated skill in formalist criticism of novels or dramatic literature. There would also be the possibility of a more meaningful horizontal integration of the various disciplines in higher education for the common purpose of preparing students for personal, occupational, and civic life. Advanced courses in a marketing major, for example, could draw explicitly on the skill of contextual analysis learned in general education courses in sociology or history.

Coherence Within Majors

There have been important initiatives during the last several years, sponsored by the Association of American Colleges and Universities and involving learned societies and departments and programs at a number of colleges and universities, to address the need for coherence in liberal arts and sciences majors (see Chapter Eleven). Many of the twelve disciplinary reports emerging from this work (Association of American Colleges, 1990) have emphasized intellectual skills development by student majors. But the reality in most fields of study at most colleges and universities is that the organizing principle is course coverage of the various subfields of the disciplines by specialists in those areas.

We do not dismiss the possibility of a department's faculty rationally planning a student's learning by dividing up the subject matter. A content-coverage curricular model can be developmental, particularly if the courses are iterative. If, for example, a history department's majors are required to complete the general education survey in U.S. history and then at least two advanced-level courses in U.S. history, these students will be studying the same subject matter in greater depth and presumably with greater sophistication. But other sequences have no such apparent logic—at least not apparent to students. To extend the example from history, the implied prerequisite of general education U.S. history for a more advanced world history elective on South Asia may be more difficult to explain developmentally unless we consider the specific intellectual skills students develop in an introductory study of history and extend and develop in a more advanced course.

If asked to confront this question of a developmental rationale, most professors of history could make a case for ways this first course assists students to think chronologically or to establish the credibility of evidence. But unless we are accustomed to talking with students about intellectual skills development in addition to presenting our portion of the subject matter of a departmental domain, the odds are not favorable that the professor will capitalize on connections between the courses to promote student learning. Some students may discover principles of coherence, but most will probably see their major courses of study as a collection of discrete topics, and in quite a few instances their perceptions will be justified. If the major lacks coherence for students, what sort of unifying rationale can they see in their travel across the borders of the liberal arts disciplines?

But when we ask each other questions focused on students and their intellectual skills, principles of curricular coherence—or their absence—come readily into view. What happens to students when they move from introductory to more advanced courses within a discipline? What kind of development takes place? Do students simply acquire more information? Is it a different kind of information? Do they use a more sophisticated kind of reasoning to raise appropriate questions about more complex information? Are the strategies for communicating about their knowledge more involved? How do they go about purposefully connecting those experiences? How should their ways of thinking be different in more advanced courses?

Concern with intellectual skills also transforms the questions we pose to ourselves about our disciplines and our own professional practice. What are the intellectual skills, rooted in the context of the discipline, that make for our own effective inquiry, interpretation, or decision making? What interpersonal skills are essential for work in the field? What particular kinds of communication skills are essential? These would have to be higher-order intellectual skills—the ability to sort and discriminate, the interpretive rules of thumb, the modes and standards of judgment—that make it possible to think and make decisions in the discipline. Until we become conscious of the relationship of intellectual skills to our own success as scholars, we can hardly be expected to see how intellectual skills are central to student learning.

The most pleasant surprise that may emerge from a discussion of these questions about intellectual skills is the number of positive discoveries that we may make about teaching and learning in our courses. The skills we explicitly identify may very well be the ways of thinking we have always hoped for and taken for granted when we ask students to write interpretive essays or solve problems. As experienced practitioners of our disciplines, we tend to view these skills as virtually transparent. We know instinctively, based on years of practice, what one ought to do to sort through data and apprehend the underlying pattern. The transparency of these skills, unfortunately, is what makes them invisible to our students. What distinguishes an intellectual skills approach from much current teaching practice is the degree to which we make expectations explicit for students and consciously address them in the design and practice of learning experiences in courses throughout the curriculum.

Beginning questions like these have led faculty at a number of institutions to lay the foundation for curricular coherence by seeking consensus about the intellectual skills that should characterize all an institution's graduates and, from among those skills, the ones essential for graduates in each field of study. Faculty dialogue may begin at either the departmental or institutional level. Our challenge is to agree on a common set of intellectual skills that will help students experience the coherence of all their educational endeavors, while at the same time preserving the rich meaning of those skills in the context of the different disciplines.

At first it might seem to be a mistake to begin within the conceptual walls of individual disciplines. If collegewide efforts to define intellectual skills have yielded scores of different definitions, how much more complexity would result if every department and program in each of those institutions would select and define the necessary intellectual skills in its own way? Would it not be simpler to start with a few very general outcomes—critical thinking, communication, teamwork, ethical decision making, citizenship—and then ask each department to respond to these? Perhaps, and perhaps not. If faculty begin with the intellectual issues associated with their own courses and the skills needed to address them, they will be less likely to view an intellectual skills emphasis as an add-on to the teaching of the subject matter of their courses. Once faculty within a department have actually named and described the essential skills students should be developing in their courses, it becomes easier to place these side-by-side with the skills identified by all the other departments, and explore the possible congruences and overlaps to create a general set of outcomes that all faculty in an institution can stand behind.

The collaborative work of a faculty to identify the essential intellectual skills for students in a major becomes in a very real sense a review of the curriculum. When we describe to each other what we hope students will be able to do in our courses at various levels, we are inductively creating a collective portrait of the intellectual development of students as a result of their progression through the curriculum. Thinking together, we can see the multiple dimensions of students in ways that we cannot as individuals. Students are already skilled in certain ways from previous learning when they enter an advanced-level course. By talking with the faculty who teach introductory courses, or better yet, by teaching these courses ourselves, we can become more aware of students' existing skills and help them to build upon those skills in the sequels.

This more comprehensive sense of student development, based on demonstrated intellectual skills incorporating mastery of information, may make it easier to articulate the developmental nature of the curriculum. We may find such development already implicit in the existing designation of courses as introductory, intermediate, and advanced. Introductory courses may, for example, require students to observe and record carefully but not to evaluate the assumptions and biases underlying different scholars' interpretations of a topic. But we may also find some courses out of place relative to an intellectual skills scheme and decide they should either be moved to another level of the curriculum or be revised so that their goals match the intellectual skills of the majority of students enrolling. Other courses may seem so essential to the development of students' intellectual skills that they will need to be elevated from elective to required status. We may also discover that important dimensions of intellectual skills are inadequately presented in the current curriculum and should be emphasized in a greater number of courses.

Faculty who have worked extensively with intellectual skills have discovered that these skills cannot be taught across the curriculum, even within a single major, unless they are articulated in developmental stages. It is not enough to specify the highest level of skill appropriate to a particular program and use it as a target for student achievement throughout that program. This becomes an exit standard. We need to visualize how students develop as thinkers, communicators, and ethical decision makers and specify how they grow in sophistication as they learn more and continue to apply those skills from course to course.

Perhaps the most serious implication of an intellectual skills emphasis for the curriculum is that faculty will likely decide that the order in which students take courses makes a great deal of difference. If one of the purposes of a course is to assist students in the development of specific intellectual skills, that purpose is defeated if the student is not prepared to perform at that level of skill or if the student is not challenged because she has already taken several courses with higher expectations. Course scheduling is undoubtedly one of the thorniest problems facing the multipurpose college or university, and an intellectual skills approach will do nothing to mitigate the course scheduling conflicts that students face. But a departmental curriculum can coordinate courses into groups, with each group emphasizing the same level of intellectual skills. This would provide some flexibility for students within each group. By requiring that they complete a certain number of courses within one group before enrolling in a course at the next higher level, the department would ensure that students build their intellectual skills in a coherent way.

Transfer of Skills Across Disciplines

Thus far we have been discussing coherence and integration within major areas of study. But major requirements are often less than half of an undergraduate's total coursework. The more important question about the curricular implications of an intellectual skills focus may be how it can assist faculty to promote coherent learning from one general education course to another and from general education in one discipline to advanced work in a different discipline. Intellectual skills create the common ground on which faculty across an institution can meet to share responsibility for student learning.

Is it possible for faculty from diverse departments to agree on a limited set of intellectual skills that all students need to develop? This should be relatively easy if the skills are defined in sufficiently general terms. But what will be the relationship between students' skill-based learning in one discipline and learning of the same skill in another? Student thinking in an art history survey and in a course in experimental psychology may both be called analytical skills, but will these skills bear any real similarities to each other? Is it possible for students to begin developing a skill in one discipline and continue to refine that skill in a later course in another discipline?

In their review of the literature on the *transferability* of intellectual skills, Perkins and Salomon (1989) suggest a compromise between those who argue that there are general (and transferable) thinking skills and those who find that intellectual skills such as critical thinking are so domain specific that they should be regarded as different skills in different disciplines. According to Perkins and Salomon, general intellectual skills develop in context-specific ways. The failure to transfer those skills from one context to another, they argue, may be more a function of the absence of conditions needed to promote transfer than of inherent domain specificity. Those conditions are primarily teaching strategies such as showing the learner how to make the transfer, directing attention to the possibility of transfer, and providing rules for making connections.

The important point about this research is not whether intellectual skills can be refined to such a degree that they become domain specific, but whether faculty can perceive and articulate meaningful connections across the disciplines for the benefit of student learning. These connections will not be established by research in cognitive science alone. Instead, they will be discovered through interdisciplinary faculty dialogue and the resulting familiarity with student learning experiences outside one's own courses or field. For example, a general aspect of *analytical thinking* is the use of heuristics, theories, or conceptual frameworks to organize the collection and interpretation of data. By learning something about the way colleagues in different disciplines talk about these tools of analytical skill, a faculty member can cue students to anticipate thinking in terms of conceptual frameworks analogous to those they have worked with in other courses. A science professor may remind students that just as different critical frameworks in the study of literature lead to different interpretations of a text, laboratory data may be interpreted differently according to different models for explaining natural phenomena. This cue should prevent students from recycling to a novice learner mode, indiscriminately gathering data in a new area of study, and instead encourage them to actively search for principles of analysis in the new discipline.

One of the most important insights faculty have gained from work to refine their curricula to emphasize intellectual skills is the need to work collaboratively. We need to have collective ownership of the ends and purposes of the degree. Our differences over the meaning of particular skills in different disciplinary and interdisciplinary contexts have to be negotiated *for the sake of our students*. By thinking aloud with each other about our different disciplines or about the connections across disciplines, we can come to a better understanding of how students encounter their education as a synthesis of the perspectives of a number of faculty, not necessarily the way any one faculty member sees it.

Implications for Teaching

In a very real sense, we have been raising questions about teaching throughout the chapter. It would be a mistake to separate the broader restructuring of curriculum from the act of teaching and to regard the latter as only what happens in an individual course. Both planning where courses fit in relationship to each other and designing those courses are just as much part of teaching as the implementation of the resulting plans in the classroom. Also an integral part of teaching is assessing student achievement—determining the degree to which each student has met the objectives of a course. An intellectual skills focus, particularly with its student-centered emphasis on performance and on the individual's long-term development of skills, has significant implications for what knowledge and skills faculty need to bring to courses, for what we and our students do in these courses, and for how we go about measuring students' achievements.

Knowledge and Skills Needed for Teaching

If an intellectual skills focus is to mean more than "students will be held responsible for writing effectively, reasoning clearly, and so on," if that focus implies the active role of faculty in helping students learn how to be skilled, then we may need to develop new ways of thinking about ourselves as disciplinary scholars. For example, we need to consider ways that our disciplines can serve as frameworks for student learning. Philosophy professors may need to give students more opportunities to philosophize on important issues, rather than concentrating only on what other philosophers have thought.

In addition, we need to develop some familiarity with areas other than our discipline specialties. If we happen to be psychologists who are teaching students to develop written communication skill in the discipline, for example, we would probably be more effective if we understood some of the principles of rhetoric or recent theory on writing pedagogy. Even if we do not have primary responsibility for teaching this skill, this background would enable us to reinforce what students have learned in previous courses and help them to adapt and refine writing strategies appropriate to the discipline of psychology.

Rather than ask the question of whether it is possible for faculty to become experts in adult learning theory and problem solving and rhetoric in addition to their discipline specialties, we should ask *how much expertise it would take* in these areas to make an impact on student learning. In the long run, the transformation of undergraduate education to emphasize intellectual skills may necessitate a related transformation of graduate school education. Graduate students might be better prepared to join us as faculty in an intellectual skills–focused environment if their graduate education included more of a reflective, metacognitive emphasis on what it meant to reason, communicate, and solve problems in their disciplines. In the near term, however, we will probably have to rely informally on each other for faculty development to enable us to integrate teaching for intellectual skills with the subject matter of our disciplines.

An intellectual skills focus will make us aware that we need to have background knowledge about our students as well as expertise in our disciplines. How do the ages, genders, races, classes, and faiths of our students affect the way they learn? How can we build upon the significant work and life experience that many of our students have had? Knowledge of how different students learn can be based in theory (see Belenky and others, 1986, and Gilligan, 1982), and on observation and common sense. If it is obvious, for example, that the ages of our students preclude most of them from understanding certain kinds of allusions or anecdotal examples that we feel comfortable using, then we should modify our habits to be more effective for our students.

Another form of teaching expertise is a familiarity with some of our students' previous class experiences. An important aspect of lifelong learning is the ability to use skills and knowledge appropriately in situations different from the ones in which they were learned. It has been our experience that students can gain a more holistic, multifaceted understanding of their skills if they develop these skills in multiple contexts. By referencing aspects of learning in prior courses, we can assist more students to make connections at earlier points in our courses. We can learn about different areas of the curriculum through informal interdisciplinary discussion, but it makes more sense to establish formal mechanisms, such as regular meetings of faculty teaching different components of the general education or core curriculum. Departments could also briefly describe their general education programs as a part of periodic program reviews for faculty from other departments to read, which would enable us to place the subject matter of our disciplines in a more interdisciplinary context.

An important implication of adopting an intellectual skills focus is the way it can affect our ongoing scholarship in our own disciplines. If, for example, we are assisting students to develop ethical decision-making skills, some of us may find ourselves shifting our research focus to consider ethical questions in our fields. Faculty who teach for the skill of perspective taking as an aspect of critical thinking may become more sensitive themselves to the way that research in their own fields is influenced by the cultural context in which it is carried out.

Teaching and Learning Strategies

Intellectual skills involve both knowledge and action—doing something with what one knows. Students also need to be aware of their skills, internalizing them as personal characteristics they are in the process of developing and that they can use in a variety of new academic and life situations. These dimensions of intellectual skills—active and experiential, self-reflective, developmental, and transferable—all will have an impact on what faculty and students do in courses.

If lecturing is our preferred or exclusive mode of teaching, we may have to vary instructional approaches. The development of social interaction skills, for example, cannot be taught through lectures, and students cannot actually demonstrate interpersonal skills by writing a paper about the theory of social interaction. We will need to create opportunities for collaborative work, find ways to observe this work, and give feedback on how to improve the skill.

Lecturing may continue but the form may change. For example, we will need more emphasis on the process of knowing and doing in the context of the subject matter of the course, and less on summarizing the results or findings of research. An effective use of lecture may be lecture demonstrations in which faculty think out loud about the way one works in the discipline. For students to be able to visualize what intellectual skills look like in performance, we may need to devote time to very explicit discussion—both about relevant intellectual skills and about the integration of knowledge and skills. However we choose to introduce and explain intellectual skills, student learning requires practice.

Students cannot effectively develop as skilled individuals simply by watching someone else perform or by talking about skills. Students will need the opportunity to practice intellectual skills under conditions where they can be observed and can receive feedback on their performance and suggestions of ways to improve it. To be sure, some kinds of practice would not require classroom time. We could ask students to analyze a text or solve a problem outside of class and to write reflectively about the thought processes they engaged in to do their work. And, of course, we could evaluate that writing and provide written feedback outside of class time. But if we wish to promote self-awareness and reflectivity during the process of engaging in problem solving, we would need to arrange for this within the classroom, by having students think through problems aloud in dyads or small groups. Our feedback and recommendations for improvement will likely be more relevant, too, if closely connected in time with students' performances.

An intellectual skills focus also increases the need for faculty to receive ongoing feedback from students. In a more traditional course with a focus on subject matter, that subject matter is not likely to change in the course of a semester. But when the focus is on intellectual skills, students' development of those skills throughout the course of a term becomes a dynamic factor. It may be important to reserve time regularly to gather information informally about what students are learning so that we can adjust our instruction as needed.

In general, regardless of the intellectual skills being emphasized, it is likely that learning will be more interactive and collaborative, like most real-life applications of intellectual skills. Accomplishing joint tasks requires that people explain what they know to others. The more that learning parallels the situations in which students will likely apply their knowledge and skills, the greater the possibility that students will be able to make that transfer from education to the world of work, citizenship, and family life.

Implications for Assessing Student Performance

The same dimensions of intellectual skills—active and experiential, self-reflective, developmental, and transferable—will also affect the way we assess or measure the achievements of students in their courses as well as the effectiveness of programs and curricula. If skills are manifested in performance, then we need to structure assessments so that we can observe students in action (Alverno College Faculty, 1994). And if we wish to promote independent lifelong learning, then we need to devise assessments that come as close as possible to the actual circumstances in which students will be using the skills assessed. In a course on differential equations, for example, mathematics students might be asked to take an ill-defined problem situation, such as the interactions over time of predator and prey animal populations, and devise mathematical models to transform it into a well-defined problem. In presenting their work, these students might be asked to address an audience of students familiar with calculus but not with differential equations, forcing them to clarify and articulate the principles and assumptions that have guided their thinking. Not every course can include a practicum or internship, but every course can include some form of simulation such as playing roles in group tasks or making oral presentations. Essay or research paper assignments can include rhetorical directions that specify audience, purpose, and context, or require students to select them, rather than simply to formulate ideas in the abstract and address them to the instructor.

For students to understand themselves as skilled persons who know how to be effective in a variety of situations, we need to promote purposeful and self-reflective behavior. Two ways of doing that in assessment are by making our expectations for successful performance explicit through public criteria prior to assessment and by providing opportunities for self-assessment in every assessment situation. Criteria need to include standards by which faculty judge students. Such standards, made explicit, assist students in visualizing the skilled performance expected of them. If chemistry students are told, for example, that they must go beyond learning formulas and replicating laboratory experiments and instead raise their own questions, test their own hypotheses, and present their findings to peers, they are likely to learn these skills more effectively. The more readily students are able to articulate criteria for effective performance, the better they are at recognizing the developmental aspects of their own performance and making specific plans for improvement.

Our sense of intellectual skills as developmental and open-ended will affect the frequency of assessment in our courses, the way we can link assessment to ongoing learning through feedback, and the way we verify and record student achievement. Since students have the potential to develop skills continuously, assessment should take place, both formally and informally, throughout a course. Students in a political science course might be asked to complete a worksheet summarizing different theories from a reading assignment on modernization. If feedback to students were specifically linked to criteria for articulating the underlying assumptions of theory, an instructor could show students, based on their own work, what it would mean to raise critical questions about theory. This early assessment and feedback become a teachable moment promoting further growth as the course progresses. Thus one of the major benefits of an intellectual skills focus is that it allows faculty to integrate their roles as teachers and as examiners continually throughout a semester.

The developmental nature of intellectual skills may, however, require that we rethink the way we measure students' overall achievement in a course. Consider the example of a student who makes a breakthrough in a course, progressing from weak to very sophisticated demonstration of intellectual skills by the end of the term. As a result of her progressive mastery of the intellectual processes required in the discipline, she has also achieved a comprehensive understanding of the subject matter. Should we average her initial performance with all her more advanced ones and characterize her achievement as moderate, or is it not more accurate to certify her performance in the course as highly skilled?

Finally, assessment can play a major role in assisting students to develop the dimension of transferability, the ability to apply their skills independently and creatively to new situations. To promote transferability, faculty will need to vary the modes of assessment as much as possible. We might engage different aspects of critical thinking, for example, in different situations. We might encourage and observe elements of reflection most readily in written assessments, while we might evoke thinking on one's feet by assessments based on oral presentations or group interactions. Asking students to create a work of art such as a poem or a graphic design may elicit different aspects of aesthetic skills than an assessment based on audience response to another's work and analysis of it.

We may also find it more effective to put students in somewhat unfamiliar assessment situations, rather than to base assessments directly on texts and materials that have already been presented or discussed. In a literature course on the short story, for example, might it not be preferable to ask students to apply their reasoning and aesthetic skills to an assessment based on a short story they have never before discussed?

We should remember, however, that all aspects of assessment, if they are student-centered, will work to promote transfer of skill and lifelong learning. Realistic assessment situations prefigure the way students will use their skills throughout their lives. Self-assessment and a clear understanding of what constitutes effective performance make students aware of what they can do. And feedback that is both diagnostic and prescriptive points students toward future learning and future performance.

Implications for Collaboration Across Levels of Education

Once faculty at undergraduate institutions begin to consider intellectual skills as a basis for student-centered education, the opportunities to make connections across educational systems will become apparent. We feel confident that very few would question the desirability of articulation across systems of education. When we focus on students, we can see clearly that many students we teach in college are the same students who went to high school a few months earlier, and some are the same who go on to professional and graduate schools and eventually to professional continuing education. As a society we cannot afford a system of education with discontinuities for the learner or with unnecessary repetitions.

An intellectual skills focus provides a vehicle for articulation. Subject matter has tended to separate elementary and secondary education from postsecondary. Intellectual skills as we have discussed them, however, are attributes of our students as they move from one level of education to another.

There is much that we can learn from each other. At present, educators in K–12 and in postgraduate professional education have done much more with intellectual skills than we have in undergraduate education. The movement for national standards in the schools in subject areas such as history, mathematics, science, and the arts has gone beyond the specification of essential content to consider the essential intellectual skills students require to be successful in these areas. The work of the standards groups and of the teachers working to implement them could make major contributions to the dialogue we are engaged in here. Professional school educators, with their experience in internships, practicums, and experiential learning, can teach us a great deal about performance-based learning and assessment. But we, as undergraduate faculty, have a key role in the overall educational process. We need to work together for the benefit of students' long-term learning. Intellectual skills form the agenda for that collaboration.

In this chapter, we have drawn on the experiences of faculty at colleges and universities who have actually worked with intellectual skills as the central focus of undergraduate education. We have not specifically described our own program or that of any other institution because each has emerged from local circumstances and needs. What is common to each program, however, is the discovery by faculty of the transforming effect of an intellectual skills focus on their practice and on their institutions as a whole. We have used our experiences to create a possible scenario for what might happen if all the faculty at an institution talked seriously with each other about intellectual skills.

This process of questioning and transformation is complex. Discursive debate of the meaning of intellectual skills as a general concept, of the nature of individual skills, and of the relationships among domain-specific aspects of those skills will take considerable time. We have stipulated agreements rather more quickly and easily in this questioning scenario than in our actual experience so that we can provide an overview of the many layers of this process in one brief chapter. We believe this shortening of the process is appropriate because we know from experience that faculty in a variety of institutional settings can reach agreement about a working definition of intellectual skills for the sake of student learning. We also hope that this vision of faculty dialogue based on a predisposition to reach agreements about teaching and learning may inspire us to move forward in a more radical transformation of education.

The serious consideration of intellectual skills represents a shift of concern from the subject matter to the student: what the student can come to know and what the student can learn to do. This shift is likely to be of seismic proportions. In systems theory, when one aspect of a system changes, everything else must change. Faculty will need to consider changes in their preparation, teaching activities, modes of assessing individual student progress as well as educational programs, and even their ways of working collaboratively with colleagues. Administrators will have to find ways to enable faculty to collaborate, as well as ways to reward faculty in a student learning–focused environment. Registrars and academic advising offices will have to assist students in planning their academic careers more coherently. Graduate school training will have to focus more explicitly on the intellectual skills basis of the disciplines. Even the physical environment of an institution may need to be changed. Social interaction and collaborative learning do not adapt very easily to rooms with fixed desk-chairs all facing forward. These changes will not occur in one wave, but each must be addressed if an intellectual skills focus is to contribute to a transformed educational system.

Intellectual skills are not a new fix for education. If our view of knowledge—as the knower's transformation of data—holds, then intellectual skills have always been central to education. Now is the time to make them part of an ongoing public dialogue in higher education, to reinforce them, and to make them an explicit part of our work.

References

Alverno College Faculty. *Student Assessment-as-Learning at Alverno College.* Milwaukee, Wisc.: Alverno College Institute, 1994.

Association of American Colleges. "Integrity in the College Curriculum: A Report to the Academic Community. The Findings and Recommendations of the Project on Redefining the Meaning and Purpose of Baccalaureate Degrees." Washington, D.C.: Association of American Colleges, 1985.

Association of American Colleges. *Liberal Learning and the Arts and Sciences Major.* Vol. 2: *Reports from the Fields.* Washington, D.C.: Association of American Colleges, 1990.

Belenky, M. F., Clinchy, B. M., Goldberger, N. R., and Tarule, J. M. *Women's Ways of Knowing: The Development of Self, Voice, and Mind.* New York: Basic Books, 1986.

Consortium for the Improvement of Teaching, Learning, and Assessment. *High School to College to Professional School: Achieving Educational Coherence Through Outcome-Oriented, Performance-Based Curricula.* Report to the W. K. Kellogg Foundation. New York: The Kellogg Foundation, 1992.

Covington, M. V. *Making the Grade: A Self-Worth Perspective on Motivation and School Reform.* Cambridge: Cambridge University Press, 1992.

Gilligan, C. *In a Different Voice: Psychological Theory and Women's Development.* Cambridge, Mass.: Harvard University Press, 1982.

National Education Goals Panel. Task Force on Assessing the National Goal Relating to Postsecondary Education. "Report to the National Education Goals Panel." Washington, D.C.: National Education Goals Panel, 1992.

National Governors' Association. "Time for Results: The Governors' 1991 Report on Education." Washington, D.C.: National Governors' Association, 1986.

Perkins, D. N., Jay, E., and Tishman, S. (eds). "New Conceptions of Thinking." *Educational Psychologist,* 1993, *28*(1), entire issue.

Perkins, D. N., and Salomon, G. "Are Cognitive Skills Context-Bound?" *Educational Researcher,* 1989, *18*(1), 16–25.

Schulte, J., and Loacker, G. *Assessing General Education Outcomes for the Individual Student: Performance Assessment-as-Learning. Part I: Designing and Implementing Performance Assessment Instruments.* Milwaukee, Wisc.: Faculty Consortium for Assessment Design, 1994.

Walker, L. (ed.). *Institutional Change Towards an Ability-Based Curriculum in Higher Education: Report of a Three-Day Conference Held in York, 3–6 July 1994.* United Kingdom Employment Department, 1994.

CHAPTER NINE

DIVERSITY AND EDUCATIONAL INTEGRITY

Caryn McTighe Musil

The metaphors available to describe higher education as it struggles to come to terms with the diversity of the United States are tangled up with those used to describe the nation as a whole. The choice of metaphor is no mere literary exercise. Each metaphor reveals a political and personal vision of the inter-relationships necessary to sustain excellence, cohesion, and integrity. All of them reveal the deep tensions inherent in our familiar national motto, *e pluribus unum*. How much can an individual or group be recognized and function, separate and apart from the whole? What is the glue, the commitment, the aspiration that can hold the many together as one? At what point is unity achieved by erasing practiced inequalities and subordinating individuals and groups, especially those who are marked as other?

Pots, Salads, Quilts, and Mosaics

Some believe deeply that America is—at its best—a melting pot, a place where one sheds one's particular identity and slides into an all-encompassing meta-identity. In *The Disuniting of America*, Schlesinger embraces the same definition of what it means to be an American that de Crèvecoeur articulated in his *Letters from an American Farmer:* "He is an American, who leaving behind him all his ancient prejudices and manners, receives new ones from the new mode of life he has embraced, the new government he obeys, and the new rank he holds. The American is a new man, who acts upon new principles. . . . Here individuals of all nations are melted into a new race of men" (Schlesinger, 1992, p. 12). Such a definition, however, presumes that race, gender, and ethnicity are invisible markers that have little influence over identity or citizenship. It also assumes that every group has an equal amount to surrender in order to conform to that image of an American citizen.

History suggests, however, that the reputed neutral identity is not neutral at all. It is, in practice, a gendered and racialized identity, deeply layered with religious, ethnic, and cultural values. To melt into this "new race of men" one must have a certain length of hair. So if you are a Native American boy at an Indian boarding school, you must cut your braids. It has a certain set of surnames. So if you immigrate to the United States as Kantrowicz, you change your name to Kaye. It has a certain language. So if you speak any other but English, you are to ban it from your lips. It has a certain skin color. So if you are Asian American, you cannot sit on a jury in 1920, or if you are African American, you cannot vote in Mississippi until 1964, and then only at great risk. When groups challenge the feasibility of constructing social relations upon such assumptions, some proponents of the melting pot metaphor become truculent. In a rather disturbing image, Bloom writes, "There is now a large black presence in major universities . . . but they have, by and large, proved indigestible" (1987, p. 91). Bloom expands his cannibalistic metaphor as he continues: "The heat is under the pot, but they do not melt as have *all* other groups" (p. 93).

In contrast to pots, others have sought some negotiated alternative either to melting into unrecognizability or to remaining stubbornly self-contained and unconnected to a larger common society. This group argues that it is not always possible or even preferable to shed one's identity or culture. Rather than labeling diversity as a threat to unity, they see it as a source of our nation's strength. While Schlesinger also sees it as a national strength, he sees a great danger in perpetuating ethnic identities and warns, "Separatism . . . nourishes prejudices, magnifies differences and stirs antagonisms" (1992, p. 12). Offering a different way to unity through fully recognizing our differences, Takaki writes, "As Americans, we originally came from many different shores, and our diversity has been at the center of the making of America. While our stories contain the memories of different communities, together they inscribe a larger narrative" (1993, p. 428). Thus, we find metaphors of salads, quilts, and mosaics as the metaphors of choice among another group of Americans.

In the search for the perfect metaphor we can see the longing for community, either of an imagined bygone era or of a nation embracing the full if complex richness of its history. Amid the sometimes heated debates about which metaphors, if any, adequately capture the fragile balance of *e pluribus unum*, the jagged remnants surface of unsettled and unsettling questions about historic inequalities and continued patterns of discrimination.

Higher education is at the very epicenter of these debates. This is as it should be but not as it has always been. Today, the academy has a unique opportunity to provide leadership for the nation as our country reconstitutes its national identity and rethinks its future commitments in light of its past legacies. The academy can be, but has not always been, the locus of national experimentation. In such a context, higher education can become a place where new conceptual frameworks for diversity can be tested, where new structures for equality and inclusion can be created, and where the possibility for face-to-face candor and understanding can teach us how to revitalize our community life. The time is ripe for such an experiment.

The intellectual ferment within higher education in the United States has rarely been more potent. The student body has never been so diverse. There is, of course, a correlation between the two. The correlation suggests that intellectual diversity, long espoused by the university, and demographic diversity, too long avoided by the university, have combined in a fertile dynamic that has already transformed the academy and promises to do so even more in the next century. While a few powerful and vocal critics have sought to link diversity with disintegration, fragmentation, and political indoctrination, the fact is that diversity has been, on the whole, a stimulus for dazzling intellectual investigations, innovative experiments in making higher education more democratic, and a new vision of community grounded not only in recognition of differences but also in commitments to shared obligations. Instead of being divisive, then, diversity is potentially unifying. Such unity is achieved not through the imposition of one view upon another, but through negotiation, reciprocal recognition, and commitment to continued dialogue.

Increasing Student Diversity

Despite public claims to the contrary, higher education has never been divorced from the gritty reality of serving particular political interests. Thomas Jefferson believed an educated citizenry was a necessary component of the fledgling republic. Eventually the country adopted universal schooling through eighth grade. Until the current century, however, higher education had long been understood to be the province of the chosen elite, who were, it turned out, usually white, usually male, and usually comfortable economically. They were understood to be more privileged. Education helped maintain that privilege. And through that privilege, the graduates of higher education had (and continue to have) influence over how the country is shaped disproportionate to their numbers.

With the founding of land-grant institutions and colleges for women, African Americans, and Native Americans in the nineteenth century, higher education began to diversify its student body and, to a more modest extent, its curriculum. The last half of the twentieth century, however, has witnessed an even more dramatic experiment in democratic practice as higher education—with intentionality or acquiescence—became one of the principal testing grounds for American pluralism. Could the academy become an inclusive intellectual community at the very moment when it was more diverse by race, class, gender, religion, ethnicity, age, and sexual orientation than it had ever been in its history? And could it at the same time maintain its commitment to excellence? The decade of the 1990s is the harvest of a half century's commitment to opening the academy to new populations. It is a harvest that some critics think is bitter. But the vast majority welcome it as a means of revitalizing the academy and the larger community beyond its walls.

It wasn't the notorious "culture wars" that were responsible for making the first major shift in higher education, but a real war: World War II. When peace was declared and Congress sought to compensate veterans with the passage of the GI Bill, the opportunity to earn a college degree was extended for the first time to large segments of working-class Americans who in prewar years had neither the financial means to attend college nor the national and local support to do so. As a result, higher education increased its population dramatically, thus leading the phalanx of expansion in higher education that would dominate the next several decades. Although among the veterans there were many new groups who had been largely absent from earlier college classes, almost all of them were male, the vast majority of them were white, and instead of fighting their way into being admitted, they were wooed, praised, and paid for by a grateful public. Nonetheless, it was the beginning of the creation of a more genuinely democratic higher education system. By introducing new voices and perspectives, the system eventually allowed scholarship to emerge in new areas.

Over time there was, for example, a new interest in labor studies, in white working-class ethnic communities, and in the role of Jews in the United States and the world. Despite new areas of investigation, however, knowledge continued to be dominated by the view that if you studied white men, you studied the whole world. It would take two other powerful movements to dislodge that position: the Civil Rights movement and the women's movement.

The overall impact of the Civil Rights movement on American life cannot be underestimated. It changed national consciousness, national policies, and became the touchstone for almost every political movement that followed it. This mass movement, which profoundly expanded our nation's democratic commitments and practices, was powered and led principally by southern African Americans, but eventually was joined by people of all colors and ages working in all corners of the country. Higher education was at the center of some of the most bitter confrontations as Governor George Wallace sought to physically impede the entrance of black students to the University of Alabama. Only the presence of armed soldiers from the National Guard deterred his opposition and offered the students some momentary protection from physical violence. The dismantling of the de jure educational segregation in the South was followed by the erosion of the de facto segregation of the North and other regions.

Because of the passage of "Title VII of the Higher Education Act" and the Civil Rights Act of 1964, the establishment of affirmative action policies and the Equal Education Opportunities Commission, the expansion of scholarship opportunities, and an increasing middle-class black population, the number of black college students increased in the 1960s and 1970s. This trend paved the way for the entrance of other racial groups who over the next decades gained greater access to higher education. Always a minority but now with a critical mass that enabled group action, new black students on campuses arrived with no illusion that to study white men was to study the world. They had already participated in and witnessed a political movement in which the powerless outsiders proved they could change the dominant culture. On campuses, many began to undertake a similar enterprise in the educational arena.

African American students assumed—and for the most part were correct—that higher education, like the larger society, had been constructed without them in mind. The lives and contributions of black people were left out of the curriculum, race was a largely unexamined category, and the faculty and administrators did not reflect anything approaching the racial diversity of the country. Black students in the 1960s demanded that the situation change. The arrival of critical masses of black students also corresponded to the emergence of black power, which fueled many young people with a determination to study their own history, redefine how black people were presented, and demand justice from the educational system. The dynamics were dramatically different from what they had been for the returning veterans. Although many black students, like veterans before them, received new sources of financial support, African Americans had entered the academy on their own initiative and only after deep resistance to providing them with equal educational opportunities. To the annoyance of some white educators, these students came not in gratitude but in a mood of proud militancy.

Intertwined with the new demands from black students to be recognized and listened to was the political awakening of a generation of students who eventually redefined their role as learners and that of education as they protested the war in Vietnam. Like the Civil Rights movement before it, the antiwar movement was among other things deeply democratic in its thrust if not always in its practice. "Question Authority," read a common bumper sticker of the period. While some saw the slogan as subversive, others saw it as suggesting an ameliorative relationship between the governed and the governing. Instead of trusting the authorities quietly and without hesitation, generation after generation of students grew increasingly wary of what the authorities presented as facts. Generating knowledge themselves, students began to participate in teach-ins, start alternative student papers, and become chief inquisitors themselves of historical claims, foreign policy decisions, and reports from the battlefield.

They learned about military ties to research funding in universities, which had long existed but had been hidden or glossed over. They demanded a curriculum that would more clearly be relevant to their lives and to explaining the social, political, and economic chain of events that led to U.S. involvement in and then perpetuation of the war in Vietnam. This was no abstract issue, but one that immediately affected their lives and the lives of soldiers and civilians ten thousand miles away. Like many of the black students, the antiwar students were often militant, insisting that they be heard and demanding new political power within the institution.

With roots in both the Civil Rights movement and the peace movement, the women's movement emerged at the end of the 1960s. It has influenced the content and context of knowledge in higher education ever since. In some ways, it has had more impact and been sustained longer than either of the other two movements because the numbers of women of all colors who were students, faculty, staff, and administrators were always far greater than those of black students and because their cause—achieving equity for women—could not be assuaged with the signing of a single peace treaty.

During the 1970s, as many schools were opening their doors for the first time to increasing numbers of black students, formerly all-male schools were opening their doors to women. Today, there are only a handful of single-sex male schools. In the 1950s, the percentage of women college students had declined to its lowest since the 1920s. During the 1960s, their numbers began to increase. By 1975, 50 percent of those enrolled in college were female. By 1981, for the first time in U.S. history, women earned the majority of undergraduate and master's degrees. Today, women make up 55 percent of the undergraduate population—and of that group, 45 percent are over twenty-four years of age (Knopp, 1995, p.1). More than one-third of the faculty is now female, although women of color are only 4 percent of the total faculty. While they are unevenly divided among the various departments and their numbers increase at community colleges and decrease at more elite schools, women have emerged as an important economic and political constituency in higher education.

Imitating the model of the black students who initiated black studies courses and programs, women insisted that the curriculum study gender as an important category of analysis and that women's stories be examined as part of human history and culture. The first women's studies courses were offered in the late 1960s, and the first documented women's studies program was formally approved in 1970 at San Diego State University. In 1973, there were 78 women's studies programs; by 1977 the number had grown to 276, and by 1990 there were more than 620 women's studies programs (McTighe Musil, 1990, p. ii). Graduate programs in women's studies continue to double in number almost every two years. By 1990, more than 102 institutions offered graduate-level courses in women's studies (McTighe Musil, 1990, p. iii). The emergence of research centers on women paralleled the growth of women's studies programs. The National Council for Research on Women includes seventy-seven research centers, both campus-based and community-based, among its members.

In the past decade, as women of all colors became the new majority of students, students of color in our colleges and universities continued to expand their numbers even though they still are disproportionately low for their population and even though they still lag behind the number of white students. According to the American Council on Education's Office of Minorities in Higher Education, "Analysis of the most recent four-year trends indicates increases of 23 to 40 percent for minority groups" (Carter and Wilson, 1994, p. 2). The total enrollment by Asian students nearly doubled over the past ten years, while the Hispanic students registered the largest enrollment growth among the four ethnic minority groups from 1991 to 1992 (Carter and Wilson, 1994, p. 3). For both Hispanics and African Americans, the increases are spurred largely because of the gains by women in those racial and ethnic groups. In a number of campuses, the demographic changes are so dramatic that there is, for example, no longer a majority of any single racial group at the University of California, Berkeley.

Such emerging visible demographic changes at the college level are magnified in elementary schools. According to one study, "In Los Angeles, over 80 languages are spoken in the school system" (Schensul and Carroll, 1990, p. 341). More than five states now have populations in which more than a quarter of their residents are people of color. According to the Census Bureau, nearly one in three Americans will be designated as "minority" by the year 2000 (Schensul and Carroll, 1990, p. 341). The 1990 census showed a 44 percent increase among Hispanics since 1980, a 65 percent increase among Asians, and a 16 percent increase in the black population (Schensul and Carroll, 1990, p. 341). The 1965 Immigration Act (Hart-Cellar Act) opened the doors to populations from Asia and Latin America previously limited in entry to the U.S. Their presence is changing the color and the culture of the United States and its educational systems. And the diversity in the United States is not only racial but religious. Today, for instance, there are more Muslims than Episcopalians in America.

During the 1960s and 1970s, higher education also witnessed the establishment of statewide community college systems in most states in the Union. Today, 40 percent of students in higher education are taking courses at community colleges. A disproportionate number of students studying at community colleges are white women and women and men of color. Community college students also tend to be older than the students in four-year schools, although the average age of students at four-year institutions has also increased with the establishment of continuing education for women programs, special arrangements with senior citizens, and the addition of night school and weekend classes. In 1993, 42 percent of all college students were over the age of twenty-four, and of those, almost three in five, or 58 percent, were women (Knopp, 1995, p. 2). Nevertheless, many institutions have not yet recognized the change and adapted their curricula to accommodate it.

In the last half of the twentieth century, then, we have witnessed the dynamic interplay between expanded student, faculty, and staff constituencies and the impact these changes have had on the content of courses as well as on the structures and policies of academic institutions. To truly educate the majority is now a far more complex task for colleges and universities than it was at the turn of the century. Moreover, those demographic changes in sex, race, class, and age, and increasingly in religion, will only lead to more diversity in the twenty-first century. What began in pre–World War II years as a relatively narrow, homogeneous student and faculty constituency with a concomitant knowledge base that suppressed existing differences and focused on a slender slice of humanity has now blossomed into a rich and textured student population, generating an explosion in new scholarship. Higher education has a historic opportunity for leadership. As Schneider put it succinctly, "Our nation's campuses have become a highly visible stage in which the most fundamental questions about difference, equality, and community are being enacted. . . . To this effort . . . the academy brings indispensable resources: its commitment to the advancement of knowledge and its traditions of dialogue and deliberation across difference as keys to the increase of insight and understanding" (Association of American Colleges and Universities, 1995b, p. xvi).

New Constituencies and Intellectual Power

The presence of expanded student constituencies has dramatically altered the knowledge base of what we study in higher education. In some cases, as with black students and women, there were demands for entirely new courses as well as insistence that old assumptions governing traditional courses be revised in light of the new scholarship on diversity. A parallel push for an expanded intellectual base was pressed and continues to be pressed by other groups like Latino and Latina students, Native American students, Jewish students, gay and lesbian students, and non-Western students. The more diverse faculty also has led over the last two decades to intellectual and curricular initiatives that capture the dynamic ferment of the new scholarship on diversity. Presses, journals, and new publications attest to its richness, a richness that has engaged the intellectual imagination of students, faculty, and administrators, whatever their group identity.

The impact of the new scholarship is so powerful that it no longer necessarily requires a markedly diverse student body before a college commits itself to incorporating diversity into its courses and policies. In a survey by the Association of American Colleges and Universities in 1992, over 63 percent of institutions surveyed had already included teaching students about diversity as a component of their mission statement. This was true whether the student body itself was particularly diverse or not. At a small Midwestern liberal arts college, where they were actively recruiting to bring students of color *up* to 2 percent of their population, they already had in place an African studies program and a general education program structured to compare three groups: a non-Western group, Norwegian Americans, and African Americans.

In a survey of 196 higher education institutions of varying types, Light and Cureton (1992) reported that weaving diversity into the intellectual and structural life of institutions was the emerging norm, not the exception. Fifty-four percent nationwide have already introduced multiculturalism into their departmental course offerings and one-third have established a multicultural general education requirement (pp. 25, 26). Such figures suggest that there is more activity at the departmental level than at the general education level, which is not surprising given that general education reform requires a more comprehensive consensus among a wider group of faculty and departments. However, the departmental activity is unevenly distributed. Some departments and divisions have significantly rethought their structures and content, while others have remained largely impervious to the new scholarship. Despite departmental variation, the survey also revealed that a majority of the institutions are actively seeking to increase their institutional expertise on diversity either through recruiting new faculty or investing in faculty development—or more typically, a combination of the two. One-third offer coursework in ethnic and women's studies, and that figure is matched by multicultural centers and institutes that provide support for multicultural students and offer an institutional locus for faculty research.

Light and Cureton's survey also revealed that four-year colleges have invested in integrating the new scholarship on diversity into the curriculum more than two-year schools, although the latter have on average a more diverse student body. That suggests that the composition of the student body alone should not restrict or replace commitment to diversifying the curriculum. Among four-year institutions, research universities lead the rest in their overall diversity efforts, and comprehensive institutions outpace liberal arts colleges on the whole. Public institutions are more responsive than private colleges in their overall efforts as well.

While there is multicultural programming in every region of the country, support varies geographically. The leading regions are the Mid-Atlantic states and the West, with strength in the Midwest as well. By contrast, the South and the Northwest are developing more slowly. In most cases, New England was nip and tuck with the South. For example, in general education requirements, 59 percent of the Mid-Atlantic region, 45 percent of the West, and 40 percent of the North Central had general education diversity requirements. But New England had only 23 percent and the South only 20 percent. Even more significant gaps surfaced in other areas. When one compared multicultural changes in the disciplines, for instance, the Mid-Atlantic figure was 77 percent, New England was 48 percent, and the South 39 percent (Light and Cureton, 1992, p. 28).

Myths About Traditional Base of Knowledge

Because of the development of significant bodies of new scholarship, the changing demographics of student populations, and the consciousness of the global village that characterizes contemporary life, several myths about the traditional base of knowledge so typical at U.S. colleges and universities in 1960 and earlier have been punctured. While some people are disturbed by the intellectual changes and call for a return to the earlier curriculum, the vast majority of people in higher education see the expansion of the knowledge base as a healthy, if daunting, new development.

It does mean, however, that certain truths that many thought were self-evident have little credence in today's intellectual arena. The earlier, largely monocultural knowledge base had been presented as complete, eternal, and universal. Its excellence was largely unquestioned, and its origin presumed devoid of contamination by any political viewpoint. The new scholarship on diversity, coupled with other intellectual movements in the last quarter century, has made it all but impossible to hold such views and still have intellectual integrity.

Completeness: While much of the previous knowledge has been sustained over time, it is now seen for the most part as a partial description of the world and its dynamics, hardly the whole. Until the most recent decades, for example, the development of the United States as a nation was taught as if the only Americans were men. With the advent of feminist scholarship, we began to look at the impact of the family on national life, of female labor production, of the social impact of women's voluntary work, of women's active leadership in major grassroots political movements like the Civil Rights movement or the labor movement, of the maintenance of religious communities through the services of women, or the involvement of women in times of war. As Collins explains it, "Each group speaks from its own standpoint and shares its own partial, situated knowledge. But because each group perceives its own truth as partial, its knowledge is unfinished. . . . Dialogue is essential to the epistemological approach," she argues, adding, "Everyone has a voice, but everyone must listen and respond to other voices" (1990, pp. 236–237).

Eternal Truth: Many of us who went through undergraduate years in the 1950s and 1960s naively believed that much of what we learned was not subject to change but represented eternal truths. In light of the new scholarship fueled by multiple voices, eternal truths seem far more contingent and conditional today, open to reevaluation and revision. Some truths can be revised, that is, modified in the face of new information. That Columbus discovered America, for instance, has been seen from multiple perspectives in the recent five-hundred-year celebration of the events of 1492 with connections between three cultures: Western European, Native American, and Asian. But some truths must be discarded; they can not be reconciled or modified in light of new information. People in the Renaissance eventually had to give up the once-eternal truth that the earth was the center of the universe around which everything else revolved. Similarly, the Age of Exploration made it impossible to reconcile the notion that the earth was flat with the notion that the earth was round.

Universality: For many years, knowledge based on the experience of a very small group of people was assumed to be universally applicable to a heterogeneous population. For instance, Kohlberg's theory of moral development was applied to girls and women as well as boys and men even though every subject that generated the original theory was male. When Gilligan (1982) began to study young women, however, it quickly became apparent that Kohlberg's theory no longer adequately explained the moral developmental patterns for all of human experience.

Unquestioned excellence: What was perceived to be complete, eternal, and universal was quite logically regarded as unquestionably excellent. The new scholarship that represents multiple voices and views about a wide range of subjects now questions the excellence of theories, assumptions, and explanations that are based on insufficient investigations. How excellent can medical advice be on heart disease when the subjects studied were exclusively male and the research design did not take into consideration the effect of hormonal differences in women? How excellent can a rendering of U.S. history be that excludes the histories, for example, of Asian Americans, Jewish immigrants, or working-class Americans?

Uncontaminated by politics: Perhaps the hardest myth to surrender about the earlier knowledge base is that it was entirely or largely apolitical. As *Classroom in Conflict: Teaching Controversial Subjects in a Diverse Society* states, "It seems more honest to examine our cultural starting point instead of pretending we do not have one" (Williams, 1994, p. 74). The argument is frequently made that only the current scholarship seeking to include formerly suppressed or excluded knowledge is political. The opposite of the politics of inclusion, however, is the politics of exclusion. What ones teaches or reads or writes is a matter of choice, choice based on what one believes is the best information. But all those choices represent a political view, are grounded in a particular set of values, and project on the world a specific way of seeing things.

The politics of exclusion was so widespread that it seemed normative. Anything that presumed to alter it, then, seemed at first glance political. But the decision to deny examination of the history, culture, and experiences of the majority of humankind surely betrays a political point of view, just as the decision to examine a more inclusive world embraces a point of view, both of them political in nature. The politics of exclusion, however, is often covert and unverbalized; the politics of inclusion is more frequently openly embraced and articulated.

Reframing the Issue of Diversity

In the United States, educators have adopted at least five major approaches toward diversity over the centuries: suppress it, segregate it, oppose it, celebrate it, and engage with it critically. There are gains and losses with each approach, and each affects different groups in different ways. Some choices are deeply bound by historical conditions. Today, we probably have all five espoused by some group and frequently simultaneously within one institution.

Suppress it: This has been the approach of choice for the greater part of higher education's history. Its most compelling advantage is the enforced sense of a shared curriculum in which the subject matter is largely studied without dispute, without conflict. There is a predetermined body of common knowledge, even if it is knowledge skewed to reflect only a very small part of human history and culture. In the suppression mode, there is a kind of feigned homogeneity that is calming to some, especially to those whose voices, experiences, and culture actually appear in the curriculum.

But even those typically excluded sometimes learned how to acquiesce to a narrower curriculum. Some never noticed the missing voices, even their own. Others learned the art of transposing their own experience onto the experience of a given curriculum. Girls, for instance, simply imagined they were Huck floating down the Mississippi with Jim or lighting out for the new territory at the novel's end. Still others resisted the negative messages that distorted what they knew to be true about themselves or their culture. To overcome potentially damaging distortions, some organized a covert or parallel curriculum of their own, typically supported by their own communities. Black communities, for example, preserved black history and offered alternative sources of knowledge to that being promulgated by the dominant culture, a culture that typically made African Americans either invisible, trivialized, or demonic.

But there are significant disadvantages to this approach to diversity, both for those whose culture is represented in a given narrow curriculum and for those whose culture has been erased or distorted. Members of the hegemonic group are deprived of access to vital information, to more avenues to truth, if you will, by eliminating alternative sources of knowledge. They are enveloped in partial knowledge they falsely believe to be whole and therefore they are ill equipped to make decisions that will take everyone's welfare into account. Members of the excluded group face the crushing impact of being subjected to a curriculum that denies their existence, suggests they never contributed to civilization, and implies that since they never shaped the past, they will never shape the future. Adrienne Rich put it this way: "When those who have the power to name and to socially construct reality choose not to see you or hear you, whether you are dark-skinned, old, disabled, female, or speak with a different accent . . . when someone with the authority of a teacher, say, describes the world and you are not in it, there is a moment of psychic disequilibrium, as if you looked into a mirror and saw nothing" (Maher and Tetreault, 1994, p. 1).

Suppressing difference, then, can only be done ultimately through some kind of violence. Typically we recognize violence when it is physical and clearly stated as it was under the Nazis during World War II toward Jews, homosexuals, Gypsies, the disabled, and the dissident. The intellectual violence of suppressing difference in education is less apparent but still has its own lethal aspects. Ultimately, it is not possible to sustain an approach of suppressing diversity in the curriculum without resorting to the physical imposition of domination. As hooks argues in *Talking Back, Thinking Feminist, Thinking Black,* "Our capacity as women and men to be either dominated or dominating is a point of connection, of commonality" (1989, p. 20). She goes on to assert, "It is necessary to remember that it is first the potential oppressor within that we must resist—the potential victim within that we must rescue—otherwise we cannot hope for an end to domination" (p. 21). Because human variation is too great and diversity is the norm and not the exception, it is impossible to carry on as if everyone were the same, unless you do so through some kind of violent suppression dependent upon domination.

Segregate it: Another alternative that has a long history in the United States is the approach that recognizes that there are differences and seeks to accommodate those differences by segregating them. For most of higher education's history, the segregation has been imposed by the dominant culture, whether that meant men, Protestants, upper classes, whites, whatever. More recently, however, some segregation is now deliberately self-chosen by groups who had formerly had segregation imposed upon them. There are profound differences in the purposes and consequences of the two. One of the most egregious fallacies in today's parlance is the mistaken assumption that the two kinds of segregation—imposed by a dominant group and self-chosen by a marginalized group—are versions of the same phenomenon. For instance, a recent newspaper headline on black residential patterns at Duke University read, "Duke More Segregated Than Ever." A colleague, who remembered that Duke's long history of racial segregation did not end until the first black students were admitted in 1963, smiled wryly when he saw the headline. He said with an edge of relief in his voice, "Thank goodness that there are finally enough black students at Duke that they could even consider the possibility of separate housing!"

Although women's colleges began as a result of imposed sex segregation when few colleges would accept women as students, the vast majority have voluntarily continued segregated because they believe women excel academically in a single-sex educational environment. Similarly, the Catholic Church set up its own network of higher education institutions in the United States in order to avoid religious discrimination but also to offer an educational experience that reflected its specific set of values. The United States has long taken pride in the expansive diversity of its baccalaureate institutions, which we see as evidence of excellence and vitality. The special challenge comes as campuses welcome and nurture diversity, whether that diversity occurs at what might at first glance look like a homogeneous group—a women's college, a Catholic institution, or tribal college—or at a public university—Berkeley, City College, Michigan—where the range of diversity is more readily apparent.

Within a given single institution, however, there is also considerable segregated education that takes a subtler form and is cause for less jubilation. Many schools, for instance, are happy to have women's studies programs as long as men don't have to teach or take the courses or think about the implications for knowledge and society as a whole. The same can be said for many similar programs—Latino and Latina studies, Jewish studies, urban studies, gay and lesbian studies. Student populations in such courses often repeat the patterns of segregation at the institution as a whole. Few whites appear in a black studies course, few Asians in a Chicano studies course, and few men in a women's studies course. To overcome such patterns, many professors and administrators have sought to integrate the new knowledge from these courses into general education and courses in the major so that students of all kinds can be introduced to and debate the merits of the new scholarship from historically segregated and understudied groups.

The unmistakable disadvantage of segregating diversity is the diminishment of the overall body of knowledge and the ease with which unexamined ideas, assumptions, and assertions can remain unchallenged. It impoverishes everyone when it could enrich all. When the segregation is involuntary or imposed from without, it also is a means of perpetuating imbalances in the power structure within society, thus keeping the outsiders marginal, weak, dismissed, and largely ineffectual.

Oppose it: I am making a distinction in this discussion between critically engaged opposition and unexamined opposition. Opposing the presence of diverse perspectives and voices undermines the fundamental purpose of education. Such a position is often appealing because it so easily and comfortably reifies one's own standards and values and ultimately one's own position. Absolutism can indeed make a complex reality seem simple. It can eliminate all apparent confusion. But it is not a defensible educational option, nor a defensible intellectual one either. Its greatest disadvantage is that it leads to a dangerous kind of thinking that prematurely eliminates opposing views, narrows the field of what one can consider, and sustains the paradigm of domination as the mode of choice.

Some who oppose diversity in the disciplines and the curriculum as a whole do so on the grounds of protecting excellence. That was certainly a key argument in the influential *Closing of the American Mind* (Bloom, 1987), which argued that by opening up the university to diversity, we had closed it to excellence. In the new framework, however, it becomes difficult to claim excellence if it excludes such a significant set of histories, questions, sources of knowledge, and perspectives that diversity generates. In a genuine intellectual community, oppositional viewpoints are an integral part of the landscape. To oppose the presence of various perspectives that inevitably derive from diversity, then, seems clearly to invert the purpose of higher education. As Taylor argues, "Nonrecognition or misrecognition can inflict harm, can be a form of oppression, imprisoning someone in a false, distorted, and reduced mode of being. . . . Due recognition is not just a courtesy we owe people. It is a vital human need" (Gutmann, 1994, pp. 25–26).

Celebrate it: This has become the most common language used by advocates of diversity in higher education. It is found in most mission statements, is frequently a rallying theme for collegiate events, and marks a positive acceptance of the gains to be made if diversity is a central educational goal. It has also proven a means of building a consensus on campus. It assumes that diversity contributes to the intellectual and social life of a given campus and is an existing part of our common lives in our nation and around the globe.

Its major weakness as an approach is that it is not fully sustainable. That is, it suggests that diversity is an easy, smooth achievement, something that everyone can feel good about. What it ignores are the painful, difficult, conflictual realities embedded in the very bones of diversity. Some diversity does not raise fundamental social, economic, or value questions. I am United Church of Christ; you are Episcopalian. I am a mother; you are single. I want to be an astronaut; you want to teach elementary school. I like skydiving; you prefer scuba diving. But some kinds of diversity derive their historic differences from profound experiences of inequality and injustices. And in most cases, those historic discriminations are perpetuated in varying degrees in continued structural inequalities. The consequence is that diversity cannot be merely celebrated; it must be grappled with in uncomfortable ways that certainly don't always feel like a celebration.

There are very different expectations of diversity depending on who you are and what your particular history has been—as the University of California, Berkeley, discovered when they did a major research project on diversity on their campus (Duster, 1992). While the vast majority of students came to Berkeley in part because they were seeking an institution that was diverse, most were dissatisfied with their experience once they got there. They might have celebrated diversity as freshman, but as seniors they were a bit unhinged by it. White students couldn't understand why hanging out with nonwhite students wasn't enough and why students of color would sometimes get angry with them and retreat to their own self-chosen racial groups. Students of color couldn't understand why more white students wouldn't help them in their attempts to achieve more systemic changes at Berkeley that would, they believed, create a more level playing field and address unresolved inequities on campus.

A white professor who had fought to end segregation at a major research institution in the South is angry and puzzled by the fact that many of the African American students there were not more grateful and insisted on changing the institution once they were admitted. A male student who has on his own initiative sought to take a women's studies course is unsettled by the fierceness of the anger at men that surfaces when the class reads a novel that includes the rape of a preteen girl. A Christian student in a class on anti-Semitism in the early Christian Church is stunned to discover how difficult it was for her Jewish friend in the class to purchase the book with the cross on its cover. A devout Catholic who has been brought up to believe that practicing homosexuality is a sin discovers that her roommate has a lesbian partner.

Celebrating diversity can be a beginning. It might ultimately even be an end. But it is not a sustainable option on its own.

Engage critically with it: This is by far the most responsible educational approach and the most viable societal approach if the end product we are seeking is greater understanding and the ability to create and sustain inclusive communities. Making a commitment to celebrate diversity, that is to value it, can be an entry point to engaging more fully with diversity. But to engage more fully with diversity is to take seriously acquiring the knowledge of other people's histories and lives. It also requires that a learner is willing to be vulnerable, to subject personal views to others' scrutiny, and to accept the fact that conflict and debate are integral to the process of gaining reciprocal understanding. It is not something undertaken as diversionary entertainment or with any illusion that it will always be done with ease. But then, education is at its core an investigative process that necessitates a certain amount of risk. Diversity when fully engaged can affirm the most fundamental commitments of higher education's purposes.

To engage with diversity is to uncover rather than suppress differences. Paradoxically, it is through uncovering those differences that a new sense of what is held in common emerges. Instead of feigned homogeneity achieved by erasing differences, a far more complex and fluid understanding of areas of commonality is illuminated once differences are fully explored. The mysterious *other* becomes unsettlingly yet comfortingly familiar. The rigidly categorized *them* disarmingly becomes blurred with *us*. *Their* history becomes irrefutably *our* history.

In the midst of emphasizing the centrality of engagement, it is important to underscore that some of the most profound insights were birthed in the confines of segregated intellectual communities where issues could be explored singly and with a common passion to understand. But these new ideas from women's studies or African American studies or gay and lesbian studies have not remained encased in a world where they never remain interrogated. Instead, they are deeply tied to major intellectual questions and paradigms in a larger arena. Their marginalized location means they are inevitably related to oppositional views, views they have questioned profoundly and views with which they are in constant intellectual conversation. The best of these insights have also moved into a more diverse arena—through integrating the new scholarship into regular courses, through team-taught courses, through interdisciplinary study—where they vigorously test the credibility of their insights, refining their arguments and altering their assumptions in the process.

One of the most significant intellectual discoveries emerging from two decades or more of producing scholarship by and about various understudied groups and issues is the complicated multiplicity in each individual, each group, each historical period, each nation. The notion of the multicultural self, which Lee Knefelkamp speaks about so eloquently, or that of hybridity that Cornel West writes about, explodes simplistic notions that there is a single woman's experience, a monolithic Latino or Latina voice, a predictable Catholic viewpoint. Each of us typically inherits a web of interrelated cultural, racial, and religious traditions and most of us freely adopt a similarly wide circle of attachments. In some cases, those multiple commitments conflict: a devout Baptist is shunned by her church because she is a lesbian but her lesbian support group mocks religion as patriarchal; a working-class professor who is economically in the affluent middle class feels at times an imposter on campus but finds he is sometimes viewed as suspect in his ethnic urban neighborhood; an African American feminist is disturbed by the unexamined racism of her women's study group but is castigated by her African American brothers for being part of the women's movement. For the most part, however, such multiple, layered, and intersecting identities open up new avenues of knowledge, new pathways for connection, and new capacities to negotiate between differences.

At such moments, we can achieve in higher education what Anzaldúa calls *borderlands.* "Borderlands," she explains, "are physically present whenever two or more cultures edge each other, where people of different races occupy the same territory, where under, lower, middle and upper classes touch, where the space between two individuals shrinks with intimacy" (Anzaldúa, 1987, preface). The task for higher education is to transform such borderland experiences into an opportunity for intellectual enhancement and personal exploration. We can not do that by suppressing differences, nor by opposing them, segregating them, or simply celebrating them. But we can do it by fully engaging in what the experience teaches us and how we can be part of teaching others in an environment of mutual exchange and enlightened self-awareness that emerges from our contact with others.

The heart of how to transform such a borderland moment is fundamentally a deeply democratic one. Little learning will occur if we take an authoritarian, absolutist stance that brooks no dissent or emphatically silences people. Rather, democratic values such as voice, open expression of views, compromise, respectfulness, and latitude that seeks flexible habits of mind and generous compassion of the heart become the vehicle for building an authentic and vibrant intellectual community on our campuses. Dissent and disagreement are normative in such communities because dialogue, tolerance, and reciprocity are normative. As *The Drama of Diversity and Democracy: Higher Education and American Commitments* argues, "In this vision of relational pluralism, each person must be prepared to venture out of the comfort zone of one community into . . . the 'contact zone . . . the space in which peoples geographically and historically separated come into contact with each other and establish ongoing relations.'. . . Dialogue become absolutely critical to this generative, relational democracy, and the civic culture becomes not simply a political process, or a marketplace of competing interest, but rather one that seeks deliberatively to reflect and address the aspirations, needs, and realities of all of its citizens" (Association of American Colleges and Universities, 1995b, pp. 32–33).

Implications of Diversity for Curricular Design and Teaching

To decide to create new intellectual learning communities on our campuses where diversity is central rather than peripheral indeed challenges us to rethink the overall purposes and current structures in higher education. If diversity were a central educational goal, what would the general education design look like? How might we restructure our major? What would we alter about how we teach our classes? In a major initiative of the Association of American Colleges and Universities called "American Commitments: Diversity, Democracy, and Liberal Learning," we developed a set of questions as a suggestive guide for higher education as it struggles to address U.S. pluralism. What is specific to U.S. pluralism could certainly also be modified to raise questions about how to address global pluralism as well. We asked the following (Association of American Colleges and Universities, 1995a, p. 7):

- What must we know and understand about the multiplicity of groups and people who have been unequally included and acknowledged in our nation?
- How are we to understand the contradictory interconnections between democratic aspiration and the persistence of unequal participation in U.S. society? How do we address them?
- Recognizing that multiplicity is a given in our societal situation, how do we foster the development of each person's sense of self, voice, particularity, and moral vision?
- What relational principles can we envision in this phase of our evolution as a democracy to guide us in forging new civic covenants and more just relations among both individuals and groups?
- What capacities must we develop to negotiate disparate and multiple commitments and communities, inherited and adopted? To encounter diversity as a resource rather than a threat?
- What are the crucial distinctions between recognizing or acknowledging difference and learning to take grounded stands in the face of difference? If both are goals for liberal learning, how can we develop both kinds of capabilities over time?

While there is an impressive array of experimentation under way in higher education to find some answers to these tough questions, we have really just begun to explore the full implications for our scholarship, teaching, and curriculum. They require that we pause to look with renewed intentionality to the purposes of our general education program, our majors, and our pedagogy.

General education: How do our general education courses introduce students to diversity? Is there a developmental model so students can revisit earlier questions later in their academic careers? Do our general education courses have a place for students to explore their own personal identities as well as their inherited and adopted communities? Do they have a place where students can compare several groups, finding commonalities as well as differences? Is there a place in the program where students can connect personal experience with course content and think about how experience can be used to build theory? Are there enough voices to suggest the multivocal and multiperspectival as an epistemology?

Academic majors: How do our academic majors assist students in their inquiries about personal identity, communities of commitment, and societal obligations? How do the majors complement and build on the exploratory work in general education? How do we introduce our students to the fundamental questions about content and methodology that arise when one begins to include the new scholarship on diversity within our disciplines? Where in the major can students connect the work of the major to the work of contributing to the larger good in society and the world as a whole?

Teaching: How can a professor help students to become more effective boundary crossers and borderland dwellers? What can an instructor do to ensure that the classroom becomes a learning community that listens to and encourages speech from everyone? That is engaged in reciprocal understandings and reciprocal conversations of respect? To provide an environment that is an affirming one for students but also one where students feel free to question, disagree, and discuss competing or discomforting viewpoints? How does one develop a learning community where students tolerate each other's ignorance and misinformation so such ideas can be aired, examined, and discarded? How does one develop a sense that we all need each other's knowledge and perspective if we are to move beyond partial knowledge? How can classrooms become spaces that allow us to analyze things that matter deeply to us?

To create inclusive intellectual communities on campus cannot be a sidebar on the list of reforms in higher education. It must be a central educational commitment. To do that will require higher education to turn its sights and redefine its responsibilities. The reward systems will need to be rethought in light of an altered sense of societal responsibility and student engagement. Promotion and tenure will need to be opened up to reflect the new institutional goals. There needs to be serious new investment in faculty development to assist faculty as they rethink what and how they teach in light of the new scholarship on diversity. While it will be difficult to suppress differences anymore, it is still relatively easy to polarize people on the basis of perceived differences. That inclination will need to be resisted and defused as much as possible. Dialogue and not demagoguery is what we need to reach for, a language of relationship not of opposition.

Whatever the metaphor we finally select to describe diversity in higher education—and it will likely be a collection of metaphors—whether quilts, salads, or mosaics, our task is how to bind ourselves to one another in a project larger than ourselves, without in the process obscuring who we are in our distinctiveness and our particularities. That can be done not through haranguing one another but through talking candidly and compassionately with one another; not by simply talking but by listening as well; not by erasing who we are but by learning how to recognize one another in our fullness, our pain, and our deepest longings. At this moment, when higher education is as diverse in its student body as it has ever been in its history and when the scholarship of diversity has amassed such a tantalizing array of information, higher education is poised to assume a leadership sorely needed in our own country and the world at large. We need only the will and the courage, the civility and the compassion to do it.

References

Anzaldúa, G. *Borderlands/La Frontera: The New Mestiza.* San Francisco: Spinsters/Aunt Lute, 1987.

Association of American Colleges and Universities. *American Pluralism and the College Curriculum: Higher Education in a Diverse Democracy.* Washington, D.C.: Association of American Colleges and Universities, 1995a.

Association of American Colleges and Universities. *The Drama of Diversity and Democracy: Higher Education and American Commitments.* Washington, D.C.: Association of American Colleges and Universities, 1995b.

Bloom, A. *The Closing of the American Mind: How Higher Education Has Failed Democracy and Impoverished the Souls of Today's Students.* New York: Simon & Schuster, 1987.

Carter, D. J., and Wilson, R. *Twelfth Annual Status Report on Minorities in Higher Education.* Washington, D.C.: American Council on Education, 1994.

Collins, P. H. *Black Feminist Thought: Knowledge, Consciousness, and the Politics of Empowerment.* New York: Routledge & Kegan Paul, 1990.

Duster, T. *Diversity at the University of California, Berkeley.* Berkeley: University of California Press, 1992.

Gilligan, C. *In a Different Voice: Psychological Theory and Women's Development.* Cambridge, Mass.: Harvard University Press, 1982.

Gutmann, A. (ed.). *Multiculturalism: Examining the Politics of Recognition.* Princeton, N.J.: Princeton University Press, 1994.

hooks, b. *Talking Back, Thinking Feminist, Thinking Black.* Boston, Mass: South End Press, 1989.

Knopp, L. *Women in Higher Education Today: A Mid-1990s Profile.* Research Briefs, Vol. 6, no. 5. Washington, D.C.: American Council on Education, 1995.

Light, R., and Cureton, J. "The Quiet Revolution: Eleven Facts About Multiculturalism and the Curriculum." *Change,* 1992, 24(1), 24–29.

Maher, F., and Tetreault, M. *The Feminist Classroom.* New York: Basic Books, 1994.

McTighe Musil, C. (ed.). *NWSA Directory of Women's Studies Programs, Women's Centers, and Women's Research Centers.* College Park, Md.: National Women's Studies Association, 1990.

Schensul, J. J., and Carroll, T. G. "Introduction: Visions of America in the 1990s and Beyond: Negotiating Cultural Diversity and Educational Change." *Education and Urban Society,* 1990, *22*(4), 339–345.

Schlesinger, A. M. *The Disuniting of America: Reflections on a Multicultural Society.* New York: Norton, 1992.

Takaki, R. *A Different Mirror: A History of Multicultural America.* Boston: Little, Brown, 1993.

Williams, J. A. *Classroom in Conflict: Teaching Controversial Subjects in a Diverse Society.* Albany: State University of New York Press, 1994.

CHAPTER TEN

STRENGTHENING PREPAREDNESS OF AT-RISK STUDENTS

Dennis McGrath, Barbara K. Townsend

There has long been a deep-seated confusion among institutions of higher education about how to respond to at-risk students, especially those who enter college without the requisite academic or cultural and social skills necessary for success. This confusion is expressed in the varied terminology used to describe and identify at-risk students, the conflicting schools of thought concerning institutional obligations to these students, the uncertain institutional position of remediation and developmental education in higher education, and the lack of adequate information on program effects.

In the 1960s and 1970s, at-risk students were primarily conceived of as those with academic skill deficiencies requiring remediation. During the past three decades, though, student bodies have diversified, with colleges and universities enrolling many low-income and minority students, returning adults, and others long underrepresented in educational institutions. These demographic and institutional changes have led to a broadening of the notion of at-risk students to include a variety of populations. The term has now expanded to cover learning disabled students, the visually and hearing impaired, those enrolled in English as a Second Language programs, as well as returning, first-generation, and underrepresented students.

While many of these populations, especially nontraditional and underrepresented students, remain concentrated in community colleges, they are appearing in substantial numbers in many four-year institutions. In consequence, providing effective responses to the needs of at-risk students has become a critical issue throughout U.S. higher education. Programs for at-risk students that try to improve their academic performance and persistence are among the most important ways that institutions can promote educational equity and ensure the democratization of education.

However, there is still little consensus about the nature or needs of at-risk students. Institutional responses include a wide range of activities, programs, and practices, alternately termed remedial, developmental, or compensatory education, as well as approaches such as supplemental instruction, specialized tutoring, advising, counseling, and retention programs. The initial response to the growing numbers of at-risk students in the 1960s primarily took the form of special courses or programs, and many institutions continue to offer specially designed instruction or support services. At a number of schools, though, the distinction between the at-risk and general student body has been blurred, with programs and services such as freshman year experiences, supplemental instruction, and retention efforts directed at all students. This diversity in programmatic responses expresses a good deal of creative experimentation, but it also reflects a lack of agreement about how to define at-risk students, what kinds of programs are most effective, or even the extent to which institutions have responsibility for the academic success and persistence of their students.

In our overview of this complex topic, we place contemporary approaches in a historical perspective, examining the various ways in which at-risk students have been defined, the types of programs and services that have been provided, the quality of evaluation data, and current principles of good practice.

History of Institutional Responses

In an earlier handbook, Levine (1978) relied heavily on Cross's (1976) influential history in tracing the development of remedial and developmental programs. Cross explored collegiate response to underprepared students by examining the evolving relationship between educational theory and institutional practice. In her sketch, the modern response begins with how-to-study courses that were voluntary, noncredit activities provided by student services for students conceived as able to do college-level coursework, but immature and in need of discipline in organizing and planning their studies. These were followed, in the late 1930s and early 1940s, by remedial reading programs for students in need of work on their academic skills in the mechanics of reading. These responses reflected the primary concern with traditional, high-ability students who were able to do collegiate work, but were performing poorly academically.

These programs, in Cross's view, influenced the initial response to the increased enrollment of nontraditional students in the 1960s, in that baccalaureate institutions were primarily concerned with distinguishing underachievers who could be helped—that is, students with good ability but poor motivation and inadequate study habits—from students of so-called low ability who could not be expected to perform at the collegiate level. This way of conceiving the problem, Cross emphasizes, was clearly inadequate to the demands placed on higher education by the waves of new students entering higher education in the 1960s and 1970s. Many of these students, as measured by test scores and classroom performance, were academically unprepared for college-level work. The typical institutional response to this new challenge was the development of remedial courses, primarily in mathematics and English, with remediation understood as attempts to alleviate deficiencies so students could enter a program for which they were previously ineligible (Cross, 1976, p. 30). Early efforts also included programs supported by federal government funds, such as Upward Bound and Special Services to Disadvantaged Students.

The initial surveys of such approaches found them to be quite ineffective—poorly designed, uncoordinated, and with little or no commitment to evaluation (Roueche, 1968). Roueche, for instance, reported that as many as 90 percent of all remedial students in California community colleges failed or withdrew from remedial courses. Cross traces the next round of efforts in the 1970s as a reaction to the failure of the initial attempts by open-access institutions to serve underprepared students. These new efforts, she argued, entailed a conceptual shift from remediation to a new understanding of compensatory education, and a programmatic move from individual courses to "total push," comprehensive programs. These programs included the now-familiar features of specially trained tutors and learning laboratory staff, counseling, and new instructional approaches, such as mastery learning, which focused on the individual needs of students. This, in Cross's view, was the correct approach, reflecting what she termed the "developmental" aim of maximizing the talents and skills of each student, rather than the remedial goal of alleviating deficiencies.

Cross's history, while quite valuable, needs to be revised in light of later developments and new understandings of the institutional response to the influx of at-risk students. Perhaps most significantly, a revised historical interpretation must account for why the move toward compensatory education, which Cross and others so strongly advocated in the 1970s and expected to predominate, has not been institutionalized in higher education.

In the 1960s, the concept of compensatory education appeared likely to become the dominant paradigm for instructing students with academic deficiencies. It was introduced into educational discourse following World War II and emphasized the need to lessen or remove environmentally induced educational deficits (Clowes, 1982). The concept gained substantial legitimacy with the passage of the Elementary and Secondary Education Act of 1965, which authorized billions of dollars to encourage schools to focus on underprepared, "culturally deprived" low-income and minority children. Title I of the ESEA provided the major source of funding for school-level projects. Funds were targeted to poor students by distributing them through state education agencies to local school districts in proportion to the number of disadvantaged children that they enrolled. The act stimulated a wide range of projects, and, by the second year of operation, more than nine million children were taking part in Title I projects conceived as efforts at compensatory education (U.S. Department of Health, Education, and Welfare, 1967). If children of the poor were to perform at levels comparable to middle-class children, it was argued, schools would have to find ways to "make up for the debilitating consequences of discrimination and poverty," to compensate for the cultural deprivation of a home environment that did not support education (Chazen, 1973, p. 35).

However, as educators and activists focused on the environmental sources of educational failure, they soon came to recognize how profound the effects of poverty were on the lives of children, and how difficult it was to provide them with real equality of educational opportunity. Compensatory education efforts were soon affected by a substantial disagreement about how to best conceive the exact nature of poor children's academic deficiencies, as well as the preferred way of remedying their problems. Perhaps most striking was the dispute over exactly what compensatory efforts should attempt to compensate *for*—whether the focus should be on the learning situation, that is, curriculum and teaching methods, or in developing new institutions to link schools with families and neighborhoods (Little and Smith, 1971). One strand of thought emphasized the need to work with teachers to improve the curriculum and the instruction offered to poor children. The other strand identified more with the community development efforts of the Civil Rights movement and Great Society programs, arguing that schools for poor children could be improved only if parents were mobilized and strong community organizations were built in economically disadvantaged neighborhoods.

Although the high levels of federal funding virtually ensured the predominance of compensatory education (in at least one of its forms) as the preferred model of intervention in public schools, it was never fully accepted in higher education. A major reason is that compensatory programs appeared to threaten colleges' traditional sense of mission. By defining the education problem in terms of the social and cultural experience of students, advocates of compensatory education encouraged the redefinition of schools as social or community action agencies, rather than as educational institutions. Within higher education, the conception of remediation was much more attractive as it seemed to offer neutral scientific and technological categories in place of controversial cultural or political ones. As the language itself suggests, remediation works on a medical model: specific weaknesses are diagnosed, appropriate treatments prescribed, and the learner evaluated like a patient to determine the effects of treatment (Clowes, 1982, p. 4). By concentrating on specific academic deficiencies of individual students, rather than on large social inequalities, remediation nestled comfortably within the traditional educational mission of higher education. Further, its diagnostic-prescriptive approach provided intellectual continuity with the long-standing practices of reading instruction and study skills programs by emphasizing that at-risk students lacked discrete mechanical skills that could be improved through the application of an appropriate educational technology.

Although remediation was the preferred conception in higher education in the 1960s and early 1970s, guiding most initial programs for underprepared students, it was significantly contested by other views. One line of criticism focused on the democratic promise implied by the new practices of open access and admission policies that favored low-income and minority students. These critics identified closely with the Civil Rights movement and the more activist strains of compensatory education. They charged that remediation programs functioned as yet another form of tracking, keeping poor and minority students from access to the benefits of higher education (Karabel, 1972; Zwerling, 1976).

A second line of criticism, advanced by what has been termed the *educational effectiveness movement* (McGrath and Spear, 1991) argued that traditional college curricula and pedagogy could not be effective with the mass of underprepared new students. But whereas the more radical critics took that failure to be a matter of public policy, educational effectiveness critics took it as a technical challenge. Advocates of this approach believed that colleges could reconstruct their curricula, student services, and pedagogy to create inviting and supportive environments for nontraditional students. In the process, educational effectiveness critics softened the issue of the relation of higher education to class structure and racial inequality, ultimately advancing a conception of students detached from their social and economic backgrounds.

Cross, for instance, disputed the left's assumptions about what the so-called new student was really like. In *Beyond the Open Door* (1974), she described these students as new to higher education in that only in an age of open admissions would they be considered college material. However, she argued against the identification of nontraditional or underprepared students with racial minorities or the poor. She held that most actually are drawn from the white working class, even the middle class: "Two-thirds are first-generation college students . . . over one-half are white, about 25 percent are black" (1976, p. 6). Further, Cross contended that it is illegitimate for public policy to shift the meaning of educational equality from individual to group mobility. Cohen and Brawer also explicitly offered a liberal response to the social goals of the left critics, arguing that no form of schooling can "break down class distinctions . . . or move entire ethnic groups from one social stratum to another" (1989, p. 353). With these arguments, the educational effectiveness critics tried to release colleges from the ideological and political debates about racial and economic equality that raged in the 1960s and 1970s. Colleges, in their view, were to be ideologically neutral, concerned only with enhancing educational opportunity for broader segments of the population.

But when the educational effectiveness critics examined what colleges were actually doing with underprepared students, they found conventional and mostly ineffective programs. Students whose previous academic performance was marginal or failing were encountering either standard college coursework for which they were clearly not ready or watered-down versions of courses taught by faculty not committed to working with underprepared students (Roueche, 1968; Cross, 1974). Remediation helped those on the borderline of acceptable academic performance, but, as Cross remarked, "We have not found any magic key to equality of educational opportunity through remediation" (1976, p. 9). This was due in significant part, according to these critics, to the way remedial efforts operated on the fringes of higher education, in isolated special courses or in only partly legitimate vestibule programs, and had not penetrated into the instructional core of colleges.

This view was supported by the initial evaluations of remedial programs. Roueche, in the first national study, found only limited commitment to remediation. Reviewing programs in the late 1960s, he noted, "As many as 90 percent of all students assigned or advised into remedial programs never completed them" (Roueche, 1968, p. 48). Roueche and Cross both applauded the comprehensive programs that were developed in the 1970s as distinct improvements. The new programs embodied what both at the time took to be the principles of best practice in remediation. Such programs offered a broad range of educational services and teaching strategies, integrated skills training into the educational experience, had a volunteer teaching and counseling staff, granted degree credit, and were often housed with separate divisions of remedial education (Roueche and Kirk, 1973). For these critics, such comprehensive programs offered a glimpse of the coming "instructional revolution" needed for colleges to be educationally effective. In Cross's assessment, remediation "started as a simple approach to equality through lowering the access barriers . . . [but] turned into an educational revolution involving all of higher education. The revolution has reached the heart of the educational enterprise—the instructional process itself" (Cross, 1976, p. 9).

The educational effectiveness critics drew on one of the strains in the compensatory education movement in public education, emphasizing improving the learning situation of underprepared students rather than extending the school's responsibility to the family and the community. They were distinctive in drawing on the then-dominant theories in cognitive psychology as the guide to improving educational practice. In their view, learning theory suggested that instruction ought to be radically individualized in order to best match instructional strategies to the needs of underprepared students. Approaches like programmed and computer-assisted learning, with their emphasis on self-pacing, active participation, clear and explicit goals, small lesson units, and frequent feedback were especially recommended. These exemplary practices would enable even significantly underprepared students to achieve success by leading them through carefully graduated learning sequences, with the difficulty of tasks always geared to the present capabilities of each student.

According to its advocates, the instructional revolution would be based on mastery learning, individualization of instruction, and new learning technologies. Starting with remedial programs, where the sense of crisis was most acute, the revolution in pedagogy was imagined as spreading throughout community colleges, and then to the other sectors of higher education. Community colleges were to be the distinctive vanguard institutions of the instructional revolution. Their commitment to the difficult project of remediation, because of their policy of open admissions, would force community colleges to innovate, and their success would encourage others to follow. As instructional innovations broadened their influence, traditional classroom practices, such as lecturing, would be replaced in the effort to enhance student achievement. Schools would be reconstructed when, as Cohen put it: "[given the] aim of engendering minimum, fundamental achievement in all students . . . all the instructional processes are then directed toward bringing students to this goal" (1969, p. 22). When this occurred, the instructional revolution would be complete. Beginning with attempts to improve the performance of underprepared students, the best of remedial practices would become the model of good instruction throughout all of higher education as all schools became achievement-oriented institutions.

In advancing these views, the educational effectiveness critics spoke from within the tradition of progressive education, which attempted to develop a science of instruction and to place it at the service of incrementalist social reconstruction. However, with the emergence of developmental programs in the 1970s, colleges turned away from the path projected by the progressives. The rise of *developmental education* greatly complicated the collegiate response to the problem of at-risk students, projecting an alternate vision of the educational task that stood in uneasy relation to the views of remediation.

Developmental educators did not define themselves in the tradition of progressive education, with its model of theory informing an ever-improved practice. Instead they drew more on the Romantic tradition, and portrayed the goal of their efforts in terms of the ideal of a fully developed, multifaceted self that successfully integrates the cognitive and affective aspects of personality. They drew their ideal of the unfettered, fully developed self from a number of sources. Frequently they turned to developmental psychology, especially the work of Jerome Bruner and Jean Piaget. From them they drew the notion of developmental stages and the readiness to acquire concepts and skills. But they leavened that scientific psychology with the humanistic teachings of Rogers and Maslow, especially their emphasis on the importance of empathetic communication in promoting personal growth, and the need for teachers to fully accept and nurture student individuality. From writers such as Peter Elbow they adapted the ideal of a collaborative learning environment in which the authority of the teacher is displaced. For many classroom teachers, the technocratic vocabulary of remediation—with its talk of "educational technology" and "intentional learning"—was rejected in favor of humanistic notions like "developing the whole person," and "helping students understand themselves and their lives."

The shift from remediation to developmental education happened quietly at most institutions, without rancor or debate. Since these conceptions rely on such utterly different accounts of proper classroom goals and methods, that is rather surprising. Indeed, often each approach explicitly defined itself against the other, portraying itself as trying to accomplish different ends by different means and for different reasons. Typically, however, the two camps talked past each other, and in any case lacked any institutional means to articulate and settle their differences. Over time, the alternatives merged institutionally and appeared to merge theoretically. In many programs, the developmental goals of personal development were no longer clearly distinguished from the remedial aims of ameliorating skill deficiencies. By the late 1970s and 1980s programs typically began to describe themselves as "remedial/developmental," and pursued a peculiar blend of cognitive gains and personal development for their students.

In these hybrid programs, remedial categories continue to guide admissions testing and placement, as well as entrance and exit criteria for precollege courses. These are all typically described in terms of the mastery of writing, reading, and computational skills; and, of course, precollege programs are dominated by reading, writing, and mathematics courses. Developmental understandings, though, deeply shape the way faculty actually teach those courses, and what they value about them. Teachers in *developmental programs* are extremely concerned with issues of students' self-esteem, personal growth, and feelings of autonomy, and these concerns are expressed in typical classroom practices (McGrath and Spear, 1991).

Developmental views are also programmatically expressed in the great emphasis on counseling. As one observer notes: "Counseling is considered almost a panacea in that it is supposed to give high-risk students the extra attention they need" (Moore, 1981, p. 20). At community colleges and other schools with large remedial/developmental programs, the support and development goals characterized by counseling have a great potential to come into conflict with the academic goals of enhancing basic skills and preparing students for collegiate work. The affinity between developmental programs and the student service function commonly results in institutional alliances between developmental faculty and counseling staff. Richardson and Bender observe that since counselors have an ambiguous relation to the academic function, these alliances pose significant institutional dilemmas. "The existence of a special cadre of [student services] staff who see themselves as protectors of the open-door philosophy for the underprepared has produced fewer academic solutions than desirable. . . . The rift between academic and student service staffs . . . can erupt into conflicts that stymie efforts to deal with the issues of academic quality and standards" (1987, p. 49).

The hybrid programs lack the clarity of vision of either the purely remedial or purely developmental, although they have appropriated much of the vocabulary and many of the practices of each. Perhaps most significantly, cognitive and affective achievements are not clearly distinguished, and are actually allowed to drift together. Inevitably, the mixing of the hard outcomes proposed by remediation with the softer ones of developmental programs has made such programs notoriously difficult to evaluate, and has muted faculty interest in monitoring their efforts. Even if few students successfully make the transition from the special precollege programs into the regular curriculum, the staff can defend such programs as encouraging the full development of students whose lives might be enriched by their participation. This tendency is part of what has been termed the remedialization of community colleges and other institutions that have seen the merging of remedial and developmental understandings (McGrath and Spear, 1991).

This trend to merge remedial and developmental understanding also helps explain the peculiar institutional position typically occupied by these programs. Although efforts to serve at-risk students are of vital importance, they occupy a marginal position in many institutions. This is due in part to the difficulty their staffs, largely unaware of the deep tensions in the remedial and developmental traditions, have in articulating their goals and in building support for their aims.

In relating the development of such programs to their origin in the compensatory education movement of the 1960s, we can interpret remedial and developmental education as emphasizing the two different dimensions of that earlier effort. Remediation drew on the concern to improve the learning environment of the school by enhancing teaching and curriculum. This was expressed in the desire to match instructional approaches to the needs of underprepared students and to reconstruct schools by promoting an instructional revolution. Developmental educators, on the other hand, identified more with the social mission of compensatory education and the desire to overcome the debilitating effects of cultural deprivation by developing the whole student. However, the institution-building dimension of compensatory education was abandoned in favor of a heavily psychological understanding of students and their needs. In consequence, neither the conventional understandings of remedial or developmental education encouraged institutional collaboration with public school systems, community organizations, or other institutions serving underprepared learners. Efforts largely remained limited within the walls of individual campuses. Even there, though, institutional mechanisms have never developed to permit a reconciling of these two emphases, so they continue to be expressed in muted and theoretically unarticulated ways.

The instructional revolution associated with the ideal of compensatory education articulated by leading theorists in the 1960s and 1970s has not been realized in higher education; nor has it been explicitly rejected. The inability to resolve the competing responses to underprepared students has greatly complicated and confused institutional responses to at-risk students. There are many more programs than existed three decades ago, but little agreement about desired outcomes, effective program features, or even how to define at-risk students. On the positive side, though, remedial education's concern with the learning environment has helped sustain the focus on teaching and learning, and has stimulated valuable instructional innovations. Developmental education's concern for the student has helped broaden the understanding of who is at-risk. This broader understanding is reflected in the greater institutional concern for groups such as women and minorities who have been traditionally underrepresented in higher education, for the special needs of students in particular majors, for the specific problems of physically challenged students, and ultimately for retention efforts directed at all students.

How Effective Are Current Approaches?

Although programs designed to meet the needs of at-risk students exist throughout higher education, and many are of long standing, it is still difficult to make confident statements about their effectiveness. Since the first national studies of programs to remediate basic skills (Roueche, 1968), researchers have complained about the lack of adequate data on program effectiveness. Evaluators who tried to assess the programs designed to respond to the first cohorts of open-access students found that most colleges could not supply data required to answer even basic questions of student completion and retention rates (Roueche, 1968; Roueche and

Snow, 1977). In the few programs that could supply appropriate data, the attrition rate was found to be as high as 90 percent (Roueche and Snow, 1977). The early goals of remedial programs were characterized as "nebulous and ill defined because no one is absolutely convinced that it is even possible to remediate" (Roueche, 1968, p. 25).

Despite many national calls for greater attention to assessment, and a growing number of state testing requirements, the quality of data routinely gathered still limits the ability to conduct carefully designed evaluation. Few schools are committed to comprehensive, ongoing, and systematic evaluation (Maxwell, 1979; Boylan, Bonham, and George, 1991). An attempt to conduct a metanalysis of outcome studies in the 1980s reviewed 504 published reports, but concluded that only sixty programs could be examined (Kulik, Kulik, and Schwalb, 1983). Another review of published reports from over 500 colleges and universities found evidence of ongoing written evaluation reports in less than one-third of all institutions submitting documentation (Spann and Thompson, 1986). A national survey conducted in 1989 reported that 97 percent of responding institutions reported conducting at least one type of evaluation of remedial/developmental programs, and 92 percent reported using at least two different methods to track program outcomes (National Center for Education Statistics, 1991). However, at most institutions, what counts as program evaluation consists of collecting student evaluations, gain scores, or analysis of course grades or (less frequently) completion rates (National Center for Education Statistics, 1991). Seventeen percent of the institutions surveyed were unable to provide percentage figures for their enrollment of freshmen in remedial courses, and 25 percent could not provide the passing rates of freshmen. Other program components are evaluated infrequently, if at all, and rarely as part of a consistent, systematic effort (Boylan, Bonham, and Bliss, 1994).

Principles of Best Practice

Although we lack the kind of systematic evaluation that would be most desirable, an inductive and conceptual review of the literature suggests a body of best practices that should be considered by program planners, curriculum designers, and teachers.

• *Institutional commitment is a key factor.* Identifying at-risk students, developing well-crafted responses to their needs, and comprehensively evaluating those efforts are time-consuming, difficult, and costly activities. Success requires senior administrative commitment that is consistent and is communicated to all levels of the institution (Richardson and Rhodes, 1983). As the history of institutional efforts suggests, one of the most significant issues is how at-risk students are defined. This may legitimately vary among institutions. Some may develop narrow definitions that focus on students who lack certain specific skills, or who have difficulty in certain highly demanding courses, while other schools may serve large number of underprepared students or engage in efforts to recruit and serve underrepresented students. But however at-risk students are defined, it is vital that programmatic responses be proportionate to the magnitude of the problem, and that staff receive adequate resources, secure funding, and consistent administrative support.

• *Programs should be as comprehensive as possible.* At-risk students typically present schools with wide diversity in their patterns of performance and behavior. Many come with a history of academic deficiencies and lack adequate social support networks. Research has consistently suggested that comprehensive programs that include a number of program features targeting a variety of student needs are more successful than single-focus programs, such as simply offering tutoring or special sections of courses (Boylan, Bliss, and Bonham, 1992; Cross, 1976; Roueche and Roueche, 1993).

• *Programs should be proactive and be available early in a student's academic career.* Studies consistently find that reactive programs are ineffective. Reactive drop-in programs—those that rely on student-initiated contacts—tend not to be widely used by at-risk students (Abrams and Jerrigan, 1984; Levin and Levin, 1991). At-risk students have difficulty in recognizing that a problem exists, and are reluctant to seek help (Levin and Levin, 1991). Further, students are most at risk of attrition early in their collegiate experience, especially in their first term (Tinto, 1987; McGrath, forthcoming). Effective proactive interventions require early identification of at-risk students and interventions that are front loaded in the first year, or even earlier. This can be accomplished in a number of ways. Successful approaches include procedures for careful preenrollment assessment and placement, and early warning systems like the one at Miami Dade Community College where faculty try to identify students experiencing academic problems early in the semester (Cohen and Brawer, 1987). There are also successful "Freshman Year Experience" courses such as those developed at the University of South Carolina, which provide a mechanism to acquaint students with available resources and promote their involvement in the institution, as well as precollegiate summer bridge programs for high school and conditionally admitted students, and also supplementary instruction attached to identified problem courses that have high rates of attrition (Blanc, DeBuhr, and Martin, 1983).

• *Cognitive skills training must be integrated into the broader academic preparation of students.* The history of remedial efforts provides ample evidence that discrete skills training is ineffective in helping academically underprepared students gain the competencies necessary for collegiate-level coursework. Contemporary research in cognitive development has also emphasized that new knowledge and conceptual skills are best acquired in a meaningful context (Sticht, 1986; Roueche and Roueche, 1993). The traditional assumption, which has guided many remedial efforts, was that certain skills are basic and must be mastered before students can acquire more advanced skills. This led to the curricular distinction between skills and content courses, and pedagogical approaches that placed heavy emphasis on practices such drilling and rote memorization. However, much research in cognitive development emphasizes that skills are best acquired when they are embedded in the context of more global tasks (Means, Chelemer, and Knapp, 1991). Students learn best when activities are intrinsically related to a relevant goal (Malone, 1981).

The integration of skills instruction within a more global and meaningful context can be accomplished in a number of ways. Supplemental instruction programs that attach instruction directly to specific courses have been developed at a number of institutions. This approach helps ensure that the skills taught are subject-specific, and skill instruction is provided in credit-bearing courses. La Guardia Community College's Integrated Skills Reinforcement program systematically builds basic skill instruction into intermediate and upper-level courses, which both reinforces earlier gains and enhances skill transfer (Chaffee, 1992). Writing Across the Curriculum programs serve to reinforce writing abilities by integrating writing instruction throughout a large number of courses (McLeod and Soven, 1992). Collaborative learning practices, such as the Mathematics Workshop developed at the University of California, Berkeley, which uses collaborative group instruction, also helps to integrate skills instruction into a meaningful context (Garland, 1993). See Chapter Eight for an in-depth discussion of skill definition, and Chapter Eighteen for more on programs that run across the curriculum.

• *The instruction of academically underprepared students must be of high quality and must emphasize high-order skills.* From the earliest remediation efforts, policy analysts have emphasized that underprepared students need effective instruction from competent and committed teachers (Cross, 1976; Roueche, 1968). However, those designing or teaching in programs for underprepared students should expect that the enriching of curricula and instruction will be a difficult and lengthy process, and will require continuous examination and evaluation. Research suggests that there is typically a substantial gap between faculty intentions, actual classroom practice, and student outcomes (Ratcliff, Jones, Guthrie, and Oehler, 1991). Even the most highly motivated faculty tend to be unaware of the actual task structures and interaction patterns in their classrooms (Erickson and Schultz, 1981; Erickson and Mohatt, 1982).

A growing body of research at the primary, secondary, and collegiate levels has discovered that classes for disadvantaged and underprepared students typically offer less challenging and more monotonous work and provide few opportunities for students to be active and engaged learners (Barr and Dreeben, 1983; Good and Brophy, 1987; Oakes, 1986). Teachers are more directive, and students have less opportunity for problem solving (Anyon, 1980), and there is an overemphasis on the repetition of content through drilling and related practices (Knapp and Shields, 1990).

Curricula and instructional approaches for underprepared students should be designed to prepare them for college-level academic tasks by enhancing their analytic and synthetic reasoning abilities, and their facility with language and quantitative reasoning. This can best be done by reviewing programs to ensure that they provide students with opportunities to focus on complex and meaningful problems, encourage multiple thinking strategies, promote communication and collaboration among students and teachers, and make dialogue rather than lecture the central medium of teaching and learning.

Issues and New Directions

American education has a unique institutional configuration among industrialized countries. It has neither the high-quality general education for all students through secondary school of Japan, nor the job training and apprenticeship system of Germany. In both those systems, testing leads to clear winnowing and academic performance has direct and visible consequences for individuals (Paris, 1994). As compared to those countries, American education provides students with neither clear incentives for performance nor clear institutional pathways to follow in continuing their education or in making the transition from school to work (Bishop, 1989). Because of these institutional factors, along with the consequences of the rights revolution of the past several decades (Glendon, 1991), we can expect to see large numbers of underprepared and otherwise at-risk students entering higher education, as well as a growing recognition of the need to reach out to and better serve currently underrepresented groups. The continuing influence of these factors will require institutions to become much more responsive and successful in meeting the needs of at-risk students. This has several implications:

• Colleges and universities must become much more attentive to issues of program design and evaluation as they try to understand the sources of academic risk for their students and identify the program features that are most effective in meeting student needs.

- Institutions of higher education must look beyond their campus walls for solutions, and join in collaborations and partnerships with other institutions concerned with at-risk students. There are a number of interinstitutional collaborations that can be looked to as models, including the Ford Foundation's Urban Partnership Program, which is developing alliances to focus on at-risk students in seventeen cities throughout the country, the American Association of Higher Education's efforts to develop school-college alliances to improve teaching and learning, and The Pew Charitable Trust's Community Compacts for Student Success, which funds collaborations to improve outcomes for poor and minority students. But whatever model is employed, any substantial effort must examine ways to build the institutional alliances needed to improve the K–16 educational pathway for underrepresented and at-risk students.

- More research is needed on the effects of new immigration patterns and the growth of ESL study on remedial, developmental, and supplementary instruction programs. Particular attention should be paid to successful program features in ESL instruction that can be transferred to other programs.

- More research is also needed on multiple-transfer students to better understand the importance of institutional fit for student success. Currently, individual colleges and universities expend a great deal of effort on retaining students and count each student who leaves their institution before graduating as an institutional failure as well as a student failure. Yet research suggests that many of these students leave to find a better fit at another institution. In other words, their departure from one college may ensure their graduation from another. Also, many students transfer several times during their college career before they ultimately graduate. Some of these multiple-transfer students are more talented academically, as indicated by SAT or ACT scores and GPA, than are students who stay and graduate from the colleges the multiple-transfer students left (Kearney, Townsend, and Kearney, forthcoming). Yet these multiple-transfer students may well have been viewed or treated as at-risk in some of the institutions they attended.

Institutional leaders need to accept that not all students will graduate from their particular institution. The institution may not be the right fit for some students. When institutional leaders adopt the perspective that all students are at risk of leaving their particular institution and make extensive efforts to retain all students, the leaders are ignoring the possibility that some students do not fit well in certain schools. Narrowing the definition of at-risk student to focus efforts upon students who lack adequate academic preparation for the particular institution may be more cost effective for the school and ultimately of more benefit for all the students an institution serves.

References

Abrams, H. G., and Jerrigan, L. P. "Academic Support Services and the Success of High Risk College Students." *American Educational Research Journal*, 1984, *21*, 261–274.

Anyon, J. "Social Class and the Hidden Curriculum of Work." *Journal of Education*, 1980, *162*, 67–92.

Barr, R., and Dreeben, R. *How Schools Work.* Chicago: University of Chicago Press, 1983.

Bishop, J. "Incentives for Learning." In Commission on Workforce Quality and Market Efficiency, *Investing in People: A Strategy to Address America's Workforce Crisis.* Washington, D.C.: U.S. Department of Labor, 1989.

Blanc, R., DeBuhr, L., and Martin, D. "Breaking the Attrition Cycle: The Effect of Supplemental Instruction on Undergraduate Performance and Attrition." *Journal of Higher Education*, 1983, *54*, 80–90.

Boylan, H., Bliss, L., and Bonham, B. "The Impact of Developmental Programs." *Research in Developmental Education*, 1992, *10*(2), 1–4.

Boylan, H., Bonham, B., and Bliss, L. "Characteristic Components of Developmental Programs." *Research in Developmental Education*, 1994, *11*(1), 1–4.

Boylan, H., Bonham, B., and George, A. "Program Evaluation." In R. Flippo and D. Caverly (eds.), *College Reading and Study Strategy Programs.* Newark, Del.: International Reading Association, 1991.

Chaffee, J. "Critical Thinking Skills: The Cornerstone of Developmental Education." *Journal of Developmental Education*, 1992, *15*(3), 2–8.

Chazen, M. (ed.). *Compensatory Education.* London: Butterworth, 1973.

Clowes, D. A. "More Than a Definitional Problem." *Current Issues in Higher Education*, 1982, pp. 1–12.

Cohen, A. *Dateline '79: Heretical Concepts for the Community College.* Beverly Hills, Calif.: Glencoe Press, 1969.

Cohen, A. M, and Brawer, F. B. *The Collegiate Function of Community Colleges: Fostering Higher Learning Through Curriculum and Student Transfer.* San Francisco: Jossey-Bass, 1987.

Cohen, A. M., and Brawer, F. B. *The American Community College.* (2nd ed.) San Francisco: Jossey-Bass, 1989.

Cross, K. P. *Beyond the Open Door.* San Francisco: Jossey-Bass, 1974.

Cross, K. P. *Accent on Learning: Improving Instruction and Reshaping the Curriculum.* San Francisco: Jossey-Bass, 1976.

Erickson, F., and Mohatt, G. "The Cultural Organization of Participation Structures in Two Classrooms of Indian Students." In G. Spindler (ed.), *Doing the Ethnography of Schooling.* Troy, Mo.: Holt, Rinehart & Winston, 1982.

Erickson, F., and Schultz, J. "When Is a Context?" In J. L. Green and C. Wallat (eds.), *Ethnography and Language in Educational Settings.* Norwood, N.J.: Ablex, 1981.

Garland, M. "The Mathematics Workshop Model." *Journal of Developmental Education*, 1993, *16*(3), 14–19.

Glendon, M. A. *Rights Talk.* New York: Free Press, 1991.

Good, T., and Brophy, J. *Looking in Classrooms.* (4th ed.) New York: HarperCollins, 1987.

Karabel, J. "Community Colleges and Social Stratification." *Harvard Educational Review*, 1972, *42*(4), 521–562.

Kearney, G., Townsend, B., and Kearney, T. "Multiple-Transfer Students in a Public Urban University: Background Characteristics and Interinstitutional Movements." *Research in Higher Education, 36*(3), forthcoming.

Knapp, M. S., and Shields, P. M. "Reconceiving Academic Instruction for the Children of Poverty." *Phi Delta Kappan,* 1990, *71,* 753–758.

Kulik, J., Kulik, C-L., and Schwalb, B. "College Programs for High Risk and Disadvantaged Students: A Meta-Analysis of Findings." *Review of Educational Research,* 1983, *53,* 397–414.

Levin, M., and Levin, J. "A Critical Examination of Academic Retention Programs for At-Risk Minority College Students." *Journal of College Student Development,* 1991, *32,* 323–334.

Levine, A. *Handbook on Undergraduate Curriculum.* San Francisco: Jossey-Bass, 1978.

Little, A., and Smith, G. *Strategies of Compensation: A Review of Educational Projects for the Disadvantaged in the United States.* New York: Center for Educational Research and Innovation, 1971.

Malone, R. "Toward a Theory of Intrinsically Motivated Instruction." *Cognitive Science,* 1981, *4,* 333–369.

Maxwell, M. *Improving Student Learning Skills.* San Francisco: Jossey-Bass, 1979.

McGrath, D. "Teaching New Students in the Community College." In J. Hankin (ed.), *Promoting New Student Success in the Community College.* Columbia: University of South Carolina, National Resource Center for the Freshman Year Experience, forthcoming.

McGrath, D., and Spear, M. B. *The Academic Crisis of the Community College.* Albany: State University of New York Press, 1991.

McLeod, S. H., and Soven, M. (eds.). *Writing Across the Curriculum: A Guide to Developing Programs.* Newbury Park, Calif.: Sage, 1992.

Means, B., Chelemer, C., and Knapp, M. (eds.). *Teaching Advanced Skills to At-Risk Students.* San Francisco: Jossey-Bass, 1991.

Moore, W. M. *Community College Response to the High Risk Student.* Los Angeles, Calif.: ERIC Clearinghouse Monograph, 1981.

National Center for Education Statistics. *College Level Remedial Education in the Fall of 1989.* Washington, D.C.: U.S. Department of Education, 1991.

Oakes, J. "Tracking, Inequality, and the Rhetoric of School Reform: Why Schools Don't Change." *Journal of Education,* 1986, *168,* 61–80.

Paris, D. C. "Schools, Scapegoats, and Skills." *Policy Studies Journal,* 1994, *22,* 10–24.

Ratcliff, J. L., Jones, E. A., Guthrie, D. S., and Oehler, D. *The Effect of Coursework Patterns, Advisement, and Course Selection on the Development of General Learned Abilities of College Graduates. Final Report.* University Park: Center for the Study of Higher Education, Pennsylvania State University, 1991.

Richardson, R. C., Jr., and Bender, L. *Minority Access and Achievement in Higher Education: The Role of Urban Community Colleges and Universities.* San Francisco: Jossey-Bass, 1987.

Richardson, R. C., Jr., and Rhodes, W. "Building Commitment to the Institution." In G. B. Vaughn and Associates, *Issues for Community College Leaders in a New Era.* San Francisco: Jossey-Bass, 1983.

Roueche, J. *Salvage, Redirection, or Custody?* Washington, D.C.: American Association of Community Colleges, 1968.

Roueche, J., and Kirk, W. *Catching Up: Remedial Education.* San Francisco: Jossey-Bass, 1973.

Roueche, J., and Roueche, S. *Between a Rock and a Hard Place: The At-Risk Student in the Open-Door College.* Washington, D.C.: American Association of Community Colleges, 1993.

Roueche, J., and Snow, J. J. *Overcoming Learning Problems.* San Francisco: Jossey-Bass, 1977.

Spann, M. G., and Thompson, C. G. *The National Directory of Exemplary Programs in Developmental Education.* Boone, N.C.: National Center for Developmental Education, 1986.

Sticht, T. "Teachers, Books, Computers and Peers: Integrated Communications Technologies for Adult Literacy Development." Monterey, Calif.: U.S. Naval Postgraduate School, 1986.

Sticht, T., and others. *Cast-Off Youth: Policy and Training Methods from the Military Experience.* New York: Praeger, 1987.

Tinto, V. *Leaving College: Rethinking the Causes and Cures of Student Attrition.* Chicago: University of Chicago Press, 1987.

U.S. Department of Health, Education, and Welfare. *Title I Year II.* Washington, D.C.: U.S. Department of Health, Education, and Welfare, 1967.

Zwerling, L. S. *Second Best.* New York: McGraw-Hill, 1976.

PART THREE

ACADEMIC DISCIPLINES AND SPECIALIZED LEARNING

Academic study has become largely a matter of specialization. Scholars created fields of knowledge that exist today as academic disciplines that organize their intellectual work. The disciplinary communities define which problems are worthy of study; advance certain central concepts, theories, or principles (and not others); embrace certain methods of investigation (and not others); provide forums for sharing research and airing controversies; and even shape professional identity and offer career paths for scholars. Intellectual progress has been marked by greater and greater specialization within fields, creation of subdisciplines, and expansion of specialties.

In colleges and universities, the academic disciplines found an organizational home in the form of the depart-

ment. Departments have become dominant ways to organize academic work, including offering the curriculum. The academic major, the most central and advanced work of the discipline taught to students who are most interested in carrying on its traditions, has become the central concern of faculty and students alike. When students are asked, "What are you studying?" they typically respond with their choice of major (or apologetically say they don't know, if they haven't decided on one), implying that all of the rest of their studies in the arts and sciences and elsewhere are insignificant.

Since their creation and spread at the end of the nineteenth and early twentieth centuries, the discipline, department, major, and specialization have become ubiquitous features of American higher education. These elements have proven to be extremely durable structures, especially given the tremendous growth and expansion of knowledge within and between fields in the last century. One might reasonably ask, are these structures developed in the nineteenth century, when the United States was still an agrarian society, still suitable for the needs of the twenty-first century?

Geertz (1983, p. 7) asserts that conventional organizations of knowledge are unrelated to much of today's intellectual work. "Grand rubrics like 'Natural Science,' 'Biological Science,' 'Social Science,' and 'The Humanities' have their uses in organizing curricula, in sorting scholars into cliques and professional communities, and in distinguishing broad traditions of intellectual style. . . . But when these rubrics are taken to be a borders-and-territories map of modern intellectual life, or, worse, a Linnaean catalogue into which to classify scholarly species, they merely block from view what is really going on." Indeed, he argues that intellectual progress today often comes not from more and more specialization but from cross-fertilization of ideas from different fields. For example, the interpretation of texts of various sorts has borrowed concepts, methods, perspectives, and metaphors from many fields, and in turn had an impact on many different disciplines. One might ask whether intellectual progress in the future will come more from new connections, interpretations, and integrations—both within and between disciplines—or from discoveries of smaller and smaller

bits of information. In contrast with Geertz, Clark (1993, 1995) argues that the disciplines are working quite well. They are creating new knowledge, generating subdisciplines, and continuing to provide the knowledge base for both undergraduate and graduate education.

In Chapter Eleven, Carol Schneider reports on a decade of work initiated by AAC&U to assess the arts and sciences major and to take steps to improve it. In a project assessing learning in majors, she notes that none of the fifty-four departments involved in the project had defined goals for students' learning in terms useful for guiding assessment. Subsequent efforts to restructure the major emphasized five key steps: create a clear, departmentwide understanding about intellectual capacities and the core of conceptual knowledge that should be developed; define the major as a vital learning community in which every student's intellectual development is both valued and sought; design a sequence of core courses that cultivate the desired capacities; introduce a culminating project or capstone course that allows students to pull together and demonstrate their learning; and develop connections between the major and other fields of knowledge.

Lyn Maxwell White in Chapter Twelve analyzes the issues in the recent national debates over the humanities. These issues include the content and methods of the humanities, the so-called culture wars, and the search for community, and extend into major programs of study and, indeed, into community and public conversations. She presents a number of examples of effective and innovative humanities programs at specific schools. In the future, she believes, we are likely to see greater inclusiveness in humanities programs, both in the professoriate and in subjects of study, new modes of cross-disciplinary collaboration, and more active engagement with the public sphere.

Mathematics and natural sciences, too, are in the midst of controversy, as Gene Wubbels and Joan Girgus demonstrate in Chapter Thirteen. They call for curriculum reform to get away from the memorizing of what Alfred North Whitehead called "inert ideas." The authors cite twelve directions for change, which include content that has fewer and larger or more important ideas, course and laboratory activities that enable and invite students to actively construct meanings, courses that make connections to other disciplines or applications, and less competition and more supportive learning communities. They describe notable curriculum innovations in the individual disciplines.

In Chapter Fourteen, Anne Hendershott and Sheila Wright discuss the social sciences, pointing out that as neither arts nor natural sciences, these studies have often struggled for recognition and acceptance. Torn between the goals of understanding the world through objective study and reflection and changing it through informed intervention, the recent development of applied studies in the social sciences seems to be reuniting these twin poles of professional atten-

tion. The authors explore the missions and emergence of the social science disciplines, their divergent purposes and paradigms, and the impact of the debate about the canon and its relation to the treatment of cultural pluralism. They conclude by asserting that study of the social sciences should leave students with both the knowledge for and the interest in taking social responsibility and participating in informed civic discourse throughout their lives.

In Chapter Fifteen, Ellen Harris declares that the arts offer students a different way of knowing the world around them and an approach to problem-solving that need not take a linear path. She explores several tensions within arts education—art as interpretation and history as opposed to art as practice and performance, curricular versus extracurricular, and professional and avocational. She describes different curricula at different kinds of institutions that rest on different choices among these tensions. Asserting that the arts are atomized into separate and isolated areas, she makes a plea for faculty to collaborate across field boundaries to offer meaningful programs of study for all students.

Lynn Curry and Jon Wergin in Chapter Sixteen analyze the growth of professional education and its marked influence on the undergraduate curriculum. They point to the emergence of professional education in apprenticeships and its current grounding in formal study of the relevant knowledge base of a field. They note the complications of assuring competent professional practice amid rampant consumerism, explosion of technical knowledge, and expansion of technologies. They identify key issues to be defining competence; measuring and certifying competence; and integrating technical knowledge, practical knowledge, and liberal learning; and they argue for sustained change in undergraduate professional education.

Darrel Clowes in Chapter Seventeen analyzes occupational education in the context of the growing practical bent of the undergraduate curriculum. He distinguishes between professional, occupational, and vocational education in terms of the relative balance of theory, technical knowledge, and liberal learning versus practice (professional is high on theory, vocational high on practice, and occupational in the middle), as well as the kind of program and the type of institutional setting where they occur. He looks at the relationship between work and learning, and questions the assumption of a tight connection between the training given and the employment obtained. After discussing some of the issues in the design and management of occupational curricula, he focuses on the trend among community colleges to shift from preemployment training in

degree and certificate programs to postemployment training to serve the employment needs of older, part-time students. The role of occupational programs, he concludes, continues to expand.

These chapters demonstrate that specialized study is alive and well in the academy and in the curriculum. In some sense, specialization is so successful that it creates problems for itself. The growth of disciplines and subdisciplines fragments fields, as seen in the split between clinical and academic psychologists. In the curriculum, specialized programs and courses spawn calls for holistic study and more connections within and between fields. In departments, faculty and students yearn for a greater sense of community. But as many have discovered, it is difficult to foster integrated learning in a dis-integrated academic world.

References

Clark, B. R. *The Research Foundations of Graduate Education.* Berkeley: University of California Press, 1993.

Clark, B. R. *Places of Inquiry: Research and Advanced Education in Modern Universities.* Berkeley: University of California Press, 1995.

Geertz, C. *Local Knowledge: Further Essays in Interpretive Anthropology.* New York: Basic Books, 1983.

CHAPTER ELEVEN

THE ARTS AND SCIENCES MAJOR

Carol Geary Schneider

Throughout the United States, the most widely touted efforts to revitalize educational purposes and practices address general education programs and courses that meet common graduation requirements. For most students, however, it is study in the major or concentration that represents the primary point of college—and therefore the primary locus of personal and intellectual investment in higher education. Symbolically, the choice of a college major expresses a student's sense of personal and often professional direction. Developmentally, it is in meeting the requirements for a major that students are most likely to internalize a concept of intellectual mastery, a feel for what it might mean to frame a personal inquiry and direction rather than remain a recipient of others' claims and findings.

If the contemporary educational reform movement is to pay the learning dividends its proponents seek, its goals must be more directly tied to what happens in undergraduate majors, liberal arts, and preprofessional alike. Those who seek to improve undergraduate learning need to ask how work in the major can be reconceived so that the major incorporates central educational objectives. Consider the capacities and habits of mind described elsewhere in this handbook as goals for undergraduate learning: writing, analytical and technological skills, interdisciplinary and integrative learning, knowledge of diversity, and ability to negotiate difference, to cite only a few. If students are really to develop these demanding intellectual capacities and inclinations, they must be asked to do so not only in their general education courses but in the one portion of their college studies where they work intensively over an extended period of time.

Liberal Education and the Arts and Sciences Major

Acknowledging the centrality of the major to the quality of students' college learning, the Association of American Colleges and Universities (AAC&U) has, over the past decade, initiated a series of national projects that address educational purposes and effective practices in undergraduate majors.

This initiative has viewed the major as a form of *connected learning,* a matrix in which the student is encouraged to integrate the several parts of his or her learning and interests in focused and purposeful ways. Although the focus of this effort has been arts and sciences fields, the ideas and recommendations that emerge from this work are also relevant to majors in professional and preprofessional fields. Many of the reports of these projects were issued under the original name of the organization, the Association of American Colleges (AAC), and are so noted in the references. The organization became the AAC&U in 1995, and we refer to it by its current acronym throughout the text.

The AAC&U is a voluntary collaboration of more than 650 colleges and universities, large and small, public and private, whose purpose is the improvement of undergraduate liberal education. It holds an ecumenical view of liberal education and has worked on liberal learning in professional fields. Here, however, we report on a decade-long effort to renew and revitalize arts and sciences majors. This work has involved such fields as history, English, foreign languages, philosophy and religion; anthropology, economics, political science, psychology, and sociology; biology, mathematics, and physics. It has also addressed newer interdisciplinary majors, including women's studies and environmental science.

These efforts to revitalize majors have touched on a large part of the intellectual terrain conventionally described as the liberal arts or the liberal arts and sciences. In effect, AAC&U has raised the question: What do we mean by the liberal arts? At the turn of the twenty-first century, does the term capture anything more than an enumeration of the increasingly disparate subject areas typically assigned to colleges of arts and sciences?

To enter this terrain is to enter a field of considerable semantic confusion. There is a long and distinguished tradition of liberal arts education in the West and an equally long tradition of high regard for such education (Kimball, 1986). Both the tradition and the regard have flourished with considerable vitality in the twentieth-century American college and university, where liberal education has been broadly viewed as education for leadership and service (Rudolph, 1977; Winter, McClelland, and Stewart, 1981). But in the main, the twentieth-century curricular programs most famously associated with the revival of liberal education have been general studies programs, rather than programs of study in specific fields. Consider, for example, the "Contemporary Civilization" course at Columbia, the Meiklejohn Experimental College at the University of Wisconsin, the Hutchins College at the University of Chicago, or the Federated Learning Communities initiated at the State University of New York, Stony Brook, and widely imitated at other institutions. Featuring general problems, primary texts, and interdisciplinary learning, none of these widely influential liberal studies programs were departmentally organized academic majors or concentrations.

Conversely, the terms liberal arts major or liberal arts and sciences majors now conventionally refer to structured programs of collegiate study organized and offered through academic departments. Appearing on most campuses in the first decades of this century, majors in arts and sciences fields emerged as an acceptable compromise between the nineteenth-century classical college curriculum, in which courses of study were absolutely and sequentially prescribed, and the elective system, which allowed students to do much of their college work in the introductory courses of different departments (Rudolph, 1977, pp. 225–230). The term *major* seems to have been first used in the Johns Hopkins catalogue in 1877–78 (Levine, 1978, p. 29), a linkage that signals the major's intimate ties to and dependence on the establishment of research departments. The major is a child of the research department, requiring faculty members with specialization in particular subject matters for its inception and sustenance.

Yet if the arts and sciences major entered the university on the organizational structures and intellectual accomplishments of the research disciplines, it also successfully appropriated a significant part of the rationale for the nineteenth-century classical curriculum that it so successfully displaced. Just as nineteenth-century educators had defended the classical curriculum's effectiveness in fostering intellectual discipline useful in all aspects of life, twentieth-century educators said much the same thing about the educational value of the disciplinary fields that displaced the classical curriculum. The organization and content of the liberal arts curriculum changed dramatically from the nineteenth to the twentieth century. But the ethos of the liberal arts lived on in the major's claim that education in an arts or sciences field provides students with sophisticated intellectual development—cultivation of analytical capacity and judgment—rather than professional or immediately practical training (Schneider, 1993, pp. 45–46; Graff, 1987, pp. 72–74). Arts and sciences majors so effectively aligned themselves with the inquiry mission of the research university that, even at the end of the twentieth century, the private research colleges and universities most sought after by applicants and their families still give pride of place to arts and sciences fields as the focus of their undergraduate curricula.

But as arts and sciences disciplines have themselves evolved, the educational purposes and effectiveness of liberal arts majors have become increasingly problematic. Enrollment figures alone signal difficulty. Despite the prestige of arts and sciences fields in a relatively small number of sought-after institutions, nationally these majors have experienced precipitous decline in the overall context of increasing baccalaureate enrollments. In 1968, 47 percent of all degrees were awarded in arts and sciences fields; by 1986, it was 26 percent (Oakley, 1992, p. 85).

Numbers, however, tell only part of the story. Notwithstanding the major's claim in principle to introduce students to a set of inquiry methods and practices basic to a field, the proliferation of subject matter and subfields in many disciplines has meant that majors are frequently organized by a principle of *coverage* rather than around intellectual mastery of particular forms of inquiry. A report prepared by the American Political Science Association (APSA) illustrates the problem:

> The content knowledge a political science department hopes to impart usually is defined by distribution requirements [within the major]. The plasticity of definitions of subfields for this purpose is extraordinary. The earliest study of political science programs (. . . 1912–16) divided the field into only four subfields: American government, comparative government, elements of law, and political theory. . . . The 1968 APSA Bibliographical Directory list grew to twenty-seven, while that for 1973 displayed sixty subfields organized into eight major categories. APSA data show that, in 1988, collectively, eight subfields were available at the 667 institutions surveyed. Each of these was either required or recommended by between 64 percent and 97 percent of them. [Association of American Colleges, 1991, p. 135]

As the example suggests, the explosion of knowledge in the disciplines has created departmental curricular structures in which students are more likely to sample disparate and loosely connected course topics than to pursue a structured, intellectually focused, and progressively purposeful course of study.

The problem is further compounded by the contemporary migration of both problems and methods across disciplinary boundaries. The psychologist may study family systems, but so too does the economist. No discipline lays solitary claim to the child, or gender, or culture, or language. The body, the mind, the evolution of the earth: all are cross-disciplinary topics. Analytical approaches have been similarly fluid. The majority of fields—those termed disciplinary and interdisciplinary alike—are in practice multidisciplinary, increasingly encompassing in their ranks the range of tensions that have traditionally divided soft humanists from hard scientists.

Geertz has incisively described the resultant intellectual ferment: "What we are seeing is not just another redrawing of the cultural map . . . but an alteration of the principles of mapping" (1983, p. 20). But what is the meaning of this remapping for the so-called liberal arts major? Or, to put it differently, what is it, at the end of the twentieth century, that establishes a course of study as a liberal arts experience, or liberal learning? Do these terms still capture a form of study that has its own distinctive style and ethos? Should they?

The initiative undertaken by AAC&U approached this question through an extensive and multifaceted examination of present practices and desirable purposes in arts and sciences concentrations. Rather than assume that whatever goes on in, say, the philosophy or psychology department is by definition liberal learning, AAC&U involved both national learned societies and hundreds of departmentally based arts and sciences faculty members in a normative and practice-oriented consideration of what liberal learning in the major should address as higher education approaches the twenty-first century.

Not everyone working for improvement in undergraduate education agrees that arts and sciences majors should be revitalized—as they see it, the problem runs too deep for that. For many contemporary critics, "the intellectual specialization represented by disciplinary study is the source of higher education's shortcomings—the academy's equivalent of original sin" (Green, 1993, p. 101). These critics have long contended that the intellectual agendas that undergird academic majors lead almost by definition to more and more attention to ever smaller twigs in the tree of knowledge (Carnegie Foundation for the Advancement of Teaching, 1977). Others are concerned that as the boundaries of scholarship become more fluid and blurred, undergraduate majors tied tightly to conventional academic fields cut students off from the most interesting frontiers of knowledge (Association of American Colleges, 1990, p. 15). The major, such critics assert, should be replaced with all due speed by more deliberately integrative designs for learning (Botstein, 1991).

Yet there is equally a case to be made for *re-form*—to use AAC&U's term—rather than displacement of undergraduate majors. The research enterprise that supports arts and sciences majors stands at the heart of the academy's mission. Majors thus are closely linked to faculty members' scholarly specializations. Faculty members necessarily stand at the center of any institution's core educational purposes. To elicit faculty commitment to these purposes, educational improvements in higher education need to connect with and build on faculty members' scholarly commitments, not proceed in diametrical opposition to them.

A focus on the major as the centerpiece of educational renewal also recognizes, moreover, the educational potential of particular communities of inquiry within the larger, more heterogeneous—and often impersonal—academy. As the generation of educational research sparked by Astin's work suggests, student involvement in educationally productive peer and faculty relationships is positively linked with both persistence and achievement in their college studies (Astin, 1992; Light, 1992; Treisman, 1992).

An important implication of Astin's "involvement" research is that the academy should work to make involvement in human-scale learning communities a lively possibility for every student. But why begin de novo to create learning communities within the academy? Departmental majors already bring together faculty members and students who share an interest in a constellation of related questions, issues, and approaches. If we accept the value of community as an important resource for students' intellectual growth and development, the role, work, and interrelations among the departmentally based communities of interest that have already formed in higher education can be a promising place to begin. For more on learning communities, see Chapter Twenty-Two.

Re-Forming Majors: An Emerging Issue

This initiative to rethink and renew arts and sciences majors has spanned nearly a decade. It has included three phases: an initial critique of prevailing practice; collaboration with national learned societies in developing a series of analytical reports and recommendations; and, since 1992, campus action to *re-form* departmental majors. The work described in this chapter, although far-reaching, is still preliminary. While it seems inevitable that the current press toward institutional and educational restructuring will directly affect departmental configurations and programs, colleges and universities are only beginning to look systemically at their majors.

In 1993, AAC&U conducted an informal survey of chief academic officers at its member institutions and follow-up telephone interviews with leaders at thirty institutions that had previously sent faculty study teams to national workshops on re-forming the major. Both the survey and the interviews confirmed that institutional leaders viewed the major as an emerging issue on their curricular agenda, the logical follow-up to general education renewal. Of 238 institutions responding to the survey, 100 indicated that they were working systematically to strengthen their undergraduate majors. Responding research universities showed the least interest (27 percent) and comprehensive institutions the greatest interest (50 percent). A closer analysis of the responses suggested, however, that many institutions were still in a planning phase for work on the major. The deans interviewed by telephone, for the most part, described themselves as gathering ideas for how to proceed.

A number of converging trends seem likely to accelerate the growing interest in restructuring majors. The regional accrediting associations' emphases on assessment frequently draws attention to departmental programs, because campuses find it easier to envision assessing learning in the major than in general education. The growing pressures to streamline divisions and departments coupled with the increasing significance of interdisciplinary programs also press faculties to view their educational organization with fresh eyes.

A number of campuses already have institution-wide reviews of their majors well under way. In 1993, Harvard University initiated a comprehensive review of all forty-two of its undergraduate concentrations. All departments were asked to address such issues as "a coherent concentration structure with sequenced requirements," "participatory small group instruction," "a synthesizing experience for all concentrations," and "strengthened advising" (Harvard University Educational Policy Committee, 1993). By 1995, a number of departments were reporting significant accomplishments and the EPC was sharing examples of good practice across the departments (Harvard University Educational Policy Committee, 1995).

In the fall of 1994, Stanford University launched a comprehensive review of undergraduate education that addressed general education and majors simultaneously. At Columbia University, faculty members wrote a comprehensive critique of majors in 1993–94, although their call for significant changes in both disciplinary and interdisciplinary programs fell victim to internal administrative changes. Northeast Missouri State University (renamed Truman State University in 1996) completed a systematic review and restructuring of all its majors in 1993–94. St. Joseph's College (Indiana), which implemented a comprehensive and widely noted eight-semester general education program in the 1970s, now has a major initiative under way that asks departments to frame sequences and outcomes for their majors and to link practices in the major to the work of the core curriculum. Milliken University has also involved all its faculty members in a simultaneous renewal of general education and rethinking of majors in relation to the university's general goals for undergraduate learning.

Beginning in 1992, the College of Charleston; Dickinson College; Iona College; Jacksonville University; Manhattan College; Rowan College of New Jersey; the University of Arkansas, Little Rock; and Western Michigan University were competitively selected to form an AAC&U consortium to work separately and collaboratively on reorganizing selected arts and sciences majors. The work of this consortium forms a major part of the discussion later in this chapter.

Critique of Prevailing Practice

In all probability, renewal of the major will prove to be, like general education before it, a multidecade, multifaceted effort that will gradually change the form and focus of undergraduate study throughout the country. The process requires a clear-sighted look at the situation as it stands.

Well into the third quarter of this century, the major was widely regarded as the success story of the twentieth-century curriculum. The Carnegie Foundation for the Advancement of Teaching keyed into this standing by using "The Major—A Success Story?" as one of the chapter titles in its 1977 report *Missions of the College Curriculum* (p. 186), although the authors expressed concern about the amount of time majors consumed in the overall curriculum and of the tendency toward specialization. Such criticisms notwithstanding, the prestige of the arts and sciences major prompted leaders of the 1980s effort to reform teacher education to issue a widely followed recommendation that future high school teachers pursue an arts or sciences rather than an education major (Holmes Group Executive Board, 1986).

In 1985, the generally favorable view of the arts and sciences major was strongly challenged. That year, a select committee of leading educators released a widely read and trenchant critique of the academic marketplace, *Integrity in the College Curriculum* (Association of American Colleges, 1985). In the context of a scorching analysis of the "decline and devaluation of the undergraduate degree," *Integrity's* authors singled out the major for special opprobrium. More a bureaucratic convenience than a purposeful educational program, *Integrity* observed, "The major in most colleges is little more than a gathering of courses taken in one department, lacking structure and depth, as is often the case in the humanities and social sciences, or emphasizing content to the neglect of the essential style of inquiry on which the content is based, as is too frequently true in the natural and physical sciences" (p. 2).

This initial critique of curricular practices in liberal arts majors was reinforced by a study prepared for AAC&U by the University of Pennsylvania Institute on Research in Higher Education. This study reviewed seniors' transcripts from all arts and sciences majors in thirty-five institutions, representing the complete range of institutional types in four-year postsecondary colleges and universities. Like *Integrity* before it, this report, *Structure and Coherence: Measuring the Undergraduate Curriculum* (Zemsky, 1989), found too little of either structure or coherent purpose in the practice of many liberal arts departments. In some departments, there was not even a single course that all students took in common.

AAC&U staff also gathered information about the state of the major through a collaborative effort undertaken (1986–1989) with eighteen colleges and universities to test external examiners as a way of assessing students' learning in the major. Organizing the eighteen institutions into clusters of three and their fifty-four participating departments into field-specific clusters, also of three, this assessment experiment asked faculty members in each cluster to serve as external examiners for students in one another's departments. The two rounds of external examinations produced several dozen faculty-developed reports from arts and sciences departments throughout the United States on strengths and weaknesses of their programs and of students' learning in those programs.

This description of gleanings from the External Examiners Assessment Project is based on internal project reports from the examiners and on an internal staff evaluation of the project. In general, faculty members who served as visiting examiners for this assessment experiment reported positively on one another's students and programs. But there were also discordant notes that added another layer of detail to the critiques of the major offered in *Integrity* and *Structure and Coherence*. Collectively, the reports highlighted a series of difficulties: missing curricular goals, absence of a clear educational structure for study in the major, and fragmentation of student learning.

Missing goals: Strikingly, project leaders found that not a single one of the fifty-four departments involved in the project had defined goals for students' learning in any terms that could usefully guide assessment. To develop the assessments, the examiners had first to determine what the departmental goals actually were. Typically, the examiners worked inductively and on their own; the initiative elicited considerable resistance to the very idea of assessment but no groundswell to articulate shared educational objectives.

Absence of clear educational structure: At the outset, this experimental assessment design called for both comprehensive written examinations that would test students' common learning and for individualized oral examinations to probe their individualized learning. In practice, because students had followed such disparate paths through their majors, the written examinations also had to be highly individualized. None of the eighteen disciplinary clusters actually offered a single, unified comprehensive examination because, field by field, cluster by cluster, even in comparatively unified fields like economics, faculty members judged that it would be unfair to do so. As the evaluators noted, commonality of content was conspicuous by its modest appearance in the departments contributing to this assessment experiment (Association of American Colleges, 1989).

Two of the eighteen participating institutions, both liberal arts colleges, had since the early twentieth century required seniors to complete culminating experiences in their majors: a comprehensive examination at one college and a senior thesis accompanied by an oral examination at the second. But these two were the exceptions. In other departments, culminating projects were an option rather than an expectation. In some, they were not even available as an option. Faculty examiners from one cluster reported after interviewing their graduating seniors that students found this absence of a formal exit process unsettling. There was, the students thought, "something odd . . . about graduating, as if one floated out of the university without feeling finished with this stage of one's learning" (Association of American Colleges, 1989).

Fragmented learning: With students taking different curricular paths through the major and few departments offering advanced synthesizing courses within the regular curriculum, several faculty reports from this assessment experiment commented that integrating learning was a problem for many of the students examined. Faculty members from three highly selective liberal arts colleges provided an especially incisive analysis of students' problems with *integrative learning:*

> What was most striking . . . was the gap between what we thought the [seniors] knew and what they knew (much less). . . . It . . . appeared the students had difficulty moving beyond the course-format to the general, open-ended kinds of questions we posed. They also seemed to have problems applying material learned in one course to issues in other courses. In other words, it seemed that the students' learning and hence thinking was specific and compartmentalized; a kind of thinking engendered by our teaching material in courses, and sufficient for performing well in class examinations, but inadequate for life outside the classroom. [Association of American Colleges, 1989]

Review by the Learned Societies

The intersecting national and campus-based reports on educational fragmentation in arts and sciences majors helped frame an agenda when AAC&U initiated a national review of both purposes and needed changes in arts and sciences fields. This second stage of work on the major began in 1988 and continued through 1991.

The core activity in this second stage of work was a broad-based collaboration with twelve national learned societies, each of which agreed to work within a charge framed by a national advisory committee of scholars and educational leaders (Association of American Colleges, 1991, pp. 1–8). The learned societies participating in the project were: American Academy of Religion, American Association of Physics Teachers, American Economics Association, American Historical Association, American Institute of Biological Sciences, American Philosophical Association, American Political Science Association, American Psychological Association, American Sociological Association, Mathematical Association of America, National Women's Studies Association, and the Society for Values in Higher Education. The latter group developed a report on and recommendations for interdisciplinary concentrations and majors.

The charge asked the learned societies to address four themes: the processes by which goals are set in the major and the adequacy of these processes in the context of an institution's overarching educational mission; the degree to which learning in the major is or should be intentionally developmental and therefore, sequential; opportunities for students to integrate and receive feedback on their learning; and the blurring of intellectual boundaries across disciplines and the implication of these developments for organizing majors. The charge also asked each field to consider the extent to which specific groups of students, whether women or ethnic and racial minorities, were underrepresented in the field and what might be done about it.

Working within the common charge, each learned society organized its own review of the intellectual purposes and current state of college majors in its field. The learned societies conducted research reviews, organized national and regional discussions, and in some cases implemented their own formal surveys of campus practice and opinion. Each published its own separate report on the purposes that ought to be addressed through collegiate study in that field and identified priorities for campus attention. Abridged versions of all twelve of the learned societies' reports were published in a single volume, *Reports from the Fields* (Association of American Colleges, 1991).

The learned society recommendations for strengthening their majors were diverse, as might be expected. Disciplinary communities have developed their own cultural patterns. Reporting on their content analysis of the learned society reports, Stark and Latucca (1993) observed that these cultural differences produced notable differences in the ways the task forces of humanists, social scientists, and scientists responded to the common charge. They note, for example, that humanists and social scientists were much less comfortable than scientists with such concepts as curricular coherence or sequential learning. Scientists, conversely, reported on their fields' resistance to the idea of encouraging students to connect the different parts of their education (p. 77).

Nonetheless, a careful reading of the twelve reports published in *Reports from the Fields* shows discernible and significant common emphases across the learned society recommendations for their majors (Association of American Colleges, 1991). Collectively, the reports marked these learned societies' acceptance of a paradigm shift away from content to be mastered and toward methods of interpretation and modes of judgment. While content was certainly discussed in every report, there was an even stronger emphasis in these reports on helping students learn to use the field's analytic or experimental approaches. All the reports called for early introduction to methods, critical approaches, or experimental work so that students would have opportunities to use these approaches throughout their studies. All accepted and addressed the call in the AAC&U charge to distinguish among purposes for introductory and more advanced work and to clarify the relations between them.

Many of the reports devoted considerable attention to the kinds of pedagogy likely to help students learn to use the approaches of the field. Most called for some kind of culminating course or project. While, as Stark and Latucca note, the concept of sequential learning initially aroused considerable suspicion among the humanities task forces, the final reports from both philosophy and history proposed ways that students could move toward progressively more sophisticated analyses whatever the content of their early and advanced courses. The learned society reports also accepted and incorporated the emphasis on integrative or connected learning proposed in the initial AAC&U charge. Most of the reports addressed integrative learning within the boundaries of the academic field but some gave considerable attention to cognate work in related disciplines. The National Women's Studies Association report made critical engagement with a range of disciplines a hallmark of women's studies. The American Academy of Religion report observed that studies in religion are by definition multicultural and require comparative and multimethodological approaches in order to be done at all. The Society for Values and Higher Education report on interdisciplinary majors urged that teaching students to integrate their learning must be a central commitment of any interdisciplinary study.

Strikingly, a number of the learned society task forces laid claim to the broad responsibilities of a liberal education as well as the analytical and content responsibilities of learning in a particular field. Several reports commented on a set of general goals for liberal education enumerated in *Integrity in the College Curriculum* and observed that their majors cultivated these broad capacities—for example, critical inquiry, historical consciousness, scientific perspective, values assessment, aesthetic judgment—as well as particular disciplinary approaches and knowledge. In other words, these scholars contended that education in a particular field can and should advance general as well as specialized ends of college learning.

While only the American Sociological Association explicitly developed a full-blown conception of the major as a learning community, all the reports implicitly treated departmental majors as purposeful communities, one of whose goals was to help students develop the ways of thinking appropriate to that community. The reports on history, religion, philosophy, economics, sociology and women's studies spelled out in considerable detail the ways of thinking basic to their field. The American Psychological Association (APA) report offered a series of alternative curricular models, each designed to help students develop "conceptual structures whereby they can 'think in psychological terms.'"

The APA report went on to frame a description of the educational theme that appears across all the fields: "We want to emphasize teaching for the transfer of learning. Our students should be able to recognize, and apply appropriately, concepts and skills in a variety of contexts. They should be able to look at relationships, to make connections, to struggle with ambiguity. To accomplish this, our curricular models emphasize students having the experience of practicing (talking, writing, doing) psychology" (Association of American Colleges, 1991, p. 164).

Following the publication of these field reports, several of the learned societies undertook further efforts on their own to foster improvements in the major. The American Political Science Association, for example, having found that half the 667 departments it surveyed had no general required introduction to politics and government, launched a project on models for the introductory course in the major. The National Women's Studies Association published curricular models from a range of institutions for its members and undertook an extensive assessment of what students were actually learning in a women's studies major. The Modern Language Association, which had declined an invitation to take part in AAC&U's collaborative national review, independently published reports on changing requirements in the English major and secured funding for a national project to encourage redesign of departmental programs. Several of the learned societies sponsored symposia and special issues of their journals on issues related to the major.

Cross-Disciplinary Review

In addition to these field-specific reports, the national advisory committee that wrote the initial charge to the learned societies prepared *The Challenge of Connecting Learning,* a general report on educational purposes in arts and sciences majors that AAC&U released in 1991. Virtually all the learned society reports stressed the importance of local autonomy in devising college majors, and *Challenge* too recognized both the disparate content concerns of different fields and the distinctive missions that mark American colleges and universities.

Nonetheless, *Challenge's* authors contended, building on the common themes in the learned society reports, that college majors can and should acknowledge a set of shared obligations, important whatever the actual subject matter of a field. "It is surely not the subject matter alone—which varies not only among departments or programs in the same field but also among student majors in the same program—that constitutes a major program as 'liberal' learning. Liberal learning describes—or ought to describe—intellectual habits fostered through and inseparable from successful completion of a course of study" (1990, p. 3).

Providing its own answer to the question of what characterizes a study in a major as liberal education, *Challenge* argued that every arts and sciences field ought to incorporate:

- A conception of the major as an inclusive learning community, in which each student's intellectual development is deliberately cultivated and supported and diverse participation in the community is both valued and sought

- A spine of developmentally sequenced common courses and experiences in every major program that teach students to use the analytic approaches of their field in dealing with complex problems and issues
- A commitment to "connected" learning that fosters:
  Integrative learning within the major
  Integration between the major and general education
  Integration between the major and the student's commitments beyond the academy
- The development of critical perspectives on the approaches of one's field, including opportunities to consider issues through multiple disciplinary lenses, with attention to the limitations of any one approach

These strong emphases on analysis, integration, and second-order critical reflection as core dimensions of a liberal arts major continued themes initially articulated in *Integrity in the College Curriculum*. What mattered, *Challenge* implied, was not how much information a student acquired but whether the student was able to use knowledge in making arguments and apply knowledge to a range of contexts and issues.

Especially important, *Challenge* contended, was the major's cultivation of critical perspectives on one's field. "Part of the articulated purpose of the major . . . is to prepare a student to be sufficiently confident in the discourse of a community to subject the major to sophisticated questions and to compare and connect its proposals with the proposals of other communities. Students must encounter the limitations of their temporary home and explore the possibilities beyond" (1991, p. 12).

This argument for critical reflection on the approaches of the field is the one theme in *Challenge* that moves substantially beyond the directions adopted by the learned societies. In practice, as we will see later in this chapter, it is the theme that proved most difficult for departments to grasp and use in contemporary efforts to reconceive college majors.

Organized Restructuring of the Major

In the third phase of its work on the major, AAC&U invited colleges and universities throughout the United States to work within this recommended framework in revising the educational purposes and structures for their majors. This phase began with a series of national conferences sponsored by AAC&U in 1991 and 1992, which disseminated recommendations for re-forming majors and provided workshops and planning time for campus teams. AAC&U also published a handbook for program review that incorporates the principles articulated in *The Challenge of Connecting Learning*, turning them into a set of questions that faculty members can use in periodic cycles of program review. This handbook, *Program Review and Educational Quality in the Major* (Association of American Colleges, 1992), provides a design for program review that centers on the connections between faculty goals for student learning and students' actual experience of the curriculum in the major.

With grant support from the U.S. Department of Education Fund for the Improvement of Postsecondary Education, eight competitively selected colleges and universities undertook broad-based efforts to change their majors. The College of Charleston; Dickinson College; Iona College; Jacksonville University; Manhattan College; Rowan College of New Jersey; the University of Arkansas, Little Rock; and Western Michigan University joined together in this AAC&U-led collaborative project. Under the direction of leadership groups established on each campus, these eight schools worked systematically to clarify educational goals, develop purposeful structures for the beginning, middle, and end of the major, and introduce various forms of integrative and hands-on learning.

Altogether, sixty-three departments took part in this effort, which lasted from 1992 through the end of 1994. Many of the departments involved are unofficially still involved in educational change efforts: some are implementing changes proposed through the project, and most are fine-tuning specific changes introduced as part of the re-forming effort.

Agenda for the Liberal Arts Major

What is the conception of the undergraduate major that emerges from this decade of work? AAC&U's "re-forming majors" initiative takes as its point of departure a conception of a robust learning community. Optimally, its recommendations propose, a major should offer students a community-centered experience of focus, grounding, and intellectual growth. A well-structured major can provide students with a locus within the larger academy, connect students with mentors who know them personally and feel accountable to guide them intellectually, and involve students in learning that links them to communities of practice as well as knowledge communities.

Notwithstanding the fears of critics that disciplinary majors are intrinsically and artificially narrow, there is no inherent reason why undergraduate learning in such a community-grounded major must be overspecialized. Majors can be communities that, as a matter of good practice, encourage integrative learning, not just within the field but between the field and other fields of inquiry. Undergraduate concentrations can be structured, for example, to encourage or even require that students engage a range of disciplinary perspectives in advanced seminars with faculty and peers. Departments might, although currently most do not, ask students to develop an interdisciplinary concentration within the major or to connect their particular interests to broader contemporary themes. Graff, a member of the National Advisory Committee that drafted *The Challenge of Connecting Learning*, has urged in a series of forceful articles and opinion pieces that fields should teach their internal disputes so that students can understand the societal implications and consequences of different claims and positions. The major, in short, can be restructured as a locus for integrative learning, a center through which students bring different parts of their intellectual explorations together, in personally and societally meaningful syntheses.

Influenced by an argument developed in the National Women's Studies Association report on the major, *The Challenge of Connecting Learning* proposes in effect that the major should be restructured as a matrix rather than a silo. So conceived, majors assume a dual obligation: to ground students in a particular set of dialogues and then to teach them how to connect those dialogues to the perspectives of other communities in the academy and in the larger society.

Once a major is defined as integrative or even interdisciplinary learning, it must be asked whether there is still a need for students' intellectual grounding in a particular field of inquiry? Why not move, as critics of traditional majors propose, directly to interdisciplinary learning? One answer is that integrative or interdisciplinary learning is an advanced, not an introductory intellectual competence. Before students can be asked to make connections, they must develop a knowledge base sufficient to support the integration.

Students of cognition have long contended that there is no such thing as critical thinking in general, only critical thinking about some defined set of questions in particular. In the same way, these proposals for the major suggest that there is no such thing as integrative, contextualized learning in general. As noted in Chapter Eight and elsewhere, *learning* is not so much a process of recording information as of interpreting it. In complex forms of learning, interpretation invariably involves connecting new content with constructs, concepts, and data the learner has previously internalized. Faculty members cannot impart these kinds of connections directly to students; they can only create the conditions in which the student's own work of interconnection becomes possible.

To engage in fruitful integrative learning, the student must develop a knowledge base about a topic that, to be usable in analysis, argumentation, and eventual integration, needs to be complex, well-structured, and accessible from multiple points of entry. The student must also develop procedural knowledge about how to frame and support an argument that will be persuasive within a particular context or knowledge community.

There is widespread emphasis in higher education on teaching students critical thinking or what many faculty members describe as logical thinking, problem solving, or higher-order reasoning. But it is misleading and even educationally self-defeating to imply that these terms refer to a general set of intellectual skills sufficient to undergird analysis and argument across very disparate fields. In the contemporary world, making persuasive arguments requires field-specific procedural or analytical knowledge as well as content knowledge and general skills (Glaser, 1984; Perkins and Salomon, 1989; Voss, Greene, Post, and Penner, 1983).

The procedures one learns to make an economic argument or solve an economic problem are very different from the rules internalized to make a psychological interpretation. Both sets of procedures will prove sorely out of context in a philosophical or literary forum. Beyond the campus boundaries, argumentation marshaled to support a scholarly analysis is likely to prove inadequate or even counterproductive in a political or organizational context. As the context changes, both the substance and the form of an argument must change with it. This is the basic insight of writing-across-the-curriculum projects: not just that writing must be taught in multiple courses, but that because writing employs different procedural rules and draws on different constitutive assumptions in different communities, the fields must themselves teach students the requisite analytical and rhetorical vocabulary (Russell, 1991). Many of the learned society reports on the major make a similar point. Learning in a field requires the student to adopt ways of thinking particular to that field. But these procedural skills are not easily developed. The research reported in *Women's Ways of Knowing*, for example, describes the difficulty with which women students surrender their previous forms of thinking to adopt the analytical approaches of their chosen fields (Belenky, Clinchy, Goldberger, and Tarule, 1986, pp. 86–124).

Seen in this light, the well-structured departmental major becomes the primary community in which students learn field-specific arts of critical inquiry, analysis, and persuasion. If appropriately organized, the major should teach students to frame questions, test hypotheses, and develop trained intuitions about arguments that hold weight and those that do not. Crucially, the student develops these capacities in the context of a working community that is charged to provide mentoring collegial assistance and feedback. Practicing new approaches within a community of peers and advisers, students can reap the benefit of colleagues who take their work seriously enough to raise real questions about it.

The field-specific major thus provides a context for the student's first apprenticeship in disciplined study. As *Challenge* proposed, the departmental major offers a home in which "faculty members . . . provide structures and languages that enhance and challenge students' capacities to frame issues, to test hypotheses and arguments against evidence, and to address disputed claims" (Association of American Colleges, 1991, p. 5).

This kind of procedural learning is, however, a means and not an end for liberal learning. It is important but not sufficient. As *Challenge* argues, the major must then assume the additional responsibility of teaching a student to connect the arguments of this home community with those of other communities. "To fulfill its role in liberal learning, the major also must structure conversations with the other cultures represented in the academy, conversations that more nearly reflect the diversities throughout our world and require patient labors of translation. Ultimately, the goal of the major should be the development of students' capacities for making connections and for generating their own translations and synthesis" (Association of American Colleges, 1991, p. 5).

Moreover, the major has a responsibility to foster critical perspectives on the approaches and assumptions of the field. *Challenge* develops this point as an extension of the metaphor of the major as a home for liberal learning. The major is but a temporary home and students must encounter its limitations if they are to be able to explore the possibilities beyond. "Any proposal from any community as to 'what is the case' is necessarily partial and bounded; any proposal is necessarily simpler than the complexity it attempts to describe and explain. This is the way that disciplines generate knowledge; it is the source of its cognitive power. But it is also a central reason that students and faculty members must work within settings characterized by an ethos of communication and contestation that ensures that no proposal stands without alternatives or arrogates to itself the claim of possessing the sole truth" (Association of American Colleges, 1991, p. 12).

In the conception of liberal learning developed in *Challenge,* it is these integrative and critical dimensions that establish a course of study as one of the liberal arts, with liberal understood to mean *boundary-expanding.* The major that simply imparts its own working concepts, procedures, and worldview, whether the subject matter be marketing strategy or literary analysis, is only providing training.

There is nothing wrong with training; learning how to do things skillfully is a necessary foundation for agency and effectiveness. Liberal learning, however, implies something more. As *Integrity* argued, "Any subject, if presented liberally, will take students into a world beyond themselves, make them again and again outsiders, so that they may return and know themselves better" (Association of American Colleges, 1985, p. 22).

The challenge to make students "again and again outsiders" implies a responsibility to organize study so that students step outside the original field of training, both to raise critical questions and to explore connections, implications, and translations beyond the boundaries of the field.

This conception of liberal learning echoes Bell's argument that the curriculum should be like an hourglass in its design: starting with broad explorations, then focusing on particular topics, and finally expanding to locate the particular topics in a broader context (Bell, 1966). The AAC&U proposals are also compatible with Boyer's argument (1987) for an "extended major." Focusing on the increasing popularity of preprofessional rather than liberal arts majors, Boyer contended that every major, whatever its subject matter, should introduce students to broader questions, both historical and normative, that require the learner to place specific interests in a broader context.

As Boyer's arguments imply, the recommendation that majors push students to place their learning in broader perspectives provides a point of potential connection between arts and sciences majors and preprofessional majors. Conventionally, arts and sciences scholars have assumed that professional majors would be improved by the addition of liberal arts perspectives but have seen little need for their own fields to seek critical engagement with alternative perspectives. Once critical perspective and connected learning are accepted as hallmarks of liberal education, however, then every field assumes a responsibility to contextualize and critique its own assumptions. From the economics department to the business program, from literary studies to teacher preparation, no field stands exempt from the requirement to help students with the challenge of connecting learning and reflective judgment across disparate communities of inquiry and practice (King and Kitchener, 1994).

Implications for Practice

What are the practical implications of these proposals for structuring majors? The approach promoted here presses departments toward new forms of intentionality. In some fields and departments, the practical implication is to move away from the state of affairs in which students take courses in no particular order toward no clearly stated goal.

For most departments, however, the practical task that follows from this work is complementing departments' existing intentionality about content and covering the main content areas of a field with a new intentionality about helping students learn first to use the field, then to gain critical perspective on it, and finally to connect the field's approaches with those of other communities.

The key shift here is away from an approach that organizes study in the major primarily as an orientation to the primary subfields of a discipline and toward an emphasis on analytic and reflective practices. As the psychology task force on the major noted: the objective is to *do* work in the field, not simply encounter it.

A second basic shift is away from the conventional notion that each course offered in a department is in some sense the intellectual property of the faculty member offering it. When a department sets clear goals, each of the faculty members and each of the department's courses assumes some measure of shared responsibility for helping students meet the goals. Minimally, faculty members need to develop:

- Departmental clarity about the intellectual capacities, the ways of thinking and reasoning, and the core conceptual knowledge to be developed through the major
- A core course or course sequence that introduces these approaches in a purposeful way to student majors, recognizing that each field has multiple methods, not one alone
- Provision in middle-level courses for practicing and developing at least some of the intellectual skills and modes of expression introduced in the introductory courses in connection with the student's particular interests
- Culminating projects or studies that foster and demonstrate a reasonable level of sophistication in using the field's approaches to solve problems and in connecting these approaches with alternative possibilities and perspectives
- Involvement throughout the course of study with a community of peers and mentors who provide feedback on each student's work and alternative ways of addressing comparable issues

Figure 11.1 illustrates re-forms undertaken in the mathematics department at Jacksonville University, showing what an energetic department can do when it sets out to provide both intellectual community and developmental support for its students. The figure also illustrates one field's translation of this very general model to its own issues and concerns, including, in this case, a concern for incorporating technology as a learning tool within a program.

Departments that make this shift toward emphasizing active and analytical learning still need, of course, to concern themselves with the organization of content. In AAC&U's re-forming majors project, several departments found ways to link a new intentionality about the intellectual tasks basic to the field with considerable flexibility about student choices in course taking within the major.

The central innovation devised in these departments was a specific delineation of intellectual tasks that students ought to practice during their course of study. These tasks were then sorted by level and assigned to different levels of course categories within the major. Tables 11.1 and 11.2 show how this was done in the history department at Rowan College and in the anthropology department at the University of Arkansas, Little Rock.

The history department at Dickinson College has developed a variant on these approaches. In this curriculum, students are introduced to historical method with a seminar taken early in the major, but after the student has had at least one content course in history. Subsequently, students take a research tutorial linked to one of their midlevel content courses. The tutorial, a small-group experience, guides the student in the practice of doing historical analysis. Every student then takes an advanced *capstone* seminar that further cultivates and demonstrates the ability to do historical research.

FIGURE 11.1. JACKSONVILLE UNIVERSITY: SUMMARY OF RE-FORMS IN MATHEMATICS.

- Revision and clarification of departmental goals and objectives
- Review of objectives of individual courses for coherence and consistency with program goals
- Addition of capstone course in problem solving as an integrative experience
- Revision of program assessment:

  Field testing of senior exit examination

  Use of capstone course as tool for program assessment

- Increased emphasis on involving students in the department:

  Revitalization of the student mathematics society

  Consultation with student groups on curriculum revision, pedagogy, and departmental activities

  Participation in the Mathematical Contest in Modeling

  Presentation of student papers at national and state conferences

  Refurbishing of student lounge

- Renewal of emphasis on undergraduate research, including:

  Early identification of talented students

  Provision of research opportunities both on and off campus

- Incorporation of graphing calculators in precalculus
- Implementation of a computer algebra system in calculus and scheduling of all calculus classes in a computer classroom
- Increased use of collaborative learning and group projects in calculus and other courses and the development of lab manuals for calculus sequences
- Piloting of experimental course combining freshman-level physics and calculus
- Revision of midlevel offerings to emphasize problem solving and to introduce students to advanced technology specific to the discipline
- Change of calculus sequence from four three-semester-hour courses to three four-semester-hour courses
- Offering of an interdisciplinary course, "The Infinite," team-taught by faculty from mathematics and philosophy
- Establishment of internships, especially with the Mayo Clinic
- Agreement to join a pilot program for a new introductory course in mathematics developed by the Consortium for Mathematics and its Applications (COMAP)

Source: Association of American Colleges and Universities, 1995, p. 20.

TABLE 11.1. ROWAN COLLEGE OF NEW JERSEY DEPARTMENT OF HISTORY (MAJOR REQUIREMENT—36 CREDIT HOURS).

Course Sequence	Portfolio Requirements
100 Level World History U.S. History to 1865 Western Civilization to 1660	Historical Essay Documentary Analysis (Essay requiring citation of primary source materials) Abstract of one document or article
200 Level U.S. History since 1865 or Western Civilization Since 1660 or a 200-Level Elective Global Field Survey-Level Course Historical Methods and Materials	Documentary analysis using multiple genres of source materials Numerical Analysis (Assessment of data, charts, and tables) Graphic Analysis (Assessment of artifacts, maps, and blueprints)
300 Level Proseminar Global Field Upper-Level Course Free Elective	Historical Abstract of a Journal Article Research Proposal Library Research Exercises Bibliographic Essays Scholarly Book Review Peer Evaluation
400 Level Free Elective Free Elective Capstone Seminar	Historical Fiction Periodic Literature Review Video Research paper in field related to history Capstone Seminar Paper

All students are required to maintain a history portfolio. Each portfolio will include seven items in order to graduate with a B.A. in history: three from the 100–200 level, three from the 300–400 level, and the required senior seminar paper.

Source: Association of American Colleges and Universities, 1995, p. 10.

TABLE 11.2. UNIVERSITY OF ARKANSAS, LITTLE ROCK: ANTHROPOLOGY DEPARTMENT SKILLS DEVELOPMENT OVERVIEW.

Courses	Skills Development
Lower-Level **Introduction to Anthropology** **Cultural Anthropology** **Physical Anthropology**	1. state a problem and ask a question 2. formulate a research question 3. write, or, more specifically, articulate and organize thoughts and abstract ideas 4. engage in informal oral presentations 5. identify current problems in newspapers, magazines, books, and other sources that might have anthropological solutions 6. critique articles through answering guided questions 7. understand some basic notions in science: hypothesis, theory, testing hypotheses, generating hypotheses
Upper-Level **Anthropological Theory** **Archaeology** **Linguistic Anthropology** Statistics Ethnographic Methods Electives **Capstone Course**	1. conduct a literature search (and use AA/AE style) 2. write an annotated bibliography 3. critique anthropological works 4. interview 5. conduct participant observation in settings to which they are strangers 6. conduct library research including formulation of a question and presentation of current knowledge on a topic 7. using research methods of physical, cultural, archaeological, or linguistic anthropology to (1) formulate and justify a research question; (2) collect, examine, and analyze data; (3) articulate conclusions in both written and oral forms

1. Student must take thirty-two credit hours. The four fields, theory, and capstone courses will be required. Statistics and Ethnographic Methods will be strongly recommended.
2. Courses in **bold** are required courses.
3. Evidence of the skills listed for upper-level courses are portfolio requirements, but we encourage students to include all their work.

Source: Association of American Colleges and Universities, 1995, p. 13.

The approach taken by the history department at Dickinson also suggests ways that students can be encouraged to develop their own thematic interests within the broad framework of departmental emphasis on historical inquiry and analysis. Each student is further expected to develop a concentration of his or her own design and choosing. Students select four courses connected either by region or by theme as their concentration; one of these courses can come from another discipline. The department thus creates a core curriculum around doing history while guiding each student in the development of a meaningful and coherent thematic emphasis within the field.

This shift toward a focus on intellectual tasks provides a road map for both faculty members and students. It guides faculty members in planning course assignments that help students learn to use the approaches of their field in ways consistent with the shared goals of the department. It further makes visible to students the department's expectations not only about what they should know but also about what they are expected to be able to do.

General Education

As the examples presented suggest, many of the sixty-three departments that worked on the re-forming majors effort made significant changes in their programs. A full report on the curricular changes implemented through this project was published by AAC&U in 1995 under the title *Changing the Major*. A subsequent report will be published in 1996 as *Re-Forming the Major: Lessons from the Fields*. New models for fostering learning community, collaborative learning, project-based and applied learning, and integrative studies were developed throughout the project. In the most interesting and promising examples, the changes made wove together a developmental program designed to teach students the intellectual practices of the field with a reaffirmation of the content emphases equally important to the field. The emphasis on analysis did not displace content—rather, it provided a new focus on teaching students to use content in more intentional and purposeful ways.

Strikingly, however, the departments that worked in this initiative did much less with AAC&U's call for the development of critical perspectives on the field and for critical discourse across fields. One especially candid dean's report summarizes what a group of faculty members said informally about this recommendation:

> Similarly, the AAC guidelines advocate introducing students to a critical perspective on the major. We did attempt some discussions of this [in the campus steering committee] but to the extent that we could even agree on what it meant—which was not great—the discussions typically came to a quick halt when some asserted that they did not want their majors to have more understanding of the discipline's disputes but believed they should fully grasp one approach before encountering any others. This . . . I believe is rooted in a conviction that we are training practitioners rather than citizens, and it is very hard to break into that. [Association of American Colleges and Universities, forthcoming]

A number of departments did develop courses designed to expand student horizons, for example, an interdisciplinary course on infinity developed by the mathematics and philosophy departments at Jacksonville University or a seminar on science, technology, and society developed at Iona College as a requirement for all science majors. But in general, providing critical or multidisciplinary perspectives on the approaches of particular fields did not become a major theme in work undertaken within the AAC&U framework on the major, despite the prominence of this theme in the guidelines provided to the campuses.

There is good reason to believe that asking students to step outside the ways of thinking they are adopting through a major is an essential dimension of higher learning, not something to be chosen or set aside. In a world of multiple perspectives, knowledgeably engaging more than one of them is surely an important purpose for undergraduate education. It may be, in fact, the university's capacity to cultivate critical reflection—and its offshoot, reflective judgment—that most firmly establishes higher education as education, and not simply training.

But it may also be that this never was a goal appropriately assigned to departments. If we compare the *Reports from the Fields* with the *Challenge of Connecting Learning*, it is clear that it was AAC&U representing the curriculum as a whole—rather than the learned societies representing their individual subjects—that was most interested in fostering critical perspectives on and dialogues across disciplines. And in the context of the curriculum as a whole, it may well be that it is general education, rather than the departments, that should assume responsibility for joining departmental communities in larger, intercommunity dialogues. If the capacity for generalizing emerges out of more specialized studies, it makes sense that the unit responsible for general or generalizing education should take the primary responsibility for eliciting those connections. Creating a curricular architecture that nurtures these generative connections in the context of advanced studies may well emerge as an agenda that seeks to purposefully connect student learning in both general education and the major.

References

Association of American Colleges. *Integrity in the College Curriculum: A Report to the Academic Community.* Washington, D.C.: Association of American Colleges, 1985.

Association of American Colleges. Unpublished internal project evaluations. Washington, D.C.: Association of American Colleges, 1989.

Association of American Colleges. *Liberal Learning and the Arts and Sciences Major.* Vol. 1: *The Challenge of Connecting Learning.* Vol. 2: *Reports from the Fields.* Vol. 3: *Program Review and Educational Quality in the Major.* Washington, D.C.: Association of American Colleges, 1990, 1991, 1992.

Association of American Colleges. Unpublished report. Washington, D.C.: Association of American Colleges, 1993.

Association of American Colleges and Universities. *Changing the Major.* Washington, D.C.: Association of American Colleges and Universities, 1995.

Association of American Colleges and Universities. *Re-Forming the Major: Lessons from the Fields.* Washington, D.C.: Association of American Colleges and Universities, forthcoming.

Astin, A. W. *What Matters in College? Four Critical Years Revisited.* San Francisco: Jossey-Bass, 1992.

Belenky, M. F., Clinchy, B. M., Goldberger, N. R., and Tarule, J. M. *Women's Ways of Knowing: The Development of Self, Voice, and Mind.* New York: Basic Books, 1986.

Bell, D. *The Reforming of General Education: The Columbia College Experience in its National Setting.* New York: Columbia University Press, 1966.

Botstein, L. "Structuring Specialization as a Form of General Education." *Liberal Education,* 1991, *77*(2), 10–19.

Boyer, E. L. *College: The Undergraduate Experience in America.* New York: HarperCollins, 1987.

Carnegie Foundation for the Advancement of Teaching. *Missions of the College Curriculum: A Contemporary Review with Suggestions.* San Francisco: Jossey-Bass, 1977.

Geertz, C. *Local Knowledge: Further Essays in Interpretive Anthropology.* New York: Basic Books, 1983.

Glaser, R. "Education and Thinking: The Role of Knowledge." *Educational Psychologist,* 1984, *39,* 93–104.

Graff, G. *Professing Literature.* Chicago: University of Chicago Press, 1987.

Green, W. S. "The Disciplines of Liberal Learning." In C. G. Schneider, and W. S. Green (eds.), *Strengthening the College Major.* New Directions for Higher Education, no. 84. San Francisco: Jossey-Bass, 1993.

Harvard University Educational Policy Committee. "On Enhancing the Undergraduate Concentration." Unpublished reports. Cambridge, Mass.: Harvard University, 1993 and 1995.

Holmes Group Executive Board. *Tomorrow's Teachers: A Report of the Holmes Group.* East Lansing, Mich.: Holmes Group, 1986.

Kimball, B. *A History of the Idea of Liberal Education.* New York: Teachers College Press, 1986.

King, P. M., and Kitchener, K. S. *Developing Reflective Judgment: Understanding and Promoting Intellectual Growth and Critical Thinking in Adolescents and Adults.* San Francisco: Jossey-Bass, 1994.

Levine, A. *Handbook on Undergraduate Curriculum.* San Francisco: Jossey-Bass, 1978.

Light, R. *The Harvard Assessment Seminars: Explorations with Students and Faculty About Teaching, Learning, and Student Life. Second Report.* Cambridge, Mass.: Harvard University, 1992.

Oakley, F. *Community of Learning: The American College and the Liberal Arts Tradition.* New York: Oxford University Press, 1992.

Perkins, D. N., and Salomon, G. "Are Cognitive Skills Context-Bound?" *Educational Researcher,* 1989, *18*(1), 16–25.

Rudolph, F. *Curriculum: A History of the American Undergraduate Course of Study Since 1636.* San Francisco: Jossey-Bass, 1977.

Russell, D. R. *Writing in the Academic Disciplines, 1870–1990: A Curricular History.* Carbondale: Southern Illinois University Press, 1991.

Schneider, C. G., "Enculturation or Critical Engagement?" In C. G. Schneider and W. S. Green (eds.), *Strengthening the College Major.* New Directions for Higher Education, no. 84. San Francisco: Jossey-Bass, 1993.

Stark, J. S., and Latucca, L. R. "Diversity Among Disciplines: The Same Goals for All?" In C. G. Schneider and W. S. Green (eds.), *Strengthening the College Major.* New Directions for Higher Education, no. 84. San Francisco: Jossey-Bass, 1993.

Treisman, U. "Studying Students Studying Calculus: A Look at the Lives of Minority Mathematics Students in College." *College Mathematics Journal,* 1992, *23*(5), 362–372.

Voss, J. F., Greene, T. R., Post, T. A., and Penner, B. C. "Problem Solving Skills in the Social Sciences." In *The Psychology of Learning and Motivation: Advances in Research and Theory.* Vol. 17. New York: Academic Press, 1983.

Winter, D. G., McClelland, D.C., and Stewart, A. J. *A New Case for the Liberal Arts.* San Francisco: Jossey-Bass, 1981.

Zemsky, R. *Structure and Coherence: Measuring the Undergraduate Curriculum.* Washington, D.C.: Association of American Colleges, 1989.

CHAPTER TWELVE

THE HUMANITIES

Lyn Maxwell White

The humanities became highly visible in the 1980s as many colleges and universities were urged to address problems in general education by moving from broad distribution requirements toward various forms of common or core curricula (Bennett, 1984; Cheney, 1989; Zemsky, 1989). The content and the methods of the humanities were central to programs organized around topics or periods in Western or world civilization or based on themes such as "the individual and the community." This renewed attention to the humanities, coupled with efforts to reach agreement on the goals and subject matter for required courses, drew widespread attention to intellectual and political controversies in humanities research and teaching.

So-called culture wars erupted in books and essays and in the public media as conservative academics and public figures claimed that radical professors were using the classroom to indoctrinate students in politically correct ideas, and members of what came to be called the cultural left responded by challenging the conservatives to acknowledge the political nature of their own cultural agendas. Pressure for radical restructuring of institutions and for political use of the classroom came from both the left and the right. By the early 1990s, a number of monographs appeared in which commentators criticized extreme positions on both right and left, proposing ways to approach the teaching of the humanities that would permit exploration of conflicting issues within the curriculum as well as collaborative efforts toward common goals.

The intellectual and political concerns that converged in the undergraduate curriculum reflected circumstances in the public sphere as well as inside the academy. As Chapters Six and Nine have described in detail, demographic shifts in the country and in education since the late 1960s had brought new perspectives—especially those of women and people of color—into the college classroom. In addition, scholarship spurred by the methods and subjects of social history and by theories derived from European philosophy offered new interpretations of the external world, individual identity, and the nature and meaning of texts. The most controversial intellectual issue had to do with commonality and difference and the tension between essential human values and values constructed within different cultural and historical contexts. While many faculty and K–12 teachers saw the curriculum as enriched by the particularity and differences of multicultural texts and perspectives, other academics and public figures argued that inclusion of these voices threatened commonly held values and displaced canonical perspectives.

These educational issues emerged as the United States responded to significant international changes including the fall of the Soviet Union, the emergence of a new world economy, and the overwhelming impact of advances in communication and information technologies. Within the country a conservative political movement had begun to oppose many legacies of the progressive era, including prevailing approaches to education. Although the debates that reached the public media tended to have political rather than intellectual agendas, they served to underline the importance of the way history, language, and culture should be taught in a changing society. Faculty and administrators in higher education who make decisions about humanities curricula began to do so with the awareness of external scrutiny as well as of sharply conflicting views on campus. This climate of intellectual and political ferment offers opportunities for creative syntheses and new modes of collaboration, but it also holds serious dangers of greater divisiveness and disintegration.

Many of the attacks on the academy in the late 1980s were launched in sound bites or in polemical language that gave little evidence of the humanities' capacity to provide insight and promote balanced judgments. Disciplines of the humanities such as philosophy, history, and literary studies offer models and methods for addressing dilemmas and acknowledging ambiguity and paradox. They can help us face the tension between the concerns of individuals and those of groups and promote civil and informed discussion of conflicts, placing current issues in historical perspective. They also give voice to feeling and artistic shape to experience, balancing passion and rationality and exploring issues of morality and value. The study of the humanities provides a venue in which the expression of differing interpretations and experiences can be recognized and areas of common interest explored.

Despite intellectual and political polarization in the last decade, humanities faculty in many colleges and universities have collaborated effectively in the on-going task of revitalizing humanities programs through newly designed courses and joint faculty study projects, sometimes in conjunction with similar efforts in the sciences and social sciences. Some institutions have developed course clusters or interdisciplinary course sequences based on Western or world cultures. New program models have been developed to improve the teaching and learning of foreign languages and cultures as well as to strengthen and broaden the study of American topics. Increasing numbers of humanities faculty members and administrators are engaged in the design of effective ways to employ the new electronic technologies for teaching as well as for better access to knowledge. Many colleges and universities are collaborating with other sectors, including two-year colleges, high schools, and cultural institutions such as museums. Some are extending the work of the humanities beyond the classroom by involving the public in campus programs and encouraging students to participate in internships or voluntary experience in the community.

What Are the Humanities?

The *humanities* are modes of examining and understanding human experience, human aspirations and achievements, and human expressions such as written texts, artifacts, and cultural practices. They permit us to look at the relationship of individuals to groups and of groups to each other over time, addressing questions of power and authority and of justice and equity. The humanities enable us to respond emotionally, imaginatively, and aesthetically to writers' expressions of inner conflicts, fears, hopes, and joys along with the details of their particular experiences and contexts.

The humanities also permit reflection on human relationships to the natural world and human beliefs about a supreme being or supernatural order in various eras and cultures. They provide tools for logical analysis and modes of discussing and debating moral and ethical questions. Recent developments in the study of the humanities enhance their ability to look at human beings as part of the natural world, to acknowledge differences as well as similarities, to compare cultures across time, to collaborate across disciplines, and to gain rapid access to information and expertise around the world.

Definitions of the humanities are always partial and provisional, and they vary over time with views of human nature and with the purposes of the speaker. The term itself is subject to a variety of misconceptions; three common ones are that the humanities are intended primarily to foster humanitarian activity, or that they are limited to appreciation of high culture, or that they promote a nontheistic religion called secular humanism. One reason for such confusion may be that the term is a generic one embracing areas of study that are more familiar to the public under disciplinary names such as history, philosophy, English literature, or foreign languages and literatures.

In discussing the humanities, one can focus on the specific disciplines included, on the content or the subject matter, and on the methods and purposes of humanistic study. The term is sometimes confused with the liberal arts and *liberal education*, but those terms encompass the sciences and social sciences along with the humanities. As curricula become increasingly connected and integrated, however, the lines between the humanities, the social sciences, and the sciences are harder to draw. Humanistic and scientific methods may both be used to examine subject matter in interdisciplinary core curricula and in fields such as environmental studies. Quantitative and empirical methods are often used by social historians to extend and reinforce humanistic understanding and interpretation. The clearest remaining distinction between the humanities and the sciences or social sciences is that the humanities neither employ experimental methods nor take replicability as a touchstone of validity.

Humanities Disciplines

The humanities are often simply defined by listing professional disciplines— typically those for which university departments and professional associations exist and for which budgets are allocated by institutions. The National Foundation on the Arts and the Humanities Act of 1965 follows this model with a few additions: "The term 'humanities' includes, but is not limited to, the study and interpretation of the following: language, both modern and classical; linguistics; literature; history; jurisprudence; philosophy; archeology; comparative religion; ethics; the history, criticism, and theory of the arts; those aspects of the social sciences that have humanistic content and employ humanistic methods" (Sec. 952–953).

Defining the humanities by listing disciplines is pragmatic and sidesteps a number of controversies, but it is not fully descriptive of the humanities as they are currently practiced in either research or the undergraduate curriculum. The organization of separate departments may vary from campus to campus, and there are associations and sometimes departments for interdisciplinary fields like American studies. In addition, the work that goes on within the traditional departments often draws on the methods and subjects of other disciplines. Scholarship in English, for example, now incorporates approaches from fields such as history, philosophy, and anthropology, while scholars in historical studies may borrow narrative and interpretative strategies from literature and quantitative methods from sociology. In many institutions, core humanities courses are extradepartmental, involving faculty and approaches from several disciplines and examining texts, topics, and materials that could be taught in a variety of liberal arts departments.

The distinction between "those aspects of the social sciences that have humanistic methods" and those that do not is increasingly difficult to make. The humanities and the social sciences now share a wider range of methods, and the humanities are increasingly likely to be engaged in reflection on contemporary life and social or political concerns that were considered the province of the social sciences twenty-five years ago. Subsequent amendments to the National Endowment for the Humanities' (NEH's) 1965 legislation have extended the definition of humanities and enabling legislation to include "the study and application of the humanities to the human environment with particular attention to reflecting our diverse heritage, traditions, and history, and to the relevance of the humanities to the current conditions of national life." An assumption of objectivity and detachment that had accompanied the establishment of the individual humanities disciplines has increasingly given way to an assumption of applicability and involvement.

Humanities Content

The content or subject focus of the humanities is typically what draws students to them and evokes the passion that can lead to a major or concentration or even to graduate study and a professional career in research and teaching. Students may fall in love with literature, with their own history and culture, or with foreign languages and the experience of different cultures. They may want to think more deeply about meaning and value, to understand human experience in an integrated and informed way, or to participate in addressing local, national, and global problems from a humanistic rather than a purely pragmatic or technological perspective.

While the subjects of study matter a great deal in the humanities, they are so broad as to defy description. The disciplines of the humanities may be brought to bear on all aspects of human experience, including human responses to that which is not human. It is therefore easier to talk of disciplines and of methods and purposes than to speak of content covered or subjects studied. Methodology and disciplines are also safer because the discussion of content treads on areas to which faculty are often still passionately committed. Even after they have acquired all the tools of a discipline and moved beyond emotional or aesthetic responses to deeper intellectual analyses and comparisons of the subjects, humanities researchers may still argue vehemently for coverage or for their view of the canon.

Participation in general education reform usually means that faculty with very different intellectual, political, and emotional commitments to subject matter as well as different disciplinary training must agree on at least some selections of themes and texts for common courses. In this context, the discussion of content can be divisive—any selections necessarily exclude other possibilities. Recent discussions of content in the undergraduate curriculum range from ways to represent or include everyone's diverse groups to arguments for an exclusive focus on Western or even Afrocentric traditions.

Originally the humanities did have a specific, limited body of content. In *Education's Great Amnesia,* Proctor (1988) points out that the term *humanities* was first used in this country in the eighteenth century to refer to the Greek and Roman classics. The *studia humanitatis* had begun in fifteenth-century Italy as "a cultural revolution calling for the study of classical Latin, and of Roman and Greek literature, history and moral philosophy as models for building an inner life" (p. xiv), and they remained the dominant focus of education in Europe and America until the late nineteenth century. Proctor suggests that the difficulty we have in defining and discussing the term humanities results from the fact that the original content no longer serves our needs and we have not yet found a new unifying focus.

In retrospect, we can see that the first volley of the culture wars took place in 1984 with the publication of Bennett's *To Reclaim a Legacy: A Report on the Humanities in Higher Education.* Bennett proposed that American education reclaim and place at the core of undergraduate education a body of content and standards of excellence from the Western tradition. Borrowing from Matthew Arnold, Bennett proposed a content-based definition of the humanities: "the best that has been said, thought, written and otherwise expressed about the human experience" (p. 17).

By the mid-1980s, many colleges and universities had begun to work toward a more inclusive content in humanities courses as well as toward comparative study of Western perspectives and those of other civilizations and cultures. Bennett's emphasis on works of the Western tradition challenged this movement toward multicultural content, which had been generated through new scholarship in the humanities. Bennett's suggestion that faculty reach consensus about the significance of readings to require of their students was applauded by some, but vehemently criticized by others who feared the exclusion of diverse voices and perspectives from the curriculum. Some institutions resolved this tension by offering programs based on paired canonical and noncanonical texts and by introducing the question of canon formation and changing tastes over time into course content.

Modes and Purposes of Humanities Study

U.S. education for most of this century has been based on progressive and pragmatic assumptions (following John Dewey) that every mind should be developed and that a liberally educated citizenry will contribute to the ongoing improvement of its institutions. In 1985, the Association of American Colleges and Universities published *Integrity in the College Curriculum: A Report to the Academic Community,* which proposed reform within this tradition. The report deemphasized specific content and offered a model for the baccalaureate degree that focused on a number of humanistic skills or experiences: inquiry, abstract logical thinking and critical analysis; literacy (writing, reading, speaking); historical consciousness; values; international and multicultural experiences; and study-in-depth. In addition, it included science and understanding numerical data (pp. 15–26).

A number of recent commentators have also urged in different ways that the focus be placed on the purposes of humanistic study as a means of moving beyond conflict over specific content and cultural approaches (Stearns, 1993; Bromwich, 1992; Arthurs, 1993). Arthurs stresses public engagement and mediating purposes outside the academy, arguing that "humanist scholars have more power both on campus and off than they are comfortable claiming" (p. 267).

Humanistic modes of inquiry, analysis, and description have traditionally been understood to be qualitative and interpretive rather than quantitative and experimental, and the purpose of the humanities has been to offer a balanced perspective that steers clear of advocacy or social action. One of the most important issues that has emerged since the publication of *Integrity in the College Curriculum* is the extent to which engagement in the active world is encouraged through the humanities curriculum, perhaps reflecting the reality of career concerns of students as much as it does changes in the humanities. A problematic side to the issue of engagement with the public sphere is the possibility of political advocacy replacing balanced consideration of alternatives in the classroom.

Conflict in the Humanities Curriculum

The reports of both Bennett and the Association of American Colleges and Universities responded in different ways to reports issued in the late 1970s and early 1980s on educational problems in the country. Concerns about disaffection and lack of achievement in high schools and lack of direction in undergraduate programs were widely shared, but differences began to emerge over causes and solutions.

Serious conflict in the humanities first came to public attention with the publication of a series of popular books by conservative authors such as Allan Bloom,

Roger Kimball, and Dinesh D'Souza. Oakley (1992), who calls some of the authors "vituperative," provides a list of the books and a general analysis in his essay "Against Nostalgia: Reflections on our Present Discontents in American Higher Education." The key conservative accusation was that radical faculty were undermining traditional values and enforcing so-called political correctness or agreement with multicultural views in the classroom.

One group of academics met at the University of North Carolina, Chapel Hill, and Duke University in 1988 to discuss conditions and practices in the liberal arts, and to begin a public response to conservative critics and to the issue of canonical versus multicultural texts raised by Bennett and others. In her introduction to the resulting volume of essays, Smith claims that media exploitation has been a major problem in the educational controversies. She notes that thoughtful academic discussions do not lend themselves to sound bites, and mentions anecdotally that the term *cultural left* (used wryly by one of the participants) was picked up as a lasting label by journalists at this meeting. "The educational problems of the nation are extensive and complex. Demons are always easier to fashion than solutions. And someone is always ready to take advantage of a communal anxiety by producing a communal scapegoat" (Gless and Smith, 1992, p. 3).

On the subject of canonical works, Smith reports that across the country— "in Durham and Palo Alto as in Cambridge and Chapel Hill"—faculty still assign classic authors like Homer, Dante, Milton, and Shakespeare because they are unique. "They do not do everything uniquely, however, and there are some worthy things that they do not do at all—which is not only why canons keep expanding but also why writers keep writing" (Gless and Smith, 1992, pp. 6–7).

In this same volume of essays, Graff introduces his much-quoted concept of *teaching the conflicts*. He argues that the way to handle differences over high and popular culture or old and new texts is to structure both sides into the curriculum. In his view, the issues do not have to be resolved before we can teach them; the tensions are dynamic and appropriate. Graff argues that consensus never really existed in the past, or existed only through the exclusion of many voices (Gless and Smith, 1992, p. 58). While subsequent commentators may disagree with Graff's specific modes and examples, a number follow his lead in bringing the contested ideas and content into the forum provided by the humanities curriculum.

War-related metaphors have abounded in the titles of books and articles on the ongoing debate over ideas, culture, and politics, reflecting the language of many of the participants. Bromwich's *Politics by Other Means: Higher Education and Group Thinking* plays on Clausewitz's famous definition and justification for war, and Carnochan calls his thoughtful historical study of liberal education and the American experience *The Battleground of the Curriculum*. Carnochan traces the crisis mongering to statements by Allan Bloom, and urges some tempering of this kind of language. "Crises engender panic and call for heroic responses. Problems call for solutions or for accommodations" (Carnochan, 1993, p. 4).

The Scylla and Charybdis of the far right and the far left have both been criticized in a number of recent works that seek accommodation and collaboration. In a recent essay, Graff and Jay turn from their usual defense of the professoriate to warn radical academics against the kind of critical pedagogy that is oppositional or fails to leave questions open for exploration. They argue for a model of education in which ideological opponents not only coexist but cooperate: "If educational institutions hope to be true communities of intellectual inquiry, reforming them will require models that respect the ethical and political dimensions of community life. This means respecting those with the 'wrong' politics, and even accepting the risk that they may change us" (Graff and Jay, 1995, p. 209).

A model in which opposing thinkers cooperate, respect each other, and remain open to new ideas is not only appropriate in a democracy but probably the only workable solution if the society remains committed to respect for the individual. Paradoxically, discussions of collaboration are currently controversial because they may be associated variously with women's studies, liberal communitarian philosophy, and postmodern cultural theories that emphasize the role of cultural context and community over individual agency and identity.

Two political theorists offer sober critiques of the culture wars and focus hopes for resolution on democratic communities. Gutmann sees those she calls the *essentialists* and the *deconstructionists* as "two mutually exclusive and disrespecting intellectual cultures in academic life." She asserts that mutual respect would require the ability to articulate and defend our disagreements, and to be open to changing our minds, because "the moral promise of multiculturalism depends on the deliberative virtues" (in Taylor, 1992, pp. 21, 24). Characteristically invoking the ideas of both John Dewey and Walt Whitman, Barber asserts in *An Aristocracy of Everyone: The Politics of American Education and the Future of America* that "a canon that cannot be reinvented, reformulated, and thus reacquired by a learning community fails the test of truth as well as of pertinence" (Barber, 1992, p. 214). He identifies a number of ways of creating community within the academy and makes a case for community-based service learning, concluding that "without community neither the almighty canon nor the almighty dollar can do much to inspire learning or to promote democracy" (pp. 253–255).

Bromwich's *Politics by Other Means* presents a counterpoint to the emphasis on community, arguing instead that needed reforms can be achieved through the development of individual minds. Writing from the perspective of literature and from a deep commitment to the liberal individualism inherited from Enlightenment thought, he objects to the emphasis of the right as well as the left on the influence of institutions and culture on individual judgment. "I have in mind a way of thinking that associates personal reflection with social morality, and that sees both as modified by a tradition that can reform itself" (Bromwich, 1992, p. 133).

In their introduction to a 1995 volume of essays, *Higher Education Under Fire: Politics, Economics, and the Crisis of the Humanities,* Bérubé and Nelson turn attention to the economic realities of the academic market and offer recommendations that would, for example, limit the size of English graduate programs. They add to previous arguments for collaborative activity the argument that humanities faculty must become more knowledgeable about their universities and about the larger social context in which they work. "Then all of us will have to build relationships with relevant constituencies. For if, as concerned faculty, students, and citizens, we do not take our stand collectively and take our stand now, we will be left without a leg to stand on" (1995, pp. 21, 23–25).

Curricular Implications of Humanities Scholarship

The last thirty years have been heady and confusing ones in the disciplines of the humanities, offering new interpretations and new implications for knowledge and society, and raising questions about content, purpose, and pedagogy in the undergraduate curriculum. Humanities scholars are now asked to defend their perspectives within their disciplines, and to explain them to colleagues in other disciplines, to undergraduates, and to the public. The increasing impact of women and people of color in the scholarly professions and in the classroom is one, but only one, of the factors leading to the rethinking of accepted views and to the inclusion of new materials in humanities courses.

Some of the key cross-cutting influences in humanities scholarship are: the impact of continental philosophers on poststructuralist theories of language and meaning, and on ideas about the nature of texts, of authorship, of reading, and of power; the study of the experience of nonelites introduced by social historians as well as an interest in *mentalities* or rituals and cultural themes; questions initially raised by women's studies about power relationships, the perspectives of readers and writers, inclusiveness, and subjectivity and identity; and new ideas about the nature of culture, the influence of cultural context on individuals, and the role of race, class, and gender.

These topics are overwhelming in their complexity and they defy summarization. Some of the conclusions drawn by scholars are positive and exciting for the classroom; some can be extremely threatening and depressing. The issues addressed in the culture wars have primarily had to do with essential versus relative values and with the political consequences of various assumptions about cultural values and about power. Scholars go far beyond these issues, however, in rethinking the effects of two centuries of emphasis on rationalism and scientific positivism. Questions are raised about objective reality, about human nature, about the relationship of mind and body, and about the very possibility of communicating with each other. Scholars with different theoretical and political perspectives disagree hotly on many of these topics.

Chodorow provides an excellent short summary of what he calls "transformations" in the humanities in an essay focusing primarily on the controversy about objectivity in history and literature. He traces its origins to the arguments of anthropologist Clifford Geertz that the observer becomes a part of the data observed. The article examines the impact of new historicism in literature, and argues that history is in less flux than literature because historians continue to insist on causal relationships (Chodorow, 1994, pp. 28–31). Another good summary of current directions in humanities scholarship is offered by Katz in an essay that emphasizes the blurring of disciplinary boundaries, using the example of his own work in history and law to demonstrate the current tendency to work across disciplinary lines. He discusses the new inclusiveness of topics considered appropriate for study and the new critical approaches developed to read these topics (Gates, Katz, and Stimpson, 1993, pp. 8–9).

In thinking about the curricular implications of recent humanities scholarship, it is important to recall that this scholarship is in great flux. It seems likely, however, that the following will persist into the next millennium along with a fair amount of controversy: greater inclusiveness, both in the professoriate and in subjects of study; new modes of cross-disciplinary and collaborative research and teaching that may contribute to a more integrated understanding of the world; and more active engagement with the public sphere. It is also quite certain that the new uses of electronic technologies and the emphasis on international concerns will continue.

Humanities Courses: Credits and Curricula

The U.S. Department of Education recently issued a new map of college courses along with an extensive analysis of college transcript files from 1972 through 1993. The thirty-five courses claiming the largest percentage of total undergraduate credits are identified as an "empirical core curriculum" representing 37.7 percent of all credits generated. The author of this study notes that the discussions of the core curriculum in the 1980s were based on what students should study. He argues that these course credit data provide empirical evidence that a core does in fact exist (Adelman, 1995, p. 229).

In the nonhumanities areas, this list shows responsiveness to the labor market, indicates continuing interest in business, and records a reduction in introductory science courses such as general biology. Geology and geography have slipped from the list as have two humanities categories: Bible studies and German. Eleven humanities courses are included—with English composition, not surprisingly, at the top of the list, followed by Spanish, which ranks seventh. The eleven humanities course categories are listed below in the order of their credit share. The first five humanities courses listed rank within the top fifteen on the overall list (Adelman, 1995, pp. 230–232).

- English Composition
- Spanish: Introductory and Intermediate
- U.S. History surveys
- Western Civilization/World History
- U.S. Government
- French: Introductory and Intermediate
- Art History
- Introduction to Literature
- Introduction to Philosophy
- English Literature
- American Literature

This list of courses indicates that a significant share of undergraduate credits are earned in traditional humanities course categories. Adelman's extensive analysis of transcript files provides further information about the share of course credits logged by different types of institutions and about the increase or decrease of credits in topical humanities courses. Adelman notes, for instance, that enrollments in literature courses declined overall, but that courses on both Shakespeare and Afro-American literature held their own (1995, p. 171).

Since these data are based on course categories as listed in transcripts, they do not provide information on changes in the content or approaches of the courses or on the curricular relationships among courses. Ratcliff (1993) has conducted a series of studies using student transcripts and assessment scores in textual interpretation (reading comprehension) and analysis to identify salient sets of course sequences, including humanities coursework. Jones, Hoffman, Moore, and Nugent (1996) have identified humanities coursework at the Pennsylvania State University associated with gains in students' reading, writing, and critical thinking abilities. Much of the concern voiced about the core curriculum in the 1980s had to do with the connectedness of learning, with approaches to the humanities, and with the ways in which cultural traditions were reflected in the courses.

Projects funded by NEH's Higher Education in the Humanities Program over the decade 1985–1995 provide useful examples of the ways courses have changed in design, content, and approach in response to current scholarship and current debate over the civic purposes of humanities curricula. The project examples listed in this section have had some form of NEH support; the information is drawn from NEH grant files and project descriptions, and in one case it is augmented by information from the Fund for the Improvement of Postsecondary Education's *1995 Program Book*.

Several specific examples are offered because each is in a different way illustrative of trends in the humanities. Projects that are effectively charting new directions in humanities courses tend to merge good institutional leadership and direction setting, solid scholarship in the humanities, and a strong commitment to the purposes of undergraduate teaching. While not all examples have all these features, they are as a group:

- Collaborative across departments, institutions, and sectors
- Comparative in their approach to culture
- Designed around engaging pedagogies and uses of technology
- Inclusive of both new and traditional materials
- Selectively focused rather than aiming for coverage
- Successful in engaging faculty and students in new learning
- Related to institutional strengths, missions, and directions

Comparing Western and Asian Traditions

Eckerd College in St. Petersburg, Florida, is a relatively young liberal arts institution that strengthened its offerings on both Western heritage and East Asia through intensive faculty study of Western and Asian texts. All faculty now teach a required freshman course that compares Western and Asian texts and perspectives. Global perspectives courses focusing on such topics as Japanese family life and Asian fiction may be taken at the sophomore and junior levels. Further, a required capstone course focuses on moral and religious issues in the cultural heritage of the West and of East Asia. Eckerd has raised funds for an endowed chair in classics to strengthen the Western offerings and hopes to complete fundraising for an East Asian chair soon. The college has involved senior professionals from the community with Eckerd faculty on an East Asia Resources Committee that offers six programs a year, and Eckerd faculty have joined area high school teachers in collaborative activities that will strengthen course content on East Asia.

Foreign Language Learning and International Studies

Oregon State University in Corvallis, Oregon, offers a degree program that allows an undergraduate in any discipline to obtain a concurrent international degree composed of seven courses from the Western Culture, cultural diversity, and global perspectives categories of the core curriculum, competency in a foreign language, and a senior project that demonstrates the international dimensions of the major field of study. The project is intended to strengthen language learning at third- and fourth-year levels in Japanese, Russian, and Chinese using proficiency-based methods and new technologies. In addition, a Foreign Language Across the Curriculum (FLAC) project has been introduced in Spanish, so that advanced students can take courses in disciplines such as history and political science in the target language.

Bridging the Sciences and Humanities

Southwest Texas State University in San Marcos, Texas, has developed an interdisciplinary and intercultural regional studies curriculum that offers a minor. Faculty ranging from historians to physicists have participated in intensive summer seminars and course development activities as they put together a two-semester upper division course sequence (including a laboratory) focusing on the relationship of the region's geography and physical ecology to its history and on the interaction of Anglo, Chicano, and Indian cultures. The program draws on the public activities of the Center for the Study of the Southwest and on the resources of its Southwest Writers Collection. The course syllabi include primary materials through which students can consider the relationship of human beings to the natural environment, such as Cabeza de Vaca's *Adventures in the Unknown Interior of America*, the earliest work on the Southwest and the first overland travel book describing the Americas, and *Texas*, an early history by Mary Austin Holley. The Center is now involved in a project financed by the Fund for the Improvement of Postsecondary Education (FIPSE) to establish a consortium of regional studies centers across the country that will participate in faculty exchanges and integrate comparative elements into these programs.

The cultural focus of this regional program offers potential exploration of larger questions of national identity. According to the NEH grant proposal, "The harsh Southwestern landscape has historically led Southwesterners to glorify an American individualism long celebrated in our national documents; . . . Anglo-American settlers entered an unknown world and saw nature as a resource for their singular use. But many minority cultures question the emphasis placed on individuality instead of community. Their response to the hot, arid land of scorpions and rattlesnakes has been to band together in communal societies that were part of a larger natural world."

Bridging Humanities and Occupational Curricula

Genesee Community College in Batavia, New York, is characterized by strong programs in computer technology and the widespread use of interactive video and computer-assisted instruction. Twenty humanities and vocational faculty members participated in a four-week study program on the changes of technology over time and the effects of these changes on thought and culture. Topics included oral traditions, literacy, and culture in ancient Greece; transformations of technology and culture in the Middle Ages and the Renaissance; and consideration of the impact of the computer on written communication and contemporary society. The intention was not to develop new courses but to broaden course content and create connections through faculty development and interaction. This project was so successful on campus that it was then offered to fifteen faculty teams from other interested community colleges.

University–High School Collaboration for Teacher Preparation

Temple University in Philadelphia, Pennsylvania, carried out a two-year collaborative project to strengthen undergraduate world history courses at selected colleges and universities in the Philadelphia area in cooperation with the city school district. The objectives were to offer substantive undergraduate courses and to arrange effective practice teaching opportunities for future teachers. This program was built on a project funded by the Rockefeller Foundation in the late 1980s to allow professors and high school teachers to collaborate in the development of the world history course in the city's schools. The high school course emphasized global comprehension of world history along with an emphasis on how we know what we know, and included eight ten-week units with syllabi that were both chronological and thematic in design. Participants in the new project met regularly in working groups to examine broad themes such as urbanization and empire building and to produce annotated primary materials for use in the college classrooms as well as essays synthesizing information on the content and methodology of the course segments. This regional collaboration among historians was intended eventually to lead to national dissemination; it was featured in the November 1995 issue of *History Teacher*, published by the Society for History Education (Spodek, 1995).

Broadening an Existing World Literature Survey

Faculty in the English department at *Clark Atlanta University* in Atlanta, Georgia, resolved in 1987 to expand their two-semester survey of world literature beyond a focus on Western literature. Over time, they prepared themselves to teach more broadly by studying African American, African, Caribbean, Asian, Arabic, Latin American, and Native American literatures in summer workshops. They then developed common syllabi with the goal of providing students with "vicarious experience of the common problems of humanity as they have been addressed by various peoples." The first semester of the course offers four units on literature before 1600, organized by genre, while the second semester focuses on three themes important in the modern world: order and rebellion, the emerging modern consciousness, and redefinition of values and identity. The only literature courses required of all Clark Atlanta students for general education, this sequence is also intended to hone critical skills.

Exploring U.S. Heritage and the Multiculturalism Debate

Lewis and Clark College in Portland, Oregon, developed a new two-semester core course called "Inventing America" to replace a one-semester course called "Basic Inquiry." It retained such features of "Basic Inquiry" as an emphasis on expository writing, collaborative learning, and participation of faculty from a variety of disciplines. The first semester of the course focuses on concepts of equality and freedom, justice and authority, and conflict and consensus in the Declaration of Independence and the Constitution. In the second semester, students examine the evolution of the democratic experiment in the light of the Bill of Rights and the 14th Amendment. Readings include key court cases and key commentators on democracy or on the American experience, ranging from Aristotle, Cicero, de Tocqueville, Thomas Jefferson, and Herman Melville to Sojourner Truth, Ralph Ellison, and Ronald Takaki.

Conclusion

While polarized views about humanities teaching have had wide play in the media, these examples illustrate the empirical reality on campus: humanities faculty have been collaborating across disciplines to develop courses and curricula that merge traditional viewpoints with new scholarship, incorporate diverse experiences and perspectives, and forge new intellectual connections among the humanities and the sciences. Colleges and universities are also working in unprecedented ways with elementary and secondary teachers, two-year colleges, and the public as they seek to preserve and explore cultural traditions, and to empower individuals through the development of their knowledge and understanding as well as their facility with words and ideas.

The accusation that enduring ideas or texts from the Western heritage or from the founders of the United States are being replaced does not appear to be accurate when one looks at course credit data or at examples from the broad spectrum of American education. The curricular reality seems to be that familiar texts are discussed in a wider context and often given new life and relevance through the greater engagement of students, through a wide range of interpretive strategies, and through collaborative perspectives.

References

Adelman, C. *The New College Course Map and Transcript Files: Changes in Course-Taking and Achievement, 1972–1993.* Washington, D.C.: Office of Educational Research and Improvement, U.S. Department of Education, 1995.

Arthurs, A. "The Humanities in the Nineties." In A. Levine (ed.), *Higher Learning in America: 1980–2000.* Baltimore, Md.: Johns Hopkins University Press, 1993.

Association of American Colleges. *Integrity in the College Curriculum: A Report to the Academic Community.* Washington, D.C.: Association of American Colleges, 1985.

Barber, B. R. *An Aristocracy of Everyone: The Politics of American Education and the Future of America.* New York: Oxford University Press, 1992.

Bennett, W. J. *To Reclaim a Legacy: A Report on the Humanities in Higher Education.* Washington, D.C.: National Endowment for the Humanities, 1984.

Bérubé, M., and Nelson, C. (eds.). *Higher Education Under Fire: Politics, Economics, and the Crisis of the Humanities.* New York: Routledge, 1995.

Bromwich, D. *Politics by Other Means: Higher Education and Group Thinking.* New Haven, Conn.: Yale University Press, 1992.

Carnochan, W. B. *The Battleground of the Curriculum: Liberal Education and American Experience.* Stanford, Calif.: Stanford University Press, 1993.

Cheney, L. V. *Fifty Hours: A Core Curriculum for College Students.* Washington, D.C.: National Endowment for the Humanities, 1989.

Chodorow, S. "Transformations in the Humanities." In S. Blackman and others, *Perspectives on the Humanities and School-Based Curriculum Reform.* ACLS Occasional Paper, No. 24. New York: American Council of Learned Societies, 1994.

Gates, H. L., Jr., Katz, S. N., and Stimpson, C. R. *The Humanities in the Schools.* ACLS Occasional Paper No. 20. New York: American Council of Learned Societies, 1993.

Gless, D. J., and Smith, B. H. (eds.). *The Politics of Liberal Education.* Durham, N.C.: Duke University Press, 1992.

Graff, G., and Jay, G. "A Critique of Critical Pedagogy." In M. Bérubé and C. Nelson (eds.), *Higher Education Under Fire: Politics, Economics, and the Crisis of the Humanities.* New York: Routledge, 1995, pp. 201–213.

Graff, G., and Warner, M. (eds.). *The Origins of Literary Studies in America: A Documentary Anthology.* New York: Routledge & Kegan Paul, 1989.

Jones, E. A., Hoffman, S., Moore, L. M., and Nugent, M. *Linking Student Assessment Outcomes and General Education with Faculty Perceptions.* University Park, Pa.: Office of Undergraduate Education, Pennsylvania State University, 1996.

National Foundation on the Arts and the Humanities Act of 1965, as amended through November 5, 1990. 20 U.S.C. Section 952(a).

Oakley, F. "Against Nostalgia: Reflections on Our Present Discontents in American Higher Education." In D. J. Gless and B. H. Smith (eds.), *The Politics of Liberal Education.* Durham, N.C.: Duke University Press, 1992.

Proctor, R. E. *Education's Great Amnesia: Reconsidering the Humanities from Petrarch to Freud with a Curriculum for Today's Students.* Bloomington: Indiana University Press, 1988.

Ratcliff, J. L. *What We Can Learn from Coursework Patterns About Improving the Undergraduate Curriculum.* University Park, Pa.: National Center on Postsecondary Teaching, Learning, and Assessment, 1993.

Smith, B. H. "Introduction: The Public, the Press, and the Professors." In D. J. Gless and B. H. Smith (eds.), *The Politics of Liberal Education.* Durham, N.C.: Duke University Press, 1992.

Spodek, H. (ed.). "World History: Preparing Teachers Through High School/College Collaboration: The Philadelphia Story, 1993–1995." *History Teacher,* 1995, *29*(1), pp. 63–75.

Stearns, P. N. *Meaning Over Memory: Recasting the Teaching of History and Culture.* Chapel Hill: University of North Carolina Press, 1993.

Taylor, C. *Multiculturalism and "The Politics of Recognition": An Essay by Charles Taylor with Commentary by Amy Gutmann, editor, Steven C. Rockefeller, Michael Walzer, Susan Wolf.* Princeton, N.J.: Princeton University Press, 1992.

Zemsky, R. *Structure and Coherence: Measuring the Undergraduate Curriculum.* Washington, D.C.: Association of American Colleges, 1989.

CHAPTER THIRTEEN

THE NATURAL SCIENCES AND MATHEMATICS

Gene G. Wubbels, Joan S. Girgus

Natural science and mathematics have long been integral to the liberal arts curriculum. When the study of the liberal arts was reestablished in the medieval universities, the curriculum consisted of the *trivium* (grammar, rhetoric, and dialectic) and the *quadrivium* (geometry, astronomy, arithmetic, and music). Thus, almost half of the classical liberal arts curriculum was what we now call science and mathematics.

The transition from medieval instruction in the subjects of science and mathematics to modern instruction followed differing paths depending on the field. Certain subfields in mathematics such as geometry and algebra show continuity from ancient to modern times, while others such as calculus and non-Euclidian geometry emerged from breakthrough discoveries. The experimental sciences shifted from the classical subject of natural philosophy, a study based on speculation loosely coupled to observation, to science, the process of relating theory to experiment or observation. These fields and instruction in them changed by what Kuhn (1962) characterized as paradigm shifts, which are abrupt changes in fundamental understanding that change whole fields. They are illustrated by the Copernican revolution in astronomy (around 1500), the revolutions in chemistry (around 1800) brought about by Lavoisier (conservation of mass) and Dalton (atomic hypothesis), the changes in biology (around 1850) brought about by the findings of Mendel (genetics) and Darwin (evolution), and the radical ideas in physics (around 1900) of Bohr (quantization) and of Einstein (relativity).

As the sciences changed, so did curriculum and instruction. Instruction in modern sciences had been added to the undergraduate curriculum by the end of the nineteenth century, sometimes in what was called applied science in a Bachelor of Science degree outside the traditional Bachelor of Arts degree. Required curricula remained the norm, however, and both degrees typically required at least one-third of student time in science and mathematics (Rudolph, 1977), whether of a classical or applied nature. Science instruction of around 1900 is often thought to have emphasized rote learning, but we think it is more accurately characterized as focused on concrete exercises, practical experience in the laboratory, and thorough recitation. By the standards of today, it was not a bad example of hands-on instruction, well-connected to contexts, and meaningful to a wide range of student interests.

Starting in about 1900, the elective and major system proliferated in U.S. colleges, which gradually freed science faculties of the necessity of making their courses understandable to the full range of students. Instruction in the sciences became more specialized within each discipline, and palatable increasingly only to deeply committed students (Rudolph, 1977). A second development occurred in the post–World War II era as the sciences grew enormously in content. As content exploded, college instruction became more abstract, replete with quantitative models and algorithms, and filled with unconnected terms and details.

The large-scale curriculum reform projects of the post-*Sputnik* era, mostly supported by the National Science Foundation (NSF), aimed to update the content of courses, to make the process of science clear to students, and to recruit more students to be scientists. In practice, this meant a substantial emphasis on and improvement of laboratory instruction, and the emergence of reform terms that are still with us such as hands-on learning and discovery approach (Jackson, 1983). While these reforms are similar to current reform efforts in that both attack the presentation of science as abstract, unconnected to contexts, and copious in received detail, significant differences also appear. The post-*Sputnik* reforms focused on science majors whereas the current reforms focus, as did the pre-1900 curricula, on reaching all students. Moreover, the decline and cessation of funding of educational reform efforts at the NSF in the 1970s and early 1980s caused the post-*Sputnik* reform efforts largely to wither before the current efforts were restarted by many private and public foundations—including the NSF—in the mid-1980s.

The twentieth-century replacement of the required liberal arts curriculum by curricula dominated by majors and electives diluted the emphasis on all the original subjects, but an important role in general education for science and mathematics remains. The vast majority of college students continue to study the natural sciences (by which we mean biology, chemistry, computer science, geosciences, and physics and astronomy), although the study of mathematics (including statistics) has been less widespread. Adelman (1992), using the National Longitudinal Study of the High School Class of 1972, reports that 91 percent of the high school graduates of 1972 who had obtained a baccalaureate degree by 1984 had at least some college credit in science or engineering. The nine other areas of the college curriculum for which transcripts were surveyed showed participation rates ranging from 18 percent to 80 percent. In contrast, the rate of participation in the study of mathematics including statistics was 69 percent, which was about average. Not only was minimum exposure to natural science and mathematics widely accomplished, considerable depth was acquired by many. About half of the baccalaureates with majors in areas outside natural science and mathematics completed more than eight credits in these areas. Thus education in science and mathematics constituted an important part of the undergraduate curriculum.

Regular, even continuous, curriculum reform is both normal and necessary in any subject, but reform of undergraduate education in science and mathematics has special urgency at this time for two reasons. First, investigational techniques and even core concepts in science and mathematics have changed rapidly in recent years, and no curriculum can be effective that is out of touch with the disciplines it represents. Second, there is a growing sense that the ways in which this content is packaged and presented need to change so as to reach students in a rapidly changing society. If we fail to engage students in these subjects, we risk producing a society with little scientific literacy at a time when such literacy is needed more than ever, and losing scientific minds essential to our future in a high-tech world.

Unique Aspects of Natural Science and Mathematics Curricula

Science and mathematics curricula for undergraduates differ in some important ways from those of other disciplines. Each of these differences has its own relation to the central questions of student learning that curriculum developers in science and mathematics should have constantly in view.

Sequence. The study of science and mathematics is more sequential than is the study of most other fields. If the learner misses something, whole areas of learning in the subject matter may be blocked until that thing is identified and mastered. Traditionally, science and mathematics curricula have been unforgiving in this regard, which contributes to high dropout rates (Adelman, 1992, p. 42). Efforts to construct science and mathematics curricula that provide more flexibility for the order of mastery of important concepts would be worthwhile. Many institutions have allowed their science and mathematics curricula to become so sequenced and specified that eight semesters of successful lockstep work are required to fulfill the major. While course sequences do promote learning and coherence (see Chapter Seven), they should be constructed to develop the broad intellectual skills of students (see Chapter Eight). They should provide clear connection with liberal learning, not just unidirectional corridors to create greater and greater specialization for majors (see Chapter Eleven). Such is a recipe for depopulated programs, and it is not necessary.

The relationship of theory to experiment or observation. This relationship is the fundamental defining characteristic of science. In instruction, however, this and the cumulative nature of scientific knowledge provide a clear and fast reality check, which means that the errors of learners are subject to immediate exposure. This can have two unfortunate consequences, which curriculum developers and instructors must guard against. First, science learning is hierarchical. The absence of real learning cannot be covered up, and the deficit is cumulative. These frightening facts must be confronted, aired, and planned for by all parties involved in curriculum development. Second, students are prone to give up and drop out because they are not aware that it is normal to make errors in the study of science and mathematics. The secret of successful students is that they make their errors early and often; they are disposed to anticipate errors and take corrective actions. Good curricula encourage and provide for this.

Quantitative skill. The study of most of science and all of mathematics requires quantitative skill. There is evidence that U.S. students in comparable grade levels and after comparable education rank near the bottom on international comparisons of mathematics achievement (International Association for the Evaluation of Educational Achievement, 1988). Learning science and mathematics in the United States may be a special learning challenge because of some uniquely American stumbling blocks. Of great significance is the attitudinal difference summarized by a former Secretary of Education: "American parents think that doing well in math is the result of natural ability, while Asian parents think it is the result of hard work" (Cavazos, 1990). Recent research supports the latter view. We are talking here about the ability to think, and no educator or educational system can address improvement of that ability starting from the presumption that the ability is innate.

Role of research. Research and undergraduate education should have a synergistic relationship. This plays out very differently, however, for different types of undergraduate institutions, which include two-year colleges, four-year colleges with few or no graduate programs, comprehensive universities with master's degree programs in most fields, doctoral granting universities, and research universities. Enrollments in science and mathematics are spread rather evenly across these institutional types, no type accounting for more than a quarter of the total enrollment. The need for action to improve the synergy and, therefore, the instruction changes from enhancement of the scholarly dimension to enhancement of the teaching dimension as one moves across this spectrum of institutions.

The connection of research or scholarship to undergraduate instruction is particularly strong in science, for three reasons. First, investigation is built into the definition of science, and no one can pretend to have learned science who remains innocent of its investigative power. Second, the content and means of doing science change rapidly; teaching programs must be up-to-date in content and facilities, which is hard to achieve if the instructors are personally insulated from research. Third, most scientific research is experimental or calculational, which means that students with reasonable backgrounds of coursework can begin to contribute to a research effort quickly by doing the hands-on work of the research, and this can be an efficient and enormously effective means of cultivating interest in and knowledge of science. Students at nonresearch institutions need active involvement in scientific research to capture the engaging qualities of these fields. Students at research institutions need to develop the capacity to see research within the context of pedadogy and learning.

Majors and nonmajors. This unhappy distinction arises sharply in science and mathematics principally because of the discriminator of quantitative skill. Nonmajors do not have enough time in the few courses they take to acquire the quantitative mastery that is needed by majors. In other words, nonmajors can learn a lot more science in those few courses if they don't have to learn all the quantitative underpinnings. Furthermore, students who do not plan to major in science or mathematics frequently lack motivation for quantitative mastery; many, in fact, have a good deal of anxiety about quantitative material and tend to avoid it as much as possible.

Thus, science—especially physical science—and mathematics present the constant problem to faculty and academic administrators of whether to retain one track or two at the introductory level. While a few institutions have made one track, most retain two tracks to cope with the differences of student skill levels and motivation. Science faculty frequently question the rigor and legitimacy of coursework designed for nonscience majors. Some shun interdisciplinary courses—such as "Values, Technology, and Society"—because interconnecting the sciences and the social sciences supposedly dilutes "true" science learning. What must be remembered is that these courses serve different groups of students with different curricular aims. In a series of studies involving transcript records of students' science enrollments and students' improvement in quantitative and analytic skills, Ratcliff showed that those enrolled in the science-for-nonscience-majors courses, and particularly those enrolled in the integrative and interdisciplinary courses involving science, showed large gains in learning (Ratcliff, 1990, 1995).

Surprisingly, the track for science majors may be more in need of reform than the track for nonscience majors (Sundberg and Dini, 1993; Sundberg, Dini, and Li, 1994). Paradoxically, introductory courses for majors are often less scientific than those for nonmajors, if one considers science to be the endeavor of relating theory to experiment. The spirit of most majors courses is: "Never mind how the knowledge in this course was won, how it applies to anything, and why you have to learn to calculate in these strange ways. We know what is good for you to learn, and it is tied to the coming sequence of ten courses. Just do the work we have laid out for you." In fact, if one imagines that introductory courses should respect and cultivate the characteristics of a practitioner, the usual majors courses select for characteristics alien to those of scientists. The damage caused by this trait of our usual introductory courses is wonderfully exposed by the observation that what makes science hard for learners is that courses provide no answer to the question, Why am I learning this now? (Tobias, 1990).

We advise working to blur the distinctiveness of these two tracks. For both, this can be done by connecting the subject matter to contexts. In general, the nonmajors track should become more quantitative as it becomes a truer representation of the real thing, and the majors track should become less fixed on plug-and-chug algorithms, manipulation, voluminous content, and drill as it also becomes a truer representation of the real thing.

Equipment. Instruction in science is distinguished by the need for laboratory or field experience and its associated equipment. Equipment costs escalated sharply in the 1960s and 1970s and the performance gap between research and educational scientific equipment increased. Computerization and other advances in technology have actually brought some relief in this area. High-performance, reliable equipment of modest cost that can do double duty for research and education is now available in most areas of science. The advances of computers, software, and networking have added further amazing capabilities for education, also at modest prices.

Institutions need to develop specific policies for obtaining and maintaining instructional equipment to have effective science and mathematics curricula. It is probably useful to distinguish three levels of equipment: routine equipment with a unit cost of less than a few hundred dollars; moderately priced, permanent equipment in the range of hundreds to several thousand dollars that is not attractive for a proposal to an external funding source; and permanent equipment beginning at about $10,000 to $20,000 per item that should be connected to specific faculty interests and competencies. The latter is almost always equipment that should do double duty for teaching and undergraduate research. The first category can be handled in one or more line items in the annual budget. The second can be handled by an internally budgeted fund for small equipment to which departments annually submit a rationalized list of candidate items. Equipment in the third category is best handled, wherever possible, as an external fundraising objective. Institutions should be slow to fund expensive scientific equipment entirely internally. The sources of outside support for these items are substantial, and asking departments or individual faculty to meet the peer-review standards of performance competency and intrinsic merit for the acquisition of expensive equipment is a sound policy. For most institutions with more than minimal holdings, it is usually more cost effective to get new equipment exclusively and to acquire manufacturer service contracts only in special cases.

Differential institutional costs for facilities and faculty time. Whether the accounting is done by cost per credit hour, cost per graduating major, or cost per course, science instruction will typically cost an institution about one-quarter to one-half again more than instruction in most other fields. This fact of life stems most directly from the extra facilities and faculty time required by laboratory and field experience, which is generally not fully recognized by the credit-accounting system. Administrators need to understand that the only real alternative to not meeting these differential costs is to have weak or nonexistent science programs.

Constructivist Learning and Its Background: The Improvement Paradigm

The paths to instructional improvement taken by curriculum improvement projects seem at first sight so multifaceted as to defy description or generalization. Yet there is an overarching model that fits virtually every improvement plan. The model—called *constructivism*—has powerful generality because it is a theory of the learning process (Forman and Pufall, 1988; Fosnot, 1989). The growing recognition that constructivism in its many guises is the wide path to improvement of college science curricula (Donmoyer and others, 1991) has been preceded by development of a consensus on this approach for precollege instruction (see Anderson and others, 1994, for an extensive bibliography).

Constructivism holds that learning consists less in recording information than in interpreting it. To interpret what is received and is attended to, the learner must personally construct meaning for it. To put the matter plainly, this kind of learning is to be distinguished from rote learning. Too often the philosophies of *essentialism* (see Chapter Seven) and *objectivism* (see Chapter Seven) have provided a convenient basis for teaching science as bits of information to be memorized. The ways that learners can construct meaning are many and can be interpreted neurologically (Anderson, 1992). This model presents a rich menu of possible improvements of curriculum and pedagogy.

Several details of this conception require elaboration. Cognitive psychologists are increasingly skeptical that the quality dubbed intelligence is the most important determiner of the ability to think. Measured intelligence, in fact, may be as much or more a manifestation of acquired thinking ability than the reverse. Learning in the opinion of these scholars requires thinking, and is an exercise of constructing knowledge for oneself (Sternberg, 1985). This requires the learner to be mentally active rather than passive, and it depends on personal, social, historical, and phenomenological contexts of the content. It also depends on the receptiveness and richness of the preexisting cognitive structure of the learner, his or her intentions and motivations, and the opportunities to try out knowledge in some context safely and to compare it with that of others.

For most science instructors, these ideas represent a codification of things long known even if unarticulated. It is not uncommon, for example, for teachers of organic chemistry or comparative anatomy to tell students that there is indeed a lot to remember in the subject, but that, if it is merely memorized, it will not be *learned* and progress in the course will stop. Instructors are also known to counsel students to make early decisions about selected material to be memorized, and to set about to do that efficiently because certain raw material must be accessible in order to start the process of making sense of it. The report of Project Kaleidoscope, *What Works: Building Natural Science Communities* (1991), asserted that natural science and mathematics educators know well enough already what works. It is instruction that is active, hands-on, lab-rich, curricularly lean, connected to contexts, and enmeshed in a community of learners—all characteristics that facilitate the construction of meaning. Since the Project Kaleidoscope report found little question of what is best, it dealt mainly with identifying exemplary practice and considering what prevents us from doing the right things.

It is important to realize that the constructivist model represents an ideal that can never be fully realized. There will always be room for improvement if one accepts this model. Moreover, the big opportunities for curriculum improvement arise with truly bad curricular and instructional practices, and their flaws are almost always attributable to the aim of rote learning. We thwart meaningful learning by teaching science and mathematics in well-sorted, airtight, bite-sized packets of information, because subjects packaged this way are clear to students, free of messy entanglements, and easy to test with multiple-choice examinations in large sections. We also thwart meaningful learning by yielding to the inclination to cover our subjects exhaustively.

If *pedagogy* is admitted as an aspect of curriculum, we encourage superficiality by maintaining what Tobias (1990) has termed a culture of competition rather than cooperation in our classrooms, and we enforce it through grading on the curve rather than grading on an absolute basis. We also encourage learner passivity through the fifty-minute uninterrupted lecture to large audiences of students, and by associating mastery of the subject with authority rather than the standards of the field.

Constructivism has many antecedents. One can find the concepts of constructivism, without that name, in the literature of cognitive psychology of the past thirty years (Ausubel, 1968). An ancient antecedent is surely Socrates's advice to the learner to "know thyself," a realization that self-knowledge is the beginning of all other knowledge. Newman's classic defense of liberal education, *The Idea of a University* ([1852] 1982), emphasizes the need for undergraduates to personally relate principles to practice.

In a famous essay, *The Aims of Education,* Whitehead (1929) scorned meaningless instruction with the term *inert ideas,* which he characterized as "ideas that are merely received into the mind without being utilised, or tested, or thrown into fresh combinations" (p. 1). Whitehead regarded the toleration of inert ideas as the central way to fail to educate.

> The solution which I am urging is to eradicate the fatal disconnections of subjects which kills the vitality of our modern curriculum. . . . With good discipline, it is always possible to pump into the minds of a class a certain amount of inert knowledge. . . . [But] the mind is never passive; it is a perpetual activity, delicate, receptive, responsive to stimulus. You cannot postpone its life until you have sharpened it. Whatever interest attaches to your subject matter must be evoked here and now; whatever powers you are strengthening in the pupil must be exercised here and now; whatever possibilities of mental life your teaching should impart must be exhibited here and now. That is the golden rule of education, and it is a very difficult rule to follow. [pp. 8–10]

In *Personal Knowledge,* Polanyi (1958)—himself a notable scientist—argues that modern thought has erred on a grand scale by ignoring the role of the knower in the knowing process, and that we tend, therefore, to misunderstand the ways in which science attains objectivity. New knowledge may be won by the mind and hands of one person, but this is trial knowledge until the knowing community of the discipline has "stood in the place" of that investigator and agrees eventually that the new version of reality is true. Polanyi argues that the formulation of science as an objective process of falsification of hypotheses is incomplete. At some stage, that is what goes on, but science relies heavily on scientists' sense of what is an interesting result, an apt or conclusive experiment, and a body of significant work. The attributes of judgment, incisiveness, and feel for reality are the key characteristics of a scientist, and they are decidedly personal. One can come to knowledge vicariously by standing in the place or seeing through the eyes of one who has come to know. These ideas offer great insight for teachers and those who would reform science and mathematics curricula.

A Lexicon for Reform

The curriculum reform projects of recent years present an initially bewildering variety of approaches. In an attempt to bring some order to this array, we surveyed abstracts from five years of NSF curriculum improvement awards, assuming that this would provide a representative sample of curriculum reform projects undertaken in colleges and universities generally in recent years. Using the perspective of constructivism, we found that most of these curriculum reform projects could be categorized into the lexicon given in this section. For each term listed, the lexicon summarizes a primary criticism of instruction and then identifies the improvement approach. Readers can regard the list as a collection of named avenues to reform.

•   *Pedagogy.* The methods of teaching in the course are not informed by what we know about how students learn. In particular, students are not induced to be active.

The solution is to develop new content, evaluation, and, especially, modes of interaction for class meetings and the laboratory, to enable and invite students to construct—rather than merely accept—meanings for the course material.

•   *Content.* The course content is too much, too detailed, and mostly too unimportant. One can learn this content and yet remain uninformed about it. Most of what passes for problem solving amounts to plug-and-chug work with algorithms, second-rate algebra, and tedious calculation. There is plenty of opportunity for error but mostly because of momentary and trivial lapses of concentration and discipline rather than flaws in cognitive structure.

The solution is to develop content having fewer and larger or more important ideas, which are examined from several perspectives and which are applied to contexts.

•   *Connections.* The course consists of numerous well-sorted, isolated, bite-sized packets of information that are unnaturally clear to learners and depend for their existence on the disciplinary insularity of the course. The packets so lack connections that they are essentially meaningless. The topics of the course are the right ones, but they need radical reworking.

The solution is to build connections to other disciplines or to applications. This process is exceedingly effective in aiding understanding of such things as material, energy, economics, technology, society, the environment, evolution, the arts, disease, history, and war, to mention a few. Students are acquainted with and curious about these subjects, and they can be used very effectively as the vehicles for learning science and mathematics.

• *Scholarship.* Our curricula for majors and nonmajors are too little connected to current scholarship of any kind. We do not refer the subjects to relevant disciplinary research, to scholarship of comparison and integration, to application, or to scholarship concerning the teaching of these subjects.

The solution to this aridity includes fostering professional studies and seminars concerning science involving scholars on our campuses from nonscience disciplines, developing portfolio-based or other means of peer assessment of instruction, developing a focus of the course on the methodology of the discipline, and developing student-faculty research collaborations connected to the techniques and other content of courses.

• *Theory.* The problem is not that we do too much theory, but that we do not take the theory we do seriously enough. We do not generate any feel for theoretical approaches, we do not do logically connected problems in these areas, and we do not explain how we know when one general theory is useful or superior to another.

The solution is to review the entire curriculum for its treatment of theory, introduce it in coherent packages large enough for understanding, and introduce investigational exercises involving theory that use modern computer hardware and software where applicable.

• *Investigation.* Current courses are boring because the material is presented as facts acquired by a mature discipline. The material is inert.

The solution is to reverse the usual order of presentation, so that phenomena or problems are presented first, perhaps in laboratory, followed by instruction on a need-to-know basis. This could include a discovery or guided-inquiry approach, or a theme of who won the knowledge and how. It is also useful to relate the concepts to current research or technology and to engage the students in actual investigation during the course.

• *Technology.* The many new means of storing and transmitting images, working with databases, and using the computer with instructional software are absent from many current courses. Ignoring up-to-date technology leaves the coursework dull and without vitality.

The solution is to use computing and other educational technology to enrich lectures, simulate and model systems, master techniques, facilitate problem solving, visualize systems or phenomena, import otherwise impossible visual aids, and promote interaction.

• *Instrumentation.* Powerful, cheap, fast analytical tools exist for acquiring and manipulating data, teaching crucial practical lessons, testing hypotheses, and exciting interest. Students are at least vaguely aware that such things exist, and soon lose interest in classes that ignore them.

The solution is to stop plodding along with twenty-five-year-old instruments and adopt some of the amazing and inexpensive tools now available for enriching laboratory work—and lecture sessions as well.

• *Examinations.* Our methods of assessing learning are so bad that they would trivialize even a perfect course perfectly taught. Specialized knowledge within the science disciplines has exploded, and the temptation is to assess students with easy-to-score multiple-choice tests of bits of information.

The solution lies at least in part with computers, which offer promise of interactive evaluation able to handle large numbers of students better than multiple-choice questions graded on the curve. Moreover, essay methods of testing, writing assignments in science and mathematics courses, and new feedback methods all offer undeveloped areas of pedagogy and virgin territory for us in our institutional outcomes assessments. For examinations to truly help students to improve in science, they must provide constructive suggestions on *where* and *how* students can improve, and they must give suggestions and guidance *when* students can do something about them—not just at the end of a term or topic.

• *Communities.* Students are now immersed in a culture of competition enforced by grading on the curve. This impedes learning by making students unwilling to ask questions or help each other explore problems.

The solution is to develop a culture that induces students to cooperate, help, and sustain each other, and teach each other across their levels of experience and acquired competence. Programs and courses that create and sustain learning communities would help everyone, but especially those from groups currently underrepresented in science, such as women and minorities.

• *Literacy.* We are too narrowly engaged in our disciplines to create scientific literacy in either the science majors or the nonscience majors that populate our courses.

The solution is to develop courses that focus on understanding science through a primary lens of real-world problems or other contexts, usually with a multidisciplinary or interdisciplinary stance.

• *Articulation.* Our courses are insufficiently mindful of high school and middle school science instruction and instructors, a matter that has become critical in the advent of national standards for mathematics and science instruction. What we do is ignorant of what the mainstream student brings to our course, and we are even worse at accommodating those with unusual backgrounds. These mismatches inhibit active learning by students in our courses.

The solution is to develop a community across the interface of college faculty and schoolteachers by beginning summer research programs involving teachers, developing joint pedagogy and curriculum seminars involving our science and education faculty and the teachers, and working to improve the preservice instruction of the students who aim to become teachers.

Notable Curriculum Developments by Discipline

We do not have space here for thorough descriptions of even a selected group of curriculum developments nationally; nor can we list the many curriculum reform projects undertaken in recent years. Activity of this type in science and mathematics is abundant, and other summaries are available (see Tobias, 1992; Project Kaleidoscope, 1991; and National Science Foundation, 1995a, 1995b). Our purpose here will be to identify, as examples of the issues described, several significant developments in each discipline and to indicate for each its particular approach.

Many of these developments began with projects supported by the NSF Division of Undergraduate Education, the Pew Science Program in Undergraduate Education, or another external funding source; others have been institutionally supported from the beginning. For each project, we have provided the name of at least one person who has worked on that development so that the reader will have a starting place to pursue more detailed descriptions. While most fit within disciplines, we have also included a section on intentionally interdisciplinary or multidisciplinary projects.

• *Mathematics.* Calculus has been a principal focus of reform in mathematics. The NSF targeted program in calculus funded a variety of projects, and reformed courses are now reaching an audience estimated at 20 percent of the nation's calculus students. For example, the Harvard Calculus Project, involving the collaboration of Harvard University, the University of Arizona, and Suffolk Community College, eschews algorithms and uses a threefold approach of graphing, analysis, and calculation to elucidate the subject matter. Project CALC, a widely disseminated approach that originated at Duke University, uses real-world examples extensively and features a lab in which students work in groups on problems. Several efforts have been supported to develop calculus instruction that uses graphing calculators extensively. A notable example, also integrating cooperative learning, has blossomed at the University of Michigan. Cooperative learning as an approach in calculus was pioneered with particular relevance to African American students at the University of California, Berkeley, by Uri Treisman. *Resources for Calculus,* by Wayne Roberts (1993) of Macalester College, is a useful guide to new developments.

Mathematics reform has also spread to precalculus. Smith College, Trinity College, and Eastern Connecticut State College have collaborated on a precalculus course in which students encounter elementary functions in realistic contexts, use a graphing utility, collaborate with classmates, and present ideas in essay-style laboratory reports. Other efforts include the Chance Project at Dartmouth College, which has developed materials for a course on probability and statistics that uses topics currently in the news, and two courses developed at Mount Holyoke College, one a hands-on introductory-level geometry course in which students investigate topics of interest to scientists and mathematicians, and the other a sophomore-level laboratory course in which students investigate some of the key mathematical concepts that they will encounter in advanced courses.

New software for instructional use is a major theme in mathematics instructional reform, and it is available for either modestly or radically revised offerings of most lower-level mathematics courses including statistics, precalculus, and linear algebra, as well as calculus itself. While the patterns of use vary, the software often liberates instruction from algorithms, substituting the possibility of asking questions and investigating.

- *Computer science.* Since computer science has only emerged on the undergraduate level recently and evolves rapidly, it has much less fossilized debris than other fields. The emergence of powerful distributed computers has enabled the discipline increasingly to be taught as a laboratory science, and has encouraged its partner discipline, mathematics, to adopt this view. For example, the University of Virginia is developing an extensive set of laboratories to lead the lectures at all levels of the computer science curriculum. Duke University has developed software titled "Visualizing Computation: An Automated Tutor" for the introductory courses for computer science majors or for science and engineering majors. The program depicts and relates programming language, machine language, and computer hardware nature and operations in new ways. The relationships are generally regarded as challenging to teach and to grasp, and the software makes a clear improvement. The State University of New York, Geneseo, has incorporated breadth into the introductory courses by focusing on three methods of inquiry: design, theory, and empirical analysis. This project uses both *closed labs* (structured, supervised computer exercises) and *gateway labs* (interactive tutorials on basic concepts). A project aimed at developing software for animation of computer science concepts is being pursued by Montana State University.

- *Physics.* The Introductory University Physics Project (IUPP) of the American Institute of Physics aims to make fundamental changes in the introductory, calculus-based physics course, and it is doing so by creating qualitatively new courses based on overarching themes. The project intends thereby to get some twentieth-century physics into the introductory course, to make it leaner and deeper in content, and to replace algorithmic work with more realistic problem solving. The IUPP courses also use collaborative learning, qualitative reasoning, and interactive computer programs to make physics appealing and understandable to a wider audience. Workshop Physics at Dickinson College and Tufts University and Studio Physics at Rensselaer Polytechnic have done away with the lecture. In these new introductory courses, all class instruction is done in the laboratory through hands-on experiments and demonstrations that rely on microcomputers for data collection and analysis, and commonly are discovery oriented. Cooperative learning is also part of this approach. The University of Washington has pioneered many significant changes in introductory physics, particularly in cooperative learning pedagogy and new modes of carrying out laboratories. Harvard University has developed a technique for interactive learning in large lecture classes in which the time is broken into short lectures on important concepts, with each minilecture followed by a concept-based qualitative question. Students first respond to the question individually, they then consult each other in small groups, and then respond individually again before the answer is given.

Colgate University and Union College have developed a set of introductory experiments that use sophisticated, inexpensive equipment that is easy to construct and manipulate. A variety of new software resources for physics courses have been developed by Robert Fuller of the University of Nebraska, and these are available in the form of CD-ROMs and video discs.

• *Chemistry.* A radically new course for the high school level called "Chem-Comm" puts contexts first, proceeds through role-playing and cooperative learning in class, and introduces the disciplinary subject matter on a need-to-know basis. This class was developed in the late 1980s by a team coordinated by Sylvia Ware of the American Chemical Society. The ACS then generated a spin-off for the nonmajors college level called "Chemistry in Context."

The University of Wisconsin has developed a course in general chemistry based on the context of physical materials, and Beloit College has developed interactive laboratories for general chemistry using materials science topics. The theory of these projects is that every student has experience of materials, that new materials are changing the world and are fascinating, and that concepts typically taught in general chemistry can be illustrated with or through materials. Montana State University and Kutztown University have developed new laboratories for general chemistry based on inexpensive sensors interfaced to computers, permitting discovery and the pursuit of experiments that are both more interesting and more scientific than traditional experiments. Stanford University has developed project-based laboratories for general chemistry using lasers. Cooperative learning approaches in the laboratory for general chemistry have been developed at Clemson University, and a similar development for the organic chemistry laboratory is in progress. An approach to cooperative learning in the introductory course based on peer mentoring and small workshop groups of students has been developed at the City College of the City University of New York.

The College of the Holy Cross has developed a discovery curriculum for general and organic chemistry that emphasizes the laboratory and engages critical thinking, scientific communication, and testing of hypotheses. Much software for visualization, lecture presentations, and tutorials has been developed at the California State University, Fullerton, University of California, Los Angeles, the University of Wisconsin, and Amherst, Mount Holyoke, and Smith Colleges. The incorporation and integration of organic chemistry in the general chemistry course is a significant trend exemplified at Trinity University. The improvement of the physical chemistry laboratory through the development of laser-based experiments has been carried out at James Madison University, Dartmouth College, and elsewhere. The Pew Physical Chemistry Project, which included chemists from ten colleges and universities in the Mid-Atlantic region, has developed and published laboratory experiments in laser spectroscopy, electrochemistry, fluorescence, electronic spectroscopy, photochemistry, and X-ray diffraction, most of which use modern computational and graphical techniques.

• *Geosciences.* The geosciences have a richer trove of informative graphics than do most other fields of science, and the power of the computer and electronic media to marshal these images in the service of education has been a theme of recent curriculum improvement. The use of electronic images and of computers has inspired changes in the introductory laboratory that permit students to explore geological phenomena, take virtual (and otherwise impossible) field trips, and conduct investigations. A representative project of this type is that of SUNY, Buffalo. The Geographic Information System (GIS) software, which permits information of almost any kind to be connected to points on a physical map and the maps to be overlaid and manipulated, has penetrated into almost all areas of geoscience education. The University of Massachusetts, Amherst, is pursuing a project to develop a SuperCard interface to dynamic digital maps of the GIS type. A project at the University of Illinois (and now at Radford University) is developing tutorial and exposition software for large courses in geology aimed at nonmajors. The University of California, Santa Barbara, has done the same for oceanography. Hamilton College has developed a new introductory course on the geology of Africa as a means of encouraging the interest of African American students in geology.

• *Biology.* Beloit College has led a large effort called BioQUEST to develop software chiefly for the laboratory that permits students to pool experimental data and to access previous data so as to conduct realistic experiments on the great themes of biology such as evolution, genetics, physiology, ecology, and gene expression. Arizona State University and Mesa Community College have developed computer software to be used in conjunction with laboratory to allow a discovery approach to concepts of biology at the introductory level. Hypertext software for an invertebrate zoology course has been developed at the Florida Institute of Technology.

Faculty from sixteen colleges and universities in New England have collected what they judge to be the seventy best laboratory experiments for introductory biology and made them available in a computer-accessible format. A consortium of college and universities in the Mid-Atlantic states, led by Swarthmore, has developed forty experiments in cell and molecular biology for use in introductory biology courses, available in manual format. The University of Wisconsin at Madison has modified the introductory course by adding props and examples aimed at attracting more women and minorities to the study of biology. The themes of this reform concern overcoming fears about biology, emphasizing science as a process, and assigning a pet microbe to each student for their investigation throughout the course.

A significant development with a focus on nonmajors is a course developed at Baruch College. It involves ten departments, serves three thousand students annually, and has the theme of the nature and implications of Darwinism. Radford University has also developed a new nonmajors course that uses historical case studies of important concepts of biology.

• *Interdisciplinary.* We use this term recognizing that some entries under it would be more accurately termed multidisciplinary. The New Liberal Arts project supported by the Sloan Foundation developed several interesting courses aimed primarily at the development of literacy in science, technology, and matters quantitative. The many course developments under this banner are nicely documented in the form of six books, fifteen extensive annotated course descriptions in book form, and approximately seventy-five course outlines in pamphlet form. Most of these had a strong contextual focus on technology, and virtually all types of technology were included.

Numerous recent efforts have been made to develop multidisciplinary courses for nonscience majors. One example is a course organized around great ideas in science at George Mason University. Another is a course on chemistry and art developed at Holy Cross College, which is laboratory-based and uses the discovery approach.

Approaches that teach mathematics as a subject integrated with other disciplines are a focus of the new NSF program in mathematics. The Rose-Hulman Institute of Technology has developed a team-taught first-year curriculum that integrates mathematics, engineering, and science; it is taken by a quarter of the entering students. The University of Pennsylvania teaches a similar course at the introductory level that integrates mathematics, physics, and chemistry.

Other significant projects target science majors. Lehman College of City University of New York has developed introductory two-semester courses that integrate mathematics and physical sciences and are run as hands-on laboratories incorporating cooperative learning and a discovery approach. A project at Nassau

Community College integrates the study of the physical and biological sciences at the introductory level. It induces active learning by emphasizing scientific inquiry, personal observation and experimentation, and collaborative problem solving. A team at New York University is working on a three-semester integrated core mathematics and science sequence that will be required of all non-science-major matriculants.

Innovation Versus Change: The Need for Comprehensive Reform

While the need for curricular reform in the natural sciences and mathematics has become widely accepted in the past decade and many excellent projects have resulted, the elements of reform are mostly isolated. Most projects are at one institution, involve one aspect of one course in one discipline, and involve only one or two investigators. The few exceptions represent several aspects of a particular course, focused efforts of small consortia of different types of institutions, cross-institutional efforts in a single discipline usually at one level, and efforts at several levels in a single institution and discipline. Because undergraduate education in the United States is richly heterogeneous, there are few systemic connections of institutions and their missions. This makes large-scale or comprehensive reform difficult. Despite this daunting scene, we conclude by glancing at the prospects of weaving together the many threads we have identified.

We are considering here essentially the difference between innovation and change, construing innovation to be the acts of one or a few persons to do something new, and change to be altered practices of a significant portion of an academic population or program. Foundations that target change are acutely aware of this distinction. The NSF has recently set up a new division specifically charged with the study and facilitation of the process of converting innovation to change through dissemination and effective evaluation of instructional developments.

We suggest that colleges and universities should seek to provide for an ongoing environment supportive of and conducive to the creation and discarding of science and mathematics curricula. (For an example, see Chapter Thirty-Three.) This requires leveraged support for improvement that we will call *entrepreneurial* and support that we will call *comprehensive*. The former constitutes most of the support mechanisms that currently exist. They are entrepreneurial in that they provide incentives and means for alert and ambitious individuals and small groups to begin an enterprise of innovation that will, at the minimum, have a desirable local effect. We currently lack significant support mechanisms that address systemic change or that support the faculty or faculty-student scholarship that a vital curriculum requires.

Recent program initiatives of the NSF Division of Undergraduate Education to reform the science gatekeeper disciplines of chemistry and mathematics are examples of comprehensive approaches centered on introductory disciplinary courses. The large projects funded in these initiatives will produce curricular products reflective of the lexicon outlined earlier in this chapter for use in all types of institutions. Grants to disseminate and extend the developments beyond the original grantee consortia will be offered in subsequent years of the programs. While both initiatives target improvement of the service of the discipline to client disciplines, the mathematics initiative includes the mathematical tools that are taught and used in other disciplines. The products of these projects are comprehensive in the sense of being integrated in approach and designed for national use, but they center on particular disciplines and involve the introductory level only.

Comprehensive curricular change projects that cut across different types of institutions confront the differing roles that faculty play in science education at their respective institutions. Effective projects need to strike a balance of contributions from faculty at each institution. The diverse types of undergraduate institutions may require innovative grant programs that target specific audiences, that define merit as a synthesis of research and teaching, or that focus on institutional or departmental development. Examples of programs that do the former, more or less, are the NSF Research in Undergraduate Institutions program (for all sciences and engineering), the NIH Academic Research Enhancement program (for health-related sciences), the American Chemical Society-Petroleum Research Fund Type B program (for chemistry and geology), and the Cottrell Program of the Research Corporation (for physics, astronomy, and chemistry). Programs that encourage faculty development are the NSF-CAREERS program of grants to young investigators, and the Camille and Henry Dreyfus Foundation grants in the Teacher/Scholar program. The efforts of the Pew Science Program in Undergraduate Education encourage synergy in research and teaching by making grants to regional consortia of colleges and universities for collaborative projects. The Howard Hughes Medical Institute program supports comprehensive improvement in biology and related disciplines at hundreds of colleges and universities. These programs represent steps to seed initiatives in the right direction, but they do not involve the resources that are necessary to sustain change.

The focus for the future in planning and funding curriculum reform in the natural sciences and mathematics should be on comprehensive reform. Curricular change must engage systems and networks in addition to individual courses. Within an institution, changes should be encouraged that involve the entire curriculum of a department or a set of related departments. They should also involve facilities, pedagogy, student-faculty research, faculty development, and support services. This effort will also require coherent linkage across institutions. The interinstitutional cooperation and partnerships implied by this concept will help to sustain communities of innovators and change agents, and provide the cross-enrichment, professional stimulation, and recognition that are essential to academic excellence.

References

Adelman, C. *Tourists in Our Own Land*. Washington, D.C.: U.S. Government Printing Office, 1992.

Anderson, O. R. "Some Interrelationships Between Constructivist Models of Learning and Current Neurobiological Theory, with Implications for Science Education." *Journal of Research in Science Teaching*, 1992, *29*, 1037–1058.

Anderson, R. D., and others. *Issues of Curriculum Reform in Science, Mathematics, and Higher Order Thinking Across the Disciplines*. Washington, D.C.: U.S. Government Printing Office, 1994.

Ausubel, D. P. *Educational Psychology: A Cognitive View*. Troy, Mo: Holt, Rinehart & Winston, 1968.

Cavazos, L. F., "Science Education." *Journal of NIH Research*, 1990, *2*, 18–20.

Donmoyer, R., and others. "The Knowledge and Pedagogical Base of Science Education: An Overview." *Teaching Education*, 1991, *3*, 57–67.

Forman, G., and Pufall, P. B. (eds). *Constructivism in the Computer Age*. Hillsdale, N.J.: Erlbaum, 1988.

Fosnot, C. T. *Enquiring Teachers, Enquiring Learners: A Constructivist Approach for Teaching*. New York: Teachers College Press, 1989.

International Association for the Evaluation of Educational Achievement. *Science Achievement in Seventeen Countries*. Elmsford, N.Y.: Pergamon Press, 1988.

Jackson, P. W. "The Reform of Science Education: A Cautionary Tale." *Daedalus*, 1983, *112*, 143–166.

Kuhn, T. S. *The Structure of Scientific Revolutions*. Chicago: University of Chicago Press, 1962.

National Science Foundation. *Profiles of Innovative Projects*. (NSF 95–71) Arlington, Va.: National Science Foundation, Division of Undergraduate Education, 1995a.

National Science Foundation. *Project Impact: Disseminating Innovation in Undergraduate Education*. (NSF 95–69) Arlington, Va.: National Science Foundation, Division of Undergraduate Education, 1995b.

Newman, J. H. *The Idea of a University*. Notre Dame, Ind.: University of Notre Dame Press, 1982. (Originally published 1852.)

Polanyi, M. *Personal Knowledge*. Chicago: University of Chicago Press, 1958.

Project Kaleidoscope. *What Works: Building Natural Science Communities*. Washington, D.C.: Stamants Communications, 1991.

Ratcliff, J. L. *Development and Testing of a Cluster-Analytic Model for Identifying Coursework Patterns Associated with General Learned Abilities of College Students: Final Report, May, 1990*. U.S. Department of Education, Office of Educational Research and Improvement, Research Division. Contract No. OERI–R-86–0016. University Park: Center for the Study of Higher Education, Pennsylvania State University, 1990.

Ratcliff, J. L., and Associates. *Realizing the Potential: Improving Postsecondary Teaching, Learning, and Assessment*. University Park, Pa.: National Center on Postsecondary Teaching, Learning, and Assessment, 1995.

Roberts, A. W. (ed.). *Resources for Calculus.* Vol. 1–5. Washington, D.C.: Mathematical Association of America, 1993.

Rudolph, F. *Curriculum: A History of the American Undergraduate Course of Study Since 1636.* San Francisco: Jossey-Bass, 1977.

Sternberg, R. J. *Beyond IQ: A Triarchic Theory of Human Intelligence.* New York: Cambridge University Press, 1985.

Sundberg, M. D., and Dini, M. "Science Majors vs. Nonmajors: Is There a Difference?" *Journal of College Science Teaching,* 1993, *22,* 299–304.

Sundberg, M. D., Dini, M., and Li, E. "Decreasing Course Content Improves Student Comprehension of Science and Attitudes Towards Science in Freshman Biology." *Journal of Research in Science Teaching,* 1994, *31,* 679–693.

Tobias, S. *They're Not Dumb, They're Different: Stalking the Second Tier.* Tucson, Ariz.: Research Corporation, 1990.

Tobias, S. *Revitalizing Undergraduate Science: Why Some Things Work and Most Don't.* Tucson, Ariz.: Research Corporation, 1992.

Whitehead, A. N. *The Aims of Education, and Other Essays.* New York: Macmillan, 1929.

CHAPTER FOURTEEN

THE SOCIAL SCIENCES

Anne Barnhardt Hendershott, Sheila Phelan Wright

Neither art nor natural science but embracing aspects of both, the social sciences have often struggled for recognition and acceptance in the traditional arts and sciences curriculum. From their very inception, the social sciences have been torn between the ideals of scientific objectivity and those of humanistic reform-mindedness. How to explain the world or how to change the world—that seems to be the question that social scientists continue to ask (Horowitz, 1994). It is also the question that many students are now asking in their social science courses.

Students arrive at universities with concepts of literature, history, biology, and mathematics embedded in their notions of education, but political science, anthropology, and sociology as disciplines—indeed, the whole field of social science—may be new to them. Not only is the content of the social sciences new to some students, but the methodology is also new, and not neatly packaged. The social sciences can be both qualitative and quantitative, both scientific and humanistic. Yet students are increasingly drawn to these disciplines.

When commenting upon the current state of the discipline of sociology, Babbie (1992) recalled Victor Hugo's reference to nothing being so powerful as "an idea whose time has come." It is useful to explore this contention and extend the analysis to the disciplines of economics, psychology, and political science in an effort to understand the coming of the social sciences and the reemergence of interest in the fields.

A Historical Perspective on the Social Sciences

The nature of society has been examined since the beginning of human history, as evidenced by the writings of some of the earliest thinkers of the ancient world. Today's social sciences continue to reflect the influence of classical thinkers such as Plato, Thucydides, and Aristotle.

The early philosophers and theologians were primarily concerned with the ideal society. But it was the rise of empiricism in Europe that grounded our current understanding of the natural and social worlds as objects of study. During the fourteenth and fifteenth centuries in Europe, a profound change began to take place in the conception of the world with the belief that the only source of knowledge about phenomena is the direct examination of a phenomenon itself. Indeed, this change led to the age of science and technology in which we now live (Gordon, 1991, p. 16).

Empiricism is important in the modern history of Western civilization because it helped to establish the principle of intellectual freedom, which was extended to areas of human thought and experience well beyond the domain of natural phenomena—to politics, economics, and even to religion. The development of natural sciences had strong effect upon the development of the social sciences. In fact, it is doubtful that the social sciences could have come into existence in their modern form without the development of the natural sciences before them.

A second crucial development during the Renaissance was the belief in progress—the idea that the present is superior to the past and that the future will be, or can be, better still. The idea of progress was the subject of a long debate during the seventeenth and eighteenth centuries—sometimes called the "ancients versus moderns controversy" or the "battle of the books" (Gordon, 1991, p. 30). Related to the idea of progress was a growing conception of "social perfection," the vision of a social order that would meet all the requirements of a just society.

The earliest social scientists attempted to apply to human behavior the new conceptions that the natural sciences had been successfully using in investigation of natural phenomena. In fact, social science as it came to be defined in the nineteenth century was the empirical study of the social world with the intention of understanding normal change and thereby being able to influence this change. Social science was not the product of solitary social thinkers, but the creation of a collective body of persons within specific philosophical frameworks to achieve specific ends. It involved a major social investment, which was never previously the case with social thought (Wallerstein, 1991, p. 18). Given the orientation of social science to the analysis of social problems, it is unlikely that it could have flourished in a static society or one in which people believed that knowledge has no influence upon events or outcomes (Gordon, 1991).

Emerging Social Science Disciplines

From the earliest days of the development of the social science disciplines, the primary aim was the examination of human characteristics and the ways in which individuals and groups are organized into a collective social system or society. Each of the disciplines—anthropology, economics, psychology, political science, and sociology—emerged from a desire to make sense of human behavior.

- *Anthropology* involves the study of human nature through investigation of variation and commonality among groups of people. Anthropologists examine variation in biological populations, society, and culture. The antecedents of anthropology trace to the speculation among theologians and philosophers, such as St. Augustine, John of Salisbury, and Thomas Aquinas, regarding the nature of human diversity (Slotkin, 1965). This speculation gravitated into two camps: the monogeneticists, who stressed the *common* nature and features of different peoples, and the polygeneticists, who gave primary attention to the description and analysis of *variation* among peoples. In modern cultural, physical, and biological anthropology there persists a dynamic between the search for universals among peoples and the examination of differences among societies and cultures.

Modern anthropology is a twentieth-century addition to the curriculum. Membership in the American Anthropological Association grew from just 408 in 1987 to more than 10,000 in 1990. During World War II, the U.S. and other governments found the expertise of anthropologists valuable in considering strategy that involved interaction with indigenous peoples in the Pacific, Africa, and Europe. The result was a dramatic growth in cultural anthropology, and the development of an extensive literature on national character produced by Margaret Mead, Ruth Benedict, and Geoffrey Gorer. These foundational writers for the discipline not only conversed among themselves, but also engaged a wider audience of academics, intellectuals, government officials, and the general public (Shore, 1992).

- *Economics* was one of the earliest social science disciplines to develop. Most historians would associate its beginnings with Adam Smith's *Nature and Causes of the Wealth of Nations* (1776). However, other historians credit a group of French writers during the reign of Louis XV with the first systematic and comprehensive theoretical model of economic processes (Gordon, 1991, p. 88). These early economists, called the Physiocrats, tried to show that there were natural laws of economics as in physics and physiology. They fostered the idea that a system of markets in which voluntary exchanges take place functions as a mechanism of economic coordination (Gordon, 1991). It is their systematic view that makes these early economists significant for today's social sciences. It reflects not only the construction of the first analytical model in the social sciences, but also the "wrapping of the model in a thick blanket of ideology" (p. 99).

• *Psychology* has always had a close alliance with the natural sciences, including physiology, neurology, and mathematics (Hothersall, 1995). In fact, for the ancient Greeks, numbers were something more than a useful tool to summarize and describe measurements; mathematics could be used to predict future events and to improve society. In *The Republic,* Plato described a utopian society with an oligarchical system of government in which a small number of people endowed with superior reason ruled under a philosopher king. Those with superior courage would be warriors; those with a superior sense of beauty and harmony would be artists and poets; those with little talent or ability would be servants or slaves. Plato believed that these qualities were localized in different parts of the body: reason in the head, courage in the chest, and appetite in the abdomen. By proposing to measure individual differences in these qualities, Plato anticipated the modern field of psychometrics (Hothersall, 1995, p. 27).

Early psychological questions were often the province of religion also. In the fourth century, knowing God was the ultimate goal of the human mind. In his *Confessions,* Saint Augustine disclosed his own emotions, thoughts, motives and memories. For this work of public disclosure, Augustine has sometimes been called the "first modern psychologist." Hothersall (1995) believes that the label was premature, but feels that Augustine's work is still of great interest for the analysis and description of the psyche.

While the Renaissance provided the foundation for psychology, it was not until the work of René Descartes, a leading French mathematician and philosopher, that the field took on something resembling its modern form. Descartes had important influence on the historical development of psychology. His clear statement of a dualism of mind and body provided a model and paradigm which has adherents even today (Hothersall, 1995, p. 49). After the Renaissance, several advances were made in philosophy that ultimately laid the conceptual foundations for empirical psychology. The early empiricists—Thomas Hobbes, John Locke, and George Berkeley—emphasized the effects of experience on a passive mind (Hothersall, 1995, p. 52). Later empiricists including Hume, Hartley, and John Stuart Mill considered the role of the active mind in the formation of association, thus setting the stage for the psychological study of learning and memory.

• *Political science* examines the ways in which governments organize individuals into collective social systems. Like the other social sciences, political science has always been, and continues to be, interested not merely in describing the structure of particular political systems but also in constructing abstract models of types of political systems, and in using such models, together with empirical data, to arrive at evaluative judgments concerning the merits of different systems by reference to general normative criteria (Gordon, 1991, p. 57). Still, debates continue between scholars who emphasize the strongly positivistic features of the discipline and those who favor normative argumentation; between those who accept only analysis based upon empirically verifiable data and those who allow room for interpretation; between those who argue for the possibility of a general framework of analysis capable of integrating the entire discipline and those who accept existing variety (Scott, 1995). This division continues to be reflected in the political science curriculum.

• *Sociology* can be traced to Auguste Comte and Emile Durkheim, who concentrated on understanding the actual functioning of society rather than imagining how it ought to be (Macionis, 1991). While they were certainly concerned with how human society could be improved, their major goal was to understand how society really operates.

The need to understand society was brought about by the revolutionary changes occurring in society at that time. Mills (1959) has suggested that social disruption fosters widespread sociological thinking. The birth of sociology coincided with striking transformation in European societies during the seventeenth and eighteenth centuries. Rapid technological innovation in eighteenth-century Europe soon led to the spread of factories and an industrial economy. Millions of people were drawn from the countryside, causing an explosive growth of cities. The people in expanding cities began to entertain new ideas about the world—leading to important sociopolitical developments. People were understandably less likely to take society for granted (Macionis, 1992, p. 13). Wolfe (1987) argues that sociology began out of a feeling that individualistic philosophies—embodied in economics or psychology—placed little emphasis on the moral ties that create community.

According to Mills's argument, the sociological perspective was sparked by this revolution. Macionis (1992) extends the analysis by pointing out that in this century, the 1930s stand out as a decade of heightened sociological awareness. Following the stock market crash of 1929, the Great Depression resulted in unemployment for about one-fourth of the labor force. Under such circumstances, most unemployed workers could not help but see general social and economic forces at work in their particular lives. The decade of the 1960s was another period when the sociological awareness of Americans was enhanced. The Civil Rights, women's, and antiwar movements all challenged accepted social patterns in a highly visible way. Students looked to the social sciences for answers. Sociology was one of the most popular majors on campus in the late 1960s and early 1970s. In 1973, U.S. universities conferred 35,996 undergraduate degrees in sociology—but by 1991, that number had dropped to 14,393, reflecting increased student interest in business and professional schools in the 1980s (Adelman, 1995).

Social science disciplines that formerly showed declining enrollments are now attracting new majors to oversubscribed classes. In a recent survey of 677 department chairs in U.S. sociology departments conducted by the National Science Foundation, more than half the respondents (56 percent) indicated that the number of majors had increased. In contrast, only 9 percent reported a decrease in the number of majors (National Science Foundation, 1992).

Associated with the increase in student interest has been a substantial growth in the numbers of sociologists who identify themselves as applied sociologists. Many of the core areas studied in sociology—communication, conflict, crime, family, mass behavior, and intergroup relations—are part of social, political, and organizational aspects of everyday life. This overlap offers sociologists, like many other social scientists, the opportunity and temptation to apply their knowledge in order to enrich the grounding of their knowledge in real-life situations. The Society for Applied Sociology reports large gains in membership and attendance at national meetings. This increase in participation corresponds to changes in the curriculum in the direction of greater emphasis on applied sociology. For example, undergraduate courses in applied research methods have been added on many campuses. A survey conducted by the American Sociological Association and the Society for Applied Sociology found that of 265 reporting undergraduate sociology departments, 184 offer from one to eight undergraduate courses in applied sociology. Fifty-seven percent of the institutions reported having an undergraduate program in applied sociology, primarily offered as an option or concentration, with only a few institutions offering a separate applied major. At least 20 percent of those colleges and universities offering undergraduate courses in applied sociology plan to add new courses within the next three years (Ballantine, 1991). This is consistent with the trend that began in the 1980s (Deutscher, 1984).

In addition to undergraduate programs in applied sociology, the fastest-growing graduate programs in sociology today are the master's degree programs in applied sociology, which are becoming increasingly competitive in many colleges and universities (Ballantine, Howery, and Pendleton, 1992). Preparing students for these applied graduate programs has led some departments to strengthen courses in research methods and statistics, and to add applied research courses in evaluation research or research internships.

Related to these developments, licensure and credentialing guidelines for graduates of applied sociology programs are currently under review by the Society of Applied Sociology and the American Sociological Association. Within the latter organization, a section process and a committee on sociological practice have been established. The group has offered extensive assistance to undergraduate sociology departments in assessment and curriculum development in the form of workshops, materials, and conferences.

Paradigms and Purposes: The Canon Debates and the Social Sciences

In the social sciences, as in other disciplines, the *canons* that have historically guided research are increasingly debated. Etzioni (1991) and Ross (1991) offer divergent views representing two poles of opinion on these debates, sociology and social science history. At issue is where the social sciences stand in relation to critiques of canonical texts and research paradigms initially most evident in the humanities (as described in Chapter Twelve), particularly those related to cultural pluralism and scientific objectivity.

Etzioni (1991) maintains that the social sciences long ago recognized and dealt with the issues of multiculturalism and ethnocentrism that lie at the core of the canonical debate in literature and history. From Etzioni's perspective, social scientists in the earliest days developed several ways to deal with biases inherent in one's cultural and status-based perspectives. As evidence, he points out that the social sciences were the first academic disciplines to include minority, women's, and Third World studies in their disciplinary bodies of knowledge, exchanges at annual meetings, and research programs. Etzioni cites, among others, *Women and Economics* (Gilman, 1966) and *The Souls of Black Folk* (Du Bois, 1939) as examples of classic works in the core of the social sciences that reflect cultures and viewpoints different from those of the dominant groups. Etzioni further argues that because the social sciences have historically incorporated scientific methodology, they have progressed further in dealing with the problems of context, relativism, and deconstruction. Because of this methodological advantage, Etzioni believes that the social sciences are better equipped and better able to deal with the issues of multiculturalism and diversity than the humanities.

In contrast, Ross (1991) argues that the social sciences are indeed implicated in the debate on the educational canon because each discipline of the social sciences attempts to set up paradigms to govern work in their disciplines; each, therefore, privileges some kinds of work and excludes others. Ross maintains that although there may be some aspects of the social science canons that are worth defending, "The social sciences are, like many of the canonical literary texts, products of modern Western culture and likely to have absorbed the structural biases of that culture" (p. 11).

Ross maintains that the social sciences are Eurocentric and that the deepest source of Eurocentric bias is the conception of history built into the framework of the social sciences at their inception. Modern society, according to Ross, is portrayed by the social sciences as a distinctive product of Western civilization. Ross cites Adam Smith's *Wealth of Nations* as evidence, wherein Smith constantly contrasts modern Western society's capability for progress, primitive societies that have never developed that capacity, and stationary societies that seem to have lost it altogether (1991, p. 11).

In addition to a Eurocentric bias, Ross argues that the social science canons have always been masculine. She recalls that in the nineteenth century, when European sociology wavered between the realms of literature and science, sociological science was repeatedly cast in masculine terms, literature in feminine (1991, p. 12). This gender-based casting has significance for Ross because when the social sciences established disciplinary foundations in the universities, the gendered language of the culture identified so-called hard facts and hard science as masculine; and sentiment, idealism, and insight as feminine. Faced with the new industrial conditions to which the inherited cultural traditions no longer seemed to apply, American social scientists embarked on a self-consciously realist, masculine course that would allow them to engage the objective things in themselves. The subsequent history of the social sciences, according to Ross, is a story of how they established legitimacy within the university curriculum against competing voices in the public arena, and claimed the right to speak in the name of universal rationality. The solution for Ross is not simply diversification of the social science canon to allow "voices from the margins" (p. 12). Instead, the solution is to attack the canons and to abolish the privileged form of societal study embodied in them.

Relevance of the Canonical Debate for the Curriculum

The canonical debate has affected the social science curriculum in two major ways: increasing attention to multicultural and gender concerns, and increasing debate over scientific realism, objectivity, and postmodern deconstructionism. Both the debate over scientific realism (as opposed to relativism) and the debate over multiculturalism have been divisive in the social sciences as in other areas of the curriculum.

• *Multicultural and gender concerns.* If one were to look only at the titles of undergraduate social science textbooks, one would say that the debate over multiculturalism has indeed mattered. For example, despite some attempts to internationalize and diversify the curriculum in sociology, until recently there were no titles of introductory sociology textbooks with "diversity" or "global" or "multicultural" in the title. Today there are over a dozen introductory textbooks with titles such as *Sociology: Cultural Diversity in a Changing World* (Bryjak and Soroka, 1994).

Introductory textbooks in psychology have long included attention to diversity and gender, with a major curriculum change effort spearheaded by the American Psychological Association in the 1980s (see, for example, Bronstein and Quina, 1988).

While many in the social sciences welcome the assistance of textbooks in integrating themes of diversity into their lower division courses, attention to multicultural concerns is not accomplished without debate. This debate can become especially aggressive when proposals for new courses and majors like ethnic studies or gender studies are presented to undergraduate curriculum committees.

Some social scientists have become increasingly alarmed as growing numbers of ethnic studies majors and gender studies majors are housed in English or literary studies departments. These programs are often supported by grants in intercultural studies, as is the case at St. Lawrence University with its new program in American Cultural Pluralism housed in the English department. Indeed, there is a growing perception that the humanities are assuming the responsibility for teaching what has historically been viewed as the domain of the social sciences.

When housed in English or literary studies, new multicultural majors may or may not include required social science courses. The result is that on some campuses, a student may graduate with a major in ethnic studies without having taken a course in demography, quantitative research methods, statistics, or immigration public policy—which many social scientists would view as necessary to understand the basis of racial and ethnic tensions and the consequences of public policy. For example, from a traditional social scientist's perspective, while a Border Poetry course can capture the essence of the individual immigrant's experience, foundational coursework in migration patterns and public policy on immigration is necessary to enable the student to understand the social structure of immigration.

An Association of American Colleges and Universities project, Engaging Cultural Legacies: Shaping Core Curricula in the Humanities, has focused on core programs that address cultural diversity in a variety of ways (Schneider, 1991; Schmitz, 1992). Although this project began as a way of helping institutions shape core curricula in the humanities, it has certainly transcended the humanities to include social sciences, alliances in interdisciplinary courses, and new discussions between and among faculty from across disciplines. The partnerships necessary to successfully engage cultural legacies have invigorated the social sciences. This project is a catalyst to the inclusion of social science concepts in humanities core curricula and the reduction of arbitrary borders.

Questioning the Value of Social Scientific Realism

Even social scientists do not agree on the value of positivism, the goal of scientific objectivity, and the privileging of quantitative methods in the social sciences curriculum. Much of the curricular debate over what some view as issues of turf between the social sciences and the humanities reflects differing conceptions of the value of scientific realism and positivism in the social sciences. Indeed, social scientists have been affected by the recent debate over what constitutes knowledge of the social world.

Some social scientists have introduced controversial social science topics, including cultural relativism and the social construction of reality, to undergraduate students. These topics may raise contradictory views in terms of the core concepts of the discipline—including the value of positivism, and the goal of scientific objectivity. Conversely, sociologists have questioned whether instructors even have an obligation to introduce complex and controversial ideas like relativism to their introductory undergraduate students. For Fredericks and Miller (1993), failure to acknowledge these issues in the introductory courses raises potential ethical concerns for the instructor.

This concern can be traced to the pioneering work of Kuhn (1962). Kuhn's analysis of what constitutes normal science is viewed by many social scientists as leading to a fundamental reanalysis of the meaning of doing science. The direct impact on the social sciences probably has been felt most acutely in the movement, often labeled *postempiricism*, to question traditional positivism (Fredericks and Miller, 1993). This has had major implications; Roth (1987) presents a complete discussion of the reactions to the decline of the positivism in the social sciences.

Ward (1995), addressing the debate in the social sciences between scientific realists and postmodern relativists, argues that instead of treating the debate as a philosophical disagreement over the status of epistemology, we should view it as a political and organizational strategy used in the historical and ongoing struggle between scientific and literary fields and camps. Ward also argues that just as scientific realism and experimentalism were used to dismiss the knowledge contributions of literary fields and to relegate them to secondary status in the seventeenth century, postmodern deconstructionism and its turn to rhetoric and textualism are now being employed as a strategy to counter the political and intellectual dominance gained by the sciences over the last few centuries.

Ward points out that "the result of recovery of rhetoric is that rationality becomes a rhetorical concept, society and economics become texts, reality becomes simulacrum, social psychology becomes deconstructed, and anthropology becomes part of an ongoing interpretive dialogue." Science begins to have literary devices and ideologies rather than philosophy, ontology, or epistemology (1995, p. 120).

In the undergraduate curriculum, some social scientists have attempted to confront, accommodate, and react to these changing conceptions of social reality (Fredericks and Miller, 1993). They believe that educators must rethink their views concerning relativism, including a reconsideration of the value of the curricular requirements of social statistics and quantitative methods courses for the social science major. In its extreme form, the rejection of positivism brings the risk that students may come to believe that the social sciences are only one of the many types of literary criticism. Most importantly, relativism severely undermines the scientific status of the social sciences and the practice of social science research.

The postmodernist attacks on the philosophical basis of the social sciences seem to have threatened the dominance of scientific explanation. Still, Ward (1995) reminds us that science is an entrenched and well-fortified network with an expansive ideology. Science has vast resources and supporting allies which extend far beyond the confines of academia to include government and popular culture. He adds that it is also important to remember that science has long held an advantage over literary intellectuals in building knowledge. But the struggle between scientific realists and postmodern textualists continues because at the university level the stakes include departmental survival, funding possibilities, and student recruitment. Thus, as some social scientists criticize the canons of social science methods, others insist on their inclusion. For sociology, the research methods course is still most likely required—but depending upon the instructor, the course may or may not include quantitative methods and statistics—and may or may not make claims as to the objectivity of social science research.

Integrating the Debates—Teach the Conflicts

Although most of the culture or canon debates have taken place in the humanities, we would argue that the very notion that culture is a debate belongs in the social science undergraduate curriculum.

It is less important that students embrace one school of thought than that they understand both the theoretical underpinnings and the conflicts between and among various positions. We therefore agree with Graff that it is important to "teach the conflicts." As Graff reminds us, "The best way to make relativists of students is to expose them to an endless series of different positions which are *not* debated before their eyes. Acknowledging that culture is a debate rather than a monologue does not prevent us from energetically fighting for the truth of our own convictions" (Graff, 1992, p. 15).

Quantitative-Applied Debate

The canon debates are not the only source of critiques of contemporary sociology. Creation of mathematical models has been so prominent in the discipline of sociology that to some observers, it seems that mathematics became an end in itself. Powell (1995) objects to this trend, observing that "quantophrenia" (quantitative

mania) is rife in American sociology departments, and that top professional journals, especially the flagship *American Sociological Review,* can be understood only by
mathematicians. As academic sociology moved toward sophisticated mathematical model creation, it was increasingly viewed as isolated from the central problems that confront society. Many sociologists feel that scientific sociology may
actually be the problem, not the solution (Powell, 1995). As Torpey notes, "For
many sociologists, if you can't count it, it doesn't count" (1989).

To some, the emphasis on modeling moved sociology far from its original mission of understanding the emotional ties that link people in communities. Some
sociologists believe that the moral dimension was lost as the discipline became
more scientific and sociologists tried to fashion their discipline into a hard science
like physics (Wolfe, 1987). Still, as we attempt to show later, it was not empiricism
itself that contributed to the decline of sociology on campuses, it was the increasing
distance between research and applications that disturbed many prospective students and sociologists.

General Education and the Social Sciences

General education has been described as the "cultivation of knowledge, skills, and
attitudes that all of us use and live by during most of our lives—whether as parents, citizens, lovers, travelers, participants in the arts, leaders, volunteers, or good
samaritans" (Association of American Colleges, 1988, p. 3). The social sciences are
implicit in several of the common goals of general education. Individual students
are to develop substantive knowledge regarding the cultural heritage of the society
in which they find themselves, as well as those of other peoples and cultures. They
are expected to develop their capacity to think logically on the basis of a careful
examination of assumptions, premises, and contexts, disposing themselves to gather
and weigh evidence, evaluate facts and ideas, and make independent judgments
about them. Students are to discover freedom of the mind, openness to new ideas,
and the ability to question authority, deal with complexity, and function effectively
within a milieu of cultural diversity. General and liberal learning seeks to impart a
historical perspective, a cosmopolitan outlook, and an understanding of the limitations of human understanding and knowledge (Bowen, 1980).

Such goals are the direct province of the social sciences. Yet the problem remains as to how to best attain these goals through social science coursework. There
is the aforementioned rift between those who seek to accomplish the goals just outlined through understanding a culture or society holistically by way of interdisciplinary coursework and those who insist on the value of student mastery of cohesive
paradigms imparted by single-discipline sequences of courses and prerequisites.

While it is clear that the social sciences give focus to general education goals of practical competence—such as leadership, citizenship, economic productivity, health, sound family life, and consumer efficiency—it is not clear what curricular design can best accomplish these aims. Open distributional requirements do not address such questions; taking twelve to twenty credits in the social sciences does not ensure that any of these aims will be met. Trends toward active learning, service learning, and the application of knowledge tend to favor the applied social sciences. Trends toward intellectual skills development and interdisciplinary studies tend to mitigate against traditional departmentally defined requirements for the social sciences. These rifts in social science philosophy, ontology, and epistemology have implications for general education as well. Curricular goals to foster rationality, understanding of the limitations of knowledge, and the capacity to comprehend the complexity of human existence (Bowen, 1980) are redefined in society when viewed as social or personal constructs. The current controversies—the study of diversity and commonality, rationalism and social constructionism; the use of quantitative and qualitative data; the engagement and application of knowledge and processes to real-life situations—not only contribute to the resurgent popularity of the social sciences in general education but also introduce new problems and challenges in defining what curricular sequences and patterns ought to be deployed to accomplish these aims.

Studying the purposes of each of this century's three revisions or revivals of general education, Boyer and Levine (1981) found fifty different reasons for the revisions. They observed that the purposes of general education really fit into two groups: those that promote social integration, and those that combat social disintegration. General education, construed in this way, can provide students with a sense of community and shared experience of what it is that binds people together—a goal closely aligned with the earliest mission of the social sciences.

The emphasis on diversity suggests that the role of general education is to promote social integration in a way that includes an understanding of social disintegration. The new emphasis on diversity and ways of knowing has brought the social sciences into a much more visible position in general education. For the foreseeable future, it is clear that issues of diversity, cultural pluralism, and gender and ethnic studies will play major roles in general education. In turn, social sciences will play a significant role in the success of general education as we move into the future.

Why the Increasing Interest?

One reason for the recent resurgence in student interest in the social sciences may be a growing realization that the world and national problems that concern us must have their solutions in the social sciences (Babbie, 1992). Social science students learn that problems of hunger and homelessness will not be solved only by improvements in agronomy or architecture. The solutions to the problems of hunger and homelessness are found in the realms addressed by the social sciences—the structuring of political and economic systems and the nature of inequality. The social sciences offer an explanation for why women continue to earn substantially less than men; why millions of people continue to die of hunger in nations that export food; and why African American infants are twice as likely to die in infancy as white infants (Babbie, 1992).

Social science courses present students, many for the first time, with the concept that their personal freedom may be inhibited by social forces (Sharkey and others, 1993). Instead of responding with anger and confusion to social problems, students in social science courses address the possibility of solutions. This is not to say that students are led to believe that the social sciences have the answers to all social problems. It is clear, however, that students are learning that many solutions in the past have focused on the wrong places.

Today, on many campuses, the disciplines of sociology, political science, economics, psychology, and anthropology are beginning to work together to address social problems inside and outside the classrooms. Indeed, curricular innovation in the social sciences reflects a reduction in the interdisciplinary rivalries that have characterized the fields in the past. Some of the most creative interdisciplinary innovations in the undergraduate curriculum couple one or more of the social sciences with the natural and health sciences, the humanities, education, and the professions in an effort to address such varied social problems as crime, juvenile violence, infant mortality, AIDS, ethnic tensions, and pollution.

Many of the curricular innovations in the social sciences point to a renewed emphasis on applications, though this attention to applied concerns is not without tension. Contentious debates characterize many undergraduate curriculum committee meetings and often center on proposed interdisciplinary courses and majors. An important contributor to the contentiousness is the way interdisciplinary planning tends to focus on the combining of entire disciplines and sometimes neglects the role of fragmentation within the disciplines. In some instances, disciplines such as psychology and sociology have become interdisciplinary within themselves. This fragmentation has resulted in the creation of hybrids at the boundaries between social science disciplines (Dogan, 1994).

Scott (1995, p. 12) recently described the tension between the applied and basic social sciences as "an important fault line" running through the landscapes of all social science fields. Still, one aspect that appears to be common to all social science disciplines, and is reflected in current disciplinary mission statements, is a return to more applied pursuits—a rediscovery of the sense of mission that the social sciences possessed in their earliest days.

Rediscovering the Mission of the Social Sciences

We have argued that the social sciences appear to grow in strength as people realize that their personal experiences are shaped by forces beyond themselves—the political, economic, and technological elements of their society. In light of the problems faced by society today, the current resurgence of interest in the social sciences is not surprising. Racial and ethnic struggles, concerns about crime and safety, poverty and homelessness, institutional challenges to education, the family, and the polity, coupled with a technological revolution that threatens to leave many in a state of permanent poverty, point to social forces that affect the lives of all.

On many campuses, the curriculum increasingly reflects these concerns. For example, the economics section of *Reports from the Fields* describes a lecture-laboratory approach to the subject developed at Denison University, where students use real-world data to develop, explore, and test economic theories. The tutorial nature of the laboratory approach creates an apprenticeship atmosphere that engages students in the subject (Association of American Colleges, 1991, p. 32). Similarly, the political science section of the same volume suggests that all political science majors should have the opportunity "not only to observe but actually experience at least one, and preferably several kinds of real life political situations off campus" (p. 139). The sociology section reinforces the view that applied experiences enhance students' learning of the traditional curricula.

The idea of providing community experiences to undergraduate social science students with the aim of increasing their understanding of community and diversity, as well as increasing their skills and employability, has spread rapidly in the United States and Canada. Supporting this trend is the belief that theories are more adequately constructed, tested, and refined when they are grounded, applied, and empirically evaluated in real-life settings. The growth of *service learning programs,* in which field experiences are linked directly to coursework in the social sciences and other disciplines, illustrates the serious attention being given to experience-based reflection as an integral part of the curriculum.

Horowitz (1994) calls for maintaining empirically driven applied research as a powerful tool for reform. He argues that sociology began as an objective social science and has become "increasingly problematically enmeshed in the politics of advocacy and the ideology of self-righteousness." Horowitz, editor of the journal *Society,* reminds us that empirical and methodologically rigorous studies of educational practices were used as evidence of the need for school desegregation in the 1960s. He recommends that this empirical rigor should be used to confront today's social problems—and that statistics and empirical methods must remain the foundation of the sociology undergraduate curriculum.

Undergraduate social science students who learn data collection and analysis skills will find themselves at an advantage competing with other liberal arts students, as a result of knowing key social factors and having a firm grasp on research design and methods. Indeed, the sociology section of *Reports from the Fields* (Association of American Colleges, 1991) argued for the importance of developing in students "a sociological perspective" that includes three central aspects: the importance of social structures and their influences on social processes, the utility of empirical analysis, and the link between the individual's experience and larger social processes. The sociological perspective enables students to understand how their lives are shaped by social forces.

Garrison (1992), past president of the Society for Applied Sociology, lamented that a large segment of the sociological profession had retreated from the issues of concern to the public and concentrated upon increasingly remote and abstract areas of specialization. Still, as Garrison pointed out, by virtue of its direct connection with major social institutions, applied sociology has the opportunity to correct this situation. For Garrison as for the current president of the Society for Applied Sociology, Iutcovich (1995), it is time now for social scientists to return to their historic role as an intellectual force by taking the initiative and generating new ideas and perspectives which will ensure that the social sciences will contribute solutions to the pressing social issues of the next century.

Conclusions

While paradigms and practices continue to be debated in the social sciences, Wallerstein reminds us that "it has taken 100 years for our present social science disciplinary divisions to institutionalize themselves, and they are now well entrenched . . . social science is a mega-colossus—even its feet of clay are large and not easy to chip at" (1991, p. 272).

A significant issue to be addressed by those undertaking curricular reform or teaching undergraduate social science majors is how to prepare students for their professional and personal lives. While it is true that most students planning on graduate school will have to demonstrate knowledge of key theorists and ideologies in order to further their studies in a more specialized manner, is such knowledge enough to prepare students going directly into the professional world of work? What must those students going into the workforce immediately upon graduation bring with them from their majors that will allow them to demonstrate proficiency in their chosen fields? We need to understand and teach theoretical and applied approaches that are useful and meaningful for people who not only will change professions several times in their lives, but also will enter fields that do not even exist today. We must provide internships, community action, service learning, study-abroad programs, and opportunities to apply theory that will facilitate students' ability to use the social sciences in ways that are both meaningful and productive.

Much of what students learn in their undergraduate experiences affects the ways in which they live. The social sciences should provide students with the knowledge base for, and interest in, social responsibility and informed civic discourse. Astin (1995) concludes that only 31.9 percent of entering freshmen say that "keeping up with political affairs is an important goal" for them. This is the lowest rate in the history of the twenty-nine-year survey. In contrast, 42 percent in 1990 and 58 percent in 1966 stated that keeping up with political affairs was an important goal. The figures demonstrate a challenge to those teaching the social sciences to undergraduates.

Is there more that can be done as we head into the twenty-first century? It seems clear that the disciplines within and outside the social sciences should be moving toward each other and not patrolling artificial boundaries. As Karl Popper reminded us, academic disciplines are largely matters of administrative convenience, because we are students of problems, and problems cut across the borders between disciplines. As we move into an increasingly complex, high-tech future, the history, purposes, and intellectual foundations of the social sciences suggest that they again represent an idea whose time has come. The social sciences, more than any other area of study, are in a position to provide the overarching framework for the innovations and partnerships necessary to develop and sustain a vital undergraduate curriculum.

References

Adelman, C. *The New College Course Map and Transcript Files: Changes in Course-Taking and Achievement, 1972–1993.* Washington, D.C.: Office of Educational Research and Improvement, U.S. Department of Education, 1995.

Association of American Colleges. *A New Vitality in General Education.* Washington, D.C.: Association of American Colleges, 1988.

Association of American Colleges. *Liberal Learning and the Arts and Sciences Major.* Vol. 2: *Reports from the Fields.* Washington, D.C.: Association of American Colleges, 1991.

Association of American Colleges. *Strong Foundations: Twelve Principles for Effective General Education Programs.* Washington, D.C.: Association of American Colleges, 1994.

Astin, A. *UCLA Report on Undergraduates.* 1995.

Babbie, E. "Sociology: An Idea Whose Time Has Come." *Footnotes, the Newsletter of the American Sociological Association,* 1992, p. 2.

Ballantine, J. "Market Needs and Program Products: The Articulation Between Undergraduate Applied Programs and the Market Place." *Journal of Applied Sociology,* 1991, *8,* 1–18.

Ballantine, J., Howery, C., and Pendleton, B. F. "Graduate Programs in Applied Sociology and

Sociology Practice." Unpublished paper prepared under the auspices of the Society for Applied Sociology and the American Sociological Association, Washington, D.C., 1992.

Bowen, H. R. *Investment in Learning: The Individual and Social Value of American Higher Education.* San Francisco: Jossey-Bass, 1980.

Boyer, E. L., and Levine, A. *A Quest for Common Learning.* Washington, D.C.: Carnegie Foundation for the Advancement of Teaching, 1981.

Bronstein, P. A., and Quina, K. *Teaching a Psychology of People, Resources for Gender and Sociocultural Awareness.* Washington, D.C.: American Psychological Association, 1988.

Bryjak, G., and Soroka, M. *Sociology: Cultural Diversity in a Changing World.* Needham Heights, Mass.: Allyn & Bacon, 1994.

Deutscher, I. "The Moral Order of Sociological Work." *Journal of Applied Sociology,* 1984, *1*(1), 1–12.

Dogan, M. "Fragmentation of the Social Sciences and Recombination of Specialties Around Sociology." *International Social Science Journal,* 1994, *46*(1), 27–43.

Du Bois, W.E.B. *The Souls of Black Folk.* Chicago: McClurg, 1903.

Etzioni, A. "Social Science as a Multicultural Canon." *Society,* Nov./Dec. 1991, pp. 14–18.

Fredericks, M., and Miller, S. I. "Truth in Packaging: Teaching Controversial Topics to Undergraduates in the Human Sciences." *Teaching Sociology,* 1993, *21*(2), 160–165.

Garrison, H. "The Uses of Sociology." Presidential Speech to the Society for Applied Sociology. Reprinted in *Journal of Applied Sociology,* 1992, *9*, pp. 1–9.

Gilman, C. P. *Women and Economics: A Study of the Economic Relation Between Men and Women as a Factor in Social Evolution.* New York: HarperCollins, 1966. (Originally published in 1898.)

Gordon, S. *The History and Philosophy of Social Science.* New York: Routledge & Kegan Paul, 1991.

Graff, G. *Beyond the Culture Wars: How Teaching the Conflicts Can Revitalize American Education.* New York: Norton, 1992.

Horowitz, I. *The Decomposition of Sociology.* Oxford, England: Oxford University Press, 1994.

Hothersall, D. *History of Psychology.* New York: McGraw-Hill, 1995.

Iutcovich, J. "Sociology in the Year 2000." Presidential address at the annual meeting of the Society for Applied Sociology, San Diego, Calif., 1995.

Kuhn, T. S. *The Structure of Scientific Revolutions.* Chicago: University of Chicago Press, 1962.

Macionis, J. J. *Society: The Basics.* Englewood Cliffs, N.J.: Prentice Hall, 1992.

Miller, S., and Fredericks, J. "The False Ontology of School Climate Effects." *Educational Theory,* 1991, *40*, 333–342.

Mills, C. W. *The Sociological Imagination.* New York: Oxford Press, 1959.

National Science Foundation. *Undergraduate Education in Sociology.* Higher Education Survey (HES 15). Washington, D.C.: U.S. Department of Education, 1992.

Powell, A. "Sociology on the Skids." *Utne Reader,* Nov.–Dec. 1995, pp. 28–29.

Ross, D. "Against Canons: Liberating the Social Sciences." *Society,* Nov./Dec. 1991, pp. 10–13.

Roth, P. *Meaning and Method in the Social Sciences.* Ithaca, N.Y.: Cornell University Press, 1987.

Schmitz, B. *Core Curriculum and Cultural Pluralism: A Guide for Campus Planners.* Washington, D.C.: Association of American Colleges, 1992.

Schneider, C. G. "Engaging Cultural Legacies." *Liberal Education,* 1991, *77*(3), 2–7.

Scott, R. Unpublished manuscript on the social sciences, 1995.

Sharkey, S., and others. "Social Structure and Personal Freedom: A Case About Teaching Introductory Social Science." *Chance,* 1993, *25*(6), 30–40.

Shore, B. "Anthropology." In B. R. Clark and G. Neave (eds.), *The Encyclopedia of Higher Education*. Tarrytown, N.Y.: Pergamon Press, 1992.

Slotkin, J. S. (ed.). *Readings in Early Anthropology*. Hawthorne, N.Y.: Aldine de Gruyter, 1965.

Torpey, J. "What's in a Number?" *The Nation*. Oct. 9, 1989, pp. 393–394.

Wallerstein, I. *Unthinking Social Science*. Cornwall, England: Polity Press, 1991.

Ward, S. "The Revenge of the Humanities: Reality, Rhetoric and the Politics of Postmodernism." *Sociological Perspectives*, 1995, *38*(2), 109–128.

Wolfe, A. "Moving from Forced Statistics to Emotional Ties." *Long Island Bay Insider*, Aug. 30, 1987, p. 34.

CHAPTER FIFTEEN

THE ARTS

Ellen T. Harris

The arts provide an important means of emotional and creative expression for all college students. Studying the history of the arts offers them insight into the long and rich history of human creativity; participating in the arts fosters their creativity and enables them to recognize, acknowledge, and capture human feeling. In an increasingly technological world, the arts offer the opportunity to learn about human dimensions, human motion, and the human frame. In this way, the arts also foster an understanding of the relation between human beings and technology; they offer the chance to understand that a simple dependence on technological solutions cannot provide all the answers, and that human relations often form an essential element in resolving a problem. The arts help individuals place themselves within the world in terms of culture, religion, and society, and as such help to define community. Through their multicultural basis, the arts also teach about diversity and difference. Often the arts provide the first and lasting gateway into the understanding of other cultures, past and present.

Goals of Arts Education

In addition to its value to the individual, arts education fosters good citizenship. Because of their value in identifying community and welcoming diversity, the arts enable the building of pride in individual ethnic backgrounds and also the building of bridges between ethnicities. Learning about and participating in the arts also prepares students to act as informed citizens in issues concerning the content of art and the freedom of expression, whether this occurs in terms of arts making or just in regard to what books belong in the libraries of our K–12 schools. Arts education prepares students to understand and assist in determining what role the government should play in terms of patronage, provoking questions both about financial support and control over the work.

The arts offer a different way of knowing. The nonverbal arts demonstrate how ideas can be expressed in images, sounds, and motion, as well as words. The practice of art offers the satisfaction of incremental improvement through developing experience and skill. All arts offer an opportunity to experiment with multiple right answers and to approach problem solving without necessarily taking a linear path.

In today's culture, these skills are of paramount importance because of the increasing stimuli with which society is bombarded. With the growing use of computers and ever-expanding media advertising, the ability to use and manipulate visual images and to discriminate among them has become a necessity. As music is relegated to the background through Muzak and headsets and shorter and shorter sound bites are used in news as well as entertainment, attentive listening over any significant period of time becomes rarer and rarer. And the ability to express oneself in words—both orally and in writing—and to evaluate the words of others increases success. The training the arts offer in the use and evaluation of spatial imaging and language, and the enhancement of aural discrimination and attentive listening skills, improves us as citizens, as consumers, and as individuals, at the same time as it offers aesthetic pleasure and enjoyment.

Contemporary Issues in Arts Education

In current educational philosophy and curriculum, the arts are often contrasted with the fields of mathematics and science as a pleasant and relaxing escape from the demands of formulae, equations, and problem sets, but this attitude places both the arts and scientific fields at a disadvantage. One can perhaps progress up to a point in science and math, as well as in art, by following a rote course of technical training, but without imagination the scientist or artist follows an impoverished if not a dead-end path. Without discipline, the path is difficult to find at all in either science or art. Despite these similarities, science and the arts are usually taught very differently. Whereas students learn math and science sequentially and historically, building skill upon skill through practice (Euclidean geometry before Newtonian calculus, for example), arts education for the majority of college students consists of passive arts appreciation. Serious incremental learning in the arts is largely reserved for students choosing professional arts careers, who then study perspective and anatomical drawing, or choral harmonization in the style of Bach, or classical ballet step by step in specialized schools or conservatories. Arts appreciation courses are offered to those who have not proceeded through such sequential learning. Too often, however, the words creative and appreciation are used to hide a lack of rigor. It is difficult to imagine a course called "Science Appreciation," and as Ackerman (1973, p. 222) points out, we do not use the term creative science.

Deficiencies of K–12 Preparation

The distinction in the college curriculum between science and art derives from different preparations in high school. Although the K–12 system suffers from serious problems across the board, the approach to science and math, however flawed and deficient, is still sequential and incremental, while the arts have been eliminated completely from many major school systems—including New York, Chicago, Los Angeles, and Boston—as well as many small-town school districts. The K–12 education plan proposed by President George Bush in *America 2000* included the goal that "U.S. students will be first in the world in science and mathematics achievement" by the year 2000 (Alexander, 1991, p. 9), but excluded all mention of the arts.

Federal emphasis has begun to shift. The current version of the K–12 education plan, *Goals 2000: Educate America Act* (1994) does include the arts. In 1992, the National Council on Education Standards and Testing called for the development of world-class standards and assessment procedures in the arts as well as six other core subject areas. In addition, the governing board of the National Assessment of Educational Progress called for a national plan for student assessment in the arts by 1996 (National Endowment for the Arts and U.S. Department of Education, 1994, pp. 4–5). Changes in preparatory education, however, are likely to be slow, especially in today's budget-cutting atmosphere, so that the current situation is unfortunately likely to obtain for some time to come and to continue to affect college curricula accordingly.

College science is devoted largely to professional education for the serious student who has sequentially mastered the prerequisite skills; students who have missed or failed to acquire this preparation are largely denied access to scientific thought. Arts education, in contrast, is primarily for the amateur, however skilled; students typically first take superficial surveys (either chronological or topical in format) and then move on to courses on targeted subjects in no particular order. Both approaches present problems for the educational system. The arts community must provide a deeper understanding of its aesthetics and philosophies to its broad constituency, and the science community must find ways to educate more informed amateurs in their field. As Oppenheimer observes of the sciences:

> In our world, many things that men do rather naturally, that they have learned to do long, long ago, have become part of the market. I think of song and sport and the arts, the practical arts and the fine arts. None of these is without discipline; and although they are very different from those that lead to the sciences, I would be slow to rate them easier. Yet people sing and make sport and practice the arts quite apart from the market, quite apart from a career. It would be a poorer, thinner life without that. Though surely we will not all burst into song, or take to skis, or pick up a chisel or a brush, some of us have done some of these things, and some of us will; and it seems a proper hope that in our education, both for the young, and for those, in growing number, who like us have kept a lifelong taste for it, we do what we can to open the life of science at least as wide as that of song and the arts. [1965, p. 278]

Oppenheimer's comments could be inverted to form an equally useful observation that, just as young people are now being introduced to the hands-on practice of science by being given an understanding of what is involved even if they don't mean to go forward in careers in the field, they need—in this age of consumer culture and MTV—to be given the practical experience of activity in the arts.

Multiculturalism

However parallel art and science may be in some ways, they differ in at least one critical aspect: the arts are multicultural and not universal. Although it is often asserted that the arts, especially the nonverbal arts, represent a universal language, this is simply not true. Universality can only be attributed with any semblance of truth to some areas of science and math, where the equations and formulae are constant from culture to culture. Indeed, one physicist has told me that he learns foreign languages by reading physics textbooks, because the equations are always the same and he knows what the text must say.

By contrast, the arts are culture-bound, by time as well as geography. A brief stroll through any comprehensive museum will illustrate the differences between European, Asian, and African art, to name only three large continents, and a closer look will reveal differences by smaller areas within those continents and differences by time within single areas. The same is true of music (the Western tonal system differs from Indian ragas and Balinese gamelan structures), theater (the West is only now becoming familiar with Japanese Noh drama and Chinese opera, for example), and literature.

Of course, one can learn to appreciate the art of a culture different in time or space from one's own—and even to prefer it. Nonetheless, art represents its own culture so strongly that cultures are most easily identified by the art they create. The educated person recognizes and differentiates Japanese screen painting, Italian Renaissance painting, and modern abstract art in terms of geography and time. Indeed, art is not, at least today, seen as teleological. Bach, Mozart, and Wagner each represent German culture at a different period. Clearly distinguishable, despite undeniable influences, the music of these three composers does not trace a linear improvement; rather, Bach represents baroque Lutheran tradition, Mozart Viennese aristocratic society, and Wagner romantic German nationalism. Because art represents culture, arts education offers an entryway into learning about difference and learning to respect it.

Art's affinity for cultural history allows the study of art to be separated to a certain extent from the study of skills for the practice of art. Unfortunately, as discussed at greater length later in the chapter, most arts programs draw much too sharp a line between historical interpretation and practice. Some things about the cultural place of art are best learned from attempting to develop the requisite skills, and some things about the production of art are best learned in a cultural context.

Challenge and Representation

Art sometimes represents a culture by challenging it. Society often responds to this challenge by ignoring or censoring the art. Molière's plays challenged aristocratic privilege in prerevolutionary France and were banned; D. H. Lawrence challenged the sexual mores of his time and his works were censored; in the twentieth century, nontonal music was considered degenerate and banned by Nazi Germany and later by Soviet Russia (for example, the works of Hindemith and Shostakovich, respectively). Political censorship of art has occurred throughout history and has been particularly rife in this century. In the former Czechoslovakia, for example, President Vaclav Havel spent time in prison for the views presented in his plays, and in Iran the Ayatollah Khomeini issued a death threat to Salman Rushdie for his novel, *The Satanic Verses*. (See Suleiman, Jardine, Perry, and Mazzio, 1990, for more on world censorship.)

The arts are also hotly debated in the U.S., and censorship thrives—especially at the local level. Herbert N. Foerstel has tried to quantify this trend by examining the annual lists published by both the People for the American Way and the American Library Association's Office for Intellectual Freedom of books banned in U.S. schools and libraries, and then by compiling the fifty "most frequently banned books in the 1990s." For each of these books, he describes a selective but proportional number of challenges. The list includes *The Adventures of Huckleberry*

Finn (number one, with nine challenges in nine different states) and *The Adventures of Tom Sawyer* (number forty-three, with two challenges in two states) by Mark Twain; *Little Red Riding Hood* (number twenty-three, with five challenges in two states) by Jacob and Wilhelm Grimm; and *One Hundred Years of Solitude* (number forty nine, with two challenges in two states) by Gabriel García Márquez (Foerstel, 1994, pp. 135–217). Critical issues for the arts therefore include the place of censorship in light of this country's commitment to freedom of speech, as well as the role of the federal government in the arts, and the future of the National Endowment for the Arts as a patron of the arts (see Harris, 1990). Arts education at all levels will influence and be influenced by the outcome of these debates.

Curricular Issues

The first problem in discussing arts education is to determine what fields make up the arts, since the term *arts* is flexible and supports multiple definitions. An art is at its most basic a skill. Thus developing technology in the nineteenth century was often referred to as the arts, and we still speak today of the industrial and medical arts. For example, the official seal of the Massachusetts Institute of Technology (MIT) includes the words science and arts, where arts clearly means what we today refer to as technology (that is, engineering and architecture). In this formulation, science refers to abstract thought, arts to the application of scientific thought. In contrast, the phrase "arts and crafts" distinguishes between the so-called fine (or, in what is now a pejorative term, decorative) arts as "arts" and the utilitarian arts such as wood-working and furniture-making as "crafts." In the modern phrase "arts and sciences," the arts represent all of the liberal arts—literature, philosophy, languages, history, and so forth. The liberal arts, or studies of language, culture, and history, are not only distinguished from the sciences (thus Bachelor of Arts and Bachelor of Science), but also from technical and professional training. Frequently, the fine arts (excluding literature) are held separate from the liberal arts.

The distinction between music and visual arts, on one hand, and literature, on the other, traces a historical separation between the visual and performing arts and the literary arts. Sometimes the terms used are the verbal and nonverbal arts, placing dance logically among the nonverbal arts. This differentiation, however, is difficult to maintain in light of growing curricular programs in theater studies and film. Even in the so-called nonverbal arts, the use of text is critical—most obviously in music, but also increasingly in visual arts.

Although the tradition of distinguishing between verbal and nonverbal arts is difficult to sustain, the literary arts are in practice rarely included in the arts curriculum. The National Endowment for the Arts and the U.S. Department of

Education (1994, p. 2) clearly identify four arts education disciplines: theater, music, visual art, and dance. The National Council on Education Standards and Testing (U.S. Department of Education, 1992) has identified the same four disciplines as the arts; English is considered a separate discipline. Ackerman's study of the arts in higher education (1973) includes music, visual arts, theater, film, and dance (notably excluding literature or writing). In contrast, Morrison (1973, 1985) includes theater, dance, film, writing, music, visual arts, and architecture as the arts disciplines. In *The Arts at State Colleges and Universities* (Prince, 1990), the fields included are dance, architecture and design, creative writing, media (film, video, radio, television, recordings), music, theater, and visual arts.

Generally, music and visual arts make up the core of the college arts curriculum. Literature, by contrast, is considered part of the humanities. Theater and dance are often relegated to extracurricular programs. Architecture is typically considered separately in terms of professional training. Media arts, where taught at all, are generally embedded in other departments—film in literature, for example. Arts outside the European-based traditions either show up at random in various curricular units or are diverted into ethnic studies or language and culture departments. All these distinctions have ramifications for the curriculum that need to be addressed, falling into five major areas: the split between the practice and history of art; the place of multicultural studies; the role of technology in the practice and study of art; the balance between curricular and extracurricular programs; and curricular issues concerning professional practice, scholarship, and avocation in the arts.

Practice and History

The split between the practice and history of art has had a major effect on the placement of the arts in university structures. In some schools, especially those emphasizing the history and interpretation of the arts, music and visual arts fall into the humanities division. In others, often those emphasizing the practice of art, the arts have a distinct division of their own. Sometimes the history of art is curricular and the practice extracurricular, as, for example, largely typifies art programs at Harvard University and the University of Chicago. Some universities divide history and practice into separate administrative units, as Yale and UCLA do in music. All these structures affect the curriculum in different ways.

As a component of our undergraduate programs, this separation of practice and history is in part a trickle-down effect from graduate programs that clearly divide between professional training for practicing artists and scholarly training for historians of art. Thus the Master of Fine Arts (M.F.A.) degree is distinguished from the Master of Arts (M.A.). The Doctor of Philosophy (Ph.D.) degree is largely reserved for scholars; practitioners usually receive alternative doctorates, such as the Doctor of Musical Arts (D.M.A.), or certificates of proficiency. These differences have in the past thirty-five years been reified by the establishment of the distinct National Endowment for the Arts (NEA) and the National Endowment for the Humanities (NEH). The NEH supports scholarship—largely postdoctoral—in fields such as philosophy, linguistics, languages, history, sociology, anthropology, and the arts; the NEA supports the professional making and dissemination of art through performances, exhibits, and publications.

In contrast to graduate programs and the national endowments, K–12 arts education (in part supported by the NEA) has moved strongly toward programs that combine practice and history. For example, the Getty Center for Education in the Arts has developed a curriculum in the visual arts entitled Discipline-Based Art Education that "integrates content from four art disciplines, namely, aesthetics, art criticism, art history, and art production, through a focus on works of art" (Clark, Day, and Greer, 1991, p. 236). Other programs, such as Howard Gardner's Project Zero at Harvard and especially Arts Propel—in the Pittsburgh, Pennsylvania, public schools—which identify "the principal components of an arts education [as] production, perception, and reflection," have pursued similarly integrated curricula (Gardner, 1991, p. 281).

Undergraduate arts education stands to benefit from the thinking that has gone into these innovative K–12 arts programs, as opposed to accepting the professional divisions of graduate training. Thinking and doing cannot be arbitrarily separated as if doing involves no thinking and thinking is doing nothing. Just as the student who writes learns something about literature that cannot be gleaned in any other way, the student who draws learns about art and the student who composes or performs learns about music. Much like the laboratory component of science courses, the practice of art needs to be integrated into undergraduate arts education.

Multiculturalism and the Cultural Study of Art

The curricular tension between production and interpretation parallels that between study of the object itself and its context. *Connoisseurship* in visual arts (or analysis in music) focuses on the intrinsic properties of the art object, those properties that give the work its structure, shape, and identity. Contextual studies, on the other hand, place the work in its historical setting and look for expressive meanings reflecting personal or societal issues.

Traditionally, the study of Western art has focused on the object. This is true of traditional Great Books programs, and the same attitude transfers to the visual and performing arts when lists of objects or repertoire are proposed as the focus of a curriculum. Most recently, Hirsch has propounded this philosophy in his argument for what he calls *cultural literacy,* which emphasizes the study of Western culture through familiarity with a specific cultural canon, including such objects as Debussy's *La Mer,* Picasso's *Guernica,* and Irving Berlin's *White Christmas* (see Hirsch, 1987; Hirsch, Kett, and Trefil, 1988).

Those, including Hirsch, who have recently argued for the reestablishment of a Western canon have responded in large part to the growing interest during the 1980s in non-Western cultures. At the center of this controversy were changes Stanford University made in its core program to encompass non-Western thought. The resultant discussions too often trivialized the issues of cultural education, by implying on one hand that multicultural education could be well served by adding this or that art object to the core curriculum, and on the other that our knowledge of Western culture could be preserved by a fixed enumeration of Western art objects in core programs. The more important outgrowth of ethnic studies has not been this often-vapid discussion of the canon, implying as it does an object-based study of culture, but rather a new contextual approach to art of all cultures (see Smith, 1990).

Ethnic studies in the arts have rarely objectified the art object as has the study of Western art. By looking at art as a product of its culture, the artwork can be seen embedded in a web of cultural meaning that enhances our understanding of the work, the culture, and the artist. Studying Western art in this way offers new insights into the meaning of any individual object without negating its intrinsic properties. The question of meaning in art is fraught with debate, and terms such as absolute music (as opposed to program music) and pure art (as opposed to, say, political art) continue to express a point of view that meaning in art is (only, purely) intrinsic, structural, and formal—and that applying extrinsic meaning is debasing.

The study of art is the study of culture. Intrinsic values still obtain, but understanding the social context completes one's grasp of the work. Studying culture rather than isolated art objects offers a better view of Western culture as one among many. Further, it allows an examination of the whole spectrum of artistic contributions across what have been called high and low, classical and popular, and formal and folk traditions. Just as Hogarth in the eighteenth century and Dickens in the nineteenth frequently made low culture the object of their work, which we regard as "high" art, so too do students and scholars need to study the full breadth of culture. Such an approach would even help to demonstrate how *La Mer* and *White Christmas,* both part of Hirsch's list, are equally part of Western culture.

Levi, in a recent discussion of the study of literature (1991), has said that "every literary work . . . is less an absolute frozen and encapsulated text than a variable with a range of values. . . . Most immediately [literature] can be taught

. . . as language, as history, and as philosophy. Any critical methodology that does not employ the full range of this humanistic spectrum is seriously flawed through atomism and partiality" (1991, p. 230). His list of "universal questions" for any literature whatsoever is equally relevant to any art.

1. What is its language?
2. What is its structure?
3. What is its style?
4. When was it written [painted, acted, or whatever]?
5. Why was it written?
6. For whom was it written?
7. What attitudes does it express?
8. What values does it assert or deny?
9. What message (if any) does it convey? [1991, p. 235]

Art and Technology

Technology has opened new avenues of learning in the arts and new artistic fields, yet there remains a distrust of technology in both arts education and criticism that needs to be overcome. To take an early example, questions about whether photography is art are now old, but still not completely settled. Philosophical issues have revolved around the lack of a unique object, whether the film needs to be developed by the artist, whether the work is the negative or the print, whether the work is any print or only the original print, and the relationship among art photography, documentary photography, news photography, and snapshots (see Benjamin, [1935] 1955). The underlying question, of course, asks where in the photographic process is the hand of the artist, where is the human touch, the human imagination. Without doubt, the recent controversies surrounding the photographic work of Robert Mapplethorpe and Andreas Serrano are due at least as much to the medium as the content, for equally challenging painted images of sexual and religious subjects from across centuries are exhibited in museums worldwide. For many, the unspoken—and perhaps unacknowledged—difference lies in whether the work is considered to be mediated by imagination or simply a "dirty picture" of a real person or thing. With the development of digital photography, the ground rules have changed once again, but the questions have not gone away (see Mitchell, 1992). And similar questions have been or are being asked about film, video, holography, radio, and television. Arts education needs to embrace these issues.

In addition to their debated role as artistic media, these technologies, along with audio recordings, the laser disc, CD-ROM, Internet, and the World Wide

Web (WWW), have had as enormous an impact on learning in the traditional arts as in other fields. With audio recordings, film, and video it is possible to access the performing arts on demand without entering the concert hall, theater, or opera house. With CD-ROM and the WWW, one can walk through a museum collection, choosing galleries and additional informational material on demand. CD-ROM technology also provides new techniques for learning. The Shakespeare Electronic Archive at MIT, for example, can bring together the original folio of a Shakespeare play and variant editions, historical information, and multiple performances, so that a student can scroll the folio text simultaneously with a performance, or screen performances simultaneously, or simply read the edited text and refer to the glossary and notes as desired.

In addition, film and video are providing broad access and education in the arts. Films of such works as Shakespeare's *Henry V* and E. M. Forster's *Howard's End* have introduced large audiences to this literature, creating peaks of interest in the original texts that often have lasting effects. Similarly, films such as *Amadeus* and *Immortal Beloved* have excited more interest in classical music than perhaps any other medium.

Arts education must recognize the importance of technology and media to its goals. It needs to examine the products of media as art objects, assess the impact on performance of recording and filming processes that eliminate the need for a continuous beginning-to-end performance and occur outside the view of a live audience, and integrate technology as a critical tool in teaching. By teaching technology as art and teaching art through technology, arts education offers students a way to assess value, filter, and judge the images and sounds with which technology surrounds—some would say bombards—us. This is not just an opportunity for arts faculty; it is a responsibility.

Extracurricular Versus Curricular

The arts both benefit and suffer from their role in recreation. Although the apparently widespread human desire to pursue the arts through creation, participation (in performance or advocacy), or attendance seems deeply rooted, this tendency has sometimes been cited as a reason to reduce the arts in education to extracurricular status only—and, more recently, to eliminate federal support for arts education and the arts. The reasoning in both cases is specious and masks a purely financial goal. On one hand, the argument that what is enjoyable does not warrant support is irrational at its root. On the other, the argument against funding the arts derives not from recreational art but from challenging art. Further, because the split between curricular and extracurricular harkens back to the divide between the history of art and artistic creation, the history of the arts sometimes survives cutbacks in undergraduate programs as part of or an extension of the humanities, whereas art making is more (most?) often made extracurricular, unless the goal is professional study. But extracurricular programs are not essentially less valuable than curricular coursework. Although undirected and undisciplined efforts in the arts are often no more than, as Ackerman (1973, p. 225) has put it, "messing around" and should not substitute for nor be equated with structured study, appropriately supervised and focused extracurricular programs play a significant role in arts education and help prepare students for lifelong learning.

Students clearly should not leave school with the fixed idea that learning only occurs in the classroom, and it is an egregious failure of education when this happens. Although the arts need to be studied both through practice and criticism within the curriculum, strong extracurricular programs are neither a weakness nor a disincentive to curricular work. Rather, extracurricular programs need to be judged as are curricular programs by standards of excellence in content, approach, and outcomes. Of course, standards need to be applied appropriately to level, but there is no reason to assume that standards cannot be applied to beginners in the arts, just as in other fields, and there is no reason to assume that standards in the arts will ruin the fun unless one believes there is not (or worse, should not be) joy in learning in all fields.

Extracurricular programs should not take over arts participation entirely, because they cannot adequately teach the material. They inevitably lack a sequential program that builds knowledge and experience, and they cannot reach a broad enough spectrum of students. A well-planned extracurricular program—better termed a *cocurricular* program—however, is neither a detriment to nor a detraction from arts education and should rather be considered an important and enviable supplement to classroom learning.

Professional or Avocational

A similar but separate issue relates to the differences between professional and avocational learning. This distinction applies most obviously to artistic practice, where, on one hand, professional schools in the arts, such as the Juilliard School of Music or the Massachusetts College of Art educate undergraduates for careers, while, on the other, similar but avocational arts training for undergraduates of liberal arts programs is usually extracurricular, if it exists at all, or only found privately off campus. The theory behind this distinction seems to be that education in the practice of art is appropriate to the curriculum only when the student has previously determined that he or she will pursue an artistic career. The flaw in the argument lies in equating educational level and intent. Not only can avocational interests reach professional standards, but also students who are professionally trained do not all go—or even intend to go—on to professional careers. Furthermore, standards lower than professional levels have intrinsic educational value. This is understood in other fields (mathematics and writing are obvious examples, but the same applies to courses related to law, business, medicine, theology, and engineering) where a professional intent is not a prerequisite for the existence of the course in the curriculum or for student enrollment.

Full professional training in the arts is sometimes accommodated at liberal arts colleges and universities by the incorporation of professional arts schools. These function on the model of other professional schools, such as law, medicine, or engineering and are usually successful. The most obvious example in the arts is architecture, especially because this field is rarely taught avocationally, but other examples exist, such as the Yale School of Drama or the Oberlin Conservatory. In addition, some professional schools collaborate with liberal arts colleges, giving the liberal arts students an opportunity to study the practice of art professionally and the professional students an opportunity to acquire a liberal arts background from a fine institution. One such collaboration exists between the Museum School of the Museum of Fine Arts, Boston, and Tufts University.

Potential conflicts between the professional arts and liberal arts education arise when museums and galleries, resident artistic companies, and large centers for the fine arts actively engage in presenting professional arts events at colleges and universities. There are tremendous advantages in having students at liberal arts colleges in direct contact with professional artists, especially through residency programs that give students an opportunity to work directly with the artist and have their work seriously examined. In contrast, having resident companies on campus offer performances for the community without organized interaction with the students offers much less educational benefit, no matter how prestigious it may be for the college or university.

The large fine arts centers, such as the Hopkins Center at Dartmouth or the Krannert Center at the University of Illinois, for example, offer first-rate performing arts programming for the surrounding region as well as the university community. This is part of what a university can offer the wider community in which it resides—a lively arts program that brings the best artists to the area. Such programming can also help support a large facility. All such centers, however, suffer from the problem of determining how the space will be shared between curricular or extracurricular programs and professional programming, and too often the professional programming wins out.

Similar questions can and should be asked about university and college museums and resident theater companies. Can these benefit the wider community and at the same time act as a resource for the curricular program? The Court Theater at the University of Chicago and the American Repertory Theater (ART) at Harvard University, for example, function largely—if not totally—as professional companies unrelated to curricular programs. ART, furthermore, has largely taken over the Loeb Drama Center, which was originally intended for student theater as well. The arts offer institutions of higher learning an important venue for reaching out to and serving the wider community, but institutions must learn to balance the educational needs of their students against their professional arts presentations.

Although the issue of professionalism in education seems obvious in the practice of art, it also applies strikingly in the humanities, where education is often confused with the professional training of an academic. The history and criticism of the arts, the practice of art, and the other humanities curricula as well need rather to be taught at the undergraduate level so as to emphasize education over training. The curriculum should be broad, rather than narrowly focused, encompassing sequentially ordered courses that permit the acquisition of specific knowledge of art objects, of cultural context, and of practice, while building aesthetic appreciation, critical judgment (of the works and also of interpretations), and historical research skills. With such a curriculum, students could progress to whatever level suited their interest—whether avocational or professional—and their abilities.

Effective Arts Programs

Because the arts are so multifaceted and schools differ so greatly, it is impossible to dictate an arts curriculum that would or could be used universally. In general terms, however, it is difficult to imagine a successful arts program that does not offer the opportunity for serious exploration of the history and practice of visual art, music, and writing. The importance of film also needs to be recognized, if not in a separate unit of media studies, then as a part of either visual art or literature. The history of architecture, if not the practice, can be and traditionally has been explored in visual art, just as the history but not the practice of theater has traditionally been part of literature. The field of dance has not been as widely accepted. Its placement within athletics is hardly satisfactory; a more academically legitimate home could possibly be found in theater or music. Such interdisciplinary collaborations could actually strengthen the arts on campus by consolidating the number of small departments that now struggle against one another. While recognizing that there are connections among all the arts (narrative qualities exist in music as well as literature, and film, like opera, can comprise narration, visual design, drama, and music) three possible interdisciplinary artistic units might be: art and architecture—the visual arts; music, theater, and dance—the performing arts; and literature and film—the narrative arts.

Core or Distribution

Courses in the arts should be offered as part of the common experience, whether that is a core curriculum or distribution requirement. Such classes need to be formulated in such a way as to demonstrate both history and practice and to examine works of art both as isolated objects and representatives of a specific time and culture. This would be a difficult task within a single course covering a single field; to try such broad coverage in a combined-field course would be nearly impossible. Although one arts course within a core is hardly sufficient, few cores allow more than one course in the arts. In the core curriculum suggested by the National Endowment for the Humanities (Cheney, 1989), the arts were allowed no separate courses, but rather were given cursory attention in the civilization sequence. The question that faces those arts educators who have the advantage of a core program that includes the arts is whether to use the brief time allotted them to attempt a deeper understanding of a single artistic field or to offer a sweeping view of all the arts. Core programs including the arts at three very different institutions can serve as examples of arts requirements within existing curricula, indicating both common and unique solutions.

- *The University of Chicago: Traditional Core Curriculum.* In the Common Core at the University of Chicago, the arts courses (defined as musical and visual arts only) are identified as part of the humanities requirement but separated out from courses based on text. Students must take a three-quarter sequence "in the interpretation of Historical, Literary, and Philosophical Texts" and one quarter of either musical or visual arts. One wonders whether this requirement could be usefully reformulated into two sequences of two quarters each, one in history and philosophy and one in the visual, performing, and narrative arts—placing the study of literature in the arts. Although the math requirement is allowed prerequisites, music and art are not—a typical situation that creates difficulties in required courses where the level of preparation is wildly disparate. Finally, the practice and history of art are clearly separated into discrete course offerings; students not only choose music *or* art, but they choose history *or* practice (University of Chicago, 1994). Despite these potential shortcomings, the strength of this approach is that at least some arts are taught seriously and well to all students. The Chicago core program in the arts is typical of general education at many of our large research universities; the programs at Columbia University (where students must take both art history and music history, but practice is not an option) and Harvard University are similar but not identical. Because of its seriousness and prevalence, it is an important model despite its limitations.

- *The University of North Carolina, Asheville: Incorporating practice.* Another model is that of the University of North Carolina, Asheville, where the arts are integrated into the humanities historically, while a separate arts requirement allows for interdisciplinary but in-depth analysis of selected works of art and hands-on experience in a single field. Students are required to take a four-semester sequence in the humanities, which emphasizes text-based fields but also includes the nonverbal arts, placing them in historical perspective in conjunction with ideas in literature, philosophy, religion, and science; furthermore, students are required each semester to attend between three and five cultural events and submit a report for each event. In addition, students must take a one-semester arts course that offers an in-depth interdisciplinary approach to understanding the arts. In one recent term, the four topics were *Hamlet* (including issues of production and film versions), musical formal design and creative choices (based on Brahms's Symphony No. 4), Picasso's *Guernica* (including discussion of the principles of design and social commentary), and Toni Morrison's *Beloved*. As part of this requirement, the students also must enroll for one of five possible arts laboratories in visual arts, drama, music, creative writing, or dance, which introduce the students to the creative process itself. Contrary to the Chicago model, students do not receive from the core itself a historical survey of any single artistic field, although such courses are available outside the core (Arts Program Faculty, 1993). The benefit is that students are not asked to choose among discrete artistic fields or between practice and history; all students are introduced to artistic thinking, the role of art in society, and some hands-on experience. This is an exemplary model.

• *Massachusetts Institute of Technology: Arts and Humanities Core.* At MIT, the Humanities, Arts and Social Sciences (HASS) core program was established in the 1940s to assure that the students—who chose MIT for its science and engineering programs—also studied culture, history, and humanistic thought. This eight-semester requirement, matching the eight-semester Science Core in length, has taken on different forms in its fifty years. The current model shows a special recognition of its position in a technological institute. Students begin by taking a three-semester distribution requirement. This is currently configured so that students must choose one course from one of three categories representing arts and humanities, one from one of two categories representing history and social science, and one from among any of the three subcategories not previously elected. The student then chooses a concentration from among the various disciplines of the humanities, arts, and social sciences; this normally comprises four-semester subjects, one of which can also be counted as a distribution subject, leaving two possible humanities electives. Students may either use these electives to continue to broaden their experience in the humanities, arts, and social sciences, or to explore their concentration in more depth, frequently leading to a minor or second major. The point of the HASS curriculum at MIT is to ensure that within a student body made up of 60 percent engineering majors and 30 percent science majors (the remaining 10 percent includes arts and humanities majors), all students are not only grounded in science through the Science Core but also acquire an understanding of the breadth of the HASS fields (the distribution requirement) as well as some deeper knowledge of a single field (the concentration requirement). However, despite the strength of the arts offerings in both history and practice in this core program, a student can graduate without ever having taken an arts subject. This could easily be changed by making the three-semester distribution requirement one subject in each of the humanities, arts, and social sciences. The HASS curriculum at MIT offers a fascinating model of a core in which all science and engineering students will also have a concentration in one of the liberal arts and all humanities majors will have taken an eight-semester sequence in science and math (Massachussets Institute of Technology, 1995, pp. 40–42).

Concentration Programs

Concentration programs in the arts exist at most of our colleges and universities; under various names (major, minor, concentration) these are programs offering in-depth experience in a single field. Concentration programs should not simply impose a specified number of courses, but should offer a structured if not sequential approach to the intellectual ideas of the field, to specific art objects, and to substantial experience in practice—preferably both in scholarship and art production, although students will naturally choose one direction or another by preference. Students whose primary interest is in scholarship should not be bereft of the experience of hands-on art; students who chose art practice should understand the historical and cultural background of their field.

Next Steps

There are several logical steps that emanate from this revival of the arts in the undergraduate curriculum. We need a cogent, coordinated, and comprehensive policy across national agencies for the arts and humanities.

National Policy and Advocacy

The arts and humanities suffer from the lack of a single federal agency to advocate and support work in the field, from K–12 initiatives through to independent work and study. The National Foundation on the Arts and Humanities might at one time have served this purpose, but the devolving of responsibility to the three discrete agencies (the National Endowment for the Arts, the National Endowment for the Humanities, and the Institute of Museum Services) has eliminated the central foundation. Since their inception, the three agencies have focused their energies more on patronage than advocacy and education, and, as a result, their very survival is now in great jeopardy. By contrast, the National Science Foundation has focused and continues to devote much of its energies on science policy, precollegiate education, undergraduate science education, and NSF Fellowships for graduate study, as well as on postdoctoral and advanced research support. Because the two Endowments and the Institute of Museum Services have not worked together on policy and educational issues, each agency is now in the position of spending its energies advocating for its survival rather than fighting for the broader field.

The lack of a central organization that can accept and disseminate information about arts education is in part a symptom of the atomization of the arts into separate and isolated areas, not to mention the greater separation within arts fields between the study of practice and the study of history. Arts educators across all fields and levels must now work together to create the collaborative energy necessary to move curricular issues forward. This is difficult within the current structures. There is, for example, no parallel organization to the National Science Teachers Association for precollegiate arts teachers. Rather, we have the Music Educators National Conference, the National Art Education Association, the American Alliance for Theatre and Education, and the National Dance Association. One may ask why music, theater, visual art, and dance need more professional separation than physics, biology, and chemistry. These professional arts groups are now working together on issues of standards and assessments; undergraduate arts educators need to do the same. It will be difficult to find a place for the arts in the curriculum if the arts themselves are in conflict with one another.

On the basis of "what you test is what you get," undergraduate arts education stands to benefit enormously by the inclusion of the arts in the National Council on Education Standards and Testing call for world-class standards in seven core subject areas. In another forward move, "the National Assessment Governing Board (NAGB), which oversees the National Assessment of Educational Progress (NAEP), agreed to begin the process of organizing a 1996 NAEP assessment of the arts" (Mitchell, 1994, p. xxvii). The arts have led the way in establishing "direct demonstrations of skill and knowledge," such as the performance and portfolio assessments that move away from one-right-answer multiple-choice and short-answer tests and that are now being used in many fields (Mitchell, 1994, p. 3). Only with appropriate evaluative measures can we hope to maintain the new standards. If states and local school boards adopt these standards and mandate appropriate assessments, undergraduate arts education will be able, for the first time, to depend on a basic level of competence in entering freshmen and move the curriculum to a higher level.

Entrance Requirements

With standards and assessment programs in place, entrance requirements in the arts for college admission will become more common, and in turn, help drive the K–12 curriculum program. One current example comes from the Academic Deans of the Commonwealth Partnership (which includes Allegheny College, Bryn Mawr College, Bucknell University, Chatham College, Dickinson College, Franklin & Marshall College, Gettysburg College, Haverford College, Lafayette College, Lehigh University, and Swarthmore College). In a brochure entitled "What We Expect: A Statement on Preparing for College," the six core areas are arts (defined as music, theater, dance, and visual art), foreign languages, history, literature, mathematics, and science. The statement reads:

> *The Arts:* Music, theatre, dance, and studio art enrich our appreciation and understanding of the world. Students drawn to the arts should take every opportunity to develop their talents. All students should learn to appreciate major artistic creations, develop an understanding of artistic sensibility and judgment, and seek to increase their understanding of the creative process. We recommend two challenging semester-long courses which introduce students to the arts of their own and other cultural traditions.

This statement regarding arts preparation for college is an important model for other colleges and universities as a strong recommendation, if not a requirement, for entrance.

Exit Requirements

Colleges also need to develop exit requirements for all students, not just for the majors; usually these will be attached to a core program of some type. More and more employers in business and industry are recognizing the importance of the arts in teaching problem solving, risk taking, and the appreciation of diversity, and in enhancing human expression and communication. General Electric in Pittsfield, Massachusetts, uses dance in its training programs (Deutsch, 1991); ARCO Chemical encourages "the energy, creativity, and imagination that comes from the arts to help us enlarge the value of science" through volunteerism in the arts (Hirsig, 1993); and the Kohler Company in Wisconsin hires artists to encourage researchers to "experiment with designs" and "try new things" (Deutsch, 1991). Just as colleges and universities help determine K–12 curriculum through their entrance requirements, so too can the needs of business, industry, and citizenship help drive college curriculum.

Financial Support

Financial support is, of course, an issue, but to frame the question by asking whether there is funding to support the arts accepts as its premise that the arts are an add-on. The question of whether there is sufficient funding for the arts will only become relevant when the question is asked whether there is enough funding for other core areas. The issue is not funding, therefore, but rather one of identity. The case that needs to be made nationally is not whether the arts should be funded, but rather why the arts are integral to education.

Roles for Arts Educators

To establish their integral place in education, the arts need to collaborate across field boundaries to encompass the breadth of the visual, performing, and narrative arts and cross the gulf between history and interpretation, on one hand, and the practice of art, on the other. They need to embrace art in the richness of its cultural and multicultural context, to integrate technology into the learning process as both a tool for learning and a source of new art objects, and to value and structure extracurricular learning as a support to curricular programs. Undergraduate arts programs must seek to expand and improve their own offerings by working closely with the new and exciting K–12 initiatives to establish entrance requirements and with business and industry in addition to professional postbaccalaureate programs in the practice and study of art in order to establish exit requirements.

When taught to the highest standards, the arts offer benefits in terms of mental training, discipline, and continuous improvement. They offer training and experience in risk taking, creativity, and imagination. They offer a way of experiencing and appreciating many cultures while understanding the universality of human expression. And they offer lifelong intellectual challenge and stimulus. Arts educators have the opportunity in their hands to make this happen for all students.

References

Ackerman, J. S. "The Arts in Higher Education." In C. Kaysen (ed.), *Content and Context: Essays on College Education.* New York: McGraw-Hill, 1973.

Alexander, L. *America 2000: An Education Strategy.* Washington, D.C.: U.S. Department of Education, 1991.

Arts Program Faculty. *General Education Arts Program Review.* Asheville: University of North Carolina, 1993.

Benjamin, W. "The Work of Art in the Age of Mechanical Reproduction." In H. Arendt (ed.), *Illuminations* (H. Zohn, trans.). Orlando, Fla.: Harcourt Brace Jovanovich, 1955. (Originally written 1935.)

Cheney, L. V. *50 Hours: A Core Curriculum for College Students.* Washington, D.C.: National Endowment for the Humanities, 1989.

Clark, G. A., Day, M. D., and Greer, W. D. "Discipline-Based Art Education: Becoming Students of Art." In R. A. Smith and A. Simpson (eds.), *Aesthetics and Arts Education.* Urbana: University of Illinois Press, 1991.

Deutsch, C. H. "What Art Can Teach Business." *New York Times,* Sept. 8, 1991, Sec. 3, p. 23.

Foerstel, H. N. *Banned in the U.S.: A Reference Guide to Book Censorship in Schools and Public Libraries.* Westport, Conn.: Greenwood Press, 1994.

Gardner, H. "More Effective Arts Education." In R. A. Smith and A. Simpson (eds.), *Aesthetics and Arts Education.* Urbana: University of Illinois Press, 1991.

Goals 2000: Educate America Act, P.L. 103–227. Washington, D.C.: U.S. Department of Education, 1994.

Harris, E. T. "It Takes Practice and Serious Thought to Learn How to Dislike Art Properly." *Chronicle of Higher Education,* Sept. 19, 1990, p. A56.

Hirsch, E. D. *Cultural Literacy: What Every American Needs to Know.* Boston: Houghton Mifflin, 1987.

Hirsch, E. D., Kett, J. F., and Trefil, J. *The Dictionary of Cultural Literacy.* Boston: Houghton Mifflin, 1988.

Hirsig, A. R. Unpublished address for the Business Volunteers for the Arts Awards Luncheon, ARCO Chemical Company, 1993.

Levi, A. W. "Literature as a Humanity." In R. A. Smith and A. Simpson (eds.), *Aesthetics and Arts Education.* Urbana: University of Illinois Press, 1991.

Massachusetts Institute of Technology. *MIT Bulletin 1995–96: Courses and Degree Programs.* Cambridge: Massachusetts Institute of Technology, 1995.

Mitchell, R. (ed.). *Measuring Up to the Challenge: What Standards and Assessment Can Do for Arts Education.* New York: ACA Books, 1994.

Mitchell, W. J. *The Reconfigured Eye: Visual Truth in the Post-Photographic Era.* Cambridge, Mass.: MIT Press, 1992.

Morrison, J. *The Rise of the Arts on the American Campus.* New York: McGraw-Hill, 1973.

Morrison, J. *The Maturing of the Arts on the American Campus.* New York: University Press of America, 1985.

National Endowment for the Arts and U.S. Department of Education. *Arts Education Research Agenda for the Future.* Washington, D.C.: U.S. Government Printing Office, 1994.

Oppenheimer, R. "Communication and Comprehension of Scientific Knowledge." In *The Scientific Endeavor: Centennial Celebration of the National Academy of Sciences.* New York: Rockefeller Institute University Press, 1965.

Prince, J. N. *The Arts at State Colleges and Universities.* Washington, D.C.: American Association of State Colleges and Universities, 1990.

Smith, R. (ed.). *Cultural Literacy and Arts Education.* Urbana: University of Illinois Press, 1990.

Suleiman, S. R., Jardine, A. A., Perry, R., and Mazzio, C. (eds.). *Social Control and the Arts: An International Perspective.* Cambridge, Mass.: New Cambridge Press, 1990.

University of Chicago. *Courses and Programs of Study: The College: For the Academic Year 1994–95.* Chicago: University of Chicago, 1994.

U.S. Department of Education. *World Class Standards for American Education.* Washington, D.C.: Office of Educational Research and Improvement, 1992.

U.S. Department of Education. *Goals 2000: A World Class Education for Every Child.* Washington, D.C.: Government Printing Office, 1994.

CHAPTER SIXTEEN

PROFESSIONAL EDUCATION

Lynn Curry, Jon F. Wergin

Not so long ago, professional schools were the country cousins of the academy. They lay (often literally) at the periphery of the campus; their faculties engaged only in applied (and thus second-rate) scholarship; and their students were getting vocational training, not real education. Even such relatively prestigious fields as medicine and engineering were regarded by the rest of the university as walled-off domains with relatively little to contribute, either to the campus culture generally or to the undergraduate curriculum in particular.

Times have changed. While some vestiges remain of the disconnections between so-called real college and professional school, professional education has had an increased influence on undergraduate education in recent years. There are several reasons for this, some of which are economic and market driven. Professional schools, especially the ones based on hard science, bring in big dollars from grants, contracts, and clinical income. It's not uncommon, for example, for a medical school today to derive less than 20 percent of its total income from state appropriations. Professional schools are also increasingly important sources of student full-time equivalents (FTEs): undergraduate students pursuing careers

Note: The bulk of this chapter has been abstracted by the authors from Curry, Wergin, and Associates, 1993, with the permission of Jossey-Bass Publishers.

in professional fields or preparing to do so increased to more than 60 percent of the college population by 1993 ("Almanac," 1994, p. 17).

But more than just market forces are at work here. Professional schools, crucibles of educational innovation for more than thirty years, have begun to influence undergraduate curricula in some direct ways. Problem-based learning in medicine, competency-based assessment in nursing, and guided design in engineering are just three examples of such innovations that are being adapted or reinvented at the general education level. Even the classic case method of teaching, which at one time was limited to law schools and business schools, has become a far more common strategy in the teaching repertoire of liberal educators. Our purpose in this chapter, however, is to go beyond simply acknowledging the growing influence of professional schools in the life of the modern university, and to analyze the critical issues for professional education and suggest ways these issues might be resolved.

We should begin with some clarification. Just what is a profession, and by extension, what is professional education? Any consensus is difficult to establish, given the diversity of professional groups and their proclivity to define the terms in their own way. Our view is that the professions encompass occupational groups that share specialized skills requiring extensive systematic and scholarly training, restrict access with rigorous entrance requirements, and because of their importance to society, claim high social prestige. Professional education is different from training for the trades and crafts because it emphasizes theory. It is different from science and graduate study because it emphasizes the use of knowledge. *Professional education* may thus be defined as a system of formal education that prepares novices for highly skilled occupations through a combination of theory and practice, and that culminates with an award of certification, licensure, or other formal credential. Just how much theory and how much practice are appropriate for a professional school has been an issue of intense debate in most professions for a large part of this century. Understanding the origins and evolution of this issue must underlie any recommendations about how to improve professional education itself, and so we turn there first.

Evolution of Professional Schools

In colonial America, professional education was almost exclusively an apprenticeship. Colonial colleges had no faculties of law or medicine, and even though most colleges were church-related and required significant time in religious studies, many young clergy entered the ministry with no college at all. As Brubacher (1962) notes:

There were two aspects of the colonial apprentice's training. On the one hand he actually performed professional duties. The physician's apprentice washed bottles, mixed drugs, assisted at operations. The lawyer's apprentice copied legal papers, filed actions, served writs. In addition to these practical duties, apprentices received theoretical training by reading the professional books of the men to whom they were apprenticed. . . . But, at best, the intellectual content of professional training was slender enough. Except for the ministry, where extended study of the classical tongues and theology were almost indispensable to expounding sacred texts, the claim of the professions to be learned was belied by the level of training provided. [p. 57]

Apprenticeship training as the central component of professional education continued well into the nineteenth century, and the methods of certification to practice remained informal, to say the least. Abraham Lincoln, as a member of the Illinois Bar, was said to have examined a young candidate by asking him to define a contract, then—after regaling him with many recollections of his own practice—to have penned the following note to the chair of the Board of Examiners: "My dear Judge: The bearer of this is a young man who thinks he can be a lawyer. Examine him, if you want to. I have done so, and am satisfied. He's a good deal smarter than he looks to be" (Woldman, quoted in Bledstein, 1976, p. 164). The candidate gained his certificate without further ado.

As the demand for professionals increased, however, and as the number of apprentices swelled to meet the demand, practitioners began to take apprentices on in larger numbers, and some came to devote large amounts of their professional energies to teaching them. Medical practitioners then took the next logical step and formed cooperatives, forming larger classes and thus reducing their teaching loads—though the terms, of course, were not then in use. Even though the instruction under these circumstances became necessarily more didactic, Brubacher (1962) notes two features of these early professional schools that distinguish them clearly from the professional schools of today. First, the lectures given in these settings were distillations of individual experience and practical wisdom, and thus largely devoid of theoretical or scientific content. Second, the schools were proprietary, the private property of the faculty. Because these schools continued to compete with more traditional apprenticeship experiences, professional standards continued to be low or nonexistent. Even in the late 1800s, formal training in a typical medical school lasted only eight months (Numbers, 1988); and even an institution as prestigious as Harvard granted its medical degree to anyone who could pass five of nine oral examinations, all given in the same day (Brubacher, 1962).

The first real prod to educational reform came from individual states, all of which passed some form of medical licensing legislation between 1870 and 1900

(Numbers, 1988). While there was some political pressure for this, stemming from the increasingly formal functions performed by physicians, licensing was pushed mostly by medical societies—to restrict access to practice. Thus was set in motion a precedent for professional self-regulation that exists to this day.

A second stimulus for reform came in 1893, when Johns Hopkins University became the first medical school to require a bachelor's degree for admission. The conditions in most medical schools were so deplorable, however, that The Carnegie Foundation for the Advancement of Teaching commissioned Abraham Flexner to undertake a national study of medical education. The Flexner Report issued in 1910 was so devastating that nearly half of all medical schools closed, some even before the report was made public (Brubacher, 1962).

The Flexner Report revolutionized medical education by holding up the Johns Hopkins curriculum as the model for all others to emulate. Schools of medicine were moved into research universities, and the scientific component of medical education was greatly increased, with two years of basic science instruction preceding two years of clinical instruction.

The idea that professional education should structure knowledge in this way soon pervaded other professions, as well. The Flexner Report led to similar reviews, first in law (Reed, 1921) and then in dentistry (Gies, 1926). Common to both reports was the recommendation that professional competence was to be grounded in systematic, preferably scientific, knowledge.

The Flexner legacy has lasted for most of this century, based on the presumption that learning must be hierarchical, that scientific theory must precede practical application. As Rice and Richlin (1993) note, "Normative for almost all career-oriented programs are the assumptions that learning precedes doing and that practice is the application of theory" (p. 81). Such a view, which Schön (1983) calls "technical rationality," is reinforced by the dominant academic culture of our universities, a culture that prizes basic research, the pursuit of knowledge for its own sake, above all other forms of scholarship. Generally speaking, the more its faculty are able to conform to this culture, the higher the professional school's status in the institutional pecking order. This is why technical rationality continues to hold sway in most professional schools, even in the face of mounting criticism that much of the professional curriculum is irrelevant to practice (for example, Abbott, 1988; Cavanaugh, 1993), and that other more powerful pedagogical models are available (Harris, 1993).

Four Critical Issues Facing Professional Schools

The issues suggested by this brief history are still with us today. What, exactly, is the nature of the social contract between the professions and society, and what is the responsibility of the professional school in fulfilling this contract? What should the role of the school be in defining what it means to be professionally competent, and in certifying the readiness of its graduates to practice? What is the relative importance of technical knowledge, practical knowledge, and liberal learning in professional curricula? And, what is the school's responsibility to maintain the skills of professionals in practice? It is well worthwhile to review these four issues from the perspective of the political and social trends of the late twentieth century, as they provide insight into areas where major changes are in order.

Understanding, Negotiating, and Meeting the Social Contract

The professions hold a simple contract with society: they will guarantee the competence of their registered members in exchange for professional control over all aspects of their profession. The professions themselves decide who is admitted to practice, the standards and methods of training, why and by what method membership is withdrawn, how members are deployed, and the nature of the work they will do.

The guarantee of professional competence, on the other hand, depends almost entirely on individual professionals' voluntarily adhering to standards of professional conduct articulated by their professional bodies. Only a few professional bodies (for example, pilots) periodically examine the competence of professionals in practice. Most have proxy indicators instead: some require passage of a knowledge test at intervals (some specialty medical societies); some require attendance at a fixed minimum of continuing professional education events (American Law Institute, American Bar Association, Institute for Certification of Computer Professionals). A number of recent changes have directly influenced the nature of the social contract between society and its professional groups.

• *Increasing consumerism.* Professions no longer have the paternal authority and deference the public once allowed them. Role expectations now require professions to advise their clients and to involve them in all decisions affecting their welfare. The public is also becoming increasingly vociferous about requiring proof of continuing professional competence, such as periodic recertification. Consumers are more sophisticated than they used to be, and thus less in awe of paper credentials.

The public is also questioning the cost-benefit value of professionals' contribution to society. This is seen in the rising numbers and support for the paraprofessions (paralegals, physiotherapy aides, nursing assistants) and the whole range of alternate providers (acupuncturists, midwives, private sector tutors for public school curricula).

The professions, forced to react to this increased public militancy, now engage in widespread discussions about the changing definitions of competence and its inculcation, measurement, and assurance throughout a practice career. The professions have also been pressured by increased government regulation and court sanctions to loosen their control procedures to better involve the public. Public representation on professional regulatory bodies has led to more public disclosure about members' competence, and about the organizations' methods of professional review, dismissal procedures, and rationales for other actions.

• *The explosion of technical knowledge.* Geometric growth in technology has led to the creation of new fields of necessary expertise. For example, the legal profession now must grapple with the intricacies of patenting not only intellectual property but new life forms. The reaction of the professions has been to further specialize and divide their spheres of work. Thus, we have physicians who specialize in "a single small part of the body (the hand, the eye, the heart), or a single disease process (infectious diseases, endocrinology, oncology), and/or a single age group (paediatrics, adolescent medicine, geriatrics)" (McGuire, 1993, p. 9). Similarly, in law, we find specialization by type of client: family law, corporate law, criminal law. Within client type there is further specialization by problem area. For example, within corporate law there are subspecialties for entertainment law, trust and antitrust law, financial law, tax law, real estate law, and even extremely rarefied subspecialties such as law applied to biotechnological patents.

• *Rapid expansion in technical capability.* The amazing increase and proliferation of capacity in technologically assisted imaging (magnetic resonance imagers or MRIs, computed axial tomography or CAT-scanning, micro-television-aided internal surgery), and communications technologies (faxes, computer modems, e-mail, the Internet, and the World Wide Web) have irreversibly changed the nature of professional practice. Tightly guarded professional monopolies were built and maintained by restricting access to specialized knowledge. All this information is now publicly accessible and often newsworthy enough to receive wide media coverage. Many professionals are challenged daily by clients who may be better informed than the professionals themselves about new breakthroughs in the pertinent professional knowledge base. Further, professionals are increasingly reliant on technicians to run the machinery now so fundamental to their practice. Lawyers rely on bibliographic technicians to search the statute databases; physicians must await the MRI technician.

New knowledge, new skills, and new attitudes are required to respond adequately to increased public involvement, the knowledge explosion, and the expansion in technological capabilities. This requires professional schools to radically alter their curriculum content and the formats for curriculum delivery. Social work students, for example, will need to learn how to gain electronic access to client records and service availabilities. Marshall (1993) argues that professionals need to devote time and energy to understanding the technologies available to them and to become proficient enough in their use to judge their contribution to professional practice.

Another direct effect will be an increasing demand for continued professional development opportunities placed on professional schools by practitioners in the field. These returning professionals will come both voluntarily and involuntarily through actions of government, professional regulatory bodies, and court action, and they will have dramatic effects on the current student body in professional schools. Some of these effects will be positive (as they share their practical experience), and some negative (as they share the cynicism they may have developed in the course of business).

Changing demographic characteristics of individuals applying to professional schools will also affect the professional schools and their curricula, both directly and indirectly. Changes have already occurred in many professions with respect to the gender balance in entering classes. In North America, the proportion of women in first-year medical classes is approaching 50 percent. This will place enormous pressures for change on the current professional medical school curricula—pressures to accommodate pregnancy and child-rearing responsibilities, for example. These issues have already been raised by the increasing numbers of female graduate and postdoctoral students in the science and engineering fields (American Association for the Advancement of Science, 1993).

Defining, Measuring, and Certifying Competence

Since the issue of professional competence is at the center of the social contract society has with professionals, one might think there would be considerable unanimity in the definition, measurement, evaluation, and certification of that competence. Like most aspects of human behavior, however, competence is elusive in definition, difficult to measure and evaluate, and troublesome to correct.

• *Defining competence.* In most practical aspects, ease of measurement has determined the functional definition of competence. For example, the current standard approach to evaluation of an individual's competence for practice as set out in the *Standards for Educational and Psychological Testing* (American Educational Research Association, American Psychological Association, and National Council on Measurement in Education, 1985) states that "for licensure or certification (credentialling), the focus of test standards is on the level of knowledge and skills necessary to assure the public that a person is competent to practice" (p. 63). This definition of competence focuses narrowly on knowledge and skills and does not address areas—such as interpersonal skills and moral characteristics—that most of the public would consider to be necessary in a competent individual. We might also prefer that the definition of competence focus more on competence in practice as opposed to competence in examinations. Finally, an acceptable definition of competence would assure the public that a professional could respond appropriately to a wide range of critical problems, even though not all would be encountered routinely in professional practice.

To meet the spirit of the social contract, competence indicators should be made available to the public and grouped into a competence profile. The advantage of a profile approach to defining professional competence is that it would allow clients to choose a professional to consult by finding a competence profile that matched their own attitudes and dispositions. Thus, if a client valued very high indicators on mastery of new knowledge, the client might be willing to accept rather low scores on interpersonal skills in making a choice of professionals to consult. A second advantage of this type of competence definition is that it allows professionals to demonstrate competence in different contexts, within different measurement systems, and according to different criteria. Using a variety of measurement methods in collecting data for the evaluation of competence ameliorates some of the competence measurement problems we currently encounter.

• *Measurement of competence.* The measurement of competence has been plagued by a series of both conceptual and practical problems. First among these is the problem of determining a criterion against which competence can be measured. The central problem here is that the competence criteria most frequently used are cumulative test scores from paper-and-pencil tests composed of a series of questions, each of which has one most correct answer. Professionals in practice, however, do not encounter problems structured into discrete questions with one correct answer. In practice, we are interested in professional judgment, temperament, insight, and style, in addition to how much book knowledge the professionals have at their command. So our present criteria for measuring competence are inadequate when compared to what we actually expect of professionals in practice.

A second conceptual problem is the assumption that a professional's competence is a stable, enduring trait that, once accurately measured, will not change with changes in context, client or patient characteristics, time available, or other details of professional life. The research evidence indicates, however, that professional competence is not a stable trait, but one that varies with the content and severity of client needs, the amount of professional preparation time available, client difficulty—and random chance (Shaw and Dobson, 1988; Stillman and others, 1986; Shavelson, Mayberry, Li, and Webb, 1990). Professional effectiveness appears to be case- or situation-specific. One suggested solution (Engel, Wigton, LaDuca, and Blacklow, 1990) is to improve the measurement of professional competence by conducting performance assessment against a wide variety of practical problems and situations rather than just on tests of what the professional knows.

A related conceptual problem with measuring professional competence is the assumption that performance on tests, which are usually conducted in controlled situations, has any direct relationship to the outcomes desired by clients consulting those same professionals in practice. McGaghie (1993) takes up this issue: "Today's competence evaluations, chiefly tests of acquired knowledge, assume that there is a link between standardized test performance and behavior in practice. However, a meta-analysis of thirty-five studies that assessed the link between performance in educational settings and performance in professional practice did not find a strong correlation. Teaching, engineering, business, nursing, medicine, the military and civil service were the professions covered in the meta-analysis. The authors of the report concluded that: 'the overall variance accounted for makes grades or test scores nearly useless in predicting occupational effectiveness and satisfaction' (Samson, et al., 1984, p. 320)" (p. 242).

Methods presently used to measure professional competence are also plagued by many technical problems. The assessment of a professional's knowledge base has become very precise and efficient using multiple-choice tests. These procedures, combined with a theory of the underlying knowledge structure, such as latent trait theory (Hambleton and Swaminathan, 1985), can yield extremely efficient, short, yet predictive written testing. The primary disadvantage of over-reliance on written testing, however efficient and accurate, is that mastery of the necessary knowledge base is given more importance in the definition of professional competence than it warrants. A few alternatives to written tests do exist (such as direct and indirect observation, open-ended problems, and simulations), but each has specific weaknesses (McGaghie, 1993).

• *Certification of competence.* The act of certifying a professional as competent is reserved by the nature of the social contract for a professional association or other professional agency. Generally speaking, these associations and agencies rely on a two-step process to award certification to an individual.

The first step is that all candidates must successfully complete a course of professional training in an accredited professional school. Although the criteria for accreditation are only loosely related to the outcomes society demands in competent professionals, most professional associations and agencies have considerable input into, if not sole control over, which schools achieve and maintain their professional accreditation.

The second step to certification is successful performance on a certification examination managed by the professional association or agency. These certification examinations invariably involve extensive paper-and-pencil measurement of the candidate's knowledge base, and occasionally an assessment of practice skills.

Some professions (such as medicine, veterinary medicine, psychology) require a government license in addition to the professional association certification. Very often these licenses are provided at a set point prior to the completion of the accredited professional certification program, to allow students to provide services to the public under supervision as part of their training program. Therefore, medical interns, veterinary interns, and psychologists-in-training all work directly with the public prior to full certification by their professions as competent professionals.

Professional competence must extend throughout a professional's practice career, of course, and some assurance of this is required by the social contract professions hold with the public. It has never been logical that certifying competence only once in a career should indemnify a professional from any further requirement to demonstrate competence, including mastery of necessary new knowledge and skills. The same pressures that are reforming the social contract with professionals have forced professional associations and agencies to expand their focus to include consideration of recertification, maintenance, and assurance of competence.

As articulated by Norcini and Shea (1993), the goals for a program of professional relicensure are similar to the goals for initial certification of competence:

- Some aspect of the evaluation should warrant the competence of the individual as demonstrated in actual practice. Ideally this goal would be achieved by an assessment of the outcomes of professional activity.
- The evaluation should warrant that a practitioner has the potential to respond appropriately to a wide range of problems, even though not all situations are commonly seen in practice.
- Recertification and relicensure should warrant the interpersonal and moral characteristics of the practitioner. [p. 82]

Professional schools find themselves in the middle of these problems of defining, measuring, and certifying competence. Often relationships between schools and professional associations compound the difficulties. The schools are generally the source of competence definitions, sometimes resulting in an overly academic orientation divorced from the concerns of competence in actual practice. Schools also invest enormous resources in measuring their students' attainment of competency— as defined by the school. Certification of competence, however, is usually reserved as a function of the professional association, which by definition reflects the concerns of its practicing members. Professional regulatory bodies represent a third layer. These bodies (for example, the medical licensing boards in each state) were established by governments to protect the public from charlatans purporting to offer professional services. This regulatory control results in a legal license to practice as a named professional, and is yet a third effective definition of professional competence.

Integrating Technical Knowledge, Practical Knowledge and Liberal Learning

In the introduction to this chapter we indicated that an emphasis on theory is what distinguishes the professions from other skilled occupations. *Theory* refers to the highly specialized technical material specific to a particular profession, such as human anatomy in medicine, mechanics in engineering, or torts in law. We have also pointed out that one legacy of the Flexner revolution, when professional schools were absorbed into research universities, has been to create a discontinuity between technical and practical knowledge. Cavanaugh (1993) explores this discontinuity in some detail, including the influences of academic culture on professional education, the dominance of discipline-based discovery research as a valued faculty activity, and the traditional organization of professional curricula along disciplinary lines.

First, professional education takes place for the most part in research universities. These strong academic institutions have a culture that places high value on the pursuit and generation of new knowledge, much more than on the appropriate application of that same knowledge in practice. This value discontinuity produces in learners an orientation toward pursuing academic rather than practice-based careers. Those choosing careers in practice must make their own translations from the values, approaches, and information they receive in the academic milieu.

Second, professional school faculty are rewarded within academic contexts for their contributions to disciplinary knowledge. This generally occurs through discipline-oriented scientific inquiry that, given the knowledge explosion in professional contexts, can be evaluated, applied, and appreciated by increasingly narrow groups of like-minded—or at least like-interested—academics. Generally these similar academic specialists are widely dispersed, so it is through international academic organizations that faculty members are rewarded and judged to have made contributions sufficiently significant to attain tenure, promotion, access to graduate students, and other rewards within the academic culture. The aspirations created by these rewards have little immediate relevance to improvement of professional practice, improvement of teaching, improvement of curriculum, or improvement of students' learning.

Finally, the academic culture approaches the body of knowledge, skills, and attitudes within the profession on a discipline basis. Disciplines have structures that may not map well onto the fuzzy presentations and phenomena that practitioners encounter in their work. Professional practice problems do not come labeled by their contributing disciplines.

According to Cavanaugh (1993), rigorous evaluation of professional school curricula would bring these discontinuities between practice and academic needs into clearer focus. Unfortunately, outcomes evaluation in professional curricula rarely occurs. There is occasional rhetoric about the necessity of outcomes evaluation, usually expressed in accreditation standards promulgated by various professional associations, agencies, and certification or licensing bodies for the professions. Nonetheless, there is little or no effort in this direction: no profession at this time requires a minimum outcomes standard for renewal of school accreditation. Without ongoing proof of efficacy, curricula can drift into structures and processes that satisfy administrative and professional preferences, and may not meet needs of students, graduates, or employers.

Another way to resolve the discontinuity between technical academic knowledge and the practical knowledge required in professional practice is to fundamentally reconsider the knowledge requirements for each profession (Cavanaugh, 1993). A new epistemology of professional practice is emerging that defines adequate professional practice as judgment and wise action within complex, unique, and uncertain situations. Thus a necessary professional skill is to think about and learn from one's own practice and the practice of others. This is referred to as reflection-in-action and reflection-about-action, or collectively, *reflective practice* (Schön, 1983, 1987, 1991; Harris, 1993). These authors state that skills in reflective self-correction must be taught and learned during professional training if they are to be practiced throughout a professional career.

Discontinuities exist also between professional education and the so-called preprofessional education required by nearly all professional schools, either as a separate degree or as a necessary requirement in the early years of college work. While it is true that all professions give at least lip service to the importance of liberal studies, the faculties in the liberal arts and professions are separated both by space and by culture. With the increased emphasis on career specialization by students, and on academic specialization by faculty, the gaps have become wider in recent years (Boyer, 1987). The result is that liberal arts requirements are "all too often viewed by students and professional faculty alike as a rite of passage, something to 'get through' as painlessly as possible before getting down to the real work of the profession" (Armour and Fuhrmann, 1989, p. 1). Under these circumstances, in which students take professional courses "over here" and liberal arts courses "over there," integration of liberal and professional curricula is almost nonexistent, and change becomes very difficult.

In an attempt to break down these curricular and disciplinary barriers, the Professional Preparation Project brought educators from eight professions together with colleagues from the liberal arts and identified ten learning goals that liberal and professional educators hold in common. Armour and Fuhrmann, two of the participants in this project, have further refined the concept of liberal learning as it applies to professional education from ten competencies to only four: "Our point of view is that liberal learning fosters thinking skills in students, provides them with an intellectual and social context for that thought, helps them to develop and question values, and provides them with the skills to communicate the results of the thought process" (Armour and Fuhrmann, 1989, p. 127).

Examining these goals within the context of what novice professionals should learn leads to some powerful conclusions about what we should be teaching them. First, professionals must be able to sift through multiple kinds of evidence from multiple sources, and make reasoned choices without letting their own biases get in the way. Second, they must do this within a context that makes sense for *them,* while recognizing the boundaries and limitations of the context they have chosen. Third, they must have well-articulated personal standards against which to measure new ideas and experiences. "Central to an understanding of values," Armour and Fuhrmann write, "is the value that views values as important to the thought process, essential to the development of our society, and always subject to challenge" (1989, p. 136). And fourth, the sharpest critical and analytic skills will do professionals little good unless they are also able to listen, to speak, and to write. Communication skills provide the critical bridge between theory and practice.

Efforts to articulate and incorporate in professional programs competencies generally relegated to the liberal arts curriculum have perhaps been most evident in accounting, where professional leaders have worked closely with educators for many years to implement a new curriculum based on analysis of the changing needs of the profession (AAA Committee on the Future Content, Structure, and Scope of Accounting Education, 1986). Objectives for the new curriculum integrate knowledge of professional concepts and tools with intellectual, interpersonal, and communication skills; ethics and values of the profession; and the capacity for lifelong learning (Accounting Education Change Commission, 1990). The Accounting Education Change Commission, supported by the six largest accounting firms in the United States, has funded curriculum innovation and assessment on over two dozen campuses nationwide. Conferences, workshops, publications, and program presentations—often co-sponsored with professional associations in accounting—have disseminated project results and resources to accounting educators in every type of institution.

In short, professional educators should no longer assume that liberal learning is the sole responsibility of the faculty over there in the liberal arts and sciences. Increasingly, we are discovering that these qualities need to be developed as part of the student's own professional self as well. Students need to learn the unique critical thinking of their future profession, the social context and values of that profession, and how they as future professionals may best communicate with clients, patients, and colleagues.

One of the most neglected foci of liberal learning within professional education is the development of professional values (Ozar, 1993). The most appropriate place to begin building awareness of ethical standards and professional conduct is in the undergraduate years, with refinement and reinforcement in professional courses. Ozar has identified six goals that should be part of each professional curriculum:

1. To enhance the modelling-imitation-habituation process that is part of all professional formation.
2. To heighten students' awareness of ethical issues in professional practice.
3. To strengthen students' moral reasoning skills, particularly in the application of norms in the profession to practice situations and in judgments of whether norms of the profession are appropriate and sufficient.
4. To develop a basic understanding of the nature of a profession and the general character of professional obligations and to develop an understanding of the content of norms of the profession.
5. To enhance the students' ability to implement careful, ethical judgments and to formulate appropriate strategies for addressing barriers to such implementation.
6. To make students more articulate in discussing the ethical dimensions of professional practice and more effective listeners when such matters are being discussed by others. [1993, pp. 153–157]

Nurturing Values of Lifelong Learning

Much of the learning in professional practice is in response to changing context or conditions; most professional practice change thus results from self-directed learning rather than traditional continuing professional education programming (Fox, Mazmanian, and Putnam, 1989). It would seem obvious then that learning how to become a self-directed learner should be a part of any professional education curriculum.

The reality, however, is that an undergraduate and professional education organized to instill and build upon the professional's commitment to lifelong learning would require a "transformation in the role of educator, from distributor of knowledge and skills to collaborator and facilitator of learner controlled changes in performance" (Bennett and Fox, 1993, p. 270). If we believe in lifelong learning, all educators must enhance the abilities of the learners to plan and manage their own learning. Formal education, undergraduate through continuing, should be designed and made available in such a manner that fits the pattern of learners' self-directed activities. Educational systems dedicated to fostering and promoting lifelong learning must provide systematic feedback designed to indicate areas of learning need, and alternatives to approach the necessary learning. By this standard, the current design for undergraduate and professional education inhibits rather than fosters independent learning.

Continuing professional education is therefore facing a fundamental choice. The first option is to continue with present models of design and delivery, which have the virtue of administrative simplicity, suitability to faculty and an unending potential for making money, at least for the designers and providers of continuing professional education. The alternative is to require providers of continuing professional education to reorient instructional content and methodology to emphasize learners' needs, intentions, and contexts and thus orient the program more toward professional practice than professional schools, more toward changing professional behavior than updating professional information.

As outlined earlier in this chapter, it is precisely this change that is demanded by the present societal renegotiation of the social contract with professions—the public wishes assurance that practicing professionals remain competent throughout their careers. In addition to improving the definition, measurement, and certification procedures for initial competence, the ability of a profession to meet this new obligation will rest on the quality and effectiveness of remediation efforts mounted once incompetence or diminishing competence is discovered. This remediation will take the form of continuing professional education that will very likely fundamentally involve the professional schools throughout the careers of professionals in practice. Some professional schools have retained their sense of responsibility for continuing professional education in addition to their primary responsibility for quality initial education. Medical schools, for example, more than professional schools of social work and law, evidence this continuing commitment.

Across all professional schools, new models of continuing professional education will have to be developed and tested. Primary among these new models will be practitioner-initiated methods of self-reflection and practice change, made more likely and sustainable through recently available technological supports. For example, electronic mail can help professionals in widely dispersed settings compile and analyze variations in professional practice. Such communication can lead to the questioning of practice norms, and to the identification of practice outliers. This personalized information is of high salience to professionals; research has shown repeatedly that the primary source of influence on professionals' practice behavior is their own colleagues (for example, Wergin and others, 1988). Other technological enhancements to professional reflection include memory prompts within an electronically displayed client chart, and client simulations, developed with increasing fidelity using CD-ROM technology. In all these areas, professional schools need to be more creative in innovation, more scholarly in evaluation, and more vigorous in adoption. They will be aided throughout by increasingly close relationships with professionals in practice.

Conclusions

What should be the priorities for approaching the changes suggested in this chapter?

Certainly, the need for change in undergraduate and professional education has become more acute. For at least the past thirty years, rhetoric has been widespread within the university community about the necessity of improvement in structure, function, and outcomes. A number of change schemes have been attempted over the years, including such business management imports as zero-base budgeting, management by objectives, and most recently, Total Quality Management (Seymour, 1992). These efforts have generally followed current fads and have been both underevaluated and short-lived. Despite a range of exciting efforts now under way ("Innovations on Campus," 1994), better efficacy would be achieved by paying attention to three fundamental priorities:

- Taking a proactive stance with regard to public accountability
- Integrating technical with practical knowledge
- Adopting a more reflective educational practice

As described earlier in this chapter, the implicit contract that professional schools and universities hold with society provides certain exclusive rights in exchange for the assurance of quality and effectiveness. Because of the technical and complex nature of these quality and effectiveness objectives, ordinary citizens historically have felt unable to pass judgment and have thus entrusted the accountability function to the professions and the universities themselves. Many players are involved in the definition, measurement, certification, and assurance of competence of professional and university graduates. Nonetheless, professional schools and universities have a responsibility to the societies that fund them to provide leadership in constantly refining these definitions of competence, improving the measurement, and ensuring the competence of their graduates.

This assurance of outcomes competence will depend centrally on how competence and outcomes are to be defined. We have suggested throughout this chapter that the current academic definitions based on assessment of knowledge bases are inadequate. The self-consciousness and self-critique necessary for competence in practice, and the ability to self-direct continuing education, must form part of the outcomes objectives for university undergraduate and professional school education. These competencies have long been held central to the objectives of liberal learning, are central to the ethics of professional practice, and go a long way toward satisfying the accountability problems in higher and professional education. In increasingly complex societies, successful professional practice and adequate university level outcomes cannot be defined simply as the ability to apply and demonstrate mastery of technical and abstract information. While this has never been the defining characteristic of higher education graduates, too often higher education has acted as if it were.

Fundamentally, what is required is a renaissance in our mental archetypes of higher and professional education. Universities are no longer insulated, privileged sanctuaries. They must either become agents of their own reform or face becoming increasingly vulnerable targets of a skeptical society.

References

AAA Committee on the Future Content, Structure, and Scope of Accounting Education. *Issues in Accounting,* 1986, *1*(1), 168–195.

Abbott, A. A. *The System of Professions: An Essay on the Division of Expert Labor.* Chicago: University of Chicago Press, 1988.

Accounting Education Change Commission. *Objectives of Education for Accountants: Position Statement Number One.* Torrence, Calif.: Accounting Education Change Commission, Sept. 1990.

"Almanac." *Chronicle of Higher Education,* 1994, *XLI*(1), 5–45.

American Association for the Advancement of Science. "Gender and the Culture of Science." *American Association for the Advancement of Science,* Apr. 16, 1993, pp. 260, 383–430.

American Educational Research Association, American Psychological Association, and National Council on Measurement in Education. *Standards for Educational and Psychological Testing.* Washington, D.C.: American Psychological Association, 1985.

Armour, R. A., and Fuhrmann, B. S. (eds.). *Integrating Liberal Learning and Professional Education.* New Directions for Teaching and Learning, no. 40. San Francisco: Jossey-Bass, 1989.

Bennett, N. L., and Fox, R. D. "Challenges for Continuing Professional Education." In L. Curry, J. F. Wergin, and Associates, *Educating Professionals: Responding to New Expectations for Competence and Accountability.* San Francisco: Jossey-Bass, 1993.

Bledstein, B. J. *The Culture of Professionalism: The Middle Class and the Development of Higher Education in America.* New York: Norton, 1976.

Boyer, E. L. *College: The Undergraduate Experience in America.* New York: HarperCollins, 1987.

Brubacher, J. S. "The Evolution of Professional Education." In National Society for the Study of Education, *Sixty-first Yearbook, Part II.* Chicago: University of Chicago Press, 1962.

Cavanaugh, S. H. "Connecting Education and Practice." In L. Curry, J. F. Wergin, and Associates, *Educating Professionals: Responding to New Expectations for Competence and Accountability.* San Francisco: Jossey-Bass, 1993.

Curry, L., Wergin, J. F., and Associates. *Educating Professionals: Responding to New Expectations for Competence and Accountability.* San Francisco: Jossey-Bass, 1993.

Engel, J. D., Wigton, R., LaDuca, A., and Blacklow, R. S. "A Social Judgement Theory Perspective on Clinical Problem Solving." *Evaluation and the Health Professions,* 1990, *13,* 63–78.

Fox, R. D., Mazmanian, P. E., and Putnam, R. W. *Changing and Learning in the Lives of Physicians.* New York: Praeger, 1989.

Gies, W. J. *Dental Education in the United States and Canada: A Report to the Carnegie Foundation for the Advancement of Teaching.* Bulletin no. 19. New York: Carnegie Foundation for the Advancement of Teaching, 1926.

Hambleton, R. K., and Swaminathan, H. *Item Response Theory: Principles and Applications.* Norwell, Mass.: Kluwer, 1985.

Harris, I. B. "New Expectations for Professional Competence." In L. Curry, J. F. Wergin, and Associates, *Educating Professionals: Responding to New Expectations for Competence and Accountability*. San Francisco: Jossey-Bass, 1993.

"Innovations on Campus." *Science*, 1994, *266*, 843–893.

Marshall, J. G. "The Expanding Use of Technology." In L. Curry, J. F. Wergin, and Associates, *Educating Professionals: Responding to New Expectations for Competence and Accountability*. San Francisco: Jossey-Bass, 1993.

McGaghie, W. "Evaluating Competence for Professional Practice." In L. Curry, J. F. Wergin, and Associates, *Educating Professionals: Responding to New Expectations for Competence and Accountability*. San Francisco: Jossey-Bass, 1993.

McGuire, C. "Sociocultural Changes Affecting Professions and Professionals." In L. Curry, J. F. Wergin, and Associates, *Educating Professionals: Responding to New Expectations for Competence and Accountability*. San Francisco: Jossey-Bass, 1993.

Norcini, J. J., and Shea, J. A. "Increasing Pressures for Recertification." In L. Curry, J. F. Wergin, and Associates, *Educating Professionals: Responding to New Expectations for Competence and Accountability*. San Francisco: Jossey-Bass, 1993.

Numbers, R. L. "The Fall and Rise of the Medical Profession." In N. O. Hatch (ed.), *The Professions in American History*. Notre Dame, Ind.: University of Notre Dame Press, 1988.

Ozar, D. T. "Building Awareness of Ethical Standards and Conduct." In L. Curry, J. F. Wergin, and Associates, *Educating Professionals: Responding to New Expectations for Competence and Accountability*. San Francisco: Jossey-Bass, 1993.

Reed, A. Z. *Training for the Public Profession of Law*. New York: Carnegie Foundation for the Advancement of Teaching, 1921.

Rice, R. E., and Richlin, L. "Broadening the Concept of Scholarship in the Professions." In L. Curry, J. F. Wergin, and Associates, *Educating Professionals: Responding to New Expectations for Competence and Accountability*. San Francisco: Jossey-Bass, 1993.

Samson, G. E., Grave, M. E., Weinstein, T., and Walberg, H. J. "Academic and Occupational Performance: A Quantitative Synthesis." *American Educational Research Journal*, 1984, *21*(2), 311–321.

Schön, D. A. *The Reflective Practitioner: How Professionals Think in Action*. New York: Basic Books, 1983.

Schön, D. A. *Educating the Reflective Practitioner: Toward a New Design for Teaching and Learning in the Professions*. San Francisco: Jossey-Bass, 1987.

Schön, D. A. (ed.) *The Reflective Turn: Case Studies in and on Educational Practice*. New York: Teachers College Press, 1991.

Seymour, D. T. *On Q: Causing Quality in Higher Education*. Old Tappan, N.J.: Macmillan, 1992.

Shavelson, R. J., Mayberry, P. W., Li, W., and Webb, N. M. "Generalization of Job Performance Measurements: Marine Corps Riflemen." *Military Psychology*, 1990, *2*, 129–144.

Shaw, B. F., and Dobson, K. S. "Competency Judgments in the Training and Evaluation of Psychotherapists." *Journal of Consulting and Clinical Psychology*, 1988, *56*, 666–672.

Shulman, L. S. "Knowledge and Teaching: Foundations of the New Reform." *Harvard Educational Review*, 1987, *57*(1), 1–22.

Stillman, P. L., and others. "Assessing Clinical Skills of Residents with Standardized Patients." *Annals of Internal Medicine*, 1986, *105*, 762–771.

Wergin, J. F., and others. "CME and Change in Practice: An Alternative Perspective." *Journal of Continuing Education in the Health Professions*, 1988, *8*, 147–159.

CHAPTER SEVENTEEN

OCCUPATIONAL EDUCATION

Darrel A. Clowes

Chapter Sixteen offers an interesting starting point for a discussion of occupational education. It defines professional education as "a system of formal education that prepares novices for highly skilled occupations through a combination of theory and practice, and that culminates with an award of certification, licensure, or other formal credential." It sharpens this definition by identifying the professions as law, medicine, engineering, and the like, and the sites for professional education as schools typically lodged in research universities. What then is *occupational education*? What are its representative fields and its usual sites?

The Curry and Wergin definition of professional education applies reasonably well to occupational education, with three reservations. The first is that the highly skilled occupations I will be discussing here are less reliant than those in Chapter Sixteen on theory over practice or technique. This is indicated by the reduced liberal education component in the training program and the less stringent technical or preprofessional preparation demanded. Thus the skills used are not as complex as those needed for professionals. The second reservation is that the mix of theory and practice is different. If professional education is described as high on theory and low on practice and vocational training as high on practice and low on theory, then occupational education takes the middle position, represented by a balance of theory and practice. The third reservation is that certification or licensure may or may not be called for by a particular occupation, and completion of the educational program and receipt of the resultant credential may not be necessary to work in a particular occupation. Thus, for practical purposes occupational education can be defined with the same words as professional education, with these three modifications in meaning.

Professional, occupational, and ultimately vocational education are best distinguished by fields and sites within postsecondary education. At one end of the continuum of programs addressed by occupational education are the advanced technologies like instrumentation specialist and fiber optics technician, which do emphasize theory over practice; at a midpoint of the continuum are programs like nursing aide and hospitality specialist, which balance theory and practice; and at the vocational training end of the continuum are programs in carpentry, truck driving, engine repair, and brick laying, which call for extensive practical experience and training but have few requirements for theory, technical knowledge, or liberal arts education. Sites for these representative programs reflect their particular blending of theory and practice. Professional education is usually housed in the research university. Occupational education is usually housed in the community college, proprietary school, or career college with some upward shift to four-year colleges—usually nonselective liberal arts colleges and comprehensive colleges and universities (Clowes and Hawthorne, 1995). Vocational training is usually the province of secondary education, proprietary schools, and adult training facilities.

Chapter Sixteen argues that professional education is characterized by *technical rationality*, where programs are structured on the belief that "learning precedes doing and that practice is the application of theory" (Rice and Richlin, 1993, p. 81). *Vocational training* may be distinguished from professional education as an area where doing precedes learning and practice is the guide. Occupational education again occupies a middle ground where learning is a roughly equal blend of learning by doing and learning from theory. In this context, occupational education shares a degree of technical rationality with professional education but differs in matters of degree.

There is another significant distinction of value. Green (1968) draws a useful distinction between *jobs* and *work*. Jobs, as he uses the term, involve labor done solely for the purpose of income for consumption with little commitment of the self. A job does not provide a sense of completion or fulfillment. Work, by contrast, Green sees as a sustained and purposeful activity that enriches or sustains life and through which the purposes and meaning of the worker are expressed. A job becomes work when it includes the "exercise of judgment, sense of style, and the practice of a sense of craft" (p. 44). This concept can be related to the continuum from vocational training to occupational education to professional education. Vocational training would be preparation for jobs. Professional training would be preparation for work. Occupational education would again be a middle ground where at the lower end jobs and training are involved, at the upper end education and work are involved, and the center shows a mixture of training and education, jobs and work. Thus occupational education is a sector of the educational world representing a tension between the training and the educating function in U.S. education. This tension may be reflected in the language by our use of *craft* as a special midway point between job and work, between useful object and art object, between utility and art. This tension will find its expression in curricular issues and in the alignment of curricula with institutional types.

Perspectives

A look at a few historical turning points and theoretical approaches can provide useful perspectives on occupational education.

History

The earliest manifestations of technical rationality in American postsecondary education should probably be credited to the proprietary schools of the colonial era. Training for work began to shift from a craft-and-apprenticeship model with the emergence of programs designed to bring a number of students together under the tutelage of a master of the field. Tuition was charged and some certification of competence provided to allow the students entry into a field. This model developed for surveying, accounting, and general business, among other fields; a blend of theory and practice was the hallmark of these programs. Apprenticeships and related forms of on-the-job training and proprietary school training remained the primary form of preparation for work. Higher education retained a classical curriculum and—except for the preparation of ministers and teachers—did not participate directly in workforce preparation (Honick, 1995).

The Morrill Land-Grant Colleges Act of 1862 is a significant marker in the emergence of a practical component in the mission of higher education. The Morrill Act provided federal support for state institutions devoted to the cultivation of the practical and mechanical arts—to technical rationality. Although it would be years, decades in fact, before the land-grant colleges were active players in the majority of states (Johnson, 1981), the Morrill Act legitimized the practical curriculum and technical rationality as part of higher education. In another sense, it made preparation for work in the sense Green used the term as a function of higher education. In a similar way, the Smith Hughes legislation of 1917 made preparation for jobs the province of the secondary schools.

Other significant historical markers were the report of the Truman Commission emphasizing increased access to postsecondary education, and the language shift from higher education to postsecondary education in 1972 amendments to the Higher Education Act of 1965. The emphasis on access and on practical education in the Truman Commission report became operationalized in the rapid expansion of community colleges in the late 1950s and throughout the 1960s. These institutions introduced a newly significant institutional type between the secondary school and traditional four-year higher education. Community colleges and the existing proprietary schools became a thermocline in the ocean of American education, lying between the lower waters represented by secondary schools and the upper waters represented by higher education. The amendments of 1972 legitimized the language shift occurring as these institutions in the thermocline began to assume a role and identity separate from the rest of higher education. In this legislation and in other ways within the field, postsecondary education began to emerge as a label for a distinct group of institutions within or apart from higher education (Clowes, 1995).

The 1990 Carl D. Perkins Vocational and Applied Technology Education Act Amendments joined a stream of Technical Preparation and School-to-Work initiatives designed to support and encourage occupational education in secondary institutions and in postsecondary institutions—usually the community college but potentially proprietary institutions and four-year institutions with an emphasis on professional and vocational preparation as well (see *Journal of Higher Education*, 1984). This pattern of legislation is a current marker for the continuing development of a practical curriculum in postsecondary institutions. A significant curricular emphasis in this legislative initiative is the integration of academic and vocational education. Although to date this is primarily a secondary school initiative, there are expectations that this integration will extend into postsecondary education.

Theoretical Approaches

Different theories can provide perspective on the role of occupational programs, particularly on the crucial link between occupational education and the job market. In many respects, this linkage provides the basis for occupational education. Schwab (1978) argued that curriculum could at best be described as eclectic activities of the practical world. He would expect theoretical formulations to provide little understanding of occupational programs; instead, he would look to social, economic, or technological forces operating on curricular content, design, and execution. In a similar vein, Kliebard (1992) has argued persuasively that vocational education in America is a "symbolic action" that has meaning only as metaphor—as an expression of our valuing of work. He asserts that "rather than seeing vocationalism as curriculum policy . . . it may be more useful to think of it as a morality play" (p. 197). In my judgment, a full answer cannot be found in theory, but various efforts do shed light.

At the macroanalytic level, these questions of theory involve the relationship of work and education and consideration of the place of work in our society. Those issues are beyond the scope of this book and this chapter. James O'Toole provides a useful entry into them in *Work in America* (1974) and *Work, Learning, and the American Future* (1977), as does Arthur Wirth in *Productive Work in Industry and Schools* (1983) and *Education and Work for the Year 2000* (1992). At a more modest microanalytic level, there are theories that are useful.

• *Functionalism* is a theoretical position that assumes a tight coupling between higher education preparation and occupational competence and employment. This position assumes that employment needs can be reasonably projected, that training programs can be geared to meeting those projected employment needs, and that trained graduates will take those positions and remain in them. However, as O'Toole (1977) reports, "The madness of the situation is that forecasters take only fairly reliable data about the supply of workers, run these against unreliable demand data in a process complicated by the cobweb effect and the substitutability of labor, and, lo and behold, produce 'the truth.' It is no wonder that manpower planning efforts to match the exact supply of workers with specific job openings simply have not worked in the past (and are unlikely to work in the future)" (p. 47).

Many observers challenge the assumption of a tight connection between the training given and the employment obtained. Wilms (1980) and Pincus (1980) criticized the functionalists' position fifteen years ago; their criticisms still hold today. Functionalism as a theory does not provide a reliable perspective on the role of occupational education.

• *Credentialism* is a theoretical position that asserts that the primary function served by schooling is to provide school completers with credentials that set them apart from the remainder of the workforce and which provide them with the credentials for entry into occupations with high status (Collins, 1979). Karabel (1972) earlier adapted this argument to the community college and argued this institution has served to raise the level of credential expected for certain occupations and thus to increase the stratification within an already-stratified society.

These arguments depend on establishing a tight connection between specific degrees earned and employment in high-status positions across a broad range of occupations. While connections can be established in fields like engineering and nursing, no such connection has been established across the broad range of occupations. These connections are especially difficult to establish in the community college because of the modest numbers of students who actually graduate and receive the credential. At best a weak general association is established between level of credentials attained and level of economic success. There is no clear evidence that even this modest association is related to the occupational education obtained rather than other factors. Thus credentialism also provides little help in establishing a theoretical basis for specific occupational education.

• *Legitimation theory* offers insight into the roles played by postsecondary educational institutions in a complex society (Roemer, 1981). This theory sees postsecondary institutions serving two important functions. First, they identify bodies of knowledge appropriate to a particular occupation or field, legitimize that knowledge area by structuring college courses and programs around it, and provide the credentials (course credits, certificates, and degrees) appropriate for the field. In this way, higher education participates in the legitimation or professionalization of occupational fields. Second, new professional roles are established, and new knowledge must be produced for the field and new professionals prepared. Both are roles for postsecondary education. While legitimation theory's operation is clearest in higher education at the baccalaureate degree level and above, it also operates to legitimize semiprofessional and technical areas appropriate to the associate degree. Examples would be the Associate of Science degree in nursing, instrumentation, fiber optics, food science, and other technologies. Thus legitimation theory helps explain the emergence of new occupational fields and degree programs and clarifies the roles of postsecondary institutions in that process.

• *Queue* theory also has explanatory power and can be argued to support legitimation (Geiger, 1980). Queue theory is grounded in the practical. This argument holds that competition for jobs causes more desirable positions to have a large queue of applicants while less desired positions have a short queue. Since most individuals act in rational ways to find a preferred place in a long queue, applicants strive to have a special qualification to set them apart and move them to the head of the queue. Postsecondary education responds to the market and produces programs to provide those special qualifications, such as the Bachelor's in Business Administration and then the Master's in Business Administration; the Associate of Science degree in nursing and then the Bachelor of Science degree in nursing. In this formulation, applicants with special qualifications displace other applicants in the queue until the market becomes glutted and the queue is full of individuals with the same credential. This is the point at which new queues must be established. Either the job market will shift, changing the mix of long and short queues for applicants to enter, or postsecondary institutions will produce even more specialized programs to provide applicants a more special qualification.

The vocationalization of postsecondary education is a fact. It is important to understand that the tight connections between manpower planning, postsecondary training, and employment assumed by functionalism and credentialing do not hold. We must look beyond mere training to understand our programs. Legitimation and queue theory provide insight into the social roles postsecondary institutions play; they do not explain the theoretical base for occupational education.

Undergirding all discussions of occupational education are concerns for the distinction between specific job-skills training and education for generic work skills, and for finding an appropriate balance between the two skill sets. The preceding discussion emphasized the loose connection existing between training and the workplace, which argues for generic forms of work skills and is consistent with most professional judgment and current legislation. Illustrative of this is the emphasis on enhanced academics and integration of academic and vocational education in the Perkins legislation—a strand that has run steadily through all American education rhetoric since the publication of *A Nation at Risk* (National Commission on Excellence in Education, 1983).

Praxis

A well-designed occupational education program would provide a carefully planned sequence of courses leading to the degree. At the same time, it would ensure that students are not locked into a curriculum or program with no alternatives. A curriculum should ideally allow a student to explore a general area (for example, nursing) with an option to move toward the next professional step (premed) without undue loss of credits. Conversely, the curriculum should allow a student who finds a specific curriculum too difficult an option to move into a less demanding curriculum (dental hygiene, for example) without undue loss of credits. This means the curriculum should first provide general education courses and general courses in the field appropriate for a wide range of related programs. Specialized courses should come late in the sequence when students are committed to a specific program.

The institution's total occupational curriculum should ensure program integration. Labs and specialized equipment are very expensive to establish and to maintain. Only the most specialized labs should be program specific. Most labs should serve two or more programs to make them economic. Service courses within occupational departments should be designed to serve several different occupational programs. In this way students from a number of programs, some large and some small, can be brought together in substantial numbers in common courses. General education courses are service courses to occupational curricula. In the same way, lab-based courses ought to serve a number of related programs.

Vertical and horizontal integration of programs pose other significant programmatic considerations. Vertical integration involves the issues of articulation with secondary school programs, the provision of courses to bring returning adults up to speed for entry into programs, and articulation with potential transfer institutions for the program graduates. Horizontal integration involves outreach to industry and other employers to provide students with related work experience through internships and co-op experiences, to ensure programs are responsive to local employment needs, and to facilitate placement of graduates with appropriate employers.

Practice in postsecondary institutions reveals two significant trends. The first is the well-documented shift toward a practical curriculum; the second is toward an increased emphasis on noncredit and work-related training activities designed for specific client groups.

• *Practical curriculum.* The shift toward a practical curriculum has been discussed in several ways already. Its impact on four-year institutions has been chronicled by historians of higher education. Rudolph (1977) explained the situation thus: "If in the nineteenth century the curriculum defined the market for higher learning, in the twentieth the market defined the curriculum" (p. 247). Nowhere was this trend more evident than in the lower prestige levels of the postsecondary arena. The transfer function steadily declined in community colleges (Grubb, 1991; Lombardi, 1979; Pincus and Archer, 1989) while the preparation-for-work function increased (Brint and Karabel, 1989; Clowes and Levin, 1989; Harris and Grebe, 1977). Nonselective liberal arts colleges were transforming their curricula from the traditional to more applied or occupationally oriented curricula. This movement was reported and analyzed relative to liberal arts and other small colleges in the March/April 1984 issue of the *Journal of Higher Education.* Campbell and Korim (1979) examined this movement and described a shift of curricula in occupational fields from two-year institutions to four-year institutions. Dickerson and Clowes (1982) described a curriculum movement in the other direction as two-year institutions developed curricula based on programs in four-year institutions. Not only was there an increasingly practical emphasis to the postsecondary curriculum, but the distinctions among the curricula of nonselective liberal arts colleges, comprehensive four-year institutions, and community colleges were breaking down.

• *Noncredit and work-related training activities.* The trend toward an increased emphasis on noncredit and work-related training activities designed for specific client groups has emerged over the past two decades. A related development has been the shift in student or client populations. Students in community colleges are increasing likely to be part-time, female, and older. This change is also occurring in nonselective four-year institutions with applied curricula. Thus we are seeing an emphasis upon occupational education and training but a shift in clients away from the full-time regular student. Indeed, there is among the community colleges a shift away from degree-seeking students as the norm. All these elements confound program planning and development for these institutions.

The community college exists on the penumbra of higher education and is more exposed to the shifts in mission and client than other institutional types. That makes the community college an excellent early warning system for the changes operating, and especially the changes that will affect the lower-status institutions like the comprehensive universities and the nonselective liberal arts colleges. Community colleges have seen an increase in numbers of degrees conferred in occupational specialties over the past decade. However, this is a weak indicator of their activity. Substantial proportions of community college students never achieve a degree (perhaps as high as 95 percent in some states), and the most frequent use of the community college is for a student to take five to six classes in a ten-year period with the majority of the classes being occupational in orientation (Adelman, 1992). With a college's curriculum and faculty organized to deliver programs for degree completers serving students who mainly take a few classes and leave, there is a clear disjunction between the curriculum of many institutions and the reality of their role. This has become increasingly apparent in the community college and has led to a series of adaptive behaviors.

Community colleges have increasingly shifted from preemployment training in degree and certificate programs to postemployment training. This fits the needs and interests of the older and part-time student body and has served to ensure a steady stream of students. The drawback is the need to constantly replace students who take only a few classes and leave. In an effort to achieve stability, many institutions have turned to business and industry as a new client group and tailored their offerings to local employer training needs. Customized training and contract courses have become standard offerings. The critical point is that, for all practical purposes, these activities are outside the degree-granting track for most students. What then is the organizing principle for the curriculum if it is not programs and courses leading to a degree or a certificate? Has Rudolph's observation come to pass? Does the market determine the curriculum?

An adaptation made by many community colleges is to protect their degree-oriented curricula—by partitioning customized training and contract courses off from the rest of the curriculum. This is accomplished in two ways. Either the activities are separated from the normal academic programs and administered through a continuing education unit of the institution or they are delivered as noncredit offerings. Because so many institutions are funded on the basis of full-time equivalent students (FTEs) in credit courses, there is often reluctance to relinquish credit for these offerings. As a result, a number of Byzantine delivery systems have emerged. However, the central point remains. These courses are partitioned off from the regular classes in some way. The practice of delivering these classes (both credit and noncredit) for a fee has become so prevalent that it has been tagged a cash cow of postsecondary education *(Chronicle of Higher Education,* 1991).

What can be learned from observing these adaptive behaviors? First, institutions have been so concerned with adapting to market forces and so concerned with the fetish of client service that they have often neglected to ask the basic questions: What business are we in? Are we actually doing what we say we do? Some community colleges, for instance, are dangerously near losing their original mission without clearly establishing a new one (see Clowes and Levin, 1989, and Clowes, 1995, for elaboration on this point). This concern over mission underscores the importance of deciding the place of occupational education in each institution.

Second, clarity about curricular components is important. The core of the enterprise is degree-granting programs designed as preparation for work, for transfer to a baccalaureate degree program, or both. A related function is providing postemployment training for individuals through planned sequences of courses leading to certificates. Another function is serving clients in business and industry by designing special programs for their employees. Determining what function or functions you choose to pursue is the first step. Next come decisions about financing the activity. Is it to be FTE-funded as a credit course? Is it provided on a fee-for-service basis and thus self-supporting or profit generating? Will you attempt a blend of the two? Another step is determining which unit of the institution will provide each function. The choices include using an academic department as the delivery vehicle, using the continuing education unit, or setting up a separate center for contract training or some other discrete function. Practice has revealed a number of new issues emerging. The worst error often is not the decisions themselves but the failure to make decisions and allowing the institution, like Topsy, to just grow.

Evaluation

Evaluation of occupational programs is complex. Basic to any evaluation effort is answering three key questions: Evaluating for what purpose or audience? Evaluating what? and Evaluating against what criteria? For occupational programs, the answers to those simple questions lead in many directions. Purpose or audience determines the form evaluation will take, a point discussed further in Chapters Twenty-Eight and Twenty-Nine. Deciding what is to be evaluated is equally important and leads directly into the dilemma presented by the multiple functions served by many occupational programs. This is exemplified best in the community college. A conventional practice is to evaluate a program in terms of the employment histories or transfer records of graduates. Yet in a community college a very modest proportion of students are graduates and many students transfer without graduating from the community college program. So evaluating program completion and completers is a poor and partial measure of program outcomes. Many students use programs for their own purposes. They take selected courses to enhance their skills and knowledge and then leave the program or the institution. Should there be an arbitrary standard established to identify students in the program? Perhaps a student who has taken five courses in a program in a three-year period ought be considered as in the program and followed as a class of student along with program completers. Cohen (1993) has proposed such a mechanism to better track transfer students who do not graduate from the community college; perhaps it is an appropriate approach in occupational programs also. Another determination must be made about noncredit and contract courses offered by the occupational program or through a continuing education unit. Are these to be evaluated? As one pursues this question of what should be evaluated, it becomes apparent that there is no easy and simple answer. The further one pursues the question, the clearer the distinctions among forms of programs become and the more focused and useful an evaluation can be.

Evaluation can be goal free, but for many purposes it is important to have clear criteria against which evaluation may occur. Yet clear and exact criteria are difficult to establish. How many graduates ought a program have? What proportion of students ought to complete a program? What is an acceptable attrition figure within a program? Given the shifting student population of many programs, these are difficult if not impossible criteria to establish. The closer one moves to the traditional college model of full-time students enrolled in programs, the more feasible, though still arbitrary, such criteria become. It may be most desirable to conduct goal-free evaluations first to establish what programs are actually accomplishing before setting artificial and perhaps unrealistic criteria.

Criteria for noncredit and contract courses are also difficult to establish. Typical course-based criteria like attrition, grade distributions, and attitude survey results can be developed, but there is a real question about whether these data or criteria relate to significant issues. Basic issues like the kind of service to the community a program offers are not addressed. Social policy issues embedded in these programs are often unaddressed through evaluation. Questions like the appropriate role for a college (public or private) in providing employer-specific training lie behind occupational training—but can be addressed best through analytic and policy-oriented discussions at the upper levels of the institution. Another such issue is the role of occupational programs in cooling out students and in diverting them from other curricular avenues that offer more potential for upward mobility. These issues too are part of the evaluation of occupational programs and ought be addressed.

Conclusion

Can one draw conclusions about occupational programs in U.S. higher education? Certainly, each of us can. However, the curriculum remains eclectic. There is no clear or tight connection between occupational curricula, the student desire for certain programs, the employer demands for certain types of graduates, and the social need for qualified and credentialed technical expertise. This leaves us with no compelling theoretical basis for occupational curricula. Occupational curricula serve a pragmatic purpose and are guided by pragmatic considerations. That seems appropriate for a nation whose core values may be grounded in pragmatism and the practical.

There are clear trends in the way we plan and deliver occupational programs. Occupational programs are moving further into higher education and becoming an established part of the curriculum. The pattern of movement reflects the Carnegie classifications, with occupational programs more dominant in the less prestigious levels of the Carnegie scheme but contesting with professional education at the higher prestige levels. The effort to compartmentalize occupational programs by assigning them to noncredit status and to off-campus delivery is clear. It is most successful at the more prestigious institutions and least successful at the less prestigious institutions. Whether financial stress will force institutions to more overtly pursue the cash-cow dimension of occupational programs may affect the programs' role in higher education institutions in the future. It is clear that a role exists for these programs and that the role is expanding.

References

Adelman, C. *The Way We Are: The Community College as American Thermometer.* Washington, D.C.: U.S. Department of Education, 1992.

Brint, S., and Karabel, J. *The Diverted Dream: Community Colleges and the Promise of Educational Opportunity in America.* New York: Oxford University Press, 1989.

Campbell, D. F., and Korim, A. S. *Occupational Programs in Four-Year Colleges: Trends and Issues.* ASHE-ERIC/Higher Education Research report no. 5. Washington, D.C.: Association for the Study of Higher Education, 1979.

Chronicle of Higher Education, May 15, 1991, p. 1.

Clowes, D. A. "Community Colleges and Proprietary Schools: Competition or Convergence?" In D. A. Clowes and E. M. Hawthorne (eds.), *Community Colleges and Proprietary Schools: Conflict or Convergence?* New Directions For Community Colleges, no. 91. San Francisco: Jossey-Bass, 1995, pp. 5–16.

Clowes, D. A., and Hawthorne, E. M. (eds.). *Community Colleges and Proprietary Schools: Conflict or*

Convergence? New Directions for Community Colleges, no. 91. San Francisco: Jossey-Bass, 1995.

Clowes, D. A., and Levin, B. H. "Community, Technical, and Junior Colleges: Are They Leaving Higher Education?" *Journal of Higher Education,* 1989, *60*(3), 350–355.

Cohen, A. M. *Celebrating Transfer: A Report of the Annual Transfer Assembly.* Los Angeles: Center for the Study of Community Colleges, 1993. (ED 358 877)

Collins, R. *The Credentialed Society: An Historical Sociology of Education and Stratification.* New York: Academic Press, 1979.

Dickerson, K., and Clowes, D. A. "Curriculum Movement of Clothing and Textile Programs from Four-Year to Two-Year Colleges." *Clothing and Textiles Research Journal,* 1982, *1,* 18–23.

Geiger, R. L. "The College Curriculum and the Marketplace." *Change,* Nov./Dec. 1980, pp. 17–23, 53–54.

Green, T. F. *Work, Leisure and the American Schools.* New York: Random House, 1968.

Grub, W. N. "The Decline of Community College Transfer Rates: Evidence from National Longitudinal Surveys." *Journal of Higher Education,* 1991, *62,* 194–223.

Harris, N. C., and Grebe, J. F. *Career Education in Colleges: A Guide for Planning Two- and Four-year Occupational Programs for Successful Employment.* San Francisco: Jossey-Bass, 1977.

Honick, C. A. "The Story Behind Proprietary Schools in the United States: The Road They Traveled to the Hinterlands of American Higher Education." In D. A. Clowes and E. M. Hawthorne (eds.), *Community Colleges and Proprietary Schools: Conflict or Convergence?* New Directions For Community Colleges, no. 91. San Francisco: Jossey-Bass, 1995.

Johnson, E. L. "Misconceptions About the Early Land-Grant Colleges." *Journal of Higher Education,* 1981, *52*(4), 333–351.

Journal of Higher Education (Special Issue on the Liberal Arts College: Managing Adaptations to the 1980s), 1984, *55*(2).

Karabel, J. "Community Colleges and Social Stratification." *Harvard Educational Review,* 1972, *42*(4), 521–562.

Kliebard, H. M. *Forging the American Curriculum.* New York: Routledge & Kegan Paul, 1992.

Lombardi, J. *The Decline of Transfer Education.* Topical Paper No. 70. Los Angeles, Calif.: ERIC Clearinghouse for Junior Colleges, 1979. (ED 179 273)

National Commission on Excellence in Education. *A Nation at Risk: The Imperative for Educational Reform.* Washington, D.C.: U.S. Department of Education, 1983.

O'Toole, J. O. *Work in America: The Quality of Life Resource Papers for Work.* Cambridge, Mass.: MIT Press, 1974.

O'Toole, J. O. *Work, Learning, and the American Future.* San Francisco: Jossey-Bass, 1977.

Pincus, F. L. "The False Promise of Community Colleges: Class Conflict and Vocational Education." *Harvard Educational Review,* 1980, *50,* 332–361.

Pincus, F., and Archer, E. *Bridges to Opportunity: Are Community Colleges Meeting the Transfer Needs of Minority Students?* New York: Academy for Educational Development and College Entrance Examination Board, 1989.

Rice, R. E., and Richlin, L. "Broadening the Concept of Scholarship in the Professions." In L. Curry, J. F. Wergin, and Associates, *Educating Professionals: Responding to New Expectations for Competence and Accountability.* San Francisco: Jossey-Bass, 1993.

Roemer, R. E. "Vocationalism in Higher Education: Explanations from Social Theory." *Review of Higher Education,* 1981, *4*(2), 23–46.

Rudolph, F. *Curriculum: A History of the American Undergraduate Course of Study Since 1636.* San Francisco: Jossey-Bass, 1977.

Schwab, J. *Science, Curriculum and Liberal Education: Selected Essays.* I. Westbury and N. D. Willkof (eds.). Chicago: University of Chicago Press, 1978.

Wilms, W. W. *Vocational Education and Social Mobility: A Study of Proprietary School Dropouts and Graduates.* Los Angeles: University of California, Graduate School of Education, 1980. (ED 183 966)

Wirth, A. G. *Productive Work in Industry and Schools: Becoming Persons Again.* Lanham, Md.: University Press of America, 1983.

Wirth, A. G. *Education and Work for the Year 2000: Choices We Face.* San Francisco: Jossey-Bass, 1992.

PART FOUR

DIRECTIONS FOR REFORM
ACROSS THE DISCIPLINES

Curricular experimentation and renewal have been staples of higher education for the last two decades. Institutions of all sizes and shapes have asked, What is an educated person? and What are the qualities we want our graduates to possess? After reaching widespread agreement about the answers, a campus then sets out to devise a curriculum that intentionally cultivates those qualities.

Although answers to those questions vary from institution to institution, several commonalities are apparent. Frequently the answers are something like this:

- Students should write and communicate clearly and cogently, and should practice and refine their skills in courses across the curriculum.

- Students should connect ideas and methods from different academic disciplines and use the disciplines to illuminate themes or solve problems.
- Students should learn about other peoples, cultures, and languages.
- Students should understand cultural diversity within America and develop the sensitivities and skills to negotiate differences of gender, race, ethnicity, and class.
- Students should develop the ability to work productively in groups and become engaged in a learning community.
- Students should become familiar with the range of new technologies and use them to advance their own learning and to solve problems.

Large numbers of colleges and universities are seeking to develop instructional programs that purposely develop students' knowledge, skills, and abilities to address these issues, and Part Four focuses on such initiatives.

In Chapter Eighteen, Elaine Maimon—an inspiration and guide for "writing-across-the-curriculum" programs—reflects on the development of what has become a veritable movement. After describing two contrasting conceptions of education and calling for students and faculty to reimagine the curriculum, she moves into an autobiographical history of teaching across the curriculum. She recounts the invention of key aspects of teaching writing across the curriculum—conducting faculty workshops, linking courses to use writing as a way to learn, and working collaboratively. Writing across the curriculum now has its own professional organization, body of literature, accepted principles of practice, and research studies, and there are hundreds of campus programs. Maimon notes that other subjects are now being approached across the curriculum, including speaking, ethics, computing, international awareness, and media criticism, and argues that such programs offer an excellent way for faculty to continue their own learning as they grow as scholars and teachers. Her chapter represents a personal history of broad-based curricular and pedagogical change.

Chapter Nineteen discusses interdisciplinary studies in the context of institutions that are organized by academic disciplines. Julie Klein and William Newell look briefly at the history, motivations,

structures, and forms of interdisciplinary study that address issues too broad or complex to be dealt with adequately by a single discipline or profession. They analyze the core concept of integration, and discuss its implications for course design, approaches to teaching and learning, and assessment. They cite the substantial gains in the theory and practice of interdisciplinary studies, including a professional association, a body of literature, principles of practice, research studies, and many campus programs.

In Chapter Twenty, Joseph Johnston, Jr., and Jane Spalding present a rationale for internationalizing the curriculum and describe the rapid growth in campus programs addressing that agenda. They analyze key aspects of the task—language study, study abroad, and education of international students. And they discuss various practical strategies and steps that institutions may take, describe several campus programs that illustrate general principles, and suggest promising courses of action. The authors argue that the many gains that have been made are still fragile and urge campus leaders, wherever they begin, to realize that internationalizing is not work of any fixed duration and that the impact of that work needs, in time, to spread throughout the institution.

In Chapter Twenty-One, Rick Olguin and Betty Schmitz examine cultural pluralism within the United States and analyze the challenges of addressing diversity closer to home. After a brief history, the authors discuss the complexities of this interdisciplinary agenda, which challenges the epistemological foundations of traditional scholarship. They identify several different concepts, each with different but complementary learning goals, that imply different curricular content. Each of the different approaches calls for faculty development and for styles of teaching that are more personal, experiential, and collaborative than the traditional lecture-discussion model. The chapter concludes with a description of elements of a successful change process.

Chapter Twenty-Two is fashioned by four leaders of what have come to be called *learning communities*—Roberta Matthews, Barbara Leigh Smith, Jean MacGregor, and Faith Gabelnick. Learning communities challenge the idea of isolated courses as the building blocks of the curriculum and point to the values of combining courses for greater educational power. After briefly tracing some milestones, the authors illustrate different forms of learning communities—in freshman year programs, general education, gateway courses (large, so-called filter courses with an expectation that many students will fail), developmental studies, honors programs, and academic majors and minors. They offer practical suggestions for developing learning communities and present strong evidence of their benefits in terms of student satisfaction, achievement, and retention. Of particular note is the benefit that faculty derive, including intellectual stimulation, professional and personal renewal, and

engagement with interesting colleagues in other departments.

James Farmer in Chapter Twenty-Three assesses the information, computer, and communications technologies that for years have promised more effective or efficient learning. He discusses the information technologies of text, audio, images, animation, video, multimedia, and interactivity and also the communication technologies. He argues that to be effective workers in an information society, all college students should: be able to access information resources found on networks such as the Internet, and be familiar with Web browsers, search services, and sources of information related to their own fields; understand indexing and searching well enough to find needed information on all types of media; be able to use word processors, spreadsheets, database management systems, and presentation software; and understand basic programming concepts well enough to make effective use of software. He concludes by discussing the use of technology for learning and instruction, both at present and in the immediate future.

Each of these chapters serves as a pathfinder for academic leaders wanting their campuses to follow these new directions. Together these chapters make clear that more change in the undergraduate curriculum is taking place than most people realize. The scale and pace of change are not apparent even to some of higher education's leaders because it takes place in different areas and in different institutions. More and more students are learning to communicate ideas, integrate knowledge, understand other peoples, deal with diversity, work in communities, and utilize technology.

Conversely, as Johnston and Spalding observe about international educa-

tion, the gains are still scattered and tentative and their cumulative impact is weak. Despite the very substantial progress in each of these areas, much more is required to embed them firmly in our institutions and to extend the benefits to larger numbers of students.

CHAPTER EIGHTEEN

TEACHING "ACROSS THE CURRICULUM"

Elaine P. Maimon

Robert Redford's 1994 film *Quiz Show*—and the television quiz-show scandals of the 1950s on which the film is based—highlight two radically different settings for public education, that is, education undertaken in public: the isolation booth, where quiz-show contestants (fraudulently, it turns out) sweat out discrete items of information in answer to questions of fact, and the college classroom, where students ask questions. In the film, quiz-show contestant Charles Van Doren, and his Pulitzer-Prize-winning father, Mark Van Doren, are both shown in their respective classrooms at Columbia University, which is presented as a culture of inquiry in contrast to the television game show.

Questions and approaches to truth across the curriculum; answers and lies in the isolation booth. Quiz shows valorize factual responses, oversimplifying and distorting what it means to be an educated person. Some approaches to teaching use a quiz-show model, while teaching across the curriculum creates a classroom in which connections are more significant than facts. The quiz-show scandals are emblematic of conflicts in American higher education that have spanned the century.

Facts Versus Connections

Higher education in the twentieth century has been the setting for conflicting assumptions about the curriculum. The conventional view, mostly unexamined and therefore even more powerful, has been that curriculum is made up of discrete units of content (answers to quiz-show questions), with writing and thinking taken for granted as entrance requirements and therefore marginalized. Most educators have assumed that thinking was for the most part unteachable, in the genes, made manifest in IQ scores.

Writing, when it was defined as related to thinking, was assumed to be likewise unteachable. Or when writing was defined, quite differently, as a mechanical transcription of speech, it was still not the business of higher education. A simplistic definition of writing justified the assumption that students would learn to do it at an early age or not at all. Throughout the century, reformers have held very different assumptions about writing, thinking, and the curriculum.

As Russell (1991) describes in *Writing in the Academic Disciplines, 1870–1990: A Curricular History,* from the Progressive Era to the end of the century, from John Dewey to James Britton, educational reformers have questioned the false distinction between content and expression. Reformers imagine the curriculum, not as individual packets of facts, but as conceptually interrelated communities. Or to use another metaphor, not as separately owned condominiums—or isolation booths—but as a house with open doors between the rooms and shared corridors and living spaces.

Russell's ostensible subject is a history of writing instruction outside general composition courses in American secondary and higher education, but it is revealing that in order to talk about writing in the academic disciplines, he must by necessity discuss educational reform. Teachers who think about writing as integral to what they are teaching, not as somebody else's business, have been the exception to the rule. A concern with writing in the disciplines also makes it difficult to adopt a quiz-show approach to teaching, to live in an isolation booth where only facts count.

Reimagining the Classroom

For better or worse, teachers teach the way they were taught. Students in the Gradgrind School in *Hard Times* would undoubtedly grow up to teach in their turn that "facts alone are wanted in life" (Dickens, [1854] 1966, p. 1). They would applaud the factual recall that is honored on quiz shows and would not be concerned with writing in the academic disciplines—unless somehow they were motivated to reexamine their assumptions about learning. As Bruffee puts it, "The way college and university teachers have been taught to think about what they know and how they know it drives the way they teach it. So teachers can change the way they teach only by changing what they think about what they know and about how they know it" (Bruffee, 1993, p. 10).

Teaching across the curriculum means revising the classroom and thereby the curriculum. Revising the classroom depends upon reimagining the classroom. We cannot become what we cannot imagine. For us to become teachers across the curriculum, we must imagine the classroom as a place of more questions than answers, more ideas than facts, more interaction than loneliness. We must imagine the classroom as a place of conversation: talking back in writing to what we read; interacting with texts and people; questioning facts rather than reciting them. We must imagine the classroom as a place of intellectual inquiry and, therefore, of wonder.

"Never wonder," says Mr. Gradgrind to Louisa, his daughter and pupil, in *Hard Times*. "Never wonder. By means of addition, subtraction, multiplication, and division, settle everything somehow, and never wonder" (p. 37). But wondering is exactly what we want our students to do. Intellectual curiosity, the itch of ignorance, can—if we manage not to repress it—be a more powerful motivator than fear of the MCATS. Wondering implies involvement. The revisions that we enact in our classrooms are directed toward that sense of wonder that is the educational elixir. We are talking about much more than writing across the curriculum or even teaching across the curriculum. We are concerned with involving students in understanding what they already know or think they know so that they can articulate that understanding and connect it with the new worlds that we explore together in the classroom.

Students come to the classroom with the resources of their own personal experiences and mental associations. It is our job to tap these resources, helping students to identify significance in what they already know and to build from there. We are not, in Gradgrindian terms, filling empty vessels with brand new facts. We are instead reminding learners of what they know already—assisting in the restructuring and reorganizing of that knowledge, empowering students to use that knowledge in new contexts. Schwarz (1974), in *The Responsive Chord*—a fascinating book that is not sufficiently well known in the education community—suggests that teachers could learn a great deal from the techniques of advertising. Advertisers understand, as if their lives depended on it, that they must connect their message to something already in the minds of the audience. Schwarz himself, the creator of over five thousand radio and TV spots, mostly political commercials, has successfully taught ideas with great effectiveness. One Schwarz teaching moment that those readers my age may remember is the anti-Goldwater commercial in 1964, showing a little girl counting the petals of a flower while an atomic bomb goes off. Never was Goldwater's name mentioned, but the pictures on the screen effectively connected with fears and images that were already in viewers' minds.

Teachers across the curriculum should not be too proud to learn this lesson of connection from advertising. If we object to the ideas taught by the advertisers, our defense must be to co-opt the power of their strategies.

Readers who cringe at a teaching example from the world of commercialism may be surprised to learn that Schwarz and Freire, who may not agree on many points, are unified in their belief that students are people who already know things. Freire argues in *Pedagogy of the Oppressed* (1970) that the conventional mode of education, which he refers to as "banking," teaches people that they are ignorant. "The more students work at storing the deposits entrusted to them, the less they develop the critical consciousness that would result from their intervention in the world as transformers of that world" (p. 60). Once again, we see a reformer breaking down educational metaphors of accumulation (deposits, discrete items of information, facts, quiz-show answers) and calling for "problem-posing" education, which becomes liberating when "acts of cognition" replace "transferrals of information" (p. 67).

The reforms that I am summarizing under the term "teaching across the curriculum" replace mere transferrals of information with active engagement of students in processes of thinking, writing, speaking, and questioning. Britton, a widely recognized forefather of writing across the curriculum, found in his large-scale study, *The Development of Writing Abilities (11–18),* that schoolchildren in Great Britain differed dramatically in their writing performance based on "the degree of involvement in the writing task" (Britton and others, 1978, p. 7). In other words, when students were required to act like bankers and provide perfunctory recitations of quiz-show answers, they did not write at their best. "When involved, the writer made the task his own and began to write to satisfy himself as well as his teacher; in perfunctory writing he seemed to satisfy only the minimum demands of the task. When a writer wrote to satisfy himself as well as to fulfil the task, he seemed better able to bring the full force of his knowledge, attitudes and language experience to bear on the writing, which was carried to a conclusion on some sort of 'rising tide'" (p. 7).

Teaching Across the Divide Between Teachers and Students

Teaching across the curriculum means connection. "Only connect," E. M. Forster advises in the epigraph to *Howard's End*. The most important connection in the curriculum is between the student and the material. When we find the living synapse between what students already know and what we are presenting, we have created a powerful teaching moment. Students will then be empowered to use the full resources of their knowledge and language to learn well and to write well.

Teaching across the curriculum means changing the geometry of the classroom, metaphorically and physically. Dickens in his description of the Gradgrindian classroom gives us a model, exaggerated in its detail, to react against.

Read the following passage aloud, as Dickens did in many public performances, to appreciate the full impact. As you do so, consider another technique for interactive teaching across the curriculum: reading to your students, allowing them to hear the human voice behind the page. I recommend interpretive reading, not just in literature classrooms, where it is essential, but in chemistry and math, where the *emphases* of an experienced reader can enter the consciousness of novices and help them to become better skilled in reading and responding:

> The scene was a plain, bare, monotonous vault of a schoolroom, and the speaker's square forefinger emphasized his observations by underscoring every sentence with a line on the schoolmaster's sleeve. The emphasis was helped by the speaker's square wall of a forehead, which had his eyebrows for its base, while his eyes found commodious cellarage in two dark caves, overshadowed by the wall. The emphasis was helped by the speaker's mouth, which was wide, thin, and hard set. The emphasis was helped by the speaker's voice, which was inflexible, dry and dictatorial. The emphasis was helped by the speaker's hair, which bristled on the skirts of his bald head, a plantation of firs to keep the wind from its shining surface, all covered with knobs, like the crust of a plum pie, as if the head had scarcely warehouse-room for the hard facts stored inside. The speaker's obstinate carriage, square coat, square legs, square shoulders— nay, his very neckcloth, trained to take him by the throat with an unaccommodating grasp, like a stubborn fact, as it was—all helped the emphasis. [p. 1]

The "vault" of the schoolroom suggests both Freire's banking metaphor and a tomb. It is also the vault that blocks from the students the vault of the sky with the sunshine of nature and truth. Isolated facts in their bare monotony are contained in the isolation booth of the classroom. The mind is a "warehouse-room" for storage, not an organ for cognition. Language is made of linear sentences and walls, rather than voices. The metaphor implicit in the commonly used term *word-attack skills* suggests walls and battering rams. The shape of the Gradgrindian classroom, all squares and sharp angles, is in stark contrast to the circles of collaborative learning and the curves of teaching across the curriculum.

An Autobiographical History of Teaching Across the Curriculum

In 1975, when I was named director of composition at Beaver College, classrooms in that small, residential college were hardly Gradgrindian. But his legacy was evident in a number of crucial ways. My promotion to composition director in my second year of part-time employment at the college (my full-time contract was not to begin until the following September) was in itself evidence that writing was regarded as less important than those college responsibilities requiring full-time, senior personnel.

Beaver was by no means distinct in assigning supervision of writing to the most junior person available. Colleges and universities all over the country were doing the same thing at that time, leading to a marvelous camaraderie among those of us who shared such youthful experiences. Our national organization, Writing Program Administrators (WPA), founded in 1976, became a setting for conducting our educations in public. We have grown into middle age with a sustained sense of wonder as we reflect on those years in the 1970s, when we thought that all we were doing was exercising common sense, trying to do well by our students, and hoping to keep our jobs. In retrospect, we see that we were participating in the creation of an educational movement: writing across the curriculum. (Our journal, *WPA*, continues to be an excellent source for information and ideas on teaching across the curriculum.)

The term *writing across the curriculum* (often abbreviated WAC) derives from "Language Across the Curriculum," Britton's contribution to the influential 1975 Bullock Report on "all aspects of teaching the use of English" in British education. Britton earned his membership in the blue-ribbon Bullock Commission by publishing a 1970 study, *Language and Learning*, which argues that language is the central organizing principle for learning across the curriculum. While working on the Bullock report, Britton was also leading the research team that produced *The Development of Writing Abilities (11–18)*. Both the government report and the results of the research project were published in 1975, the *annus mirabilis* for writing across the curriculum.

On December 9, 1975, *Newsweek* published a cover story on "Why Johnny Can't Write." That same week, when I answered a summons to the office of the academic dean, he threw the magazine at me and asked me what I was going to do about it. Three weeks later—on a cable car in San Francisco, during a break from the 1975 annual meeting of the Modern Language Association (MLA)—I knew.

I had just come from a hotel ballroom where Mina Shaughnessy had delivered a talk titled "Diving In" (Shaughnessy, 1976). The august MLA had for the first time in generations provided ballroom space for a forum on the teaching of writing, and Shaughnessy, a writing instructor from City College in New York, had issued a call to a standing-room-only crowd, several of whom were poised to lead across-the-curriculum movements at their respective universities. Most of the listeners held Ph.D.'s in English literature from traditional university departments. Shaughnessy appealed to us as scholars who had the opportunity to apply our research skills and our intellectual habits of mind to the frontier of teaching writing and thinking to new populations of students.

City College and the entire City University of New York (CUNY) had instituted open admissions in 1970. Even though CUNY restricted that policy during the city's fiscal crisis in the mid-1970s, during the years leading up to Shaughnessy's talk, CUNY had become a crucible for the problems and opportunities inherent in educating a diverse population of first-generation college students. Reacting to conservative academics who recommended "guarding the gates," and "converting the natives," Shaughnessy urged us to dive into the intellectual challenges and the social responsibilities uniquely before us.

She told us about *Errors and Expectations*, her work-in-progress about teaching basic writers. That book calls for WAC in simple and direct terms: "Ways ought to be found to increase students' involvement with writing across the curriculum. This does not mean simply persuading more teachers in other subjects to require term papers but making writing a more integral part of the learning process in all courses. Writing is, after all, a learning tool as well as a way of demonstrating what has been learned" (Shaughnessy, 1977, pp. 87–88).

To say that writing can be an integral part of the learning process, rather than merely a means for testing the retention of facts, runs counter to the quiz-show philosophy of education. I left that San Francisco ballroom inspired as I had never been before. I was leaving the isolation booth. I was ready to dive in to teach new populations of students. And I knew that I did not have to do it alone. Writing across the curriculum made sense, not only because literacy could not be the domain of one or two English courses, but because writing was a powerful tool for learning in all disciplines.

As the cable car ascended and descended, I thought of the cross-curricular projects we had already initiated at Beaver College. During the previous spring semester, I had tossed aside what I considered the boring anthology of readings that was used in most composition sections. After learning from the registrar that the anthropology course "Marriage and the Family" had the largest freshman enrollment and assuming that the enrollment in my two composition sections would have some overlap with that course, I approached the anthropology instructor with a proposal for an experiment. I would adopt for my composition classes whatever book of readings she had already selected for her course. All my students would write in response to assigned readings in this text, and the students whom we taught in common would be given the opportunity to participate in drafting-across-the-curriculum. Those students would be required to prepare a draft of a paper based on the readings and submit the draft to either the anthropologist or to me. The first reader would provide the students with written comments and questions to help with the assigned revision. The final draft with comments would be submitted to the other instructor for a grade. The single grade would stand for both courses.

Participants in this experiment were delighted with the results. The anthropologist found that the students who were in my composition course read the anthropology essays with a sophisticated sense of context. Since I was in no position to teach anthropology, I asked students to read the fine print in the footnotes and to bring different expectations to an article that had been first published in the *Journal of Marriage and the Family* than to one that had first appeared in the *Ladies' Home Journal.* The anthropologist and I found that we each learned a great deal from reading the other's comments on drafts. I developed a sense of what were the important questions and issues in an anthropology paper, and she learned more about commenting on students' work-in-progress so that they would be prepared to reconceptualize material and to go beyond what they had thought and written at first. The students were, of course, delighted that the same paper could count for two courses, and later some even understood the importance of revision in the writing process and the power of writing as a learning tool. Students also seemed amazed that two of their instructors were talking to each other across the curriculum. Each instructor had stopped being the master of ceremonies on a separate quiz show. And the students were not sweating in separate isolation booths.

Since the composition-anthropology experiment proved so successful, the next semester we tried it with similar good results with "Introduction to Psychology," another large freshman course.

As I thought these thoughts on the lurching cable car, I caught the eye of another passenger who had been in the audience at Shaughnessy's talk. Harriet Sheridan, dean of Carleton College in Northfield, Minnesota, invited me for a drink so that she could tell me what Carleton was doing about writing across the curriculum.

In January 1976, I returned to the spring semester at Beaver College with what we then called the Carleton Plan. In the summers of 1974 and 1975, Carleton had conducted two-week workshops for faculty members in all disciplines to discuss the assignment and assessment of writing. The underlying principle was that the liberal arts faculty as a whole, not just one academic department, was responsible for students' writing and reading. No longer was writing trivialized or marginalized. To assist instructors who agreed to take writing seriously in their courses, Carleton trained a group of undergraduates as *writing fellows,* students who would provide peer support to others during the writing process. At its March 1976 meeting, the Beaver College faculty unanimously approved the Carleton Plan, accepting the broad outlines it set for full-faculty responsibility for writing and for peer tutoring.

In January 1977, Harriet Sheridan led the first faculty writing workshop at Beaver College, using Aristotle's *Rhetoric* as the first text. The following July, the National Endowment for the Humanities (NEH) funded a program at Beaver to create a liberal arts college committed to teaching writing in all parts of the curriculum. At the heart of the program were faculty seminars—two weeks in January, five weeks in the summer. To qualify for the summer stipend, faculty members had to volunteer for the preliminary January seminar. During each week a specialist in rhetoric and composition would visit for three or four days. But we always reserved one or two days each week for assessment and application. The seminar leaders ranged widely in background and perspective: Edward P. J. Corbett, Janet Emig, Linda Flower, John R. Hayes, Lynn Bloom, Harvey Wiener, Donald McQuade, James Kinneavy, Kenneth Bruffee, Richard Young. The list reads like a catalogue of major contemporary rhetoricians and researchers. No one presented a programmatic heuristic for writing across the curriculum, since none existed at the time. Leaders discussed their current work on writing and thinking. The Beaver faculty participants could then develop program plans from this scholarly feast.

Principles and Practices of Writing Across the Curriculum

Beaver College became what Russell calls "the most influential of the early private, liberal arts WAC programs" (1991, p. 284) because its emphasis was always scholarly. We created a culture in which faculty members could see writing as integrally related to their intellectual inquiries, within and across their disciplines. We were changing what we thought about what we knew and thereby changing the way we taught. The workshops allowed faculty members to become learners without becoming schoolchildren. The workshops created a new kind of space in the academy—not a committee meeting, not a postdoctoral seminar, not a party—but somehow incorporating the best features of each. And the workshops were not hierarchical. The seminar leaders did not adopt the role of expert and did not treat the faculty participants as novices. The outside guests were interested in participating in the creation of something new—writing across the curriculum. Everyone involved was both teacher and learner.

This history of the Beaver program demonstrates a major principle of writing and teaching across the curriculum. Curricular change must be based on intellectual exchange among faculty members. We teach as we are taught. Changing the instructor's role from quiz master to mentor requires new experiences for the instructor. One of the most important contributions of WAC has been the creation of the interactive faculty workshop. The geometry of the workshop eschews all Gradgrindian squares and sharp corners. Circles, ovals, and curves predominate. Typically, sitting around a table, faculty members from various disciplines read a sample student work-in-progress and find within it most of the issues in higher education, from the definition of evidence in various fields to the application of multicultural viewpoints. The seminar leader's job is to draw from the faculty members what they know from their own scholarship that might contribute to student learning.

The Beaver program also pioneered two other important WAC features: the *course cluster* and collaborative learning. Building on the early experiments with "Marriage and the Family" and "Introduction to Psychology," we loosely linked groups of courses, either thematically or through a text (for example, we linked history, biology, and English literature through Charles Darwin's *On the Origin of Species)*. Interdisciplinary teaching might occur as serendipity, but the major goal was to provide occasions for faculty members to plan ways to make writing a natural part of each class meeting.

Beginning with freshman composition, students were taught explicitly to assess their own work-in-progress and then to ask for advice from peers. The Writing Center changed radically from a clinic to a center where peer tutors read and commented on drafts, although as the Writing Center posters said, "The pencil is always in the hand of the writer, not the tutor." Tutors were trained to ask questions, not to give answers or fix papers. Faculty members across the curriculum assigned students to write prefaces and acknowledgments that explained the intellectual development of projects and thanked those who had made suggestions or read and commented on their work-in-progress. Students were assigned to read authors' published acknowledgments and then, in writing their own, better understood the subtle connections between originality and intellectual community. Just as the faculty workshop enabled cross-curricular conversation among faculty members, the acknowledgment page was the ticket out of the isolation booth for students.

Developing a National Movement

The late seventies was an exciting time in higher education. The National Endowment for the Humanities helped to move writing instruction from the margins to the center. NEH approval encouraged many college professors to remember that writing instruction has its roots in the ancient art of rhetoric, which was itself central to the classical and medieval curricula. Before 1977, NEH viewed writing as a mere mechanical skill and not under the purview of the humanities endowment. In July 1977, in addition to approving the Beaver program, NEH funded the National Writing Project, which expanded the model of teacher workshops from the Berkeley/Bay Area Project.

In the 1980s, NEH funded a national dissemination program called Writing in the Humanities, enabling Beaver College to host a national group of multidisciplinary college professors and administrators who were required to complete the team with colleagues from secondary schools in their area. Through this project, writing and teaching across the curriculum were disseminated to sites from Texas to Puerto Rico, from Virginia to California. Partnerships were encouraged among faculty in different disciplines within colleges and universities and between those faculty members and secondary school teachers in neighboring schools. The four-year program culminated in the first national conference on writing across the curriculum, held in Philadelphia in 1986 and attended by over five hundred participants. Any history of teaching across the curriculum should recognize that at a crucial point in educational history, NEH raised the level of the national conversation.

In addition to private liberal arts colleges, several large public institutions were pioneers in WAC. The Michigan Technological University program refined the faculty workshop to a setting for intellectual conversion. Other early programs were those at the University of Michigan, the University of Maryland, and the University of Washington. The University of Michigan developed the model of writing-intensive courses in disciplines other than English. The University of Maryland instituted a junior-level writing requirement in the major. The University of Washington linked writing courses to large lecture classes.

The Ivy League also made a number of early contributions to WAC. When Harriet Sheridan left Carleton College for Brown University in the early 1980s, she established a Writing Fellows program there that has become a model for the nation. Yale instituted a large-scale training program for graduate students in the disciplines to prepare them to transform discussion sections into writing sections. Many of these former graduate students are now professors in colleges and universities across the country. The University of Pennsylvania, my alma mater, invited me to design their Writing Across the University program, which still thrives today.

Sources of Information

Russell (1991) reports that "the WAC movement far surpasses any previous movement to improve writing across the curriculum, both in the number of programs and in the breadth of their influence. McLeod's 1987 survey of 2,735 institutions of higher education found that, of the 1,113 that replied, 427 (38 percent) had some WAC program, and 235 of these had a program in existence for three years or more" (p. 291). Most of these programs are supported internally, rather than by grant dollars, attesting to their place in the infrastructure of colleges and universities. Christopher Thaiss at George Mason University has established the National Network of Writing Across the Curriculum Programs, which prepares a directory of WAC programs, meets annually at the Conference of College Composition and Communication, provides a computer bulletin board, and contributes a column to the *Composition Chronicle* (edited by Bill McCleary, Viceroy Publications).

One sign that WAC has achieved a degree of success unusual for educational reform movements has been the controversy stirred by newcomers to WAC about whether conventions of specific disciplines or the student's personal voice should be given primacy. Speaking as an *enfant terrible* who is no longer so *enfant,* I find it amusing—and irritating—to read lengthy discussions in the composition journals about what I consider false dichotomies (Maimon, 1990). As Russell says, "Britton, Maimon, Fulwiler, and Charles Bazerman, as well as other WAC proponents espouse varying theories and pedagogical approaches, but all favor students doing personal and public writing at various stages of their writing and learning. They agree that learning to write is part of a dialectic between self and society, which can transform both, but only if students learn how disciplines are constituted through discourse" (1991, pp. 294–295).

Research and scholarship in writing across the curriculum encompass principles, evidence of effectiveness, common problems, and guidelines for developing institutionwide programs. Readers may wish to consult a number of excellent essay collections edited by Griffin (1986); Fulwiler and Young (1990); McLeod and Soven (1992); and Herrington and Moran (1992), which outline both the debates and the shared principles. Soven's *Write to Learn: A Guide to Writing Across the Curriculum* (1996) is a concise guide to teaching writing in the disciplines and to developing a campuswide program. An earlier guide is Walvoord's *Helping Students Write Well: A Guide for Teachers in All Disciplines* (1986). Also useful is Walvoord's *Thinking and Writing in College: A Naturalistic Study of Students Writing in Four Disciplines* (1991).

Bazerman's rhetorical analysis of scientific writing (1988) is one demonstration of the scholarly underpinnings of writing across the curriculum. Maimon, Nodine, and O'Connor's *Thinking, Reasoning, and Writing* (1989) presents scholarly approaches to writing from the disciplinary perspectives of cognitive psychology, applied logic, and rhetoric. Bizzell's *Academic Discourse and Critical Consciousness* (1992) powerfully presents and debates underlying theoretical issues. Gaudiani's *Teaching Writing in the Foreign Language Curriculum* (1982) remains the best guide to the teaching of writing in that field. McQuade's bibliographic essay, "Composition and Literary Studies" (1992) places writing across the curriculum in the context of English studies. And *Writing in the Arts and Sciences* (Maimon and others, 1981) and *Readings in the Arts and Sciences* (Maimon and others, 1984) are textbooks coauthored by professors in English, history, biology, psychology, and philosophy that explain to students the varying contexts for academic writing and thinking.

Active Learning Across the Curriculum

WAC has from the beginning been shorthand for active learning across the curriculum. Morrison may not be aware of WAC as a national educational reform movement, but she writes eloquently about the empowerment of taking a writer's approach to reading: "As a reader (before becoming a writer) I read as I had been taught to do. But books revealed themselves rather differently to me as a writer. In that capacity I have to place enormous trust in my ability to imagine others and my willingness to project consciously into the danger zones such others may represent for me" (1993, p. 15). As a reader, Morrison read passively, "as she was taught to do," in classrooms, presumably, that unconsciously adopted the banking–quiz-show mode of instruction. But as a writer, she finds that the page is no longer a wall to batter down but a chorus of voices inviting her into "danger zones." As a writer, she is never alone when she reads. Even in the privacy of her study, she is sitting in the midst of a crowd. The writer of the text she is reading is, of course, there in person. Morrison talks about techniques with her colleague. Others are present in Morrison's study, too—generations of readers, reading the text from the perspective of unexamined assumptions compelled by gender, race, class, and family history.

Unlike Morrison, uninvolved students, reading as they are conventionally taught to do, read in lonely passivity. Students who are involved in their own learning through WAC read, study, and think actively in good company, even when alone. When we transform the classroom into a place where every reader is a writer, then we have a chance to help students understand the paradox of creative thinking—the individual alone at her desk can think something original only when she can conjure up and respond to the voices of others. As a writer, Morrison reads actively by imagining the writer of the text, who is not herself, and by imagining other readers and readings. WAC, defined broadly, educates the imagination.

Such education of the imagination is crucial to teaching students from diverse cultural, ethnic, and racial backgrounds to imagine otherness, to respect difference, and to create shared public space. The five-hundred-student honors program I direct at Queens College, where sixty-six native languages are spoken, creates a free zone in the classroom where students can form a community that crosses neighborhood borders. The eight courses in the program are connected through WAC, collaborative learning, and cross-curricular approaches to speaking, computing, problem solving, and ethical decision making. At this commuter institution, students have telephone partners with whom they are assigned to discuss particular assignments. They read classmates' work-in-progress in writing groups, and they write pages of acknowledgment. The curriculum is imagined, not as individual packets of facts, but as conceptually interrelated communities. Neither faculty members nor students live in isolation booths.

Enriching Courses From Within

The Queens College program is only one example of programs designed explicitly to teach concepts, ideas, and ways of thinking across the curriculum. Reformers quickly understand that the connection between writing and learning makes WAC shorthand for *teaching* across the curriculum. At Brown University, for example, Nancy Dunbar, chairperson of Speech, Theatre, and Dance, after participating in writing across the curriculum, instituted a connected program in speaking across the curriculum, with undergraduate fellows prepared—like their counterparts in writing—to assist classmates in oral communication. The Poynter Center at Indiana University is now working with the support of the Lilly Endowment on a program for all its four-year colleges on ethics across the curriculum, examining the ethical issues inherent in the subject matter of all fields. It may not be a coincidence that Indiana University has also been a leader in writing across the curriculum.

Many undergraduate institutions are now using an enlightened approach to the challenge of revising curriculum to encompass the rapidly expanding world of knowledge and concepts. Teaching across the curriculum offers an escape from playing a zero-sum game, in which the addition and subtraction of course units constitute the only form of curricular mathematics. Members of a faculty curriculum committee may agree, for example, that ethical problem solving is essential to the educated person of the twenty-first century, but they may also see that merely adding a required course title to the list of distribution requirements can be facile. Teaching across the curriculum, enriching courses from within, may be the better solution, enabling students to work actively within existing courses to grapple with ethical implications. Covering new ideas with a proliferation of new courses may be covering up opportunities to reform the curriculum.

In the lexicon of WAC, the "A" may be the most important letter. *Across* implies connection, rather than isolation. When we hear about programs of speaking, computing, international awareness, and media criticism across the curriculum, we are encountering a clear sign that the faculty members who have formulated these programs do not imagine that the goal of a college education is to master discrete units of content. They have examined underlying assumptions and concluded that writing, speaking, international awareness, and media criticism cannot be left to someone else. They understand that teaching across the curriculum means forming conceptually interrelated communities and helping students to make connections between what they already know and care about and new frontiers of knowledge and ideas.

We teach not only as we are taught but also as we continue to teach ourselves and our colleagues through the ongoing interaction of seminars, workshops, and corridor conversations. Faculty members who learn across the curriculum also teach across the curriculum. Intellectual exchange leads to curriculum change. As we learn to increase our own knowledge of writing, speaking, computing, ethical problem solving, and so on, we will enrich courses and curricula—if we are willing to take the risk of encountering something new, of exploring undiscovered countries. In other words, if we are willing to be scholars as well as teachers.

In *Quiz Show,* a pivotal scene—the one preceding Charles's confession to his father—occurs as the son waits in a Columbia University classroom as students ask his father questions about *Don Quixote.* How is it, one student asks, that Don Quixote, old and decrepit as he is, can believe he is a knight? Paul Scofield (as Mark Van Doren) tells the student that if he thinks he is a knight then he needs to act like a knight. And, by implication for his son's benefit, if you don't want to be a fraud, then don't act like one.

If we wish to teach across the curriculum, then we, too, must act like those who do, examining our assumptions, learning from colleagues across the curriculum, making connections, giving up the role of game show emcee and opening the doors of the isolation booths.

References

Bazerman, C. *Shaping Written Knowledge: The Genre and Activity of the Experimental Article in Science.* Madison: University of Wisconsin Press, 1988.

Bizzell, P. *Academic Discourse and Critical Consciousness.* Pittsburgh: University of Pittsburgh Press, 1992.

Britton, J. *Language and Learning.* London: Penguin, 1970.

Britton, J., and others. *The Development of Writing Abilities (11–18).* Urbana, Ill.: National Council of Teachers of English, 1978. (Originally published 1975.)

Bruffee, K. *Collaborative Learning: Higher Education, Interdependence, and the Authority of Knowledge.* Baltimore, Md.: Johns Hopkins University Press, 1993.

Dickens, C. *Hard Times.* Norton Critical Edition, G. Ford and S. Monod (eds.). New York: Norton, 1966. (Originally published 1854.)

Freire, P. *Pedagogy of the Oppressed.* (M. B. Ramons, trans.). New York: Continuum, 1970.

Fulwiler, T., and Young, A. (eds.). *Programs That Work: Models and Methods of Writing Across the Curriculum.* Portsmouth, N.H.: Boynton, 1990.

Gaudiani, C. *Teaching Writing in the Foreign Language Curriculum.* Washington, D.C.: Center for Applied Linguistics, 1982.

Griffin, C. W. (ed.). *Teaching Writing in All Disciplines.* New Directions for Teaching and Learning, no. 12. San Francisco: Jossey-Bass, 1986.

Herrington, A., and Moran, C. (eds.). *Writing, Teaching, and Learning in the Disciplines.* New York: Modern Language Association of America, 1992.

Maimon, E. "Reexamining False Dichotomies." Paper presented at the Conference on College Composition and Communication, Chicago, Mar. 1990.

Maimon, E., Nodine, B., and O'Connor, F. (eds.). *Thinking, Reasoning, and Writing.* White Plains, N.Y.: Longman, 1989.

Maimon, E., and others. *Writing in the Arts and Sciences.* Cambridge, Mass.: Winthrop, 1981.

Maimon, E., and others (eds.). *Readings in the Arts and Sciences.* Boston: Little, Brown, 1984.

McLeod, S. H. (ed.). *Strengthening Programs for Writing Across the Curriculum.* New Directions for Teaching and Learning, no. 36. San Francisco: Jossey-Bass, 1989.

McLeod, S. H., and Soven, M. (eds.). *Writing Across the Curriculum: A Guide to Developing Programs.* Newbury Park, Calif.: Sage, 1992.

McQuade, D. "Composition and Literary Studies." In S. Greenblatt and G. Gunn (eds.), *Redrawing the Boundaries.* New York: Modern Language Association of America, 1992.

Morrison, T. *Playing in the Dark: Whiteness and the Literary Imagination.* New York: Vintage, 1993.

Russell, D. R. *Writing in the Academic Disciplines, 1870–1990: A Curricular History.* Carbondale: Southern Illinois University Press, 1991.

Schwarz, T. *The Responsive Chord.* New York: Anchor Books, 1974.

Shaughnessy, M. "Diving In." *College Co*

Walvoord, B. *Helping Students Write Well: A Guide for Teachers in All Disciplines.* (2nd ed.) New York: Modern Language Association, 1986.

Walvoord, B. (ed.). *Thinking and Writing in College: A Naturalistic Study of Students Writing in Four Disciplines.* Urbana, Ill.: National Council of Teachers of English, 1991.

CHAPTER NINETEEN

ADVANCING INTERDISCIPLINARY STUDIES

Julie Thompson Klein, William H. Newell

When Levine's *Handbook on Undergraduate Curriculum* appeared in 1978, the era of innovation and reform that marked the late 1960s and early 1970s had passed. For interdisciplinary studies (IDS), it had been a watershed era. New interdisciplinary universities, cluster colleges, programs, and courses documented the growth and diversification of IDS. By 1978, the euphoria had passed, and retrenchments were cutting deeply into once-heralded experiments. Even as the death knell of IDS was being sounded, however, a rebirth was already under way in the form of new integrated approaches to general education, new interdisciplinary fields, and integrated problem solving. This chapter is a result of those developments. The 1978 *Handbook* contained only a few scattered references to IDS. Today, not only is there an entire chapter devoted to the subject, the rhetoric of interdisciplinarity pervades the entire book.

Conceptualizing Interdisciplinary Studies

Approaches vary and disputes over terminology continue. Broadly speaking, though, *interdisciplinary studies* may be defined as a process of answering a question, solving a problem, or addressing a topic that is too broad or complex to be dealt with adequately by a single discipline or profession. Whether the context is an integrated approach to general education, a women's studies program, or a science, technology, and society program, IDS draws on disciplinary perspectives and integrates their insights through construction of a more comprehensive perspective. In this manner, interdisciplinary study is not a simple supplement but is complementary to and corrective of the disciplines.

Origins and Motivations

IDS can no longer be defined by pointing to a few exemplary practices and program types. Levine's typology encompassed interdisciplinary, field, and joint majors. His leading examples of interdisciplinary majors were American studies, applied mathematics and psychology, modernization, urban studies, art and aesthetics, social psychology, and environmental studies. Since the 1970s, interdisciplinary studies have expanded in kind as well as in number. Diverse structures and practices emanate from diverse motivations and purposes. This diversity was already apparent in the late 1960s, when the Organization for Economic Cooperation and Development (OECD) conducted the first international survey of interdisciplinary activities. The OECD found five major origins of interdisciplinary activity: the development of science (knowledge), student needs, the need for professional training, original needs of society, and problems of university functioning and administration (Center for Educational Research and Innovation, 1972, pp. 44–48).

When we ask the same questions today—the what and the why of interdisciplinary study—familiar motivations reappear alongside new ones:

- General and liberal education
- Professional training
- Social, economic, and technological problem solving
- Social, political, and epistemological critique
- Faculty development
- Financial exigency (downsizing)
- Production of new knowledge

Traditional IDS

In the first half of the century, the most prominent interdisciplinary presence was in general education. The most influential models were programs at Columbia, Chicago, and Wisconsin; the most influential thinkers were Hutchins, Meiklejohn, and, to a lesser extent, Dewey. Data continue to reveal that general and liberal education programs remain prominent sites of IDS, from Levine's 1976 study of college catalogues (Levine, 1978) to Klein and Gaff's 1979 survey of 272 colleges and universities (Klein and Gaff, 1982) to Newell's 1986 questionnaire results from 235 interdisciplinary programs. The most recent data, gathered by Newell for *Interdisciplinary Undergraduate Programs: A Directory* (1986), indicated that a renaissance of IDS was under way across geographical locations, institutional types, and curricular areas. The greatest increases were in general education, followed by honors and women's studies. The greatest growth in subject-matter areas of general education encourages interdisciplinary curricula in areas such as international studies, American multicultural and gender studies, and the inherently synoptic areas of historical consciousness and ethical understanding (Casey, 1994, p. 56).

IDS Today

Despite the continuing prominence of its role in general education, IDS today includes a great deal more. The fuller extent was noted in 1990, in the first authoritative national report on IDS. Emanating from the three-year study of the undergraduate major by the Association of American Colleges, the report of the Interdisciplinary Studies Task Force highlighted the evolution of new fields of knowledge in a history that spans the rise of American and area studies in the 1930s and 1940s; women's, urban, and environmental studies in the 1960s and 1970s; and the current expansion of cultural studies, cognitive science, and science, technology, and society. The task force found a wide range of interdisciplinary majors, including international and public policy studies, area studies, labor and legal studies, programs in human ecology and social ecology, neuroscience, biochemistry, and molecular biology, environmental sciences and marine biology, and cognitive and information sciences. They also found numerous individual courses in disciplinary departments, such as a physics course designed to familiarize students with cutting-edge research connecting theoretical physics and biology, as well as courses bridging business and law or history and political science (Association of American Colleges, 1990, 1991b).

The task force findings also confirm a widely held belief that knowledge has become increasingly interdisciplinary. The reasons include new developments in research and scholarship, the continuing evolution of new hybrid fields, the expanding influence of particular interdisciplinary methods and concepts, and the pressing need for integrated approaches to social, economic, and technological problems. The growing inclusion of new elements in professional courses and programs is another important indicator. Management studies are appearing in engineering, social analyses in medicine, and foreign language or computing applications in professions.

This development and the problems of interrelating constituent elements in these fields are usually discussed in terms of companion notions of integration and coordination, not interdisciplinarity per se. The problems at stake are largely pragmatic or organizational, not theoretical (Squires 1992, pp. 206–207). At the same time, interdisciplinarity is conceived in theoretical terms. The claims of theory differ, from general systems theory, holistic paradigms, and transdisciplinary schemes to critiques of knowledge and culture in Marxism, feminism, and post-structuralist practices that reformulate as they cross disciplinary boundaries. As we move into the twenty-first century, pragmatism, holism, and critique will all continue to be influential in conceptualization of interdisciplinary approaches. Marking this trend, multiple conceptualizations have been prominent in major reports on the undergraduate curriculum over the past decade.

The National Institute of Education report *Involvement in Learning* (1984) urged that liberal education requirements be expanded and reinvigorated to ensure that content is directly addressed not only to subject matter but also the capacities of analysis, problem solving, communication, and synthesis. Students and faculty alike should be able to integrate knowledge from different disciplines, both in the academic setting and in real-life situations. *Integrity in the College Curriculum* (Association of American Colleges, 1985) called, additionally, for curricula capable of enabling faculty to escape departmental confines, to attain contextual understanding, to assess multifaceted problems, to gain a sense of the complexities and interrelationships of society, and to examine the human, social, and political implications of research. In 1990, in *The Challenge of Connecting Learning*—a report framed by a widely noted blurring of disciplinary boundaries—the Association of American Colleges highlighted the need for curricular coherence while extolling promising practices that enable connection making and interdisciplinary skills of synthesis.

Clearly, the strong intellectual and educational value of IDS has been a major theme of modern educational reform. However, because the structure of higher education has been dominated over the course of the twentieth century by disciplines and departments, interdisciplinary study was often regarded as additive or separate from the main business of higher education. The increase in the sheer amount of interdisciplinary activity strains this concept. Financial belt tightening will continue to create pressures to return to basics, construed in terms of traditional disciplines and departments. What is new since the 1978 *Handbook* is the perception that interdisciplinary approaches have become essential, not peripheral, in thinking about institutional structure, about curriculum, and about faculty development.

Interdisciplinary Forms and Structures

The coexistence of older and newer interdisciplinary activities has created greater heterogeneity and complexity in higher education. These conditions are apparent in the variety of forms and locations where interdisciplinary study occurs today—in traditional, formal, and visible structures—and involves a wider, more heterogeneous, informal, and nontraditional set of activities.

From Simple to Complex Structure

General systems theory suggests a fruitful metaphor for conceptualizing what has happened and its implications. The structure of higher education is shifting from simple systems to complex ones. *Simple systems* may have multiple levels and connections arranged in a hierarchy, but they still operate according to a single set of rules. *Complex systems,* in contrast, are nonhierarchically structured. They obey multiple conflicting logics, employ both positive and negative feedback, reveal synergistic effects, and may have a chaotic element. To understand them, linear and reductionist thinking must be replaced by nonlinear thinking, pattern recognition, and analogy. Simple structures still exist, but the multiplicity of hybrid interdisciplinary forms has fueled a change in the way many faculty members think of knowledge and the academy.

Metaphors for describing knowledge have shifted from foundational and linear structures to networks, webs, and complex systems. Correspondingly, IDS is no longer a simple matter of adding a few formal interdisciplinary programs to the existing structure of the institution. (For a parallel view of science and research, see Gibbons and others, 1994.)

We describe the difference in terms of two categories. The first category comprises traditional and familiar bridging structures typical of simple systems:

- Free-standing institutions
- Autonomous and cluster colleges
- Centers and institutes
- Interdisciplinary departments
- Interdisciplinary majors, minors, and concentrations
- Mainstream and alternative general education programs
- Individual courses within disciplinary departments
- Tutorials
- Independent study and self-designed majors
- Travel-study, internships, and practicums

These structures have yielded exemplary models and practices that span hybrid specialization (the Social Ecology Program at the University of California, Irvine, and the Consciousness and Culture Program at the College of the Atlantic), interdisciplinary degree programs in the liberal arts tradition (Eugene Lang

College at the New School for Social Research and the State University of New York (SUNY) College at Old Westbury), general education in the tradition of Great Books and great ideas (St. John's College and Shimer College), and the clustering of disciplinary courses around a common integrative seminar (the Federated Learning Communities at SUNY, Stony Brook, and the loop sequencing of traditional courses with a third bridging course at California Lutheran College). In addition to honors and general education programs, Newell's 1986 *Directory* called attention to long-standing American studies programs (the University of Minnesota and University of Texas at Austin), free-standing interdisciplinary institutions (Evergreen State College and Hampshire College), and cluster colleges surviving from the late 1960s and early 1970s (Watauga College at Appalachian State University, the Paracollege at St. Olaf College, and the Hutchins School of Liberal Studies at Sonoma State University), as well as science and society programs, women's studies programs, self-consciously interdisciplinary world studies programs, and environmental, ethnic, and urban studies.

From Visible to Invisible Forms

The second and growing category encompasses hybrid communities and interactions that are less visible, if not invisible, on organizational charts:

- Learning communities of students and of faculty
- Problem-focused research projects
- Shared facilities, databases, and instrumentation
- Interdisciplinary approaches and schools of thought
- Enhanced disciplinary curricula to accommodate new developments in scholarship and research
- Subdisciplinary boundary crossing
- Educational functions of centers and institutes
- Training in collaborative modes and teamwork
- Interinstitutional consortia and alliances

The Washington Center for Improving the Quality of Undergraduate Education epitomizes the second category. An interinstitutional consortium of over forty public and private colleges and universities in the state of Washington, the center was founded in 1985. The idea of a *coordinated studies program,* or learning community design, is at the core of the center's work. Learning communities are envisioned as a low-cost, holistic approach to curriculum restructuring and reform, faculty development, and assessment (see Chapter Twenty-Two). Faculty cite the revitalization afforded by the interdisciplinary environment, *team-teaching,* and interactions with students in learning communities. Maintaining a nonbureaucratic approach in its retreats, workshops, and conferences, the center has expanded to include a range of innovative pedagogies linked with collaborative learning, cultural pluralism, and respect for diversity.

The second category also includes the host of study groups, interest groups, and networks that enable faculty to stay abreast of developments in research and in higher education. Most of these hybrid communities do not appear on organizational charts, but they are vital sources of faculty learning as well as new programs, centers, and reformulations of departmental curricula. Faculty are involved, additionally, in interinstitutional and community-based projects that cross the traditional boundaries separating the academy, government, industry, and the community. These structures indicate that curricular reform is not simply a matter of courses and programs for students. It also entails the continuing education and development of faculty. As a result of the complexity and heterogeneity of both knowledge and faculty activities, interdisciplinary structures may be interconnected in a shifting matrix, replete with feedback loops and unpredictable synergistic relationships. The evidence is familiar.

The same faculty member may be involved in multiple activities: a scientist teaching in a new basic science course while conducting research in molecular biology, an engineer conducting problem-focused research in an industrial partnership program while working with members of the business school to restructure the business curriculum, a social scientist teaching a capstone course in the sociology department and holding a joint appointment in a center for urban studies, a member of the English department serving as a member of a planning group for a new cultural studies program, a member of the history department teaching in a women's studies program while collaborating with a colleague in the art department on representations of women in early American painting, a political scientist gathering support for a new environmental studies program while studying the history of environmental legislation, a faculty member teaching French while designing a minor in Canadian studies and team-teaching a section of a general education core curriculum, or a faculty member teaching Spanish while designing a new course on the U.S.-Mexico borderlands and conducting research on settlement patterns in the Southwest.

The lesson of complex structure has powerful implications for institutional change. Managing a complex system requires recognizing the coexistence of multiple activities and their essential heterogeneity. Whether the context is a large research university, a comprehensive institution, a small private liberal arts college, or a community college, there are often several roles, forms, and sites of interdisciplinary study.

Institutional Change

Two principles of institutional change apply in thinking about IDS. The first and most important principle is the importance of listening to the system to find out what is actually happening. Rather than imposing a single model or making a priori assumptions about what will work best, administrators and curriculum planning groups should identify what motivations exist and what changes are desired. Recent institutionwide efforts to make campus climates more conducive to interdisciplinary education and research reveal an added lesson of complex structure: there will be more interdisciplinary activity and interest than initially supposed.

The second principle is that interdisciplinarity will not be a matter of agreement, conceptually, practically, or politically. Interdisciplinarity is a complex concept. Attitudes are shaped by differences of disciplinary worldview, professional training, and educational philosophy. Given this diversity, a vital first step is to clarify what each group means by the concept and its related terminology. This step may be taken with the aid of an outside consultant or as part of the planning process through discussion of the literatures on IDS and pertinent fields of knowledge. The goal is twofold: to promote a general climate of innovation in which a variety of activities can coexist and to foster an agreement on a common language and conception of the outcomes envisioned from any given activity.

Conceptual and Organizational Variables

In taking the next steps in curriculum planning, participants need to realize that between motivations and structures, a number of intervening variables are at work in curriculum change:

- The nature of the institution (size, mission, financial base)
- The institutional culture (past experience with curricular reform, patterns of interaction among faculty and administration, the nature of the academic community, and assumptions about the learning styles of students)
- The level of the desired change (institution-wide, program, or course)
- The nature of the desired change (general education, interdisciplinary majors and concentrations, department and program enhancement, bridging research and the classroom, learning communities)
- The extent of faculty capabilities and interests
- The variety of academic cultures within disciplines, professional fields, and interdisciplinary areas

Institutional contexts vary greatly. Some—for example, the University of Chicago, Hobart and William Smith Colleges, and the University of California, Irvine—have strong traditions of interdisciplinary work. At others, the institutional mission may be highly compatible with a given initiative. The Human Development and Social Relations Program at Earlham College is a case in point. The program was founded in 1976 to provide interdisciplinary, values-oriented preparation for the helping professions, in addition to a focused *liberal education* that draws on the social sciences and philosophy. It combines team-developed and team-taught interdisciplinary courses with a base of disciplinary courses and a senior seminar that synthesizes theory and practice while providing a bridge to careers. The same type of program will also reflect local needs and philosophies. The University of Hartford's guidelines for interdisciplinary general education seek to place learning for students in a contextual framework that unites knowledge and human experience with such courses as "Living in a Social Context" and "Living in a Scientific and Technological World." Bradford College seeks to link liberal and professional education and the world of work (Casey, 1994, pp. 58–59).

Size is an added factor. In a large university, a new curriculum may take years to work its way through various planning and policy committees. In a smaller institution, change may come more quickly. Even in a large institution, however, comprehensive change may occur in a relatively short time scale. At Michigan State University (MSU), the necessity of shifting from a quarter system to a semester system provided an opportunity for recasting an older program of general education into a new set of college-level schools of Integrative Studies in the Social Sciences, Humanities, and Sciences. The schools are attached to MSU's colleges of Social Science, Arts and Letters, and Science.

The MSU example raises another important consideration. Change occurs at different levels and on differing timescales, even in the same institution. Regardless of institutional size and mission, regardless of the particular activity, a number of questions should be addressed early in the planning stages:

- Does the program or course require small, limited, localized, and incremental interventions or more global, comprehensive, or even radical actions?
- Does it entail a modification of existing structures or the creation of new ones?
- Are existing material resources and personnel adequate for the change, or are external consultation and financial support necessary?
- Who are the key administrative and faculty personnel for the initial development?
- What is the appropriate administrative structure?

Fostering Communication and Collaboration

To foster communication and collaboration, interdisciplinary curricula need clearly defined administrative responsibility. In small liberal arts colleges, responsibility might be assigned to an associate provost or a dean; in a large institution, a dean for undergraduate studies. A central office or coordinating structure has tremendous value. Names and formats vary: Office of Interdisciplinary Studies, Division of Interdisciplinary Programs, Interdisciplinary Activities Committee, or Chair of Interdisciplinary Studies. A central office facilitates coordination of resources, effective use of facilities and instrumentation, and provisions for annual reports and program evaluation. It also ensures greater visibility and protection for individual programs while illuminating the whole context of interdisciplinary activity on campus. One of the first functions of such a body should be an inventory of existing activities and interests, an initial step toward establishing an information clearinghouse. A central office can also sponsor an interdisciplinary forum series and coordinate visits to campus by outside scholars. Quite often, featured speakers in departmental lecture series and seminars represent cutting-edge research and new developments that are interdisciplinary in nature.

A central oversight office or body can aid in another important way, providing an adequate resource base for all interdisciplinary activities on campus. In conjunction with the main library, individual departments and programs, and a center for teaching and learning, a central office can build a library of publications and teaching materials, including a bank of syllabi and program models. The office can also aid in literature searches and publish a newsletter keeping the campus informed of local and national developments, including news of funding agencies that support participation in pertinent conferences, seminars, workshops, postdocs, and summer fellowships. The office can also manage an internal electronic bulletin board for interdisciplinary conversations and information.

Examining the existing structure for mechanisms that stimulate and support IDS is another important means of fostering communication and collaboration. Sabbatical and other professional leaves may be used for faculty development in interdisciplinary areas. Curriculum- and research-development programs are excellent sources of seed money that may lead to external funding. Release time from teaching one or more classes is the most common means of enabling faculty members to develop new competencies and possibly to prepare for collaborative teaching. Cross-listing of courses enables wider student participation, and joint appointments formally recognize faculty participation in a wider array of activities. The eternal problem of budget and teaching-load credit can be handled in several ways, by doubling, splitting, or rotating course credits. Not all support for interdisciplinary activity, moreover, requires large financial outlays. Budgeting a few hundred dollars for lunch or social gatherings goes a long way toward facilitating the dialogue that is crucial to interdisciplinary interaction. For more substantial stimulus, new seed grants, challenge grants, and curriculum-development funds may be established and, if possible, resident or visiting professorships may be established using endowment funds.

Visibility and Legitimacy

Visibility and legitimacy must be considered from the outset. On too many campuses, good interdisciplinary programs are minimally visible in catalogues and bulletins. Correspondingly, they are underrepresented in admissions and counseling. All internal documents should be examined for inclusion, with separate material developed for each program articulating its mission, structure, relation to the larger institution, and sources of further information. Interdisciplinary activities need to become part of the way the institution represents itself to students, faculty, and the community. Just as excellence in disciplinary and professional study is recognized, interdisciplinary study should be recognized by means of prizes, awards, and public celebration at graduation and convocations.

From a faculty standpoint, the bottom line is inclusion in the reward system. An institution gets what it rewards. Even the most valued and stimulating curriculum will dwindle or fail if faculty participation is not rewarded. This is an especially pressing issue in institutions that weigh research more heavily than teaching in making decisions about tenure, promotion, and salary. Participation in interdisciplinary activity needs to be spelled out explicitly and continuously—in the initial interview, in the letter of hire, and in formal guidelines for tenure, promotion, and salary. Matrix evaluation is an approach that specifies, explicitly, how much an activity counts and at which levels it is counted. Evaluative categories are determined interactively by the institution, the individual, and the program so as to recognize and thereby sanction the kinds of activities the faculty member engages in. These matters are of particular concern when junior faculty are borrowed from departments where they hold their primary appointments, though even senior faculty permanently assigned to interdisciplinary programs may find themselves subject to tensions between programs and academic departments. Lessons derived from general systems theory would suggest that complex structures are most likely to succeed when they stimulate interaction among disciplines and IDS units and reward faculty who engage in such activity. Because faculty are engaged increasingly in greater numbers and kinds of activities that are not adequately accounted for in traditional organization charts or evaluated by a single set of global criteria, institutions of higher education need to respond appropriately.

Teaching and Learning

The acid test of IDS is the extent to which integration is achieved in the learning experience of students (Squires, 1992, p. 206). Ever since the 1970 OECD seminar, the degree of interdisciplinary integration has been indicated by labels such as multidisciplinary and interdisciplinary. The difference is important.

Integration

In *multidisciplinary* courses, faculty present their individual perspectives one after another, leaving differences in underlying assumptions unexamined and integration up to the students. In *interdisciplinary* courses, whether taught by teams or individuals, faculty interact in designing a course, bringing to light and examining underlying assumptions and modifying their perspectives in the process. They also make a concerted effort to work with students in crafting an integrated *synthesis* of the separate parts that provides a larger, more holistic understanding of the question, problem, or issue at hand. Smith's iron law bears repeating: "Students shall not be expected to integrate anything the faculty can't or won't" (quoted in Gaff, 1980, pp. 54–55).

Armstrong's definition of four levels of integration and synthesis clarifies levels of curricular integration. At the first level, students take a selection of courses from different departments, counting them toward a specific major. This is the cheapest, least demanding, and usually the most easily achieved variant but, from an interdisciplinary standpoint, probably the least effective. At the second level, students have an institutionally provided opportunity to meet and to share insights from disciplinary courses, often in a capstone seminar. Responsibility for achieving integration, however, may be left largely to the students. At the third level, a significant change occurs as faculty join students in the process of synthesis. This level implies creation of courses focused on interdisciplinary topics and may require the participation of more than one faculty member. Even at this level, though, the degree of interaction varies. In many team-taught courses, individual faculty simply bring their disciplinary wares to the class. At the fourth and highest level a conscious effort is made to integrate material from various fields of knowledge into a "new, single, intellectually coherent entity." This step demands understanding the epistemologies and methodologies of other fields and, in a team effort, requires building common vocabulary and assumptions (Armstrong, 1980, pp. 53–54).

Integration is not a strictly linear process, either in education or in research. Most interdisciplinary programs use a combination of disciplinary courses, multidisciplinary formats, and interdisciplinary elements and approaches. A number of mechanisms facilitate integration:

- Courses and course segments clarifying the concept of interdisciplinarity
- Capstone seminars
- Capstone theses, essays, and projects
- Coordinated alignment of parallel disciplinary courses
- Clustering of disciplinary courses around a common integrative seminar or discussion groups
- Organizational structure based on a topic, theme, issue, problem, or question
- Specific integrative approaches, theories, or concepts (such as systems theory, feminism, Marxism, textualism)
- Course learning portfolios and academic career portfolios
- A specific learning model
- Common living arrangements, shared facilities, and equipment
- Field work, work experience, travel-study

These mechanisms have yielded exemplary practices in strikingly different contexts. The Interdisciplinary Studies Program (ISP) at Wayne State University begins with a seminar that introduces its student population of working adults to interdisciplinary study through sequenced orientation to the concepts of disciplinarity and interdisciplinarity. The ISP also clarifies what IDS means in its promotional material. The Department of Human Development at California State University, Hayward, uses sequences of videotaped disciplinary lectures, symposia, and modules for use at home or in a listening center. These elements are integrated through student- and instructor-led seminars, as well as team-teaching and group learning in separate IDS courses. In the context of travel-study, Cultural History Tours at Eastern Michigan University employ teams of faculty from history, art, literature, and political science who form mobile residential colleges with students. Interdisciplinary learning occurs in the dialogue that develops not only in formal meetings—often at the actual sites of museums, monuments, and ruins throughout Europe and Asia—but also in the sense of community that evolves through sharing meals and traveling together.

Hursh, Haas, and Moore's (1983) model of an interdisciplinary solution to a given problem in general education has the widest generic value in the curriculum. The model identifies two levels in interdisciplinary process: *identification and clarification* of salient concepts and skills to be used, then *resolution* of differences. A course on U.S. energy policy, for example, may draw on the geology of coal and oil formation, the chemistry of energy storage, the physics of energy release and transformation in a power plant, the chemistry of air pollution, the biology of low-level ionizing radiation, the economics of energy pricing, and the politics of big oil. The concept of efficiency, central to combining these disciplinary insights into policy, is defined differently in physics, economics, and political science. They all recognize efficiency as a measure of output per unit input, but vary in what they include as input and output. By contrasting the ambiguities and assumptions of individual definitions, one can construct a higher-order, comprehensive meaning, accommodating discrepancies and integrating around identified commonalities. Resolution does not mean a false consensus or unity, as differences are neither reduced nor blurred. Instead, resources are marshaled for the task at hand.

Course Design

In designing courses, planning groups and faculty need to consider a number of issues. Most interdisciplinary courses are organized around a particular topic, theme, problem, question, issue, idea, person or persons, cultural or historical period, or world area or national region. Once curricular purpose has been clearly established, the first task is to select the organizing principle of the course and determine how it will be defined. If the course is part of a program or a sequence of courses, its relationship to other components of the program needs to be clarified. The next task is to determine what knowledge and information—out of all that is possible—will be presented and what texts used. The final task is to define the sequence of the course and how the interdisciplinary process will be addressed. Interdisciplinary courses, like the interdisciplinary process itself, require achieving a working balance among breadth (to ensure a wide base of knowledge of information), depth (to ensure the quality of requisite knowledge and information for the task at hand), and synthesis (to ensure integration of knowledge) (Association of American Colleges, 1990, pp. 65–66).

Achieving synthesis requires proactive attention to process. That means examining how the elements to be synthesized are obtained and interrelated. The skills involved are familiar ones: differentiating, comparing, and contrasting different disciplinary and professional perspectives; identifying commonalties and clarifying how the differences relate to the task at hand; and devising a holistic understanding grounded in the commonalities but still responsive to the differences. The worldview and underlying assumptions of each discipline must be made explicit. By doing so, an interdisciplinary approach promotes "strong sense critical thinking," going beyond logical skills to become critically reflexive of discipline and self (Newell, 1992, p. 220). Students and faculty are able to structure a framework flexible enough to allow for shifting groupings of information and knowledge, to define adequate depth and specificity as well as breadth and general connection, to identify salient concepts and global questions, then to use them in an integrative manner to clarify and present results for mutual revision (Klein, 1996). An important part of course planning, therefore, is determining how and when comparative analysis of pertinent methods and tools takes place, and ensuring that the goals of both depth and breadth are explicitly defined and pursued (Association of American Colleges, 1991b, p. 74).

The tendency in designing interdisciplinary courses is to try to cover too much content, especially in general education curricula that place greater value on the breadth part of the breadth-depth-synthesis triad. An interdisciplinary course needs to be conceptualized as covering disciplinary perspectives the way a disciplinary course covers subject matter. A narrower topic leaves more time to apply diverse disciplinary perspectives and increases the likelihood that those perspectives confront the same issues instead of talking past one another. The narrower the topic, the more complex its examination can be and the more the various perspectives themselves can be probed. The choice of topic further requires balancing faculty expertise and student interest. Since the topic is often shaped for the disciplines it introduces and the skills and sensibilities it cultivates, as much as by faculty interest, it is important to distinguish between this subtext, which constitutes the real course for faculty, and the common-sense understanding of the course by students (Newell, 1994).

Pedagogy and Team-Teaching

One of the first questions faculty ask is what constitutes *interdisciplinary pedagogy.* There is no unique interdisciplinary pedagogy. IDS typically draws on innovative pedagogies that promote dialogue and community, problem-posing and problem-solving capacities, and an integrative habit of mind. Collaborative work is one way of achieving a sense of community, usually through exercises and small-group projects. Because collaborative inquiry alters the strict hierarchy of teacher and student, traditional roles are redefined in the process. Discovery- and praxis-based learning, as well as game and role-playing, also encourage making connections, while dialogic and process models of learning heighten awareness of the role of critical thinking. Learning portfolios encourage integration of subjects as well as personal synthesis of knowledge and experience. Lectures are used, especially in core curricula that combine large plenary sessions with small discussion workshops. In interdisciplinary settings, however, the lecture format may not be useful. A teaching team may engage in dialogue in the middle of a classroom discussion, interrupting each other for clarification and questioning their definitions and assumptions. Faculty in the American studies program at Tufts University have a self-imposed ten-minute rule that restricts lecturing to imparting necessary information. The Tufts team also uses *dyads,* exercises between two students focusing on course issues and tasks. In addition, many interdisciplinary courses also use free-writing exercises to stimulate thinking.

Team-teaching is frequently associated with interdisciplinary study, though more often courses are team planned but individually taught. A team may teach together for the initial offering of a course; then, as individuals become more comfortable with the perspectives and contributions of other disciplines, they may teach sections individually. Team-teaching is more expensive than individually taught sections of a team-designed course. For that reason, the University of Maine's program in general education brings six faculty members together for course development and lectures to promote dialogue and community within each course, but then splits them up into teams of two for separate seminar sections.

Generally speaking, even members of the same teaching team tend to lack consensus on a definition of interdisciplinarity and engage in little philosophical discussion. Through pragmatic faculty discussions in the classroom, different operational and implicit definitions evolve. Whether a course is team-taught or team-designed and individually taught, a regular meeting of the teaching faculty is vital for tending to day-to-day operations. Discussions tend to center on topics to cover, passages in assigned readings to emphasize, issues to raise, concepts and theories to master, sensibilities and skills to develop the next week, and effective pedagogy. Presemester and postsemester as well as summer workshops afford more time for evaluation, reflection, and bringing new faculty on board. Collaborative construction of course portfolios, with teaching versions of syllabi and readers, are excellent means of focusing on definitions and the evolving shape of courses. (See Davis, 1995, for a comprehensive guide to the subject shaped by organizational and group theory, practical wisdom, and program models.)

Interdisciplinary curriculum development and teaching are vital forms of faculty development. Individuals contribute their own expertise, but they grow intellectually through exposure to other viewpoints and the interrogative learning that ensues. Faculty seminars, workshops, and study groups are the primary mechanisms. Whether scheduled during the academic year or in summer, on a voluntary basis or in connection with an internal or external grant, whether self-directed through reading of common texts or in conjunction with seminars with visiting scholars, they are cost-effective investments in the intellectual life of an institution. The key to stimulating interaction is providing nonhierarchical structures that foster dialogue, self-criticism and risk taking, trust and mutual respect, and a sense of mutual ownership. This environment aids in the essential and sometimes thorny task of bridging disciplinary and professional worldviews, styles of working, and ways of dividing up subject matter.

Assessment and Evaluation

Criteria for assessment are the least understood aspect of IDS, partly because they have been least studied and partly because multiple motivations and tasks militate against any single standard. The recent appearance of a comprehensive discussion of the issues involved in assessment of interdisciplinary learning provides a much-needed clarification (Field, Lee, and Field, 1994).

Assessment of Learning

The traditional conceptual focus of assessment has been on acquisition of knowledge in established curricular areas, usually using nationally normed tests. By their very nature, though, interdisciplinary programs tend to be unique. No standard curriculum provides an index, and many veterans of interdisciplinary teaching find acquisition of knowledge alone a questionable goal. Lack of a standard curriculum is often held to be a major disadvantage. Yet, it may well be an advantage, because it requires a shift in focus from a fixed body of information to the students' cognitive development and integration. Field, Lee, and Field (1994) suggest that intellectual maturation and cognitive development may, in fact, be the most appropriate conceptual frameworks for assessment. (For more information on assessment, see Chapters Twenty-Eight and Twenty-Nine.)

Some standardized instruments are useful. The College Outcomes Measures Project (COMP), developed by the American College Testing Program as an evaluation of learning in general education, measures a wide range of intellectual skills instead of specific intellectual content. The School of Interdisciplinary Studies at Miami University has used COMP for pre- and postcourse testing of students. The General Intellectual Skills test, currently being developed by the Educational Testing Service (ETS), will measure critical thinking and communication skills, with grading by local faculty equipped with ETS protocols. The more discipline-oriented ETS instrument, the Academic Profile, measures college-level reading, writing, mathematics, and critical thinking in relation to the humanities, social sciences, and natural sciences. Either a long or a short form may be used. Field, Lee, and Field note additional measures such as the Test of Critical Thinking, the Reflective Judgment Interview, the Watson-Glaser Critical Thinking Appraisal Test, the College Student Experiences Questionnaire, the Measure of Intellectual Development, and ACT ASSET. Yet they caution that many of these instruments are not standardized and lack full validation. For interdisciplinary majors and concentrations, instruments or parts of instruments that test knowledge in pertinent subject areas will also be relevant. Still, the limits of standardized, quantitative instruments underscore the importance of local control.

A number of recommendations emerge from the 1990 report of the Interdisciplinary Studies Task Force and from Field, Lee, and Field (1994). The keys to appropriate assessment are taking a developmental perspective, applying multiple strategies, combining qualitative and quantitative measures, and devising locally designed measures tied to local goals. Using multiple, ongoing instruments and methodologies balances the weaknesses of any one instrument and addresses the full range of IDS goals. The locally designed measures in Field, Lee, and Field's exemplary models—the School of Interdisciplinary Studies at Miami University, the Evergreen State College, and the Interdisciplinary Studies Program at Wayne State University—include contextualized use of quantitative measures, portfolio analysis of student work in individual courses, comprehensive multiyear portfolios, written and oral performance in capstone seminars and theses, entry and exit interviews, courses focused proactively on the nature of interdisciplinary process, regularized faculty feedback on student capabilities, data on graduate- and professional-school placement, career placement, and retrospective evaluations by alumni. Faculty and administrators should also consider whether standard measures can be adapted to local needs or new qualitative measures must be designed. Regularly updated, accessible data are crucial to quantitative tracking of students, though plans should not be more ambitious than local resources allow or so complex they become ends in themselves. When an assessment plan is being formulated, goals should also be articulated early in the development process and feedback loops incorporated, leading back to improvement of both teaching and curriculum design.

Until recently, hard evidence on the outcomes of interdisciplinary education was rare in the published literature. Interdisciplinarity was almost never a factor included in major educational studies. In their massive compendium of research on higher education over the last twenty years, Pascarella and Terenzini (1991) do not even include interdisciplinary studies or integration in the index, though they report that "A second general conclusion is that change in a wide variety of areas is stimulated by academic experiences that purposefully provide for challenge and integration. . . . [A] curricular experience in which students are required to integrate learning from separate courses around a central theme appears to elicit greater growth in critical thinking than does the same curricular experience without the integrative requirement" (p. 619).

In *What Matters in College?* Astin (1992) related the number of interdisciplinary courses, the number of faculty teaching them, and student satisfaction with opportunities to take interdisciplinary courses. While in general he discovered that what is taught in college and how the curriculum is structured have much less impact on students than active learning pedagogies, student-orientation of faculty, and students' interaction with peers, the one major exception was interdisciplinary studies. Astin reported that "the true-core interdisciplinary approach to general education, in which all students are required to take precisely the same set of courses . . . does appear to have generally favorable effects on many of the twenty-two general education outcomes" (pp. 424–425).

In particular, he discovered that interdisciplinarity has widespread effects on cognitive and academic development, including knowledge of field as well as general knowledge, critical thinking, GPA, preparation for graduate and professional school, degree aspirations, intellectual self-concept, and performance on MCAT, LSAT, and NTE examinations. He also determined that IDS has extensive impact on affective development, including all self-reported growth measures except job skills and foreign language, and virtually all diversity outcomes. The next task for studies of higher education is to probe the precise mechanisms through which interdisciplinary study has such widespread effects.

Program Review

Evaluating the effectiveness of the curriculum should be an ongoing process tied to feedback loops from assessment measures. Carefully designed instruments can play an important role in testing claims about attainment of program goals. The St. Andrew's College general education program uses multiyear comparison both within and across individual courses of the program. Student evaluations include targeted questions about the effectiveness of particular texts, lectures, workshops, the syllabus, the reader, and teaching strategies. Aided by this data, discussions of program effectiveness combine quantitative measures with qualitative impressions, without undue balance of one over the other.

Every five years, a more formal review should be conducted and external evaluators involved. In addition to following the procedures stipulated by a local institution for program review, interdisciplinary program review should also address the following questions:

- How effective are the faculty? If faculty are borrowed from departments, are there problems of availability and rotation? Whether they are borrowed or resident in an IDS program, is their interdisciplinary teaching (and research) adequately evaluated and rewarded?
- Is there an adequate system of faculty development? Are there adequate resources available on campus for curriculum development and learning in pertinent fields?

- Do the organizational and budgetary procedures of the institution facilitate and enhance interdisciplinary programs and other forms of interaction and collaboration? Do programs have secure budgetary lines in hard money, thereby integrating them into the life of the campus? Is there sufficient flexibility to allow shifting groupings of faculty and courses as topics and projects change? Are there incentives to encourage this?
- Is the breadth-depth-synthesis triad fully and adequate addressed? Is there sufficient specificity as well as sufficient breadth? Is adequate attention paid to integrating elements to ensure adequate synthesis?
- How effective is the counseling and information system? Do students understand the goals and structure of the interdisciplinary program? Are they aided in articulating their interdisciplinary experience when they apply for graduate, professional, and career placement (Lynton, 1985, pp. 144–150)?

Additional Resources

The difference between 1978 and 1996 is striking in a final respect. In 1978, no comprehensive bibliographies on IDS existed. Since then, Klein (1990, 1994) has identified core literatures, and Klein and Doty (1994) have provided overviews of the literatures and strategies for locating resources, program administration, course design, assessment, and networking. The latter source is a good beginning point for administrators, curriculum committees, and faculty seeking information about all points of program life cycle, from planning and implementation to review and revitalization.

The ready availability of resources underscores the recommendation of the Interdisciplinary Studies Task Force that faculty be formally prepared for IDS. The quality of interdisciplinary program design and teaching is directly related to development of a shared body of knowledge and a shared sense of what is at stake, both conceptually and pragmatically. Echoing the importance of networking, relevant professional bodies—disciplinary, professional, and interdisciplinary— are also vital sources of information, contacts, guidelines, and intellectual community. For continuing developments, the Association for Integrative Studies (AIS), a national professional organization for interdisciplinarians, functions as a clearinghouse for information, pertinent professional groups, consultants and external evaluators.

To reiterate the importance of an adequate resource base, colleges and universities seeking to provide better support for interdisciplinary needs and interests can use the holdings in the King Library of Miami University as a defining touchstone for collection building. To gain access to the library's on-line catalogue via Internet, type Sherlock@lib.muohio.edu, then log in as "library." In case of technical difficulties, phone the reference desk at 513–519–4141, then ask for the current liaison to the School of Interdisciplinary Studies. Interdisciplinary material appears under many subject headings, but the most fruitful for searching in the King collection, in local collections, and in electronic databases are *interdisciplinary approach in education* and *interdisciplinary approach to knowledge.* In addition, the Institute in Integrative Studies, located at Miami University, houses an archive of syllabi generated by participants in the institute's seminars and workshops on interdisciplinary methodology, pedagogy, and curriculum design.

Conclusion

Making use of the abundance of resources available today is all the more imperative when the current financial strains on higher education are considered. As Eckhardt observed in 1978, "The intelligent management of change is never easy, and it becomes particularly difficult at a time when change no longer implies an overall growth in size" (pp. 2–3). Eckhardt's caveat rings even truer today as colleges and universities are expected do more with less, attempting to maintain existing offerings while devising new structures to accommodate a wider range of students. The cost-saving measure of downsizing raises an issue that will loom larger in the future. In cases where departments have been combined and modular approaches to the curriculum developed, IDS has been seen as a way to achieve greater efficiency in allocating faculty resources. This strategy can provide a partial solution for financially strapped institutions, but it is not a sufficient condition for interdisciplinarity. Simply combining disparate units is unlikely to produce integration in the curriculum. At the other end of the scale, collapsing interdisciplinary programs back into disciplinary departments with assurances their interests will be protected is a naive hope. Combining interdisciplinary programs into a unit of interdisciplinary studies is a better solution than collapsing them altogether.

As we move from the twentieth into the twenty-first century, IDS is no longer considered marginal to the curriculum, from K–12 through higher education. Interdisciplinary studies will continue to promote greater coherence, focus, and connectedness in order to mitigate the costs of fragmentation. Interdisciplinary approaches to research will continue to promote effective problem solving at the same time they stimulate the production of new knowledge and propel the critique of existing intellectual and institutional structures. The lessons of interdisciplinary history are clear and abundant. The challenge now is to use them wisely.

References

Armstrong, F. "Faculty Development Through Interdisciplinarity." *Journal of General Education,* 1980, *32*(1), 52–63.

Association of American Colleges. *Integrity in the College Curriculum: A Report to the Academic Community.* Washington, D.C.: Association of American Colleges, 1985.

Association of American Colleges. *Liberal Learning and the Arts and Sciences Major.* Vol. 1: *The Challenge of Connecting Learning.* Washington, D.C.: Association of American Colleges, 1991a.

Association of American Colleges. "Interdisciplinary Studies." In *Reports from the Field.* Washington, D.C.: Association of American Colleges, 1991b. Excerpted version of the Report of the Interdisciplinary Studies Task Force. Complete version appears in "Interdisciplinary Resources," *Issues in Integrative Studies,* 1990, *8,* 9–33 (special issue).

Astin, A. W. *What Matters in College? Four Critical Years Revisited.* San Francisco: Jossey-Bass, 1992.

Casey, B. "The Administration and Governance of Interdisciplinary Programs." In J. T. Klein and W. Doty (eds.), *Interdisciplinary Studies Today.* New Directions for Teaching and Learning, no. 58. San Francisco: Jossey-Bass, 1994.

Center for Educational Research and Innovation (CERI). *Interdisciplinarity: Problems of Teaching and Research in Universities.* Paris: CERI/Organization for Economic Cooperation and Development, 1972.

Davis, J. *Interdisciplinary Courses and Team Teaching: New Arrangements for Learning.* American Council on Education. Phoenix, Ariz.: Oryx Press, 1995.

Eckhardt, C. D. *Interdisciplinary Programs and Administrative Structures: Problems and Prospects for the 1980s.* University Park, Pa.: Center for the Study of Higher Education, 1978.

Field, M., Lee, R., and Field, M. L. "Assessing Interdisciplinary Learning." In J. T. Klein and W. Doty (eds.), *Interdisciplinary Studies Today.* New Directions for Teaching and Learning, no. 58. San Francisco: Jossey-Bass, 1994.

Gaff, J. G. "Avoiding the Potholes: Strategies for Reforming General Education." *Educational Record,* 1980, *61*(4), 50–59.

Gibbons, M., and others. *The New Production of Knowledge: The Dynamics of Science and Research in Contemporary Societies.* Newbury Park, Calif.: Sage, 1994.

Hursh, B., Haas, P., and Moore, M. "An Interdisciplinary Model to Implement General Education." *Journal of Higher Education,* 1983, *53,* 42–59.

Klein, J. T. *Interdisciplinary: History, Theory, and Practice.* Detroit: Wayne State University Press, 1990.

Klein, J. T. "Finding Interdisciplinary Knowledge and Information." In J. T. Klein and W. Doty, eds. *Interdisciplinary Studies Today.* New Directions for Teaching and Learning, no. 58. San Francisco: Jossey-Bass, 1994.

Klein, J. T. *Crossing Boundaries: Knowledges, Disciplinarities, and Interdisciplinarities.* Charlottesville: University Press of Virginia, 1996.

Klein, J. T., and Doty, W. (eds.). *Interdisciplinary Studies Today.* New Directions for Teaching and Learning, no. 58. San Francisco: Jossey-Bass, 1994.

Klein, J. T., and Gaff, J. *Reforming General Education: A Survey.* Washington, D.C.: Association of American Colleges, 1982.

Levine, A. *Handbook on Undergraduate Curriculum.* San Francisco: Jossey-Bass, 1978.

Lynton, E. "Interdisciplinarity: Rationales and Criteria of Assessment." In L. Levin and I. Lind (eds.), *Inter-Disciplinarity Revisited: Re-Assessing the Concept in the Light of Institutional Experience.* Stockholm: OECD, Swedish National Board of Universities and Colleges, 1985.

National Institute of Education. *Involvement in Learning: Realizing the Potential of American Higher Education.* Report of the Study Group on the Conditions of Excellence in American Higher Education. Washington, D.C.: U.S. Government Printing Office, 1984.

Newell, W. H. *Interdisciplinary Undergraduate Programs: A Directory.* Oxford, Ohio: Association for Integrative Studies, 1986.

Newell, W. "Academic Disciplines and Undergraduate Disciplinary Education: Lessons from the School of Interdisciplinary Studies at Miami University, Ohio." *European Journal of Education,* 1992, *27*(3), 211–221.

Newell, W. "Designing Interdisciplinary Courses." In J. T. Klein and W. Doty, eds. *Interdisciplinary Studies Today.* New Directions for Teaching and Learning, no. 58. San Francisco: Jossey-Bass, 1994.

Pascarella, E. T., and Terenzini, P. T. *How College Affects Students: Findings and Insights from Twenty Years of Research.* San Francisco: Jossey-Bass, 1991.

Squires, G. "Interdisciplinarity in Higher Education in the United Kingdom." *European Journal of Education,* 1992, *27*(3), 201–210.

CHAPTER TWENTY

INTERNATIONALIZING THE CURRICULUM

Joseph S. Johnston, Jr., Jane R. Spalding

Once a marginal activity on most campuses, international education has emerged as a leading imperative of curriculum reform for the 1990s and the beginning of the twenty-first century. At institutions of all types, there is heightened interest in what can be done to create environments for teaching and learning as well as research and service that reflect and address the increasingly interdependent nature of our world. Solid programmatic accomplishments and promising initiatives abound. Viewed as a whole, however, the current internationalization of higher education is, as Groennings (1990, p. 29) has described it, essentially, "a disorderly development, lacking clear definitions, boundaries or framework." The gains made are still scattered and tentative and their cumulative impact is weak. Given that the need is for "arguably the most powerful substantive re-direction in the history of American higher education" (Groennings, 1990, p. 28)—far more powerful than the internationalization accomplished in earlier decades—it will only be met if our campuses greatly strengthen their commitment and attention to internationalization and increase both the number and the quality of their efforts.

Those who would lead or take roles in this work at their institutions face a host of questions. What is the rationale for international education? What are its possible goals and elements? What strategies can be effective? Where, generally, do we begin? Reviewing these questions can provide campus practitioners—

faculty members, academic administrators, and other institutional leaders—a sense both of what they can accomplish and the approaches that might serve them best.

Rationale

Why, first of all, is international education important? The success of a campus's reform efforts may depend, in part, on its willingness to answer this question in more than a perfunctory way. During the last half century, each of two arguments for internationalizing higher education has had its day. The first major pressures for U.S. colleges and universities to develop more international expertise emerged after World War II in response to arguments of national security and the country's newfound role as leader of the free world; these led to the development of centers of international expertise—particularly area studies and language programs—and the involvement of faculty in assistance programs overseas, but they did little to make entire institutions more international in character and outlook (Groennings, 1990, pp. 16–17; Goodwin and Nacht, 1991, pp. 3–4 and 110–111). Today, with the fall of the Soviet Union, concerns about the effectiveness of public education, and the emergence of an increasingly integrated world economy, economic competitiveness provides the dominant rationale. This argument for international education has considerable force. Already 33 percent of U.S. corporate profits and four of every five of the nation's new jobs are generated by international trade. America's ability to hold its own amid challenges from a host of established and emerging economic powers will have a large part in determining, for good or ill, its future.

As a rationale for internationalization, however, economic competitiveness is a narrow formulation of the national interest. It excludes other dimensions of our relations with foreign countries and their peoples and the acute worldwide need for more cooperation in the solution of common problems (Pickert and Turlington, 1992, p. 105). Within the academy, many faculty members are uninterested in manufacturing and balances of trade and regard these matters as irrelevant to their work (Hayden and Muller, 1990, p. ix). It is not surprising that, given their relative enrollments, business programs have done disproportionately more to internationalize in recent years—and programs in other areas disproportionately less.

The strongest rationale for international education arises not from forces external to the university but from interpreting the aims of liberal education. Our species has been described as "biologically and culturally adapted to the near-at-hand," (McConaghy, 1990, pp. 646–648) and overcoming parochialism, broadly understood, always has been one appropriate goal of schooling. To be educated is to have a general knowledge of the larger world, some understanding of the array of individual cultures that constitute it, their interdependence, and the place of one's own culture among them. It is to have some sense of "the complexities of religion and ethnicity, the nuances of power, and the forces at work in the long, complicated histories of many nations" (Marden and Engerman, 1992, p. 42). It entails, by some definitions, having deeper knowledge and understanding of at least one foreign culture, including the skills to negotiate the challenges of life there as a speaker of its native tongue. At another level, education is a matter of attitude and habits of mind—including those of valuing other cultures and their distinctiveness and seeing things from the perspective of peoples other than one's own.

Research on the effects of international programs and global education goals within the undergraduate curriculum is minimal, largely anecdotal, and confined to single institutions. Nevertheless, proponents of international education assert that it produces an array of outcomes, as well as other desirable qualities and kinds of learning. International education may help undermine received opinions of all types, and this can be unsettling and challenging. At its best, however, it fosters personal growth through reflection on assumptions, values, and moral choices. It may challenge students to confront the relativity of things, but also to make their own grounded judgments. It is often active and experiential, putting a premium on competence—on putting what one has learned into effective practice. It may accommodate and integrate work and service. It may be the best context in which to learn and appreciate the need for multidisciplinarity—for looking at things comparatively, in context, and in their full complexity. International education, as Stoltzfus (1992) has nicely put it, is good education. Although only a small fraction of the American undergraduate population incorporates some form of international education in their program, we believe that it can be beneficial for all students, not just specialists-in-training, or the self-selected (and often self-financed) group that chooses to study abroad. It is no less true in a school of business or engineering than in a college of arts and sciences. Indeed, the rationale for internationalizing our colleges and universities will likely not only endure but grow long after today's economic circumstances have passed into history.

Key Elements of International Education

As background and context for local analysis and planning, we offer now a brief account of the challenges faced by U.S. higher education generally in several key areas of international education: language study, study abroad, the education of foreign students, and the internationalization of the curriculum. In several of these areas, as we shall see later, reform efforts are beginning to produce good examples and even make a difference. But in all of them, daunting work remains to be done.

Language Study

Americans are notoriously hapless language learners, and their underperformance derives in large part from systemic problems in their schools and colleges. Only 17 percent of public elementary schools offer any form of language instruction (Commission on International Education, 1989, p. 8), and barely one-third of all high school students study any language other than English (Kilpatrick, 1991, p. 10). Only 8 percent of colleges and universities require a foreign language for admission (Gardner, 1990, p. 10), and fewer than 9 percent require one for graduation (Commission on International Education, 1989, p. 8). It is no surprise, then, that at any time only 9 percent of our undergraduates are in foreign language classes (Marden and Engerman, 1992, p. 43). Those that are typically study only for a year or two; very few ever attain even basic proficiency (Pickert, 1992, p. 13).

Also of concern is the relative inattention of our schools and postsecondary institutions to languages other than French, Spanish, and German. Among the so-called less-commonly-taught foreign languages are Arabic, Chinese, Japanese, and Russian—arguably among those most important for Americans to know in coming decades. This group of languages, taken together, accounts for less than 1 percent of all language enrollments at the K–12 level and between 5 percent and 8 percent of those in college. French, German, and Spanish, on the other hand, account for 90 to 95 percent of all language enrollments—although these languages are spoken by only 14 percent of the world's population (Walton, 1992, pp. 1–7).

Study Abroad

If study abroad is to fulfill its vast potential as a component of international education, several key problems must be overcome: the small scale of the enterprise; its lack of diversity in terms of participants, locations, and program types; and its lack of integration with the rest of the student's and institution's academic experience.

The percentage of all U.S. undergraduates who study abroad in any given year has been negligible—less than 0.5 percent (Commission on International Education, 1989, p. 2). Although a small minority of institutions have claimed to send at least 10 percent of their students abroad at some point in their undergraduate years—and a few can cite participation rates of up to 90 percent—the numbers nationally have been abysmally low (El-Khawas, 1992, p. 13).

Among those who have gone, females have outnumbered males two to one (Advisory Council for International Educational Exchange, 1988, p. 25). Liberal arts majors (excluding those in math and the sciences) have outnumbered students in all other fields by approximately the same margins (National Endowment for the Humanities, 1992, table 3). Those who have *not* been well represented include males, minorities, science majors, working adults, and (business majors somewhat excepted) professional students (Advisory Council for International Educational Exchange, 1988, pp. 7–10). The inflexibility of most current programs—70 percent are of a semester's or summer's duration, virtually all are traditionally academic in nature, and most are completed during the junior year—prevents them from attracting and meeting the needs of currently underserved populations (National Task Force on Undergraduate Education Abroad, 1990, tables 6, 5, and 4).

Perhaps the most dismal failing of U.S. undergraduate study abroad has been its thorough Eurocentrism. Nearly 80 percent of students pursuing programs abroad have done so on the European continent. By one recent count, far more undergraduates (27 percent) have studied in the United Kingdom alone than in Asia (5 percent), Africa (1 percent), the Middle East (3 percent), and Latin America (9 percent) combined (National Endowment for the Humanities, n.d., tables 1 and 2; National Task Force on Undergraduate Education Abroad, 1990, p. 6).

Unlike students from other countries' universities, American undergraduates—when they have studied abroad—have tended not to enroll directly in a foreign institution. Eighty percent have enrolled instead in programs sponsored by a U.S. institution (National Task Force on Undergraduate Education Abroad, 1990, p. 8); too many of these programs, in turn, have created American enclaves abroad and have not encouraged a full engagement with and immersion in the host culture. There are reasons—if not always acceptable ones—for this situation, including U.S. students' inadequate language preparation and difficulties in the transfer of credit. But these characteristics call the quality and impact of these programs into question.

So too, finally, does the unconnectedness of study abroad with the rest of a student's program of study and the academic life of his or her home institution. Too seldom are students adequately prepared for immersion or encouraged to take full academic advantage of their time abroad. Their period of study in another country is often seen by them and their professors as time away from the real work of their major field of study and hence as carrying an opportunity cost that makes it doubly expensive. Perception further becomes reality, of course, when upon a student's return his or her new interests and knowledge are not shared or developed or used as the basis for further academic work.

International Students

If the United States has a competitive advantage in international education, it is surely because our colleges and universities have enrolled far more foreign students than those of any other nation. The nearly 450,000 foreign students enrolled here in 1990 constituted a cohort about six times as large as that of U.S. students studying abroad. The 47 percent of them who studied at the associate or bachelor's level constituted 2 percent of undergraduate enrollments in this country (Zikopoulous, 1992, pp. 1–3).

The foreign student population has had characteristics that have shaped and constrained its potential for assisting the internationalizing of U.S. campuses. One characteristic has been the numerical dominance of Asians, who have made up nearly 60 percent of the whole; nine out of the top ten countries of origin have been in Asia. Europe, by contrast, has accounted for only 13 percent, and Latin America, the Middle East, and Africa for 10 percent, 7 percent, and 5 percent, respectively (Zikopoulous, 1992, p. 15).

Foreign students have tended disproportionately to choose certain fields of study. In 1993–94, for example, the preferred fields were business (with 19 percent of students enrolled), engineering (17 percent), physical and life sciences (10 percent) and mathematics and computer science (8 percent). They were commensurately underrepresented in the social sciences and humanities (Zikopoulous, 1992, p. 30).

As these statistics suggest, their countries of origin, native languages, and academic interests have limited the extent to which many foreign students have been linked with other elements of internationalization on U.S. campuses. Because most speak Asian languages, their native language skills have gone largely unused. Nor have foreign students been well represented in courses and programs with international content where they could make important contributions. Most of these offerings—too high a proportion, in fact—are in the arts and sciences rather than in the tightly structured professional, scientific, and technical curricula in which most foreign students have enrolled (Lambert, 1992, pp. 26–31).

The Curriculum as a Whole

Here, too, there is impressive evidence of the work to be done. More and more institutions have indeed declared the importance of internationalizing their courses and programs. Many are developing plans. A growing number have accomplished real changes. Observations and surveys, however, suggest that far too few faculty are active agents of international education. A recent survey of colleges and universities found that although nearly two-thirds of all institutions claim increasing faculty involvement in overseas activities, only a very small fraction of faculty members do research involving other countries and just 3 percent supervise students abroad or participate in faculty exchanges. Only one in three institutions claims that even 10 percent of its courses contain international materials (El-Khawas, 1992, pp. 12–14).

One teaches what one knows and what one is rewarded for teaching. It is unfortunate, then, that the academy has not always been hospitable to internationally minded scholars. The sociology of the disciplines traditionally has not afforded the status enjoyed by their mainstream counterparts to international studies or peace or world order studies. Some faculty members in more traditional fields regard these explicitly international or global fields as lacking in rigor or prone to ideological bias; they may argue that students should gain their international understanding within the rigorous framework and by using the conceptual tools of the traditional disciplines (Pelikan, 1992, p. 33; Groennings, 1990, p. 27). These same faculty members, paradoxically, often shy away from comparative issues in their own courses. Many feel they lack the necessary skills to do this work or are discouraged by its marginality to what is perceived as the real work of their disciplines.

Yet we are increasingly aware that these disciplines give us views that are at best partial if we limit their enquiries to the study of the near-at-hand. A prized conclusion can depend too much on domestic data, on assumptions that do not travel. Subjected to conditions abroad, theories and models thought to be universally applicable can lose their explanatory power. What we don't know can hurt us, prompting simplistic analyses that compromise the quality and credibility of our scholarly judgment—and through our teaching, the education our students receive.

Addressing the Challenge

There are a number of useful guides and handbooks available to those wishing to understand what they, their programs, and their institutions can do to achieve a more international perspective. They are, moreover, largely in agreement on essential steps. We summarize several of these steps very briefly here.

As Wollitzer has observed, "The fact is that most institutions of higher education start to internationalize *ad hoc* via targets of opportunity, individual initiatives and sometimes even by accident." This, he adds, "does not diminish the advisability of having a plan." As with any campuswide reform, senior administrators, faculty, and students should all be involved in such a plan's formulation and help ensure that its elements address their overlapping but distinctive needs and purposes. There is much hard thinking to be done at the institutional level, where these needs and purposes need to be brought into synthesis. How broadly will the college or university understand its goals in international education? To what extent will they relate to the institution's hopes for a future position within a rapidly evolving global educational landscape? To its intended contributions to society through research, education, training, and service? To the aim of preparing its graduates for productive work and citizenship? To what extent do the institution's geographical location, the ethnic and socioeconomic characteristics of its students, or the current strengths of its faculty suggest that some goals may be more important or attainable than others? To what extent does the institution aspire to offer all its graduates awareness of international and intercultural differences, direct exposure to them, a deeper understanding of them, and real competence in negotiating them? Different approaches and different levels of resources are implied by each goal. Difficult as achieving agreement may be, it is essential to do so. The resulting institutional articulation, as Wollitzer points out, can provide an indispensable framework for rational decision making and priority setting at other levels (Wollitzer, 1995, p. 10).

When divisions, departments, programs, and other functional units address the question of how they can best contribute to the overall institutional goals on internationalization, they must reflect on several factors. Among these should be the extent to which teaching and research in particular disciplines might, now or in the future, transcend nationally and geographically limited—and limiting—frames of reference. Of course, some fields—international studies, area studies, peace or world order studies—are explicitly devoted to examining international or global questions. Other disciplines—geography and anthropology, for example—are also intrinsically transnational in concern. Still others—archeology, botany, geology, linguistics, zoology, entomology, and a number of comparative specialties in the social sciences and humanities—extend their knowledge bases in direct proportion to their access to new sites and materials. Even in highly abstract fields such as physics, mathematics, and computer science, understanding advances as practitioners come into contact with the work of colleagues in other countries. Professional fields such as business, law, and medicine are shaped by developments outside the United States as surely as they contribute to them (Groennings, 1990, p. 2; Lambert, 1986, pp. 125–126). Volumes Three and Four of *The Encyclopedia of Higher Education* (Clark and Neave, 1992) provide descriptions of the evolution of each major discipline from an international comparative perspective, and are an excellent resource to departments and programs. Virtually all fields afford international dimensions. A large part of the work to be done in many settings will be to identify these and encourage their development.

Particular disciplines may well see their opportunities differently. Engineering educators, for example, may have a special interest in Germany and Japan—two highly developed industrial economies—and in study-abroad opportunities that emphasize internships in manufacturing concerns. Educators in the health sciences, social work, and the helping professions may want to explore language study and service-learning focused on large domestic minority groups.

Social scientists, to cite a final example, might heed Heginbotham's judgment (1994, pp. 33–40) as to the diminishing demand in our post–cold war era for area studies–type programs providing in-depth knowledge of specific countries per se, and the growing importance of problem-focused programs that prepare students to deal with the "challenges of building more effective social economic and political systems" in a wide variety of regions of the world, to programs such as those the traditional social sciences have much to offer—and much to learn, as well.

Setting goals and recognizing opportunities are, of course, one thing; helping faculty members find the motivation to change their teaching and research is another. Institutional efforts to encourage faculty members to activate their natural curiosity about the larger world might take many forms. Within reason, institutional policies affecting hiring, promotion, and tenure, as well as curriculum, should be revised to remove disincentives to the incorporation of international perspectives. Faculty members taking leave abroad, for example, should not have to forgo salary increases or be placed at a disadvantage for promotion and tenure because they publish at a somewhat slower rate or have peers unsympathetic to comparative or international scholarship (Tonkin and Edwards, 1990, pp. 14–17).

More positively, promotion and tenure decisions should be recognized as opportunities to retain and advance internationally minded faculty members—just as every academic search should be considered an opportunity to secure new ones. The creation of permanent or visiting positions designed for scholars from other countries, the replacement of faculty members away on Fulbright scholarships or sabbaticals by visiting foreign faculty members, and the use of joint appointments to both traditional departments and interdisciplinary international programs are other effective strategies (See Christensen, 1988, pp. 27–30).

Curriculum committees can be powerful agents of internationalization. They can review the international dimensions of institutional offerings department by department and course by course. They can question, where appropriate, the absence of international content in existing and proposed courses and challenge faculty members to justify syllabi that focus only on the United States (Tonkin and Edwards, 1990, p. 16).

Institutions wishing to internationalize the faculty should actively promote faculty and curriculum development. There are many ways of doing this. Faculty members can be encouraged to spend periods of leave in other countries, participate in international development projects and foreign conferences, or undertake joint research with foreign scholars; sources of funding for study and research abroad can be publicized on campus; faculty members can be offered summer salary and foreign study expenses to develop new internationally oriented courses; release time during the academic year can be provided to faculty members introducing international courses; and, finally, institutions can encourage— as well as train and pay—a wider circle of faculty members to design and lead study-abroad programs.

Few strategies have wider impact on a campus than organizing internationally oriented workshops for groups of interested faculty members. These might take the form of seminars on areas or issues, such as sub-Saharan Africa or global hunger; intensive language study; or a combination of two or more of these approaches. Programs of this kind can be especially effective if they are sustained by the institution, involve a period of group travel abroad, and carry an expectation that participants change their courses to reflect what they have learned. Institutions with minimal faculty turnover may find such workshops an especially helpful way to keep faculty members current and motivated. Workshops tend to be most effective when they are an integral part of a campus plan for globalizing the undergraduate program, rather than as isolated, one-time events.

A useful variant is the development of workshops or training programs under consortial auspices. This can prove especially practical in the case of less-commonly-taught languages or areas, or where particular institutions have special resources or interests they can share with faculty members from other colleges and universities, perhaps on a reciprocal basis.

Even this brief an overview of processes and means by which an institution can try to make its programs more global should mention the potential power of technology. Effective low-cost educational technologies have brought distance learning within the reach of virtually all institutions, increasing numbers of which are now sending or receiving educational programming or otherwise linking their students and faculty with peers across national borders. The Internet, for example, has already established its effectiveness as a medium for communication among students and faculty internationally. Its value is now being enlarged by the World Wide Web, which offers users full graphical and multimedia capabilities. These and other means of teleconferencing and distance learning have obvious potential, for example, for students studying abroad, who can continue to receive instruction from the home campus. They open up exciting possibilities, as well, for language instruction, especially in the less-commonly-taught languages in which an institution would not be able to hire its own faculty.

Curricular Examples

The remainder of this chapter very briefly describes some specific curricula and a number of initiatives. We have chosen our examples to illustrate the premise that every institution—regardless of its history, resources, size, control, and location—can do something to make its curriculum more international. The starting point can be anything from the creation of one new course to the reconception of an entire general education curriculum around international issues. The programs highlighted by no means exhaust the possibilities, but we hope that they suggest how various those possibilities are.

One caveat before looking at operational programs: curricula exist to further specific learning goals, and acquiring global perspectives is not a unitary concept. In fact, one study (Barrows, Clark, and Klein, 1980) found three quite distinctive kinds of learning: *knowledge* (a student's grasp of facts about international events), *affect* (attitudes and values about other peoples), and *language* (foreign language ability and attitudes toward foreign language study). Programs that serve one type of learning may contribute little or nothing to other types.

1. *Develop one course that draws on existing faculty expertise.* At the University of Michigan in Ann Arbor, an economist and a professor of Asian languages and cultures have created "Global Interdependence," a multidisciplinary course for nonspecialists from all parts of the university. The course, which has no prerequisites, fulfills an undergraduate general education requirement and is taught by more than ten professors drawn from as many different disciplines. The first two lectures frame the course's theme—the complex interdependence of economic, political, historical, geographical, and cultural forces at the local, national, and international levels. The course unfolds in four units: The History of International Trade; International Economic Relations; Culture and International Competition; and One World: Technology, Health, and Environment. Discussion sections after each unit and two final lectures help students with the difficult task of integrating the many different perspectives to which they have been exposed. One of the course developers reports that students who take the course become more open to the idea not only that business is a major factor in world affairs today but that it is a necessary force for progressive change. For institutions interested in creating similar courses, the University of Michigan has developed a book of course readings.

Goucher College's year-long freshman core course, "The Common Intellectual Experience," also draws on faculty members from different disciplines. During the first semester, students explore recent American history using the thematic framework of the individual and society. In the subsequent semester, they explore the same themes in Greek and Japanese culture. Plans call for an expansion of this course to include Islam. Ten Goucher faculty from the social sciences and humanities collaborate on this course, which requires them to teach sometimes unfamiliar material in unfamiliar historical and cultural contexts. The college has secured grant support for workshops to help the faculty with these challenges of interdisciplinary and international and intercultural teaching.

2. *Offer language study across the curriculum.* In Minnesota, St. Olaf College helps students make significant use of second languages in their study of the humanities, behavioral and natural sciences, and mathematics. St. Olaf students with at least advanced intermediate proficiency in a foreign language are allowed to take courses in other disciplines with an Applied Foreign Language Component (AFLC). In courses so designated, students substitute texts in a foreign language for a number of assigned English-language course readings. They also participate in a special weekly discussion session conducted in that second language, led jointly by a foreign language department faculty member and the course instructor. Successful completion of two such courses is recognized on student transcripts by awarding an Applied Foreign Language Certification. Each course with a language component carries additional credit.

Syracuse University has a slightly different take on language across the curriculum. Here the concept has been expanded to include its study-abroad programs. At three of its International Programs Abroad sites, Syracuse is attempting to bridge the gap between language and discipline study. One-credit language modules taught in the host language are linked to three-credit, discipline-based courses taught in English. The objective is for students to strengthen linguistic competency in their major discipline by using authentic materials in the host language. Examples of courses currently being taught this way include international relations, contemporary Italian history, Italian cinema, women's studies, and fine arts.

3. *Develop an intensive foreign language study program.* For thirteen summers, Beloit College has offered instruction in less-commonly-taught languages (Russian, Japanese, Chinese, and Hungarian) in an intensive, personalized program through its Center for Language Studies. Students from across the country enroll; on average one in four are Beloit undergraduates. Organizers of this program believe its small size enables it to be competitive by responding quickly to challenges and opportunities. For example, a course in second-year Spanish was added to the summer program in 1992 largely because five students needed to attain a greater degree of proficiency in Spanish so that they might study in Ecuador during the fall. This summer program, which complements Beloit's regular language offerings, is also contemplating the addition of new languages, including Portuguese.

4. *Add a new dimension—and coherence—to an existing set of courses through a "region-across-the-curriculum" approach.* In the fall of 1989, the University of Southern

California mounted a campuswide curricular and cocurricular effort to educate its students about the region of Southern Africa. Eighteen courses in fourteen departments were identified as including—or modified to include—relevant material. Approximately 2,100 students enrolled in these offerings, taking courses in business, urban and regional planning, and—as a core course—freshman writing. The campus hosted visiting artists from South Africa and Mozambique during the semester. In addition, the drama division produced two South African plays, and about twenty films dealing with South African issues were shown on campus.

At Maui Community College, which is part of the University of Hawaii system, faculty began by reconceiving what was originally a one-semester course on world regional geography. They decided to make it a two-semester course and modify it in such a way that it would complement and reinforce another two-semester course on world literature. The two courses focused in a coordinated way on a sequence of world regions: India, China, and Japan during semester one and Europe, the former Soviet Union, and Africa during semester two. More recently, a course on world religions and an art survey course have been modified to parallel the geography and literature courses and also to permit concurrent registration.

5. *Combine study abroad with service abroad.* By the time they graduate, approximately 80 percent of Goshen College students have participated in a thirteen-week Study-Service Term (SST) in countries with cultures significantly different from that of the United States. The SST, which is part of Goshen's general education requirement, begins with a brief period of on-campus orientation. It then combines seven weeks of language and culture studies abroad with six weeks of field work, usually in a rural area of the host country. Thirteen weeks, program organizers believe, is long enough for the students to begin adjusting to a new culture and short enough to allow their other academic pursuits to continue more or less uninterrupted.

Students take part in the SST in groups of twenty students and one faculty leader. Most SST locations are in the Caribbean and in Central America, where students live in the homes of nationals and eat at least two meals a day with their families. To date, about 50 percent of all Goshen faculty members have led an SST unit abroad. The SST is viewed and valued at Goshen as both a study program committed to learning with and from hosts in a mutual, collaborative intercultural effort, and a service program committed to ministering to the needs of both parties.

Warren Wilson College's International Development Program also combines academics with work and service. In this program, students carry out a voluntary work project in a Third World country, but only after completing a semester of required courses on campus. Predeparture courses include language and culture instruction, sociology, and a course on journal writing. Eight- or sixteen-week projects are designed and led by faculty members for groups of between ten and twenty students. All work projects take place on a village level and employ technology appropriate to regional economic development.

6. *Focus on groups usually underrepresented in study-abroad populations.* The University of Maryland and Lancaster University in Great Britain have developed a program of year-long exchange for science and engineering students—both groups traditionally underrepresented in study-abroad programs. Because of the careful attention program developers have paid to course design and content as well as to the transfer of all credits earned, participating students do not need to extend the length of their already lengthy and largely prescribed undergraduate programs.

From 1988 to 1991, Hampshire College received external funding to conduct January term science courses in Third World settings. Groups of students undertook small-scale projects in Argentina, Nicaragua, Belize, and Sri Lanka. Among other tasks, students took measurements on radon and radiation in areas of Sri Lanka and performed an animal census in Argentina, where others studied overgrazing and other environmental hazards. This initial brief exposure led some students to plan related semester-long projects in these same locations for their senior theses.

Recognizing the value of having minority students speak to peers about their study-abroad experiences, the Council on International Educational Exchange (CIEE) and the National Association of Foreign Student Affairs' (NAFSA's) Association of International Educators has created a national database of study-abroad advisers who maintain a list of minority students who have studied abroad. The database is a project of CIEE's Forum for Minority Participation in Education Abroad.

7. *Create the capacity for internationalizing courses by further developing the faculty.* When the leaders of Bentley College decided to develop international education on their campus, they started with the faculty, because relatively few faculty members had significant international experience. Today, more than a quarter of the full-time faculty members have been directly involved in the college's multifaceted international program. They take part in faculty development seminars, exchange programs, foreign study, and travel with Bentley students. In addition, they teach groups of foreign students on the Bentley campus and consult with institutions of higher education abroad. To provide an even more extensive network for faculty exchange and cooperative projects, Bentley has taken the lead in setting up the new International Consortium for Business and Management Education, which counts among its other members institutions in the United States, France, Spain, Belgium, Estonia, Egypt, Mexico, Brazil, Australia, and New Zealand. Faculty involvement internationally has now reached a point where it cuts across all departments of the college.

Earlham College, recognized nationally for its teaching of Japanese and Japanese studies, decided in 1990 to develop its faculty in the area of Hispanic culture and language. Specifically, Earlham wanted to broaden a number of courses by including units with a Latin American perspective. To achieve this end, the college developed a multiphase project, beginning in the spring of 1991, in which ten faculty members from the departments of English, literature, religion, philosophy, psychology, peace studies, biology, physics, and history studied the Spanish language. In June, the group participated in eight days of intensive predeparture orientation sessions. Then it went to Mexico, where intensive language instruction continued and faculty began to work on self-designed projects, including studies of such topics as ancient musical instruments, museums in Mexico, liberation theology, family planning, conservation, and medicinal plants. Participants gathered materials for use in their courses at the same time that they underwent an experience that allowed them to see firsthand the value of Earlham's foreign study initiatives for their students.

8. *Target professional education for internationalization and arrange for international internship placements.* At the University of Rhode Island (URI), faculty members in German teach a sequence of classes composed entirely of—and designed entirely for—undergraduate engineers. These courses stress oral skills and everyday, as opposed to literary, German. They also integrate basic vocabulary from fields such as physics, computer science, chemistry, and mathematics. The courses are part of URI's International Engineering Program (IEP), which enables students to combine the study of German with engineering and to graduate after five years with both a B.S. in an engineering discipline and a B.A. in German. The key elements of the program are the tailored German-language courses over the first three years of study; a six-month paid internship in an engineering firm or research institute in a German-speaking country during the fourth year; and in the fifth year, both traditional upper-level German language courses and a special interdisciplinary engineering course taught in German by bilingual engineering faculty members.

Students and faculty members regard the internship as the focal point of the program. It is a key motivation for students in the first three years, as well as a powerful educational experience that brings each student's interests and preparation together. It also has been one of the most challenging elements of the program to arrange and administer. Working through new and preexisting contacts both here and abroad, the program directors have, over time, developed a growing international network of businesses willing to offer placements.

Finally, while the program directors have been studying the possible expansion of this program into other language areas—including French, Chinese, and Japanese—they have launched a similar initiative in cooperation with URI's college of business administration. URI is now helping its business faculty learn German in preparation for six-semester, team-taught sequences of German courses focusing on issues pertinent to careers in international business.

The good news at Worcester Polytechnic Institute (WPI) is that foreign study is thriving. Each WPI student must complete in the junior year a nine-credit Interactive Qualifying Project (IQP). Because of its timing and duration, the IQP lends itself to international study. Yet few students would choose to tackle projects abroad if it were not for other types of support they receive. The first factor is the enthusiasm of the faculty—for whom the supervision of IQPs is a basic teaching responsibility. A second essential support is the growing international network of project centers and programs in Europe (England, Ireland, and Italy) and Asia (Thailand, Hong Kong, and Taiwan). Two new centers soon will begin operation—one in Puerto Rico and the other in Ecuador. In addition to these project centers and programs, WPI also has an array of bilateral educational exchange agreements with institutions in Germany, France, Switzerland, and Sweden, as well as membership in the International Student Exchange Program.

WPI conceives of foreign study as a form of purposeful service learning. The list of recent projects abroad includes studies of the safety regulations governing high-rise apartment construction in Hong Kong, the societal impact of Taipei's new mass transit system, and the public policy implications of a toxic spill in the Rhine River. In 1994, about 30 percent of WPI juniors conducted their IQPs at foreign sites.

9. *Identify and use local community resources to enhance and complement efforts to internationalize.* The Culture and Commerce program at the College of Staten Island of the City University of New York is noteworthy for its combination of undergraduate study in the liberal arts and business and for its emphasis on experiential education. It also exemplifies a particularly effective use of location—in this case, proximity to Manhattan and its immediate location in the predominately ethnic borough of Staten Island. Culture and Commerce is a four-year course of study, equivalent in length to a very substantial academic minor. It allows students majoring in the arts and sciences to develop fluency in Italian, French, or Spanish; complete a sequence of courses in international business; spend a semester studying abroad; and complete a semester's internship—typically in the New York office of an international business.

In the program, students take eight to twelve credits in a foreign language of their choice and then up to twelve more credits during their semester abroad. Before, during, or after this semester—which usually occurs in the junior year—they also take one or more courses in the history of civilization of the country or countries in which their chosen language is spoken. The professional component of the program is a six-course sequence including one course each in computing and economics, an introductory business course, and three courses in international business. With an emphasis on political, economic, technological, and cultural influences, the international business courses explore how financial, marketing, and other management decisions are made in an international context.

Study-abroad sites—universities in Spain, Italy, France, and Ecuador—are the same for most students, but internships are carefully designed to fit each individual student's academic background, language skills, and career interests. This tailoring of internships is as distinctive and important a feature of the program as its aggressive outreach to neighboring employers. Students value the program's internships as opportunities for testing their career interests and the applicability of their academic preparation, as well as for acquiring international work experience.

10. *Organize general education program around an international theme.* St. Lawrence University's Cultural Encounters general education program is a vertically organized alternative general education track for fifty students. The heart of the program is a series of two courses, a study-abroad experience, and a senior seminar. All the core components include Western and non-Western subject matter, are highly interdisciplinary, and are writing intensive. The first-year course, "Level One: Conceiving the World," is comparative and topical in its approach. Students learn about several cultures, only one of which is Western. They focus on a number of dimensions of the human experience, including death, work, gender, and healing. "Level Two: Cultural Encounters" is organized historically, emphasizing multiplicity and cultural diffusion. It introduces the concepts of hegemony, colonialism, appropriation, and resistance, and focuses on how cultures change through contact with other cultures. This second course also serves to prepare students for their upcoming study abroad. The final piece, a senior seminar, engages students in an examination of contemporary global issues such as hunger, AIDS, the environment, and peace. The purpose of this seminar is to help students reflect critically on how their studies, both abroad and on campus, have enlarged their perspectives and increased their knowledge about different ways of living. In addition to these four components, students are required to complete two semesters of foreign language study.

It is important to note that St. Lawrence's program explicitly addresses the relatedness of international education to domestic pluralism education. Although often viewed as competing interests on our campuses, they are regarded at St. Lawrence as two perspectives existing along the same continuum. Students in this general education track are asked to reflect on the cultural traditions from which they derive their own identities and at the same time on traditions from different parts of the world, as they engage in a critical evaluation of cultural relativism and universalism.

At Fifth College at the University of California, San Diego, an international general education curriculum provides students a coherent, integrated core program that emphasizes cross-cultural studies in the humanities, social sciences, and fine arts. Like students elsewhere, Fifth College students complete distribution requirements of two courses each in the natural sciences and in mathematics or computer science, and meet an upper division writing requirement. The international emphasis appears in a stipulation that one of two required fine arts courses be an exploration of non-Western art, music, or theater—as well as in a language requirement of a full year, regardless of previous study. Each Fifth College student also must take three courses constituting a regional specialization in one of the following geographical areas: Africa, Asia, Europe (classical and medieval, modern, or Russian studies), the Middle East, or Pan-America.

The heart of the Fifth College curriculum is "The Making of the Modern World," a two-year sequence of six required courses taken in the freshman and sophomore years. This distinctive core program involves students in "longitudinal, cross-cultural study of both Western and non-Western civilizations." It employs numerous perspectives from the humanities and social sciences, with history as the integrating discipline. In learning how different traditions developed and led to the modern world, students take "Prehistory and the Birth of Civilization"; "The Great Classical Traditions"; "The Medieval Heritage"; "European Expansion and the Clash of Cultures"; "Revolution, Industry and Empire"; and "Our Century and After." Using an approach that cuts through much contentious national debate about the relative claims of Western and non-Western legacies, the courses all follow both Western and non-Western timelines and emphasize multiple traditions and cultures.

Students find the sequence demanding, with its extensive readings, its sweep from primates to postmodernism, and its substantial writing requirements. They take a special pride, however, in the knowledge and perspective it gives them and see it as an important influence on their subsequent work.

11. *Make use of educational technology.* The University of Hawaii at Manoa is newly funded to pioneer a distance education program in Mandarin Chinese over interactive television and the Internet in collaboration with Peking University and the Beijing Film Academy. The program employs distance education as a strategy for meeting the demand for a less-commonly-taught foreign language education both economically and across a wider geographical area. The project will eventually include the creation of opportunities for U.S. students to study language and culture in China.

A project that began with a homemade dish antenna on the roof of the sculpture lab at Creighton University in Omaha is now SCOLA, the Satellite

Communications for Learning Association—a nonprofit consortium that receives television signals from countries around the world and makes them available as instructional materials. It transmits foreign newscasts, in their original languages, to four hundred colleges and universities, nine thousand primary and secondary schools, and several other institutions twenty-four hours a day. SCOLA broadcasts programming in twenty languages from forty countries. Many of the programs are broadcast live; others are taped and airmailed to SCOLA to be broadcast within thirty-six hours. SCOLA Channel One is devoted to news broadcasts. Plans for Channel Two include a wide variety of documentary and entertainment programs in a number of languages. A nominal affiliation fee, based on an institution's student FTE, is all that is required to join this international network of learners.

Conclusion

No matter where a college or university begins—and again it is most likely to be in selected areas and in response to particular opportunities—it should realize that internationalizing is not work of any fixed duration and that the impact of that work needs, in time, to spread throughout the institution. Although a strategy of selective excellence, of promoting the development of particular strengths, will always have its place, the standard of good educational practice with respect to international education will increasingly be one of balance across all programs. Appropriately internationalizing both general education and the major, giving basic attention to all world regions, leaving students in no discipline without language and study-abroad options, and attending adequately to both international and more properly global issues—these are the appropriate long-term commitments for institutions wishing to offer the best education possible and to position themselves for the future.

References

Advisory Council for International Educational Exchange. *Educating for Global Competence.* New York: Council for International Educational Exchange, 1988.

Barrows, T. S., Clark, J. L., and Klein, S. F. "What Students Know About Their World." *Change,* May–June 1980, pp. 10–17.

Christensen, G. C. "International Curriculum for the Professions." *National Forum,* Fall 1988, pp. 27–30.

Clark, B. R., and Neave, G. (eds.). *The Encyclopedia of Higher Education.* Tarrytown, N.Y.: Pergamon Press, 1992.

Commission on International Education. *What We Can't Say Can Hurt Us.* Washington, D.C.: American Council on Education, revised draft, Apr. 1989.

El-Khawas, E. *Campus Trends, 1992.* Higher Education Panel Report No. 82. Washington, D.C.: American Council on Education, 1992.

Gardner, D. P. "Internationalization: The State of the Institution." *Educational Record*, Spring 1990, p. 10.

Goodwin, C. D., and Nacht, M. *Missing the Boat: The Failure to Internationalize American Education.* Cambridge, England: Cambridge University Press, 1991.

Groennings, S. "Higher Education, International Education and the Academic Disciplines." In S. Groennings and D. S. Wiley (eds.), *Group Portrait: Internationalizing the Disciplines.* New York: American Forum, 1990.

Hayden, R. C., and Muller, K. E. "Preface." In S. Groennings and D. S. Wiley (eds.), *Group Portrait: Internationalizing the Disciplines.* New York: American Forum, 1990.

Heginbotham, S. J. "Rethinking International Scholarship." *Items*, 1994, *48*(2–3), 33–40.

Kilpatrick, J. J. "Illiterates Abroad: Our Neglect of Foreign Languages Must End." *Annapolis Capital*, Oct. 10, 1991, p. 10.

Lambert, R. D. *Points of Leverage: An Agenda for a National Foundation for International Studies.* New York: Social Science Research Council, 1986.

Lambert, R. D. "International Challenges for American Higher Education: Student Flows and the Internationalization of Higher Education." Paper presented at the meeting of the Consortium on Financing of Higher Education, Cambridge, Mass., Oct. 1992.

Marden, P. G., and Engerman, D. C. "In the International Interest: Liberal Arts Colleges Take the High Road." *Educational Record*, Spring 1992, pp. 42–43.

McConaghy, T. "Global Education: Learning to Think in a New Way." *Phi Delta Kappa*, April 1990, pp. 646–648.

National Endowment for the Humanities. *National Security Education Program Report*, March 16, 1992, Tables 1–6.

National Task Force on Undergraduate Education Abroad. *A National Mandate for Education Abroad.* Washington, D.C.: National Association of Foreign Student Affairs, 1990.

Pelikan, J. "Essential Embrace." *Yale*, Mar. 1992, p. 33.

Pickert, S. M. *Preparing for a Global Community: Achieving an International Perspective in Higher Education.* ASHE-ERIC Higher Education Report No. 2. Washington, D.C.: George Washington University, 1992.

Pickert, S., and Turlington, B. *Internationalizing the Undergraduate Curriculum: A Handbook for Campus Leaders.* Washington, D.C.: American Council on Education, 1992.

Stoltzfus, V. Presentation to International 50 meeting. Beloit, Wisc., 1992.

Tonkin, H., and Edwards, J. "Internationalizing the University: The Arduous Road to Euphoria." *Educational Record*, Spring 1990, pp. 14–17.

Walton, R. A. "Expanding the Vision of Foreign Language Education: Enter the Less Commonly Taught Languages." *National Foreign Language Center Occasional Paper 10*, Feb. 1992, pp. 1–7.

Wollitzer, P. Unpublished document for Association of American Colleges and Universities annual meeting, San Francisco, Jan. 1995.

Zikopoulous, M. (ed.). *Open Doors 1991/92; Report on International Educational Exchange.* New York: Institute of International Education, 1992.

CHAPTER TWENTY-ONE

TRANSFORMING THE CURRICULUM THROUGH DIVERSITY

Enrique "Rick" Olguin, Betty Schmitz

Cultural conflict is a basic characteristic of the times in which we live. Global politics have become increasingly multipolar, rife with ethnic conflict and cultures poised in confrontation. In the United States, we are coming to recognize that we live in a society of many cultures, if not to appreciate the implication that our very economic and political survival may rest on our ability to understand and benefit from cultural differences and to reach compromise in matters of governance and social policy when parties hold fundamentally irreconcilable points of view.

These issues affect education. If the future leaders of the United States are being educated on today's campuses, how do we fulfill our obligation to prepare them for the world they face? As Takaki puts it in *A Different Mirror: A History of Multicultural America*, "Americans have been witnessing ethnic strife erupting around the world. . . . Is the situation here different, we have been nervously wondering, or do ethnic conflicts elsewhere represent a prologue for America? What is the nature of malevolence? Is there a deep, perhaps primordial, need for group identity rooted in hatred for the other? Is ethnic pluralism possible for America?" (1993, p. 5).

There can be no doubt that faculty members and institutions nationwide have embraced the challenge of teaching cultural pluralism as a central focus of undergraduate education. According to an internal report by the Association of American Colleges and Universities (AAC&U), 63 percent of campuses already include in their mission statements some reference to diversity as an educational goal. Twenty-two percent have models for multicultural studies that they feel may be of value to others, and 28 percent have focused that exploration principally on American pluralism. These curricular changes indicate that we are developing a new consciousness about our evolution as a multicultural society peopled by citizens who trace their roots to pre-European conquest and to all parts of the globe.

These changes have not gone uncontested. Student protests, criticism by constituencies external to campus, and deep divisions among faculty members about the content of the curriculum have brought considerable strife to many institutions (Carby, 1992; Graff, 1992; Scott, 1992). Even when there is a consensus on campus about the need to teach about cultural pluralism in general education, curriculum committees and faculty governance bodies may spend inordinate amounts of time debating the focus and content of proposed courses—for example, whether to focus solely on U.S. peoples of color or to include international studies—without tying their discussions to assessment of the present state of research in the disciplines, faculty expertise, current outcomes of curricula, and student needs and interests.

To evaluate the subject in this chapter, we draw primarily upon the experiences of sixty institutions participating in the AAC&U project "Engaging Cultural Legacies, Shaping Core Curricula in the Humanities" (Schmitz, 1995). We also consider the twenty-seven institutions participating in a statewide Cultural Pluralism Project, funded by the Ford Foundation, jointly sponsored by the Washington Center for Undergraduate Education, Evergreen State College, and the University of Washington (Washington Center for the Improvement of Undergraduate Education, 1996); the American Commitments Initiative, a project of the AAC&U that includes one hundred institutions nationally (Association of American Colleges and Universities, 1995b); and our own campus experiences in the development of new curricular requirements and faculty development seminars.

Cultural Difference and the American Intellect

"So we went to school to copy, to imitate; not to exchange language and ideas, and not to develop the best traits that had come out of uncountable experiences of hundreds and thousands of years of living upon this continent. Our annals, all happenings of human import, were stored in our song and dance rituals, our history differing in that it was not stored in books, but in living memory. So, while the white people had much to teach us, we had much to teach them, and what a school could have been established upon that idea!" (Standing Bear, [1933] 1978, p. 236).

Cultural diversity as a curricular issue is as old as higher education in America itself. The first college in the colonies, William and Mary, began its existence as an institution dedicated to the cultural assimilation of Virginia's Indian peoples. In 1774, Boston's Quaker community established a school for the city's free black population. In the North, furthermore, leaders in black communities established library societies with the purpose of promoting literacy and knowledge about black history and achievements. The subsequent history of private colleges for African Americans is one of debating, and experimenting with, the relationship between culture and curriculum. These associations and colleges were interested not just in developing the intellectual skills of the black community, but also promoting knowledge of the achievements and history of black people. The ultimate goal was to create in the black community the capacity for full democratic participation (Reed, 1984).

But mainstream efforts to provide education for both African Americans and American Indians sought to assimilate them into European American culture. In the late 1800s, the United States government began establishing off-reservation boarding schools for American Indian children as part of its grand civilizing plan to assimilate native peoples into mainstream society. Boarding school curricula mixed religious proselytization with industrial education, stripping Indian children of their native language, names, dress, and food (Lomawaima, 1994; Standing Bear, [1933] 1978). American Indians had no control over curriculum. As a consequence, these institutions did not receive the kind of challenges to incorporate culture-specific content that the New Negro movement brought to the black colleges, although spokespersons for culture-specific curricula, such as Standing Bear, favored industrial education along with bilingual education and the incorporation of Indian history into the curriculum.

Du Bois also advocated culture-specific education because he wanted African Americans to lose the debilities imposed by slavery; he favored teaching blacks fundamental industrial education and general knowledge of society and culture to impart to future generations. Du Bois also urged classical training for black intellectuals. He suggested in his essay on the talented tenth that the elites are to help black children enter into the white world, arguing that the education of children happens in the life of black society as well as in school (Du Bois, 1903b). Du Bois suggested that education for African Americans is not just about learning to be American, but about America as a whole learning about its African Americanness, the same position taken by Standing Bear in relation to American Indians.

Du Bois elaborated this idea in "The Field and Function of the Negro College," a commencement speech given at Fisk University in 1933, laying out the goal of black colleges in a manner consistent with today's most advanced work in African American studies (Du Bois, 1973). He argued that black education was no different in principle than German or French or any other national education. For Du Bois, the black college should teach universal truth as it manifests itself in African American life, just as the German university taught Western philosophy in order to impart to students their cultural legacy. In his view, teachers in the black colleges are obliged to articulate a genuinely African American interpretation of American culture. Du Bois lauded the ideal described by Frederick Douglass as "ultimate assimilation *through* self-assertion, and on no other terms" (1903a, p. 49). Thus the contemporary tension between imparting classical education to new groups for purposes of assimilation and forging a new curriculum out of the multiplicity of cultures has roots in the educational philosophy of the late nineteenth and early twentieth century.

Ethnic Studies and the Teaching of Difference

The students trained by Du Bois's talented tenth came of age in the 1960s. Their quest was twofold: to bring the knowledge from the university back to the neighborhood, the barrio, and the reservation; and to transform the university—and ultimately the definition and content of knowledge. The development of culture-specific American ethnic studies, as well as women's studies, gay and lesbian studies, and so forth, provided a base from which to generate new scholarship and pedagogy that would enable the academy to fulfill the challenges of curriculum transformation. (We use the term *American ethnic studies* for ethnic-specific programs and departments in African American studies, American Indian and Alaskan Native studies, Asian Pacific American studies, and Hispanic, Puerto Rican, Chicano and Chicana, and Latino and Latina studies, as well as comparative study of these populations and their histories singly, in relation to each other, and in relation to European Americans.)

One of the founding goals of culture-based fields was to establish interdisciplinary approaches to scholarship to reconfigure concepts, ideas, and frameworks so as to develop theory and scholarship that elucidate the experiences of their respective populations. Central to the epistemology of these fields is the meaning of plurality of worldviews. Since Aristotle, Western tradition has been based on the principle of duality, that a proposition is either true or false. Many other traditions reject the idea of binary opposition as a fundamental aspect of thought (Olguin, 1991). In an essay on curriculum transformation through ethnic studies and women's studies, Butler (1991) delineates a "both/and" worldview, which she distinguishes from the "either/or" approach of European epistemology, and illustrates through the West African proverb, "I am because we are; we are because I am" or "I am we" (p. 76). The promise of the both/and approach is its emphasis on reconciliation; it recognizes the intersection and interaction of difference and sameness. Both/and thinking recognizes the interconnected nature of opposition. Both/and criticism does not call for rejection, but rather for integration, of that which is criticized. Key to this epistemology is the reconceptualization of the relationship between individual and community.

Another central challenge of these interdisciplinary fields is to come to see the self as multiple and fragmented, not as an integrated whole. Contemporary theorists, especially those inhabiting multiple identities, such as Anzaldúa (1987), illustrate the power of the recognition of multiplicity. Discussing a person in her village said to be a woman six months of a year and a man the other six, she writes, "Contrary to some psychiatric tenets, half and halfs are not suffering from a confusion of sexual identity, or even from a confusion of gender. What we are suffering from is an absolute despot duality that says we are able to be only one or the other. It claims that human nature is limited and cannot evolve into something better. But I, like other queer people, am two in one body, both male and female. I am the embodiment of the *hieros gamos:* the coming together of opposite qualities within" (p. 19).

Anzaldúa feels and understands her identities as a Chicana in a Euro-American literary establishment, as a woman in a patriarchal society, and as a lesbian in a homophobic culture. Her writing is her effort to bring a sense of purpose to her fragmented selfhood. Anzaldúa does not seek unity of identity, she seeks room to be a manifold subjectivity. Gates (1993) points out that "identities are always in dialogue, they exist only in relation to one another and they are sites of contest and negotiation, self-fashioning and refashioning" (p. 11).

These and other cultural worldviews bring complex theoretical challenges to the epistemological foundations of Western tradition. Some of the most vital scholarship today focuses on the borderlands of culture—the physical, psychological, social places where cultures meet, coexist, and overlap, and on the cultural tensions, exchanges, and transformations that emerge from these places.

The field of *multicultural education* emerged in tandem with ethnic studies. Multicultural education refers to an idea or concept, an educational reform movement, and a process of institutional change (Banks, 1994, p. 3). One of its major goals is to change teaching and learning approaches so that *all* students have equal opportunity to learn in educational institutions. It embeds the idea that cultural difference has consequences in the classroom, that some differences have traditionally been privileged over others, and that educational reform is necessary to bring equity into education. As a curricular approach, multicultural education characterizes the manner in which U.S. cultural pluralism has been engaged over the past three decades: the introduction of new content into the curriculum, the study of the knowledge construction process, of new pedagogies, of curriculum change processes, and of educational institutions as social systems. Multicultural education includes single-group studies as well as comparative studies. Not a self-esteem curriculum for marginalized groups, as it has been characterized in the media, it seeks to create undergraduate curricula that reflect multiple voices and perspectives.

Many scholars who have called for transformed curricula have critiqued ways in which multicultural education has been interpreted and implemented as a reform of educational practice. In particular, they criticize multicultural approaches that ignore race and racism as causal factors in political and economic structure—that is, those that leave out the history of power relations and of sociocultural positionality (Bensimon, 1994; Carby, 1992; Gates, 1993; McCarthy, 1993; San Juan, 1991). Bensimon, for example, distinguishes "human relations multiculturalism," which focuses on awareness and appreciation of other cultures, from "critical multiculturalism," which encourages students to raise questions about who is represented in official knowledge and why, and to forge ideas for a different kind of future (pp. 12–14). Implicit, then, in the challenge of teaching cultural pluralism is a reexamination of basic assumptions of what "America" is, what it means to be a citizen, and what kinds of interconnections exist and can exist among groups socially and politically defined by difference.

Defining Curricular Content

The issues institutions encounter in defining multicultural curricula revolve around three questions: how to define the intellectual content of the curriculum; what form the curriculum will take; and how to implement change, especially faculty preparation to teach the new curriculum.

The most effective efforts to transform curriculum are those that begin with a discussion of the knowledge, habits, and skills the institution wishes its graduates to possess. Shaping a new curriculum means translating the campus's *why* into a definition of *what:* what students ought to know, ought to be able to do, and ought to aspire to display as citizens.

One of the first set of choices curriculum planners must negotiate has to do with what areas to study within the broad rubric of cultural pluralism. Where and how should the study of so-called non-Western cultures be addressed? Where does U.S. pluralism fit within Western and world studies? Where and how should curricula include the study of U.S. pluralism, and how to address race, gender, ethnicity, class, sexual orientation, religion, and other dimensions of human identity. How and where do concepts of power and conflict in relation to difference enter such a curriculum? To what extent do local or regional cultures help define answers to these questions for a particular college or university? The categories discussed in this section represent some of the areas institutions have identified as essential and hence integrated into the liberal arts curriculum.

Non-Western and World Studies

Campuses participating in the AAC&U Engaging Cultural Legacies project have each developed different approaches to teaching multiple traditions. Some include units on Western history and culture but embed them in larger narratives that show the West as part of a larger world community. Others take the world cultures or world systems as the organizing principle. Both approaches rely heavily on comparative methods. All approaches shape, and in turn are shaped by, the educational aims of the institution.

Hampton University's "Enduring Human Values and Cultural Connections" is a two-semester interdisciplinary course that introduces students to Western and non-Western cultural legacies through the study of works of art, literature, and music from antiquity to the present. The focus is on exploring cultural contact and collision—the impact of the West on other cultures and other cultures on the West. Multiplicity is the organizing principle; in the first term, for example, students analyze the role of epics in forming human values by reading the *Odyssey*, the *Iliad, Gilgamesh,* and *Sundiata.*

Those who make the world rather than the West the organizing framework for core courses argue that their approach best responds to the global challenges confronting today's students, who must come to see themselves and their nation as linked to others economically, ecologically, and politically. This model allows more attention to the dynamics of change and to interrelationships among different societies; it is less oriented to multiple meanings within particular societies at particular moments in time. Queens College of the City University of New York developed a four-semester sequence that combines the study of particular societies with a world-systems approach. In the first semester, "Interpreting the World," Queens College students—themselves often from families recently arrived in the United States—study examples of migrations and cross-cultural encounters. The objective is to help students develop an understanding of different strategies, humanistic and social scientific, for understanding cultural transactions and interactions. In the second semester, the course turns to the ancient world, focusing in particular on concepts of cosmos and nation from prestate societies to the rise of empires. The third course—which spans the period from the age of exploration to 1945—emphasizes intercultural contacts among civilizations: for example, Mexico and the arrival of Spanish colonizers. The fourth course explores the development since 1945 of an increasingly interactive world community as seen from different historical, ideological, and cultural positions and different disciplinary perspectives.

Multicultural Humanities

Humanities fields have been transformed by new theories, concepts, and content about cultural pluralism globally. Courses have begun to incorporate texts and topics that introduce students to the political and legal histories of different peoples, to their literature, art, and music, and to their worldviews and definitions of self and community. Most humanities departments nationwide include at least one course that covers these topics, either focused on particular groups or comparative, often cross-listed with American ethnic studies, African American studies, Asian American Studies, Chicano or Latino studies, Native American studies, women's studies, or a similar interdisciplinary field.

Through these kinds of courses, faculty members wish to help their students grasp and negotiate these transforming interrelationships by grounding them in the historical context of U.S. pluralism. They want their students to have a context for analyzing complex cultural issues such as those embedded in the development of organized white supremacist groups, conflicts over fishing rights and development on tribal lands, or Supreme Court rulings on civil rights law. Curriculum planners who believe this knowledge is central to an undergraduate liberal education articulate these kinds of goals for student learning:

- To understand and appreciate the diversity of knowledge traditions within the contemporary United States, and to understand the central role of cultural, racial, and ethnic differences in the formation of U.S. national identity
- To evaluate how men and women of diverse origins have shaped their visions of self and community, and of the interrelationships of self and community
- To consider ways various social groups within a given society participate in the culture of their society
- To identify, explore, and evaluate concrete examples of the students' own cultural heritage in relationship to other heritages
- To develop in students the ability to read a culture through its cultural expressions, and also the ability to see relationships, contrasts, parallels, commonalities, and interactions among various cultures

The attainment of these goals demands a comparative approach to the study of different cultures, as illustrated by several courses taught by the Seattle Community Colleges. Requirements for the A.A. degree now include five credits each of U.S. cultures and global studies. Courses under the former focus on the comparative and relational study of two or more of the following cultures: African American, Asian American and Pacific Islander, European American, Latino and Latina American, Middle-Eastern American, and Native American. Goals include study of the internal diversity of these groups, the historical and contemporary confusion of the concepts of race and culture and changing constructions of race. Students also consider how U.S. culture continues to emerge and be shaped by the interaction of people with different views, origins, and experiences. Aspects of power and privilege are also part of the learning goals. At Seattle Central Community College, a team of faculty members teaches a coordinated studies program titled "Speaking for Ourselves: Cross-Cultural Visions and Connections" using the disciplines of art, history, sociology, writing, and literature.

Theories of Difference

American racial and ethnic studies, postcolonial studies, gay and lesbian studies, and women's studies have also produced an enormous body of scholarship on the social construction of race, gender, ethnicity, class, religion, and sexual orientation. These kinds of analyses help develop critical thinking in students by strengthening their ability to identify hidden assumptions and perspectives in knowledge construction.

Goals for student learning include:

- To develop increased self-awareness of what it means in our culture to be a person of their own gender, race, class, ethnicity, and religion as well as an understanding of how these categories affect those who are different from themselves
- To develop an understanding of how categories of race, ethnicity, gender, social class, religion, sexual orientation, and so on intersect and overlap
- To develop an understanding of the complexity, multiplicity, and fluidity of identities determined by self and other
- To expand ability to think critically and with an open mind about controversial contemporary issues that stem from the gender, race, class, ethnic, and religious differences that pervade our society

A good example of required courses incorporating the study of multiple variables of human identity is the "American Pluralism and the Search for Equality" program at the State University of New York (SUNY), Buffalo. After taking a required year-long course in world civilizations, students are required as sophomores to select a course under the American Pluralism requirement. Unlike most courses outside ethnic studies and women's studies programs, the "goals and standards" statements for these courses include expectations for in-depth analysis of gender, race, class, ethnicity, and religion, and their intersections in both individual and group identity (Schmitz, 1992, p. 35). The courses developed for the core are taught by many different faculty members, including specialists in ethnic studies and women's studies. Each of the courses that fulfill this requirement examines the multicultural, multiethnic nature of U.S. society and also addresses the study of power and difference by providing undergraduate students with an intellectual awareness of the causes and effects of structured inequalities and prejudicial exclusion in the United States—and of the processes leading to a more equitable society.

Power and Difference

The study of structures of domination that have differentially shaped people's lives, choices, and sociocultural, economic, and political participation brings the issue of power into central focus. Social science courses have traditionally taught these topics, but often from a point of view that describes minority groups with blame-the-victim formulations rather than as agents and that uses categories of analysis formulated by the dominant culture (for example, in the construction of the notion of an underclass). Social scientists in ethnic studies and women's studies have formulated new theories that challenge notions of choice and social group relations and experiences in light of structural inequities.

Goals for student learning in this category might include:

- To develop an awareness of the causes and effects of structured inequalities and prejudicial exclusion in our society, and to understand notions of difference, discrimination, bias, and privilege
- To study differing perspectives on the past and diverse visions of the future as well as processes leading to a more equitable society
- To provide concepts and tools for understanding the social realities and problems in this moment in history

A good example of this focus is the "difference, power and discrimination" requirement at Oregon State University. It is a three-credit course, complementing a Western culture requirement and a cultural diversity requirement. Courses fulfilling this requirement must address a range of historical and contemporary examples of difference, power, and discrimination in the United States across sociopolitical systems; and the origins, operation, and consequences of different types of discrimination, including structural and institutional discrimination. At Lemoyne-Owen College, a six-hour social science sequence "Power and Society" and "Uses and Abuses of Power" explores issues of cultural pluralism and diversity globally and includes examinations of race, gender, class, and ethnicity through the lens of justice and distribution of power (Association of American Colleges and Universities, 1995a, p. 31; see also description of Temple University's Studies on Race requirement, on p. 31).

Civic Competencies

Cultural diversity has immensely complicated issues of civic literacy and competency. Traditional emphasis on preparation for citizenship needs to be redefined in light of cultural pluralism. Morris (1989) identifies central issues about how we will work to ensure that the different voices get heard and expressed in the democratic system, and about how to create the mechanisms and forums for new multicultural conversations. He wonders whether learning experiences ought to vary for students in the current dominant group in our society and those of culturally diverse groups; and he wonders how important is it going to be for folks to truly encounter people who are different from themselves.

These issues also call attention to another category of decision making in relation to student learning: What qualities of citizenship should the curriculum inspire? What civic competencies should be taught?

Morris's list of necessary new civic competencies includes interdependence, collaboration, holistic vision, cross-cultural communication, multicultural awareness, consensus decision making, community and global thinking, and bilingualism and multilingualism. Disciplines that have begun to incorporate these competencies include communications, education, psychology, and language. Much of the new scholarship in these areas comes, however, from interdisciplinary programs and courses such as cross-cultural studies, intercultural studies, environmental studies, global studies, peace studies, and so forth.

Goals for student learning include the development of:

- A sense of informed, active citizenship for effective participation in a society of increasing diversity
- Intercultural competencies for effective participation in organizations with diverse employees
- Competencies necessary to negotiate disparate and multiple commitments and communities
- The ability to take grounded and ethical stances in the face of significant differences

In the "Multicultural Issues: Culture, Communication and Change" course at Shoreline Community College, students learn to communicate effectively in multicultural settings, identify multicultural issues and engage in problem solving using alternative strategies, and understand and respect different viewpoints and behaviors. A major goal of the course is to create a classroom climate that encourages healthy intellectual conflict and its resolution, while assisting students to build their own personal views of a culturally diverse society.

The "American Commitments" initiative of the AAC&U represents a thematic way of developing curricula around the idea of civic competencies. This initiative brings together two major strands of contemporary scholarship—the scholarship of difference emerging from American ethnic studies and women's studies, and the scholarship of democracy, in particular, communitarian arguments engaging the question of rights versus responsibilities. As framed by AAC&U, the diversity-democracy paradigm offers the role of community in a democratic society as an organizing principle for the study of U.S. pluralism. This emphasis, as described in the program's brochure, has the advantage of recognizing "the fluidity of U.S. cultural relations, identities and intersections over time," and "stresses the importance of reciprocal commitments, shared histories and owned obligations as important both to the quality of human experience and to democratic vitality" (1995b, p. 2).

Courses categorized under the initiative's "Experiences in Justice Seeking" (Association of American Colleges and Universities, 1995a, p. 35) include Pitzer College's social responsibility requirement, which stipulates that students complete a semester of social service community work. In the course "Social Responsibility and Community," for example, students participate as observers, mentors, and teacher aides in local school districts. At Rutgers University, the Civic Education and Community Service Program offers a number of courses integrating classroom work with community service.

While this list scarcely exhausts the range of potential topical areas and student goals, it calls attention to the importance of establishing purposes *before* designing curricula. Having an agreed-upon set of goals helps give direction when making choices about subject matter for courses.

Pedagogical Approaches

Faculty members experimenting with new content on cultural pluralism have also explored new pedagogical approaches, and often more interactive, learner-centered modes of teaching. Faculty members act more as facilitators than as experts, and their role is to guide students in their exploration of texts, not predetermine what is of interest and importance. The role of faculty member as facilitator or co-learner rather than expert resonates with the new focus on the individual as interdependent with the community. Faculty members model effective relationships within a community (the classroom) characterized by those who are diversely situated relative to status and power. Students also learn to listen to their peers and gain insight into different perspectives on topics under discussion. For example, one of the learning goals for Seattle Central's Speaking for Ourselves program (described earlier) is for students to practice working and talking cooperatively with others. Active learning encourages students and faculty members to discover cross-cultural connections that build respect for multicultural voices.

Proponents of teaching cultural pluralism have repeatedly pointed out how well the complexity of the scholarship on difference lends itself to the development of critical thinking skills (Schmitz, 1992). Engagement with the realities of cultural difference can foster the development of skills of analysis, interpretation, and judgment by challenging root assumptions, paradigms, and values upon which cultures are built and calling into question the construction of meaning within cultures. One approach to development of critical thinking skills proposed by Graff (1992) is that of "teaching the conflicts." He argues that coherence and focus can be brought to the undergraduate curriculum out of the "lively state of contention" over cultural difference. The solution to culture wars is to make the conflicts the source of energy in undergraduate courses, not to reimpose common culture as a principle of order.

What this approach does not address, however, is the analysis of power and privilege in the classroom. All students are assumed to be coming to the debate with the same vested interest in the outcome of the debate. Different positions in relation to a discussion of Indian fishing rights or the restoration of artifacts to tribal governments can be debated dispassionately by some students and not by others, for whom stakes of religious freedom and economic survival are paramount.

Another approach is the comparative, relational approach to teaching U.S. pluralism, that is, teaching the conflicts through the prism of connections (Butler, n.d.). This approach is one based in conceptual frameworks for community that emerge simultaneously from differing worldviews of racial and ethnic groups coexisting in the United States *and* from the struggles for justice and democracy in U.S. history. Butler asserts that the understanding of both difference and connection—or relationship—is at the heart of the kind of curriculum change necessary today. This framework provides a positive, productive context for the exploration of communality, conflict, and shared values necessary to a new U.S. national identity.

The comparative and relational approach to curriculum development (embedded in the Seattle Community Colleges A.A. requirement described earlier) engages multiple perspectives on the same set of events or dimensions of human experience, cultural dialogues and exchanges, or cultural encounters and conflicts. In so doing, this approach assists students in understanding how their historical and cultural positions are connected to and different from those of other peoples in the United States.

Curricular Options for Cultural Pluralism

The primary curricular avenues for incorporating the wealth of material and perspectives delineated here are the traditional ones: general education and departmental and program offerings (including major and minor programs). In addition, special lecture series and student programming, organized around critical issues of social diversity or celebrations such as Black History Month, the *Cinco de Mayo*, or Women's History Week, can be used in systematic ways to enrich formal classroom study. An analysis of what is currently taught on campus—a kind of mapping of the curriculum of cultural pluralism—will elucidate what should be the focus of requirements and what areas are the most in need of curriculum transformation projects.

 • *General education and diversity requirements*. Current efforts to incorporate cultural pluralism in general education curricula generally follow three complementary models: specialized courses from new interdisciplinary fields, for example, international studies, regional studies, American ethnic studies, Third World studies, and women's studies; theory, content, and pedagogy from ethnic, women's, and area studies incorporated into all courses fulfilling general education or requirements; and new interdisciplinary courses that focus on the multiplicity of cultural experiences in the United States, whether a menu of courses under a single rubric with common elements, or one course with multiple sections.

The educational rationale for the first model points to significant new scholarship on the traditions, cultures, and histories of peoples formerly erased or marginalized in the curriculum. The existence of this base of scholarship provides an indispensable foundation for student learning and therefore warrants a place in general education.

The advantages of adopting a requirement of a specialized course are many. These courses are taught by faculty members whose educational training and scholarship are in the area of culture-based interdisciplinary fields; these faculty are skilled in the analysis of race, class, and gender and in the pedagogy of the field. They understand the classroom dynamics that occur around the introduction of material that challenges traditional frameworks and know how to handle tensions in the classroom. A considerable amount of the material includes attention to historic and contemporary issues of racism and prejudice, but this material is taught from a perspective of agency rather than victimization, based on the assumptions, paradigms, and methodologies inherent in the field. These courses also allow for in-depth study of a particular area, so that students acquire some sophistication in their understanding and analysis of subject matter. This form of requirement also supports strengthening of these fields because it necessitates the hiring of faculty members in these areas.

There are some disadvantages with requiring a course in American ethnic studies as the campus diversity requirement, however. If this requirement is not reinforced by curriculum transformation in general, it conveys a message of separatism. The study of diversity becomes the agenda of people of color, rather than the educational philosophy of the entire faculty. Students are confronted with completely different worldviews in these courses and are left on their own to integrate this knowledge with what they learn in other courses.

This kind of requirement can become diluted during faculty deliberations about which courses will be included in the list of courses fulfilling the requirement. Disparate courses often are added to a multicultural menu when political compromises rather than student learning goals dictate curricular choices. In forging a diversity or multicultural distribution requirement, for example, faculty members may combine distinct content areas—lumping together all otherness—by requiring students to take a course on minority groups in the United States *or* a course on women *or* a course on non-Western culture *or* a foreign language. Students hardly learn what they need to know about U.S. populations of color by taking a course about a non-Western civilization in its golden age, or by studying Russian. A course on Chinese philosophy has educational purposes that are quite different from a course on Native American women, and both differ fundamentally from a course on racism, sexism, anti-Semitism, homophobia, and other forms of prejudice and discrimination. Any or all of these courses may provide valuable learning experiences for students on a particular campus, but they attend to very different learning goals (Schmitz, 1992).

This kind of requirement also strains resources in these programs. It cannot be successful without financial support to staff the number of courses needed to serve the student body, as well as majors and minors in the fields.

The second model—incorporating the study of cultural pluralism across the curriculum, or curriculum transformation—acknowledges that the new scholarship of ethnic studies and women's studies has contributed to and changed the knowledge base in many fields and courses. To be educationally and intellectually sound, the curriculum in all fields must include relevant theory and new knowledge.

This model presumes that faculty members and students see cultural pluralism as central to education. It brings the study of cultural pluralism into every course where there have been significant new scholarly developments. But to be successful, this kind of requirement requires extensive faculty development. Faculty members who have not specialized in American ethnic studies need time and support to read, reflect, and revise courses in an intellectually sound and coherent way. This is particularly difficult because the new material challenges the assumptions and perspectives of previous work in the field. There are more questions than answers, necessitating a new kind of pedagogy. It takes two to three years of reading and teaching for faculty members to achieve a sense of real comfort with the new material. A campus cannot undertake this kind of requirement unless it provides support for faculty development in relation to the expectations placed on the faculty.

The third model—the development of new, interdisciplinary courses on cultural pluralism especially designed for general education or core curricula—provides courses that exist outside current frameworks. It thus avoids the problems associated with the other models, which draw upon departmental or program-based courses. There is more freedom to develop structures and topics for courses. An advantage of developing new, interdisciplinary courses is that they allow faculty members from many different disciplines to start with discussions of goals for student learning and how they might be achieved through new courses. Discussion of this kind fosters collaborative work and comparative examination of content in different disciplines and its relationship to learning goals. Often these courses include new pedagogical approaches and integrate development of writing and critical thinking skills.

However, these courses are costly, because they require faculty members to work with peers to design curricula and staff courses effectively. During the teaching of the courses, all faculty members in a given course have to meet regularly to ensure coherence in the different sections of a course.

• *Departmental majors.* No matter which of the goals for student learning in the area of cultural pluralism, or which approach to general education is used to meet these goals, general education requirements cannot alone meet the needs for serious attention to cultural pluralism in undergraduate liberal arts curricula. Although individual students may choose to explore cultural pluralism in more depth through their choice of electives, learning must be expanded and reinforced through courses in the academic major if all students are to develop a solid base of understanding.

The scholarship from women's studies and ethnic studies is pushing the boundaries of traditional knowledge in academic fields, yet few departments have undertaken an analysis of the cultural pluralism knowledge and skills base within their respective disciplines. A report of the Association of American Colleges, *Liberal Learning and the Arts and Sciences Major* (1990, 1991), demonstrates how departments can undertake a review of how knowledge and skills are or could be sequenced in the academic major through introductory, intermediate, and advanced or integrative courses, and guidelines for inclusiveness that address issues of cultural pluralism in departmental reviews of curricula. An analysis of who is teaching what in the area of cultural pluralism can enhance a departmental faculty's understanding of the present and potential impact of their courses on student learning and contribute to campus discussions of curriculum change.

Implications for Faculty Development

A striking characteristic of preparing faculty members to incorporate the teaching of cultural pluralism is the necessity of in-depth study of both new content and new pedagogies. New curricula on cultural pluralism ask faculty members to venture outside their own specialties and acquire knowledge of new cultures and texts, competence in comparative studies, skill in interdisciplinary practices, and—in many cases—skills in the techniques of encouraging active student learning. To prepare faculty members to meet such ambitious expectations, campuses must commit themselves to strong faculty development programs and develop reward structures that appropriately recognize the contributions faculty members make to curriculum development.

From our description of the content and structure of new curricula, it is clear that faculty members engaged in curriculum change need opportunities to develop their own knowledge and skill base. This can include learning new conceptual frameworks and approaches; historical and comparative understandings of diversity; critiques of core values, issues of race, gender, inequality; theories of institutional, curricular, and personal change; and methods of course and curriculum design.

In addition, a range of pedagogical issues present themselves when teaching cultural pluralism: how to establish one's own position in the classroom; how to deal with tensions that arise from guilt, defensiveness, anger, or pain; how to deal with an incident of bias or prejudice in the classroom; how to assess bias in patterns of interaction in the classroom and intervene successfully; how to advise students of color; and how to advise students who feel threatened, angry, or confused by attention to multicultural issues.

Campuses organize faculty development activities in a variety of ways: summer institutes, term- or year-long study seminars, workshops or individual study supported through stipends, release time, or travel. As an example, from 1992 through 1994 the joint Washington Center for Undergraduate Education (Evergreen State College) and the University of Washington Summer Cultural Pluralism Institutes engaged faculty and professional staff members from twenty-seven Washington colleges and universities in ten (first two years) or eight (final year) days of intensive study aimed at curriculum transformation. The cornerstone of the institutes was the intense focus on studying the history, literature, and experiences of American ethnic groups of color and European Americans through focus groups and plenary sessions that provided fundamental scholarship, texts, and methodological approaches with the goal of preparing participants for further research and course revision and development. They drew on the fields of history, literature, sociology, psychology, economics, and political science to elaborate worldviews and content paradigms.

Plenary sessions employed a comparative, relational approach to teaching U.S. pluralism, an overview and introduction to comparative ethnic studies, and a forum for the exploration of questions arising from focus group study and comparative perspectives. Themes included: comparative worldviews, the social construction of race and ethnicity, legal histories and their implication for deconstructing ways of viewing race, double consciousness and identities, European American ethnicity and multiculturalism, and new frameworks for viewing U.S. people of color and U.S. ideals (Schmitz, 1995). Part of each institute was devoted to pedagogy, course design, institutional change, and social and cultural activities; institutional teams had the opportunity to meet and design a plan for curriculum change at their institution.

Other institutions have accomplished similar ends through activities conducted during the academic year. At Skagit Valley College, faculty and staff created "American Me/American We: Creating a Plural Classroom Community," a seven-session seminar designed for faculty who wanted to revise one or more courses to make their teaching methodology or course content more pluralistic. The seminar was designed to move from a discussion of perceptions and understandings of ethnicity, race, and pluralism in the United States to their manifestations in specific histories and cultures in the United States. In the second half of the seminar, these discussions were brought into focus in terms of the local community, including its history and current culture. Seattle University used a similar approach, developing a five-year plan of faculty-staff study groups that focus on a different U.S. group each year, including European Americans.

These examples illustrate the systematic, long-term faculty development efforts required to incorporate cultural pluralism. The programs described here recognize that faculty members need considerable time and support to transform courses and curricula. Acquiring knowledge of new paradigms, theories, and texts—and new, interactive pedagogies—demands intellectual energy, commitment, and risk taking on the part of faculty members. But the results are well worth the effort. Program evaluations report that these projects result in significant revision of courses to incorporate content and pedagogy learned through the projects—and in many cases to new multicultural requirements and a strengthening of ethnic studies on campus (Washington Center for the Improvement of the Quality of Undergraduate Education, 1996).

Elements of a Successful Change Process

The contextual richness of curriculum transformation in American higher education makes it difficult to draw general conclusions. Yet, while no cookbook is possible, there are identifiable elements of successful curriculum transformation efforts that can be seen from campus to campus.

A crucial condition for curriculum transformation is a clear focus on student learning. Discussions of cultural pluralism and the curriculum can bog down or run amok if faculty lose sight of the central educational questions of what students need to know and need to be able to do, and what they need to value as principles of citizenship in a multicultural society.

Second, administrative leadership and support for curriculum transformation are essential. While faculty are the ultimate arbiters of educational practice, the diversity of faculty members by discipline and background is so great that clear and sustained commitment and support from the administration helps overcome sometimes overwhelming divisions in faculty preferences for content and approach. Sufficient resource allocation is a crucial element of administrative support. The design of educationally solid and worthy curricula requires the investment of time and energy by faculty, staff, administrators, and students. To do their work well, those involved in the process need to be funded from conceptualization through proposal discussion and adoption to design and implementation of new courses and programs.

Third, a core of leaders from all levels and segments of the campus is necessary. It is not enough for a few faculty leaders to convince their colleagues of the timeliness of change. And it is not enough to direct change efforts at the curriculum alone. Curriculum transformation must go in tandem with institutional transformation. If the messages students encounter through the campus climate are inconsistent with those of the curriculum, the curriculum will seem fraudulent. Hiring and retaining a diverse faculty and staff and designing processes so that multiple voices are present and heard at all levels are both essential parts of institutional transformation.

Finally, on those campuses where major curricular initiatives have been successful, project leaders presented their plans as they would have any other plan in the campus governance process. While critics of cultural pluralism in the curriculum often assert that the development of new courses and curricula and other diversity initiatives are the result of administrative fiat in response to social activists, this has not been the case in our experience. The change process on campuses we have observed proceeds through needs assessment to proposals, and then to review, adoption, revision, or new proposals. Campus constituencies have been able to make their views known and the hopes and concerns of the many, not the few, have been incorporated into the process.

These are just a few of the factors that contribute to a successful change process. In the end, every campus community will have to sit down and chart its own course through frequently troubled waters. The wisdom and experience of other campuses is useful in planning. Each campus will face unexpected challenges—and receive unexpected support—in its efforts to come to terms with the changing profile and needs of America's college population.

References

Anzaldúa, G. *Borderlands/La Frontera: The New Mestiza.* San Francisco: Spinsters/Aunt Lute, 1987.

Association of American Colleges. *Liberal Learning and the Arts and Sciences Major.* Vol. 1: *The Challenge of Connecting Learning.* Vol. 2: *Reports from the Fields.* Washington, D.C.: Association of American Colleges, 1990, 1991.

Association of American Colleges and Universities. *American Pluralism and the College Curriculum: Higher Education in a Diverse Democracy.* Washington, D.C.: Association of American Colleges and Universities, 1995a.

Association of American Colleges and Universities. "Boundaries and Borderlands: The Search for Recognition and Community in America." Seminar descriptions and topic bibliographies. (2nd ed.) Washington, D.C.: Association of American Colleges and Universities, 1995b.

Banks, J. A. *Multiethnic Education: Theory and Practice.* Needham Heights, Mass.: Allyn & Bacon, 1994.

Bensimon, E. M. (ed.). *Multicultural Teaching and Learning: Strategies for Change in Higher Education.* University Park: National Center on Postsecondary Teaching, Learning, and Assessment, Center for the Study of Higher Education, Pennsylvania State University, 1994.

Butler, J. E. "Transforming the Curriculum: Teaching About Women of Color." In J. E. Butler and J. C. Walter (eds.), *Transforming the Curriculum: Ethnic Studies and Women's Studies.* Albany: State University of New York Press, 1991.

Butler, J. E. (ed.). "Introduction." *Generative Practice: Teaching and Diversity.* Unpublished manuscript.

Carby, H. V. "The Multicultural Wars." *Radical History Review,* 1992, *54*(2), 7–20.

Du Bois, W.E.B. *The Souls of Black Folk.* Chicago: McClurg, 1903a.

Du Bois, W.E.B. "The Talented Tenth." In *The Negro Problem* (no editor given). New York: Pott, 1903b.

Du Bois, W.E.B. "The Field and Function of the Negro College." In H. Aptheker (ed.), *The Education of Black People: Ten Critiques, 1906–1960.* Amherst: University of Massachusetts Press, 1973.

Gates, H. L., Jr. "Beyond the Culture Wars: Identities in Dialogue." In *Profession 93.* New York: Modern Language Association, 1993.

Graff, G. *Beyond the Culture Wars: How Teaching the Conflicts Can Revitalize American Education.* New York: Norton, 1992.

Lomawaima, K. T. *They Called It Prairie Light: The Story of Chilocco Indian School*. Lincoln: University of Nebraska Press, 1994.

McCarthy, C. "After the Canon: Knowledge and Ideological Representation in the Multicultural Discourse on Curriculum Reform." In C. McCarthy and W. Crichlow (eds.), *Race, Identity and Representation in Education*. New York: Routledge & Kegan Paul, 1993.

Morris, M. "A Work in Progress: The New Civic Competencies." Paper presented to the National Society for Internships and Experiential Education, Santa Fe, N.M., Oct. 1989.

Olguin, R. A. "Towards an Epistemology of Ethnic Studies: African American Studies and Chicano Studies Contributions." In J. E. Butler and J. C. Walter (eds.), *Transforming the Curriculum: Ethnic Studies and Women's Studies*. Albany: State University of New York Press, 1991.

Reed, A. L. "The Political Thought of W.E.B. DuBois." *Political Theory*, 1984, *13*(3), 445.

San Juan, E., Jr. "The Cult of Ethnicity and the Fetish of Pluralism: A Counterhegemonic Critique." *Cultural Critique*, Spring 1991, pp. 215–229.

Schmitz, B. *Core Curriculum and Cultural Pluralism: A Guide for Campus Planners*. Washington, D.C.: Association of American Colleges, 1992.

Schmitz, B. *"Mean Spirit . . . NOT: Lessons Learned from the Curriculum Pluralism Project."* *Washington Center News*, 1995, *9*(2), 8–16.

Scott, J. W. "The Campaign Against Political Correctness: What's Really at Stake." *Radical History Review*, 1992, *54*(2), 59–80.

Standing Bear, L. *Land of the Spotted Eagle*. Lincoln: University of Nebraska Press, 1978. (Originally published 1933.)

Takaki, R. *A Different Mirror: A History of Multicultural America*. Boston: Little, Brown, 1993.

Washington Center for the Improvement of Undergraduate Education. *Cultural Pluralism Project: Final Report*. Olympia: Washington Center for the Improvement of Undergraduate Education, 1996.

CHAPTER TWENTY-TWO

CREATING LEARNING COMMUNITIES

Roberta S. Matthews, Barbara Leigh Smith,
Jean MacGregor, Faith Gabelnick

A growing literature suggests that for undergraduate students, powerful educational settings result from factors beyond the form and content of the curriculum. Rich, rigorous learning environments, active participation on the part of students and faculty, and a sense of community make a positive, often profound difference in fostering student success (Astin, 1992; Kuh, Schuh, Whitt, and Associates, 1991; Light, 1990, 1991; Tinto, 1987). The challenge revolves around how we create rich educational environments; how we build a sense of community on commuter campuses where many students and a large proportion of the faculty are part-time and how we provide students with a coherent educational experience in the face of increasing fragmentation and specialization in the curriculum. More pointedly, we must learn how to actively engage students in increasingly large classes designed for fiscal efficiency rather than student involvement. Sadly, the structure and political economy of many of our colleges are increasingly at odds with our deeply held values about educational effectiveness.

The learning community is one reform effort that addresses these challenges (Gabelnick, MacGregor, Matthews, and Smith, 1990). *Learning communities* are conscious curricular structures that link two or more disciplines around the exploration

Note: Some of the material in this chapter appeared in slightly different form in Gabelnick, MacGregor, Matthews, and Smith, 1992; Matthews, 1994; and Smith, 1991, 1993.

of a common theme. They occur as paired courses, as clusters of three or more courses that constitute the entire course load for students, or as coordinated studies that serve as the entire educational experience during a given semester for both the students and the faculty involved. Learning communities facilitate increased communication around shared interests among faculty and students. In learning communities, students and faculty members might examine, for example, technology and human values, war and peace, the Renaissance, or American pluralism. In all, however, students and teachers experience courses and disciplines as a complementary, connected whole, not as arbitrary or isolated offerings. Because learning communities intentionally rearrange time and space, they provide an extended, focused opportunity for teachers and students to learn together. This kind of restructuring includes and makes more powerful other approaches to educational reform discussed in this book.

Early Roots of Learning Communities

Learning communities are a structural approach to educational reform. While these initiatives have proliferated in the 1980s and 1990s, the rationale behind them is not new. Learning communities draw on significant theory as well as actual experiments that began to appear in American higher education as early as the 1920s.

The Meiklejohn-Tussman Legacy

At the University of Wisconsin, Meiklejohn sharply criticized the prevailing structure of the undergraduate curriculum, and went on to invent an alternative. He believed that the course itself was the university's troubling structural flaw because it was too superficial, too short for meaningful learning. Short, discipline-based courses divided the world into economical units for study, he observed, but they deprived real-world problems of their complexity and interdisciplinary roots. Instead, Meiklejohn proposed a full-time program of study (Meiklejohn, 1932). In 1927, he launched the Experimental College as a two-year undergraduate experience in which students and their faculty explored the values and ideals of democracy by reading and discussing classic works of ancient Greece in the first year, comparing that culture with the study of contemporary America in the second year, and grounding their understanding in community-based research.

The Wisconsin experiment foundered and died in the Depression years. In the 1960s, Tussman developed a similar program at the University of California, Berkeley. Tussman's analysis of undergraduate education paralleled Meiklejohn's.

The Berkeley experiment also swept away courses in favor of a fully integrated, team-taught program built around reading and discussing classic texts and probing interdisciplinary themes. Like the Wisconsin experiment, Berkeley's did not endure, but both the program and Tussman's classic account of it, *Experiment at Berkeley* (Tussman, 1969), influenced later interdisciplinary learning community programs.

Evergreen State College

The Meiklejohn-Tussman legacy reemerged in 1970 when the Evergreen State College was established. The planning faculty for this new public college in Washington was already interested in designing a college around interdisciplinary study; when they read Tussman's description of his Berkeley endeavor, they adapted the vision of full-time, team-taught, year-long coordinated studies programs as the overall curricular structure for the entire institution (Jones, 1981; Smith and Jones, 1984). Each coordinated studies program would be staffed by three or four faculty members working with sixty to eighty students. A theme or problem would guide the curriculum design and provide a holistic multidisciplinary perspective. Having students and faculty work together for an entire academic year, with no other academic commitments, would offer the opportunity for deep engagement.

Evergreen's innovative coordinated studies curriculum, now twenty-five years old, endures as a dynamic model for addressing many of the issues facing higher education: curricular coherence, connections among the disciplines, active and collaborative learning, faculty involvement outside of their own disciplines, and student retention (Hill, 1985). However, Evergreen not only purposefully changed the structure of the curriculum by substituting programs for courses; it also decentralized curricular planning responsibility and put it into the hands of small teams of faculty who, each year, invent and teach something new.

SUNY Stony Brook—Federated Learning Communities

Few institutions could make as radical a commitment to curriculum restructuring as Evergreen. It remained an open question whether there were practical ways to adapt Evergreen's ideas about structure and pedagogy to traditional institutions. In the mid-1970s, SUNY Stony Brook introduced a powerful model, the Federated Learning Community, that could capitalize on and live within the structure of a large research university (Hill, 1982). Supported by grants from the Exxon Educational Foundation and the U.S. Department of Education's Fund for the Improvement of Postsecondary Education, these learning communities were originally conceived as a faculty development project to encourage better teaching and more involvement among the faculty. Rather than creating faculty teams to teach interdisciplinary programs, Hill created miniature federations of existing courses in the curriculum around interdisciplinary themes such as "World Hunger," or "Social and Ethical Issues in the Life Sciences." About forty students were invited to co-register for the federated courses, and additionally to enroll in an integrating seminar. Hill did not ask the teachers of the federated classes to teach their classes differently; instead, he added a new faculty member to the learning community, a *master learner* (preferably not in the disciplines of any of the federated courses) released from usual teaching commitments to take the classes with the students, to facilitate the integrating seminar, and to give occasional feedback to the faculty teaching those classes. The Federated Learning Community model proved immediately powerful for students and for the faculty member in the master learner role. Other institutions adapted the model, among them Lesley College, the University of Maryland, College Park, and Rollins College.

Clusters at LaGuardia Community College

Another early learning community model emerged about the same time at La-Guardia Community College, part of the City University of New York system. Beginning in 1978, LaGuardia Community required all day students in the liberal arts programs to take an eleven-credit cluster of courses including "English Composition" and "Writing the Research Paper" and two additional courses in either the social sciences or the humanities. Eventually, a one-credit integrating seminar was added, increasing the cluster to twelve credits. These clusters adopted themes appropriate to the focus and mission of LaGuardia. For example, "Work, Labor, and Business in American Life," is especially relevant to a college populated by large numbers of first-generation Americans and known for its commitment to cooperative education-work internships. At LaGuardia, the students travel as a group to all the courses in the cluster. Rather than being a subgroup of larger courses, this cohort constitutes the total population of the clustered courses. The faculty do a good deal of team planning of the cluster syllabi, but do not team-teach the courses. Rather, they meet throughout the semester to create connections among the courses (Matthews, 1986). Moreover, a weekly seminar also provides an opportunity for one or two faculty members to enrich and explore connections with the students they teach.

Linked Writing Courses at the University of Washington

Also in the late 1970s, the University of Washington developed a modest but highly effective learning community approach, its Interdisciplinary Writing Program.

The IWP represents one of the earliest and most successful efforts to link writing courses with large general education classes. Students are invited to take an expository writing class linked to any one of about sixteen general education classes. The students enroll as a cohort in each course, which carries equal credit. The writing instructor audits the linked general education class and creates writing assignments that incorporate the material and the mode of written discourse in the linked class. There are now over seventy of these linked writing classes each year at the University of Washington, involving over forty general education classes and upwards of eighteen hundred students. Throughout the country, writing-across-the-curriculum initiatives use various models of linked courses to further their goals. Chapter Eighteen describes this program in great detail.

Learning Communities Proliferate

Reports on higher education in the mid-1980s called again for an examination of the ways that students were taught, the ways the curriculum was constructed, and the ways the faculty were educated as teachers and scholars. Learning communities, because of their unique approach to rethinking and connecting prevailing curriculum structures, were cited as a flexible, efficient, and imaginative response to these challenges (Study Group on the Conditions of Excellence in American Higher Education, 1984). Major foundations such as the Fund for the Improvement of Postsecondary Education, the National Endowment for the Humanities, the National Science Foundation, the Exxon Education Foundation, the Pew Charitable Trusts, and the Ford Foundation have supported the development of a variety of learning community initiatives at both two- and four-year institutions. From the early prototypes, then, dozens of adaptations of linked, clustered, or federated classes, and of coordinated studies programs, have developed and continue to develop on all sizes and types of campuses.

The most ambitious learning community initiative beyond single institutions is led by the Washington Center for Improving the Quality of Undergraduate Education, founded in 1984 with initial support from the Exxon and Ford Foundations. The Washington Center, a state-funded public service initiative of the Evergreen State College, is a consortium of forty-four colleges and universities in Washington. Among other initiatives, it has supported the development of learning community programs with technical assistance, small seed grants, annual conferences and curriculum planning retreats, faculty exchanges, and assessment efforts. Over the past decade, thirty-four campuses in the state of Washington have offered learning communities and twenty-four feature learning communities as an enduring aspect of their curriculum. The Washington Center models ways to build and nurture a statewide commitment to undergraduate educational reform.

Purposes of Learning Communities

Colleges initiate learning communities to serve a variety of purposes and student populations. Learning communities have targeted mainstream students, honors students, and the underprepared. They may be launched to address a particular issue on campus, for example, retention of first-year students, general education, the teaching of writing, student success in gateway courses, developmental or basic skills courses, honors programs, or coherence in the major or minor. These programs seem to succeed when they are incorporated into the curricular mission, not tucked way in the corner of an institution or program. At their best, learning communities are delivery systems designed to achieve a variety of clearly stated educational goals.

Freshman Programs

Colleges and universities throughout the nation are exploring ways to make the first term in college engaging and successful for entering students. Many different learning community models have been designed for freshmen. One particularly successful model at large universities, Freshman Interest Groups, was developed by the Universities of Oregon and Washington. This model invites students to enroll in groups of about twenty-five in a set of classes linked by a theme such as "Spectrum of Behavior," or "Politics, Communication, and Society." All classes fulfill general education requirements. In addition, each Freshman Interest Group enrolls in a one-credit proseminar led by an upper division peer adviser. The student leader of this proseminar helps the students make connections across the course material and familiarizes them with the services of the university during their first term, when they are most in need of a sense of community and connection. Faculty members teaching interest group classes do not change their courses or meet regularly, but the students attend the common seminar and often study together. Freshman Interest Groups have been successful in attracting and retaining first-year students (Tokuno and Campbell, 1992; Tokuno, 1993; Tinto and Love, 1994).

General Education

General education programs often turn to learning communities to provide coherence to core courses perceived as fragmented and disjointed. By their very nature, learning communities juxtapose diverse perspectives and diverse disciplines, often creating rich social, cultural, and intellectual linkages. They naturally lend themselves to addressing interdisciplinary topics of our times. For example, "Peoples of the World," a cluster offered at the Lee Honors College of Western Michigan University, involved general education courses in English, anthropology, and geography. This learning community, while immersing students in the ways different disciplines illuminate a topic, also addressed issues of cultural pluralism. Assignments examined the cultural biases in ethnographies, the impact of geography on cultural identity, and the power relationships among different cultures and how they became expressed through religion, gender identity, and economic decisions.

Using learning communities as part of a general education reform effort has a number of advantages. The learning community model economically incorporates preexisting courses, helping students understand relationships among these courses without costly curriculum revisions. Potential course clusters already embedded in the general education curriculum may be more pointedly focused to address contemporary issues and campus concerns. The social and intellectual experience of learning together for a whole term makes learning communities an ideal arena for active learning and the development of multiple perspectives.

Gateway Courses

Learning communities have been used to turn around attrition rates in gateway or critical filter classes that large numbers of students typically fail, such as calculus and introductory mathematics and science courses. National reform efforts are under way to create curricula that pump students through calculus into advanced work rather than filter them out—especially important in a course that is the gateway to many other fields. The precalculus-calculus program at Seattle Central Community College and the biology–study skills program at Spokane Falls Community College exemplify learning community projects specifically designed to foster student success in these critical courses.

Developmental and Basic Studies

Similarly, many institutions have developed learning communities in developmental and basic studies, another area with high student attrition. Many of these programs link mathematics, writing, speech, reading, and study skills courses with each other and with selected content courses to help students make systematic connections between skills learned in one course and their application in another.

At LaGuardia Community College, the theme of relationships in a developmental learning community, New Student House, combines reading, writing, speech, and counseling so students improve language skills in a context where instructors and counselors build on a common multicultural curriculum and co-ordinate instruction. At Edmonds Community College, "Chemath" links inter-mediate algebra and general chemistry to enable students who are underprepared or lacking background in chemistry to move successfully into science curricula at the college.

Honors Programs

Honors programs have traditionally included interdisciplinary courses and have advocated incorporating experiential and service learning in honors curricula. Since the 1960s, such programs have offered special seminars that are often team-taught. With the advent of learning communities in the late seventies, the University of Maryland, College Park, and other honors programs began offering a variety of learning community models. One of the most extensive and fully in-stitutionalized has been developed at the Lee Honors College of Western Michi-gan University, where all first-year students must take two learning communities before the end of their sophomore year. These may be two- or three-course clus-ters that often connect to the students' general education requirements and to their majors. Most WMU honors students fulfill the university general education re-quirements through this alternative program. With the Honors College offering more than a dozen learning communities each year, upwards of 20 percent of the full-time university faculty have been involved in the program since its begin-ning in 1988. The program has become one of the attractions for recruiting bright students to the university. Learning community clusters now include opportuni-ties for undergraduate research, for community service, and for computer-based pedagogy. The influence of this curriculum has been shown through higher re-tention rates and greater involvement of the students in the Honors College and in the university as a whole.

Work in the Major or Minor

Learning communities may also be used as foundation blocks for majors and minors in the liberal arts and professional programs. The latter, which often block students into related courses during given semesters, are a fertile ground for the more conscious development of learning communities. Although much interest has been expressed and some initiatives are under way, few colleges thus far have turned to learning communities to provide coherence within the major. The Uni-versity of Washington has begun a modest effort that offers "Transfer Interest Groups" in several majors as a strategy for developing community and coherence for transfer students entering large majors at the university. At George Mason University, a newly created college plans to offer its students learning communities throughout their careers, and specifically looks toward the junior and senior years as the time to consciously combine courses in the major as well as in the minor.

Implementing Learning Communities

To implement learning communities effectively, faculty and administrators need to be clear about what they expect to accomplish. Learning communities will not address, much less solve, every issue on campus. Different communities situated in different places need to be assessed in terms of realistic local goals. Grand visions of learning communities as instant promoters of multicultural understanding and as experiences that prepare participants to function effectively in a democracy may be realized in many cases, but not in all of them. Learning communities are as bound by the vagaries of personality and discipline as are the courses they contain.

The choice of learning community models is often shaped by other than purely academic considerations. The size of the available student cohort, the size of participating programs and the established patterns of course offerings, the number of faculty available and willing to participate—all these practical considerations go into the decisions that shape the learning community. When Potsdam College (SUNY) created its version of coordinated studies, called "The Adirondacks," some participating instructors fulfilled their entire load teaching in this model, others made a half-time commitment, and still others taught only one of their courses within that structure. Such an arrangement does not make for a pure model, but does reflect a thoughtful approach that takes into account local resources.

Sometimes, however, even flexible models may tax available resources unacceptably. Small departments that offer essential required courses often have difficulty indulging in the apparent luxury of releasing one of their colleagues to teach in a learning community. The arrangement may result in what faculty perceive as a hardship situation. Necessary courses might have to be covered as unwelcome overload, and splitting course hours between two faculty members may result in unwelcome fragmentation. All the best intentions notwithstanding, some departments may be uncomfortably stretched when one of their members participates in a learning community. Colleges need to acknowledge these types of situations prior to the implementation of a learning community, and if creative (and local) solutions cannot be found, may have to go back to the drawing board and involve other courses and departments.

The ultimate structure of a particular learning community is less important than its informing principle of intentionality. It is important to find a carefully chosen combination of courses or contents that gives students a coherent educational experience. Forms that do not attract students or that flounder in the wake of other priorities need to be reconceived to support local needs and realities.

When teaching first-year students, faculty are particularly challenged. Some, accustomed to teaching experienced students—majors or students taking electives because of particular interest in the subject matter—may be in for a rude shock confronting a classroom full of new students who tend to be relatively immature and uninvolved with the academic culture. Teachers of new students need to facilitate the boundary crossing that must occur and consciously contribute to the development of survival skills and necessary behaviors. Faculty members who have spent their careers assuming the existence of such skills and behaviors will need to switch gears radically if they and their students are to succeed. Expectations and prior experience need to be discussed by participating faculty prior to implementing a learning community or the disjunctures might prove fatal.

Creating a learning community should be a community-building experience. Success depends on the cooperation of many different members of the college community and the coordination of myriad aspects of the scheduling, advisement, and registration processes. The first time through is often exasperating, because learning communities usually go against the grain of established procedures. Savvy learning community implementers involve people in critical support areas and communicate frequently. Exhibit 22.1 summarizes the various questions that need addressing when a learning community program is undertaken.

Learning communities do not happen spontaneously. They must be structured intentionally and attended to throughout the quarter or semester. Faculty need to engage in fairly substantial planning to address the sequence and interconnections that can be made with the course material, experiential learning activities, class assignments, and group process. Because learning communities lend themselves to participatory pedagogies, teachers will need to prepare students whose previous education may have been in a noncollaborative, individualistic, and competitive environment. Once oriented, students engage in group work in the class and often beyond the regularly scheduled meeting times. They may spontaneously form study groups and help themselves and each other to achieve higher grades. *Collaborative learning* occurs as texts are discussed and science labs are conducted, because the emphasis is on connecting individual learning and group learning. Faculty members also learn to work together in learning communities and begin to challenge their assumptions about disciplinary ownership, shared assignments, the so-called objective nature of knowledge, and even their role as authority figures in the classroom. Those who take leadership in developing learning communities must address faculty development implications and student needs.

EXHIBIT 22.1. CHECKLIST FOR LEARNING COMMUNITY IMPLEMENTATION.

1. What design will be used? In what curricular areas? What themes, if any, will provide the focus for the learning community?

2. Which faculty members will be involved? How will broad involvement be encouraged? Do those who are involved represent the leadership on campus? Who will coordinate the effort in the short and long term?

3. What are the current initiatives on campus? How might learning communities fit with initiatives already under way, such as general education reform, diversity, writing across the curriculum, critical thinking, or others? Are there any members of the learning community effort connected with these initiatives? Will the learning community be seen as furthering these initiatives?

4. Who needs to be involved with implementing the learning community? Which administrative and support service people should be brought together to discuss implementing the learning community? How can key administrators support this effort? Where are the obstacles?

5. What resources are available to support the project? What is a reasonable time frame if outside funding is needed?

6. How will the learning community be promoted and marketed? How will the students be recruited? What are the appropriate media to use in recruitment?

7. How will the learning community effort be institutionalized? Who will lead the long-term effort in the faculty and in the administration? How will future programs and teams be selected? How will the learning community be evaluated?

8. What kind of feedback loops can be put in place so that the work is evaluated and improved? What kind of mechanisms are there for disseminating efforts within the institution?

Source: Gabelnick, MacGregor, Matthews, and Smith, 1992, p. 51.

Do Learning Communities Deliver What They Promise?

A growing body of research demonstrates that learning communities are successful because they help build a sense of group identity and community. They contribute to the transition into the social and academic communities so essential for retention and success in college (Tinto, 1987). They create community among students in at least two ways. Socially, participation in a learning community helps students feel comfortable, make friends, and develop a support network. Academically, the learning community experience facilitates communication between students and faculty and virtually guarantees the establishment of a working relationship with a faculty member around a shared interest. Retention is usually high in learning communities because students become committed to each other and to the coursework. Productive teacher-student partnerships naturally arise from the learning community experience, and students are initiated into the academic culture through their participation with teachers and peers in a common endeavor. The learning community process, in itself a collaborative activity, facilitates other kinds of collaborative activities to create a special seriousness of shared purpose. The classroom environment is less alien and more inviting than that of individual classes filled with strangers and managed by faculty who rarely refer or relate their content to other subjects students might be taking. Students of all types and levels of ability give high marks to their learning community experiences.

A comprehensive study of learning communities, *Building Learning Communities for New College Students* by Tinto, Love, and Russo (1994), presents the results of longitudinal studies conducted by the National Center on Postsecondary Teaching, Learning, and Assessment to evaluate the impact of collaborative pedagogies and learning communities on student learning and persistence at the University of Washington, Seattle Central Community College, and LaGuardia Community College. The report concludes as follows:

1. Participation in a collaborative learning group enables students to develop a supportive community of peers that helps bond students to the broader social life of the college while also engaging them more fully in the academic experience.... Students were able to meet two needs, social and academic, without having to sacrifice one in order to meet the other.

2. Students were influenced by participating in an intellectually enriched setting in which sources of learning came from a variety of perspectives beyond that of one faculty member.... At the same time, as students connected their personal experiences to class content and recognized the diversity of views and experiences ... of the classroom, the academic conversation was opened to many voices, empowering students and validating their ability to contribute to the progress of the course.

3. Students in those settings were ... more positive in their views of the institution and their own involvement in college.... They perceived an improved quality of learning in the collaborative settings and saw themselves as having made greater intellectual gains while in college than did students in regular classes. And perhaps most important ... students were more likely to stay in school.

4. These "effects" were as prevalent among "remedial" students as for their "non-remedial" peers. Learning communities work for many types of students, including those typically excluded from the mainstream of academic life because of deficient academic preparation.

This research fills a critical gap in the previous work of Astin (1992), Tinto (1987), and others who have explored the importance of student involvement to student success and persistence. While reaffirming the fact that involvement matters, our research provides empirical documentation of a number of ways in which that involvement arises in three different educational settings. In so doing, it moves the conversation about involvement beyond the recognition of its importance to the practical issue of how involvement can be generated in settings where it is not easily obtained (Tinto, Love, and Russo, 1994, pp. 17–18).

Various Washington Colleges

A wealth of other studies affirm these findings. The Fall 1991 *Washington Center News* (published by the Washington Center for Improving the Quality of Undergraduate Education at the Evergreen State College) summarizes a variety of assessment projects on the impact of learning communities in Washington state on the participating students and faculty (MacGregor, 1991). These studies indicate that learning community students are pretty typical of students in general, but retention, achievement, and intellectual development are significantly higher for students in learning communities than for their counterparts in regular college classes. This finding applied to learning communities composed of many different types of students.

A study of intellectual development in learning communities, involving co-ordinated studies programs at the Evergreen State College and several Washington community colleges, indicates that students in learning communities made significant and unusual leaps in intellectual development. The study used the Measure of Intellectual Development, an essay-writing test derived from and scored along William Perry's positions of intellectual development. The study concluded that after their learning community experience, new college students were "significantly more developed than their counterparts. . . . The meanings these learning community students are making of their academic environments are more typical of college juniors and seniors" (MacGregor, 1987, pp. 6–7). Studies of other learning communities in Washington state (University of Washington, North Seattle Community College, Skagit Valley College, Seattle Central Community College) consistently demonstrate that students in learning communities are retained at a higher rate, are more likely to complete a degree, and are more academically engaged than students in traditional individual-study programs (Tokuno and Campbell, 1992; Tokuno, 1993; Wilkie, 1990; Skagit Valley College 1992).

LaGuardia Community College

Early and ongoing clusters in the liberal arts at LaGuardia Community College continue to flourish with the same positive results about retention and completion that have consistently been gathered since 1979 (Matthews, 1986). Since 1990, La-Guardia Community College has collected data on learning communities offered through its Enterprise Center, which focuses on students in business and computer career programs, and supports academic innovation through the introduction of collaborative learning strategies, including group work and case studies. These practices occur either in thematically linked learning communities or in sections of high-risk courses that are enhanced by student-led study groups. The college has also collected data on learning communities developed and offered for the more general student population through its Freshman Year Initiative (FYI) program. Between 1990 and 1992, data collected on over a thousand students who had participated in Enterprise and FYI learning communities offered further proof that participation in learning communities increased grade point averages and completion and retention rates (Sussman, 1991, 1992a, 1992b). The data support students' self-reporting that the learning community experience increased their confidence in their ability to succeed in college (Sussman, 1991): "This was truly an experience. I have taken other college courses, but the cluster linked each class with the other and made me feel the teachers were close to the students. . . . Also, traveling with the same students allowed many of us to get close together. This cluster is a wonderful system which helps students function better" (p. 3).

The Lee Honors College

The Lee Honors College at Western Michigan University began collecting data in 1988. Over a five-year period (1988–1992), students consistently gave the program high marks for establishing a sense of community. Retention was close to 100 percent. Student demand for more cross-disciplinary involvement and more faculty collaborative efforts increased. Many students expanded their learning community studies to develop their honors thesis or to do undergraduate research. Given these results, it is not surprising that faculty never refused to participate for a second or third time in an honors learning community (Gabelnick, Reish, Wyer, and Wyrwa, 1988–1992).

Daytona Beach Community College

Longitudinal studies of the well-established Quanta program at Daytona Beach Community College, Florida, a coordinated studies program combining psychology, English, and humanities and featuring collaborative learning, suggest that "many students . . . believe that had they not been enrolled in a program like Quanta, they would not have made it through their freshman year" (Avens and Zelley, 1993). One student comment suggests the academic richness of the Quanta experience: "In Quanta, where we get to explore the basic tenets of the individ-ual disciplines and simultaneously discover the 'big picture' of complexity and in-terconnectedness, I have found a learning experience which is not only worth the effort but is irresistible! My personal learning style has flourished in the setting of looking at subjects from multiple perspectives and interrelating [them] . . . I have learned that learning is a challenge and I want to continue the quest!" (Avens and Zelley, 1993).

Temple University

Temple University made an institutional commitment to implement learning com-munities and launched its effort in the fall of 1993 with 180 students enrolled in nine communities. Like many of the more recently established programs, Temple made the wise decision to invest immediately in evaluation and assessment. The first Evaluation Report contains extensive data of various kinds that support the following conclusions:

- Students in Learning Communities received higher average grades . . . than their peers. . . .
- The rate of persistence from Fall '93 into Spring '94 for first-year students overall . . . was 87.58 percent. For Learning Community students, the rate of persistence was 95 percent.
- Many students expressed fear about coming to Temple . . . not knowing anyone . . . about the large size of the university . . . of getting lost in the crowd. . . .
- What students liked most about Learning Communities was meeting people, and the personal interactions they had with their peers. [Love, 1994]

Although different studies at different institutions focus on a variety of issues, all reach the same conclusions: the learning community experience contributes to enhanced academic achievement, higher persistence, increased satisfaction, de-velopment of a sense of community, and more involvement in learning.

Learning Communities and Faculty Revitalization

Learning communities engage and excite faculty members as well as students. In-spired by the rich possibilities for connecting disciplines, the collaborative plan-ning of syllabi, or the possibility of team-teaching, faculty members view learning community teaching as a special faculty development opportunity. Faculty mem-bers remark on how participating in learning communities immerses them in different approaches to teaching, new scholarship and ideas, and new collegial relationships (Finley, 1990, 1991; Tollefson, 1991). Teachers find learning communities that involve team-teaching valuable and enduring; they often report an acute sense of loneliness when they go back to teaching their stand-alone classes.

At many colleges, the tedium and burnout that may occur from repeatedly assuming the same roles and teaching the same courses is an important and neglected issue. As one faculty member put it after sixteen years of teaching, "When you reach a certain level of proficiency, you get afraid that you are losing your edge if you don't seek new challenges" (Gabelnick, MacGregor, Matthews, and Smith, 1990, p. 78). Learning communities rekindle the creative side of teaching and provide new challenges for well-established teachers. Another faculty member commented that learning communities "work because they turn everyone into a learner again. They remind us why we went into this business in the first place." For this reason, learning communities have been particularly attractive to mid-career faculty members, which suggests readiness on their part to assume larger and different roles.

By asking faculty members to recreate the curriculum, learning communities establish a climate of growth, trust, permission, and personal responsibility—key elements in self-renewal. Learning communities demand that we again become professors who *profess* what we think is worth teaching while providing a creative, coherent, and supportive teaching and learning environment. Learning communities promote a creative decentralized process of curriculum design rather than a process of political negotiation through curriculum committees.

As learning communities are created, some tension and difficult dialogue are inevitable. Authority relationships change among faculty and between faculty and students. Many faculty members report a shift in their approach and understanding of their disciplines and in the ways they teach these disciplines. Students find that they are making connections among some of their other courses and building a more coherent perspective on their major or their general education course work. They also face the challenges of taking more responsibility for their learning and of the highs and lows of working in collaborative learning environments. It is hard to imagine a passive learning community. The synergistic effects of individuals grappling with salient issues or challenging tasks influence the entire enterprise.

Faculty vitality, empowerment, and boundaries are critically engaged with questions about the balance between responsibility and control. Cross has noted that it is only when faculty are able to see themselves as reformers within their local spheres of influence that undergraduate education will change. Unfortunately, institutional environments seldom foster that attitude. Learning communities, on the other hand, give faculty members and students an immediate sphere of influence in which to immerse themselves deeply, learn collaboratively, and assume more responsibility.

Some years ago, Katz and Henry (1988) noted, "Continuous learning on the part of the faculty seems to be a prerequisite for the needed transformation of teaching." We would build on his insight to say that associative structures supporting continuous learning on the part of groups of faculty seem to be a prerequisite for the needed transformation of our colleges. Learning communities are one of these associative structures. They are a cost-effective way of building more coherence into the curriculum and of providing faculty development opportunities across the institution. Learning communities enrich the educational experience of students and faculty wherever they are located.

Conclusion

Many institutions are struggling with the challenges of accommodating increases in the diversity of the student body, the turnover rate among faculty (as a large proportion of the professoriate reaches retirement), and the number of part-time faculty, while they also face declining fiscal resources. The success of learning communities demonstrates that we can create educational reform initiatives that rely more on the development of communities of people than on the massive infusion of new resources. Where they have had most impact, learning community efforts are comprehensive reform efforts, not simply isolated or ephemeral innovations in teaching and learning. They provide a practical way of integrating many of the approaches mentioned elsewhere in this book. They also provide a tangible and creative way of building our connections as a community.

In the ubiquitous debates over educational reform, the character of our communities and our ways of making decisions are too often neglected. We see a need to examine our willingness to trust one another to experiment within reasonable boundaries, and to explore ways to build on our common identity while still respecting our increasing diversity. Learning community programs are a modest but powerful form of educational restructuring. Their success suggests that we can be smarter about our resources, more creative about our structures, and more intentional about building connections between our disciplines, with each other, and with our students.

References

Astin, A. W. *What Matters in College? Four Critical Years Revisited.* San Francisco: Jossey-Bass, 1992.

Avens, C., and Zelley, R. "A Report on the Intellectual Development of Students in the Quanta Learning Community at Daytona Beach Community College 1989–1990." Unpublished report, Daytona Beach Community College, 1993.

Finley, N. "Meeting Expectations by Making New Connections: Curriculum Reform at Seattle Central." *Educational Record,* 1990, *71*(4), pp. 50–53.

Finley, N. "What Differences do Learning Communities Make with Faculty? An Inside-Out View: Conversations about Curriculum Reform at Seattle Central." *Washington Center News,* 1991, *6*(1), pp. 11–12.

Gabelnick, F., MacGregor, J., Matthews, R., and Smith, B. L. *Learning Communities: Building Connections Among Students, Faculty, and Disciplines.* New Directions for Teaching and Learning, no. 41. San Francisco: Jossey-Bass, 1990.

Gabelnick, F., MacGregor, J., Matthews, R., and Smith, B. L. "Learning Communities and General Education." *Perspectives,* 1992, *22*(1).

Gabelnick, F., Reish, J. G., Wyer, J., and Wyrwa, J. "Annual Report of the Lee Honors College." Prepared for the provost and vice president of academic affairs, Western Michigan University, 1988–1992.

Hill, P. "Communities of Learners: Curriculum as the Infrastructure of Academic Communities." In J. W. Hill and B. L. Kevles (eds.), *Opposition to the Core Curriculum: Alternative Models of Undergraduate Education.* Westport, Conn.: Greenwood Press, 1982.

Hill, P. "The Rationale for Learning Communities." Keynote address at the inaugural conference on learning communities of the Washington Center, Oct. 1985. Olympia, Wash.: Washington Center for Undergraduate Education, Evergreen State College, 1985.

Jones, R. *Experiment at Evergreen.* Rochester, Vt.: Schenkman, 1981.

Katz, J., and Henry, M. *Turning Professors into Teachers.* New York: American Council on Education and Macmillan, 1988.

Kuh, G. D., Schuh, J. H., Whitt, E. J., and Associates. *Involving Colleges: Successful Approaches to Fostering Student Development and Learning Outside the Classroom.* San Francisco: Jossey-Bass, 1991.

Light, R. *The Harvard Assessment Seminars: Explorations with Students and Faculty about Teaching, Learning, and Student Life.* Cambridge, Mass.: Harvard University Press, 1990.

Light, R. *The Harvard Assessment Seminars: Explorations with Students and Faculty About Teaching, Learning, and Student Life. Second Report.* Cambridge, Mass.: Harvard University Press, 1991.

Love, A. G. "Learning Communities Fall 1993 Evaluation Report." Unpublished report. Philadelphia, Pa.: Temple University, 1994.

MacGregor, J. *Intellectual Development of Students in Learning Community Programs, 1986–1987.* Washington Center Occasional Paper #1. Olympia, Wash.: Washington Center for Undergraduate Education, Evergreen State College, 1987.

MacGregor, J. "What Differences Do Learning Communities Make?" *Washington Center News,* 1991, *6*(1), 4–9.

Matthews, R. "Learning Communities in the Community College." *Community, Technical and Junior College Journal,* 1986, *57*(2), 44–47.

Matthews, R. "Enriching Teaching and Learning Through Learning Communities." In T. O'Banion and Associates, *Teaching and Learning in the Community College.* Washington, D.C.: Community College Press, American Association of Community Colleges, 1994.

Meiklejohn, A. *The Experimental College.* New York: HarperCollins, 1932.

Skagit Valley College. "Learning Communities: A Study of Types of Learning, Retention, and Perceptions of Students and Faculty in Linked and Coordinated Courses at Skagit Valley College." Unpublished report. Mt. Vernon, Wash.: Skagit Valley College, 1992.

Smith, B. L. "Taking Structure Seriously." *Liberal Education,* 1991, *77*(2), 42–48.

Smith, B. L. "Creating Learning Communities." *Liberal Education,* 1993, *79*(4), 32–39.

Smith, B. L., and Jones, R. (eds). *Against the Current: Reform and Experimentation in Higher Education.* Rochester, Vt.: Schenkman, 1984.

Study Group on the Conditions of Excellence in American Higher Education. *Involvement in Learning: Realizing the Potential of American Higher Education.* Washington, D.C.: National Institute of Education, 1984.

Sussman, M. "Evaluating the Experience of Students and Faculty in Enterprise: An Analysis of the Cohort in the 1990–91 Academic Year." Unpublished paper prepared for the Office for Academic Affairs, LaGuardia Community College, Long Island City, N.Y., 1991.

Sussman, M. "Freshman Year Initiative, 1991–92: A Review Survey." Unpublished paper prepared for the Central Office for Academic Affairs, City University of New York, 1992a.

Sussman, M. "Vocational and Technical Education Act: Final Report 1991–92." Unpublished paper prepared for the New York State Education Department, 1992b.

Tinto, V. *Leaving College: Rethinking the Causes and Cures of Student Attrition.* Chicago: University of Chicago Press, 1987.

Tinto, V., and Love, A. G. "Freshman Interest Groups and the First-Year Experience: Constructing Student Communities in a Large University." *Journal of the Freshman Year Experience,* 1994, *6*(1), 7–28.

Tinto, V., Love, A. G., and Russo, P. *Building Learning Communities for New College Students: A Summary of Research Findings of the Collaborative Learning Project.* Syracuse, N.Y.: National Center on Postsecondary Teaching, Learning, and Assessment, Syracuse University, 1994.

Tokuno, K. "Long Term and Recent Student Outcomes of the Freshman Interest Groups." *Journal of the Freshman Year Experience,* 1993, *4*(1), 7–22.

Tokuno, K., and Campbell, F. "Freshman Interest Groups at the University of Washington: Effects on Retention and Scholarship." *Journal of the Freshman Year Experience,* 1992, *4.*

Tollefson, G. "What Differences Do Learning Communities Make with Faculty? An Outside-In View: Faculty Views of Collaborative Learning Communities in Washington Community Colleges." *Washington Center News,* 1991, *6*(1), 10.

Tussman, J. *Experiment at Berkeley.* London: Oxford University Press, 1969.

Wilkie, G. "Learning Communities Enrollment Study, 1986–1990 at North Seattle Community College." Unpublished report, North Seattle Community College, 1990.

CHAPTER TWENTY-THREE

USING TECHNOLOGY

James Farmer

Curriculum has been defined as "the subjects that are studied or prescribed for study in a school" (Allen, 1990). Rapid changes in technology have had major impact on every aspect of that definition—the subjects themselves, the methods of study, and even the nature of schools. The development of technology, especially computer and communications technologies, creates new areas of inquiry and expertise, offers new methods of learning and instruction, and creates new ways to access knowledge and manipulate information. Inevitably, these changes are challenging the way college and university educators think about the curriculum.

Technology affects the curriculum initially by accelerating the need for basic technological literacy, and by creating new areas of professional and technical specialization related to technology itself. The most profound changes, however, arise because technological advances have catapulted us from an industrial to an information era. Technology allows us to create new information at an astonishing rate. For example, we can analyze scientific measurements so voluminous that they can only be stored in huge databases. Communication technology also allows widespread access to information from the world hours or even seconds after it is created.

At the same time, we are in the midst of an economic shift from manufacturing to design, engineering, and customer service. Responsiveness in the marketplace increasingly requires knowledge links between designers, producers, and consumers of goods and services. This trend has created what President Clinton refers to as a "fault line" between knowledge workers, who manipulate symbols and information, and workers whose tasks require them to follow routine procedures designed by others. Knowledge workers are valued for their ability to identify and solve problems and to innovate, which is dependent upon research skills. To become effective knowledge workers, students will need to develop information literacy, that is, the capacity to be fluent users of the information tools made available through new technologies. As defined more specifically for the American Library Association, "an information literate person [is] one who can recognize when information is needed and has the ability to locate, evaluate, and effectively use the needed information" (Breivik, 1992, p. 8). Educators, in turn, are called upon to provide knowledge and skills appropriate for an information-rich and technologically dependent global society.

As technology expands information access and use, the way we think about, obtain, organize, and use knowledge is changing as well. Thus we can anticipate corresponding changes in the way curriculum is structured and presented, equivalent in scope to the creation of new fields of study and new institutions as described in Chapter Two. The creation of hybrid interdisciplinary specializations, for instance, suggests that boundaries in formally defined curricula are shifting, possibly toward more problem-centered, interdisciplinary, or competence-based structures. One university, for example, has a curriculum in blood bank technology that combines courses in chemistry, biology, health sciences, and business. The content of the courses reflects the specific needs and priorities of blood banks. Similarly, a technology institute has a curriculum in packaging design that includes art and photography, printing, business, and design in courses geared toward those who design and produce packaging for consumer products.

New Curricular Content

Technology has become so integral to daily life that faculties have been compelled to discuss the place in the curriculum of technological skill and understanding. Locating technology in the undergraduate general education curriculum has been problematic, in large part because it is not well understood (Ferren, 1993). Faculty often recognize technological literacy as important, but they must also address other, more entrenched subjects competing for curricular resources. As Ferren's case studies suggest, technological literacy often succumbs to the academic penchant for further study. The curriculum in professional programs more readily accommodates technological advancement required to do the work of the profession, to the extent that resources and faculty expertise permit.

Basic Technological Literacy

Technology has advanced in sophistication and declined in cost to the extent that many students enter college with at least a working knowledge of basic computing tools. These tools include the ubiquitous personal computer; associated software; and peripheral devices such as CD-ROM drives, scanners, printers, and modems. Regardless of the major discipline, every student needs to develop fluency in using these fundamental technologies. *Technological literacy* may include knowledge of technological tools, skill and comfort in their use, ethical issues related to technology, and an understanding of technology's impact on society.

However, as Labor Secretary Robert Reich and others have pointed out, a wide gap exists in the United States between those who have ready access to technology and those who do not. Thus curriculum planners increasingly need to cultivate technological literacy at levels from beginning to fairly advanced. Each institution must assess its students' technological abilities and needs, and decide for itself which goals are most relevant to the students enrolled in its programs. The goals of a curriculum to develop basic technological literacy include the ability to:

- Use basic computing applications such as word processors, spreadsheets, database management systems, and presentation software
- Use information retrieval tools to gain access to information resources found on electronic networks
- Understand basic programming concepts

Many students are going beyond word processors, spreadsheets, and electronic mail packages to become familiar with Internet search tools such as World Wide Web browsers and search services on commercial networks. A more structured approach to learning about these tools would help students become more effective researchers and learners.

Still, these subjects are not without challenges for curriculum design. The Internet is an excellent resource, but to make full use of information networks requires an understanding of how information resources are stored and can be retrieved and used, and knowledge of communication technologies for information access. The ability to use electronic information resources implies knowledge of indexing and sufficient search skill to find needed information on all types of media within the exponentially expanding electronic resources. Indexing is a well-developed art but an underdeveloped science. Librarians have developed on-line cataloguing into an effective—but currently expensive—tool. Unfortunately the volume of publications has overwhelmed the art. Many information resources are virtually unavailable because they are unknown and unknowable to the average researcher.

Students would gain a better appreciation for information technology and could be more productive users of professional tools if they had some understanding of programming and how software works. Key to this appreciation is the description of information processes and their representation in various information processing systems. Processes have been described in text for centuries and by flow charts for decades. Now processes are described in languages; languages that extend the capability of word processors and spreadsheets, languages that drive workflow applications, and languages that underlie transaction processing applications found in business. The curriculum need not require specific programming languages but should provide opportunities for students to understand the underlying logical relationships of programming, how they can be represented, what they make possible, and what limitations they impose.

Field-Specific Technology

Access to basic computing tools and guidance in their use across the curriculum is important for students' general technological literacy, but the curricular impact of technology does not end with general knowledge and skills. Advances in technology continually provide specialized discipline-specific and professional tools that must be incorporated into the curriculum as well. Today, instead of a brush or pencil, many artists will choose a computer mouse or a stylus on a digital tablet to draw or paint. Lawyers use personal computers for on-line access to the text of laws and regulations and court reports instead of searching through shelves of law books. Writers use word processing software instead of typewriters. Instead of searching through card catalogues at their local library, researchers use the global electronic network referred to as the Internet to access library catalogues around the world and to obtain information that is as current and complete as it is at the source.

Technological advances such as these have already had an impact on the undergraduate curriculum. For example, in chemistry, computer-based microlabs such as ChemLab (developed by Harvey Long, now a faculty member at George Mason University, while he was at IBM) allow students (even in introductory-level courses) to conduct experiments without costly and possibly dangerous use of large quantities of chemicals. Most business schools now routinely include the use of computerized spreadsheets in accounting and finance courses. Students in undergraduate social science and communication programs learn to use on-line databases for literature searches and computerized statistical tools for data analysis. With increasing familiarity, declining costs, and wider access (and, often, with help from students), faculty are incorporating more of these tools to enrich the curriculum.

Technological literacy also implies increased attention to lifelong learning skills, both for learning new technologies and for managing the vastly expanded and growing information resources made accessible through technology. The importance of these learning-to-learn skills is recognized by the recent publication of a guide for incorporating them in the undergraduate curriculum in accounting (Francis, Mulder, and Stark, 1995).

Course and Curriculum Development

Curriculum design and development must reflect the changing and often conflicting priorities within the disciplines and in the rapidly growing interdisciplinary fields of study. The rate and complexity of knowledge growth means that frequent and perhaps continuous curriculum redesign becomes increasingly necessary.

Managing Information Resources

New information technologies have already begun to help faculty manage the tremendous growth and restructuring of disciplines evident throughout the curriculum and highlighted in this volume. For example, traditional methods of information access can now be supplemented. Even in fields such as philosophy, art, and music, CD-ROMs (compact discs storing vast amounts of easily accessed visual, auditory, and text information) now enable faculty to search lengthy texts, large image collections, film libraries, and musical libraries complete with scores, sound, and background information. These searches can be conducted with unprecedented speed and accuracy. Recently, a peripheral device has been introduced that allows users to create their own CD-ROMs on their personal computers. The cost of this technology (currently about $1,000) is likely to drop rapidly as competing products come to market. Furthermore, CD-ROM technology about to be released will increase the storage capacity of these handy four-inch discs by a factor of five or six.

Such rapid, extensive, and flexible access to resources means that the curriculum can be enriched or changed in ways that would have been difficult at best in the traditional classroom setting. Updating or elaborating content, or creating alternative paths through a subject area, are just two examples of the responsiveness new technologies enable in course and curriculum development.

Enabling Student Learning

Information and computer and communications technologies have, for many years, offered the promise of more effective learning and instruction. Current and near-future instructional technology is making this promise a reality. It seems likely that we could see improvements of 20 percent to 30 percent per year over the next five to ten years.

Existing technologies have already demonstrated their capacity to enhance student learning in several ways. First, they allow instructors to offer more options to accommodate students with different educational backgrounds, learning styles, or objectives. For example, instructional technology can give students access to background knowledge not usually addressed directly in the curriculum, yet essential for academic and professional success. Second, instructional technology can also accelerate the pace of learning, facilitating acquisition of the increased knowledge needed to master a field of study. Third, because instructional technology permits learning independent of time and place, even students who cannot readily take advantage of traditional classroom learning opportunities can have access to learning resources in a variety of formats and modes. For example, two-way interactive video conferencing facilities let workers at a remote site sit in on classes with students in a studio classroom on a distant campus. Students at multiple locations can see and hear each other, so dialogue can take place among them. Students with physical disabilities can use specially adapted computerized hypermedia to explore a subject in full color and sound.

One might expect that the use of instructional technologies would have little impact on the curriculum because they affect the how of learning and instruction rather than what is studied. Yet in a practical sense, the impact can be substantial. Technological tools not only add a new dimension to what students must learn in particular subject areas; they also change the nature of what is taught and alter the relationship between instructor, student, and content. To understand how this occurs, we examine trends in technology as they relate to learning and instruction, with attention to curricular implications.

Overview of Technologies

It is helpful to distinguish two broad categories of technology related to learning: information technologies and communication technologies. Information technologies store, retrieve, organize, and present information, most often in digital form. Computers, software, and associated devices such as video monitors are prototypical information technologies. Communication technologies use electronic means to transfer information from one location to another.

Computer-based training and similar forms of instructional technology have been available for three decades. Advances in information, computer, and communication technologies have improved presentation and interactivity with the user, and have reduced costs. These advances make learning and instructional technologies efficient; implementation, in turn, affects the curriculum as new tools dramatically increase the range of options available for defining and presenting content and skills.

Telephone systems and computer networks are familiar forms of communication technologies. Communication technologies support *distance learning*—that is, using one-way broadcast and two-way interactive audio and video as well as e-mail and bulletin boards to transmit class material. Advances in communication technologies now make distance learning cost effective, giving educators an opportunity to offer instruction to students who otherwise might be unable to participate. The Internet and similar communication networks permit access to electronic text by literally millions of people; this access has, in turn, encouraged governments, institutions, businesses, and individuals to make materials available in electronic form. Much of this information is publicly available at no cost; for example, the University of Delaware supports Oceanic: The Ocean Information Center, "which provides access to information about current marine research around the world, datasets of oceanic research observations, schedules of research cruises, and an electronic directory of marine studies professionals" (Blurton, 1994, p. 201). As the volume of information continues to expand, information technologies such as automatic indexing and retrieval systems will make this information more readily accessible to faculty and students.

Information and communication technologies can enrich learning and improve outcomes achieved by a given curriculum. They also allow greater learner control over the learning process. This discussion will focus on major developments with potential to alter the way curriculum is conceptualized and made available to students.

Technologies for Learning

Applications of technology designed specifically to facilitate learning can be divided into six categories:

- Computer-based presentation and training systems
- Intelligent tutoring and coaching systems incorporating learning models that change the content and presentation based on the student's use of the system
- Multimedia and hypermedia that can structure information based on knowledge of how the student assimilates information
- Computer-supported collaborative learning, for example using e-mail and electronic bulletin boards
- Experiential simulations such as flight simulators, business simulation programs, and virtual reality

- Computer-based tools as learning enablers such as intelligent agents for searching the Internet to locate and display information for the user (Dede and Lewis, 1995)

Technological advances in three areas have dramatically enhanced the flexibility and reduced the costs of each of these forms of instructional technology: multimedia, hypertext and hypermedia, and Internet access. These three advances have significant implications for curriculum development and implementation.

Multimedia

In recent years, the term *multimedia* has come into use, referring to the combined use of graphic images, text, audio, video, and animation. Multimedia instructional presentations can supplement classroom presentations to make them more effective while retaining all the advantages of an instructor in the classroom.

Assembling multimedia materials for classroom use will eventually be as familiar as editing text with a word processor. Like text, each medium has a representation in digital form that permits it to be stored as a data file and processed by computers. For example, digital recorders can record audio, video, text, and images as data files. With suitable software and specialized devices such as speakers, sound cards, and video decompression chips, the files can be presented in a way that is recognizable to the user. The required devices have become inexpensive peripherals or components of a personal computer system, and are now found in more than 80 percent of the personal computers being sold for home use. Editing capability for each of these media components has also improved and costs—even of previously cumbersome or costly video editing—have dropped to the point where desktop editing is practical in virtually every medium. Also, as noted earlier, CD-ROMs with multimedia capability are widely available, inexpensive, and easy to use, and about to undergo a substantial leap in memory capacity.

Appropriate, well-designed multimedia instructional presentations used to supplement lectures and discussions can increase the rate of learning and course completion. Between 1992 and 1995, for example, completion rates in an introductory biology course increased from about 60 percent to over 80 percent. In 1993, the biology faculty began to focus on retaining students in the course, with an immediate increase to about 70 percent. Completion rates in both the traditional and multimedia courses increased over this period, but increases were greatest for a section that was taught using graphic media, first in a linear format, and subsequently in a hypermedia format to permit immediate changes in response to student needs and interests. In 1995, the multimedia section achieved a completion rate of 85 percent, compared with 80 percent for the traditional section

(Tilton , 1995). Similar results were reported for accounting courses (Terry Lovell, personal communication, February 1995).

Multimedia instructional presentations can be made available to students for independent or small-group study. The presentation can be modified and extended through test questions and navigation to a computer-based training module. This evolution may be an effective path for implementing instructional and learning technologies in college and university settings.

Hypertext and Hypermedia

Three technical developments have made text more useful. Large-capacity, economical forms of digital information storage (such as CD-ROMs) make it possible to store the text of literally hundreds of books on a single, easily portable disc. For access, computer programs are available that automatically index text and can retrieve text based on user requests or the pattern of previous use. In addition, nonlinear, user-controlled access to text is now possible through the medium of *hypertext*.

In hypertext, the order of presentation of text depends upon the choices of the reader at the time the text is being read (Nielsen, 1990). A common example of hypertext is computer help files where clicking the mouse on a highlighted or specially identified term or phrase (called a *node* or *link)* will transfer the reader to a new point in the text related to the term chosen. If you use a Macintosh or a Windows-based program on a PC, you can see an example of hypertext simply by selecting the help option for your system. Hypertext links are usually underlined or displayed in a different color from the remaining text. Selecting one of these links instructs the program to display a particular page or document, usually with more detailed information on the topic you have chosen. Hypertext allows users to find immediate answers to questions or problems without handling volumes of irrelevant material.

When a file consists of different types of media and contains links, it is called a *hypermedia* document. The popular World Wide Web pages typically include images such as photographs, drawings, and icons, as well as links to other documents or resources to encourage continued exploration of the topic (Morris, 1995). Links can be indicated by highlighted text, or by graphic images *(icons)*, photographs, or other visual cues.

Hypertext and hypermedia are important resources for curriculum development. They offer opportunities to create individualized learning by permitting students to follow threads of their own choosing through a subject. Hypermedia materials also offer limitless opportunities for hands-on, active learning experiences. Materials to be explored can include original documents, taped interviews with experts, laboratory experiments, and video or film footage of actual locations. Instructional materials can be prepared or recommended by the instructor; or students can be encouraged to use search tools to locate and assemble materials in response to their own questions. Because the learner chooses a path through the subject, the sequence of materials need not be specified in advance by the designer, simplifying the design process. Finally, hypermedia curricular materials facilitate interdisciplinary learning (Semrau and Boyer, 1994).

Computerized interactivity in multimedia classroom presentations permits the instructor to respond quickly to class interests and needs by modifying the sequence of presentation. Interactivity in learning materials improves learning speed, comprehension, and retention. Backer and Yabu (1994) point out that hypermedia-based instruction may increase learner understanding and build cognitive flexibility by allowing information presentation to depend on learner needs and individual knowledge structures.

But interactive hypertext and hypermedia can present difficulties to the learner (Backer and Yabu, 1994). Students can get lost in their exploration of a topic. Following links as they appear can lead to information overload, making integration of knowledge difficult. Some students prefer a linear approach to learning. It is also difficult to predict learning outcomes of interactive designs. Good design requires a balance of instruction and freedom to explore (Backer and Yabu, 1994). Instructors can provide guidelines and checklists to structure student research, and they can promote integration of knowledge by requiring students to discuss and write responses to descriptive, comparative, or critical questions about the materials they have identified (Semrau and Boyer, 1994).

To improve the quality of the learner's investigation of curricular resources, software designers working with each of the multimedia and hypermedia technologies are developing techniques that enable users to *navigate* the information resources available, that is, to determine the sequence in which materials are presented. Navigation techniques and associated software allow users to select text, images, or audio and video presentations on complex applications, to record notes about what they learn, and to keep a record of their path.

Incorporating interactivity can be beneficial but remains both costly and time consuming. Development of interactive, multimedia instructional materials requires skill and expertise well beyond traditional mastery of a discipline. A major curriculum development project requires a team with expertise in the content to be taught, the learning problems and processes associated with the subject, the technology to be used, and the students to be reached. As the level of interactivity goes up, development costs and required skills of the development team increase. A typical three-unit college course has 45 hours of instruction. Using available ratios, developing multimedia materials for a college course could take from 2,250 hours to 27,000 hours, or from one to fourteen person-years in addition to the time required to define the course objectives and research and to organize the content—tasks now typically done by a faculty member. Adding interactivity to a course represents a significant cost and a major commitment of development resources beyond those of the faculty member (Eugenio and Habelow, 1994).

Clearly, instructional media technologies increase the initial cost of course development. However, they can decrease the long-run unit costs of instruction when materials are designed for repeated and extensive use. The flexibility of new interactive multimedia does promise some savings in the design process, given that (as noted earlier) a linear or branching sequence of presentation need not be spelled out by the designer. On the other hand, good design will require an understanding of how people learn the subject and how they are likely to use the technology. Faculty members often understand the former quite well, but the latter is relatively uncharted territory for most.

Internet Access

New communication technologies based on digital technology have made low-cost, fast, accurate Internet-based communications a reality using high-speed modems costing under $200. Networking on campuses is becoming an attractive recruiting feature sought by prospective students. Digital communications underlie the current Internet and promise an Internet of much higher capacity and lower unit cost in the immediate future. The use of digital technology means the communications network can support audio, video, and data using the same communications network and equipment. As implemented in ISDN telephone connections and soon-to-arrive modem–cable television links, this technology permits error-free, high-speed digital communications to be delivered to the home and office at costs that are likely to be little higher than current voice communications.

Trends in communication technologies suggest:

- Internet capabilities will be extended to real-time voice and video, with faster display of images and text. This enhances the Internet as an information resource.
- Instructional materials can be delivered cost-effectively from central sites to many locations at the same time. This will enhance distance learning. Colleges and universities that have developed courses and programs using this technology have begun to export them to other institutions.
- Digital communications will be available in the home at costs comparable to current telephone service, permitting faculty and students to work and learn from home as readily as if they were on campus.

A major development in Internet use is the availability of complex multimedia applications through the World Wide Web. User-controlled navigation on the Web is made possible through a relatively accessible text editor called HyperText Markup Language (HTML) (Morris, 1995). HTML allows the creation of documents for the Web that will appear to advantage when viewed on a wide range of personal computers, and that will carry embedded links between pages of the document and between different locations or destinations and resources on the Web. HTML editors are readily available over the Internet (often at no cost), greatly simplifying the creation of Web pages or on-line destinations that can be organized around curricular themes, course topics, student research, or other instructional materials. The use of these editors offers astonishing capabilities; for example, faculty or students can locate resources such as artworks in the National Gallery or the Chagall Museum or images from the Hubble Space Telescope, then save them as files on their own hard drives for later use as part of an HTML document. Students will need instruction in source documentation more than ever under these circumstances—and copyright issues arising from such use will no doubt create a new specialization within the legal profession.

Curricular Implications

Clearly, new instructional technologies offer vast potential for enrichment of existing curricula. As the brief overview presented here suggests, both faculty and students will have faster, easier access to much wider information resources.

Curriculum Design Processes

A curriculum provides specifications for learning objectives and the instructional materials. Instructional designers use the curriculum as the basis for developing a design for learning and instructional materials, whether using old technology or new. More and more as computer access spreads, we will see audio, video, and multimedia professionals, as well as writers, editors, and graphic artists, developing or producing the instructional or learning materials from the instructional design under the guidance of an instructor. In this context, *curriculum* and *curriculum development* take on new purpose, broader scope, and different meaning. Although clarity about learning goals is important for any curriculum, the curriculum design for instructional media must rely on much greater precision about what is to be learned.

Computer-based multimedia curriculum development requires major investments. Developing multimedia instructional materials requires knowledge and skills and time not available to most faculty members. Depending on the subject and the format selected, curriculum development may require teams including content experts, production specialists, educational specialists, and production managers, and may also require specialized production facilities. However, many instructors will find they can affordably enrich existing courses by using readily available technologies such as e-mail, Internet and Web research, and CD-ROMs containing rich information resources.

In addition to the cost of developing instructional materials, there are costs associated with designing and equipping classrooms and laboratories for multi-media presentations and computer-based learning. While these costs are declining, they are still beyond the reach of many institutional budgets.

Many institutions have taught authoring languages to faculty and audiovisual staff, believing that multimedia courses would result. Most have been disappointed. Because the development of instructional materials (with the possible exception of textbooks) is not considered a scholarly activity, colleges do not provide faculty with incentives to develop these materials. For faculty to participate more fully in the development and use of instructional materials, it may be necessary to change the reward system to recognize the integration of knowledge, teaching, and service required to develop technologically based curricula.

Formal and Informal Aspects of Curriculum

The educational value of instruction has traditionally focused on the number of hours in the classroom and laboratory and other assignments—the familiar Carnegie units. This emphasis on the number of hours of instruction and study obscures the value of other learning experiences in the college setting: informal exchanges between students and faculty and among students, the activities and re-sources found on or near a typical college or university, and the sharing of a learn-ing culture these experiences and resources imply. In a classroom, instructors can respond immediately and productively to specific interests and needs of students. Faculty members also provide role models representing the perspectives and val-ues of their disciplines. Although these learning experiences are not found in the formal curriculum of a teaching institution, their benefits are real and well doc-umented; however, not all students have equal access to these experiences.

When instructional media are used to convey or support the formal curricu-lum, these informal experiences may be overlooked or their character altered. In-structional design with technology should recognize the educational value of the teacher-student relationship in the traditional classroom and the role of the teacher as an adviser—strengths that are difficult to emulate with instructional technol-ogy. At the same time, the use of instructional media may allow greater attention to these informal aspects of learning, and reduce the gap in access to their benefits.

Instructional material specifications can include learning that arises from classroom interaction as part of the finished product. For example, a multimedia project in the introductory biology sequence at Yavapai College began with the instructor's syllabus and accompanying materials. Observation suggested, though, that the instructor was teaching much more than what was represented in these materials. To learn more about what was actually taught in the class, the designer videotaped two semesters of the course showing, in one half of the image, the faculty member, chalkboard, and projection screen, and in the other half, the students. The videotape revealed that the instructor defined and explained about 1,200 words and phrases to the class (Justin E. Tilton and Jon Feriks, personal communication, 1995). During a single semester, the class asked more than five hundred questions that led to materials that were not in the instructional outline, but were related to the course. The instructor was unaware of the scope of the additional material he was presenting in the classroom interaction.

The designer incorporated into this interactive multimedia project the additional concepts offered by the instructor in response to class questions. He included an on-demand glossary to respond to student questions about terms and an on-screen index and pull-down menus of materials that could be used to respond to requests for further explanation. He also attempted to provide materials that the instructor could locate and present within the fifteen seconds necessary to hold class attention. Subsequent use of the instructional materials indicated that the developers anticipated most questions and had developed relevant multimedia materials. The glossary and supplementary materials could also be made available to students for independent use. This example illustrates the detailed analysis needed to design instructional materials rich enough to respond promptly to students' curiosity.

New technologies have also been adapted in attempts to emulate the lively exchange of a face-to-face campus environment. In the traditional classroom and its associated activities and in other campus activities, students learn from each other. Depending on how new instructional and learning technologies are organized and used, they may limit or even eliminate this interaction, resulting in loss of peer learning. These limitations can be partially overcome by creative use of electronic bulletin boards and e-mail. For example, a physics professor requires students to explain concepts to him in e-mail messages and to post their questions on a bulletin board. The resulting dialogue is lively and engaging, and helps the professor clarify difficult aspects of the subject (Kasten and Clark, 1993). Glendale Community College in the Maricopa County, Arizona, Community College District has successfully used electronic bulletin boards and e-mail, and Brennan (personal communication, January 1996) recommends video-conferencing between students and faculty to supplement classroom instruction for students taking courses by interactive instructional television.

Increased Interdisciplinary Learning

The availability of interactive hypermedia and Internet access invites learners to cross disciplinary boundaries, thus accentuating the interdisciplinary character of knowledge. New technologies will ultimately make possible complete customization of curriculum to address individual learners' interests and needs. Many learners seek education for its relevance to career objectives, and knowledge useful in those terms does not always confine itself to disciplinary boundaries, so significant shifts in the structure of the curriculum are likely to occur, extending the evolution of education away from its classical origins.

We may well see a profound (if gradual) shift in the organizational paradigm of higher education. Knowledge will be restructured by application area to be usefully organized. Traditional disciplines will be taught in the context of students' objectives. As an example, students will study biology and chemistry as these subjects apply to health care or chemical engineering as contrasted to learning general biology and chemistry. This type of change will reflect growing recognition that one knows (or uses) a subject primarily as it is applied to a specific area—say, chemistry as applied to a subset of medicine or engineering. No one person can now know chemistry or any other subject; the field is too big. Similarly, if the student's objective is an engineering job designing chips, instruction on computer-aided design and manufacturing (CAD-CAM) will respond to this objective by emphasizing chip technology rather than attempting to cover a broad spectrum of CAD-CAM applications.

To the extent that students' objectives come to drive the curriculum, traditional departments may well be replaced by new structures. The organizational paradigm at colleges and universities will be application of knowledge to jobs in a profession or industry—a new form of apprenticeship.

Future of Instructional Technology

The application of instructional technology to corporate training is being fueled by global competition and advances in all technology. These experiences will, in turn, benefit schools and colleges as they implement instructional technology where it is applicable. At the same time, these advances are reducing the educational and training monopoly once held by colleges and universities. Corporations are making tremendous investments in instructional technology to support training and education. A new institutional type on the horizon is the *corporate university* represented by such serious enterprises as Motorola University, National Semiconductor University, and Sun University.

These developments suggest possible scenarios:

• Colleges and universities may be divided into two groups: the major research institutions may become knowledge factories where graduate students serve as apprentices and cheap labor. Other institutions may become approved instructional delivery vehicles (because of quality control and accreditation) or learning centers focusing on knowledge that cannot be effectively taught by instructional technology (such as critical thinking).

• Because many colleges and universities will be unwilling or unable (depending upon their reward systems, financial condition, and entrepreneurial capacity) to fund the development of curriculum, curriculum development may shift to the private sector.

• An instructional design and development industry will arise out of the traditional textbook publishing business. Course development may cost between, say, $500,000 and $2,500,000 for a typical three-hour course. (Compare that to the cost of authoring a textbook.) These materials may be licensed to teaching institutions on a per-student basis roughly equivalent to 30 percent of tuition—which will continue to increase.

Aside from these curricular changes, social and economic developments related to the information society will continue. Society may be further divided between those who can and will learn—they will become the knowledge workers—and those who do not. (That is, Clinton's "fault line" will be a reality.) One group would be well paid, the other would receive subsistence wages. Formal learning may become bankable, financed initially by students and their parents through loans, grants, and personal savings, and subsequently by their employers as continuing education.

In summary, the accelerating pace of technological innovation creates a flood of information, which in turn creates the need for workers and citizens who can obtain and use information inventively. Students therefore need skills and understandings related to information literacy as well as knowledge of specific technologies. In the foreseeable future, we can expect to see dramatic changes in the ways the curriculum is created and implemented and in the ways students acquire the knowledge and skills they seek.

References

Allen, R. E. *The Concise Oxford Dictionary of Current English*. (8th ed.) Oxford, England: Clarendon Press, 1990.

Backer, P. A., and Yabu, J. K. "Hypermedia as an Instructional Resource." In D. F. Halpern and Associates, *Changing College Classrooms: New Teaching and Learning Strategies for an Increasingly Complex World*. San Francisco: Jossey-Bass, 1994.

Blurton, C. "Using the Internet for Teaching, Learning, and Research." In D. F. Halpern and Associates, *Changing College Classrooms: New Teaching and Learning Strategies for an Increasingly Complex World*. San Francisco: Jossey-Bass, 1994.

Breivik, P. S. "Education for the Information Age." In D. W. Farmer and T. F. Mech (eds.), *Information Literacy: Developing Students as Independent Learners*. New Directions for Higher Education, no. 78. San Francisco: Jossey-Bass, 1992.

Dede, C., and Lewis, M. *Assessment of Emerging Educational Technologies That Might Assist and Enhance School-to-Work Transitions*. Washington D.C.: Office of Technology Assessment, United States Congress, May 1995.

Eugenio, V., and Habelow, E. "Is All Multimedia Created Equal? Differentiating Between Four Types of Multimedia Products." *Journal of Instruction Delivery Systems*, Winter 1994, pp. 20–24.

Ferren, A. "General Education Reform and the Computer Revolution." *Journal of General Education*, 1993, *42*(3), 164–177.

Francis, M. C., Mulder, T. C., and Stark, J. S. *Intentional Learning: A Process for Learning to Learn in the Accounting Curriculum*. Accounting Education Series, Vol. 12. Sarasota, Fla.: Accounting Education Change Commission and American Accounting Association, 1995.

Kasten, W. C., and Clark, B. L. The Multi-Age Classroom: A Family of Learners. Katonah, N.Y.: Owen Publications, 1993.

Morris, M.E.S. *HTML for Fun and Profit*. Mountain View, Calif.: SunSoft Press, 1995.

Nielsen, J. *Hypertext and Hypermedia*. San Diego: Academic Press, 1990.

Semrau, P., and Boyer, B. A. "Enhancing Learning with Interactive Video." In D. F. Halpern and Associates, *Changing College Classrooms: New Teaching and Learning Strategies for an Increasingly Complex World*. San Francisco: Jossey-Bass, 1994.

Tilton, J. E. "Bio 180 Instructor Analysis." Report presented to Doreen Dailey, president of Yavapai College, May 22, 1995.

PART FIVE

ADMINISTRATION AND ASSESSMENT OF THE CURRICULUM

Without effective and sensitive leadership, curricular effectiveness is unlikely. Without effective means of course, program, and institutional assessment, the effectiveness of the reforms can only be conjectural. This section examines innovations in the management of undergraduate curriculum and current practices in assessing program effectiveness and student learning. As noted in Chapter Twenty-Eight, on first glance it may seem unreasonable to put assessment together with administration. Yet assessment provides the qualitative and quantitative information that must be interpreted and used to make substantive changes in courses or programs, and indeed, in the entire undergraduate curriculum. Rather than looking upon the mechanics of assessment, each author examines its role as a communication device—between teacher and student, faculty and academic leaders, and the academy and the external constituencies it serves. Assessment is essential to the management and continuous improvement of the curriculum.

In Chapter Twenty-Four, Frederick Janzow, John Hinni, and Jacqueline Johnson examine the administrative structures prevalent in the undergraduate curriculum and provide examples of innovative approaches. They note the existence of hierarchial structures, putting the chief academic officer at a distance from the workings of the curriculum. They point to the rise of new midlevel administrative positions—directors of writing or intercultural affairs and coordinators or deans of general education, for example—to provide hands-on leadership of key components of the curriculum. These positions, typically part-time, supplement the usual array of heads of departments, programs, and schools. The chapter closes with a series of what-if questions to stimulate thinking about administrative structures that are prerequisite to managing the curriculum to promote student learning.

Increasing numbers of students and decreasing revenues have forced many colleges and universities to cut back on educational programs. In Chapter Twenty-Five, Michael Reardon and Judith Ramaley offer a refreshing and innovative strategy for containing costs and developing community. Drawing on the literature regarding the improvement of undergraduate teaching and learning as well as their own experience in guiding curricular innovation and reform at Portland State, they show us how to release resources that are locked into fixed costs currently embedded in the design (or lack of design) of our current academic programs. Arguing that innovation, change, and curricular transformation are preferable to continual downsizing and institutional anorexia, they call for academic leaders to recognize the upfront investment costs of change. Even while struggling to contain costs, academic leaders can increase coherence and quality according to sound pedagogical practices and reinvigorate the faculty in the process. The chapter argues that transforming the curriculum is beneficial economically, pedagogically, and collegially.

In Chapter Twenty-Six, Ann Ferren continues the examination of the undergraduate curriculum through an economic lens, applying the concepts of efficiency and effectiveness to the undergraduate curriculum. She argues that, in an ideal world, coursework could be provided proportionally to student demand, thereby optimizing efficiency. Colleges override market demand, interfere with supply and demand through requirements, prerequisites, scheduling, and so on, and therefore are less efficient than they might be. Individual faculty and departments, and programs focusing on their particular interests often create inefficiencies that can be observed in the curriculum as a whole. The provost's office and institution-wide faculty committees can gain access to the information and take the broad view that enables efficient and effective direction of the curriculum.

Transfer is a fundamental part of today's college curriculum—most students now construct their undergraduate education from multiple institutions. In Chapter Twenty-Seven, Judith Eaton examines the role of transfer across institutions, highlights issues such as coherence in regard to transfer, and profiles what she calls the Academic Model, an exemplary strategy to facilitate transfer. She concludes by noting that as students move from institution to institution gathering credits for their degrees, they call into question traditional policies and practices of allowing individual institutions to set often conflicting policies. She asks whether general education can remain subject to campus-based policies or whether some interinstitutional arrangements might improve quality and coherence.

In Chapter Twenty-Eight, Barbara Wright reviews the development of assessment as a mechanism for improvement of instruction and for accountability. She gives particular attention to the use of assessment within courses as a means of feedback and evaluation to students and faculty. Examining closely the differences between traditional grades and testing and newer forms of assessment, she outlines some effective and promising approaches—performance assessments, portfolios, capstone projects, classroom assessment techniques, and student self-assessment—that can be used in courses.

As a key component of curriculum design, assessment is equally important at the program level. In Chapter Twenty-Nine, Donald Farmer and Edmund Napieralski review five purposes to which program assessment and evaluation may be applied. They describe several approaches to program assessment, clarifying the behavioral and humanistic methods. They provide an analysis of the movement from quantitative to qualitative procedures, from summative to formative evaluation, and from an emphasis on inputs to an emphasis on outcomes. They conclude with a list of helpful principles for designing and doing program assessment.

In Chapter Thirty, Peter Ewell concludes with an examination of the indicators of curricular quality within and across institutions. Noting the emphasis of the new accountability on efficiency as well as effectiveness of educational programs, he delineates and exemplifies how indicators promise to be effective tools for assessing both process and outcomes of the undergraduate curriculum. Providing practical parameters, Ewell illustrates how indicators can be used to monitor curricular coverage, disciplinary concentration, sequence and structure, expectations placed on students, and skills coverage within courses and programs. Ewell concludes with a discussion of the future prospects for the use of indicators.

Together these chapters point to important issues in the management of a curriculum and suggest a variety of organizational supports for a curriculum that promotes student learning and does so efficiently.

CHAPTER TWENTY-FOUR

ADMINISTERING THE CURRICULUM

Frederick T. Janzow, John B. Hinni, Jacqueline R. Johnson

In *New Life for the College Curriculum*, Gaff (1991) points out that in curricular decisions the shared authority characteristic of academic institutions often becomes a political quagmire for both faculty and administrators. As Gaff puts it, "It is no accident that colleges are underachieving their educational potential; the absence of strong educational leadership from the top administrators combines with the diffusion of authority among the faculty. Together they hasten the fragmentation of the curriculum and, ultimately, the educational experience of students." He continues, "If general education is to be strong, institutional leaders need to assume responsibility for it" (p. 169). His comments regarding general education are equally applicable to the management of undergraduate curriculum as a whole. If the curriculum is to be intellectually vigorous, relevant to society's needs, and programmatically coherent, it requires robust academic leadership.

Because the curriculum emerges from the bureaucratic structure of the college, administering the curriculum is not a simple task. Due to long-standing traditions, deep-seated and tenaciously held faculty values, and the intellectual interests of the faculty, disciplines, and departments, curriculum management has always been a lively field of intellectual and political discussion. Heated debates about the vocational and liberal missions of education, about Western and multicultural emphases, about traditional disciplinary and interdisciplinary approaches to knowledge, and about modern versus postmodern views of knowledge are indisputable evidence that the curriculum is an inherently fractious arena in which faculty, students, and professional staff play out intellectual, social, and political agendas. Furthermore, the paradigm shifts from a focus on faculty and instruction to a focus on students and learning (Barr and Tagg, 1995) and from a narrow to a broader definition of the faculty scholarly role (Boyer, 1990) challenge widely held assumptions about the faculty's role in delivering the curriculum. For an academic administrator, this can make working with the curriculum an exciting opportunity to help faculty develop and deliver intellectually rigorous and stimulating learning experiences for students.

The charters of early American colleges stipulated that a lay board was to develop institutional policy and appoint presidents to carry out policy and administer the institution. For example, the charter of Harvard College, approved by the General Court of Massachusetts in 1650 (Burns, 1962), described the organization of the college that included a president, fellows, and a bursar as well as overseers, the first American institutional policy makers. This basic pattern of policy-determining governing boards, selecting chief executive officers to be responsible for administering the institution, and ensuring that the central mission of learning takes place is found in virtually every institution today.

As the need to educate more students developed, colleges and universities increased in size and complexity. Institutions expanded their institutional missions, added programs, increased resources, and constructed new facilities. As a result, chief administrative officers were no longer able to govern the system effectively themselves. New administrative structures and positions developed as institutional leaders attempted to ensure effective implementation of policy in order to guide the expanding curriculum and attendant administrative structure of the institution. Over the three-hundred-and-fifty-year history of American higher education, colleges and universities formed units for finance, planning, development, student affairs, faculty governance, libraries, exchange programs, government relations, alumni activities, athletics, public relations, job placement, records, student aid, counseling, health, admissions, recruiting, and others, which often were staffed by experts with high levels of professional qualifications. Many of these units were specifically designed to support the teaching-learning process, while others were important in addressing other institutional goals. Today, no chancellor or president of a large institution could be directly responsible for the administration of all these units. From an original position of first among peers, often a rotating assignment, the presidency has become a true chief executive office receiving information and directing policy to and from many sources in a complex administrative structure.

In the public sector today, the governance system frequently extends beyond the institution to include systems made up of multiple institutions; these systems have their own administrative structure. To coordinate all elements of a state's postsecondary offerings, coordinating and governing boards exist with varying degrees of authority to approve and support academic programs.

Not only have growth and complexity affected the administration of higher education, so too has a fundamental shift of authority. A critical transfer of institutional responsibility from president to faculty took place during the first part of the twentieth century (Jencks and Riesman, 1968). After many struggles, the faculty gained authority over the academic program by virtue of their expert knowledge, arguing, for example, that only a physicist knows what a physicist needs to learn. Bensimon, Neumann, and Birnbaum (1989) note that this new faculty authority was formalized in the Joint Statement of the American Association of University Professors ([1966] 1984) and agreed to by other associations. This statement confers on faculty the authority for "curriculum, subject matter and methods of instruction, research, faculty status, and those aspects of student life [that] relate to the educational process" (Bensimon, Neumann, and Birnbaum, 1989, p. 2). One of the reasons that the administration of the curriculum is such a ticklish matter is that the faculty guard their authority jealously and are vigilant for any intrusion by an administrator in what they regard as their territory.

Key Roles in Curriculum Administration

Nonetheless, the faculty and administrators are both crucial to an effective curriculum. In the words of one national report, "Presidents and deans must first confront the obstacles to faculty responsibility that are embedded in academic practice and then, in cooperation with the professors themselves, fashion a range of incentives to revive the responsibility of the faculty as a whole for the curriculum as a whole" (Association of American Colleges, 1985, p. 9). An effective curriculum requires the joint support of the faculty and the administration. There is work for all.

Presidents or Chancellors

The president presides over all institutional activities, and is hence the most visible of the main players in the administration. In colonial colleges, the president was directly responsible for the operation of all aspects of the institution, but as administrative units multiplied, the president became an executive instead of a hands-on manager. Today a brief glance at job vacancy advertisements in the *Chronicle of Higher Education* reveals a stunning array of qualities and responsibilities required or expected of applicants for the position of university president. The president must demonstrate qualities desired by all constituencies in the institutional community, qualities too numerous and varied to be realistically addressed. Hahn suggests that we seek impossible indicators of success in presidents in part because we tend to believe "such a person could exist," and that our very ideas of leadership are unclear (1995, p. 13). Herein lies the paradoxical role of the president. However defined, presidential leadership needs power to be effective—and yet the exercise of that power is limited by factors such as institutional mission, nature of the governing board, external mandates, the availability of resources, the nature and extent of the bureaucratic structure of the institution, and the diversity of the student body and the service region (see McLaughlin, 1996).

The modern president then is expected to be all things to all constituents but is limited by a variety of constraints, one of the most important being faculty ownership of the instructional program. Just because the faculty are responsible for the curriculum, however, this does not mean that there is no presidential role. But what should characterize the president's role in regard to the curriculum? A general answer to this question is difficult, because local traditions affect how a president works with the curriculum. In some places, any curricular suggestion from the president may be a kiss of death to the innovation for the faculty. In other places, curriculum review has little credibility unless it is initiated by the president.

But generally, the president is expected to play three roles: provide vision and oversight of the curriculum as a whole, ensure that the faculty and curriculum are current and responsive to the changing environment, and secure financial resources for a high-quality instructional program. Specifically, presidents have often used the considerable powers of the office to influence the curriculum by appointing a committee to review the curriculum, creating new initiatives, praising and rewarding curricular leaders, even arguing for or against proposals or elements in the curriculum. But it is ultimately the faculty that designs, approves, implements, and translates the curriculum into patterns of teaching and learning. Perhaps the most important role the president can play is to support the faculty so that it, with all of its differences, can collaborate in creating a quality curriculum as a whole.

Hahn (1995) suggests that the successful president is one who "leads without flash and fanfare, who handles crises calmly, manages pressures well, and supports people in line positions, giving them credit for what they do—an executive with no need to be perceived as superhuman" (p. 16). In regard to the curriculum, the president should understand and support its central role in the institution, acknowledge curricular quality where it exists, and appropriately recognize the individuals responsible.

Chief Academic Officers

Chief academic officers (CAO)—provosts, academic vice presidents, and vice chancellors—are the persons with administrative responsibility for the curriculum. Of the many tasks of the modern CAO three are fundamental: managing the budget, attending to personnel matters, and academic planning. Each of these three tasks is directly and intimately related to the curriculum. Ensuring that resources are in place, that the quality of instruction is appropriate, and that the curriculum remains consistent with institutional goals and mission receives the major attention and energy of the effective CAO.

The CAO must assume an institution-wide view of the curriculum. The position provides a good vantage point for observing the workings of the general education program, the effectiveness of schools and departments, and such matters as enrollments, student retention rates, and test scores. This information and perspective are reasons why CAOs have played leadership roles in the reviews and revisions of general education in the 1980s (Cross, 1993). Successful revisions of these curricula have depended on two essential conditions: strong administrative support, especially from the CAO, and considerable faculty involvement. Similarly, attention to current calls for accountability of the curriculum and of teaching require strong administrative support from the CAO to mobilize faculty in developing effective assessment efforts.

Wolverton (1984) describes the multiple responsibilities of the CAO from the perspective of the view up (reporting to the Chief Executive Officer), the view down (supervising), sideways (interacting with other executive-level administrators), and obliquely (the variety of other institutional administrators that are essential to the academic mission). He summarizes the qualities important in a CAO and mentions responsibilities that require constant attention, the first of which is the curriculum.

Deans

As higher education evolved from the ninth to the seventeenth centuries, students and teachers formed guilds known as *universitates*. Within these guilds, the teachers further organized into guilds of their own called *facultates*, which elected deans to serve as managers. Meanwhile, the students elected councilors to serve as leaders. As Westmeyer (1985) points out, "What would be more natural than that the deans and councilors, the guild leaders, should form a council and elect a sort of supreme head, a chancellor? So, there was in the cathedral schools of Europe an organization not unlike that which exists in American universities today" (p. 9).

The position of dean appeared in American colleges and universities in the nineteenth century (McLaughlin and Riesman, 1993) in response to increasing enrollments, faculties, and curricula. Today the dean is the chief academic officer in many small institutions and is responsible for an academic college or school in others.

The dean is expected to demonstrate many of the skills of a CAO, as well as strong leadership qualities with respect to faculty and chairpersons. A thorough understanding of the academic programs in the school or college is essential, as is an understanding of related regional, national, and global trends. The dean must engage in planning and budgeting activities, as well as in faculty hiring, review, and development, and in program review—all with an eye on the quality of the course of study. The dean may initiate curriculum reviews, hold a retreat for faculty leaders to address interdisciplinary topics, stimulate a faculty study group on cultural diversity, or fund a group of faculty to experiment with learning communities, for example. It is particularly important for the dean to watch over the academic departments of the school or college that interact with and contribute to general education, as well as other programs that may cross departmental and college boundaries and over initiatives such as writing across the curriculum, interdisciplinary studies, and the like.

Department Chairpersons

In the ideal university, the informed governing board makes policy, the competent CEO uses the considerable resources available to administer that policy, the CAO—also having considerable power and resources—ensures that the curriculum is addressed, and the dean (with fewer resources and less power) is more intimately responsible for the curriculum and instruction. Each of these individuals has access to opportunities for their professional development offered by a wide range of organizations and associations (the *Directory of Higher Education* lists more than four hundred), which—together with workshops, meetings, and forums—collectively combine to provide information and support for managing the curriculum. The CEO, CAO, and dean generally have little or no teaching responsibilities; they may teach an occasional course as a way to keep in touch with teaching and students. Given the press of administrative responsibilities, such efforts to remain an active teacher are not always successful. These positions also carry a level of discretionary funding that enables innovation, the creation of new initiatives, and the capacity to reward others.

The department chairperson is not so fortunate. Chairs outnumber all other administrators combined, have the fewest resources, the least power, and the most limited support in terms of organizations, associations, workshops, and other forms of continuing education. Further, senior administrators tend to view department chairs as administrators (thus expecting them to carry out institutional policies), and department colleagues often see chairs as "one of us" (in order to advance the interests of the unit)—an impossible position at worst, a difficult one at best. The chair is thought of as first among equals and must respond to every new institutional curricular initiative—often without advantage of firsthand collaborative participation in its development.

The chairperson is the front-line administrator in curricular matters—and a critical one. Because today academic programs are vested largely in departments and can be no better than the faculty responsible for them, the chair is in a critical position to ensure success of the curriculum. In large part this is because she or he has the most intimate knowledge of faculty strengths and weaknesses and an overview of the department's major program and other course offerings. Therefore, if curricular initiatives gain support from chairs, they are more likely to succeed. If chairs fail to support a new curricular initiative, it will surely founder.

Efforts to improve institutional curricula or teaching must focus attention on the role of the chairperson. Because the role and leadership skills of the chairperson are critical to the vibrant curriculum and have become increasingly complex with time, we believe that institutions should consider the following ways to enhance the position:

- Provide monetary and other rewards for taking on leadership responsibilities.
- Recognize the critical administrative role.
- Implement policy to ensure involvement in early planning stages of all new initiatives that affect the curriculum, teaching, and resource allocation.
- Provide discretionary funds.
- Reward participation in national organizations, attendance at workshops, and other forms of continuing education focused on higher education administration.
- Create a national organization similar to the American Conference of Academic Deans and Council of Colleges of Arts and Sciences for deans.

Given the complex problems confronting higher education, it is no longer advisable to have the position of chairperson in a trickle-down situation that promotes reaction rather than proaction. Tucker (1981) describes leadership styles of chairpersons in some detail and suggests ways chairs may determine their own patterns of leadership.

New Administrative Positions

Many new administrative positions are appearing on the organization charts of institutions to provide greater support for key curriculum components. Indeed, the three authors of this chapter hold or recently held administrative positions that did not exist a decade ago. Consider the institution that establishes freshman seminars or a program of writing across the curriculum, for example. Often it is wise to appoint faculty members who are knowledgeable about and interested in the focus of the programs to direct those programs. Whether they serve in these roles on a part-time or full-time basis, such individuals recruit faculty from across the departments, develop guidelines for courses, provide support for course development, serve as advocates for the programs, explain the rationale to students, hear student grievances, and conduct assessments—the kinds of things that chairs of academic departments do. Without someone to attend to the range of activities associated with cross-disciplinary curricular initiatives, such innovations are often less than successful.

One of the innovative positions is administrator of the entire general education program. General education is almost always the largest academic program, and, unlike the smallest department, has not had a head, a faculty, or a budget. Such matters were not necessary when general education was considered to be simply breadth or exposure to various fields. However, as noted in Chapter Seven, recent years have seen institution-wide general education programs revised to be more purposeful and more coherent. Campus leaders have recognized that they need someone attending to these matters solely or primarily. Variously called coordinator, director, or dean of general education, these new administrators help to sustain the common vision and secure the connections and support of the individuals, offices, and resources that are needed for the curriculum to achieve its purposes.

Not surprisingly, leaders in these new positions have banded together to create networks of support and formed new organizations. The authors of this chapter helped to found the Council of Administrators of General and Liberal Studies in 1995, and it has nearly three hundred members as of early 1996. In this respect it mirrors the Writing Program Administrators and similar groups of leaders of other curriculum components.

Theories of Leadership and Organizational Behavior

Those who administer the curriculum face interesting and challenging tasks. To understand better how to be most effective in meeting the challenges of specific curricular problems, administrators can learn from some of the recent work on leadership and organizational behavior. The fundamental question to answer is, What explains the observation that some administrators have been very successful in administering the undergraduate curriculum while others have not?

Although academic administrators have usually come from the faculty and thus have spent much of their lives in the day-to-day operation of a college or university, they may have little knowledge of the principles of organizational and leadership theory. Chairpersons, deans, and even executive-level administrators are often chosen because of their success in teaching and research, not because of evidence of their administrative effectiveness or their knowledge of organizational theory applied to academic settings. In one sense, despite the existence of graduate programs in higher education administration, the profession's approach to administration resembles the do-it-yourself approach to home electrical repair. Learning about the job is accomplished on the job—with the high likelihood of a few surprising jolts before the task is finished.

Although a growing amount of research about academic administration provides some answers to questions about administrative effectiveness, much of the evidence regarding successful academic administrative leadership is descriptive and even anecdotal. A review of several recent works that report empirical and theoretical studies of leadership and organizational theory applied to academic administration thus may be helpful to those interested in academic administration. This section summarizes major theoretical perspectives and two empirical studies of academic organizational behavior, and presents questions about viewing administrative problems regarding the curriculum from these perspectives.

In a study of academic administration, Astin and Scherrei (1980) used multivariate analyses to identify characteristics of the leadership styles of college presidents and their relationships to types of administrations. Because these leadership styles and types of administrations were statistically related to certain faculty and student variables, the findings in this study have important implications for how administrators approach curricular problems.

Astin and Scherrei identified four administrative styles: bureaucratic, intellectual, egalitarian, and counselor. They found that bureaucratic leadership was negatively associated with student satisfaction, and that faculty and students perceived bureaucratic presidents as remote and relatively uninterested in their welfare. In contrast, egalitarian leaders were positively associated with student and faculty satisfaction and faculty emphasis on teaching. Intellectual leaders were focused mainly on faculty and academic issues, and not much involved with students. Counselor leaders were characterized by personal and informal interactions with others as the main means of dealing with people and issues. The counselor style was positively associated with student satisfaction with personal, health, and job placement services.

Along with these four presidential styles, Astin and Scherrei (1980) describe five types of administrations: hierarchical, humanistic, entrepreneurial, insecure, and task-oriented (Table 24.1). Each of these types was associated with certain presidential styles and faculty and student variables. For example, hierarchical administrations were associated with faculty spending less time on teaching and being less satisfied with their interactions with students, while faculty working with humanistic administrations are more satisfied with their interactions with students. Similarly, student satisfaction with curriculum advisement was positively associated with humanistic administrations but negatively associated with hierarchical administrations. At institutions with task-oriented administrations, faculty spend more time teaching than doing research and are generally satisfied with their jobs. Students at these institutions were satisfied with personal and job placement services. As Astin and Scherrei point out, some of these relationships can be explained by institution size and student characteristics, but these findings suggest important questions about how to best serve faculty and students as administrative decisions must be made about curricular issues. For example, if the current emphasis on student learning outcomes and student satisfaction continues, should institutions make a concerted effort to train academic administrators to use the behaviors and strategies of humanistic and task-oriented types of administrations? When colleges are searching for a chairperson, dean, vice president, or president, should the search criteria focus on the characteristics of the egalitarian and counselor styles that are associated with student satisfaction?

In *Making Sense of Administrative Leadership: The "L" Word in Higher Education,* Bensimon, Neumann, and Birnbaum (1989) summarize the major theories that attempt to explain leadership and organizational behavior and apply them to the academic setting. They cite six theoretical approaches to understanding leadership: trait theories, power and influence theories, behavioral theories, contingency theories, cultural and symbolic theories, cognitive theories (Table 24.1).

Each of these theoretical views of leadership provides insight into factors that contribute to effective leadership and raises interesting questions about academic

TABLE 24.1. SIX THEORETICAL EXPLANATIONS OF LEADERSHIP.

Theory	Source of Leadership
Trait	Leaders have certain personality traits that cause others to follow them.
Power/Influence	Leadership results from effective use of power to influence others.
Behavioral	Effective leaders are characterized by certain behaviors.
Contingency	Leadership emerges from needs of specific situations that happen to match the skills of a specific person.
Cultural/Symbolic	Leadership is a matter of helping the group make meaning of experience by interpreting organizational events.
Cognitive	Leadership is a cognitive invention of followers to explain why events happen.

Source: Bensimon, Neumann, and Birnbaum, 1989.

leadership. For example, from the power-influence perspective one might ask how best to train administrators to use power to accomplish curriculum goals effectively. Or from the cultural-symbolic perspective one could ask, "What myths about the curriculum exist and what must an administrator do to help faculty evaluate the assumptions underlying those myths if curricular change is to occur?"

Using Bolman and Deal's (1984) classification of four types of organizational models, Bensimon, Neumann, and Birnbaum (1989) summarize the structural, human resources, political, and symbolic views of organizations (Table 24.2). Each of these perspectives on organizations emphasizes different values and processes that may be conflicting but are not necessarily mutually exclusive. If one were to combine the various models' viewpoints, colleges and universities could be described as groups of people with deep-seated intellectual values, individual needs that should be satisfied to improve individual performance, and bureaucratic units that compete politically for limited resources. An administrator who understands that colleges and universities have these various facets and tries to incorporate them in the process of making decisions about the curriculum is more likely to be effective. Viewing curriculum matters from only one or two of these theoretical perspectives can easily result in not seeing a problem that, left untended, can block a needed curricular change. For example, making a decision to change a curriculum without attending to the time-consuming steps necessary either to adapt the innovation to the academic culture of the institution or department or to

TABLE 24.2. BASIC CHARACTERISTICS OF THEORIES OF ORGANIZATION.

Theory	View of Institution	Administrative Concern
Bureaucratic	A formal hierarchical structure designed to rationally and efficiently solve problems	Position of unit and appropriate use of procedures to make rational decisions
Human Resources	A community of people that is most effective when people's needs are served in the pursuit of institutional goals	Making the institution's form meet the needs of its people
Political	A dynamic system of power block groups that have different interests and compete for limited resources	Negotiation and compromise that lead to a decision acceptable to power groups
Symbolic	A culture with deeply entrenched traditions and tenaciously held values	Using shared values, symbols, and rituals to give meaning to actions and accomplish goals

Source: Bensimon, Neumann, and Birnbaum, 1989.

change that culture may lead to failure. Ultimately, lack of attention to the literature on leadership and its insights can lead to considerable friction between administrators and faculty.

Friction between administrators and faculty often occurs because the two groups hold conflicting views of the organization. For example, Peterson and White (1992) report statistically significant differences in faculty and administrators' perceptions of key characteristics of the institution. They report that, in contrast to faculty, "Administrators see their institutions placing greater emphasis on all areas: academic management practices, support for academic innovation, fostering a challenging and professional work setting, having supportive administrators, and having more available educational resources and facilities" (pp. 195–196). They conclude that although faculty and administrators have similar views of commitment to undergraduate education, administrators tend to have a more idealized view of the climate and processes of the campus. Interestingly, this study revealed that faculty and administrators had a similar organizational model: a bureaucratic hierarchy in which academic administrators support faculty commitment to undergraduate education. Faculty reported, however, that their satisfaction was more related to a culture of teamwork (collegiality) and institutional commitment to leadership in undergraduate education. In contrast, administrators attributed faculty satisfaction to rational decision making through the political processes of the institution.

In the context of the views of leadership and organizational structure and function described thus far, one can ask a number of questions:

- If important differences exist between faculty and administrator views of the campus climate and culture, what, if anything, should an administration do to reduce the difference?
- If a more coherent view of the institution is desired, what leadership strategy should be used to produce it?
- If faculty value teamwork and a humanistic administrative style, what administrative approach should be used in planning and implementing curricular changes that inevitably receive resistance from departments and their faculty?
- How can understanding the various theoretical viewpoints on leadership and types of administration be used to involve students, faculty, and administration in improvement of the curriculum?

An Example

The revision of general education at Southeast Missouri State University illustrates ways in which the various aspects of leadership and administration resulted in successful curricular changes over a decade-long revision process. It is useful to review highlights of administrative actions that led to successful implementation of a new general education curriculum.

• The provost provided funding to educate the revision committee about the substance of general education and the process of revision. This demonstrated that top administrators were committed to the program.

• Administrators and the faculty revision committee encouraged approval of the program in stages, attending to the faculty's need to not have large change occur all at once. Leaders also attended to the faculty's need to control change and provided time to incorporate the change into the campus cultural value system. They accepted that extended time is essential for institutional acclimation to a significant curricular revision.

• The political need to include all key power blocks that have ownership experience with the curriculum was addressed by scheduling meetings with the faculty senate, the faculty at large, students, alumni, and student affairs staff to allay concerns and obtain advice regarding the curriculum revision. Key administrators helped guide the approval process through campus and state approval bodies.

• The administration created and staffed an administrative unit, the School of University Studies, to be responsible for the new program. The new school had a dean and two half-time positions, and a budget to support faculty and course development. This provided an appropriate organizational home for the program and gave it ongoing visibility.

• Key executive administrators acquired state funding for the new program, thereby preventing concerns about damage to existing programs and reducing political conflicts over limited financial resources.

• The provost and dean supported and regularly affirmed the shift from a program based on delivering subject matter to a student-centered program that emphasizes the development of skills.

Questions for the Future

In administrative evolution, one obvious trend that emerges is the creation of new positions and increasing responsibilities for all positions as institutions grow, change missions, and respond to external demands for accountability and accreditation. Clearly, the amount of administrative work increases as new institutional initiatives are added to old administrative tasks.

How should institutions respond to this trend? Releasing faculty for administrative work, a strategy commonly used to handle increased administrative workload, is often counterproductive to a vibrant curriculum; also, such practices may be prohibited or limited by collective bargaining contracts. It may be more productive to consider new ways to think about administrative roles in addressing curricular issues. One approach to this is to ask, What are the administrative implications if we shift the institution's emphasis from the instructional delivery model to the learning-centered model? Following the suggestion of Barr and Tagg (1995), let us suppose that we were creating such a university today. The questions that arise include:

- Given the sophistication of instructional technology, accountability, distance learning, and the knowledge explosion, what administrative forms would we create if emphasis were placed upon student learning rather than instructional delivery?
- How can a learning-centered curriculum be managed?
- In our newly created university, if we evaluate administrative performance at all levels in terms of its impact on student learning, how might this change administrative leadership regarding the curriculum?
- How would the faculty reward system have to change to reflect an emphasis on learning rather than on instructional delivery?
- What changes in administrative approaches to faculty workload and budget allocations would be necessary in a system focused on student learning outcomes?
- What assessment and institutional research needs arise in dealing with changing accreditation guidelines?
- How would staffing patterns change in a system where student learning outcomes are more important than student credit hour productivity?

Given the magnitude of the many tasks confronting administrators in higher education, it is time to rethink the structure and function of administrative roles as they relate to the curriculum. The changing student body, emphasis on accountability, attention to diversity issues, and the creation of new technologies to deliver the curriculum require new thinking about what the curriculum is and how it should be supported and delivered. To administer the curriculum effectively is thus complex and challenging work, requiring an understanding of the various ways to view administration and its role regarding the curriculum. It requires as well that one accept that the curriculum is a dynamic intellectual entity that, if healthy, is always developing. Most often this lively quality of the curriculum has been seen as a battlefield—or, as Carnochan described it, as a "fault system still heaving and buckling with aftershocks of an earlier, larger rupture" (1993, p. 1). Although it is accurate that an effective administrator must occasionally dodge verbal bullets and be skilled at bouncing back after being knocked down, the traditional metaphors all conjure up visions of wounds, scars, and structural damage.

We believe it is helpful to view administration of the curriculum from another metaphorical vantage point as well. The curriculum may be seen as an intellectual ecosystem that is always undergoing secondary succession. As external and internal forces cause perturbations in the system, an administrator has exceptional and rewarding opportunities for working with faculty to stimulate the intellectual succession of ideas that give the curriculum its lively and evolving character. From this view, the curriculum that is not in some turmoil as it is influenced by its changing environment is dead.

References

American Association of University Professors, American Council on Education, and the Association of Governing Boards of Universities and Colleges. "Joint Statement on Government of Colleges and Universities." In *Policy Documents and Reports.* Washington, D.C.: National Education Association, 1984. (Originally published 1966.)

Association of American Colleges. *Integrity in the College Curriculum: A Report to the Academic Community.* Washington, D.C.: Association of American Colleges, 1985.

Astin, A., W. and Scherrei, R. *Maximizing Leadership Effectiveness.* San Francisco: Jossey-Bass, 1980.

Barr, R., and Tagg, J. "A New Paradigm for Undergraduate Education." *Change,* 1995, *27*(6), 13–25.

Bensimon, E., Neumann, A., and Birnbaum, R. *Making Sense of Administrative Leadership: The "L" Word in Higher Education.* ASHE-ERIC Higher Education Report No. 1. Washington, D.C.: School of Education and Human Development, George Washington University, 1989.

Bolman, L., and Deal, T. *Modern Approaches to Understanding and Managing Organizations.* San Francisco: Jossey-Bass, 1984.

Boyer, E. L. *Scholarship Reconsidered: Priorities of the Professoriate.* Princeton, N.J.: Carnegie Foundation for the Advancement of Teaching, 1990.

Burns, G. *Administrators in Higher Education: Their Function and Coordination.* New York: HarperCollins, 1962.

Carnochan, W. B. *The Battleground of the Curriculum: Liberal Education and American Experience.* Stanford, Calif.: Stanford University Press, 1993.

Cross, P. "Improving the Quality of Instruction." In A. Levine (ed.), *Higher Learning in America: 1980–2000.* Baltimore, Md.: Johns Hopkins University Press, 1993.

Gaff, J. G. *New Life for the College Curriculum: Assessing Achievements and Furthering Progress in the Reform of General Education.* San Francisco: Jossey-Bass, 1991.

Hahn, R. "Getting Serious About Presidential Leadership." *Change,* 1995, *27*(5), 13–19.

Jencks, C., and Riesman, D. *The Academic Revolution.* New York: Doubleday, 1968.

McLaughlin, J. B. *Leadership Transitions.* New Directions for Higher Education, no. 93. San Francisco: Jossey-Bass, 1996.

McLaughlin, J., and Riesman, D. "The President: A Precarious Perch." In A. Levine (ed.), *Higher Learning in America: 1980–2000.* Baltimore, Md.: Johns Hopkins University Press, 1993.

Peterson, M., and White, T. "Faculty and Administrator Perceptions of Their Environments: Different Views or Different Models of Organization?" In J. C. Smart (ed.), *Research in Higher Education*. New York: Human Sciences Press, 1992.

Tucker, A. *Chairing the Academic Department: Leadership Among Peers*. Washington, D.C.: American Council on Education, 1981.

Westmeyer, P. *A History of American Higher Education*. Springfield, Ill.: Thomas, 1985.

Wolverton, R. "The Chief Academic Officer: Argus on the Campus." In David G. Brown, ed., *Leadership Roles of Chief Academic Officers*. San Francisco: Jossey-Bass, 1984.

CHAPTER TWENTY-FIVE

BUILDING ACADEMIC COMMUNITY WHILE CONTAINING COSTS

Michael F. Reardon, Judith A. Ramaley

The Herculean labor now confronting institutions of higher education can be defined as simultaneously improving the quality of undergraduate education and developing a greater sense of community among faculty while accomplishing budget reductions and achieving long-range cost containment. A growing literature defining this task reveals a myriad of possible changes, but one salient issue that emerges is the relationship between the nature and structure of the curriculum and its cost. This chapter draws on the experience of a medium-sized, public, urban university to address ways to manage the task by focusing on curricular transformation. The issues considered, responses generated, and lessons learned may be applicable at other types of institutions.

Context for Curricular Transformation

Many colleges and universities have been put on a revenue diet, involuntary as it may be. In such times it is difficult to imagine significant curricular change, but it is such conditions that may make these institutions most conducive to change (Green, Levine, and Associates, 1985).

For many states, the revenue diet began in the early 1980s. Colleges and universities raised tuition, imposed austerities, deferred maintenance and repairs, distributed administrative cuts, and began across-the-board reductions in academic programs as well as selective program eliminations. The second phase of the revenue diet—the stage of doing more with less—is now upon most institutions. At this stage, campuses reduce academic programs selectively, looking for unnecessary duplication either on the campus or within a system of institutions. Various cost-reduction strategies and productivity enhancements are initiated, all meant to streamline campus procedures and contain costs. In the process, many institutions have adapted techniques originally developed in manufacturing industries facing the need to design and distribute high-quality products at attractive prices. This quality movement, traced back to the work of Deming in the 1940s and generally referred to as *Total Quality Management* (TQM), intends the streamlining and redesign of how work is done to either reallocate resources from campus operations to academic programs, or to offset as much as possible of the impact of budget cuts by doing more with less.

Unfortunately, the combined effect of the first two phases of the diet creates a dangerous condition; as Hamel points out, "This continuous downsizing—it is corporate anorexia. You get thin but it's no way to get healthy" (1994, p. 64). Most colleges and universities will soon come to the end of what they can achieve by means of cost reduction and productivity enhancements without undertaking the fundamental rethinking of institutional design.

At this point, an institution must enter an era of innovation and change. In the rethinking of institutional design, change and innovation may mean the release of resources that are locked into fixed costs largely embedded in the design (or lack of design) of our academic programs. While administrative cost reduction must precede major alterations in the academic area, the problem of cost and the current structure of academic programs must inevitably be confronted. And when that confrontation occurs, attempts to introduce quality management concepts and techniques to the faculty often meet immediate resistance. "We are not manufacturing processes," the faculty retort. "We do not sell a product." "We do not have customers." "We will not prostitute ourselves to trade!"

These are typical—and not inappropriate—faculty responses. The challenge is to identify the correct analogy to quality management within the academic mission; consultants and experts from industry very often fail in this regard. What the faculty produce and manage is the curriculum. By focusing on the curriculum as a product and as a design problem, the faculty can find an appropriate analogy for a quality initiative. Perhaps equally important, the task can then be undertaken using not the language of TQM—which inevitably meets resistance if not consternation and horror—but the language of academic culture itself. In engaging the faculty in change to achieve quality, we will be well served by turning to Nietzsche and keeping Deming in the background. As one who was both a product and participant in the emerging culture of the academic professional, Nietzsche offered sound advice:

This has given me the greatest trouble and still does: to realize that what things are called is incomparably more important than what they are. The reputation, name, and appearance, the usual measure and weight of a thing, what it counts for—originally almost always wrong and arbitrary, thrown over things like a dress and altogether foreign to their nature and even to their skin—all this grows from generation unto generation, merely because people believe in it, until it gradually grows to be part of the thing and turns into its very body. What at first was appearance becomes in the end, almost invariably, the essence and is effective as such. How foolish it would be to suppose that one only needs to point out this origin and misty shroud of delusion in order to destroy the world that counts for real, so-called reality. We can destroy only as creators. But let us not forget this either: it is enough to create new names and estimations and probabilities in order in the long run to create new things. [(1882) 1974, pp. 121–122]

Nietzsche's admonitions not only serve to underscore the need to speak to the faculty in the discourse of the academy and not of the market but also to remind us of something very significant about the curriculum itself, which we claim as the proper analogy to the manufacturing model.

Indeed, there may be no better example of Nietzsche's analysis of words and things. The original event in which the word *curriculum* was first applied to a course of study is indeed lost to us, shrouded in mist. At some point someone—one suspects a very harried student—must have referred to the seemingly fruitless pursuit of education as tearing in circles about a racetrack; one early meaning of the word *curriculum* is a light racing chariot. That metaphor sang and stuck, but further it became, as Nietzsche tells us, the thing itself. We also know that it was given weight and gravity in the language of the Calvinist universities of Scotland, where it appears as an official term. It should then come as no surprise to us that the word *curriculum*, already a metaphor, is most easily described in our current literature by other metaphors: cafeteria, battlefield, junkyard, even disaster area. But as Nietzsche tells us, "Truth is a mobile army of metaphors" (Bizzell and Herzberg, 1990, p. 891).

The choice of the term *curricular transformation* is purposeful; it is meant to convey the analysis and definition provided by Toombs and Tierney (1991). They point out three different approaches to curricular change: modification, integration, and transformation. *Modification* is the long-familiar approach of adapting new knowledge, techniques, and practices to existing disciplines and professional fields, which has the goal of preserving existing compartmentalization of learning into the disciplinary-departmental structure. This mode is in and of itself debilitating, being achieved by adding new disciplinary specialties—which in turn require new faculty lines to cover each new or more specialized aspect of the discipline. Modification requires increased financial resources and by its nature drives up costs.

The second approach, *integration*, responds to the laudable desire to provide students with a sense of the unity of knowledge, a larger scope of study, and the connections between the disciplines and throughout the curriculum; the desire for integration is reflected in part by the now-common adage, "Society has problems, universities have departments." But while providing more coherence in some areas of the curriculum, this approach is partial in its impact and frequently creates marginalized interdisciplinary programs that are only suffered to exist. These programs can play a more important curricular role if the third mode of change is enacted.

The third approach, *transformation*, encompasses elements of modification and integration but differs in its recognition that there are new issues the curriculum must cope with, and that many of these issues are not yet fully defined. In our current situation, gender equity, ethnicity, globalism, multiculturalism, and ethics, as well as environmental, health, and educational policy, are issues of profound importance for the curriculum. The service learning opportunities and social engagement demanded by these issues represent activities that the curriculum must provide for students. These issues and activities together pose questions and make urgent demands, which current disciplines and professionalized programs of education only partly engage. They compel the university toward activities that departments and schools are not organized to support (Toombs and Tierney, 1991, pp. 7–9).

If transformation is the most effective type of change, then a concept of what is being transformed is also necessary; the term *curriculum*—while the correct marker—is vague and carries diverse meanings. For the purposes of our analysis, Toombs and Tierney provide a useful definition of what the curriculum should be: "The curriculum is an intentional design for learning negotiated by faculty in light of their specialized knowledge and in the context of social expectation and students' needs" (1991, p. 21). This definition captures essential elements that must be kept in mind: that the curriculum should be not only the substantive knowledge that is taught but also the formal arrangements of classes, sequences, programs, majors, and so on. Further, this perspective correctly emphasizes that the curriculum should be constructed by faculty and that it should reflect both history and the larger collective experience of higher education, but it necessarily does so as the construction of a unique faculty for certain students at a particular institution.

In universities and colleges with a distribution model of general education, overly specialized majors, and large numbers of disconnected electives, there is most likely little sense of real community or faculty responsibility to function other than as individual agents of their particular specialization who do not consider university-wide curricular issues as of high priority or deserving their time and energy. The threat to an education of quality produced by many of our current curricular models, and the accompanying faculty culture both producing and sustained by them, has been identified for some time; the list of compelling voices warning of this threat is extensive. Perhaps Levine's term *junkyard curriculum* is the most effective metaphor:

> In short, the curriculum at most colleges and universities has grown by accretion in a haphazard fashion for some fifty years. Today it is blurred and confused, misshapen and bloated. It has taken the appearance of a junkyard, littered with the reforms of five decades and the assorted legacies of 350 years of collegiate history. . . . Colleges are more confident about the length of an undergraduate education than they are about its content. In fact, most colleges ask little more from their students than that they scrounge around the yard for four years, picking and choosing from among the rubble in accordance with the minimal house rules. . . . The real problem is that at many schools the curriculum lacks a purpose . . . the junkyard curriculum hurts. It is a liability to colleges in hard times. It is not only expensive but it lacks educational merit. A junkyard curriculum costs more to maintain than a leaner more carefully thought out alternative. A junkyard curriculum has a leveling effect on quality. It encourages mediocrity. [1985, p. 128]

For institutions facing budget reductions, a number of stopgap responses are inevitable. Transforming the curriculum requires a major commitment from all areas of the institution. When all possible tinkering has been done—when the low-hanging fruit has been picked and yet the need for further reductions remains—the university community may finally realize that it is time, in the interest both of reducing budgets and controlling costs, to analyze all major factors that drive costs. From this point of view, the undergraduate curriculum is a vital nexus: it is both a significant cause of cost increase and a point of opportunity for cost control through collective institutional decisions and actions. Recent studies of the economics and costs of higher education support this contention (Breneman, 1993; Massy and Zemsky, 1990; Massy and Wilger, 1992; Johnstone, 1993). Summarizing much of the analysis of curriculum and cost, *Policy Perspectives* states,

> The most difficult, most important and least considered part of the task is to achieve academic restructuring, which means defining a curriculum that is focused and coherent and that distinguishes clearly between core knowledge and periphery in its learning requirements. One can argue the need to sharpen and tighten the curriculum to ensure that graduates of an institution receive a

meaningful combination of learning experiences. An even more pointed reason to simplify the curriculum is to reduce costs—to realize savings that can be invested in programs, technology, and other emerging needs. The central lesson the "academic ratchet" teaches is that faculty specialization—and the discretionary time necessary to fund it—are the principal drivers of collegiate costs. When standing faculty teach primarily their own research specialties, they set in motion a process that yields course and hence cost proliferation on the one hand, and, on the other, the need for adjunct and other part-time faculty to teach the curriculum's core and required courses. ["To Dance with Change," 1994, p. 10A]

If the reduction and control of cost are potential benefits from a transformation of the curriculum, another major benefit is an improvement in the learning experience for students. The curriculum is designed explicitly to further student learning that the faculty believe is most valuable. Yet another benefit is the potential to reestablish faculty involvement in the central purpose of the institution and to recreate a sense of community. However, unless the transformation of the curriculum is guided by sound principles—above all, the principle that the change will improve quality—then it should not be used as a mode of cost control or reduction.

The accretion shaping the curriculum is the result of multiple causes: the enormous growth of higher education, the vastly increased demand for higher education, the breakdown of a common idea of what constitutes an educated person, the growth of knowledge with corresponding demands for new subject areas and new issues to be added to the course of studies, the intensifying process of the professionalization of the faculty, the ascent—or descent—to paradigmatic power of the research model of the university. Perhaps above all else this junkyard accretion suggests that it was easier simply to appease and accommodate everyone than to fight the battles within the academy. Financial crises may well enable us to unravel the complex web of motivations that led to our present curricular morass; they may well motivate us to beneficial changes. One immediate caveat (an indeed important warning), however: if curricular transformation is the royal road to cost containment, improved quality, and a renewed sense of community, it can only be accomplished as a short-term investment strategy to achieve long-range goals including fiscal reduction and restraint.

Undertaking curricular transformation as an investment strategy requires the articulation of a clear institutional sense of mission that can then be reflected in the curriculum. The curriculum is the nexus through which our scholarly activities relate us to our immediate colleagues and to the larger academic community. Curriculum change must reflect a clear and distinct mission, achieving an appropriate balance between an inherited order of knowledge and new areas that provide students with the knowledge, methods, and skills demanded by the world of work. The mission and therefore the curriculum will differ from institution to institution; hence curricular transformation, while being guided by national developments, must start with a sound analysis of the immediate institutional context.

Many institutions plunge into curricular change without taking the time to develop a shared understanding of the institutional mission and the context in which change will take place. An understanding of the mission, the student body, the institutional environment, and the nature and use of the existing curriculum is essential; only on that basis can a clear design for transformation be developed.

While it is true that our current challenges reflect recent economic, political, and social causes, we should not lose sight of the longer-term processes that are operating. In his study of European higher education in the last two centuries, Fritz Ringer points out that between 1870 and 1910 major structural changes transformed the European educational systems, changes accompanied by conflicts within education and wide-ranging public debates about education. Ringer argues that these transformations created institutional patterns still in effect. As he reminds us:

> One way to describe the changes of this critical period is to point out that they brought secondary and higher education into closer interaction with the occupational system of the high industrial era. Primarily involved on the side of the educational system were certain younger and less prestigious institutions and curricula that were considered "modern," "technical" and "applied," and thus potentially fruitful contributors to economic and technological progress. Primarily affected on the side of the occupational system was a range of younger professions that came to require more education than their earlier industrial precursors, yet arguably more relevant to commerce and industry. The partial and sectoral convergence between the educational and the occupational systems that began in this way during the late nineteenth century has continued, through recurrent crises, ever since. [1992, p. 29]

Extending Curricular Transformation

As we attempt to align our curriculum to current needs within current constraints, and as we seek to reawaken a sense of community within our faculties, we must also seek to maintain our perspective and realize that we are going through one of the recurrent crises of the last hundred years of higher education. This is not to suggest that such crises do not significantly alter the enterprise, but rather to remind ourselves that higher education has been—and will continue to be—transformed as significant structural changes occur in society. Like the changes of the 1890s, our current changes require that we develop our institutional missions with a profound sensitivity to the relation between our educational and occupational systems.

Most institutional mission statements, while long and noble, offer little help in describing what the institution really hopes to accomplish and how it will move to assess its performance. A mission must derive from some basic defining characteristics of the institution and its context. As an example, an urban public university can be characterized as committed to excellence in undergraduate education, providing access to graduate and professional programs appropriate to the needs and opportunities of its metropolitan area, responsive to the particular needs of working urban students, committed to the improvement of the quality of life in its community, promoting an academic research network through collaboration with other agencies in its community, supporting a network of educational institutions in the area to provide access and support student success, seeking partnerships and collaborative ventures at the graduate and professional level with other institutions of higher education in its community, and designing its scholarly agenda to respond to community needs. With these characteristics defined, a general education program suited to the institution can be designed as a significant part of a curricular transformation, undergraduate business and engineering programs can employ workplace experiences for student teams, or appropriate degree programs, minors, or course clusters can be developed such as urban environmental planning or community development, or child and family studies.

We still frequently encode a particular type of student in much of the language of higher education, for example, freshman, sophomore, junior, senior, or those in four-year degree programs. One recent report asks, "What kind of people do we want our *children* and *grandchildren* to be? What kind of society do we want them to live in?" (emphasis added) (Wingspread Group on Higher Education, 1993, p. 167). At many institutions, however, the four traditional student levels, the traditional time to degree, the designation of students as our children and grandchildren do not correspond to any reality. Institutions must begin discussions of curricular change by clearly discriminating who their students really are. Traditional college students, the eighteen- to twenty-two-year-olds who matriculate directly from high school, are already a minority among students in American higher education. The new majority is increasingly diverse in terms of gender, age, and ethnicity. If seeking a degree—not the universal goal—many students may attend a number of different institutions, take longer than four years to complete the baccalaureate, and require substantial amounts of financial aid (Institute for Research on Higher Education, 1995). It is unlikely that one curricular model can accommodate this new majority, either across institutions or within the same institution. As a movement toward national service evolves as a means of obtaining financial aid, institutions will need to develop greater flexibility and sensitivity in coordinating community service opportunities with the design and goals of academic programs.

Successful curricular change derives from research, both national and specific to the institution. The research should provide information about student success. What plans do students have when they first arrive? Do they intend to graduate, or to study for a time and then transfer? If students transfer or drop out, why? What percentage of students graduate in five years, six years, more than six years? Is this pattern different for students who enter as first-time college students from high school compared to students who have transferred to the institution? Is the institution doing better or worse than other schools with similar mission, environment, and student population?

Significant studies of higher education curriculum are an essential part of defining the larger context of educational reform; they can provide a sound basis for formulating productive research questions for institution-specific needs. For example, the Curricular Assessment project conducted by Zemsky (1990) provides valuable insight into the major disciplinary divisions—the humanities, social sciences, and natural and physical sciences—and the current state of their curricular structures. This research also identifies what portion of the curriculum provided to students is actually used by them to achieve their academic goals. Assessment of the impact of curricula on student learning is provided by Ratcliff (1992). This important work demonstrates the failure of the distribution model of general education and the effectiveness, by contrast, of the development of clusters of courses responding to diverse educational goals and providing developmental learning and skills acquisition. Astin (1992) adds important considerations about the relation of students' academic success and their involvement with the campus community. All these studies on the undergraduate curriculum can be used to frame campus-specific research, both to determine accurate student profiles, and to understand the functioning of specific curricula.

This research also assists us in formulating a program of inquiry that will enable faculty to understand the curriculum they offer as a product (or, if one prefers the term, an *artifact)*. We can then begin to judge whether that artifact is indeed a design, collectively and intentionally negotiated by the faculty to promote the learning of both specialized and general knowledge in response to student needs and social expectations, or whether it is (unhappily) a "junkyard of accretions" developed haphazardly out of individual faculty choices, reflecting the desire to teach one's specialty or research interest.

A program of inquiry into a curriculum should consider the following questions:

- To what extent do the institution's undergraduate programs respond to student learning goals?
- Has there been a proliferation of undergraduate course offerings because of the dominant influence of the field coverage model in disciplinary majors?
- Do undergraduate majors, particularly in the arts and sciences, reflect heterogeneous student intentions (that is, to begin advanced study of the subject, to pursue an interest unrelated to career intentions, or to prepare for graduate education in a profession outside the immediate scope of the subject)?
- Are there aspects of the curriculum that integrate or synthesize diverse fields of knowledge, or is each course or program a self-contained unit?
- Are students in each major or specialization directed to those areas of study outside the major that are most appropriate, most complementary to their academic goals?
- In what way are liberal arts and professional study integrated by the curriculum?
- Has the curriculum incorporated new instructional technologies?
- Can the curriculum be made more efficient and more flexible through differing course structures?
- Is there effective administrative oversight to assure that students can navigate the curriculum with minimal difficulty?
- Does the curriculum provide a purposeful general education experience?

A careful program of inquiry can also guide a taxonomy of the existing curriculum, which in many cases comprises not only a distribution model of general education, but also an array of disciplinary majors and professional programs, an assortment of minors, some interdisciplinary programs, and a random seasoning of electives. What we generally uncover through directed inquiry into the curriculum is the underlying assumption that the purpose of the curriculum is to give faculty the means to deliver knowledge (often envisioned as a static object, a mass of fact and data) and students an arena in which to acquire that mass of knowledge. The transfer of knowledge from this perspective is frequently a highly individualized activity in which an individual faculty member presents an organized fund of data, and students acquire that data, performing as individuals. The quality of the exchange is largely defined by input, and the curriculum is the result of individual faculty decisions; at best it approaches the status of a collective design only at the departmental level. Thus the curriculum is envisioned and realized as the transfer of information (in discrete and disarticulated units of knowledge) by autonomous persons to other autonomous persons.

If these are typical features of the normal curriculum, its transformation must be undertaken with the goal of changing these features (although this should surely not be our only goal). It is our contention that the transformation of these features is beneficial pedagogically in relation to student learning, economically in relation to institutional costs, and collegially in its promotion of a greater sense of community. Transformation should seek to change the curriculum from the packaging and transfer of discrete quanta of knowledge into a process of learning that enables students both to acquire knowledge and to apply it. Transformation must therefore provide a curriculum that augments the traditional isolated teaching and learning experience with opportunities for collective and collaborative learning and teaching, and, as well, one that augments the traditional evaluation of isolated performance (the midterm or final exam) with the opportunity for students to be assessed in the performance of collaborative learning. Transformation must allow quality to be determined not only by measuring inputs but also by measuring results. Transformation must seek to engage the faculty in designing the curriculum as a collective effort at every possible organizational level; it must seek a design that overcomes disconnection and fragmentation of the learning process.

In calling for institutions to undertake a top-down design and simplification of the undergraduate curriculum, the *Policy Perspectives* article "To Dance with Change" emphasizes the necessity for the faculty collectively to own the transformed curriculum and the strategies in teaching and learning that deliver it. To achieve this faculty commitment is a major undertaking and one that we have to carry out in a climate in higher education that is characterized by a loss of community. "Faculty are seen by themselves and others as acting as independently of one another, teaching their own courses, conducting their own research, making their own way. The kind of curriculum we have in mind cannot be delivered by a collection of independent contractors" (p. 11a). The lament over the loss of community, collective action, and responsibility is loud and frequent. While it is undoubtedly the case that the professionalization of the academy has led to the current situation, we must also recognize that the highly individual nature of university work has been a feature of academic life for some time. Haber, in his study of the American professions, describes the professoriate of the late nineteenth century in the early stages of its development into a modern profession:

> The leading professors of this era seem to have been a quirky lot who did not take easily to being drilled to even a common agreed upon end. Put together on any sort of parade ground, they often went marching off in all directions, while their democratically elected sergeant bellowed helplessly.
>
> As a result, the professor transformed independence to autonomy. This set him apart, somewhat, from the self-employed professionals, for the professor's

independence did not mean complete freedom from external control but rather that the most essential commands would not come from his own will or from the organization of which he was a part, but from exalted values beyond the reach of both. He would largely be self-directed and, at the same time, responsible. He would be sovereign and, at the same time, subject. This was the source of the dignity that was associated with the burgeoning profession of the professoriate. [Haber, 1991, p. 293]

In recommending curricular transformation as a process that can achieve greater responsiveness to our environment and community, and concerted action on the part of the faculty, we do so in full appreciation of Haber's analysis, its reminder that the modern faculty member during this century is a paradoxical being for whom individual action is culturally encoded. Community will not be harmony or consensus; it will be negotiated collective action. We shall arrive—if we can—at an *agonistic* community where struggle is the accepted norm. The competition of disciplines is at the heart of the curriculum and is embedded in the academic community. As Graff (1992) has persuasively argued, one of the problems with our current curricula is their ability to allow us both to disengage from our natural *agon* and to veil the conflict from our students:

Insofar as controversy is the life and soul of an intellectual institution, the consequences of avoiding or muffling it could only be *harmful* to the curriculum, which was left without a means of connecting subjects, perspectives, and courses and thus of confronting its own most urgent disagreements. Instead of becoming centers of continuous intellectual discussion, universities quarantined the intellectual life within the hours of class time, creating a great disjuncture between the intellectual intensity of the classroom and the social life of the campus. It was not the existence of the bureaucratic fields in themselves that was the problem, or even the idea that these fields should be covered, but the failure to develop a principle of connection that would have opened up a dialogue among them. . . . One of the advantages of the field coverage principle of organization was that it made departments and curricula virtually self-administering. Once the conventional spread of the fields was fully staffed and the courses were accordingly distributed and assigned, larger questions about the aims of the humanities and sciences and the relations of disparate periods, methodologies, and values seemingly took care of themselves. [1992, p. 140]

Curricular change that continues the tradition of adding on to cover the field, or that seeks to find connections and meta-reflections on the disciplines through special programs for a few students, enables the faculty to remain largely detached from the vital issue of designing an overall curriculum appropriate to the mission of a particular institution. However, a process capable of realizing and achieving such a design will have to involve almost all faculty and in doing so will produce a greater sense of community and responsibility.

Transforming the curriculum can improve undergraduate education and it can engage the faculty, but can it assist in facing fiscal and budgetary trends that force reductions or at best require cost containment? It is our contention that such transformation is essential in achieving the financial results we urgently need. One of the structural problems with the distribution model of general education is that it is an inflationary driver of cost.

The field coverage approach to disciplinary majors, and the increasing specialization of course topics it produces, combines with the development of interdisciplinary courses and programs to worsen the course proliferation already embedded in the distribution model of general education. For legitimate reasons on the part of individual faculty or on the part of department or programs, courses proliferate—but we have rarely monitored course development according to a well-designed overall curriculum. The result of course proliferation has been, as both the American Association of Colleges Curriculum Assessment Studies and the National Center for Postsecondary Teaching, Learning, and Assessment Differential Coursework Patterns Project argue, a significant proportion of total course offerings (between 20 percent and 25 percent) are underutilized by students in completing their undergraduate programs.

To transform the current curricular models into more cost-effective (and indeed better) programs for student learning, a significant proportion of the faculty must be engaged in the endeavor. To accomplish this engagement a number of different strategies must be employed responding to the diverse interests (and in fact the diverse motivations) of the faculty.

Portland State: One Institution's Strategy

It is clear that each institution must design the curriculum appropriate to its own mission and context, and the strategies for faculty engagement must therefore also be contextual. Nonetheless, a description of the strategy we employed at Portland State can illustrate the process.

Background and Problem Definition

The distribution model at Portland State University (quarter system with three-hour classes) required students to complete a total of fifty-four credit hours, consisting of eighteen credit hours divided between two departments in each of the three distribution areas (Science, Arts and Letters, and Social Science). The university further required that eighteen of the total credit hours must be in upper division coursework, divided between two of the major distribution areas. There was a six-hour diversity requirement that could be fulfilled by taking courses from an approved list. In addition, six hours of English composition and three hours of health education were required. This general education program was structured completely around departmental, disciplinary courses; so much so, in fact, that courses that did not carry a departmental prefix did not fulfill general education requirements. Although having its own peculiarities, this is not an uncommon model.

As an urban school with a large part-time student population and an overall student population with diverse demands of work, family, and school, we strive to accommodate our students with course offerings from 8 A.M. to 9 P.M. To enable that student population to fulfill our distribution requirements, we had to try to offer all our courses at all possible times, in a variety of patterns, and in duplicate section offerings. In other words, the distribution model—to be effective in meeting student curricular needs—required an inordinate number of courses and sections and thus required the investment of disproportionately large percentages of the overall budget in personnel costs. This experience vividly illustrated Zemsky's point that the acceleration of cost occurs where there is "an underutilization of teaching capacity [class enrollments smaller than considered optimum for the class] compounded by lower than average teaching loads and a commitment to increased scope [field coverage]" (1990, p. 30). These factors are a structural part of the distribution model of general education.

In 1990, Portland State's president began a strategic planning process. Faculty and administrators who had been at the institution for any length of time emitted a collective groan, since the campus community had already repeatedly been planned (at roughly decade-long intervals), yet had never seen any tangible results from the effort. This time the process yielded better results. A two-sentence mission statement was crafted after discussion with many constituencies:

> The mission of Portland State University is to enhance the intellectual, social, cultural, and economic qualities of urban life by providing access throughout the life span to a quality liberal education for undergraduates and an appropriate array of professional and graduate programs especially relevant to the metropolitan area. The University will actively promote development of a network of educational institutions that will serve the community and will conduct research and community service to support a high quality educational environment and reflect issues important to the metropolitan area.

We then proceeded to lay the groundwork for curricular redesign in anticipation of the goals of this mission.

We began the process of curricular design by asking the faculty senate to address the issue of undergraduate education, by holding open meetings to discuss general education, and by selecting sixty faculty members to discuss possible innovations in interdisciplinary education. As anticipated, the attempts on the part of the faculty senate to conduct discussions on undergraduate education were unsuccessful. The discussion on general education with self-selected faculty resulted in the appointment of a committee charged with reviewing and recommending a general education program appropriate to our mission. From the discussion on interdisciplinary education, ten projects, those that were seen as integrating the mission and the curriculum, were defined. A critical factor in achieving success in these two ventures was an accompanying development program. Funding was provided to send faculty to national meetings that addressed undergraduate curriculum, as well as to bring consultants to campus. Within less than a year, we had a proposal for a major transformation of general education and six interdisciplinary proposals, ranging from degree programs collaboratively developed with local community colleges to options that integrated liberal and professional education.

The general education proposal was presented to the faculty senate, approved by a sizable majority, and moved to implementation. A very valuable technique emerged from this process, one that we have adapted to the subsequent stages of our transformation process. As well as bringing to bear the substantial national research on general education, we researched our own institutional history of general education reform. The construction of that history was one of the powerful tools for neutralizing the inevitable force of faculty inertia; it confronted us with the history of our own failures to effectively construct a meaningful program of general education.

New General Education Program

Portland State University adopted a general education program called University Studies, which marks a significant departure from distribution area requirements. University Studies serves the contemporary student with a more coherent and cohesive curriculum, with the ultimate goal of producing graduates with the attitudes and skills to pursue lifelong learning. In addition to an overall enhancement of the undergraduate experience, this research-based program is designed to develop collaborative ability in and provide teamwork experience for our students. It should also address our current low retention and degree completion rates, build coordination with secondary schools and community colleges, and improve relationships with the community through a required community learning experience. Our research and discussion in the field of general education scholarship led us to identify several key attributes of a program responsive to particular needs of Portland State students:

- Team-teaching
- Interdisciplinary programs and course clusters
- Integration of academic skills within course content
- Inclusion of diversity and multicultural themes across the curriculum
- Student community service and learning
- Enhancement of student-student and faculty-student interaction

Table 25.1 lists the current and new general education requirements. The new program is being phased in over a four-year period beginning in the fall of 1994. For this university, these changes are significant and indicate the depth of the commitment of this faculty and administration to the improvement of undergraduate education.

Four elements are expected to be common to all courses in the program, so as to emphasize four educational goals: communication, diversity and multiculturalism, inquiry and critical thinking, and ethical issues and social responsibility.

The capstone experience consists of interdisciplinary student teams, led by faculty, conducting community-based projects. The intent is to provide an opportunity for students to apply their skills to problems in the metropolitan community and for them to experience problem solving in a team setting. This requirement means that all graduates of Portland State University will have at least one community-based learning experience as part of their undergraduate education. This is a significant innovation for this university. Portland State University annually awards some 1,900 undergraduate degrees. This means that each year somewhat more than 2,000 students will be participating in some 250 different Capstone projects. This is a major undertaking and reflects this university's commitment to fulfilling its urban mission. The three main objectives of the senior capstone experience are: to provide an opportunity for students to apply the expertise learned in the major to real issues and problems; to give students experience working in a team context, necessitating collaboration with persons from different fields of specialization; and to provide the opportunity for students to become actively involved in this community.

Redesign of the Majors

With our general education program approved and on the way to implementation, we then turned to changes in majors. Following our earlier strategy, we solicited volunteers and started with five departmental majors and the undergraduate business program.

The five departments that have undertaken a revision of the major are history, sociology, mathematics, physics, and English. The revisions have varied, but they have had three commonalities: (1) fewer lower division hours were re-

TABLE 25.1. PORTLAND STATE UNIVERSITY REQUIREMENTS— BEFORE AND AFTER SEPTEMBER 1994.

Previous Requirements	Credits	New Requirements	Credits
1 Basic: 18 credits from each of the three academic distribution areas, in two departments per area. Of this total, 18 credits must be earned upper division coursework in the academic distribution areas with no more than 12 in one department.	54	1 Freshman Inquiry: Three 5-credit courses	15
2 Two courses (6 credits) of diversity coursework from the approved list. Courses must be taken from two different departments. These credits may be included in the 54-credit distribution requirement.		2 Sophomore Year: Three 4-credit courses selected from different interdisciplinary programs or general education cluster.	12
3 Writing 121	3	3 Junior or Senior Years: Complete one interdisciplinary program or general education cluster (four 3-credit courses).	12
4 Writing 323	3	4 Senior Capstone Experience	6
5 PHE 295	3		
(Minimum)	63	(Minimum)	45

quired for each major; (2) there was an attempt to build the educational goals defined in general education into courses required for the major, particularly writing and computer skills; and (3) there was an attempt to provide more direction for ancillary coursework outside the major. All of these revisions have been implemented and we continue to bring more departments into the review process. We have also undertaken a study to define the goals of liberal education for students completing majors in the arts and sciences, and we expect a faculty task force's recommendations by fall 1997.

Bringing It All Together

Rather than the a priori attempt to design a new curriculum, we have proceeded by soliciting and supporting endeavors to change each of the main components of the structure: general education, professional degree programs, disciplinary majors, and electives. Our goal is to achieve a design that has a general education program that is competency-based, developmental over four levels of learning, and mission-related through a significant collaborative learning experience in the community. Writing, mathematical skills, and diversity goals are integrated into the program and are not presented in free-standing courses. We have also reduced the general education requirement from sixty-three to forty-five hours (White, 1994, pp. 168–229). We are reducing the number of lower division courses required for departmental majors and are asking departments to develop a clear purpose for lower division disciplinary courses. Where possible, we have asked departments to seek to achieve this purpose through more comprehensive lower division foundation courses that will serve more than one discipline. We are using pilot projects in selected majors that can demonstrate streamlining the major and asking that electives be seen as connectors and students advised on the appropriate use of elective courses. Interdisciplinary courses and options are designed to fit general education goals and therefore be more integral to the curricular design. Finally we are providing incentives, training, and the upgrading of classrooms to introduce more instructional technology and forms of interactive learning into the curriculum.

Our process of curricular transformation at Portland State is a work in progress but we are able to identify what has been accomplished to date and what results we are beginning to see. The first three years of the program have been implemented and we are developing the community-based learning courses for the fourth-year capstone. Although it is early, we have seen 20 percent increases in retention rates in the first cohort of students. We are seeing extensive faculty interest; to date a hundred faculty members are participating in designing and delivering courses. More important, that cohort of faculty have increased by 20 percent the amount of time they spend in planning, discussing, and evaluating their work in the program. Over eighty faculty members have participated in special workshops on instructional technology, pedagogy, and assessment. Finally, we have had 75 percent of our departments revising departmental offerings in relationship to the new general education program.

We have also seen greater faculty involvement in engaging two critical issues. We have a faculty task force studying the concept of liberal education and its redefinition in terms of our institutional mission and a faculty task force engaging in a two-year study, "Defining Faculty for an Urban University in the Twenty-First Century." In addition, forty-five faculty members have successfully secured curricular development, assessment, and pedagogy grants that within two years have brought in $2.8 million in external funding. While not all of our faculty have been directly involved, there is a large, active, involved group of faculty committed to aligning their work with institutional priorities.

In the case of the Portland State example or in any other attempt to achieve curricular transformation, the ultimate cost savings can only be achieved by an investment of resources to provide for faculty development, to support the transition from the current curriculum to the new design, and to establish the administrative structure that will enable the new design to work. Curricular designs calling on faculty to develop new skills (for example, the ability to incorporate the use of new technology, or to design new forms of faculty-student interactions such as collaborative learning or community-based service learning) can only be effectively introduced if the campus creates appropriate support structures. We were able to offer both technical assistance in the design of new courses and curricula and support for collaborative and joint projects with community agencies, public and private, and with other educational institutions. Such investment requires the institutional budget to be examined with a view to identifying funds for short- and long-term support for a new curricular design. This will probably require rethinking campus operations and administration to free resources for the transformation until savings can be obtained from within the instructional budget.

Conclusion

The labor of curricular transformation is indeed immense but it is also undeniably a task essential to the continuing improvement of our undergraduate programs—and therefore central to all of our missions. Such a labor cannot be accomplished immediately, but it can begin immediately and proceed expeditiously. In undertaking it, we will be responding to the requests of external agencies and we will be serving the needs and interests of our students. In *The Battleground of the Curriculum,* Carnochan concludes his analysis with this compelling admonition:

> Lacking adequate criteria of purpose, we do not know how well our higher education works in practice or even exactly what working well would mean. We could do better on both counts. The Universities need not only to understand their own history better and how that history intersects with the larger history of the nation but also to understand what they have been trying individually and collectively to do and then, as good sense may suggest, take steps needed to bring ends and means into closer alignment. . . . Finally, in the large social arena where educational questions come into play, more charitable habits of mind would not be a bad thing either. [Carnochan, 1993, p. 126]

References

Astin, A. W. *What Matters in College? Four Critical Years Revisited.* San Francisco: Jossey-Bass, 1992.

Bizzell, P., and Herzberg, B. *The Rhetorical Tradition: Readings from Classical Times to the Present.* Boston: St. Martin's Press, 1990.

Breneman, D. *Higher Education: On a Collision Course with New Realities.* Boston: American Student Assistance, 1993.

Carnochan, W. B. *The Battleground of the Curriculum: Liberal Education and American Experience.* Stanford, Calif.: Stanford University Press, 1993.

Graff, G. *Beyond the Culture Wars: How Teaching the Conflicts Can Revitalize American Education.* New York: Norton, 1992.

Green, J. S., Levine, A., and Associates. *Opportunity in Adversity.* San Francisco: Jossey-Bass, 1985.

Haber, S. *The Quest for Authority and Honor in the American Professions.* Chicago: University of Chicago Press, 1991.

Hamel, G. "Seeing the Future First." *Fortune,* 1994, *130*(5), 64.

Institute for Research on Higher Education. *Change, the Landscape, the Educational Journey of Transfer Students.* Philadelphia: Institute for Research on Higher Education, University of Pennsylvania, 1995.

Johnstone, D. B. *Learning Productivity: A New Imperative for American Higher Education.* Studies in Public Higher Education, no. 3. Albany: Office of the Chancellor, State University of New York, 1993.

Levine, A. "Program: A Focus on Purpose and Performance." In A. M. Levine and J. Green (eds.), *Opportunity in Adversity.* San Francisco: Jossey-Bass, 1985.

Massy, W., and Wilger, A. "Productivity in Postsecondary Education: A New Approach." *Educational Evaluation and Policy Analysis,* 1992, *14*(4), 361–376.

Massy, W., and Zemsky, R. "Cost Containment: Committing to A New Economic Reality." *Change,* 1990, *22*(6), 16–22.

Nietzsche, F. *The Gay Science* (W. Kaufmann, trans.). New York: Vintage Books, 1974. (Originally published 1882.)

Ratcliff, J. L. (ed.). *Assessment and Curriculum Reform.* New Directions for Higher Education, no. 80. San Francisco: Jossey-Bass, 1992.

Ringer, F. *Fields of Knowledge, French Academic Culture in Comparative Perspective, 1890–1920.* Cambridge: Cambridge University Press, 1992.

"To Dance with Change." *Policy Perspectives,* 1994, *5*(3), 1A–6A.

Toombs, W., and Tierney, W. *Meeting the Mandate: Renewing the College and Departmental Curriculum.* ASHE-ERIC Higher Education Report No. 6. Washington, D.C.: School of Education and Human Development, George Washington University, 1991.

White, C. R. "A Model for Comprehensive Reform in General Education: Portland State University." *Journal of General Education,* 1994, *43*(3), 168–229.

Wingspread Group on Higher Education. *An American Imperative: Higher Expectations for Higher Education.* Racine, Wisc.: Johnson Foundation, 1993.

Zemsky, R. "Curriculum and Cost." *Liberal Education,* 1990, *76*(4), 26–30.

CHAPTER TWENTY-SIX

ACHIEVING EFFECTIVENESS AND EFFICIENCY

Ann S. Ferren

After addressing early signs of potential financial trouble during the 1980s by raising tuition, expanding programs, and increasing enrollment, higher education administrators and faculty are finding sobering the rising costs, severely limited resources, and tougher competition of the 1990s. Many colleges and universities, struggling with straitened finances, wonder how long they can continue to "do the same with less" much less hope to "do more with less" before they are forced to "do less with less." Guskin captured both faculty and administrator attention with his two-part series "Reducing Costs and Enhancing Student Learning" in *Change* magazine when he suggested economizing through significant restructuring of both the administration and the role of the faculty. Guskin not only urged an end to raising tuition to cover budget challenges, but also asserted that "doing less" need not harm student learning (Guskin, 1994b, p. 19). He called for eliminating outdated activities so as to increase productivity, stating, "The key to dealing with lower revenue while maintaining quality lies in rethinking the nature of the work being done" (Guskin, 1994a, p. 27).

One particularly difficult area to rethink in its entirety is the curriculum. Indeed, a college president recently confided to a group of colleagues that with downsizing, cost containment, reengineering, cross-functional teamwork, and budget reallocations, he has gone as far as he can go to balance the college budget. His cost-cutting and efficiency strategies include new technology for registration, streamlining cleaning services, outsourcing the bookstore, eliminating some midlevel managers, reducing travel funds, deferring maintenance, and curtailing program development. The biggest single expense in the budget, however, remains faculty salaries, a cost that has hardly been touched. His current efficiency strategies do not include the curriculum, yet he suspects that there are courses that do not have to be taught and faculty resources that could be reallocated or eliminated.

His concern illustrates the key reason why the curriculum cannot readily be managed for fiscal efficiency; it is well insulated from the levels of institutional decision making focused on costs and budgets. While the curriculum was once under the authority of the board and the president, the responsibility for curriculum has been delegated to departments, programs, and individual faculty members. Consequently, those responsible for developing courses and curriculum—the faculty—are not in close contact with those responsible for managing costs and assuring the financial stability of the institution—the central administration.

Today, two consequences stemming from this distributed responsibility are producing harmful effects on both effectiveness and efficiency. First, curricula tend to be fragmented and driven by the interests of specialists. Faculty members often think of educational issues in terms of their own discipline and department, rather than in terms of the needs of students or the overall configuration of institutional offerings. While a decade of reform activity focused on general education and the undergraduate curriculum has helped faculty members identify common values and create programs that provide more coherent educational experiences for students, these reforms typically touch only a part of the curriculum (Gaff, 1991). Widespread criticism of the quality of higher education remains based on the claim that student learning, not faculty interests, should be at the center of the enterprise.

The second consequence of distributed responsibility is that faculty members develop courses and curricula to match their interests and without much concern for issues of cost. The faculty, individually and in departments, tend to protect their turf, add specialized courses that represent new developments in their fields, and advocate lower teaching loads. Although incorporating new knowledge or seeking more time for research is important and often defensible, these actions drive up costs. The long tradition of changing the curriculum through addition of courses, rather than through substitution, has left the curriculum bloated and cluttered with the former interests of faculty members.

The faculty often are guided by a conception of quality that they are trying to achieve, but there is no comparable analytic framework to evaluate efficiency— leaving the curriculum unmanageable by academic vice presidents, financial officers, and presidents who are responsible for the financial health of their institutions. Administration efforts to review faculty workload or raise class sizes as a measured attempt to control expenditures are deemed intrusive and insensitive to faculty and student interests. Program review, with carefully designed quality indicators, promotes effectiveness but seldom contains sufficient financial criteria to improve efficiency, and recommendations to cut programs—whether because of quality or cost—are resisted. Invariably, faculty members and administrators are seldom in the same room to discuss both the vitality and the viability of the curriculum.

To respond to the current pressures to both improve and economize, these two constituencies and two quite different lines of thought and action must be drawn together. Management concerns such as competitiveness and accountability must be directly linked with educational improvement issues such as educational purposes and assessment of outcomes. To date, the management and improvement agendas have been on very different tracks and have involved very different people. The management agenda is led by presidents, financial officers, and planners on campus with the encouragement of coordinating boards, governors, and legislators off campus. The improvement agenda is led by faculty members, academic administrators, and student affairs staff on campus with the support of leaders in foundations and educational associations off campus. These separate initiatives focused on cost and quality must come together, and a new combination of leaders needs to become involved in the conversation about curriculum, both nationally and on each campus, if we are going to rethink the nature of the work being done.

Central to this effort must be clear definitions of the terms of the conversation. If curriculum is defined as every course offered, then effectiveness (producing the desired results, accomplishing specified outcomes) means meeting course objectives and passing rates, and *efficiency* (using resources to meet goals with no waste, ideally, a high ratio of output to input) can be measured in terms of enrollments and cost per student. If curriculum is defined as an integrated course of study such as general education or the major, then effectiveness can be measured in terms of performance on program goals, learning outcomes, and progress toward a degree, and efficiency can be measured in terms of cost of all resources used to support the program per number of students who successfully complete the program. If curriculum is defined as the overall offerings of the institution, all programs of study, then effectiveness can be measured in terms of graduation rates, career placement, and alumni satisfaction, and efficiency can be measured in terms of cost per student to graduation, instructional costs as a portion of overall costs offset by increased revenues from tuition, and external support attracted due to the quality of the programs.

In the final analysis, however, if we endorse Guskin's view, the concept of curriculum will change, the role of the teacher will be redesigned, and learning will not be measured in courses and credits. With learning productivity and not faculty productivity as the focus, both effectiveness and efficiency will be achieved when faculty create an optimal learning environment that is motivating, focused, and experiential, and challenges individual learners to meet their highest potential (Guskin, 1994b, pp. 18, 19). Curriculum is then a dynamic process that cannot be separated from pedagogy, input is meaningful only if linked to outcomes, and effectiveness and efficiency are both redefined in terms of how much and how well students learn.

The Curricular Marketplace

Faculty and administrators have easy access to the literature on curriculum and pedagogy that focuses on improvement. Guidance on efficiency in higher education is less available and focuses primarily on restructuring administration. Even less is written to synthesize our understanding of effectiveness and efficiency focused on curriculum. This volume describes the many efforts under way to enhance the effectiveness of the curriculum. This chapter describes what current behaviors get in the way of greater efficiency and then discusses the challenge of achieving both effectiveness and efficiency. The basic economic concepts of supply and demand can help frame the rethinking of the college curriculum by clarifying the difference between faculty and student interests.

Curriculum development has traditionally relied on what faculty want to offer. Faculty believe they know best what students should learn and how they should learn it. Courses are designed, credit hours assigned, class sizes set, prerequisites selected, and requirements approved based on assumptions of the faculty about what content and structure will promote learning. To students, the curriculum represents a variety of choices, and demand is most concretely expressed through selection of institution, declaration of major, and enrollment in courses. Observers of the curricular reform movement note, "Campus initiatives have focused disproportionately on the programs we *provide* . . . the 'supply side' . . . and have largely ignored the 'demand side'" (Johnston and others, 1991, p. 181). They argue that this is detrimental to effectiveness; it is also detrimental to efficiency.

Zemsky's (1989) work on transcript analysis makes clear how complex and diffuse the idea of a curriculum is. He notes that curriculum is neither the supply of courses nor what the individual student takes. The real curriculum, he argues, can best be understood by looking at the intersection of aggregate supply and demand (Zemsky, 1989, p. 14). To maximize both effectiveness and efficiency, the narrowest possible gap would be desirable. In other words, the faculty would design a coherent, well-structured, and meaningful curriculum, which would be exactly what students experience. Unfortunately, his research reveals in many institutions a "remarkable disjunction between faculty activity and student activity" resulting in, as an extreme example of inefficiency, students concentrating "80 percent of their course credits in less than 30 percent of the total number of courses" (pp. 14, 16).

Theoretically, a market mechanism applied to the curriculum would optimize resource allocation and student choice, match supply and demand, and result in greater efficiency. A wide variety of accepted practices in higher education, however, regulate the academic marketplace in ways that impede efficiencies in the curriculum. The market mechanism described by economists is the arrangement through which buyers and sellers interact and price and quantity are determined. At equilibrium, no shortages and no surpluses are found. The market solves the basic issues of what will be offered, for whom, and how. Campuses, however, apply educational principles and assumptions to override allocational decisions, shape supply and demand, and otherwise modify the market mechanism. The resulting imperfect match of supply and demand may either drive up the per-unit cost of education or result in such scarcity of courses that students are delayed in meeting graduation requirements.

To understand the inefficiencies in the curriculum, we have to look at the ways in which both demand and supply are manipulated, and then ask to what extent the decisions are defensible because they lead to greater effectiveness and a better undergraduate education. On the demand side, for example, we do not allow complete student freedom of choice; rather, programs of study are prescribed, general education requirements are laid out, and the choice of majors is fixed. Structure is imposed without efficiency in mind because faculty believe a good education or effective curriculum makes students learn some things they might not choose. Anyone who has participated in curriculum building knows that most of these requirements have intellectual and educational integrity. Some requirements, however, are a result of turf protection and political compromise. Indeed, requirements are sometimes adopted to assure that a department's or a faculty member's courses are enrolled. In this way, demand is created artificially and, instead of a curricular marketplace, there is a political marketplace on the campus. With a free market, demand would surely drive out some products and some producers.

Conversely, demand can be suppressed. Faculty members wishing to lighten their teaching load can offer their courses at unpopular times such as 8 A.M. on Monday, knowing that few students will enroll. Demand is further affected when faculty are allowed to set limits on class size, for few registration systems record and systematically analyze expressed demand through recording first and second choices or establishing a course waiting list. Consequently, few campuses know what the unfilled demand for a course is. At the program level, the institution often intervenes in the market mechanism by setting limits on particular programs, for example, engineering, pharmacy, physical therapy, and clinical psychology. Students competing for limited spaces are forced to take second-choice programs or go to another institution.

The legitimate concern of administrators, of course, is that if curricula were totally demand driven, overall balance in the college or university would be lost, one program would overwhelm another, and certain areas of study would be driven out altogether due to lack of demand. Faculty members and deans often defend these controls in the face of student demand for professional programs by arguing that the liberal arts and their centrality to the institution must be preserved. These actions might well be justified as instances where educational effectiveness is endorsed as more important than efficiency.

Faculty prerogative and individual interest also create interventions on the supply side of the curriculum. At the course level, faculty become used to owning the courses they offer year after year, despite shifting student interest. If faculty do not keep up in their fields or become increasingly specialized, they cannot easily change their course offerings. When a new area of study emerges, instead of reassigning a faculty member, the department argues instead for hiring someone new. Typically, departments make the argument for additional specialists as a measure of quality, as they equate a wide variety of course offerings with excellence.

Departmental self-interest emerges most strongly when budget reductions threaten to reduce the total number of faculty positions. Any excess capacity is deliberately hidden since departments recognize how hard it is to get back a faculty tenure line once it is lost. Department enrollments are divided into many courses and sections to keep all faculty occupied. Every retirement is viewed as a risk of losing a faculty line, and departments argue for resource replacement even if the faculty position might be more productively used in another department or unit. The heavy hand of the central administration is criticized for market adjustments or reallocations of resources.

Certain disciplines with unstructured majors, such as history and literature, have adopted an open enrollment strategy and offer many elective courses with no prerequisites to compete for students and use excess capacity. If faculty are feeling adventurous or innovative, there is little to restrict what they want to offer. Numerous experimental and special-topic courses, not subject to standard procedures for review, show up in the curriculum—providing wonderful intellectual opportunity for faculty, adding more choices for students, but further stretching resources. Arguments develop over whether the number of enrollments should supersede number of majors as the measure for competing for scarce resources, and some departments may find their service load both reassuring and an unwelcome burden. Under all these circumstances, as faculty and institutional interests conflict, it is difficult to address systematically either effectiveness or efficiency of the curriculum, and student learning is often given second priority.

Further complications develop as campuses, recognizing the limitations of trying to manage declining budgets through cost cutting alone, adopt an entrepreneurial spirit and create new programs for new populations. These efforts to generate new revenues also affect both effectiveness and efficiency of the curriculum. New product lines such as adult education programs, designed to keep institutions competitive and in the black, place additional pressures on the curriculum as programs proliferate in an effort to capture new markets. New majors are created by clustering courses to meet the needs of returning adults or businesses committed to on-site opportunities for their employees. Adjunct and temporary faculty are used to lower costs and maintain flexibility. The effectiveness and efficiency criteria for these new initiatives are even murkier than for the traditional curriculum because they are seldom subjected to full cost accounting and held to a budget bottom line. Nor are they always created and managed through the normal academic channels with the requirement that they match the mission of the institution and have clearly established standards for quality review.

Clearly, interference with a market mechanism can affect what courses are offered, lead to oversupply, and drive up costs of the curriculum. With small classes and low student/faculty ratios, the unit cost of instruction increases. Class size and faculty workload are not the only measures of efficiency, however. The cost of the curriculum must also be measured in terms of overhead and the list of uncounted costs of the curriculum are many, usually showing up aggregated on separate balance sheets for library, physical plant, or the computer center rather than attached to individual departments and programs. If total costs were carefully calculated, and that were the only measure of comparative efficiency, many colleges and universities might well give up teaching undergraduate science, for example, because of the high overhead for such programs compared to other courses of study.

Even if the actual dollars spent on all inputs including faculty are fully measured, this would still not provide an accurate index of the true costs of the curriculum. Campuses generally fail to apply the economic concept of *opportunity cost*, and this means they do an inadequate job of evaluating allocation of resources no matter how carefully they track expenditures. There are choices for every dollar and every hour spent. If spent on salary, the dollar cannot be spent on technology. Similarly, if time is spent on teaching, it cannot be spent on research. Few curricular decisions are made with a clear idea of alternatives or opportunities forgone for either faculty or students.

Only recently has the concept of opportunity cost for students received any attention. Astin argues that student time is the most important resource and that we need to increase involvement in learning and actual time on task. Johnstone (1993), an advocate for shortened degrees and more self-paced learning, encourages higher expectations as well as more flexibility so that students are better prepared and sooner out in the workforce. He calls for less "fun," "drift," and "easy rides" so that students can learn more and faster (pp. 9–13).

To some extent, the concept of opportunity cost has been distorted as resources have diminished and institutions have created programs on the backs of faculty, expecting their energy to be stretched to meet the need. Further, we have deferred maintenance of classrooms, hoping that the physical plant would retain most of its asset value even if neglected—and have not measured the cost of tuition forgone when students choose not to attend because of the shabby environment. Ignoring scarcity and trying to stretch diminishing resources across all the same programs and courses eventually lead to diminishing productivity and effectiveness.

During the boom years in higher education, there were no fiscal incentives to change faculty or student behavior or to view the curriculum as a whole. The first waves of budget reductions often exempted academic units and faculty as colleges and universities resisted the very notion that they should manage faculty resources. Staff and administrators were cut first. As financial concerns deepened, however, pressure shifted to unstructured programs and affected faculty resources. Typically, leaders first imposed reductions across the board, creating systemic weakness in both strong and weak areas. If this was not enough, then attention turned to what was easiest to cut, such as positions vacated through retirement or entire programs that were small or experimental. Coupled with increasing tuition, this response to financial pressures appears to have gone as far as it can. It is now time to align resources with educational needs. This requires undertaking the difficult task of rethinking the whole.

Intersections of Effectiveness and Efficiency

To rethink the curriculum as a whole requires a better understanding of how the principles that currently shape the design and structure of the undergraduate curriculum also form the multiple points where effectiveness and efficiency intersect—at the level of the course, the program, the department, and the overall educational offerings of the college or university. Examples from a variety of campus experiences will demonstrate how difficult it is to maximize both educational quality and the allocation of scarce resources.

Principle #1: There are certain skills that all students should develop.

Colleges and universities have long assumed that one of their key roles is to develop a wide variety of basic skills. This goal is pursued in a variety of ways, including separate formal courses, noncredit support services, and skill instruction embedded in courses across the curriculum. A significant number of campuses use the model of required writing and mathematics courses for all entering freshmen taught in small sections to support effective learning. Given that these are required courses for a captive audience, maximum efficiency in faculty and facility use should also be achievable through assigning specialized faculty resources, filling each section before opening another one, and distributing sections across time slots to fill out classrooms efficiently. In reality, effectiveness and efficiency can end up pitted against each other.

One university, for example, decided to teach the required mathematics courses in sections of forty-five to conserve faculty resources because experience showed that by midsemester, an average of only thirty-five students remained in each class. Unfortunately, the final grades revealed that only an average of twenty-five of the original forty-five enrolled in each section received the required C grade to earn credit for the math requirement. While offering the course in large sections appeared efficient, in reality it was neither effective nor efficient because students were not successful and 40 percent of the students repeated the course, which placed demand on faculty resources a second time. Offering the course in smaller sections based on careful placement to improve student success would be both better for the students and a better use of resources. Redesigning the program around technology, tutoring support, or a collaborative learning approach (as discussed in Chapter Twenty-Two) may appear costly but could further add to both learning effectiveness and efficient use of faculty resources and student time.

Any campus focused on both quality and cost of basic skills instruction will want to ask some key questions:

- What faculty resources (full-time, adjunct, graduate student, temporary) promote both effectiveness and efficiency in basic skills instruction?
- Do basic skills courses serve a function in persistence, thus retaining students at significant economic benefit to the institution in terms of tuition dollars and other revenues?
- Can basic skills be integrated into all courses and thus strengthen the effectiveness of basic skills learning as well as eliminate faculty resources devoted only to basic skills instruction?
- Are there noninstructional investments that will lead to greater curricular productivity as measured by student success?

- What are the true costs of underresourcing basic skills programs in terms of learning productivity throughout the curriculum?

Principle #2:   Students should study a variety of disciplines to learn different modes of inquiry and acquire a broad general education.

Many of the curricular innovations in the 1980s sought to counteract loose distribution requirements from which students ended up with an amorphous education made up of little more than a major and introductions to a number of disciplines. The resulting reform debate and planning on campuses created an array of general education programs reflecting the diversity of institutions in terms of content, structure, credit hours, pedagogy, and management. Despite the variety, the new programs shared a common goal. They provided students with a more limited and coherent set of offerings in an effort to increase program effectiveness. A brief analysis of a typical model of general education illustrates how difficult it is to manage the curriculum for both effectiveness and efficiency.

A common model of general education is a structured set of requirements in which students select from designated courses across the whole range of disciplines. The courses are designed to meet the distinctive goals of the general education program, but may also meet requirements for the major. Departments are credited with the enrollments, which is a boon for departments with a small number of majors. Even though the program is structured, there is substantial choice so that if a faculty member is on leave or a course section is full, students can select another course. The effectiveness of the program is bolstered by having full-time faculty teach in the program, build on their individual strengths, and use carefully designed syllabi that meet the overall goals of the program. This model also appears to maximize efficiency, as it uses the resources already available on campus to support the program without detracting from other departmental offerings. Section sizes are set to match incoming student enrollments and the number of courses is adjusted as pipeline shifts in enrollments occur. There is no opportunity cost caused by faculty retraining to teach outside their discipline.

Sustaining this balance over time, however, can be difficult. One program director notes that, although the program is highly efficient, he is now concerned about effectiveness and program drift. New faculty are beginning to reshape the uniquely designed general education courses to look more like major requirements. Upperclass students are taking the courses as electives while others put off taking the required courses until they can get their first choice, resulting in more and more juniors and seniors taking courses designed for freshmen. Class sizes are creeping above the averages in other courses as departments try to reduce the departmental resources committed to the university-wide program. Transfer coursework is more liberally matched with program requirements to attract more transfer students to the university. Clearly, even with a well-planned program and close management of resources, departmental behavior and student behavior can alter both the available resources and the way in which a program is experienced, potentially reducing learning.

As campuses renew their general education programs and work to sustain them at a time of limited resources, they will face a number of questions about how best to balance effectiveness and efficiency:

- Can investing in the administration of general education (a director, staff assistant, faculty advisory committee) both maximize efficiency through planning and enrollment management and improve effectiveness through faculty development and assessment?
- Do limits on course availability force students to take courses in patterns that do not match the intentions of the program designers?
- Does allowing general education courses to count for the major lead to efficient use of faculty resources or distort the course purposes?
- Does allowing students to take general education courses as electives use valuable spaces in these small classes or does it reduce the need for broad course selection throughout the curriculum?
- Do strict transfer agreements protect the integrity of the program or screen out courses that should be accepted for general education, thus causing the host institution to teach too many general education courses and the students to repeat coursework, thus wasting both faculty and student resources?

Principle #3: Students should study one area in depth.

Traditionally, departments have designed majors with requirements to help students develop a full understanding of the mode of inquiry and scope of knowledge in a particular discipline and its related fields. In addition to an introductory course, the major is often structured around a few required core courses, a choice of upper-level courses, and, more recently, a culminating capstone experience. While colleges and universities set minimum credit requirements for majors, over time curriculum creep sets in, as first one requirement and then another is added. Eventually, through accretion, a major that was once thirty-six credits may become forty-five or more. Understandably, faculty want to offer a full range of subspecialties to meet their interests and those of the students. Programmatic accreditation associations may insist on certain courses, credits, and laboratory or clinical experiences in order to grant program recognition. Ideally, this internal differentiation is prompted by faculty perceptions about effectiveness of the major;

in practice, it can result in courses with overlapping content and fragmented enrollments. Despite general commitment to a sequential structure, there is no real clarity about the purposes of these intermediate courses referred to by one observer as the "muddle in the middle" (Association of American Colleges and Universities, 1995). When there are few if any prerequisites, nonmajors with little or no preparation can take a so-called advanced course, potentially diluting the effectiveness that might result from true sequenced learning (Adelman, 1995, pp. 36–38).

Deans and department chairs charged with oversight of the major may limit their analyses to a few gross measures to determine how things are going: overall departmental enrollments, average class size, number of majors, and faculty satisfaction. Program review aimed at assuring quality routinely asks questions about faculty research productivity, space, and use of technology, yet seldom asks fundamental questions about the intellectual structure and the scope of the major. Only the recent work of the Association of American Colleges and Universities (as described in Chapter Eleven) has addressed the meaning of the major in any systematic way. Conclusions from a national study are that, overall, the major—the central commitment in the undergraduate curriculum—lacks "collective purpose," "a discernible sense of progression," or agreement on the "intellectual tasks" of introductory, intermediate, or advanced coursework (Association of American Colleges and Universities, 1995, pp. 1–2). These findings suggest that student learning outcomes and not the structure of course offerings should be the focus for achieving effectiveness. Letting go of meaningless structures would, in turn, open up new ways of assessing the costs and efficiency of the major.

Two examples can illustrate the ways in which efficiency is challenged by the current curricular structure of major requirements. The first example focuses on a traditional discipline-based major. As student interests shift, some majors once very vital, such as classics, geography, or linguistics, are virtually abandoned. Left behind may be a fully tenured faculty with a set of courses to teach for which there is diminishing demand. With low enrollments, the per-student cost of instruction in major courses increases, although a large service component, perhaps in general education courses and the introductory course, may be used to balance the individual faculty member's workload and meet university standards for faculty productivity. When the program review process flags these declining enrollments and questions whether the French major, for example, should be continued, the response is, predictably, "What kind of liberal arts college would we be without a French major?" When encouraged to restructure the major to take better advantage of student interest, faculty resources, and related fields, the department is likely to respond, "Our major will not remain 'respectable' if it does not have the same structure as every other French major at every other institution." In short, defenders of the major claim the effectiveness of the institution is at stake with no consideration of cost.

Because there is no agreement on which majors are essential nor on how each must be structured, such departmental assertions cannot be tested. A number of actions could increase departmental efficiency while still retaining many of the educational benefits of the discipline. The department might rotate course offerings over a two-year cycle, reduce the number of choices at the intermediate level, offer the senior capstone as an interdisciplinary course supported by several small majors, or, conceivably, eliminate the major and offer only a minor. Many a department has created more flexibility by eliminating the concept of faculty ownership of courses, supporting retraining to overcome specialization, and rotating faculty through the introductory courses to eliminate the need for sabbatical and retirement replacements.

In an effort to retain the major for a very small number of students, some departments have come to expect faculty to teach the upper-level courses as uncompensated overload without measuring the long-term costs to faculty, including burnout. If one of the goals of the major is to create a community of scholars, effectiveness as well as efficiency is questionable without a critical mass of students. At some point, if the rigid discipline-based major cannot be recreated around student learning, program elimination may be best for both the institution and the student.

Increasing numbers of students are ignoring traditional majors and seeking specially designed majors and flexible interdisciplinary programs to match their interests and maximize their potential career-related skills. Far ahead of faculty with their innovative views, many students do not hold sacred the disciplinary boundaries and want to combine fields such as design, communication, computer science or business, languages, and area studies. Some students resist highly structured majors or the prospect of taking a double major because they want enough flexibility to fit internships, study abroad, and a variety of electives into their program. Increasing numbers of students transfer, collecting courses at several institutions. Broad interdisciplinary majors called social sciences or liberal studies become the easiest way for these students to complete requirements for a degree. Campuses concerned about enrollments are particularly vulnerable to the temptation to create a major to match any student's interests.

Self-designed or unstructured majors challenge traditional notions of effectiveness for it is unclear whether they really represent study in depth, the purpose of the major. They have many elements that enhance learning, including extensive choice, individualized support, and application—but assessing learning outcomes can be difficult if the program goals are idiosyncratic or unspecified.

Measuring efficiency is also complicated, as such incoherent student demand tests efficient use of resources both in terms of opportunity costs for faculty providing individualized courses of study and in direct costs for creating an office of interdisciplinary studies or providing additional advising. Program proliferation and flexibility make it difficult to attribute costs and predict, plan, and match course enrollments to faculty resources. It is far more efficient to track students into structured programs.

The nature of the disciplines, structure of majors, and purposes of the programs must be considered when trying to accomplish both effectiveness and efficiency in the department-level curriculum:

- How many majors can an institution support? Must a campus offer a certain number of traditional majors to be credible in its Carnegie classification?
- How might the structures of majors, based on traditional disciplinary structures, evolve to meet new needs and better use resources?
- Should some departments offer only service courses and not a major, and if so, how would both effectiveness and efficiency of the institution be affected?
- Can administrative costs be reduced by eliminating duplication of support services, advisers, and chairs, and managing curricula collaboratively through advisory boards rather than departments?
- Can efficiency be created by managing course offerings on a two- or three-year cycle to maximize enrollments while still preserving student choice and allowing faculty to teach specialties?
- Might the approval for inclusion in the major of related courses from other departments maximize class sizes while still meeting curricular goals of relatedness, depth, variety, and student choice?

Principle #4:   Students should have choice in their course selection appropriate to their individual needs and interests.

At one time, the rule of thumb for a student's course of study was approximately one-third of the program would be for breadth, achieved through general education; one-third would be for depth, represented by the major; and the remaining third would be for individual interests, accomplished through electives. Many factors have affected that formula over the years and, at some institutions, prescribed distribution or general education requirements may take up to half the credits for the degree. Some majors require more than half the student's time. Students often complain that there are almost no free electives in their program. During the curricular reforms of the last decade, little attention was given to the role of electives. We do know that students do not take advantage of the breadth of the curriculum; instead, they select courses close to their major field of study (Boyer and Ahlgren, 1987, p. 441). This may reinforce their learning in the chosen field but also narrows their overall perspective. Nonetheless, the elective course is assumed to be an important element of the undergraduate experience in support of the goal that college should develop individual interests and skills that lead to lifelong learning.

Even in highly structured programs, students can exercise choice in general education courses, choice in courses related to the major, and choice among experiential opportunities such as internships, cooperative education, service learning, independent study, and study abroad. Faculty recognize that students appear to learn more because they are far more committed and involved in courses that they choose than in courses that they have to take.

Market demand drives student choice of electives. Market theory would suggest that student choice alone would maximize efficiency within the undergraduate curriculum. Yet a pure market of electives does not truly exist, because it is influenced by requirements in general education, major, and minor. There is no comparable indication, however, that choice leads to efficient use of resources. The measure for efficiency for electives remains an elusive concept. Theoretically, if all the elective courses chosen are discretionary, that is, they are not a required part of any program, and there is excess capacity elsewhere in the curriculum, the total number of different courses available could be reduced to create more efficiency overall without severely limiting student opportunity to pursue personal interests.

Offering students a broad choice of special-interest courses in the undergraduate curriculum puts pressure on resources as well as program quality. A striking example is the role physical education activity courses play on campuses that do not have a physical education requirement. Because of growing societal awareness of health issues, many students are interested in taking weight training, aerobics, and other fitness courses as a way of rounding out their education. Faculty and administrators recognize the importance of these courses but also raise quality concerns about such issues as appropriate credit, number of activity credits to count toward the degree, and academic rigor of these courses. In contrast, students often complain about the amount of work expected, claiming, "It's only an elective." The bold efficiency question is whether a campus should continue to commit faculty and capital resources to formal instruction in swimming or first aid and CPR when virtually the same training is available through community resources at little or no cost. A more complex analysis would look at opportunity costs including what is lost when portions of the athletic facility, in order to hold class, have to be closed to faculty, students, staff, and community members who would use it for recreational purposes. The analysis could also test whether the Student Affairs programming could incorporate stress management and other health-related topics at lower cost and with greater impact. When overall student learning productivity resulting from wellness programs is added to the cost-benefit analysis, there may be a strong case for continuing the investment.

Any effort to improve effectiveness and efficiency related to electives requires documenting the reasons why students make course choices and then determining whether reducing the scope of the curriculum and rationalizing offerings will reduce costs without adversely affecting student learning and satisfaction.

- How much choice does a student need?
- How much variety in course offerings can a campus afford?
- What kinds of courses should be available to students as electives?
- Might the need for choice be accommodated at least, in part, by having students choose from among the courses offered as part of required programs?
- Could effectiveness of the curriculum as well as efficiency be enhanced by offering a managed set of elective courses that also reflect important educational commitments of the institution (for example, "Conflict Resolution" or "Cross-Cultural Communication")?
- Given increasingly diverse needs of students, should curriculum be more or less structured?

Questionable Assumptions

The five principles that currently structure the undergraduate degree are grounded on assumptions about what assures a high-quality education—skill development, coherence, breadth, reinforcement, and integration of learning experiences, to name just a few. The implicit assumption about effectiveness, of course, is that students take the programs exactly as designed by the faculty and approved by the institution. However, the most powerful data available, student transcripts, reveal that in reality students earn the baccalaureate degree through coursework that does not match faculty expectations about structure and selection. This reality must be part of the effort to rethink the curriculum.

If students do not experience that curriculum as designed, it could be argued that faculty should try to make them do so, by enforcing requirements and prerequisites before giving up on their current version of the curriculum. A review of student petitions for exceptions to academic policy may demonstrate, however, a range of reasons for accommodating student needs and interests; many may be closely related to the students' ability to finish a program of study in a timely way—one measure of efficiency. Making students take the program only as it is offered might result in far fewer students' enrolling in and completing programs—

affecting efficiency of institutions. Rethinking the curriculum based on what we know about student course-taking behavior and the ways in which they cluster the courses they take can open up new possibilities for curriculum design and allocation of resources.

There are other assumptions that also get in the way of rethinking the curriculum as a whole, many of them implicit rather than explicit:

- The more specialized courses a department offers, the better it is.
- Every faculty member ought to have the opportunity to teach one or more specialties.
- The curriculum should be both fixed and changing at the same time.
- Courses should be offered to satisfy all available markets and emerging interests.
- Enrollments are a measure of a department's success.
- Reducing class size will improve quality.

There is limited evidence to support these claims, yet such assumptions unwittingly shape the context for discussing curricula and get in the way of new ideas that could lead to change and increased learning productivity.

A parallel discussion of the curriculum with students might reveal competing claims about what leads to a quality education:

- There should be fewer requirements.
- Students should always get their first choices of class.
- Courses should be available at convenient times.
- There should be more opportunities for independent and individualized study.
- Coursework should help students get good jobs and have career mobility.

Students can provide valuable contributions to the difficult task of designing curricula that maximize both learning and resource use; such involvement may also create a better understanding of the conflicting perspectives on the curriculum.

Rethinking the curriculum requires laying out all the assumptions that guide institutional and individual behavior, for it is beliefs, values, and philosophies that shape the curriculum as surely as content, structure, and resources. Clearly, if it were easy to rethink the curriculum as a whole, more campuses would be doing so. Chapter Twenty-Five describes the multiyear process that helped one institution clarify its mission, identify its assumptions, and create common ground so that the curriculum could be structured around enhanced student learning and better management of resources. Campuses not yet engaged in such a comprehensive process are using a number of other approaches aimed at creating curricular efficiency without sacrificing quality. While several focus on how to reduce inputs and faculty labor costs, the ideal is to seek ways to increase outcomes as well.

Managing the Curriculum to Achieve Effectiveness and Efficiency

Quality has been the driving force behind faculty commitment to curricular renewal over the last decade. The result is a myriad of new structures, transformed content, and innovative pedagogies to enhance student learning and nurture the lifelong transforming power of education. Because of concern about the staying power of reforms, attention has also been paid to the institutional conditions and administrative structures necessary to sustain changes in the undergraduate curriculum (Association of American Colleges, 1994). New economic imperatives require that the cost of the curriculum and the impact of budget reductions on the curriculum also be assessed. Colleges and universities that wish to remain vital, relevant, and responsive to individual and societal needs should be committed to both quality and value, especially in the curriculum and the classroom.

To achieve both effectiveness and efficiency requires collaboration and new approaches that merge careful administrative leadership with faculty creativity and support. The approaches to effectiveness still are given the greatest attention, yet strategies to achieve greater efficiency deserve equal consideration. Stronger management, elimination of waste, reducing overhead, careful planning, better data, and greater flexibility in resource use are the foundation for maintaining quality with diminished resources in the short run. In the long run, however, only significant rethinking of what we do and how we do it, the faculty-student interaction and the medium for learning, will make it possible to sustain the twin goals of quality and value.

The first and most direct short-run approach a campus can take to increase efficiency while maintaining effectiveness is a *managed* curriculum. This approach makes either the individual course or a single program the unit of analysis and aims to optimize faculty resource use. Efficiency in this case is defined as "the distribution of students across courses such that actual enrollments per course (or course section) taught by a regular member of the faculty equal the ideal class size for the pedagogy used for that course (or section)" (Zemsky, 1990, p. 26). Application of this approach requires identifying the appropriate class size for each course, calculating the number of students who want that course, and offering only the number of seats that are likely to be fully enrolled. To maintain learning effectiveness, the faculty or department chairs must know what ideal class size matches content and pedagogy. This is not easy. Indeed, when faculty are asked merely to define a small class, the range may be from ten to fifty. When asked to estimate the number to whom they can lecture effectively, they report a range from thirty to three hundred. If these ideal student-faculty ratios can be established and learning outcomes monitored, the curriculum can be managed for efficiency without detracting from outcomes.

In contrast, many of the initial efforts to manage curriculum efficiency were limited to an examination of the faculty member and the program through analyses of workload and credit-hour production; indicators of learning effectiveness or the potential for restructuring the learning experience were not considered. This curriculum management approach is attractive because it is easy to impose via decision rules—for example: no class with fewer than ten students can be offered, every faculty member must teach six classes averaging thirty students per year, and no program below a certain income/expense ratio can be continued. However, to avoid fragmentation due to focusing solely on the individual course, the individual faculty member, or the individual program as the level of analysis, the relationships among the components of the curriculum must be considered. To assure that effectiveness and efficiency receive equal attention, the *managed curriculum* must be defined in the context of the rich research literature on learning environments and learning outcomes and not by numbers alone (Astin, 1992; Pascarella and Terenzini, 1991; Erickson and Strommer, 1991).

Any effort to manage the curriculum needs also to take into account faculty culture and legitimate concerns about autonomy and equity. Questions about individual faculty productivity as a basis for curricular efficiency directly challenge the faculty prerogative to determine what they teach, to whom, how, and when. This principle is not just an expectation based on past practice, rather it is a clear policy on many campuses. One faculty handbook states it this way: "Insofar as is possible, faculty should be permitted to teach the courses they prefer in the areas of their particular expertise, providing that student needs are met. Scheduling of courses and determination of examination policies should, insofar as possible, reflect the wishes of the department members teaching those courses." Better management of the curriculum would require both a change in policy and full faculty involvement to create support. Even when optimizing behavior is anchored to student learning, it still may be met with resistance similar to that of faculty on a unionized campus who began to wear "Stop Work—Speed-Up" buttons in response to budget reductions and workload adjustments that were imposed across the board.

A second tool a campus might use, based on actual enrollments and credit distribution, is to examine students' course choice and demand as the unit of analysis. This process seeks to identify the *discretionary curriculum*—courses that are not a requirement for any major, nor a general education requirement, nor a prerequisite for any required higher-level courses. These courses are not unimportant, yet they are subject to choice and therefore represent a resource that could be allocated in a different way and according to different priorities.

To identify these discretionary courses, institutional researchers select a sample from a graduating cohort for study, code the transcripts to identify courses taken as electives and not required for any program, calculate the proportion of credits earned in such courses, and test for substitutability, that is if the course were not offered, could the student select from among the other offerings in the curriculum in a related field and find space. The elimination of these courses would force redistribution of students to unused capacity in ongoing programs and courses and reduce the gap between supply and demand. Removing a percentage of those courses from the curriculum would not affect the effectiveness of programs, though it would modestly curtail student choice and faculty initiative. The greater the reduction in disparity between courses offered and the concentration of student credits, the greater the savings in faculty resources.

Unfortunately, a few areas of the curriculum can be especially hard hit by using this approach. It is hard to justify, for example, the continuation of several less common foreign languages such as Hindi, Swedish, and Dutch when there are few enrollments and many other options for foreign language study. Similarly, many special-topic courses such as "Oliver Stone's America" and "Children in Classical Antiquity," though perhaps enriching to the overall curriculum and to the faculty who create them, are hard to defend as institutional priorities when there are scarce resources to be allocated. One option to maintain some of the richness is to merely limit the number of special-topic courses to a certain percentage of the curriculum. Some campuses have limited costs by using only adjunct faculty to offer special-topic courses, however, this approach relegates full-time faculty to repeating the same required courses again and again and detracts from their development over time. A promising approach that meets faculty, student, and institutional needs is for several institutions to form a consortium to share curricular offerings and faculty resources, to pool enrollments, and thus continue to offer collectively a wide variety of courses and programs through cross-registration while eliminating duplication of effort on each campus.

A third approach to increasing efficiency uses the program and the institution as the units of analysis and focuses on reducing costs by *redesigning the curriculum to be taught by fewer faculty*. Many campuses are already refraining from filling positions vacated through resignations and retirements. This approach has the drawback that the impact on the department and overall curriculum is not altogether rational because the positions are randomly scattered throughout the institution. In some cases, retirements are bunched in a single unit reflecting a department demographic profile that matched programmatic developments in the 1960s or 1970s. It would be preferable to reallocate positions rationally, as it has been clear for at least a decade that faculty distribution across the various disciplines does not match current enrollment patterns. Occupational and professional majors, for example, have increased faster than the available faculty while the traditional arts and sciences majors have decreased, leaving an excess of tenured faculty. ("Tracking the Undergraduate Major," 1985, p. 33). Reallocating positions other than as they become available through resignations and retirements, however, is very difficult for most campuses due to strict guidelines for treatment of faculty if programs are eliminated.

A rational approach to reducing faculty expenditures is based on campus data that show approximately 10 percent of the faculty is away at any one time on sabbatical or other kinds of leave. Thus the curriculum could be redesigned to be handled by 90 percent of the faculty positions on the books. No temporary, visiting, or adjunct faculty would be hired to take the place of faculty on leave, which would effectively reduce the number of faculty. A 10-percent reallocation of students among remaining classes would mean that the average class size would go from twenty to twenty-two, for example, generally a manageable change for the faculty. Assuming multiple sections, the full range of course offerings would be reduced by something less than 10 percent. The major savings is achieved through the elimination of replacement faculty and overload expenses. Using the same principle, some campus observers have suggested redeploying faculty resources to enhance learning by reducing committee sizes by 10 percent, reducing meetings by 10 percent, and more.

It has long been assumed that tenure is a cause of inefficiency, guaranteeing employment in a narrowly specialized job with no flexibility to meet changing conditions. Economists trying to understand the impact of tenure come to conflicting conclusions, however, arguing on one hand that low turnover lowers cost and job security promotes effectiveness, while claiming, on the other hand, that tenure forces specialization and results in mismatching of employees and positions that raises costs (McPherson and Winston, 1993, p. 110). Recent discussions about tenure, sponsored by the American Association of Higher Education, reveal that many campuses are planning for a more flexible future by reducing the number of tenure lines and hiring faculty only on term contracts. One incentive is that faculty who are not eligible for tenure can handle larger teaching loads because they have no research responsibilities. Already there is concern, however, that over time this will have an impact on the tenure-track faculty, who will carry a disproportionate load in self-governance and service to their professions, with consequent negative impact on service to students.

A fourth approach to efficiency emphasizes the role of *faculty development* to promote greater flexibility in the deployment of faculty resources. Faculty inflexibility may be the major cause of the rigid supply problem, underutilization of some faculty, and inability to reshape programs over time. For this strategy, the unit of analysis is not just the individual faculty member but also the department and the entire institution. This long-range view regards the institution as seeking to create greater flexibility in faculty assignments to match emerging programmatic needs so that faculty resources can be deployed to accomplish the highest levels of curricular effectiveness. It also recognizes that faculty are a resource in constant need of renewal and support to maintain high-quality teaching.

The enormous success in retraining faculty to teach interdisciplinary general education courses and interdisciplinary majors such as environmental science and women's and gender studies is ample evidence that faculty can successfully expand their teaching repertoires. Indeed, faculty report being energized by the new opportunities and studies of faculty careers demonstrate that faculty are quite resilient and shift interests and priorities over the course of a career (Blackburn and Lawrence, 1995). To date, few institutions have fully developed that flexibility to institutional needs and have allowed differential contributions from faculty.

The new fiscal conditions require a different kind of faculty development, breaking from the past when teaching workshops, seminars, and consultation were all aimed at helping the faculty member become better at what he or she chose. The new faculty development approach asks each individual to identify an individualized contribution to the overall mission of the department or program. It also asks what specific support will be needed to maximize that contribution, and sets out how that contribution will be rewarded. Theoretically, each faculty member can have a different profile building on strengths and including a different mix of advising, teaching, administration, research, community service, and more. The department chair serves as negotiator, broker, and coach to bring all the resources of the unit together and prepare people to fill new roles as they are identified. This proactive faculty development model can place both student learning and institutional productivity at the center.

A fifth approach to efficiency frames the whole institution as the unit of analysis, uses *strategic planning,* and requires sophisticated use of data management systems to provide appropriate information to review past performance and then project out five to ten years. There is general agreement that institutional adjustments have come many years after events. The downturn in career opportunities for engineers or teachers or Ph.D.'s rippled through institutions, taking six to eight years before colleges and universities reactively adjusted their curriculum and faculty resources to declining student enrollments. Similarly, colleges and universities are slow to spot trends suggesting increasing need. To be efficient, institutions must be more nimble, and able to adjust proactively to the environment and changing needs. Some of this planning—especially in state systems expecting rapidly increasing enrollments—must begin at the system level, where alternatives for better utilization of resources can be modeled that expand access and preserve quality based on different roles for each campus (Jordan, 1992).

Strategic planning aims to make proactive curricular adjustments based on a realistic appraisal of strengths and weaknesses compared to competitors and identification of future opportunities that make the most of available resources. Strategic planning requires a partnership between the institutional research office and academic affairs to conduct regular environmental scanning and then link the information to institutional data. Idiosyncratic evolution of the curriculum is replaced with planned change and renewal through substitution. Involving faculty in the comprehensive planning process not only reduces the suspicion faculty have of institutional data that contradicts their disparate anecdotal and experiential data, but also engages them directly in the responsibility for institutional well-being.

Both internal and external data are essential to model for effectiveness and efficiency. Internal data include, for example, tracking student applications, admissions, matriculants, retention, and numbers of graduates by major. Trend analyses can be developed for key ratios such as the number of students to number of majors, number of students to number of courses, and number of full-time faculty to number of students. External data include, for example, demographic trends, career needs and employment opportunities, and economic forecasts. Projections based on changes in parameters of the models encourage analysis of alternative scenarios and support systematic change efforts rather than trial-and-error decision making. Proactive curricular renewal is based on enrollment modeling, faculty succession planning (considering projected retirements as well as retraining needs), planned reduction in expenditures coupled with increases in revenue, systematic strategies for effective resource allocation and reallocation, and assessment of student outcomes.

To make this approach effective requires replacing periodic five-year planning with continuous planning and replacing periodic program review with annual review. Identifying key questions for analysis and assembling comprehensive data renews the authority of deans, department chairs, and curriculum committees to reconcile course supply and demand, eliminate inefficient use of faculty time and facilities, and rebalance individual faculty commitments among teaching, research, and service. It also allows an institution to reallocate limited resources to fund new initiatives and to create risk capital for new programs that expect to bring greater educational returns.

Finally, a strategy most appropriate for the long run is the application of *quality principles* to rethink, restructure, and transform the curriculum as a whole. This strategy aims to create a self-renewing organization with high faculty and student satisfaction by developing a powerful shared vision, simplifying procedures, eliminating bureaucratic structures, creating teamwork, delegating decision making, defining measurable outcomes, and gathering performance information on all parts of the system as a basis for continuous change. The curriculum is shaped for both effectiveness and efficiency within the parameters of a sharp and compelling mission for the institution. Attention shifts from resources to results.

Rethinking the curriculum in this strategy requires rethinking pedagogy as well. The role of the faculty is restructured to take advantage of new technologies, peer learning, and new pedagogies that "maximize the essential faculty-student inter-action" (Guskin, 1994b, p. 19). To manage with fewer resources while sustaining quality requires that faculty think less about teaching and more about learning, seeing themselves less as supervisors and more as facilitators of learning. Faculty workload productivity measures and average class size analyses are set aside in favor of measures of student productivity. New ideas about when and how students learn replace credits, courses, and semesters as the units of learning (Johnstone, 1993). To do this, faculty have to raise questions about the fundamental purposes of the curriculum, clarify their vision of the learning students will need for the future, and then consider how to deploy valuable resources in new ways to accomplish those student-focused goals.

Documenting results of the curriculum is an essential part of the continuous improvement process. To date, faculty have been relatively reluctant to engage in comprehensive assessment because they are not persuaded of the value of assessment. If faculty can tie data to answering important questions about how well their students are learning and how they fare after graduation, assessment activities become meaningful. Careful cost-benefit analysis can be applied to programs and help set benchmarks for both effectiveness and efficiency.

One aspect that needs to be restructured as part of rethinking the curriculum is the administration of the curriculum and the process by which it is changed. The current departmental and college structures on campuses create competition rather than teamwork. The separate decision-making processes make it hard to evaluate proposed curricular changes by institutional criteria. The many layers of review for significant curricular change, designed presumably for quality control, are more rigid and bureaucratic than ever intended, keeping the institution from being nimble. A new proactive and efficient design based (see Chapter Thirty-Three) on forecasting environmental and student needs (see Chapter Six) can still preserve faculty initiative.

Simply recognizing the need for greater curricular efficiency, or the conflicts and overlaps between effectiveness and efficiency, or the possibility that resources allocated to faculty can be pared back without damaging student learning does not tell a campus what to do next. Asking the right questions and identifying change strategies that match the culture of the campus are essential first steps. It takes hard data, consultation, and deep consideration of what it means in the long run to "rethink the whole." Faculty who manage the curriculum cannot be expected to make decisions that are in their individual interest, the students' interests, and the institution's interests without information, incentives, and feedback. The administrators who manage resources cannot assure the quality and efficacy of academic programs without establishing a clear vision about learning and trusting the faculty. In short, the curriculum cannot be reshaped responsibly without a partnership between the faculty and the administration. To fully untie the knot of curricular effectiveness and efficiency, faculty and administrators need to have enough confidence in each other that they will both let go of the string.

References

Adelman, C. *The New College Course Map and Transcript Files: Changes in Course-Taking and Achievement, 1972–1993*. Washington, D.C.: Office of Educational Research and Improvement, U.S. Department of Education, 1995.

Association of American Colleges. *Strong Foundations: Twelve Principles for Effective General Education Programs*. Washington, D.C.: Association of American Colleges, 1994.

Association of American Colleges and Universities. *Changing the Major*. Washington, D.C.: Association of American Colleges and Universities, 1995.

Astin, A. W. *What Matters in College? Four Critical Years Revisited*. San Francisco: Jossey-Bass, 1992.

Blackburn, R., and Lawrence, J. *Faculty at Work: Motivation, Expectation, Satisfaction*. Baltimore, Md.: Johns Hopkins University Press, 1995.

Boyer, C. M., and Ahlgren, A. "Assessing Undergraduates' Patterns of Credit Distribution: Amount and Specialization." *Journal of Higher Education*, 1987, *58*, 430–442.

Erickson, B. L., and Strommer, D. W. *Teaching College Freshmen*. San Francisco: Jossey-Bass, 1991.

Gaff, J. G. *New Life for the College Curriculum: Assessing Achievements and Furthering Progress in the Reform of General Education*. San Francisco: Jossey-Bass, 1991.

Guskin, A. E. "Reducing Student Costs and Enhancing Student Learning." *Change*, July/Aug. 1994a, pp. 23–29.

Guskin, A. E. "Reducing Student Costs and Enhancing Student Learning." *Change*, Sept./Oct. 1994b, pp. 16–25.

Johnston, J. S., Jr., and others. "The Demand Side of General Education: Attending to Student Attitudes and Understandings." *The Journal of General Education*, 1991, *40*, 180–200.

Johnstone, D. B. *Learning Productivity: A New Imperative for American Higher Education*. Studies in Public Higher Education, no. 3. Albany: Office of the Chancellor, State University of New York, 1993.

Jordan, S. M. "Enrollment Demand in Arizona: Policy Choices and Social Consequences." In J. I. Gill and L. Saunders (eds.), *Developing Effective Policy Analysis in Higher Education*. New Directions for Institutional Research, no. 76. San Francisco: Jossey-Bass, 1992.

McPherson, M. S., and Winston, G. C. "The Economics of Academic Tenure: A Relational Perspective." In M. S. McPherson and others, *Paying the Piper: Productivity, Incentives, and Financing in U.S. Higher Education*. Ann Arbor: University of Michigan Press, 1993.

Pascarella, E. T., and Terenzini, P. T. *How College Affects Students: Findings and Insights from Twenty Years of Research*. San Francisco: Jossey-Bass, 1991.

"Tracking the Undergraduate Major." *Change*, Mar./Apr. 1985, pp. 31–33.

Zemsky, R. *Structure and Coherence: Measuring the Undergraduate Curriculum*. Washington, D.C.: Association of American Colleges, 1989.

Zemsky, R. "Curriculum and Cost." *Liberal Education*, 1990, *76*(4), 26–30.

CHAPTER TWENTY-SEVEN

PROMOTING COHERENCE IN TRANSFER PRACTICES

Judith S. Eaton

Conversations about curriculum and discussions about transfer have been staple features of higher education discourse for many years. For the most part, they have been held separately, focusing on different issues and conducted by different participants. They have varied in their importance to the higher education community, with the curriculum garnering a great deal more attention than transfer. Recently, however, these conversations are beginning to overlap, producing an opportunity for more thoughtful dialogue about transfer and its role in higher education.

Curriculum is the ultimate statement of what higher education values. It expresses the hopes and expectations of dedicated education professionals for the millions of students they engage daily. Curriculum gives shape to an institution's particular intellectual beliefs and aspirations; it graphically illustrates the academic choices that faculty have made for students. Curricular conversations have been going on for centuries; they are as enduring as the collegiate institutions in which they have been taking place.

Transfer is the primary strategy by which students navigate the varying demands of the 3,600 autonomous institutions that make up the current higher education enterprise. Reliance on transfer is reflected in student enrollment patterns that regularly include attendance at more than one institution to obtain the baccalaureate. Transfer has become a key strategy in addressing social justice concerns especially for some low-income and minority students, many of whom find it essential to begin their collegiate work in a two-year institution on their way to the baccalaureate. Transfer has also become an accountability strategy with growing public demand that colleges and universities document educational attainment—and this includes the contribution of transfer.

Setting the Stage: Understanding Transfer

Transfer refers to the movement of students from one institution to another. Students take certain packages of academic experiences from one institution and request that another institution formally recognize these packages—whether made up of courses, programs, or degrees. Transfer is a complex activity involving not only students but faculty, administrators, at least two institutions, many departmental interests, and perhaps even state regulations.

Millions of the students who attend more than one college or university on their way to the baccalaureate use the *standard transfer* practice: they start at a two-year school and move to a four-year institution to complete their undergraduate work. Other students engage in *reverse transfer:* moving from four-year to two-year institutions. Some use additional transfer alternatives: moving from one four-year institution to another or attending two institutions simultaneously.

Logistics of Transfer

Transfer is not easy. Students seeking to transfer immediately confront the decentralized and complex character of the American higher education enterprise.

This enterprise is structured to sustain differences among institutions and thus is not user friendly to those with transfer in mind. The United States has no ministry of education that centrally determines what is to be taught, ensuring some continuity of instruction across institutions. The varied institutions that make up the collegiate enterprise are not formally connected through national governance or funding mechanisms. The relationships among institutions are voluntary, created through institutional discretion that may or may not include serious attention to transfer.

This decentralization is sometimes advantageous, sometimes disadvantageous for transfer students. Advantages include the many choices of institutions—public and private, two- and four-year, undergraduate and graduate—that they may attend. The diversity of institutions is accompanied by diverse funding streams and governance patterns, creating a richness and energy in the enterprise. In spite of the absence of a national structure for higher education, there *is* some sharing across institutions: for example, virtually all subscribe to a credit approach to earning a degree, and degree requirements and course content are remarkably similar across institutions. Transfer students rely heavily on these similarities. Disadvantages include quality levels that can vary greatly; transfer students sometimes find, for example, that an A grade means doing a great deal of difficult work at one institution and much less at another. Students—and the public—cannot be assured that baccalaureate recipients from different institutions will have similar skills. The financial support for different institutions is radically uneven: students at public institutions, especially nonselective ones, will not be assured the same support per student that is found in the private sector.

Most students who rely on standard transfer begin their collegiate education in one of the country's 1,300 public community colleges: two-year institutions offering liberal arts and career education culminating in an associate degree. Standard transfer students are frequently low income and minority—those who are least well served by higher education. To address standard transfer thus means much more than just focusing on the academic relationship among institutions; it is a social and economic justice issue as well. For these students, transfer is not an option; it is a necessity to earn a degree. This necessity may be driven by a student's limited funds, which leads to attendance at a lower-priced public two-year institution. It may be the result of inadequate academic preparation, requiring assistance from two-year college developmental education programs. Or it may result from the need to hold a job while going to school—this places constraints on time and location options for students.

Transfer Effectiveness and Efficiency

For standard transfer to work effectively and efficiently, students need to move from one institution to another with a minimum of bureaucratic difficulty; they should make intellectual gains in the two-year coursework that are roughly comparable to the expected gains in the same courses in the four-year institution; and they should sustain a minimum loss of credit for coursework toward the baccalaureate. Although we do not have a comprehensive description of standard transfer that enables us to judge whether it meets efficiency and effectiveness expectations, we do have some valuable information.

Standard transfer involves an estimated two hundred thousand students per year across the country—roughly 22 percent to 24 percent of community college students who are first-time college-goers and who earn twelve credits or more in four years (Cohen, 1994). Three-quarters of those who transfer do so after earning forty-nine credits and approximately 37 percent transfer with the associate degree (Palmer, Ludwig, and Stapleton, 1994). Whether a particular community college has a high or low transfer rate makes a big difference to all the students it enrolls. A high-transfer-rate college, for example, sustains that rate for both minority and white students (Cohen, 1993). This contrasts with other findings that confirm differences in educational attainment among racial and ethnic groups. For example, although associate degree attainment varies some by race, this variation is not nearly so pronounced as with baccalaureate attainment, where blacks and Hispanics earn far fewer degrees than Asians and whites (National Center for Education Statistics, 1993).

Information about standard transfer from states and institutions is spotty at best. Some state departments of education collect data on transfer students, but do not establish state benchmarks or expectations of annual transfer activity. Individual community colleges do have some data on transfer, particularly about transfer to a primary receiving institution. Many, however, are not yet routinely calculating transfer rates. Private four-year colleges and universities are paying more attention to numbers of transfer students. Transfers are increasingly important to their attendance levels and are also an important additional strategy to bring minority students into their institutions. They are just beginning to develop some transfer information.

There are, to date, few clearly stated public expectations about a desired number of transfer students, either at the state or federal level. State legislatures express growing concern that more students should be transferring—without indicating what "more" means. In California, for example, transfer is essential to minority students who begin their collegiate work in a community college, and successful transfer is viewed as a key access strategy. Yet the state has not specifically defined its expectations in this area. In other states, there is a consensus among legislators that more transfer would mean that community colleges are more accountable, efficient, and effective and that four-year institutions are more sensitive to social justice concerns, but these elected officials are not explicit about their desires. Neither have legislators become sufficiently concerned to offer financial support for transfer initiatives, either through additional assistance to institutions that take more transfer students or to the students themselves. Congress and the U.S. Department of Education have not addressed either benchmarks for transfer or financial support earmarked for transfer.

As data collection improves, transfer rate calculations become commonplace, and public expectations are clarified, thoughtful judgments about the efficiency and effectiveness of transfer will emerge. Data collection on transfer needs to be accurate and routine, transfer benchmarks need to be set at institutional, state, and federal levels, and some policy direction is required to structure the role of transfer in undergraduate education. Much work remains to be done.

Dominant Strategies for Transfer

Two strategies have traditionally dominated transfer efforts in community colleges: a student support strategy and an administrative strategy. These efforts date back to the earliest days of the two-year college, when much of its work was preparing students to move to a four-year institution.

Student Support Strategy

A student support strategy focuses on providing transfer information, counseling, and advice to students. Almost all community colleges use this strategy to assist students who want to transfer. Typically, a student who is interested in transfer can go to an advising office, a counseling center, or a transfer center. Catalogues, course equivalency guides, and specially prepared transfer materials offer information about graduation requirements, how specific courses transfer, and grade requirements for entry to a four-year institution and its individual schools. Today this information is available electronically as well as in pamphlets, brochures, and other print materials.

Some community colleges hire counselors and advisers who specialize in transfer information. Students are encouraged to visit with these staff members to learn more about transferring to various institutions. Transfer counselors and advisers keep current on the changing requirements and curricula at four-year institutions. They stay in contact with key personnel at four-year schools. They develop Transfer Centers where students can find transfer-related materials and where counselors and advisers who specialize in transfer are located.

The student support strategy sometimes includes exchange of personnel between two- and four-year institutions through transfer days—four-year counselors and transfer coordinators will visit the community college at scheduled times, bringing information about their institutions and taking time to talk with prospective students. Some two- and four-year institutions arrange for student visits to four-year campuses to further acquaint students with the environment. Four-year institutions sometimes provide orientation programs for transfer students once they have arrived on campus.

Administrative Strategy

An administrative strategy regulates transfer through formal rules, agreements, and even legislation. The regulation covers the associate degree or other blocks of credit that are evaluated by a four-year school. Most community colleges enter into *articulation arrangements* with four-year institutions—agreements that detail the rules for transferring degrees and credits. These rules typically include the conditions under which a four-year institution will accept the associate degree and how credits earned in the associate degree can be used toward the baccalaureate.

Articulation agreements may be developed at the state level, generally by a department of education or state community college board working with other state coordinating or governing boards. Articulation agreements are also developed at a system level. Higher education systems made up of two- and four-year institutions will have articulation arrangements governing schools within the system. Higher education systems composed of only four-year institutions will sometimes enter into a systemwide arrangement that determines transfer conditions for its member schools as they deal individually with community colleges.

Many individual community colleges develop several articulation agreements. In addition to their agreements with primary receiving institutions—a four-year college that most transfer students attend, community colleges develop agreements with other receiving institutions that may take students in specialized program areas or have some special service to offer students. Sometimes groups of two- and four-year schools will develop regional arrangements.

Articulation agreements can be distinguished by the *level* at which they are developed (state, system, institutional); they can also be differentiated by the *scope of education* they cover. Some articulation arrangements govern *degrees:* they describe conditions for transfer of credits earned with the associate degree. Others govern the transfer of *programs,* for example, nursing or other health-related programs. Yet other articulation arrangements cover the transfer of *individual courses*—whether, for example, "Introductory History" transfers as a humanities or social science course. In general, the more narrow the scope of the agreement, the more accurate it is as a guide for students. Agreements covering degrees, for example, often do not stipulate how individual courses will transfer, leaving the student to negotiate this with individual departments and faculty members at four-year institutions.

Community college administrators report that they rely heavily on the student support and administrative transfer strategies (Terzian, 1991). This reliance is not accompanied, however, by ongoing assessment of the value of the strategies. As indicated earlier, sufficient data are not available to determine the extent to which the strategies contribute to transfer effectiveness and efficiency.

Curriculum Conversations and Transfer Discussions

The *Academic Model* is an institutional change strategy developed through the National Center for Academic Achievement and Transfer (NCAAT), a national project to strengthen transfer funded by the Ford Foundation and sponsored by the American Council on Education from 1989 to 1994. The model provides one example of how curriculum conversations and transfer discussions can come together.

The Academic Model is built on the assumption that a student's academic experience is central to success in transfer. The elements of this experience are the curricula pursued by the student, the academic expectations or performance standards the student must meet, and the teaching and learning strategies of which the student is a part. While those who support this model acknowledge the value of support services and administrative oversight provided in the dominant strategies, they believe that focusing intently on curriculum, standards, and teaching and learning is essential to penetrating to the heart of the transfer issue. Thus, this model focuses on students' intellectual gains from their courses and programs at the two-year institutions, seeking to ensure that they have the academic experiences that are critical for moving to a four-year college and achieving the baccalaureate. It calls for two- and four-year faculty to address the need for adequate similarity in lower division course content and standards across their institutions.

The Academic Model has five elements:

- Concentration on curriculum and expectations of performance for students
- Emphasis on faculty leadership in curriculum development and determination of performance standards
- Encouragement of two-year–four-year faculty collaboration
- Affirmation of the need for administrative leadership and support for faculty-led efforts
- Monitoring of the transfer population to determine transfer effectiveness (Eaton, 1990)

The Academic Model calls for faculty to examine curriculum content and standards across institutions and locate the curriculum discussion between the two- and four-year institutions—rather than isolating it on individual campuses. The curriculum and transfer discussion does not need to be confined to courses as the primary curriculum-bearing structure. It can include blocks or clusters of credits or general education expectations.

The Academic Model faces major obstacles. Bringing curriculum conversations and transfer together flies in the face of the academic culture of most colleges and universities. This culture, driven by the historical decentralization of higher education, fuels high expectations of autonomy—for both the institution and the faculty and especially in the area of curriculum. Institutional autonomy means that colleges have traditionally enjoyed the freedom to set academic standards, decide degree programs, and set prices for their services. Their primary regulatory bodies, voluntary peer-review agencies, reinforce this autonomy. Although federal and state policy makers are demanding more and more accountability from colleges (as, for example, with the Student Right-to-Know Act of 1990), they have made few inroads to date on this autonomy and self-regulation, and it is not clear that they should.

Faculty enjoy even greater freedom than their institutions. Tenure and academic freedom ensure that faculty are free agents in the classroom; faculty make curricular decisions through their departments; they set academic expectations. Faculty autonomy is viewed as a variant of individual freedom and little pressure is put on faculty members to approach their work as part of a team enterprise.

One result of this autonomy is that colleges and universities and their faculties do not feel pressured to invest a great deal in interinstitutional cooperation—to work across institutions for some common purpose. To work with another institution is complicated and constrains local freedom of operation. Institutions and faculty would be forced to limit the degrees of freedom they are able to exercise to ensure that their preferred academic decisions prevail. In the absence of any compelling reason to move beyond the campus either physically or psychologically, it is understandable that academic culture remains essentially place-bound.

Curriculum-Based Initiatives Across Institutions

Although obstacles exist, the Academic Model has sparked a modest number of curriculum-based *transfer initiatives* across the country. These efforts have been based on two assumptions: that dealing with curriculum is essential to effective transfer and that the greater the similarity in curricular content and standards across institutions, the easier it will be for students to transfer. These initiatives may be arranged in four groups based on their areas of primary attention: focus on courses, focus on distribution requirements, focus on integrating traditional support services into the classroom experience, and focus on general education. Some of these initiatives were developed through NCAAT, which provided support to two- and four-year institutions to work together to strengthen transfer through curriculum change—especially for low-income, black, and Hispanic students.

A transfer initiative that focuses on courses would call for faculty at two- and four-year institutions to come together to examine syllabi, course requirements, and classroom teaching practices. Their primary purpose is to align individual courses so that there is adequate similarity of content and performance expectations to meet two goals: students move to the four-year institution with sufficient background to continue their progress toward the baccalaureate, and faculty in upper division courses have some reasonable assurance that the transfer students are prepared for the material and assignments encountered in the new four-year setting. Courses on which faculty can profitably concentrate are those that large numbers of students will need for transfer. In the NCAAT, for example, the Houston Community College District and the University of Houston created teams of faculty from both institutions to examine course objectives in three disciplines: English, mathematics, and history—courses that are frequently needed for transfer from a range of program areas (Eaton, 1992, 1994). Faculty might also address courses in specific program areas in which there is considerable transfer, such as business or health-related programs.

Transfer initiatives that focus on distribution requirements involve the same coming together of faculty, but this time the focus is the entire block of lower division coursework that students need to graduate from a four-year school. This might be a collection of discrete courses, a general education program, or an interdisciplinary program. Faculty would need to agree on curricular content and academic standards for this block of work. Transfer initiatives that address distribution requirements are more ambitious than those addressing courses because many colleges view these requirements as a definitive statement of what they expect from baccalaureate recipients. It is not easy to align these requirements when the two institutions involved have different missions and purposes. The NCAAT provided support to Borough of Manhattan Community College (BMCC) and Hunter College to take on this challenge. These institutions focused on mathematics and science coursework needed to fulfill liberal arts requirements for students transferring from BMCC to the Hunter College teacher preparation program in early childhood and elementary education (Eaton, 1992).

Transfer initiatives that integrate student services into the classroom experience include having counselors working directly with classroom faculty in specific program areas. The counselors are present to help pinpoint student problems with coursework and to work with teaching faculty to enhance student achievement. Other efforts include using the classroom to offer tutoring, career planning, and individualized instruction as a course with both counselors and faculty involved. Faculty from the University of Arizona and the Pima Community College District in the NCAAT project, for example, jointly developed a course in transfer strategies and a transfer summer institute. Both the course and the institute helped students acquire information about the university's transfer criteria, admission policies, and orientation procedures. Mentoring and peer advising were available as well (Eaton, 1994). Many of these transfer initiatives take place in two-year colleges, but they could easily be adapted to a four-year setting.

General Education and Transfer

Discussions about *general education* have dominated much of the ongoing curriculum conversation and need to be addressed when examining the curriculum-transfer overlap mentioned at the beginning of this chapter. General education discussions concentrate on the shape and substance of curriculum, with the hope that students involved in various curricula develop certain cognitive capacities, create an information base for themselves, and become participants in what is loosely called the shared understanding of our society. General education discussions are focused on questions such as What do we want students to know? and What constitutes an educated person? There are many answers to these questions and many general education programs throughout the country.

General education programs vary in their focus. Some programs emphasize the development of certain skills and abilities. Others concentrate on curricular content. Yet others stress distribution requirements. Some mix all of these. Most of these approaches are consistent with definitions of general education such as "the cultivation of the knowledge, skills, and attitudes that all of us use and live by during most of our lives" (Association of American Colleges, 1988, p. 3).

General education programs are primarily institution-based. Individual colleges and universities develop their unique general education programs to produce the skills, information, and shared understanding that each deems desirable for students. Faculty on these campuses generally have three expectations that guide their development of general education programs. Faculty want the programs to be coherent and comprehensive, and to ensure commonality or connectedness. *Coherence* is ensured if faculty have carefully designed the general education program so that the parts hold together and protect against fragmentation of coursework. *Comprehensiveness* is the expectation that the faculty envision the curriculum as a whole rather than as the sum of its parts (Gaff, 1991). Comprehensiveness might also be viewed as the expectation that a general education program includes an opportunity for students to develop a full range of skills and capacities they all need to function in society.

The expectation that general education programs can yield *commonality* or connectedness is based on a hope for shared understanding within the society. This commonality is sometimes contrasted with individuality, urging that the country's historic emphasis on individuality be mediated by strengthening common bonds. Much of Boyer's work during the past twenty years has stressed this notion of "common learning" and its importance to society (see, for example, Boyer and Levine, 1981). The themes of commonality, connectedness, and shared understanding are prominent most recently in discussions of multiculturalism. Schlesinger (1992), for example, makes a strong case for retaining commonality and connectedness even as we struggle to accommodate and respect the varied cultural origins of our diverse population in the development of various forms of multiculturalism.

A vibrant transfer function poses major challenges for general education. It raises questions about whether or not general education can continue to be campus-based. Transfer highlights the need for consensus across institutions, calling for agreement that involves even more faculty, even more views about general education, and perhaps even greater diversity in the student population than would be found in a single-campus setting. Transfer challenges general education thinking to expand beyond institutional initiatives to embrace programs across institutions and still attempt to meet the tests of coherence, comprehensiveness, and commonality. Comprehensiveness, coherence, and commonality are expectations developed for individual institutions—involving a tacit acknowledgment that the *institution* is the appropriate framework for general education demands.

The Academic Model is useful to deal with the pressure that transfer places on general education programs that are institution-based and attempt to achieve the expectations of coherence, comprehensiveness, and commonality. First, the Academic Model's emphasis on two-year–four-year faculty collaboration and working together provides a useful forum for discussion and development of general education programs. Second, the model's concentration on curricula and standards ensures discussion of issues central to general education. Third, the model's call for faculty leadership and administrative support locates the discussion with the professionals who have the skills, interest, and resources to bring about change in general education.

Using the Academic Model will force faculty to rethink comprehensiveness, coherence, and commonality in light of another institution as well as their own. Their response to, for example, What is an educated person? will need to broaden and include academic experiences that students may have in other educational settings. A single institution could no longer answer this question solely through the curricular experiences it offers. Whether or not this can be successful depends heavily upon whether faculty at both two- and four-year institutions are willing to undertake this rethinking and accept some reduction in the autonomy to which they are accustomed.

There are two major threats to achieving success with interinstitutional general education programs. The first threat is that the faculty at the different institutions will simply be unable to agree. All their discussions may not yield a shared general education initiative. The second threat is that faculty actually reach agreement, but in a way that trivializes any program that emerges. An interinstitutional general education program has been trivialized if it is nothing more than a long list of course options at two different institutions unaccompanied by a structure that provides rationality and coherence to the options. It has been trivialized if the general education goals are very broad and do not provide a focus and character to the interinstitutional program. What emerges is lip service to general education, not a thoughtful program. These threats can be avoided. Reaching agreement may take time, but it can be done. The trivializing can be avoided as faculty see the importance of the work they are doing and how it is meaningful to students—and insist upon carefully structured programs.

A few states and institutions have begun to grapple with the challenge of interinstitutional general education programming. Virginia and Minnesota, for example, have been experimenting with statewide general education cores. All students would need to complete certain courses or clusters designed by statewide teams of faculty and administrators. The NCAAT supported Memphis State University (now the University of Memphis) and Shelby State Community College's multiyear effort to revise the general education core at each institution through bringing together two- and four-year faculty to work on transfer core areas. The center also supported Essex Community College and Rutgers University, Newark, as they began an interinstitutional review of coursework in the general education curriculum: English, history, biology, physics, and mathematics (Eaton, 1992, 1994).

Possible Futures for Curriculum and Transfer

Connecting curricular conversations and transfer discussions is a positive development in higher education. The importance of curricular conversations increases the significance of the transfer discussion. While we cannot predict the future behavior of students, there are some indications that transfer will increase among students as they make their way to the baccalaureate. This will require additional attention to transfer strategies and to the assumptions we make as we develop undergraduate curricula.

Students are taking more time to earn a degree and they are making education an ongoing part of their lives and work—rather than confining it to a preparatory experience. Students find it convenient to attend two institutions simultaneously or go back and forth between institutions. Students who pause during their collegiate work may return to a different institution from the one at which they started their undergraduate program. All of this increases the use of transfer as a strategy for degree completion or other academic work.

This increased movement of students among institutions will continue to put pressure on campus-bound academic programs and single-institution general education initiatives. More and more, faculty will be forced to examine their institutional curricular decisions in light of student attendance patterns that incorporate educational experiences from at least two institutions. The curriculum-transfer connection is one means to examine these decisions and meet the challenge that these attendance patterns pose for faculty determination of a desirable undergraduate experience.

References

Association of American Colleges. *A New Vitality in General Education.* Washington, D.C.: Association of American Colleges, 1988.

Boyer, E. L., and Levine, A. *A Quest for Common Learning.* Washington, D.C.: Carnegie Foundation for the Advancement of Teaching, 1981.

Cohen, A. M. *Celebrating Transfer: A Report of the Annual Transfer Assembly.* Los Angeles: Center for the Study of Community Colleges, 1993. (ED 358 877)

Cohen, A. M. *Analyzing Community College Student Transfer Rates.* In A. M. Cohen (ed.), *Relating Curriculum and Transfer.* New Directions for Community Colleges, no. 86. San Francisco: Jossey-Bass, 1994.

Eaton, J. S. "An Academic Model of Transfer Education." *Transfer,* 1990, *1*(1), 40–43.

Eaton, J. S. (ed.). *Faculty and Transfer: Academic Partnerships at Work.* Washington, D.C.: National Center for Academic Achievement and Transfer, American Council on Education, 1992.

Eaton, J. S. (ed.). *Strengthening Transfer Through Academic Partnerships.* Washington, D.C.: National Center for Academic Achievement and Transfer, American Council on Education, 1994.

Gaff, J. G. *New Life for the College Curriculum: Assessing Achievements and Furthering Progress in the Reform of General Education.* San Francisco: Jossey-Bass, 1991.

National Center for Education Statistics. *Digest of Education Statistics 1993.* (NCES 93–292) Washington, D.C.: Office of Education Research and Improvement, National Center for Education Statistics, U.S. Department of Education, 1993.

Palmer, J. C., Ludwig, M., and Stapleton, L. *At What Point do Community College Students Transfer to Baccalaureate-Granting Institutions?* Washington, D.C.: National Center for Academic Achievement and Transfer, American Council on Education, 1994.

Schlesinger, A. M. *The Disuniting of America: Reflections on a Multicultural Society.* New York: Norton, 1992.

Terzian, A. L. "Good Practices in Transfer Education: A Report from Two- and Four-Year Colleges and Universities." *Transfer,* 1991, *2*(7), 1–8.

CHAPTER TWENTY-EIGHT

EVALUATING LEARNING IN INDIVIDUAL COURSES

Barbara D. Wright

All the curriculum reform in the world is ultimately useless if students do not learn what faculty teach. Assessment is a response to the realization that—curricular reform, new teaching technologies, testing and grading, and ever-higher tuition notwithstanding—college graduates do not seem to be learning at a level that matches the expectations of employers, parents, or the general public.

If assessment is to improve undergraduate education, it must be a faculty-defined, faculty-controlled activity. Yet in this handbook, assessment comes under the rubric "administration and assessment." At first glance, this would seem to be exactly the wrong place to classify assessment efforts. Yet assessment practitioners also know by now, from more than ten years of experience in the postsecondary assessment movement, that campus assessment efforts are doomed without strong administrative support. In reality, both faculty and administrators have indispensable roles to play in academic assessment if it is to help students and enhance programs. Thus, this chapter on assessment in the course and in the classroom is intended to provide guidance for faculty and administrators alike.

Background on Postsecondary Assessment

Postsecondary assessment is part of a national reform agenda for education with twin roots in the academy and in the public policy arena. Within the academy, the stage was set for the contemporary assessment movement with the appearance in the mid-1980s of a series of reports on undergraduate education. These included *To Reclaim a Legacy* (Bennett, 1984), *Integrity in the College Curriculum* (Association of American Colleges, 1985) and most significantly, *Involvement in Learning* (National Institute of Education, 1984). *Involvement in Learning* called for high standards, student involvement in learning, and—a new element—assessment and feedback. This last recommendation was based on the assumption that both students and institutions could learn from such feedback and continuously improve their performance in response to it. As Ewell argues, also implicit in these reports was the need for new ways to assess that would provide more specific and robust feedback than that available through the standardized multiple-choice instruments commonly used for college or graduate school admissions (1991, p. 3).

Meanwhile, off campus, state governments became increasingly concerned in the mid-1980s about the escalating costs of higher education and the apparent simultaneous decline in the quality of postsecondary education. Parallel with the reports that appeared in academic circles, another series of reports appeared, including *Transforming the State Role in Undergraduate Education: Time for a Different View* (Education Commission of the States, 1986) and *Time for Results* (Alexander, Clinton, and Kean, 1991). Motivated in part by a desire to stimulate academic improvement, but even more by a desire for accountability and tangible returns on investment, states began to mandate assessment. Within a few years, the number of states with mandates had risen from three or four (1982) to fifteen (1987) to twenty-seven (1990). The nature of the mandates varied, with earlier ones tending to be more prescriptive and test-based while later mandates insisted that postsecondary institutions do something but left the design of a plan and choice of methods to individual institutions (El-Khawas, 1982, 1987, 1990).

Assessment, then, has not only twin roots but also twin purposes: educational improvement, from the perspective of educators within the academy; and accountability, from the perspective of politicians, employers, and the general public. Traditionally, accountability and improvement have been regarded within the education community as mutually exclusive: at assessment conferences, newcomers have been repeatedly warned that the same methods cannot and should not be used for both purposes. Yet the two cannot be so readily separated. Clearly, from the beginning of the assessment movement in the early 1980s, there has been a desire on the part of the public and politicians to improve the quality of education—and institutions that focused on educational improvement have found that their assessments also provide them with a new tool for accountability, along with a more complex understanding of accountability. They can now talk more concretely to the public about their educational goals, how well the goals are being achieved, and what the institution is doing to improve its effectiveness. The assessment process has also helped institutions accept their own accountability to their students, and faculty have come to understand the accountability they owe one another as educators and colleagues (Hutchings and Marchese, 1991, p. 71).

Thus it is important not to perpetuate a false dichotomy between improvement and accountability, but rather to view assessment as an activity that can serve both purposes. Good assessment helps institutions to focus on teaching and learning and to ask meaningful questions about what students know and what they can do with that knowlege. Assessment insists that such questions be answered not intuitively or anecdotally, but on the basis of evidence. Next, assessment interprets the data, turns it into useful information, and considers the concrete changes that may improve results. Finally, assessment uses the evidence and interpretations: it follows through with change. And then the process begins again—asking, among other things, whether the change leads to the expected improvement.

Trends in Assessment

Postsecondary assessment done right must be rooted in the course and in the classroom—in the individual cells, to speak metaphorically, where the metabolism of learning actually occurs. Recent trends in campus-based assessment reflect that; they call, for example, for performance-based assessments in naturalistic settings approximating what students will be required to do in their civic or professional or personal lives: perhaps giving an oral presentation, teaching a class, taking a medical history, or making an aesthetic judgment. Such performances require not only factual knowledge but also skills, and they require the integration of knowledge and skills in complex performances. The growing importance of such activities represents a real shift from the early years of the movement, when the operational understanding of assessment was standardized tests, divorced from courses, administered to large groups, and taken by students—sometimes poorly motivated—who saw little connection between the test and their formal studies or personal lives.

A second trend in the assessment movement is increasing reliance on qualitative as well as quantitative approaches to assessment. That is, judgments about the quality of an individual's performance are increasingly made on the basis of a wide variety of evidence, not merely test scores or other numeric data; and the evidence is evaluated narratively and multidimensionally for strengths and weaknesses not merely in command of factual information or concepts but in terms of skill levels and qualities such as creativity, risk taking, persistence, meticulousness, ethical or social consciousness, empathy, cultural sensitivity, and the like. This interest in qualitative approaches has come as a response to what many faculty view as the reductionist or trivializing character of standardized testing and scoring.

A third important trend in the evolution of postsecondary assessment has been increasing acceptance of local approaches that respect the particular emphases of local curricula and the strengths and interests of local faculty, as well as the unique missions and special clientele of particular colleges. One of the great strengths of American higher education, after all, is its extraordinary variety of institutions and curricula; and one of the major reasons for faculty resistance to assessment has been the fear that assessment would mean the imposition of mandated, uniform curricula. Yet it makes little sense, if we truly value this variety, to homogenize education through the imposition of misguided assessments.

A fourth trend, finally, is the emergence of embedded approaches—that is, assessments that make use of student work samples and performances generated through regular coursework that can be examined not only to assign the student a grade, but also to see what they reveal about the effectiveness of the teaching-learning process. Using such "classroom artifacts" (as they are called by Schilling and Schilling, 1993) gets around the problem of poor student motivation. It requires little extra time from faculty or students (in contrast to add-on assessment activities), it is cost efficient and minimally intrusive (in contrast to large-scale testing, for example), it is authentic (unlike paper-and-pencil activities from which only inferences can be drawn), and it presents student efforts in all their variety and complexity (instead of reducing them, for example, to a simplistic model of linear progress). In addition, the embedded approach respects the variety of disciplinary cultures. It encourages assessment activities that make sense in the individual discipline, given its traditions of inquiry, its traditional subjects, the questions it poses, and its definition of knowledge. Embedded assessments therefore have face validity for faculty. The insights gained from an examination of student work samples, in turn, are more likely than other kinds of assessment results to be immediately useful in the classroom. In other words, slippage is minimal.

Testing, Grades, and Assessment

As it evolves along the lines described here, postsecondary assessment is becoming ever more closely aligned with good, innovative curricular and teaching practices. Does this growing alignment mean assessment as such is redundant? Not at all. Precisely because assessment is evolving in this direction, it is important to understand the very real ways in which assessment is not identical with teaching or its traditional byproducts, testing and grading.

Differentiating the Terms

On many campuses, when assessment is introduced, the first reaction of many faculty is to view it as redundant and unnecessary. After all, they already test and assign grades; they uphold standards by failing students who do not meet course requirements; they assume that assessment is synonymous with testing; and they wonder quite legitimately why, then, assessment is necessary at all.

Assessment to improve teaching and learning is certainly related to testing students and assigning grades for their performance, but it is by no means identical with that process. There are some fundamental contrasts. First, when faculty test and assign grades, they are looking for demonstrations of learning achieved; in other words, tests and grades are primarily summative. Assessment, conversely, looks for achievement but also monitors the learning process; it is both summative and formative. Second, in testing and assigning grades, the focus is on judging the student's work; in assessment, however, faculty members turn the focus on themselves as well as students to ask how curriculum and instruction can become more effective, and to search purposefully for information that will lead to improvement.

Grading is by nature a judgmental, occasionally punitive activity that students often anticipate either with anxiety or cynicism; the spirit of assessment, in contrast, is supportive and respectful. It calls for the instructor to sit next to the student (indeed, this is the original etymological derivation of the verb "to assess") and offer feedback. Of course, traditional testing and grading can also serve this purpose, but if they do, it is as a side effect. And while the teacher or student may respond to the feedback from a test or a grade, this response is likely to be individual, informal, even arbitrary.

Second, testing and grading tend to focus on rather small units of learning: this chapter, this problem set, the first half of this course. Assessment, on the other hand, takes both a narrower and a broader view. Day to day, the classroom assessment techniques of Angelo and Cross (1993), for example, can be used to determine how well students are learning new material introduced in weekly lectures. But assessment allows more. It can seek to understand, for example, what students bring with them in the way of prior knowledge or biases or expectations, on the assumption that if the instructor is fully aware of these things, he or she can teach with them and to them, instead of against them. Assessment can also ask larger questions about the students' educational experience: how does what is taught in this course relate to what the student learned last semester or is learning in another course right now? What do the curriculum and cocurriculum all add up to for the student? In other words, assessment seeks coherence and reinforcement of the educational experience beyond the limits of the individual course.

Testing tends to be a very private affair, between a single faculty member and student. There is real reluctance to discuss publicly individual student grades or criteria for grading. Informally, of course, the faculty member may complain to colleagues at lunch that the last batch of quizzes was a disaster, and there has to be a better way to teach whatever; students, too, may get together informally to discuss their grades and try to psych out the instructor's grading criteria. But the point is that such discussions are informal, almost furtive, not open and actively looking for the collaboration of colleagues. Assessment, on the other hand, assumes a collective faculty responsibility for improving the educational experience; and the assessment process, if it is properly implemented on campus, provides a formal setting in which colleagues gather to work systematically on improvement. Assessment can (and should) also involve students directly in the conversation.

Just as testing and grading essentially represent a judgment on the student, so too the onus for improvement lies entirely with the student. Classroom instructors assume that students will take their test results and grades as indicators of the aspects of the course that they need to work harder on. For the benefit of those students who have done poorly, the faculty member generally announces a willingness to help—whatever that may mean—and reminds students of his or her office hours. But beyond that, and whatever feedback the instructor has gleaned from the test (feedback that may or may not find its way into the next lecture or the next iteration of the course), with testing and grading there is no formal commitment to change and improve, no framework to ensure it happens. Data collection, in other words, remains haphazard, rather than systematic and routine. The changes or improvements that flow from that information are similarly uncertain and intuitive, rather than flowing from shared analysis and commitment to follow through. Assessment, however, views tests or other examples of student work as sources of important information, and then incorporates that information into an intentional process of interpretation, design of improvements, and implementation.

Finally, testing and grading are iterative for the student, and cumulative when they add up to a final grade in the course or a graduating GPA. But the faculty member is under no obligation to take an iterative look at, say, mastery of foreign language speaking skills over a period of years and ask whether the upper division composition and conversation course is becoming more or less effective over time. Assessment for educational improvement, on the other hand, requires precisely that kind of longitudinal view. Ideally, assessment leads to better instruction the very next time the class meets—but assessment also needs to operate over much longer periods of time.

In testing and grading, the efforts of both students and faculty remain individual or—in the case of faculty—at best, departmental. In assessment, however, faculty work together while academic administration provides a supportive context. Administration expects assessment efforts but gives faculty the lead in designing them. Meanwhile administration promotes faculty assessment efforts in many ways: with philosophical support for forms of assessment that are perhaps unconventional but compatible with campus culture and that make sense to faculty; with political support for campus efforts, both on campus and to outside audiences; and with financial rewards and professional support for contributing faculty—for example, opportunities to attend conferences or invite consultants to campus. On a campus that is engaged in successful assessment, the campus as a whole embraces a process of improvement that has the potential to transform campus culture.

Both testing and grading of students and student evaluations of faculty are aimed at pronouncing a judgment on the success or failure of a particular actor in the educational process. They are not, however, focused in a nonjudgmental way on describing, understanding, or improving the educational process itself. Confusing assessment with individual faculty evaluation is particularly pernicious because it destroys the trust and candor—between faculty and administration and among faculty members—that are essential for meaningful assessment.

Some Effective Assessment Methods

By asking a new set of questions from a different perspective, assessment opens the classroom door and establishes new lines of communication about the skills, knowledge, dispositions, values, and behaviors that all areas of the institution are committed to fostering. Course and classroom assessment allows an institution, first, to take the pulse of the educational experience and establish what its student learning outcomes actually are, and second, to discover what students believe is helping or hindering them in their learning. Only when leaders understand the why as well as the what can an institution make positive changes.

The methods discussed in this section represent some of the most promising practices in the field. They are adaptable to individual institutions, provide provocative evidence for conversations about educational improvement, are not reductionist, get at the knowledge and skills faculty value and that students must be able to demonstrate in real life, and are respectful of the complexity of the educational process.

Portfolios. Portfolios are collections of student work. They vary enormously and are adaptable to many different situations and questions about students' progress. Borrowed from the arts, portfolios may be cross-sectional, that is, they may contain examples of a student's best work in a variety of forms at a given point in time—for example, as a job search begins. More commonly, however, academic portfolios are organized longitudinally to show the student's development over time. Portfolios vary in selectivity, depending on the purpose they are to serve. For example, they may function as an inventory and contain virtually everything the student produces in a particular course or set of courses; or they may include only the student's best work; or selected sets of products—say, writing assignments plus earlier outlines and drafts. Often, the portfolio is focused to show a particular kind of intellectual development, say, in writing skills, critical thinking, or ability to carry out a variety of library research tasks. The contents of the portfolio may be determined by the instructor, the program, the student, an assessment committee, or some combination of these. The portfolio may be discipline-specific, focus on general education, or show integration of the major with general education. It is most likely to contain written work, but audiotapes, videotapes, graphics, and other products are equally appropriate for inclusion. Often, the portfolio is accompanied by a reflective essay, written by the student, discussing his or her progress over the time span covered by the portfolio and using examples from the portfolio as documentation. Many faculty maintain that assembling the portfolio and then discussing its contents is in itself an extraordinarily valuable educational experience for students.

Normally we think of portfolios as a way to capture the knowledge and skills of an individual student, but portfolios can also be composed of samples from a student population—say, students representing different ability levels, or general education students, or graduating majors—and used to provide a picture of a course or a program as a whole. A program-level portfolio can supplement other measures typically used in program assessment (described in more detail in Chapter Twenty-Nine).

Portfolio assessment provides a basis for informed discussions of how to strengthen curriculum and instruction. Assessment content aligns with what actually happens in the course or program, and faculty obtain a rich, textured picture of student progress. When students submit commentary on how progress was achieved, they reflect on themselves as learners, building a foundation for lifelong learning. Portfolios yield a kind of data that does not lend itself to the invidious statistical comparisons that many faculty fear, for themselves or their campuses. Yet portfolios do offer vivid examples to stimulate faculty thinking about improvement, and incidentally they can also provide material for effective communication with a variety of publics: for example, prospective students, parents, employers, and legislators (Schilling and Schilling, 1993).

Originally used primarily in writing programs, portfolios can now be found in a wide range of disciplines from languages to math, in general education programs, in majors, and even as a way to show the synthesis of general education with the major or professional studies. Countless faculty use portfolios today as a standard teaching device and as the foundation for assessment of courses. The student portfolio has been accompanied by the emergence of the teaching portfolio as a way for faculty to demonstrate teaching effectiveness.

The *assessment* component of the portfolio lies specifically in the evidence it offers regarding overall program strengths and weaknesses, as well as the stimulation that the evidence provides for change. The usefulness of the portfolio, however, depends, as it does with all assessment methods, on how effectively the portfolio is used to support the entire educational improvement process—a process that includes not only gathering evidence but asking tough questions about educational quality, interpreting the evidence, and making changes as a result.

Capstones and Senior Projects. The *capstone,* as the name suggests, is a course that comes at the conclusion of a student's program of study and caps prior coursework. It is usually not designed to convey new information, although that, too, may well occur. Rather, its purpose is, first, to provide an opportunity for students to synthesize what they have learned in their major, and perhaps to fill in gaps; and second, to apply what they have learned in some kind of project appropriate to the discipline or professional program in which they have majored. The nature of the project, usually determined by faculty in the department or program, can range from the fairly traditional, for example, a scholarly paper involving library research; to the less conventional, for example, a history research project requiring the use of primary sources at a local museum; to team projects that mimic the students' future workplace, for example, a marketing campaign for a new product on which four or five marketing majors work; or the design of a new bridge by a group of civil engineering students, who must not only provide technical specifications but demonstrate skills of teamwork and communication.

As the last example suggests, capstone courses can also provide an opportunity for students to synthesize knowledge in their major with skills and knowledge developed in their general education coursework. The bridge project, for example, may require students to confront such issues as the aesthetic appeal of the design and its harmony with the style of the town's historic district; economic impact on the town's main street; ecological impact on nearby wetlands; and what graphics, written materials, or oral communications are appropriate for technical or lay audiences.

The impact of the capstone, both as a learning experience for students and as an assessment opportunity for faculty, can be increased if products are displayed publicly for students and faculty in the campus community, and if external judges are brought in to help critique student efforts. Such external judges may include faculty from other departments within the college, faculty in the same discipline from neighboring institutions, practitioners from the community, and potential employers of the graduating students. Students can thus receive feedback on their work from not only the instructor of record for the capstone course but from a range of professionals, including practitioners whose words provide a reality check and may have greater credibility for students than their instructors' comments. The public display of projects and critique of work also provide concrete models for less advanced students of what will be expected of them in a few years' time.

The capstone can thus function as an extremely powerful learning experience for students. At the same time, it can be an equally powerful assessment opportunity for faculty. The collective discussion among faculty in the department of what this year's crop of graduates has produced, and where, collectively, its strengths and weaknesses lie; the comparison with previous graduating classes; the reactions of colleagues outside the department; the feedback from instructors at other institutions; and, not least of all, the feedback from practicing professionals—all can help the department to take stock of its curriculum and pedagogy and develop specific plans for improvement. External feedback can also lend the assessment effort greater credibility with legislators and other outside audiences.

The capstone project (and more recently, the capstone activity, for example, an internship or field work) has been used at a range of institutions, from the University of Tennessee, Knoxville, and Virginia Commonwealth University to Northeast Missouri State University. King's College in Pennsylvania requires a "senior integrated project" of all graduating students.

A more recent spin-off of the capstone is the *cornerstone course,* which, as the name implies, has the purpose of providing a foundation for later work. The cornerstone course reinforces intellectual skills and knowledge that students should have brought from high school and prepares them for college-level work. The projects, performances, and other work samples produced in a cornerstone course allow assessment of where students are as they begin college, and what areas of knowledge or skill will require particular attention from faculty, academic support personnel, and others on campus. Such student work also provides a benchmark against which to measure future intellectual growth.

Performance Assessment. Portfolios and capstones can document some kinds of student performance in the form of essays, models, slides, and the like; but there are other dimensions to student performance, and other activities may be needed to capture them.

What matters, as college educators have come to understand with increasing clarity over the last decade or so, is not just what students know, but what they can do with what they know. Colleges have been criticized for focusing too much on the transmission of knowledge and too little on training students to act on their knowledge; similarly, paper-and-pencil tests have been criticized as inadequate indicators of how students will perform in a real-world setting—an office, a clinic, or a classroom, for example. Thus there is a growing trend toward the creation of activities that are either real performances or realistic simulations (that is, an assessment center approach modeled after business). Such activities provide important opportunities for practice and feedback for the student, and an opportunity for faculty to see how effectively they are preparing students on both theoretical and applied levels. Faculty assisting students in preparing for performances also helps to replace the teacher-as-authority–student-as-empty-vessel model of education with a more supportive coach-novice relationship.

Performances, whether assessed live or in recorded form, provide an ideal opportunity for students to demonstrate their ability to integrate the knowledge, skills, and values taught by a course; simultaneously, a performance can reinforce learning. Moreover, by requiring students to apply what they know in new situations, performance promotes lifelong learning skills. Focusing on a complex, integrated performance as an important outcome also offers a way for faculty to test the relevance of the curriculum. High-quality performance as a goal, whether at the course or program level, can make the curriculum more transparent, coherent, and meaningful for faculty and students alike. Clarity and meaningfulness, in turn, can be powerful motivators for both faculty and students, particularly if the performance is a public one. And public performances provide models for other students.

Tasks for performance-based assessment may range from the fairly predictable (for example, oral presentations, live interviews, or debates) to more creative academic activities (for example, the General Intellectual Skills tests developed for the New Jersey College Outcomes Evaluation Project and since taken over by Educational Testing Service) to presenting music or dance recitals, catering an event, teaching a class, interacting with clients in human service settings, repairing a malfunctioning automobile, or carrying out in-basket exercises in accounting or office management. Such activities, real or simulated, call upon students' knowledge of their field and require on-the-spot critical thinking, problem solving, creativity, judgment, ability to function under pressure, and other skills or personal attributes that are essential in the workplace.

Performance assessment is appealing because it makes so much sense. However, it does have drawbacks. One is the difficulty that important liberal arts disciplines, particularly the humanities, usually experience in attempting to design an appropriate performance for their discipline. Just what, they may ask, is a history performance supposed to be? Struggling with this question can provoke useful department-level conversation about faculty members' goals for graduating majors, goals that under normal circumstances remain implicit, undiscussed—and may diverge considerably. In addition, such departments can usually find help close by, in the professional programs on campus; many of which already have years of practice in observing student performances and rating them according to a uniform set of criteria.

Performance assessments also require a considerable investment in the design of tasks and scoring format and the definition of standards; and they require careful training of all those who will be involved in scoring the performance. This includes training of any visitors from outside the campus—potential employers, field supervisors, and so on—who may join faculty in rating the performances. Such training, in turn, while it may be time-consuming, does provide faculty with a valuable opportunity to create some understanding for the complexity of education, to discuss learning goals and outcomes with the future employers of the college's graduates, to get feedback on what employers are looking for in their employees—and to discuss the appropriateness of the department's scoring criteria. Not least of all, the work that goes into creating such criteria pays off in clearer communication to students about what faculty are looking for in a quality performance. Faculty are forced to move beyond an intuitive—perhaps very accurate but nevertheless undefined—sense of "I know a good performance when I see it" to greater specificity.

Alverno College has set the standard for campuswide performance assessment; performance assessment is common in professional fields, particularly the health care professions. Clayton State College (1993) has developed an elaborate set of descriptors for various aspects of the general education curriculum. College faculty could learn, too, from work done on performance assessment at the K–12 level (Wiggins, 1993), and from the College Board's Thinking Series, which describes student performances in mathematics, foreign language, history, literature, and the arts.

Student Self-Assessment. Self-assessment flows directly from performance assessment and ideally is closely integrated with it. Self-assessment provides an opportunity for students to assess their own performance, to reflect on the learning process, and to become fully conscious of the changes and growth they have undergone. Students' assessments may or may not be tied to a specific set of criteria and then matched against the assessments of faculty, fellow students, potential employers, or other external examiners.

Self-assessment may range from questionnaires or simple checklists of accomplishments and facts learned to conferences or interviews about performance to various kinds of self-reports: brief written descriptions, journal entries, learning narratives, or elaborate reflective essays. The writing may accompany a portfolio or capstone project, be assigned as part of a course, or serve as a graduation requirement in itself. It can even occur in a separate course devoted entirely to students' self-assessment of learning in the rest of their coursework (Waluconis, 1993).

Self-assessment is a method that allows—indeed forces—students to take stock of and analyze their own learning. As such, it can be not only an evaluative tool but an educational process in its own right. Waluconis, creator of the self-assessment course at Seattle Central Community College, argues that students who self-assess become more responsible for their learning, more motivated to engage in lifelong learning, more aware of diverse perspectives and the reasons behind varying judgments, and less likely to drop out of college. Students acquire a broader conceptual understanding of subject matter; they come to see more clearly how current learning can be applied in future, at school, in their personal lives, or on the job; and they develop their own strategies for mastery. Students in his course, like those in a project that relied heavily on student self-assessments to gauge the effectiveness of women's studies programs (McTighe Musil, 1992), reported finding their voices, learning to speak out, and taking greater ownership of their education as major benefits of the process.

There are benefits not only to students but to the institution from such self-assessment. When students are integrally involved in the assessment process, they value it and support it, and that in turn helps to change campus culture. In addition, Waluconis cites greater curricular coherence, with more integration of learning across the curriculum, and enhanced faculty development. He even suggests that quantitative appraisal of student's self-reflective essays can provide numeric scores as evidence of student learning (Waluconis, 1993, p. 228).

But student self-assessment poses challenges, as well. To begin with, students often respond negatively when asked to self-assess, their reactions ranging from anxiety to resentment. Many students are apparently uncomfortable at the prospect: either they are inexperienced at self-evaluation and unsure of what they must do, or they believe that it is appropriate for faculty members to assess, but unfair to ask this of students. Such reluctance, Alverno College has found, disappears as students become more mature, develop a reflective disposition, internalize criteria and procedures, and sharpen their own assessment skills. Once under way, student self-assessment can uncover many different kinds of changes in students, far more than any standardized survey could anticipate; but it can also highlight discrepancies between students' nonlinear development and educators' overwhelmingly linear expectations for student progress. Student self-assessments may reveal that students learned things never intended by the instructor; or that important goals of the teacher were not shared by students. Another difficulty noted by Waluconis is the "tenuous relationship" of the student's "learning story" to his or her grades. In short, Waluconis warns, "if the axis of power is shifted and students are given the control to describe their own learning, teachers must be prepared to be surprised, even dismayed" (1993, p. 255).

Classroom Assessment. *Classroom Assessment* is a learner-centered, teacher-directed approach designed to improve student learning in the individual classroom (Angelo, 1991; Angelo and Cross, 1993). It uses a variety of techniques for eliciting information from students about what they know and how they are experiencing the course, day to day. Classroom Assessment emerged from two simple yet profound insights: first, that students were by far the best source of feedback to an instructor about whether students are learning what the instructor is trying to teach in a class; and second, that regular use of such feedback could improve both teaching and learning. *Classroom Research*, in turn, takes advantage of the classroom as a laboratory for study of the learning process. In Classroom Research, the results derived through Classroom Assessment become the subject of longer-term efforts aimed at larger findings in the realm of discipline-specific learning theory.

Classroom Research and Classroom Assessment arose in the mid-1980s: a context characterized by concern about the quality of postsecondary teaching and learning both within and beyond the academy, by the education reports described above, and by state mandates calling for mass testing with off-the-shelf instruments—an approach to assessment that most educators consider at best ineffective and at worst a direct threat to educational quality. Cross's approach, in contrast, deliberately located assessment in the classroom and put control of the process into the hands of individual classroom teachers. Classroom Assessments are "created, administered and analyzed by teachers themselves on questions of teaching and learning that are important to them . . . [hence] the likelihood that instructors will apply the results of the assessment to their own teaching is greatly enhanced" (1988, p. xiv).

The lessons learned from Classroom Assessment are numerous and provocative, and to some extent they overlap with insights gained from other classroom-based approaches to assessment. For example, Classroom Assessment techniques can be used to assess a wide range of goals, from content mastery to critical thinking skills and affective responses to the material. But here, as with other approaches to assessment, faculty need to adapt, not adopt, the techniques to suit the requirements of their discipline and their course. Classroom Assessment feedback, like other assessment results, may challenge teachers' firmly held assumptions; but as Cross and Angelo point out, the most dismaying or surprising feedback may ultimately prove the most useful. And Classroom Assessment, like other forms of assessment, works best when students are actively involved in the process and results are shared with them.

Classroom Assessment, like other assessment approaches, can have a powerful effect on students and teachers alike. Regular use of Classroom Assessment techniques has enabled college teachers to become more systematic and sensitive observers of learning; and it has stimulated collegial interaction. As for students, Classroom Assessment has increased interest in learning and changed attitudes and behaviors. Through the continuous monitoring provided by Classroom Assessment techniques, students have become more engaged and self-reflective learners. As students get used to being asked what they are learning, and expressing what they have learned, it appears their metacognitive development is enhanced. Classroom Assessment seems to increase cooperation in the classroom, both between teacher and students and among students, and helps to turn the class into a learning community. Classroom Assessment also seems to send a powerful message about instructors' commitment to student success, increase student satisfaction, stimulate more use of office hours and other resources, and improve course completion rates (Angelo, 1991, 1995).

Since publication of the first handbook in 1988, the Classroom Research Project has been extraordinarily successful in spreading the word about this approach to assessment. Its proponents have produced videotapes and edited teachers' descriptions of their experience with Classroom Research (Angelo, 1991). There have been numerous articles written on the approach, and hundreds of workshops have been conducted at national and regional gatherings. Dissemination of the concept has been so successful, particularly via consortia at the two-year college level, that today it is practically impossible to visit a U.S. campus where someone has not experimented with Classroom Assessment.

Classroom Assessment was originally intended to give the classroom teacher complete control over the assessment effort. Assessment would take place within the individual classroom, students would respond anonymously, and faculty would not be required to share the results with anyone. Thus the process would be confidential and safe, and a major cause of campus anxiety regarding other forms of assessment—namely, that faculty members would be exposed or scapegoated in some way—was removed. But Cross and Angelo soon discovered that faculty did not mind discussing their discoveries with one another; in fact, they seemed to thrive on it. Cross and Angelo have since developed the Teaching Goals Inventory (or TGI) to help departments clarify their shared, top-priority departmental teaching goals; Classroom Assessment Techniques (CATs) can then be used across the program to assess how well these specific goals are being realized. Or Classroom Assessment can be used across the institution to assess general education goals, as has happened at Winthrop University. Still other institutions, such as Quinnebaug Valley Community College, have made Classroom Assessment the basis of their comprehensive institutional assessment plan.

Finally, Classroom Assessment, with its continuous monitoring of and responsiveness to the needs of a particular set of "customers," namely the students in the class, is the closest classroom equivalent to another trend in assessment circles, Total Quality Management (TQM) or Continuous Quality Improvement (CQI). Although there is the possibility of a real synergy between Classroom Assessment and CQI (Arcaro, 1995; Wolverton, 1995), the latter does not seem to have captured the hearts or imaginations of postsecondary educators.

All the approaches described here—portfolios, capstones, performance assessment, student self-assessment, and Classroom Assessment—share a focus on student work and student experience as the single most important source of information for understanding and improving the teaching-learning process. They raise similar questions: for example, about the proper relationship of coverage to comprehension; about the relative importance of command of subject matter versus development of more generic intellectual skills; and about the level of time, effort, or energy that assessment requires versus other institutional demands on faculty. These approaches to assessment also have their limitations; however, they will not provide statistical information about retention, for example, or tell an institution about alumnae satisfaction, or provide data for comparisons with other institutions.

The great strength of these approaches is that they focus directly on the artifacts of real learning, produced in the process of learning, in the classroom, where much learning begins. Indeed, these approaches suggest that almost any well-conceived teaching activity, not only those specifically mentioned here, can also serve as an assessment—if the instructor or the department takes the time to look at that student performance not merely for what it says about the student but also for what it says about the effectiveness of the course or program. If what we really care about is not generating numbers for reports, not getting legislators or accreditors off our backs, but genuinely improving teaching and learning, then this is where assessment efforts must begin.

Conclusions

Assessment is becoming increasingly embedded in standard classroom assignments. Capstone courses and senior projects are being used both to provide a grade for the student and to provide information on the success of the course or program for instructors and departments. Classroom testing procedures, conversely, have benefited from the assessment conversation, which has compelled faculty to define more specific criteria for what we expect from students, emphasizing that it matters less what students know than what they can do with what they know. Assessment has encouraged and assisted in the move away from total reliance on paper-and-pencil tests and toward authentic or performance-based tests in more naturalistic settings.

The tendency to view education in student-centered terms of learning outcomes, however achieved, and to define faculty productivity, too, as student learning rather than traditional courseloads or hours of physical presence in front of a group of students—this trend, too, will most likely grow stronger as computers and various forms of communication technology become more ubiquitous in higher educational settings, moving from the margin to the mainstream (Gilbert, 1995).

Assessment practices will likely prove a fruitful source of new testing and grading techniques that will transcend the physical classroom. Classroom-based assessment, with its more naturalistic, performance-based techniques, has made us more conscious of the fundamental artificiality of the classroom, just as program-level assessment has helped us to distinguish and define the essentials of learning. In short, an unintended benefit of course and classroom assessment may well be to help faculty move more effectively into the era of virtual classrooms and online learning (Ehrmann, 1995).

The American Association for Higher Education (AAHE) Assessment Forum began watching assessment in the mid-1980s, as mandates began to come down from state boards and legislatures. AAHE has always insisted, without dismissing the importance of accountability, that assessment must ultimately serve educational improvement; otherwise, accountability alone would prove destructive of educational quality. This central commitment to students, classroom instructors, and improvement of teaching and learning has characterized the nine national conferences on assessment sponsored by AAHE annually since 1987. In recent years, topics more appropriate for administrators have been evident on the program: for example, systems thinking, planning and budgeting, state and national perspectives, and connecting the campus with business. This shift in emphasis is reiterated with a growing sense of urgency in articles such as Ewell's on the "new accountability" (1991) and on the continuing dissatisfaction of corporate leaders and policy makers with the rate of change in the academy (1994). The AAHE Assessment Forum for several years has also produced a number of publications that it makes available to people for use in thinking about the issues surrounding assessment.

Are we looking here at an emerging bifurcation, a conflict, even—or a useful synergy? This chapter has documented a clear and growing emphasis within assessment practice on embedded, in-class methods that are inexpensive and elegant, closely keyed to what students are supposed to be learning in the classroom, and maximally useful in terms of feedback to instructor and student. In other words, with the lively and growing interest in portfolios, capstones, student performances, and the like, we find a closer, more effective linkage between assessment on the one hand and teaching and learning on the other. But at the same time, we find more administrative, state, and national perspectives of limited interest or utility to the classroom teachers who are ultimately responsible, one on one, for educational improvement. This despite the fact that much of the rhetoric in administrative, business, and government quarters these days is about decentralization and the need to push responsibility downward and horizontally to the people on the front lines.

Theoretically this rhetoric ought to empower the classroom teacher. But will it? Are systems thinking and the inclusion of administrators or policy makers in the conversation a sign of the maturing of the movement? Do they demonstrate that assessment is acquiring a structural foundation and becoming institutionalized in the best sense of the word? Or does assessment run the danger of turning into an empty bureaucratic agenda item, straying fatally from the grass roots that gave the movement its elan and where any real hope for educational improvement ultimately resides?

The answer probably depends on how all the players involved respond. National and state policy makers need to listen carefully to the stories of assessment done right, understand the complexity of the educational process, champion good educational practices, and resist simplistic, crowd-pleasing alleged solutions. Campus administrators need to "walk the talk" of empowerment and respect for frontline experience. They need to turn teaching and learning into administrative priorities. Classroom teachers, meanwhile, need to keep clearly focused on the benefits of course- and classroom-based assessment. At all levels, from the capitol to the classroom, assessment is an indispensable tool in educational transformation.

And that, perhaps, is the answer to a final conundrum. At every assessment conference, there are a few sincere but skeptical faculty members sitting at the back of the room during the closing keynote, thinking dark thoughts. Is assessment really necessary? Or is it merely another manifestation of the convoluted, neobaroque self-reflexivity that seems to characterize our intellectual style in the late twentieth century? Are we caught, as we consider such questions as "assessing assessment," in an infinite, self-indulgent regress with diminishing returns? Would our students and the cause of education be better served if we educators emancipated ourselves from process and fads, as Gagnon (1995) has argued, and devoted ourselves to real content?

But that frames the choice in a deceptively simple way. First, is assessment just another in a long line of trendy gimmicks? The movement has been going strong now for over a decade, with no sign of fading and with enough structural support—in the form of accreditation standards and mandates from boards of higher education—to keep it around for a long time to come. And there is the genuine enthusiasm of faculty who have seen assessment work. All that suggests that assessment is no ephemeral educationist fad. Beyond that, although Gagnon (1995) is enormously informed about education in the United States and at the same time brings a salutary international perspective to the debate, we need to recognize that the choice, at the college level at least, is not between empty fads and real content, but rather between competing visions of content.

As knowledgeable, committed educators agonize over that choice, assessment is no mere distraction. Used properly, as a tool and not an end in itself, assessment can force the conversation among faculty, students, employers, and other stakeholders about those content choices. Assessment, more powerfully than anything else that has appeared on the postsecondary horizon in decades, can pull faculty out of their disciplinary isolation and guide them into engagement with a larger world—a world of other disciplines and of broader educational, social, and professional needs. To speak in a parable, are we educators, like our colleagues of three hundred years ago, perhaps sitting around a table, arguing with reddened, choleric faces about the merits of this dogma or that, even as a crowd of young Enlightenment types gathers outside the door? If indeed we run that danger, assessment is probably the tool most likely to make us look up and then invite those pesky souls into the room.

References

Alexander, L., Clinton, B., and Kean, T. H. *A Time for Results: The Governors' 1991 Report on Education.* Washington, D.C.: National Governors' Association, 1991.

Angelo, T. A. *Classroom Research: Early Lessons from Success.* San Francisco: Jossey-Bass, 1991.

Angelo, T. A. "Reassessing (and Defining) Assessment." *AAHE Bulletin,* 1995, *48*(3), 7–9.

Angelo, T. A., and Cross, K. P. *Classroom Assessment Techniques: A Handbook for College Teachers.* (2nd ed.) San Francisco: Jossey-Bass, 1993.

Arcaro, J. *Creating Quality in the Classroom.* Delray Beach, Fla.: St. Lucie Press, 1995.

Bennett, W. *To Reclaim a Legacy.* Washington, D.C.: National Endowment for the Humanities, 1984.

Clayton State College. *General Education at Clayton State College.* Morrow, Ga.: Clayton State College, 1993.

Cross, K. P. *Feedback in the Classroom: Making Assessment Matter.* Washington, D.C.: American Association for Higher Education, 1988.

Ehrmann, S. C. "Asking the Right Questions: What Does Research Tell Us About Technology and Higher Learning?" *Change,* 1995, *27*(2), 20–27.

El-Khawas, E. *Campus Trends Survey.* Washington, D.C.: American Council on Education, 1982, 1987, 1990.

Ewell, P. T. "To Capture the Ineffable: New Forms of Assessment in Higher Education." In G. Grant (ed.), *Review of Research in Education.* Washington, D.C.: American Educational Research Association, 1991.

Ewell, P. T. "A Matter of Integrity: Accountability and the End(s) of Higher Education." *Change,* 1994, *26*(6), 24–29.

Gagnon, P. "What Should Children Learn?" *Atlantic Monthly,* 1995, *276*(6), 65–78.

Gilbert, S. "The Technology 'Revolution': Important Questions About a Work in Progress" (editorial). *Change,* 1995, *27*(2), 6–7.

Hutchings, P. *Behind Outcomes: Contexts and Questions for Assessment.* Washington, D.C.: American Association for Higher Education, 1989.

Hutchings, P., and Marchese, T. "Watching Assessment: Questions, Stories, Prospects." In American Association for Higher Education, *Reprise 1991. Reprints of Two Papers Treating*

Assessment's History and Implementation. Washington, D.C.: American Association for Higher Education, 1991.

McTighe Musil, C. (ed.). *The Courage to Question: Women's Studies and Student Learning.* Washington, D.C.: Association of American Colleges and National Women's Studies Association, 1992.

National Institute of Education. *Involvement in Learning: Realizing the Potential of American Higher Education.* Report of the Study Group on the Conditions of Excellence in American Higher Education. Washington, D.C.: U.S. Government Printing Office, 1984.

Schilling, K. M., and Schilling, K. L. "Professors Must Respond to Calls for Accountability." *Chronicle of Higher Education,* Mar. 24, 1993, p. A40.

Waluconis, C.J.M. "Student Self-Evaluation." In T. W. Banta and Associates, *Making a Difference: Outcomes of a Decade of Assessment in Higher Education.* San Francisco: Jossey-Bass, 1993.

Wiggins, G. P. *Assessing Student Performance: Exploring the Purpose and Limits of Testing.* San Francisco: Jossey-Bass, 1993.

Wolverton, M. *A New Alliance: Continuous Quality and Classroom Effectiveness.* Washington, D.C.: ASHE-ERIC, 1995.

CHAPTER TWENTY-NINE

ASSESSING LEARNING IN PROGRAMS

D. W. Farmer, Edmund A. Napieralski

On September 23, 1742, John Winthrop, Governor of the Massachusetts Bay Colony, presided over an assessment of student learning outcomes for graduating seniors at Harvard College. The assessment itself was conducted by the college's external Board of Overseers (Harcleroad, 1980, p. 1). Academic program assessment is not a new phenomenon in American higher education!

Colleges and universities have regularly conducted internal program reviews in a variety of formats. Evaluation has been viewed as intrinsic to the process of maintaining the curriculum. Periodic monitoring is generally accepted as necessary to determine what knowledge should form the substance of education, how it should be organized in a curriculum, and how it should be communicated to students.

The idea that program review should be conducted to demonstrate accountability to external groups is a more recent development. Academic program review has intensified during the last decade due to the recommendations of national commissions regarding curriculum and teaching, changing expectations of accrediting bodies, and the call for accountability and reallocation of resources by state boards of higher education and legislators. The changing demographics and economic conditions challenging colleges and universities have added force to the concern. Accordingly, academic program assessment has gradually become more systematic and formal as it has come to be viewed as a key ingredient in institutional long-range and strategic planning efforts. Program review has become a necessary component of the assessment of institutional effectiveness.

Consequently, a broad range of expectations now exists for academic program reviews in higher education. This poses a significant challenge to those charged with conducting such reviews because it is difficult to address multiple purposes in a single study, especially when the purposes in question are as potentially incompatible as program improvement, resource reallocation, and program termination. Reviews conducted for the purpose of program improvement rarely result in the reduction of resources, and quite often identify additional resources needed (Barak, 1986, p. 53). Investigators have also discovered the importance of establishing congruence between the stated purpose and anticipated outcomes of a program review. A clear definition of purposes and outcomes appears to be helpful to those seeking an appropriate model and methods of review.

During the last two decades, state boards of education have become deeply involved in reviewing existing academic programs and approving new programs. Such external program review has increasingly become useful in cases where programs are examined for possible discontinuance as part of a process of demonstrating accountability to external constituencies (Conrad and Wilson, 1985, p. iii). At the same time, the higher education community has witnessed the increased frequency and sophistication of internal review. Internal reviews conducted primarily for the purpose of improving existing academic programs are the focus of this chapter.

A study commissioned by the American Council on Education in 1986 indicated the existence of a broad consensus among college and university administrators regarding the purpose of internal academic program assessment. Over 90 percent cited instructional improvement as the primary purpose; baccalaureate colleges also noted the additional purpose of improving overall institutional effectiveness (El-Khawas, 1986, p. 5). This same sense of common purpose for assessing academic programs is reflected in publications of regional accrediting agencies that expect schools to clarify the relationship between assessing institutional effectiveness and improving academic programs.

Approaches to Academic Program Assessment

The literature of program evaluation is rich with "true models" and "true methods" for conducting academic program *assessment*. The belief that there is a single and universally applicable model, however, is one of the myths associated with program review (Barak, 1986, p. 53). An approach to assessment that is successful on one campus will rarely work on another campus without significant modification. The most successful program reviews are those that have been developed with a sensitivity to an individual institution's culture, with a choice of an evaluation methodology appropriate to circumstances, and with reasonable probability that the evaluation will serve a specified purpose. Moreover, designing an evaluation is a continuing process. Flexibility is required to permit the evaluator to pay closer attention to more relevant questions as the field work proceeds (Cronbach, 1983, p. 7).

In designing an approach to academic program assessment, it is helpful to be familiar with a variety of models or approaches. Each has different assumptions, constraints, and anticipated results. Although there may not be any one best model, components of several approaches can be brought together creatively to develop an appropriate design for an institution. Such hybrid models are abundant in higher education. The most prominent assessment models can be classified according to five different definitions or purposes: evaluation as measurement, evaluation as the achievement of program goals, decision-oriented evaluation, evaluation as professional judgment, and goal-free or responsive evaluation (Gardner, 1977, p. 571).

The influence of the scientific method on evaluation is clear in the first three classifications, while the remaining two represent more humanistic approaches. Both the scientific and humanistic approaches have been present together continuously in evaluation. They provide not only alternative methodologies but also differences in definition, purpose, and approach for conducting academic program assessment.

The synthetic works of more recent researchers (House, 1978, 1982; Conrad and Wilson, 1985; and Barak, 1990) confirm the usefulness of these classifications and show how consistent approaches to evaluation have been for a relatively long period of time. Rather than an evolution in approaches to evaluation, these works represent changes in the way key concepts and stages in the process are defined. What has occurred in recent years, however, has been a decided shift in emphasis from scientific to more humanistic models. The following analysis of approaches to evaluating relies heavily on Gardner's original classification (1977).

Evaluation as Measurement

Approaches to academic program assessment that emphasize measurement place great weight on the reliability of evidence discovered by quantitative social science techniques (House, 1982, p. 7). These approaches tend to be formal and systematic, focusing on data and the instruments used to collect the data. The basic assumptions for the measurement approach to evaluation are that the academic program to be evaluated has measurable characteristics and that instruments can be designed to measure them validly (Gardner, 1977, p. 576). The data generated are usually compared to a standardized scale and include such items as test scores, graduation rates, or comparative cost analysis studies.

The measurement approach exhibits two principal weaknesses. The first is that communication between the evaluator and the program participants or academic administrators is usually limited to discussions to clarify the measurement goal before the evaluation, and a formal report afterwards to display numerical data derived from the instrument used (Gardner, 1977). The second weakness relates to equating evaluation with measurement. House cites systems analysis as illustrating that measurement is too narrow an approach. Educational programs seldom lend themselves to being measured by a few simple quantitative outcomes because the judgment of worth requires going beyond the measurement and reporting of data: "Test scores often do not capture the essence of most programs, and cost benefit ratios leave too much unsaid. The evaluation is often based on a few available measures that have no credibility, particularly for the people in the program being assessed. Complex, multiple, even conflicting goals are standard in education, and maximizing one outcome often distorts others . . . a highly reliable measure might be invalid as an indicator of program quality" (House, 1982, p. 8).

Evaluation as Achievement of Program Goals

The goal-based evaluation model is one of the major approaches to evaluation in higher education (Conrad and Wilson, 1985, p. 20). Approaches to academic program assessment that emphasize a discrepancy or a congruence between actual performance and goals or standards of performance are usually associated with *summative evaluations* intended to make a judgment about the worth of an academic program. Models that fall under this classification focus on establishing goals and criteria for measuring performance; they aim to identify appropriate tools for collecting data and comparing that data with a set of previously identified program goals. The basic assumption of this approach to evaluation is that the most important decisions regarding the academic program will relate to its success or failure in achieving its goals (Gardner, 1977, p. 578).

House cites the behavioral objective approach to illustrate how actual performance is measured against standards. Frequently the objectives state expected student performances that can be reduced to specific observable behaviors, which, in turn, can be measured by tests. Behavioral approaches reflect a scientific methodology that reduces overall behavior into small steps in a technological or engineering approach characteristic of an assembly line (House, 1982, p. 10). Both the systems analysis and behavioral objectives approaches cited by House base their claims to authority on the social science quantitative methods of inquiry they employ—psychometric measurement, rigorous experimental design, and statistical methods of analyzing data.

Surveys are frequently used as part of data gathering. Survey-oriented reviews are designed primarily to collect information on a program as reported by faculty, students, and alumni. The survey instruments may be either self-developed or commercially developed. Either type requires the identification of questions or issues that need to be resolved by the evaluation process. Commercial surveys have many advantages: they are developed by experts in the field, usually field tested and revised, and frequently provide comparative data. It is also true that commercially produced surveys may not meet the identified needs of the evaluation process as well as a locally developed instrument. Barak and Breier caution, however, that—despite their apparent suitability—many self-developed survey instruments produce meaningless results due to ambiguous or biased questions and are frequently difficult to analyze even when the questions themselves are relatively clear and unbiased (1990, p. 31).

The literature includes a variety of criticisms of the measurement of performance against goals approach. The first relates to the difficulty of clarifying goals and measuring performance when academicians are concerned with highly complex activities as well as with ambivalent goals and standards of performance. A second criticism is that this approach is most frequently used in summative evaluation, resulting in feedback that reaches program personnel—if at all—too late for them to make changes to improve the program. A final criticism concerns the tendency to focus on those goals for which measurement reports are available, which results in assessing what is easiest to assess rather than what is most important to assess.

Decision-Oriented Evaluation

Approaches to academic program assessment that emphasize decision-oriented evaluation focus on collecting useful information for decision makers to judge alternatives. Decision-oriented approaches establish an institutionalized feedback mechanism that provides a continuous basis for assessing information required for decision making. Efforts to implement decision-oriented evaluation systems in higher education can be found in attempts to implement principles of management information systems across institutions (Gardner, 1977, p. 580). Ideally, this produces continual communication between evaluators and administrators regarding relevant information needed to judge decision-making alternatives. A comprehensive and systematic database is required to support this approach to assessing academic programs. Barak and Breier (1990, p. 31) suggest that data-oriented reviews are most frequently employed as a screening process to identify problem programs that require an in-depth review using other approaches.

In decision-oriented evaluation the interpretation of data is usually the responsibility of an administrator. One of the major criticisms of the decision-oriented approach is the significant cost of collecting masses of data that may not play a role in the decision-making process. Gardner (1977, p. 590) argues that this approach involves questionable assumptions: that rationality is always present in decision making, that decision makers are willing to use the data collected, and that institutional decisions occur cyclically so that systematic data collection can inform them.

Evaluation as Professional Judgment

A tradition of humanistic approaches to academic program assessment has existed simultaneously with the scientific approaches discussed earlier. Whereas scientific approaches emphasize method, humanistic approaches emphasize experience. Approaches to academic program assessment that emphasize evaluation as professional judgment use a qualified professional to serve as an evaluator for an academic program. The consultant-evaluator in the role of an expert judges the quality or effectiveness of the academic program. This approach assumes that the best judge of an academic program is an outside expert who renders a judgment based upon personal experience as a professional within a specific discipline.

The consultant-oriented review is similar to the connoisseurship model in which the external evaluator becomes the "primary instrument of measurement" (Conrad and Wilson, 1985, p. 28). Data collection, analysis, and interpretation are guided primarily by the subjective judgments of the connoisseur rather than by any evaluation design. Both the consultant-oriented and connoisseurship models usually involve the program staff by having them engage in self-study prior to the visit. Outside expert judgment is compared with that of the staff as a means of continuing the process of self-examination. The self-study approach is usually employed when the intent of the review is program improvement.

The principal criticism of the use of professional judgment as an approach to evaluation is its subjectivity. Criteria that serve as the basis for rendering such an expert judgment are frequently not explicitly stated.

Although some individuals may certainly qualify as experts in a given field, the absence of clearly articulated and publicly presented evaluation criteria may undermine the validity of the academic program assessment (Gardner, 1977). Nevertheless, such professional review may provide insights not readily available through other approaches (House, 1982, p. 11).

Goal-Free or Responsive Evaluation

A goal-free or responsive approach to academic program assessment engages in an evaluation process that is not limited to the program's stated goals. The intent of *goal-free evaluation* is to discover and to judge the actual effects of the program, including its unintended or accidental effects. This approach assumes that unintended side effects of a program may be as important as its intended effects.

Related to goal-free assessment is responsive evaluation: a process of collecting, analyzing, and interpreting information about a program in light of the concerns and issues of audiences that have a stake in the evaluation (Conrad and Wilson, 1985) whether or not these concerns and issues relate to the stated program goals. Responsive assessment resembles House's case study approach (1982, p. 11) in which the story of the program is frequently told in the words of those interviewed. In contrast with the professional judgment approach, goal-free or responsive evaluation places more emphasis on the evaluator's expertise in using qualitative assessment techniques as opposed to expertise in a specific program discipline (Gardner, 1977, p. 591).

The chief criticism of the goal-free or responsive approach is that its lack of emphasis on formal measurement techniques allows for subjectivity to shape the results. An effective evaluation using this form of professional review, however, will incorporate the perceptions of both the program's proponents and its detractors (House, 1982, p. 12).

Rethinking Approaches to Academic Program Assessment

The past decade has seen a significant rethinking of the approaches to academic program assessment. Although many aspects of the traditional approaches are still in use, clear shifts have appeared in both purpose and methods of academic program assessment. Three transitions epitomize this change: from quantitative to qualitative approaches, from summative to formative evaluation, and from reliance on inputs to emphasis on outcomes.

Quantitative methods emphasizing measurement and deemphasizing value judgments have traditionally characterized approaches to evaluation in higher education. Moreover, the quantitative approach to evaluation was until very recently reinforced by the expectations of regional accrediting agencies and state boards of education. Quantitative methods reflect scientific-evaluation models relying on numbers, measurement, statistical analysis, and verification of congruence between program goals and program performance. Methodological techniques include the use of questionnaires, test results, program records, and objective indicators or criteria.

Academic program assessment has gradually changed from an externally driven, summative evaluation process relying on quantitative methods to an internally driven *formative evaluation* process relying on qualitative information. This transition represents a change in focus from judging the worth of programs to providing feedback to program personnel for the purpose of improving programs. Quantitative data can still be used in combination with quantitative methods to provide a holistic program assessment related more to a humanistic rather than to a social scientific paradigm.

Humanistic qualitative methods rely on discovery, subjectivity, naturalistic inquiry, description, interpretation, and holistic analysis. Methodological techniques include personal observation, interviews, field study, and other unobtrusive measures.

Fundamental to the qualitative approaches available is the search for the insider's perspective (Fetterman, 1991, p 1). Qualitative assessments aim at discovering what people associated with the program think and at identifying their basis for holding such views. Although subjective views may depart to some extent from objective reality, they influence the way program participants think and behave.

Qualitative methods for assessment are free from the design and evaluation criteria used to gather and analyze data in quantitative approaches. Evaluators attempt to discover underlying patterns from a variety of information sources and then to verify those patterns by further observation and interviews. Interviews, therefore, are central to the qualitative approach to academic program assessment. Questions are usually open-ended, aiming to elicit the insider's perspective. Evaluators also strive to avoid being immersed in the life of the people in the program under review, in an effort to maintain reasonable detachment.

Qualitative methods used in academic program assessment also draw heavily upon *anthropological approaches,* especially the ethnographic interview (Tierney, 1991, p. 7). The interviewer does not have a specific agenda for the interview, but rather explores the spectrum of concerns identified by those being interviewed as they come up in conversation. The interviewer pursues interesting leads, "allowing imagination and ingenuity full reign" (Becker and Geer, 1972, p. 133) and trying to develop new hypotheses and test them during the course of the interview. The open-ended interview is frequently used in anthropology as a means of gaining a holistic understanding. Prior to initiating a series of interviews, the anthropologist develops a set of general questions that need to be covered, but is free to take the interview in any direction that appears fruitful. Open-ended questioning in program review helps the evaluator to uncover perceptions and attitudes that may later be helpful in arriving at recommendations for program improvement.

The anthropological approach appears especially suitable for evaluating liberal education. Because liberal education is difficult to define and has multiple referents, evaluations based on the scientific, experimental model often fail to command the respect of liberal arts faculty. Such faculty seek "intellectual complexity, not simplification; credibility, not certainty; discovery, not verification" (Rogers and Gamson, 1982, p. 231) as an evaluation design. The anthropological approach encourages greater reliance on observation, interviewing, journal entry, group discussions, and critical incident reporting. These methods provide the basis for analyzing connections between the process and outcomes of liberal education.

The change in emphasis from quantitative to qualitative approaches in academic program assessment parallels the change from summative to formative evaluations. Summative evaluation is conducted for a program that has been in operation for a period of time to determine its success or failure. It views program development and evaluation as linear. Formative evaluation, on the other hand, is conducted during the course of program development to provide guidance to the program's developers and implementers. Formative evaluation is not a linear activity at the end of the implementation process; rather, it forms a dialectic, developing and changing throughout the process (Craven, 1981, p. 434). Its purpose is clearly not to judge the worth of a program but rather to improve a program. Formative evaluation can give program personnel an idea of what summative evaluation would look like and can allow time for personnel to engage in program improvement to influence the outcome—particularly useful when summative evaluation may lead to terminating the program (Salasin, 1974, p. 12).

The change in emphasis from quantitative to qualitative approaches is also reflected in the shift from relying on the quality of program inputs to assessing the quality of program outcomes both in terms of intended effects and actual or unintended effects. There may be no necessary relationship between inputs and the eventual outcomes of a program. Astin notes that evidence suggests the relationship between learning and resources is a loose one, at best. Moreover, an evaluation needs to recognize the important difference between the accumulation of resources and the effective use of resources to further the educational development of students (Astin, 1982, pp. 11–12). Consequently, increasing emphasis is being placed on incorporating assessment of actual student learning outcomes into program reviews as well as on the use of goal-free evaluation strategies to discover unanticipated outcomes.

Assessment of student learning outcomes contributes most directly to improving academic programs when multiple assessment activities are administered frequently and regularly throughout the entire curriculum. Ideally, assessment results in meaningful feedback, which faculty and students can use to improve both teaching and learning. Assessment criteria provide qualitative standards for judging student performance holistically. Samples of student work juxtaposed with the criteria can be reviewed by external evaluators to determine if faculty expectations are sufficiently high and if the range of student performance conforms to the criteria.

Goal-free evaluation also focuses on actual program outcomes. By not exaggerating expected outcomes directly related to program goals, goal-free evaluation examines the actual effects of the program to identify outcomes that might otherwise be overlooked. It provides a more holistic view of what a program is actually accomplishing. Goal-free evaluation is primarily formative evaluation intended to help program developers and implementers to revise or improve a program (House and Allarie, 1982, p. 12). In a summative framework, the effects uncovered by the goal-free approach would have little or no value to evaluators.

New Directions in Current Practice

The significant transitions in academic program assessment—from quantitative to qualitative approaches, from summative to formative evaluation, and from reliance on inputs to emphasis on outcomes—are very much evident in the current practice of institutions across a wide spectrum: two-year and four-year, small and large, public and private.

While quantitative data still represent one requirement of reviews, departments or programs can be freed from the burden and responsibility of providing such data by personnel equipped and ready to supply it, operating out of institutional planning, registrar, and alumni offices. (American University and King's College have adopted such programs.) Faculty, then, are free to concentrate on the qualitative information that they generally believe to be more important and feel capable of defining more effectively. Even state commissions or boards (such as Emporia State, Kansas) have begun to recognize the value of qualitative measures and have developed formats for their reporting.

The shift from summative to formative evaluation parallels the shift from the focus on quantitative data to qualitative information that can contribute to program improvement. The formative emphasis has also affected the composition of groups involved in a program review. Formerly, department faculty might conduct their own self-study and report to an administrator. Currently, more constituencies who have a stake in the program's success become actively involved in the review. Representatives of key committees like curriculum and finance (as at American University) or even an academic affairs committee of a board of directors (as at King's College) might make up a review board to which a department submits its self-study. In other cases, the process includes focus groups of students (as at Union College) or of faculty from cognate disciplines (as at Western Carolina). The formative thrust has also led to a wider sharing of review results as, for example, in a summary report published for the entire academic community at American University. Formative evaluation has allowed for greater participation in a conversation that aims at the improvement not only of the department but of the institution as a whole. Further, such participation in the process and in communicating results indicates a movement toward having program review reflect a campus culture where widespread involvement is valued.

The third major shift, from inputs to outcomes, is very much evident as the results of the assessment of student learning become essential ingredients of program review. Assessment information includes a definition of program goals and indicators of the extent to which students are meeting these goals. (Johnson County Community College, King's College, and Winthrop University all have programs along these lines.) A review may require further an articulation of how program goals contribute to the goals of the institution as a whole (as at Ball State University). Reviews at regular intervals may also lead programs to concentrate only on selected goals and corresponding student learning outcomes and to ask questions clearly aimed at ongoing improvement, for example, whether goals are high or demanding enough (as at King's College).

All these shifts in interest and emphasis indicate as well a belief that review should influence both planning and budgeting that can respond in a more timely fashion to program needs. Such responsiveness may be difficult in cases where, for example, state boards use only headcount or FTE information to determine allocations or where reviews occur only every five to seven years.

Because of the widespread belief that reviews should more immediately influence planning and budget, institutions such as American University, Johnson County Community College, and King's College are finding ways to effect a more timely connection. Simplified annual reviews that feature selected information on student learning outcomes may provide one means to help decision makers respond to urgent program needs for the sake of ensuring and fostering quality.

Assessing Quality

Assessing the quality of academic programs poses a special challenge and has generated much confusion and debate. Although national conference themes and sessions often refer to quality in higher education, it is a concept frequently regarded as elusive—despite the judgments about the quality of academic programs that are made virtually every day (Astin, 1982, p. 10).

One source of difficulty in understanding quality is that many assume there should be a single measure for judging it. Quality is multidimensional; it cannot be assessed by unidimensional measures, and the search for the one true measure of quality is reductionist and inappropriate. Another source of difficulty can be found in viewing quality as an adjective, as in "quality program," when in fact it is a noun (Scott, 1980, p. 19).

Quality is defined by a number of characteristics such as a program's effectiveness in achieving its goals and the appropriateness of the goals themselves. These characteristics need to be public and the indicators signaling their presence must be acknowledged. Discussions with faculty on a variety of college and university campuses reveal considerably more agreement regarding what constitutes quality than one might expect. The ultimate meaning of quality lies in the nature of the effect an academic program has on the growth and development of students as learners. This implies that quality is cumulative over time (Stark and Lowther, 1980, p. 286) and that qualitative rather than quantitative approaches will provide evaluators with the greatest insight as well as the best sense of how to modify a program to enhance student learning.

Judgments about enhanced student learning result from qualitative evaluation. Program quality—as opposed to program costs, enrollments, student-faculty ratios, and data inputs—is not quantifiable. No matter how much quantitative data may be part of a program review process, the conclusions result from the exercise of judgment (George, 1982, p. 52). Quantitative measurement and quality assessment are simply different kinds of evaluation (Olscamp, 1978, pp. 510–511).

Priorities for Improving Assessment

Ironically, the frequency of conducting academic program assessments stands in stark contrast to the common lack of satisfaction with the results. If evaluators are more concerned with the process of evaluations—the doing of evaluations—than with the use of assessment findings in making decisions, their attitude may reinforce organizational inertia (Baker, 1978, p. 60).

A critique of the practice of academic program assessment suggests two priorities for improving its effectiveness: increasing the use of assessment findings for decision making and linking assessment with the planning-budgeting process.

The failure to use the results of assessment in making subsequent decisions undermines the value of the process itself. This gives rise to the well-founded perception of faculty that program evaluation is a waste of time and a bureaucratic exercise. One of the reasons for a failure to use assessment findings is the lack of clarity about the purpose of evaluations. Clarity of purpose needs to be shared by all participants in the process, and that understanding must separate the evaluation of teaching from academic program assessment. Program reviews conducted primarily to make decisions about program termination will be quite different from those designed to improve program quality. Not surprisingly, researchers report that when program improvement is the clear purpose for academic program assessment, faculty are more open and constructive participants than when assessment occurs under conditions of threat (Arns and Poland, 1980, p. 281).

A second reason explaining the failure to use assessment results is that the approach to assessing does not address the concerns and issues of the stakeholders and that the information generated, although statistically significant, is judged not to be valuable (Guba and Lincoln, 1981, p. xix). Effective evaluation must begin with the real concerns of the stakeholders and result in useful information and recommendations relating to the purpose of the evaluation. The usefulness of evaluation findings depends on the degree to which stakeholders become aware of the findings, accept them, and develop insights upon which to base an action plan (Cronbach, 1983, p. 311). This requires a form of program assessment that provides an alternative to measurement-oriented approaches. Such alternative approaches have become known as *responsive* evaluation. An assessment approach is responsive if it relates more directly to program activity than to program intent and if it addresses the issues and questions raised by a program's participants. For any assessment program to be successful, there must be a payoff to faculty. For most faculty, the acceptable reward, if not the desired reward, is action that leads to enhancing teaching and learning in the academic program.

Related to the failure to use assessment findings is the failure to connect the assessment process with the planning-budgeting process. Just as planning needs to be done before budgeting, so also does program assessment need to be done to aid planning. An effective assessment should be able to identify changes needed to improve a program. Effective planning should be able to prioritize these desired program changes in an institutional context. Effective budgeting should in turn be able to reallocate resources in response to changing institutional planning priorities. This series of sequential relationships provides a blueprint for a strategic planning process that argues against incremental budgeting and instead encourages academic program initiatives.

Principles for Conducting Effective Assessments

Examples of successful academic program assessment reveal several common principles that can serve as a basis for defining guidelines for conducting effective assessments:

- *Establish clear goals.* Recognizing the complexity of academic programs, the number of stakeholders, and the variety of possible purposes for assessment, academic program reviews should have a single defining purpose clearly articulated for all participants. A necessary prerequisite for establishing goals is conducting a feasibility study for the review to clarify the underlying issues and determine exactly why an academic program is to be evaluated. Successful evaluations begin by recognizing that there are decision-making issues that justify the effort involved.

• *Be flexible in construction and approach to assessment.* There are no fixed protocols for choosing an approach to academic program assessment (Arns and Poland, 1980, p. 278). No single approach is best for all decision-making purposes, because no two programs are alike. Attempts to use an existing model without significant modification for a specific campus environment will generally be unsuccessful. The assessment design must be constructed to serve the information needs of those who will be involved in the subsequent decision-making process.

• *Use a self-study process.* A self-study process is perhaps the most effective means of involving participants of a program in academic program assessment. Although guidelines for conducting the self-study are usually set forth by those conducting the review or in conjunction with the decision makers, it is important that the guidelines not be so restrictive as to limit the ability of program participants to present their perspective on issues and on what data mean. Also, an institutional research office's supply of needed data can allow authors of the self-study to spend more time on the qualitative assessment of the academic program. One of the chief benefits of conducting an effective self-study is to help program participants differentiate between and reflect upon what they are doing and what they should be doing.

• *Avoid information overload.* Although information is needed for effective assessment, too much information can paralyze those conducting the evaluation. Data collection needs to address the major goals, issues, and questions identified as the reason for conducting the assessment. The quality of information needed for the subsequent decision-making process rather than the quantity of information available should inform data collection.

• *Ensure credibility of the assessment experience.* Little positive value can result from an academic program assessment unless it has credibility in the eyes of the participants and decision makers. The assessment process must be regarded as unbiased, fair, and reasonable (Barak and Breier, 1990, p. 9). *Lack of bias* relates to the rigor of the assessment process and broad participation among those who have a stake in the program. *Fairness* relates to the use of multiple criteria and the availability of relevant data, and *reasonableness* relates to developing a shared understanding of the purpose for assessment and of the possible decision alternatives that will follow.

• *Maintain open communication.* Open communication among program participants, reviewers, and decision makers throughout the course of the assessment process is crucial for maintaining harmony and fostering a positive attitude. Information needs to be widely shared in relationship to the issues and questions under review. The goal of keeping the lines of communication open should be to keep the people who will be responsible for making decisions and implementing recommendations informed and involved in the process. Any evaluation requires good communication to avoid surprises at the completion of the review. The way a review is conducted can frequently be as important as the actual assessment findings, and frequently determines success or failure when program participants are implementing recommendations.

- *Link program assessment to other organizational decision-making processes.* Too frequently, directives to conduct reviews come down from on high, but the recommendations resulting from the review seem to play no role in subsequent decision making. The linkage between assessment and decision making in an organization is not something that occurs naturally (Conrad and Wilson, 1985, p. 71). That link must be established when constructing an approach to evaluation and must be constantly looked after to bring it to fruition.
- *Effect closure.* The assessment process needs formal closure. This should take the form of a written action plan following the decision making. The action plan, sometimes called a *memorandum of understanding*, contains a set of agreements among all parties to the review (Arns and Poland, 1980, p. 280). It details what actions will be taken, who is responsible for implementing each action, and the time frame in which the actions will be carried out. A memorandum of understanding helps to suppress the common tendency to write an evaluation report instead of implementing change. Only the actual use of assessment results in academic program development brings closure to the process.

Conclusion

The most successful reviews are likely to result when planners and participants exhibit a sensitivity to their particular institution's culture and an openness to creative combinations of approaches to design and process that reflect that culture. For internal program assessment intended to improve an existing academic program, particularly its effectiveness in enhancing student learning, the following guidelines may prove useful:

- The purpose of the assessment—to improve an academic program—should be clear and clearly distinguished from other forms of assessment such as the evaluation of teaching.

- Important quantitative data should be supplied not by the program under review but by departments in the institution better equipped to provide it, such as alumni, planning, or registrar's offices.
- The faculty of the program to be assessed should be in charge of the self-study; they should, however, invite the active participation of constituencies that have a stake in the program, such as students, alumni, and faculty in cognate departments.
- Academic programs should include assessment information in the self-study, especially a public definition of program goals, an articulation of the relationship between these goals and the goals or mission of the institution, and indicators of the extent to which students are meeting program goals.
- The assessment design should be practical and flexible—constructed to reflect the special nature of the academic program and to serve the needs of those making subsequent decisions affecting the program.
- The assessment should include goal-free or open-ended interviews that can provide information for qualitative and holistic analysis.
- A spirit of open inquiry and communication should characterize the conduct of the assessment; the results of the assessment should likewise be broadly shared.
- Recommendations resulting from the assessment should include a list of actions to be taken, an assignment of responsibility for such actions, and a time frame.
- The assessment must make a difference and must have some impact on institutional planning and budgeting.
- The faculty of the program should find the reward for careful self-study and program assessment in action that leads to enhanced teaching and learning.

References

Arns, R. G., and Poland, W. "Changing the University Through Program Review." *Journal of Higher Education*, 1980, *51*(3), 268–284.

Astin, A. W. "Why Not Try Some New Ways of Measuring Quality?" *Educational Record*, 1982, *63*(2), 10–15.

Baker, E. "Evaluation Dimensions for Program Development and Improvement." In S. B. Anderson and C. D. Cobes (eds.), *Exploring Purposes and Dimensions*. New Directions for Program Evaluation, no. 1. San Francisco: Jossey-Bass, 1978.

Barak, R. J. "Seven Common Myths on Program Review." *Educational Record*, 1986, *67*(1), 52–54.

Barak, R. J., and Breier, B E. *Successful Program Review*. San Francisco: Jossey-Bass, 1990.

Becker, H. S., and Geer, B. "Participant Observation and Interviewing: A Comparison." In W. J. Filstead (ed.), *Qualitative Involvement with the Social World*. Chicago: Markham, 1972.

Conrad, C. F., and Wilson, R. F. *Academic Program Reviews: Institutional Approaches, Expectations, and Controversies.* ASHE-ERIC Higher Education Report No. 5. Washington, D.C.: Association for the Study of Higher Education, 1985.

Craven, E. "Evaluating Program Performance." In P. Jedamus and M. Peterson (eds.), *Improving Academic Management: A Handbook of Planning and Institutional Research.* San Francisco: Jossey-Bass, 1981.

Cronbach, L. J. *Designing Evaluations of Educational and Social Programs.* San Francisco: Jossey-Bass, 1983.

El-Khawas, E. *Campus Trends, 1986.* Higher Education Panel Report No. 73. Washington, D.C.: American Council on Education, 1986.

Fetterman, D. M. (ed.). *Using Qualitative Methods in Institutional Research.* New Directions for Institutional Research, no. 72. San Francisco: Jossey-Bass, 1991.

Gardner, D. E. "Five Evaluation Frameworks: Implications for Decision Making in Higher Education." *Journal of Higher Education,* 1977, *48*(5), 571–593.

George, M. D. "Assessing Program Quality." In R. Wilson (ed.), *Designing Academic Program Reviews.* New Directions for Higher Education, no. 37. San Francisco: Jossey-Bass, 1982.

Guba, E. G., and Lincoln, Y. S. *Effective Evaluation.* San Francisco: Jossey-Bass, 1981.

Harcleroad, F. F. "The Context of Academic Program Evaluation." In E. C. Craven (ed.), *Academic Program Review.* New Directions for Institutional Research, no. 27. San Francisco: Jossey-Bass, 1980.

House, E. "Assumptions Underlying Evaluation Models." *Educational Research,* 1978, *7*, 4–12.

House, E. "Alternative Evaluation Strategies in Higher Education." In R. Wilson (ed.), *Designing Academic Program Reviews.* New Directions for Higher Education, no. 37. San Francisco: Jossey-Bass, 1982.

House, E., and Allarie, S. "Goal Free Evaluation." *State Evaluation Network,* 1982, *2*, 9–12.

Olscamp, P. J. "Can Program Quality Be Quantified?" *Journal of Higher Education,* 1978, *49*(5), 504–511.

Rogers, T. H., and Gamson, Z. F. "Evaluation as a Developmental Process: The Case for Liberal Education." *The Review of Higher Education,* 1982, *5*(4), 225–238.

Salasin, S. "Exploring Goal-Free Evaluation: An Interview with Michael Scriven." *Evaluator,* 1974, *2*(1), 9–16.

Scott, R. A. "Quality: Program Review's Missing Link." *The College Board Review,* 1980, *118*, 19–21.

Stark, J. S., and Lowther, M. A. "Measuring Higher Education Quality." *Research in Higher Education,* 1980, *13*(3), 283–287.

Tierney, W. G. "Utilizing Ethnographic Interviews to Enhance Academic Decision Making." In D. M. Fetterman (ed.), *Using Qualitative Methods in Institutional Research.* New Directions for Institutional Research, no. 72, San Francisco: Jossey-Bass, 1991.

CHAPTER THIRTY

IDENTIFYING INDICATORS
OF CURRICULAR QUALITY

Peter T. Ewell

In the atmosphere of fiscal uncertainty and intellectual restlessness faced by most of those charged with managing curricula in the 1990s, a principal imperative is simply to know what is going on. The explosion of knowledge itself, together with multiple and insistent challenges to traditional canons of content and delivery, has led to accelerating curricular diversity both within and across institutions. The resulting size and complexity of today's curricula make them less and less easy to administer by touch and feel. At the same time, the need to stretch increasingly scarce resources across this growing territory has led to equally pressing demands for curricular consolidation and coherence to achieve greater efficiencies. Here as well, the managerial need is for more and better information about how things are working, and how they might be made to work better. If this were not enough, pressures for the public disclosure of such information are escalating as funders and accreditors focus increasingly on outcomes and effectiveness. Given these forces, growing interest in the topic of quality indicators both as tools for academic management and as key ingredients of the new accountability should come as no surprise.

Definitions and Purposes

The term *indicator* has been used for many years in social and economic policy circles to describe a relevant, easily calculable statistic that reflects the overall condition of an enterprise, or the progress of a particular set of events (Burstein, Oakes, and Guiton, 1992). Among the most prominent national examples are the Department of Labor's unemployment rate and the Department of Commerce's report on gross domestic product, both of which are used to assess the nation's overall economic health. More recently, statistical indicators have been used in industry to monitor processes of manufacturing and service delivery and to provide a reliable base for tracking and improving quality (Gitlow and Gitlow, 1987). Examples here are varied, but include such things as component failure rates for manufactured products, cycle times for responding to customer requests, and the like. Many similar indicators are beginning to be used in such areas as student registration or business operations in college and university settings (Seymour, 1991; Sherr and Teeter, 1991).

To be useful as an indicator, a particular piece of data must communicate something important about what is happening in a complex domain. It is not necessary for the statistic to be causally related to the phenomenon of interest. The infant mortality rate, for instance, is commonly used as an indicator of the overall health of a nation or culture, but it would not be appropriate to concentrate all resources on delivering prenatal health care in an attempt to improve the overall situation. Indicator statistics are thus often labeled proxies or indirect measures of condition or attainment, and cautions on their use are advised. For similar reasons, indicators are best used in combination. In higher education, as in any field, the best indicator systems are carefully constructed to provide mutually reinforcing measures that together provide an appropriate picture of what is occurring (Ewell and Jones, 1994).

What lies behind the growing prominence of performance indicators of this kind in national discussions of academic efficiency and effectiveness? A first stimulus comes from state and federal authorities—as well as institutional accrediting bodies—who in the last decade have become far more specific in their demands for information. In the early to mid-1980s, such demands centered largely on the unexplored and controversial territory of academic outcomes, and helped spark the kinds of institutional assessment approaches described in previous chapters. More recently, such demands have become more focused—centered prominently on the need to allocate scarce public resources and to inform individual consumer choices among colleges or universities (Ewell, 1994). Two things have happened as a result. First, the external market for performance information has gradually expanded from an exclusive concern with outcomes to address core questions of instructional organization and delivery. Second, the particular form in which information of all types has been requested by external actors has become increasingly terse and truncated, placing a premium on quantitative, easily compared measures of condition and performance (Ruppert, 1994). Combined, these two phenomena have yielded a growing number of statistical report cards prepared by sources ranging from state governments to *USA Today*.

A second stimulus for the use of performance indicators is internal. Faced with growing fiscal pressures and unabated student demand, many colleges and universities are beginning to adopt new management approaches based on Total Quality Management (TQM). Initially confined to administrative support functions, TQM concepts (though with many caveats) are gradually finding their way into academic functions as well (Seymour, 1991). In contrast to assessment's apparent emphasis on inspection at the end, such approaches emphasize continuously gathering data about how core processes are actually working, and focus especially on the ways apparently different functions are supposed to fit together to achieve common ends (Ewell, 1993). This particular emphasis is quite consistent with curricular reform themes of the last decade, which stress coherence and integration. But it also demands concrete information to monitor such connections, and to determine where appropriate improvements can be made.

Consistent with both stimuli, quality indicators are effective for some things and not for others. In general, indicators of quality or performance are particularly useful for three purposes in higher education settings: to quickly compare relative performance across units, institutions, or settings; to monitor what is happening within a particular unit, institution, or setting over time; and to explicitly examine the effects of intervention or policy change—either across settings or over time.

In all three applications, moreover, important caveats apply. First, indicators should not be used singly or in isolation. As noted, the most effective systems consist of multiple indicators designed to be mutually reinforcing. At the same time, the information contained in a given indicator always lies in comparison of values for it—across different settings, at different points in time, or before and after intervention. Basing any conclusion on a single observation can be dangerous. Second, the specific settings across which indicators are compared must be sufficiently similar to allow meaningful conclusions to be drawn. It makes little sense, for instance, to directly compare the student retention rates of a community college and a selective liberal arts college; these two types of institutions have substantial differences in mission and student clientele. At the very least, additional indicators should be constructed that reflect these differences, so that they may be taken directly into account in interpreting performance (in the example noted, for instance, an additional indicator of entering student ability might be constructed). Third, indicators are at their best when used to raise questions or identify potential problems; they are not very good at rendering summative judgments about adequacy or performance. As a result, quality measures of the kind described in this chapter should always be used in conjunction with the in-depth assessments described in other chapters. Nonetheless, the increasing use of indicators in academic settings testifies to their growing utility to academic managers when used for appropriate purposes.

Indicators of Curricular Quality: Some General Issues

Until recently, the idea of managing the curriculum was rare. Since the mid-1980s, however, a number of forces have coalesced that render explicit attention to curricular management issues imperative. One is a growing concern about curricular coherence and integration, especially in the realm of general education. Here such documents as *Integrity in the College Curriculum* (Association of American Colleges, 1985) and *Involvement in Learning* (National Institute of Education, 1984) marked a major resurgence of interest in designing curricula to achieve common, cross-cutting learning objectives, and helped to stimulate strong interest in assessment. Increasingly, however, attention has shifted from exclusive concern with curricular design and outcomes to include the mechanics of curriculum delivery. In part, this shift has been due to growing recognition that what goes on inside the classroom is at least as important in achieving coherence as the way curricula are designed. And in part it is due to a new awareness, based on experience, that simply implementing new curricula does not ensure that the courses and sequences they contain are deployed as designed.

Assessment, of course, represents another visible stimulus to the development of curricular quality indicators. As institutional assessment approaches became more sophisticated, institutions began collecting data about student experiences and inputs to explore the dynamics of outcomes (Ewell, 1991). Most discovered that it made little sense, beyond accountability, to collect detailed outcomes data without simultaneously knowing something about the stimulus conditions that might be responsible for such outcomes, and that might be susceptible to change. Astin's (1991) Input-Environment-Outcomes (I-E-O) schema for assessment both summarized and stimulated such trends, and has proven especially helpful in guiding more comprehensive approaches to curriculum evaluation at the institutional level. Because they are covered in Chapters Twenty-Eight and Twenty-Nine, this chapter will intentionally exclude topics related to the direct assessment of learning outcomes—probably the best bottom line for assessing quality. But following Astin's (1991) admonition, readers should be cautioned that information drawn both from assessment (on outcomes) and from curriculum monitoring (on processes) is needed to inform improvement.

New demands for efficiency constitute a final impetus for developing indicators of curricular shape and structure. Since the late 1990s, most institutions have been under substantial financial pressure and have begun actively searching for ways to deliver equivalent instructional content at lower unit cost. Naturally, attention has turned to methods for streamlining curricula—delivering in three years what was formerly taught in four, reducing or cutting underenrolled classes, or eliminating duplicative or overlapping course offerings (for example, see Zemsky, Massy, and Oedel, 1993; or Massy and Zemsky, 1992). While early attention to curricular modifications of this kind was unsophisticated, consisting largely of pruning the curriculum, more recent efforts have turned to more far-reaching and complex forms of restructuring (State Council on Higher Education in Virginia, 1994). Prominent here have been attempts to rethink curricular delivery in terms of common outcomes and efforts to carefully monitor student course-taking patterns to determine specific student markets for particular course sequences and to discover where modifications might be made to accelerate student progress.

It is curious that the new demand for efficiency has caused modifications in curriculum often surprisingly consistent with earlier and more academic concerns about coherence. Both require clear objectives, careful monitoring of delivery, and mapping actual patterns of course content and student flow to determine if course sequences are working as intended. Indicators of curricular quality and delivery, of course, can play a major role in this process.

Another important conceptual issue affecting the development of indicators in this domain is exactly what is meant by *curriculum*. As Stark and others (Stark and Lowther, 1986) have pointed out, institutions may have multiple curricula in place—designed, taught, and experienced by students—that have little to do with one another in content, coverage, or effectiveness. For purposes of indicators development, therefore, it is useful to operate with at least four distinct conceptions of curriculum, each of which might independently be assessed across a number of domains:

• The *designed* curriculum, consisting of catalogue and syllabus descriptions. This curriculum tends to dominate faculty attention, regardless of whether it has reality in practice. While increasingly recognizing explicit learning outcomes as part of the design, the bulk of attention here remains focused on content and course sequence, as defined by institutional or departmental policy.

• The *expectational* curriculum, consisting of the specific assignments and levels of performance expected of students and the manner in which student performance is assessed. This reflects what is more often the student's view of a given curriculum—based not on course content but rather on the requirements that must be met and the levels of performance needed to meet them. Though an aspect of design, examining expectations can also be revealing for curriculum assessment. For instance, a stated objective of the general education curriculum may be to develop students' oral communications proficiency. An examination of required performances across general education courses reveals that students are rarely asked to demonstrate this proficiency in class and are never evaluated on it.

• The *delivered* curriculum, consisting of what faculty actually teach and the consistency with which they do so. In contrast to design, this curriculum is behavioral, and may vary significantly across classrooms and from original design specifications. For any established curriculum—especially in general education—the phenomenon of course drift occurs: as new faculty teaching assignments to a given course are made, both content and teaching methods may vary increasingly from the vision embodied in the original design. Similarly, significant unintended variation may occur from section to section in a multisection course. Typically, institutions know very little about the extent and impact of such variations beyond simply acknowledging that they occur.

• The *experienced* curriculum, consisting of what students actually do. This curriculum is also behavioral and can usefully be separated into two quite different components. One concerns student course-taking patterns—especially when these occur within a distributional or elective design. Formal structure may prescribe particular arrays of courses that meet specific requirements, but how do different types of students in fact act out these requirements in the actual course choices that they make? A second aspect of the experienced curriculum is student learning behavior. Regardless of what a syllabus analysis might indicate, for instance, how much writing do students typically engage in to meet their class assignments? What kinds of writing do they really need to employ? How much actual exercise of oral communications skills do they report as having occurred in the classes that they take? Again, institutions typically know very little about such matters—though they often devote meticulous up-front attention to them in the design process.

All four aspects of curriculum are important in assessing quality, and appropriate indicator systems should be designed to reflect them all. Indeed, the best such systems are especially configured to detect discontinuities among these four aspects—examining, for instance, the ways in which particular elements of design are not being effectively translated into teaching practice and student experience.

Indicators can in principle be developed for virtually any dimension of curricular structure or performance, but they are especially suited to particular domains. From the outset, moreover, a distinction must be made between indicators designed to compare performance across institutions and intended primarily for accountability, and those focused on internal curricular functioning and intended primarily for local monitoring and improvement.

Comparing Curricula Across Institutions

Curricula differ in many ways from institution to institution, and the choice of which aspects to compare depends upon one's purposes. For purposes of accountability, attention has centered primarily on standards and student experiences. Concerned about what they perceive as declining quality and eroding levels of customer service to students, public policy makers are interested in such topics as what is expected of students and whether students are obtaining real access to faculty or getting the courses they need to graduate in a timely manner. Another typical perspective for comparison is that of an individual institution seeking peer-based information about curricular structure and delivery for purposes of accreditation or internal review. Principal dimensions of interest here typically center on coverage and content, or the overall shape of the curriculum with respect to numbers of electives and required courses.

Regardless of perspective, a fairly limited number of aspects of any curriculum are suitable for the development of comparative indicators. Indicators in each of these domains can also be monitored over time within a given institution to uncover long-term trends in instructional delivery, or to examine the impact of particular curricular policies.

• *Content and coverage.* What in particular is covered, and at what level of detail, constitutes probably the most commonly discussed and compared aspect of any curriculum. Detailed specifications of coverage with explicit standards, as embodied in the traditional *trivium* and *quadrivium,* are as old as the academy itself. Their more modern incarnations are present in the highly detailed course coverage and sequence specifications often used by professional accreditation bodies. More recently, coverage concerns have partially shifted away from disciplinary content toward the development of specified skills that cut across courses. Occurring principally in the realm of general education (and in part stimulated by assessment's demand that curricular outcomes be identified explicitly), the most common cross-cutting skills embrace areas such as writing and critical thinking (see Chapter Eighteen). The process of developing indicators development in this domain is conceptually straightforward, though operationally challenging. In essence, it addresses a single question: How much of what is taught where?

• *Sequence and structure.* Another classic basis on which to compare curricula is their degree of structural elaboration. Some, especially in the sciences and in technical fields, are highly specified with respect to sequence and structure—the familiar lockstep design. Others allow considerable flexibility and choice as the student progresses. Attempts to capture such notions empirically, however, have been rare. Among the most useful are those based on concepts of breadth and depth (for example, Zemsky, 1989)—in essence the proportion of total coursework in a given curriculum (either on paper or as recorded empirically through an analysis of transcripts) that is delivered within or outside of a particular discipline or academic area. In the realm of general education, where breadth is usually intended by definition, the more common question is one of coherence: to what degree does curricular structure embody courses intended to fit together or to induce students to make connections across disparate disciplines? Behind both approaches are several specific components of curricular design suitable for the development of indicators. One is concentration—in essence, the degree to which a single field or discipline is dominant. Another is choice, or the degree to which specific courses are mandated or students are free to elect them. A final dimension is linearity, or the degree to which specified prerequisite sequences or requirements are present.

• *Exposure versus application.* This domain reflects somewhat newer concerns about the balance between the traditional concept of delivery of disciplinary content and a more recent emphasis on the ongoing application or practice of learned skills. The most visible curricular features related to application include internships, practica, or capstone experiences—settings in which students are expected to actively deploy and demonstrate what they have learned. Quite naturally, such applied curricular features have been especially emphasized in professional programs. Increasingly, however, hands-on experiences and exercises are being emphasized as a part of active learning in all fields—whether they are formally included as a discrete curricular component or are built into existing coursework in the form of assignments or applications exercises. Indicators development in this domain concentrates principally on the presence or absence of such curricular features. Naturally, these are easier to detect when they are present as formal catalogue requirements that can be counted. But based on syllabus review or student self-reports, useful indicators can also be developed that reflect the degree to which the general delivery of coursework stresses opportunities for practical application.

• *Incidence of good practice.* As attention to articulating common curricular outcomes increased throughout the 1980s, so did concerns about effective instructional practices. Partly this was due to contemporary reforms in pedagogy that went beyond teaching to emphasize active, collaborative approaches to learning. Partly it was a natural extension of wider assessment-for-improvement initiatives, which quickly recognized that information about instructional processes and student experience would be critical in making sense of any data about outcomes (Astin, 1991). The specifics of instructional good practice were given a powerful vehicle for dissemination in "Seven Principles for Good Practice in Undergraduate Education" (Chickering and Gamson, 1987), which not only succinctly codified the majority of these practices but also provided concrete inventories for assessing the degree to which they are actually engaged in (Gamson and Poulsen,

1989). Growing interest in Classroom Research (Angelo and Cross, 1993) has given further impetus to these developments, as well as providing an additional set of good practices to count. Building good indicators within this domain, however, can be complex as it generally entails digging deeper than the visible aspects of curricular design. As a result, most work in this area has relied on faculty and student reports of their own behavior.

Indicators in all four of these domains have in some fashion been developed for purposes of peer comparison or public reporting. Probably the most visible are those contained in state performance indicators reports for public institutions now in place in some fifteen states (Ruppert, 1994). While the majority of these provide basic statistics on institutional activity—for instance, graduation rates or time-to-degree—many include measures of curricular delivery as well. South Carolina, for instance, requires institutions to report on levels of undergraduate student apprenticeship in faculty research activities, while Florida monitors the amount of writing required in a student's first year. Proposals currently being finalized in Virginia (and already in place in the Minnesota State University System's "Q-7" program, a seven-step quality improvement initiative) include measures that reflect the proportion of students engaging in capstone integrative experiences (State Council on Higher Education in Virginia, 1994). At the same time, a range of curricular good practice indicators have been proposed for postsecondary education at the national level (National Center for Higher Education Management Systems, 1994).

Beyond accountability, the use of indicators for peer comparison centers largely in the areas of structure and good practice. Projects of such organizations as the Association of American Colleges and Universities in general education, for instance, incorporate measures of overall breadth and depth (Zemsky, 1989), while new scales are currently being developed for the widely used "College Student Experiences Questionnaire" (Pace, 1984) to better reflect student-faculty contact and active learning experiences.

Monitoring Internal Curricular Design and Delivery

Indicators in the above domains, of course, can be equally useful at the institutional level for monitoring trends in the curriculum. Particularly prominent here have been attempts to develop local indicators of good practice (for example, Winona State University, 1990; Ewell and Jones, 1996). But a far more frequent application of the indicators concept for internal planning and evaluation has been in connection with assessment. As institutions increasingly develop comprehensive outcomes assessment models to inform improvement, their needs have increased for information related to instructional experiences and delivery. Not surprisingly, one of the first findings is that the curriculum is not being delivered or received as intended (National Center for Higher Education Management Systems, 1991). Consistent with this experience, two particularly useful additional domains for the development of institution-level indicators arise:

• *Conformity with objectives.* A key question for any institution or department is the degree to which the curriculum as designed, delivered, or received is in fact aligned with the learning objectives it is intended to develop. So long as the principal concern in curricular design was content coverage, answers to this question were straightforward. Courses themselves tended to be organized in neat content packages that could easily be monitored. From the typical faculty standpoint, moreover, the question of content coverage was both legitimate and immediately intelligible. Curricular discussions about conformity with objectives, therefore, tended to be informal and routine. As such discussions throughout the 1980s increasingly centered on the development of identifiable common outcomes or the provision of specific learning experiences, however, the question became more complicated. In general education courses, for instance, faculty might be called upon not only to teach their discipline but to foster critical thinking or provide collaborative learning experiences as well. Often such additional, apparently noncontroversial, objectives were adopted quickly without much thought about what they might mean operationally. As assessment proceeded, however, it became reasonable to ask whether, where, and in what manner such objectives were being addressed in the classroom.

• *Internal articulation.* A parallel question is the degree to which the curriculum is actually working as intended—particularly with regard to the connections intended among its individual courses. In even the most loosely designed curricular structure, students are expected to be able to effectively apply knowledge and skills learned in the context of one course to that of another. The most visible aspect of this expectation is a structure of prerequisites, but many less formal such connections may be expected as students progress. To what degree are such connections actually operating as intended? At least two dimensions of this question can be used to guide the development of indicators. First, are designed prerequisite structures and curricular sequences actually manifested in patterns of student course-taking behavior, and what are the consequences if they are not? This is on one hand a question of longitudinal curricular flow involving identification of the overall degree of variation from expected paths that might be occurring. On the other hand, it is a question of the impact of such patterns if identified: do they lead to lower student performance or do such violations of sequence appear to not really matter very much? If the latter is the case—that is, if students fail to follow intended paths and it does not affect their ultimate success—it may be legitimate to ask why such requirements should be maintained.

A second dimension of internal articulation concerns the fit between important pairs of courses. Partly this is a more specific question of content and coverage: for instance, how much and what particular aspects of what is taught in a calculus sequence delivered by the math department, or a freshman composition course delivered by the English department, are really required for effective performance in, say, a third-year engineering course or a second-year sociology course for which these two lower-level courses serve as prerequisites? Identifying these specific areas of common ownership may be critical to fostering cross-departmental conversations about relative teaching priorities. At the same time, articulation of this kind involves a question of performance: can students work effectively in subsequent courses, and what types of errors do they make? Here, appropriately designed indicators can help point to the particular prerequisite sequences that need attention, and can help identify some of the specific deficiencies to be corrected.

The development of indicators for domains such as these, as might be expected, is generally part of a larger approach to curriculum improvement or redesign. Often this approach itself is explicitly guided by a continuous quality improvement philosophy that aims at achieving better outcomes and greater efficiencies simultaneously by eliminating unneeded curricular paths, and by cutting down on the need to repeat particular topics or skills that were not learned appropriately the first time (Baugher, 1992; Harris and Baggett, 1992). In other cases—especially in two-year college settings—curriculum improvement indicators are consistent with wider efforts aimed at improving student retention and success rates (O'Banion and Associates, 1994).

Sample Indicators and Their Construction

Indicators of curricular quality can be derived from many specific data sources, and the best approaches draw information from a range of methods. As might be expected, moreover, some of these approaches are more suited to providing data for some domains than they are for others. While a complete catalogue of the many specific indicators that can or have been used to assess curricula is well beyond the scope of this chapter, it is feasible to present concrete illustrations of some of the major types.

For a variety of reasons, this task is best undertaken by a data source. Not only does this allow a more systematic treatment of the many different methodologies available, but it also helps highlight the ways that information drawn from different sources can be mutually reinforcing.

- *Indicators based on catalogue or syllabus review.* Probably the most straightforward method for developing useful indicators of content and coverage or conformity with objectives in the designed curriculum is based on published descriptions of courses. At the broadest level, this approach allows the construction of indicators for the overall structure and coverage of the curriculum. For example, the following simple ratios and percentages can generally be constructed using available catalogue material:

Proportions of total general education credits or courses allocated to particular areas of study, or to the development of specific prerequisite skills (writing, math, oral communication, and so on)—a measure of curricular *coverage.*

The number of courses available among which students may choose to fulfill a given curricular requirement, divided by the number of courses needed to meet the requirement—a measure of *choice.*

The proportion (or absolute number) of total credits needed to complete a given major program of study that must be completed in the major discipline—a measure of *disciplinary concentration.*

The proportion of courses needed to complete a given major program of study broken down by the total number of prerequisite and implied prerequisite courses associated with each (that is, the percentage for which no prerequisites are required, the percentage for which at least one is required, two, and so on—taking into account the entire chain of implied prerequisites for each required course)—a measure of *sequence* and *structure.*

Tapping the rich array of individual syllabus material available on most campuses can yield data on the ways in which the curriculum is actually being delivered. Additional calculations such as the following become possible:

The average amount of writing required to complete a given program of study, based on an analysis of assignments—a measure of *expectations* and of *skills coverage.*

For each identified outcome or goal of general education, the number of courses that identify this intended outcome explicitly as a course goal, the number addressing the goal implicitly in what is covered (or how it is covered), or the number explicitly assessing students on achievement with respect to this outcome—a measure of *conformity to objectives* (often presented in matrix form, as in Ewell and Lisensky, 1988, Chapter Two).

At the highest level of detail, it is possible to match syllabus material to explicitly identified levels of competency on core outcomes in order to physically map the specific places in a curricular sequence at which these levels are developed, required, and tested. An excellent illustration of this process is provided by the "competence growth plans" prepared by individual departments at King's College (Farmer, 1988).

• *Indicators based on transcripts or student records.* Transcript records provide what is probably the most comprehensive basis on which to determine the shape of the behavioral curriculum. Unfortunately, they are also one of the most intractable sources of information available, as student records systems at most institutions are not designed to aggregate or otherwise analyze student course-taking patterns. Fortunately, some progress has been made in two arenas. First, useful national standards for coding samples of transcripts have been developed that allow comparisons across quite different institutions and settings (Adelman, 1990). Second, some general course-taking measures have been developed that allow reduction of extremely complex transcript records into a few broad behavioral patterns (Zemsky, 1989). Using approaches such as these, even a simple coding of longitudinal course enrollments can yield indicators such as the following:

> Percentage of students graduating (by field) never having enrolled for a course in a foreign language—a measure of specific *disciplinary or skills exposure.*

> The proportion of courses in a given discipline for which at least three-quarters of enrollments were generated by students in the same academic year of study (Zemsky, 1989)—a measure of *temporal focus.*

> Percentage of enrollments (by course or discipline) violating current placement policies or prerequisite sequences—a measure of the *implementation of curricular policy.*

> The average length of time (by course or discipline) occurring between particular course enrollments and the prior completion of any established prerequisite course requirement—a measure of the actual *realization* of a given sequential curriculum design.

The two latter measures, of course, are useful not only as indicators in themselves, but as factors to be associated with student performance. Transcript files can also allow some measurement of performance in the form of grades earned or subsequent courses passed. If individual assessment results are also included in the institution's records system (or can be matched to individual student records via an identifier), more powerful indicators of curricular performance can be constructed:

The average GPAs (or alternatively, the proportion passed with a grade of C or better) of students taking a given set of upper-level courses under varying prerequisite conditions (such as having met or not met such prerequisites, the amount of time elapsed since completing prerequisite courses, or the actual prior performance in prerequisite courses)—a measure of the *adequacy of prior curricular preparation*.

Specific types or clusters of courses taken by students that are associated with gains in achievement on external assessment measures such as standardized tests, certification or licensure passage, and so on—a measure reflecting the different *contributions of particular curricular components* with respect to outcomes (see Ratcliff, 1993).

Detailed methods for conducting analyses using combinations of student transcript record and assessment data are available from several sources. One example is the "differential coursework methodology" developed by the National Center on Postsecondary Teaching, Learning, and Assessment at Penn State (Ratcliff and Associates, 1988). Another is the approach used by Astin (1992) in the Exxon Study of General Education to identify specific curricular experiences linked to student gains in self-reported achievement.

  • *Indicators based on reports from faculty and students.* What faculty say they do and value, and what students say is delivered or experienced, constitute the most straightforward methods available to get at the behavioral aspects of curriculum. Indicators of curriculum quality based on student self-reports, for instance, are ideally suited to assess good practice. While syllabi and transcript records can record levels of expectations and patterns of attendance far more accurately and completely than student recollections, students themselves are probably in the best position to report on such matters as their own levels of effort, whether or not they spoke in class and how frequently, and the degree of group work they might have engaged in.

Currently, of course, most institutions already use such methods to evaluate individual classes through the familiar mechanism of student ratings of instruction. But such instruments are generally aimed at a single purpose: evaluating instructor behavior for purposes of promotion and tenure. Increasingly, however, such questionnaires are being reconfigured to capture students' own behavior or perceived learning as well (Ewell, 1991). This trend has been given a powerful impetus by the Classroom Research movement (Angelo and Cross, 1993) described in Chapter Twenty-Eight, but is different in the sense that the results of Classroom Research are not intended to be codified or shared widely across the institution. An important caution involved in using information from such sources for indicators development, therefore, is to ensure a proper level of aggregation in reporting the resulting information. It is generally inappropriate, for instance, to report student testimony on such matters on a class-by-class or instructor-by-instructor basis.

Some of the specific indicators that have been developed using this approach are:

The average number of out-of-class hours per week spent studying reported by students in different types of classes—a measure of *student quality of effort.*

The percentage of students reporting high levels of discussion with peers on topics related to the course, or the percentage reporting at least three face-to-face conversations with faculty on topics related to course material outside of class—measures of *engagement* and *active learning.*

The number and types of self-reported connections made by students between material or ideas presented in a general education course and some other course they are taking at the same time—a measure of *connected learning.*

The percentage of students reporting that they almost always receive graded assignments back from instructors within a week—a measure of *frequent feedback.*

While all these examples are suitable for (and have been used in) end-of-course questionnaires, similar items on self-reported behaviors are equally appropriate for inclusion in broader questionnaires administered periodically to larger samples of students. The most prominent national examples of such instruments are the Cooperative Institutional Research Follow-Up Survey (Astin and Associates, 1992), administered to nationally normed samples of students for research purposes, and the College Student Experiences Questionnaire (Pace, 1984), now available through Indiana University. Most institutions, however, design and administer their own such instruments and, where present, these provide an excellent vehicle for collecting information about reported curricular experiences.

Reports from faculty constitute a similar but less well-tapped source of information about the delivered curriculum. Some such surveys have been designed to document common instructional practices—for instance, the model instruments designed to assess use of the "Seven Principles of Effectiveness in Undergraduate Education" (Gamson and Poulsen, 1989). Others are more oriented toward determining broader underlying instructional values or attitudes toward teaching (for example, Astin, 1992). Among the specific indicators that can be developed using such sources are:

Percent of faculty time per week allocated to teaching, advising, and other instructional support tasks—a measure of *teaching investment.*

Percent of faculty reporting that support and encouragement for teaching innovations are strongly present in or strongly supported by their departments—a measure of *instructional climate.*

Percent of faculty reporting that they frequently engage in a set of identified classroom practices in their teaching, such as group work, active learning techniques, or classroom research—a measure of *classroom behavior.*

With self-reports of any kind, of course, questions about validity often arise. These are generally of two kinds. One is the credibility of self-reports themselves. Faculty, for instance, are more likely to serve as credible witnesses of the general value placed on teaching in their departments than they are about their own behaviors. Similarly, students are usually better judges of what they have done (that is, how they spent their time) than they are of how much they have learned. A second difficulty with self-reported data—especially relevant to the construction of indicators—is that data based on surveys rarely yield usable point estimates of performance. The fact that 58 percent of students majoring in biology said they were extremely satisfied with instruction in their major, for instance, is far less useful in itself than knowing that this value was 76 percent for last year's graduating class, or that a difference of 15 percent separates the men from the women. As a result, the best uses of such data rely strongly on analyses of trends over time or of the differing experiences of particular student subpopulations. (For an excellent example of how survey analysis of this kind can paint a compelling picture of the curriculum as experienced, see College of William and Mary, 1994.)

- *Indicators based on direct assessment.* Direct assessment of cognitive or affective development, of course, provides the most convincing evidence of curricular effectiveness, and such methods are discussed in Chapters Twenty-Eight and Twenty-Nine. Quite properly, direct assessment indicators are focused on the two extremes of the teaching and learning continuum—determining overall patterns of institutional goal-attainment and guiding the process of learning within individual classrooms. But most treatments of this topic ignore two additional roles of direct assessment that can be used to examine curricular functioning.

One is the often considerable amount of information that can be gained about real curricular content using assessment techniques. Long-time observers of assessment in action have particularly emphasized the indirect benefits of the process in clarifying goals (Banta and Schneider, 1988; Banta and Associates, 1993). Others have noted how assessment evidence often has as much to say about curriculum structure as it does about outcomes—or more (Ewell, 1991). A common example is the increasingly popular portfolio approach to assessment, in which student work samples are systematically compiled to determine the degree to which cross-cutting curricular outcomes like writing or critical thinking are being accomplished. In more than a few cases, institutions have found these exercises more valuable in determining what faculty are really assigning, and the alignment of these assignments with curricular goals, than in directly documenting student attainment (for example, Northeast Missouri State University, 1994; College of William and Mary, cited in Ewell, 1991).

Among the specific indicators of curricular functioning that might arise as by-products of direct assessment are the following:

Numbers of written assignments in general education courses compiled from student portfolios that contain multiple or cross-disciplinary references—a measure of *integration in the delivered curriculum.*

Proportion of written assignments in all disciplines compiled as part of a portfolio process that require students to display such analytical skills as comparing or contrasting different situations or determining flaws in an argument—a measure of *coverage in the delivered curriculum.*

A second underattended application of direct assessment in examining curricular functioning is to determine more precisely whether intended connections among courses designed into a given sequence are in fact occurring. Much evidence on this topic, as noted earlier, can be compiled through transcripts and student enrollment records. But more direct methods are available for determining the degree to which previously learned content and skills are being effectively deployed in new contexts. One such approach is to embed pretests and posttests directly into specific course sequences, designed especially to determine if prerequisite skills present at the end of one course are in fact present in the next (for example, see Farmer, 1988). Another is the use of common assignments in paired courses—taken simultaneously by students—explicitly designed to assess multicontextual skills. Specific indicators of curricular functioning consistent with these approaches might include:

Numbers and types of errors in applying previously learned statistical techniques occurring on pretests (or in portfolios of subsequent assignments) in a given set of social science courses for which statistics is a prerequisite—a measure of *curricular integration.*

Relative performance on pretests of prerequisite skills administered in a given set of courses between students who actually took required prerequisite courses and those who placed out of such requirements by other means—a measure of current *academic policy.*

In closing, it is important to reemphasize that the most powerful approaches to assessing curricular quality make use of both outcomes and process measures.

In developing appropriate indicator systems for purposes of either external accountability or internal curricular improvement, institutions are well advised to pay equal attention to both.

Future Prospects

Evidence strongly suggests that incentives for paying more systematic attention to documenting and monitoring curricular functioning are here to stay. On one hand, demands for greater accountability show no signs of diminishing. Indeed, they are markedly shifting in character from the predominant concern with outcomes evident in the late 1980s to a growing interest in instructional processes and student experiences (Ewell, 1994). At the same time, growing fiscal pressures and the consequent inability of colleges and universities to do everything for everybody are inducing more and more institutions to contemplate serious curricular restructuring—often guided by approaches drawn from continuous quality improvement. In both arenas, increasingly, the coin of the realm is statistical. Performance indicator approaches have permanent appeal to public officials because of their succinct and comparative nature. At the same time, they are seen as an appropriate response to growing pressures for information to inform consumer choice. In parallel, serious restructuring demands concrete information about the functioning of key processes to keep it on course—and this information must be regularly collected and easily understandable at all levels of the organization. Both trends suggest that indicators of curricular quality will be with us for the long haul.

Recognition that indicators are not a fad, however, does not imply that they are a panacea. As in the early days of assessment, the tyranny of numbers can easily overwhelm reasoned analysis of complex bodies of evidence. Because of their apparent concreteness, indicators systems in any field are particularly susceptible to such perversion. While recognizing their power to inform action, therefore, academic leaders should be constantly vigilant to ensure that any indicators of curriculum are multiple, mutually reinforcing, and appropriate. Above all, they should ensure that at every level, such data are used to raise questions and not to provide final answers.

References

Adelman, C. *A College Course Map: Taxonomy and Transcript Data.* Washington, D.C.: Office of Educational Research and Improvement (OERI), U.S. Department of Education, 1990.

Angelo, T. A., and Cross, K. P. *Classroom Assessment Techniques: A Handbook for College Teachers.* (2nd ed.) San Francisco: Jossey-Bass, 1993.

Astin, A. W. *Assessment for Excellence: The Philosophy and Practice of Assessment and Evaluation in Higher Education.* New York: ACE/Macmillan, 1991.

Astin, A. W. *What Matters in College? Four Critical Years Revisited.* San Francisco: Jossey-Bass, 1992.

Astin, A. W., and Associates. *Cooperative Institutional Research Program (CIRP).* Los Angeles: Higher Education Research Institute (HERI), University of California, Los Angeles, 1992.

Banta, T. W., and Schneider, J. A. "Using Faculty-Developed Exit Examinations to Evaluate Academic Programs." *Journal of Higher Education,* 1988, *59,* 69–83.

Banta, T. W., and Associates. *Making a Difference: Outcomes of a Decade of Assessment in Higher Education.* San Francisco: Jossey-Bass, 1993.

Baugher, K. *Learn: Student Quality Team Manual.* Birmingham, Ala.: Samford University, 1992.

Burstein, L., Oakes, J., and Guiton, G. "Education Indicators." In M. Alkin (ed.), *Encyclopedia of Educational Research.* (6th ed.) Old Tappan, N.J.: Macmillan, 1992.

Chickering, A. W., and Gamson, Z. F. "Seven Principles for Good Practice in Undergraduate Education." *AAHE Bulletin,* 1987, *39*(7), 3–7.

College of William and Mary. *Assessment of Undergraduate Liberal Education.* Interim summary to the State Council on Higher Education in Virginia. Williamsburg, Va.: College of William and Mary, 1994.

Ewell, P. T. "To Capture the Ineffable: New Forms of Assessment in Higher Education." In G. Grant (ed.), *Review of Research in Education.* Washington, D.C.: American Educational Research Association, 1991.

Ewell, P. T. "Total Quality and Academic Practice: The Idea We've Been Waiting For?" *Change,* 1993, *25*(3), 49–55.

Ewell, P. T. "Developing Statewide Performance Indicators for Higher Education: Policy Themes and Variations." In S. S. Ruppert (ed.), *Charting Higher Education Accountability: A Sourcebook on State-Level Performance Indicators.* Denver: Education Commission of the States, 1994.

Ewell, P. T., and Jones, D. P. "Pointing the Way: Indicators as Policy Tools in Higher Education." In S. Ruppert (ed.), *Charting Higher Education Accountability: A Sourcebook on State-Level Performance Indicators.* Denver: Education Commission of the States, 1994.

Ewell, P. T., and Jones, D. P. *Developing Indicators of "Good Practice" in Undergraduate Education: A Guide to Implementation.* Boulder, Colo.: National Center for Higher Education Management Systems, 1996.

Ewell, P. T., and Lisensky, R. P. *Assessing Institutional Effectiveness: Redirecting the Self-Study Process.* Washington, D.C.: Consortium for the Advancement of Private Higher Education, 1988.

Farmer, D. W. *Enhancing Student Learning: Emphasizing Essential Competencies in Academic Programs.* Wilkes-Barre, Pa.: King's College, 1988.

Gamson, Z. F., and Poulsen, S. J. "Inventories of Good Practice: The Next Step for the Seven Principles for Good Practice in Undergraduate Education." *AAHE Bulletin,* 1989, *42,* 7–8.

Gitlow, H. S., and Gitlow S. J. *The Deming Guide to Quality and Competitive Position.* Englewood Cliffs, N.J.: Prentice Hall, 1987.

Harris, J. W., and Baggett, J. M. *Quality Quest in the Academic Process.* Birmingham, Ala.: Samford University, 1992.

Massy, W. F., and Zemsky, R. "Faculty Discretionary Time: Departments and the Academic Ratchet." *Pew Policy Perspectives.* Philadelphia: Pew Charitable Trusts, 1992.

National Center for Higher Education Management Systems. "Enrollment Analysis and Student Tracking: What We Have Been Learning." *NCHEMS Newsletter*, Summer 1991, pp. 2–3.

National Center for Higher Education Management Systems. "A Preliminary Study of the Feasibility and Utility for National Policy of Instructional 'Good Practice' Indicators in Undergraduate Education." Washington, D.C.: Office of Educational Research and Improvement (OERI), U.S. Department of Education, 1994.

National Institute of Education. *Involvement in Learning: Realizing the Potential of American Higher Education.* Report of the Study Group on the Conditions of Excellence in American Higher Education. Washington, D.C.: U.S. Government Printing Office, 1984.

Northeast Missouri State University. *Report of the Committee on the Liberal Arts and Sciences Core.* Kirksville: Northeast Missouri State University, 1994.

O'Banion, T., and Associates. *Teaching and Learning in the Community College.* Washington, D.C.: Community College Press, American Association of Community Colleges, 1994.

Pace, C. R. *Measuring the Quality of Student Experiences: An Account of the Development and Use of the College Student Experiences Questionnaire.* Los Angeles: Higher Education Research Institute, University of California, 1984.

Ratcliff, J. L. (ed.). *Assessment and Curricular Reform.* University Park: National Center on Postsecondary Teaching, Learning, and Assessment, Pennsylvania State University, 1993.

Ratcliff, J. L., and Associates. *Development and Testing of a Cluster-Analytic Model for Identifying Coursework Patterns Associated with General Learned Abilities of Students (Progress Report #6).* Ames: College of Education, Iowa State University, 1988.

Ruppert, S. S. *Charting Higher Education Accountability: A Sourcebook on State-Level Performance Indicators.* Denver: Education Commission of the States, 1994.

Seymour, D. T. *On Q: Causing Quality in Higher Education.* Washington, D.C.: ACE, 1991.

Sherr, L. A., and Teeter, D. J. (eds.). *Total Quality Management in Higher Education.* New Directions for Institutional Research, no. 71. San Francisco: Jossey-Bass, 1991.

Stark, J. S., and Lowther, M. A. *Designing the Learning Plan: A Review of Research and Theory Related to College Curricula.* Ann Arbor: National Center for Research on Postsecondary Teaching and Learning, University of Michigan, 1986. (ED 287 439)

State Council on Higher Education in Virginia. *Summary of Restructuring Processes in Virginia Public Universities.* Working Document. Richmond: State Council on Higher Education in Virginia, 1994.

Winona State University. *Indicators for Improving Undergraduate Instructional Quality.* Winona, Minn.: Winona State University, 1990.

Zemsky, R. *Structure and Coherence: Measuring the Undergraduate Curriculum.* Washington, D.C.: Association of American Colleges, 1989.

Zemsky, R., Massy, W. F., and Oedel, P. "On Reversing the Ratchet." *Change*, May/June 1993, pp. 56–62.

PART SIX

CHANGING THE CURRICULUM

Changing the curriculum is a task of paradoxes. The curriculum is forever dynamic, expanding with changes in society, knowledge, and student populations. Yet orchestrated and mindful restructuring of the curriculum is a tender and vulnerable affair, prone to derailment, diminution, and abandonment. The distinctive college with its strong foundations and traditions is at once the most unique and the most resistant to change; the strength of its norms and values hold it to past practices (Clark, 1986). The complex university hosts multiple organizational forms and aims devoted in varying degrees to teaching, research, and service; it is easier to alter a small enclave than to realign the values and direction of the institutional whole (Levine, 1980). Curriculum committees and academic leaders contemplating change are best advised to begin by examining past efforts to effect change in light of prevailing values and traditions, asking where those embedded beliefs support or run counter to the contemplated change.

Change, however, is inescapable as we enter the twenty-first century. Institutions are being pressured to serve more students better with fewer resources, and to cut courses and programs to economize. They stand on the brink of a great transformation in the available forms of educational technology. As medieval universities befriended the Gutenberg press, will today's colleges incorporate the microcomputer into the mainstream of the curriculum? As the knowledge base expands, abandons old canons, and seeks new narratives within the fields of knowledge, will we once again find common ground, or will the new knowledge paradigms function as did those of the academic revolution—disintegratively and expansively? These questions are inescapable for colleges today. They illustrate the imperative to change the curriculum. We should come to the task with humility and resolve. Many innovations fail, and the dynamics of the curriculum insist that we revisit these challenges regularly rather than try to find the one best educational program for all time.

In this final section, we consider change and the future of the undergraduate curriculum. We begin with Jack Lindquist's enduring treatise on change strategies, Chapter Thirty-One. He challenges the assumptions of rationality upon which we often approach the change task. The majority of our colleges are not merely motivated by the intrinsic merits of innovation, though the rational change paradigm provides a systematic way to plan curricular renewal and reform. He urges us to reflect on our social networks as conduits of both advocacy and resistance to change. He calls us to recognize the underlying interests, routines, rituals, fears, and prejudices that call for skilled intervention in the organizational life of the college to bring about change. Noting that no one model of change fully explains the dynamics of the organization, he points to prevalent roles for each change strategy over the life of an innovation—from inception to institutionalization.

In Chapter Thirty-Two, Jan Civian and her colleagues relate their experience and research on how innovations are undertaken, what barriers arise during the change process, and what are some common positive and negative consequences of curricular change. They describe one of the inherent challenges as encouraging faculty to relate the courses they teach to the larger view of program, major, minor, or general education aims, processes, and outcomes. The broader the curricular change, the more difficulty it poses in cutting across disciplinary and departmental lines. Change is especially difficult when faculty feel threatened and when they are already overburdened. The chapter notes that modest curricular change is easier to achieve than dramatic, sweeping reform. Addressing what they call "the treacherous terrain of curricular change," the authors urge curriculum committees to rejoice in smaller accomplishments, approaching large-scale reform in waves rather than all at once. They conclude with eleven principles to guide change initiatives.

Roger Sell and Barbara Lounsberry, in Chapter Thirty-Three, illustrate the relationships between curriculum development and change, faculty development, and organizational development. They argue that curricular innovation can best be effected when faculty development and organizational development initiatives support the reform or transformation of the curriculum. They review the hierarchical model of academic governance and its role in inhibiting and atomizing change, and point out that, by contrast, several strategies support both curriculum and faculty development, including practice-centered inquiry, outcomes assessment, strategic planning, faculty development centers, and instructional enhancement grant programs. The chapter concludes with an examination of how each strategy can be used to support curriculum innovation and change.

In his epilogue, Chapter Thirty-Four, Jerry Gaff draws upon his more than thirty years of experience with undergraduate curriculum innovation, reform, and renewal to place in context cross-currents of trends, forces, threats, and opportunities, and to forecast future directions for the undergraduate curriculum. He notes how colleges and universities are bound by their past, by the countervailing forces of the research values of the academic revolution and the impulse to innovation for the improvement of student learning. He notes the parallel and paradoxical twin trends toward improving the curriculum and fostering accountability and efficiency. He asserts that these trends are coming together today, and asks us to innovate for greater learning productivity. He sees within the academy trends to counteract the proliferation of courses, to foster greater reflection on the enterprise, and to seek a sense of common purpose. These trends portend increased integrity and efficiency for the system. What has been represented in this closing decade of the twentieth century as a paradox or a dichotomy—the competition between the effectiveness and the efficiency of the curriculum—can be seen as a tension between tradition and innovation. Driven by strong social and economic forces, all types of colleges and universities are moving—often haltingly and irregularly, to be sure, but still moving—toward the goal of putting students and learning at the center of the enterprise.

References

Clark, B. R. *The Higher Education System: Academic Organization in Cross-National Perspective.* Berkeley: University of California Press, 1986.

Kelly, R. L. *The American Colleges and the Social Order.* New York: Macmillan, 1940.

Levine, A. *Why Innovation Fails: The Institutionalization and Termination of Innovation in Higher Education.* Albany: State University of New York Press, 1980.

CHAPTER THIRTY-ONE

STRATEGIES FOR CHANGE

Jack Lindquist

We carry in our heads, and lower, basic notions about how to bring about change. Some of these models, or strategies, are rather simple-minded, such as those based on carrot-and-stick assumptions: they promise to provide more of what the target of your change efforts wants, or they threaten to take away some source of security or status. Some are elaborate. Orchestrating a major change in the curriculum or a Total Quality Improvement initiative takes extensive understanding and skill to pull off.

Basically, however, four very different assumptions about what leads people or organizations to change are represented by four rather different change strategies. I call them the Rational Planning, Social Interaction, Human Problem-Solving, and Political approaches to planned change. The first three emerge from the seminal scholarship of Havelock and his associates (1971) at the University of Michigan's Center for Research on the Utilization of Scientific Knowledge. They

Note: Before his much-too-early death, Jack Lindquist was a pioneering scholar of the fine art of changing colleges and universities. The editors believe that the first chapter of his pathbreaking book, *Strategies for Change* (1978), remains the best overview of the theory of planned academic change. As a tribute and memorial to Jack, we have decided to reprint it posthumously; it is a fitting way to keep his ideas alive and available to those who seek to improve undergraduate education, one of the passions of his life. To make the text more contemporary, we updated the examples and removed references to dated material, but virtually all his own words remain. Reprinted by permission of CIC.

observe that all change strategies emphasize one of three particular aspects of the basic communication act: I create a message, which I deliver in such a way that the receiver (another person or a whole organization) accepts it and acts on it. One set of strategies, which Havelock calls Research, Development, and Diffusion (R&D), and which I call Rational Planning, concentrates mainly on developing a terrific message. Another set, called Social Interaction or Communication of Innovations, emphasizes the process and factors by which the change message gains the attention and acceptance of the receiver. It focuses on the social act of communicating new notions. A third group of studies and attendant theory, called Problem-Solving by Havelock, focuses upon how the receiver comes to feel the need and then the willingness to change. The Political model dwells on this same part of the communication act, but with quite different assumptions about how to generate change than those of the Problem-Solving model.

Havelock and later theorists see effective planned change as a combination of these approaches. But the separate models are well worth elaborating, for they represent strong differences in the ways academic and other changes are undertaken.

The Assumption of Rationality

Since we change on the basis of reason and evidence, the best way to obtain alterations in attitudes and behavior is to invest in systematic research and development of new knowledge, new practices, new products. Apply a rational process to attain a rational end. If the research is correct and the development sound, the proposed change will sell itself. That is the assumption that leads to heavy investment in basic and applied research and to considerable investment in the formulating, testing, and packaging of innovations based on research. Watson (1972) found these assumptions at work in the R&D efforts of AT&T Corporation. Clark and Guba (1965) found a similar rational sequence at work in the development and diffusion of educational innovations. Guba (1968) particularly stresses development, "which is at the heart of change, for while research may make change possible, it is development that actually produces an innovation that may be adopted."

Havelock and others identify five basic assumptions about change that underlie the Research and Development strategy:

First of all, the R&D model suggests that dissemination and utilization should be a rational sequence of activities which moves from research to development to packaging before dissemination takes place. Secondly, this model assumes that there has to be planning, and planning really on a massive scale. It is not enough that we simply have all these activities of research and development;

they have to be coordinated; there has to be a relationship between them; and they have to make sense in a logical sequence that may go back years in the evolution of one particular message to be disseminated. Thirdly, there has to be a division of labor and a separation of roles and functions, an obvious prerequisite in all complex activities of modern society, but one that we sometimes slur over. Fourth, it assumes a more or less clearly defined target audience, a specified passive consumer, who will accept the innovation if it is delivered on the right channel, in the right way, and at the right time. The particular process which is supposed to assure this happening is scientific evaluation, evaluation at every stage of development and dissemination. Fifth, and finally, this perspective accepts the fact of high initial development cost prior to any dissemination activity, because it foresees an even higher gain in the long run, in terms of efficiency, quality, and capacity to reach a mass audience. [1971, p. 5]

We can see around us plenty of examples of the rational change model. Cars and planes and other material products are made and sold that way. In postsecondary education, self-instructional systems such as computer hardware and software manuals are common. The development of instructional materials such as movies or videocassettes, or even the creation of whole televised courses such as those developed by the Annenberg project of the Corporation for Public Broadcasting, are other examples. The U.S. Department of Education has employed R&D assumptions in supporting an array of university-based centers to conduct research on various aspects of education, evaluate innovations, and then disseminate the results to supposedly eager recipients. Most foundations take Guba's advice and invest mainly in the development of model programs, which others supposedly will learn about and adopt.

Local schools, colleges, and social agencies also use the rational model, although high investment in R&D is usually not part of the scheme. Change in such organizations is often supported by encouraging individuals or committees to formulate proposals based on the best reason and evidence available. Review bodies, whether collegial governance or administrative heads, then judge these proposals and decide for or against, ostensibly on the basis of rational considerations. Although we all know too well that good reason and sound evidence are not the only grounds on which decisions to change are made, the formal system, the one we put on organization charts and admit in public, stresses the rational model. We formally act as if we all approach change rationally. Especially in universities, which Parsons and Platt (1973) claim are the fiduciary institutions for "cognitive rationality," it is hard to admit other approaches. Proponents of this approach claim that administrators need to establish more rational research and planning sequences, whether it involves assessment of student learning or preparation of strategic plans for an institution. Certainly, there should be participation by those whose attitudes and behaviors are supposed to change, particularly faculty and students in colleges. But the emphasis in time and dollars is on generating an impressive change message.

Research and theory, however, have found the rational model inadequate in several respects as a way to go about the introduction of change in human attitudes and behaviors, the changes at the heart of academic innovations. In the main, criticism has focused on the isolation of R&D from its audience, the people who supposedly are going to use these newfangled ideas or behaviors. Rational systems may be good ways to research and develop change, but they do not explain all the motivations and activities by which those new things get used (Gross, Giacquinla, and Bernstein, 1963).

The dynamics of local implementation are especially critical to the actual use of planned change (Zaltman, Duncan, and Holbeck, 1973; Berman and McLaughlin, 1975). Organizations, like the individuals and groups in them, do not operate simply as rational systems thoughtfully buying the latest innovations. If a change proposal threatens individual or group security and status, it is in trouble no matter how elegant its reason. If faculty and students cannot do the new behavior, or are not committed to it, watch out. Informal systems of communications and social status may be far more potent than formal communications in persuading members whether or not to do the new thing. Certainly reason and evidence are part of the change equation. One will not get very far on lousy evidence and flimsy reason. But as many would-be curriculum reformers can attest, an adequate strategy for change must include much more than clear and compelling reason.

Social Interaction

We live in social networks. One connects us to professional colleagues; another unites us with family and friends. Through these connections we get news and views about what is happening in the world around us. We gain security, status, and esteem from these informal systems, just as we do from formal organizations. Some researchers maintain that these contacts are essential to change, for new ideas get communicated and validated through social networks; agricultural extension agencies are the organizational units that best represent this approach, in contrast with research and development centers.

Rogers, one of the originators of this school of thought, and his colleagues (Rogers and Shoemaker, 1971; Rogers, Agarwala-Rogers, and Lee, 1975) find that most empirical studies of innovation identify a few consistent types of "potential adopters" and a few specific stages in the adoption of new ideas, practices or objects. In every organization or community, there will be a few innovators, eager to try new things and usually uncomfortable with the status quo (which in turn is uncomfortable with them). A second group, somewhat larger than the first but still rarely more than 12 percent to 15 percent of the organization, are the Early Adopters, usually cosmopolitan in contacts and open to new ideas, though not as eager as the Innovators. Following in sequence of adoption is the Early Majority, making up perhaps a third of the population; these are the cautious followers of the Early Adopters. Then comes another third, the skeptical Late Majority, which wants pretty impressive evidence that this new practice is possible, effective, and rewarded before it ventures a try. Finally, about 15 percent of most systems will be made up of Laggards, who probably will resist change until everyone else is already doing the next new thing. Each successive group needs substantially stronger persuasion in order to change. Researchers also find that while change messages delivered through impersonal channels (books, articles, formal addresses, memoranda, written proposals) can persuade Innovators and Early Adopters, as well as increase awareness generally, later adopters need more personal communication and contact in order to be willing to change. Although it can take a short time for a change to move from one category of adopters to another, several years is more common for new educational behaviors and several decades for new ideas such as progressive education. Clearly, the change advocate who thinks he or she can gain acceptance and use of new human behaviors or ideas by impersonal communication over a short period of time to a whole organization is in for bitter disappointment unless the group can be coerced and carefully controlled. College authorities just do not have that leverage over their semiautonomous professors. Frankly, Ford doesn't have that kind of leverage over assembly line workers, either.

Innovation diffusion researchers find that the best route into an organization or community is through Opinion Leaders, those persons (or institutions) to whom others turn for advice. As Hovland and Weiss point out, the most persuasive communicators are those whose expertise, experience, or social role establishes them as credible sources of information. Harvard University is an institutional opinion leader on almost anything. I found in a state university that a few professors and administrators rated high by their colleagues in academic expertise and experience and often placed on key academic committees were most frequently asked their opinions on current proposals for academic change. In fact, I saw faculty senate meetings turned toward a decision by the remarks of key opinion leaders while conducting research for my dissertation (Lindquist, 1972). Effective change strategists find out who the opinion leaders are, then seek to persuade them to persuade others.

Social interaction researchers also find that certain attributes of innovations besides impressive reason and evidence influence their adoption. Does the innovation have clear *relative advantages* for our particular situation, whether those advantages are better ability to meet institutional objectives, reduced costs, higher status, or greater enjoyment? Is the innovation *compatible* with our values, our structure, our skills and styles? Is the innovation *divisible* so that we can adopt only the parts we like, or adopt in some easy sequence, rather than buying the whole change at once? Is the new thing *simple* to understand and do? Does it involve *low risk and low uncertainty?* Can we *observe* it and *try it out* so we know better what we are getting into? Whether it is a professor's lecture or a proposal to change the whole curriculum, these ingredients will be important. Yet it is difficult to assess the relative advantages of academic innovations. They often clash with traditional academic values and structures. Professors and students rarely are trained to use them. Often, a whole, complex curricular reform package is laid on the faculty at once, with little promise that it will reap positive rewards. And such proposals are usually paper descriptions, not visible experiences that faculty can see and try before accepting. Small wonder significant academic change is such a rare occurrence.

Resolution of Human Problems

Parsons (1974, p. 271) has noted that "institutionalization [of a change] is imbedded in the non-rational layers of motivational organization. It is not accessible to change simply through the presentation to an actor of rational advantages in the external definition of the situation." Hagen (1970, p. 17) adds that as social change theory matures, "the units of analysis of society will not be roles, or persons, or social units. These are useful concepts only in the presentation of a descriptive framework. Rather, the units will be, within personality, such qualities as need for dependence, need for autonomy, and intensity of anxiety." There is, in short, a psychological dimension to change to which neither the Rational nor Social models do justice. Rational planning and social interaction do form part of the equation, but, as Watson (1972) observes, underlying interests, habits, fears, and prejudices compose the bulk of the iceberg. We often pretend that the essential aspects of planned change are out in the open, in our plans and public discussions. We know better. And if we seek a strategy for intentional change that will work, we need to get at these hidden sources of resistance. Human Problem-Solving approaches offer some assistance.

The general strategy is familiar enough to most people—change is a process of solving problems. Something is not going right, so we diagnose the problem, set some objectives, find a solution, make a decision, implement it, and evaluate its worth. Simple. It really is the Rational approach. But not if the problem is my need to have control, your fear of a change that may endanger your security, or our general distrust of one another. Then, say advocates of Human Problem-Solving strategies, we need skilled intervention. We need someone or some process that can help us confront and reduce these hidden obstacles to change. Intervention may come in the form of leadership training (Blake and Mouton, 1969). It may involve building an effective problem-solving team (Sikes, Schlesinger, and Seashore, 1974). It may focus on the department (Boyer and Crockett, 1973) or on the relationship of the whole organization to its environment (Lawrence and Lorsch, 1969). Some intervention tactics, such as group therapy or role-playing, are quite psychological in their focus (Bennis, 1969). Others, such as survey research or focus groups, with appropriate feedback of the results, are more sociological (Bowers, 1973). But all aim to help us deal with the human resistances to change that we may otherwise avoid.

The Human Relations school of business administration, from Elton Mayo and Chester Barnard in the 1930s to Rensis Likert and Chris Argyris in the 1960s and 1970s, has used this strategy extensively in efforts to improve the functioning of business and industry. Such persons as Ronald Boyer and Walter Sikes have applied this general notion, called "applied behavioral science," to college and university change. In his synthesis of the literature in this field, Havelock and his associates (1971, p. 13) identify five basic tenets of this approach:

(1) That the users' world (the person who is to adopt a new idea or practice) is the only sensible place from which to begin to consider utilization; (2) that knowledge utilization must include a diagnostic phase where user need is considered and translated into a problem statement; (3) that the role of the outsider is primarily to serve as catalyst, collaborator, or consultant on how to plan change and bring about the solution; (4) that internal knowledge retrieval and the marshalling of internal resources should be given at least equal emphasis with external retrieval; and (5) that self-initiation by the user or client system creates the best motivational climate for lasting change.

There frequently also is an assumption that collaboration and openness, rather than competition and closedness, are preferred ways to behave. Consensus is sought over majority rule or authoritative decree. Those who must carry out the charge need to own it as their solution to their concerns. Trust between the persons attempting change and the people to be changed is deemed crucial to genuine change. In all these assumptions, you can see the influence of humanistic psychology. Essentially, applied behavioral science takes a clinical model and applies it to groups and organizations.

This strategy for change is far more controversial in colleges and universities than R&D or Social Interaction, if for no other reason than that it probes sources of resistance we prefer to leave buried. Also, because it focuses at least part of its attention on our emotional needs, it conflicts with the claim that academicians are the protectors of *cognitive rationality.* We would like to think we are above all that. Even if we are rather irrational at times, we prefer not to admit it. Do bankers admit they sometimes lose things? Still, applied behavioral science is beginning to be used in postsecondary education. If Parsons and Hagen are right, we will not get very far toward effective strategies for change unless we face the human barriers to change that human problem-solving interventions confront.

The Political Approach

If we follow the Rational model, the route to change is to build and argue an impressive case. The Social strategy takes that case, puts it in terms attractive to its audience, personally introduces it to Innovators and Opinion Leaders, then, through them, to their various reference groups. The Human Problem-Solving path reduces the resistance to change within us and makes change our solution to our concerns. All well and good. There is much to learn from the experts in these three general schools of thought. But what if Laggards block the road, blind to our eloquent presentations and determined to let no touchy-feely interventionist get into their locked closet of fears, prejudices, and selfish desires? Not a few deans, members of curriculum committees, or faculty members have been characterized as obstructionists by those who want to turn their heads in new directions.

The most common answer is political power. Build coalitions among influential persons and groups, then seek an authoritative decision that requires others to comply with the new idea, employ the new behavior, or use the innovative product. Easton (1965) gives us a picture of the political process that depicts the course of intentional change in political systems, and organizations such as colleges certainly do have political systems. First, some range of gnawing concerns, some *wants,* arise. Things are not as they should be for some persons in a community or with influence over it. Unless these various wants are felt strongly by influential people, and the people who hold them bring together various subgroups, no change is likely. People are usually upset about something or other but not sufficiently so to press authorities into a decision. But if the income/expenditure gap widens alarmingly or if students become agitated over a racist or sexist event on campus, a demand to rectify the situation may be in the offing. Then, if those concerned feel they can make authorities take notice and have "confidence in the possibility of a more desirable state of affairs" (Lippett, Watson, and Westley, 1958), they may take action. A high administrator probably has such a "sense of efficacy" (Gamson, 1968), as did student activists after the initial success of the Free Speech movement at Berkeley and African Americans after the initial successes of the Civil Rights movement.

Once a demand is made, it must gain access to the formal decision-making system if it is to become a change in policy or program. Key here is a sympathetic gatekeeper, a person or group to put the demand on the authorities' agenda. Without a supportive gatekeeper, demanders must be powerful enough to break the gate down and be willing to take that risk. Faculty committee chairpersons and deans can play gatekeeping roles concerning demands for academic policy change. Once on the agenda, the demand gets deliberated. It is studied and debated, often modified or changed, usually in some committee. If it survives this buffeting, it emerges as a formulated proposal for change, which then gets reviewed, modified, revised, reduced, and in general worked over by all the persons or groups concerned about its potential impact on their vested interests. Will this new curriculum give our department more students and faculty or less, more status or less, more autonomy or less? Usually, coalitions of interest form pro and con. Compromises are made to get some decision approved. Much of the debate may focus on the proposal's soundness of reasons and evidence, but savvy observers know that the issue is who gets what coveted goodies. Important to the survival of change proposals in this river of nibbling piranhas are the persistent efforts of highly influential "issues sponsors" who are determined to carry the change through. Without such determined advocates, the status quo powers will defeat any change attempt.

In organizations such as colleges and universities, academic change proposals can take the short route if the demander is a president who goes ahead and exercises formal authority to set policy, or they may take the long route through layer upon layer of governance committees. In either case, the outcome is not yet change. It is an authoritative decision to change. Now comes the problem of making it stick. Usually, an executive instructs organizational units and individuals to carry out the new idea or behavior. Unless, however, that executive can force units and individuals to comply, identify whether or not they are complying, and get rid of noncompliants, the Political model breaks down in implementation. The formal authorities turn out not to be the real authorities. In colleges, academic departments and professors have considerable autonomy as expert professionals; if they do not like a new academic policy, they often can avoid serious implementation and, meanwhile, build a new coalition to get the policy rescinded. As Baldridge (1971, p. 96) discovered: "The system has a remarkable tendency to solve one set of problems only to generate another set; to give advantage to one group, but to disadvantage another; to eliminate one structural strain; but to create another. The political processes are self-generating, and there is constant feedback effect as the resolution of old conflicts creates new ones." The process is not one of open collaboration seeking consensus. It is instead a constant struggle for control. Losers of today's battles do not give up. They mount a new demand.

If vested interests and power were everything involved in planned change, an effective political strategy would be all one would need. But reason and evidence are sometimes heeded even by those whose vested interests are somewhat challenged and who have the power to ignore rational persuasion. Social dynamics are at work, and the more the change agent knows about how to make them work, the better. Often, it is more effective to seek to reduce resistance to change by human relations strategies than to try to overwhelm that resistance by force. If motivation researchers are correct that we all have need for achievement and affiliation as well as for power, we need a change strategy that speaks to all these motivations, not just to power.

Combining Change Strategies

Is it not possible to entertain the notion that humans are rational, social creatures who want to solve their hidden problems but also want to protect and enhance their vested interests? If we make such an assumption, we must combine our strategies for change. Rational research and planning are not enough. Nor is connecting innovations to opinion leaders in all the right ways. Nor is skilled intervention to diagnose human needs and to reduce resistance. Nor is the most effective political maneuvering. We must do it all.

Havelock was one of the first to provide a general change model that joined previously separate traditions of thinking (Havelock and others, 1971). He called his concept "linkage." Planned change starts with a "felt need" on the "potential user's part," on the part of the person, group, or organization that might change. Something is wrong; something needs improvement. A diagnosis is conducted and a problem statement emerges. Then there is a search and retrieval of alternate solutions both inside and outside the user. Some solution for the local situation then is developed and approved. Application follows. Often this implementation raises another need, which starts the cycle all over again.

Meanwhile, outside the potential user of a new idea, behavior, or practice is an external resource system of other persons or organizations, R&D centers, extension agents, consultants. They may be engaged in trying to solve a similar problem, either because it is their problem too or because they have a direct relationship to the user, say as its funder or consultant. They go through a similar problem-solving process.

If the external problem solver comes up with a solution in isolation from the potential user, that solution is apt not to fit local needs and circumstances nor to be of much interest to the user. If the internal problem solver develops a solution without contact with external resources, that solution is apt to be as inadequate, for it does not benefit from broader expertise, experience, and needs. Students can solve some problems on their own, but professors and books can help. The professor may be able to induce some change in students without paying much personal attention to them, but getting to their needs, their ways of thinking, their background and circumstances, can help. So it is, too, with the R&D center and the organization, the consultant and the client, and the committee making a proposal and those who must approve and implement its proposal.

Havelock's synthesis of planned change process is also a synthesis of planned change factors. Seven key ingredients in successful change efforts emerged from his and his associates' review of the literature. Applied to academic change, these guidelines would encourage several actions.

- Faculty, administrators, students and relevant outsiders (like trustees and funding agencies) should be well linked to each other and to information concerning problems and solutions.
- There should be an active openness, a real reaching out, to new information and new people across departmental and institutional boundaries.
- Change efforts should be well organized and there should be specific responsibility for follow-through, perhaps through efficient research, planning, governance, and implementation structures.
- Initiatives should enjoy capable leadership, skilled facilitation, and adequate time and materials.
- Useful information and other resources for change should be brought close together.
- Change efforts, at all stages of problem solving, should be rewarded.
- Change attempts should be numerous, various, and redundant.

This Linkage model for intentional change is very appealing in the abstract. It is far more complex than the carrot or the stick, and it has stronger evidence and logic to support it. On the rational level, it makes good sense. In the years since Havelock's synthesis, no other model for planned change has emerged that is as comprehensive and promising. It has provided a helpful way to view the academic innovation process and the faculty development process (Lindquist, 1974, 1975). It is quite compatible with the "mutual adaptation" model that emerged from the Rand studies of major federal educational innovations (Berman and McLaughlin, 1975). The authors find that local use of model programs occurs when the local institution and its members change to fit the innovation and when the innovation changes to fit local circumstances. If proposed change and potential user do not adjust to each other, actual change is unlikely. Indeed, one investigator could not even find traces of $40 million given to ten experimental schools in New York several years ago, let along find traces of change.

But Linkage has several obstacles between theory and practice. One problem is its abstractness. Just what should we do differently than we do now if we plan to implement this approach? Zaltman and his colleagues (1973) have addressed this question generally. Another and very significant problem is that Linkage has not been tested in any multi-institutional, longitudinal study of just how intentional change does occur. A major contribution of [Lindquist's] book (1978) is to fill that gap, as it contains seven detailed case histories of attempts to introduce various academic changes into five liberal arts colleges and two universities. If Linkage or one of the four other basic change assumptions explains effective planned change, we can see it for ourselves in those cases.

Summary

What brings about changes in attitudes and behaviors? Some believe that humans are essentially rational, so reason and evidence should do the trick. Intentional change, therefore, takes the form of a rational sequence of activities to produce a change message based in theory and research, then developed and tested empirically and logically and finally accepted because of its sound evidence and reason. Research and Development centers, institutional research and planning offices, and formal governance systems are designed to operate as if change is mainly a rational process.

Others find that humans are social creatures. New attitudes and behaviors, though they may be developed by rational processes, raise awareness, interest, trial, and eventual adoption through a process of social interaction and persuasion in which opinion leaders and reference groups are influences perhaps as significant as the rational soundness of the change message itself. Intentional change under these assumptions puts time and skill into linking innovative ideas, practices or products to potential adopters through social networks. Professional associations, information clearinghouses, learning resource centers, conferences, workshops, and extension agencies use this strategy.

Still others feel that the main obstacles to change are not impressive messages nor social influences. Psychological barriers are the problem. What is needed is the skilled intervention of human relations consultation in order to diagnose and facilitate the reduction of those barriers. Leadership training, clinical counseling, application of group dynamics, and Organizational Development are examples of this assumption at work.

Yet another group maintains we are political animals at base, busy protecting and strengthening our vested interests. In order to accomplish change, we need to build powerful coalitions among interests and obtain authoritative decisions that will be enforced by requiring people to change their attitudes and behaviors. That strategy is visible in the informal governance process and in such administrative controls as policies concerning program and personnel.

Recent theorists find that all these assumptions hold, probably in varying degrees depending on the issue, the situation, and the people involved. Havelock's Linkage theory was an early attempt to combine change assumptions. More recent planned change theories confirm his general model and suggest that combining all strategies for change is wise. Despite the fact that scholars may disagree about details of different models and more research may make refinements, these basic ideas provide academic leaders with practical information about how they may succeed with the complex and intricate task of changing the curriculum.

References

Baldridge, J. V. *Power and Conflict in the University.* New York: Wiley, 1971.

Bennis, W. *Organization Development: Its Nature, Origins, and Prospects.* Reading, Mass.: Addison-Wesley, 1969.

Berman, P., and McLaughlin, M. *Federal Programs Supporting Educational Change: The Findings in Review.* HEW No. R–1589/4. Washington, D.C.: U.S. Department of Health, Education, and Welfare, 1975.

Blake, R., and Mouton, J. *Grid Organization Analysis.* Reading, Mass.: Addison-Wesley, 1969.

Bowers, D. "OD Techniques and Their Results in Twenty-Three Organizations: The Michigan ICL Study." *Journal of Applied Behavioral Science,* 1973, *9,* 31–34.

Boyer, R., and Crockett, C. "Introduction, Special Issue on Organizational Development in Higher Education." *Journal of Higher Education,* 1973, *44,* 339–351.

Clark, D., and Guba, E. "An Examination of Potential Change Roles in Education." Paper delivered at Symposium on Innovation in Planning School Curricula, Airlie House, Warrenton, Va., Oct., 1965.

Easton, D. *A System Analysis of Political Life.* New York: Wiley, 1965.

Gamson, W. *Power and Discontent.* Belmont, Calif.: Dorsey Press, 1968.

Gross, N., Giacquinla, J., and Bernstein, M. *Implementing Organizational Innovations.* New York: HarperCollins, 1963.

Guba, E. "Development, Diffusion, and Evaluation." In T. L. Eidell and J. M. Kitchell (eds.), *Knowledge Production and Utilization in Educational Administration.* Eugene, Oreg.: University Council on Educational Administration and Center for Advanced Study of Educational Administration, 1968.

Hagen, E. *The Predictive Power of Social Change Theory.* Ann Arbor: University of Michigan, 1970.

Havelock, R., and others. *Planning for Innovation Through the Dissemination and Utilization of Scientific Knowledge.* Ann Arbor, Mich.: Institute for Social Research, 1971.

Lawrence, P., and Lorsch, J. *Developing Organizations: Diagnosis and Action.* Reading, Mass.: Addison-Wesley, 1969.

Lindquist, J. D. "Political Life in the State University: A Systems and Community Power Analysis." Unpublished doctoral dissertation, University of Michigan, 1972.

Lindquist, J. "Political Linkage: The Academic Innovation Process." *Journal of Higher Education,* 1974, *45,* 323–343.

Lindquist, J. "Institutional Services for Teaching Improvement: Combine Your Change Assumptions." In C. Steward and T. Harvey (eds.), *Strategies for Significant Survival.* San Francisco: Jossey-Bass, 1975.

Lippett, R., Watson, G., and Westley, B. *The Dynamics of Planned Change.* Orlando, Fla.: Harcourt Brace, 1958.

Parsons, T. "Stability and Change in the American University." *Daedalus,* 1974, 103.

Parsons, T., and Platt, G. *The American University.* Cambridge, Mass.: Harvard University Press, 1973.

Richman, B., and Farmer, R. *Leadership, Goals, and Power in Higher Education.* San Francisco: Jossey-Bass, 1974.

Rogers, E. M., Agarwala-Rogers, R., and Lee, C. C. *Diffusion of IMPACT Innovations to University Professors.* New York: Exxon Education Foundation, 1975.

Rogers, E. M., and Shoemaker, F. F. *Communication of Innovations.* New York: Free Press, 1971.

Sikes, W., Schlesinger, W., and Seashore, C. *Renewing Higher Education from Within: A Guide for Campus Change Agents.* San Francisco: Jossey-Bass, 1974.

Watson, G. "Resistance to Change." In G. Zaltman, P. Kotler, and I. Kaufman (eds.), *Creating Social Change.* New York: Henry Holt, 1972.

Zaltman, G., Duncan, R., and Holbeck, J. *Innovations and Organizations.* New York: Wiley, 1973.

CHAPTER THIRTY-TWO

IMPLEMENTING CHANGE

Jan T. Civian, Gordon Arnold, Zelda F. Gamson,
Sandra Kanter, Howard B. London

Higher education institutions have evolved into complex, decentralized organizations. These organizations have a mission that guides all campus activities and an endemic culture that further defines the relationships among faculty, administrators, and students. Like any organization, colleges and universities respond to economic conditions within and beyond themselves, and they do so in a framework of existing political agendas on campus. Navigating the political realm of curricular change is particularly treacherous because it involves attention to both the texts and the subtexts of the institution. The texts include all the obvious interests of the institutional players involved. The subtexts, however, are less readily known.

Note: The authors are grateful to the Exxon Education Foundation, which funded the Project on the Implementation of General Education from which this chapter draws. We deeply appreciate the continuing support of the foundation's former program officer, Richard Johnson, now of the Alliance for Higher Education in Dallas, Texas. Caryn Korshin has been an able successor as program officer. Coordinated by the New England Resource Center for Higher Education at the University of Massachusetts, Boston, the project was a field study designed to identify successful elements in the design and implementation of general education curriculum reform in comprehensive universities and liberal arts colleges. The study included a telephone survey of chief academic officers at seventy-one institutions followed by site visits at fifteen campuses. Several articles (Gamson, Kanter, and London, 1992; Gamson, 1992; Kanter, London, and Gamson, 1991) and working papers (Kanter, 1991; Kanter, London, and Gamson, 1990), as well as a book (Kanter, Gamson, and London, forthcoming) provide a fuller discussion of the results of the project.

Impediments to Change

Accomplishing curricular change is a feat; one must consider both the academe's general norms and cultural constraints and the economic, structural, and political constraints on the institution. We consider these domains separately because they each pose a potential impediment to curricular change.

General Constraints

Faculty are accustomed to freedom to do what they want in the privacy of the classroom. Protective of their classroom autonomy, faculty resist even hints of erosion in their freedom to teach what they want in the ways they deem appropriate.

Yet most curricular change requires, at least at the planning stage, that faculty relate the courses they teach to a larger view—to the discipline, to the department, to the college, to the institution as a whole. Faculty are typically more willing to make changes in their teaching if their discipline is moving in certain new directions. For instance, the requirement that undergraduates in sociology courses analyze computerized datasets has become de rigueur in most sociology departments. But even with disciplinary changes, no guarantee exists that individual faculty members will want to change. In disciplines like English, where there is much contention about new subfields and epistemologies, many faculty members resist changing the curriculum.

An important source of curricular change is the department, which in the majority of institutions is closely related to a discipline or professional field. Faculty even in small colleges view their departments as home, and they are likely to accept change emanating from their departments. They may agree to teach a new course or undertake an interdisciplinary or team-taught course for the fun of it, to help out a colleague, or to bring in more students. Of course, faculty may resist change emanating from the department if the change portends their departure or requires their retraining.

Faculty are most resistant to college or institution-wide curricular change. It is here that they feel most put-upon and most likely to defend the status quo. This is because the pull of colleagueship and of disciplinary requirements becomes attenuated the further away from the department one goes. Institutional loyalty and a sense of shared collective culture across the disciplines and between the faculty and administration have become weaker across the sectors of higher education in the last thirty years. The lure of the research culture, the creep of bureaucracy, and increased state control have weakened faculty community. Since college and institution-wide curricular change requires faculty to engage with one another beyond their departments, in this arena resistance is greatest.

Economic Constraints

Curricular change beyond the department is organizational change. This means that it plays into the political economy of colleges and universities in which enrollments determine—more or less directly—the number of faculty lines in a department. New curricula mean that some departments gain and others lose in this economy. No wonder, then, that despite the best intentions, departments get into turf battles over curricular change in which the winners are more likely to support change and the losers to oppose it.

Even if a new curriculum does not change faculty lines, there are increasingly severe economic constraints on change. After all, opportunity costs are involved in changing from one curriculum to another. If faculty are required to teach a new subject matter, employ new pedagogies, or team-teach, they must become prepared to do so, which takes time. And if faculty are already overemployed, there is little incentive for them to change. Certain departments like English and mathematics are stretched to the limit trying to cover remedial courses and general education requirements. Popular departments, like business or communications in the last decade, often find themselves with more students than they can handle. Their faculty may not be available, even with the best of intentions, to take on a new curriculum.

What about the departments whose faculty are underemployed? If they are willing to acknowledge this—and typically few are—they are likely supporters of a curriculum change that would bring students to their departments. But even here economic constraints are often severe. Faculty who have the time to devote to a new curriculum need support to learn unfamiliar material and pedagogies. And support for faculty development of this sort is in short supply, as institutional resources shrink and competition for external funds—for instance, from the National Endowment for the Humanities, the National Science Foundation, and private foundations—grows ever sharper.

Structural Constraints

We have already noted that for most faculty, the department is home. It is where colleagueship is likely to be strongest, and in disciplinary matters, where people can speak in incomplete sentences. This is because the modern American college and university are organized, in almost all cases, following the model of bureaucratic rationalism. Dominant in American organizations since the nineteenth century, this type of structural arrangement divides workers into departments according to competency, specialty, and shared knowledge. In the case of higher education, faculty are expected to be legitimate experts in their respective domains, and such legitimacy only comes with credentials demonstrating a thorough training in the given field. This characteristic of organizational structure influences the shape of undergraduate educational curricula in important if not always apparent ways.

First, training in a specialty, especially if it involves doctoral study, provides a good deal of socialization regarding not only a shared body of knowledge, but also common attitudes, values, understandings, customs, and assumptions. Of course, within any discipline there is apt to be wide-ranging opinion about the particulars, but it would nonetheless be quite unusual to find, for example, a group of historians arguing about whether or not history was important. Thus the distribution of faculty among departments gives rise to departmental points of view as well as competing interests in the allocation of resources, so that coordination among departments is difficult to achieve. The implications for undergraduate curricular change are clear—increased departmentalization has made it more difficult for experts to understand each other and to share in each other's concerns, yet the creation and implementation of an undergraduate curriculum require such communication.

This is particularly problematic because all disciplines are subject to a chronic strain first defined by Hughes (1973). The professions claim to have knowledge and even the solution to mysteries that cannot be understood or used by anyone not properly initiated through a course of study and the learning of a common disposition toward the field. This claim leads to exclusiveness—only a biologist can say what, exactly, the contents of the required biology course ought to be, only the historian may do the same for the history courses, and so on. The second claim, however, is that their expertise rests upon some branch of knowledge that is universal, and that at least the rudiments of it can and ought to be learned by all students. This claim leads toward integration with the world of higher learning.

Yet on campuses where faculty already have difficulty communicating across departmental lines and where worldviews on matters academic may not be shared, how is the integration of disciplines to be determined? For example, the idea that some knowledge of cultures other than the dominant one is desirable is an attitude held widely in many disciplines, particularly in the humanities and social sciences, and so one can find examples where an undergraduate curriculum stresses such an awareness. However, persons trained in fields such as mathematics or physics, while they may agree with this idea generally, may recoil at the suggestion that they should include multicultural features in their own courses—arguing (probably correctly) that their fields, being more international in organization than most of the humanities and sharing a tighter agreement about scope and methods, are already more multicultural than many if not most of the humanities and social sciences.

Because the coordination of viewpoints across departments is difficult to achieve, colleges and universities tend to be what are called "loosely coupled organizations" (Weick, 1976); that is, the various departmental (and other) sub-units are not as tightly controlled at the day-to-day level as is sometimes the case in bureaucratic systems. Thus, while a dean might control a department's budget, or while the administration might override a recommendation on a matter of tenure, administrators have little or no control regarding what is taught in individual courses, what courses will be taught, or how they will be integrated with other courses.

On the other hand, while loose coupling proves an impediment to interdisciplinary change, it actually promotes curricular innovation at the disciplinary level. Because the various departments are relatively autonomous and disconnected, they can quickly respond to disciplinary changes, trends, and discoveries in their respective fields, and any decline in the fortunes of one department need not threaten the entirety of the organization.

Political Constraints

In the real world of academe, the design and implementation of a curriculum can be highly political. Trade-offs are made in which parties mutually agree not to oppose the addition of courses from their respective departments. Trained as specialists, however, faculty usually prefer to teach their specialty rather than more general, introductory offerings. Thus, staffing an introductory course can become more difficult. A quick scan of the *Chronicle of Higher Education* position announcements reveals how often a willingness to teach introductory courses is viewed as a requirement to be fulfilled rather than a perquisite of the job. (Thankfully, not everyone sees it this way!)

The implications of this are significant, as the quality of a course is closely tied to the quality of instruction. Agreeing to have a new course added to the curriculum is a Pyrrhic victory if it is taught unenthusiastically by a senior faculty member filling out her load, or by an inexperienced graduate student who is poorly trained and supported.

Subtexts can also confound curriculum change. That is, alongside the discussion of how one or another curricular reform would be good for students, there is a parallel conversation regarding the hidden agendas of individuals or groups that can best be understood in relation to an institution's history and present struggles. Said differently, subtexts are formed by the joining of individual needs, institutional circumstances, and the historical moment. Examples of subtexts include how a curricular innovation might reverse a declining student enrollment, attract donors to the campus, assist in the consolidation of programs or campuses mandated by (in the case of public institutions) a state authority, thwart a threatened loss of accreditation, bolster a sagging college reputation, help faculty acquire more influence over the academic life of the community, or bring students to a department so that faculty jobs will be retained. In our study of general education reform, we identified another and more subtle subtext: using general education reform as the vehicle through which a cohort of midcareer faculty attempts to gain political and cultural ascendancy on campus.

Changing a general education curriculum was, we found, often seen as a route to resolving more than one of these organizational problems. In organizational sociology, this is regrettably called the *garbage can* phenomenon (Cohen, March, and Olsen, 1972), the phrase referring to the assortment of problems thrown into one vessel, with the hope that if they cannot be carted away, their mixture will suggest a useful next step for an institution.

This is not to lose sight of the more intellectual reasons for curricular reform. The struggle for power within academic units and across a campus can include demands for the inclusion of new perspectives—feminist thought, multiculturalism, ethnic studies, or environmental studies—or conversely, for the preservation of tradition. Behind these issues, in turn, lies another organizational problem having to do with the social role of higher education, specifically whether the campus is to emphasize the conservation of knowledge or the fueling of social change. In extreme cases, the polarization that results can be substantial—the inclusion of certain ideas in the curriculum lends legitimacy not only to those ideas but also to those espousing them. Thus the competition among various voices in the academy for dominance, or at least a place at the table, can lead to difficulties that are largely unforeseen in curricular design and implementation. These difficulties are not easily sorted out.

The Treacherous Terrain Of Curricular Change

Given the enormous impediments to change, curricular innovation occurs with varying degrees of success. Some kinds of curricular change are easier to accomplish than others. Curricular changes within the major are more easily accomplished than institution-wide curricular changes. Structurally, higher education is better configured to promote innovation at the departmental level, and change occurs much more easily there, where it can be based in the departmental faculty culture. This is not to discount the presence on nearly every campus of some fractious departments, nor to say that change at the department level takes place without struggle. Issues of professional accreditation, allocation of course loads, disagreements about discipline-related matters, as well as various subtexts can come into play. But these can all be addressed within the language and culture shared by faculty members who teach in the same discipline.

Changing a general education curriculum is considerably more difficult than curricular change within a department. First, it requires disparate parties to agree on the value of particular courses or arrays of courses—or, if they are not valued, to agree at least to allow their presence. Second, with the exception of only a very few elite campuses, this must occur when institutional resources are scarce, and the curriculum, if markedly different from its predecessor, will undoubtedly require money for proper implementation. Third, changes in a general education program can dramatically alter students' course-taking patterns, thus affecting the status of some departments and their claim on institutional resources. Where professional programs exist, turf wars often erupt as faculty in these departments oppose general education requirements that encroach on the number of credit hours required by accrediting associations, or that threaten to reduce the few electives their students have left. Before it reaches the president's desk, a new general education program is likely to face most of the complications and impediments outlined earlier in the chapter.

Just as departmental change is apt to meet fewer obstacles than change in general education, modest curriculum change is easier to accomplish than dramatic change. Virtually all the campuses in our study that attempted major change failed to accomplish it in the face of enormous political and financial pressures. Embittered visionaries involved in the failed change frequently retreated from active campus participation, so great was their disappointment in the compromises reached. Campuses in our study that attempted more modest change were much more likely to be successful in implementing an improved curriculum. Such programs—while obviously less innovative—are less threatening, less costly, and less likely to become lightning rods for insurmountable campus subtexts.

Where dramatic change is desirable, it is best accomplished in modest stages. Incremental changes can substantially improve a curriculum, but a failed comprehensive change benefits no one. Regular program reviews can keep the process of incremental change moving. The feedback loop helps in the resolution of unanticipated implementation problems and allows for ongoing discussion of the goals of the program.

Obviously, the primary goal of curricular change is to improve student educational outcomes. One of the unexpected positive byproducts of curricular reform, however, is not related to student outcomes at all, but to the faculty. By and large, faculty members who have been involved in curricular change report that they find the process of designing and implementing new curricula to be intellectually stimulating and professionally satisfying (except, of course, in extreme cases where the reform process has led to alienation). They enjoy being delivered from the routine of their teaching duties to participate in lively discussion about educational goals and curricular alternatives. When a program is at long last hammered out, the sense of accomplishment is palpable and enhances feelings of community. If the process has been well modulated, participants are left with energy to continue the reform process through implementation, evaluation, and reconfiguration stages.

However, our study found that an implementation process can leave many casualties. Faculty members or administrators who choose to crusade for programs that dramatically alter the status quo are not only unlikely to succeed, but may end up bitter and disillusioned. In worst-case scenarios, administrators have lost their jobs when they tried to force dramatic curriculum change. Faculty members may end up retreating to a cloistered campus existence, giving up active campus participation. In some cases, these individuals may actually have managed to get some of their ideas adopted. Not only do these particular individuals become victims of the politics of the academy, but their programs cannot be sustained when others who must deliver them do not believe in them.

Adequate attention to implementation issues must occur during the program design stage, including a realistic assessment of the resources and new structures needed to maintain it. It is not unusual for faculty committees to invest hours in designing a new curriculum, yet fail to think through the implementation issues necessary for its survival. Most often we found that campuses failed to anticipate the cost and coordination necessary to implement a new curriculum. Costs associated with a new curriculum typically include professional development activities for faculty in new skill areas such as interdisciplinary teaching. Additionally, faculty release time and new staff hires are necessary elements of successful implementation where new courses are part of the curriculum package. Finally, depending on the complexity of the new program, resources are sometimes needed to fund a coordinator who will attend to the details of program implementation. Another important implementation issue that may or may not have financial implications concerns student advising. Failure to educate faculty and students about the revised requirements creates headaches for registrars and heartaches for students when graduation draws near. Failure to anticipate the multiple needs of curriculum revision will mean that the programs never realize their full potential and may eventually fail.

Lessons from the Field

Two cases from our general education study serve to illustrate our points. At Plymouth State College (in New Hampshire), the faculty became dissatisfied with the existing loose distribution system of general education requirements. An ad hoc committee composed of respected senior faculty members hammered out the framework for a new general education curriculum, and, aided by faculty liaisons from each department, further refined the new program. The curricular revisions were not extravagant: distribution requirements were tightened so that students had less choice in the content they took, a freshman seminar was instituted to introduce students to the college culture, and students had to take at least one new team-taught interdisciplinary course.

Much went well during Plymouth State College's change process. Faculty talked about being in control of the process. Administrators were seen as allies in the effort to improve the curriculum. Everyone felt consulted and informed: department liaisons worked diligently to keep lines of communication open, a committee member was given release time to act as an ambassador-negotiator, and the ad hoc committee published a newsletter to inform faculty about its thinking and solicit input. Faculty reported that the reforms were energizing and had made them better teachers and colleagues. They believed that the curricular changes had improved students' educational experience. Additionally, a great deal of attention was paid to issues of implementation including allocation of resources and structures to support the new program. Workshops for faculty in writing across the curriculum and interdisciplinary teaching were enthusiastically received.

Some matters of implementation proved difficult, however. Staffing and scheduling were problematic early in the program. Not enough science labs were provided for students to meet the science requirement in a timely manner. According to faculty, some courses were oversubscribed and too many adjunct faculty had been hired to teach the general education courses. Faculty interest in the freshman seminar waned after a while and few could be recruited to teach it despite substantial monetary incentives. Finally, the program suffered somewhat from a lack of formal assessment as to what worked and what needed improvement.

While Plymouth State faced some difficulties implementing the new general education requirements, their program remains relatively strong and their process a model for others. The goals of the new program were well understood by the community, program design included high levels of consultation with the faculty, professional development opportunities were adequate, and the specific elements of the program were realistic for the campus (that is, the committee rejected ideas that were unrealistic in terms of budget or student characteristics, such as a foreign language requirement).

At the University of Massachusetts, Boston, an administrative edict was the catalyst for reform. The university had two colleges, each with its own philosophy of education. College I was liberal and permissive in its requirements for graduation, an outgrowth of the 1960s. College II was traditional; the canon took center stage. After a budget shortfall in the early 1970s, the two colleges were forced to merge and the new dean appointed a faculty committee to design a single liberal arts curriculum.

The faculty committee was large and included people from almost every point in the university's political spectrum. A group of faculty pushed for an innovative curriculum that emphasized critical skills as much as if not more than content. Despite opposition from traditionalists, the new curriculum, with a substantial number of new courses, was adopted.

Serious implementation problems soon arose despite thoughtful efforts to launch the program. While a Ford Foundation grant was acquired to train faculty and a new Center for the Improvement of Teaching was established to support the new curriculum, these efforts fell short. Many faculty believed that the multiple goals for each of the required core courses were impossible to attain; no one class could enhance academic skills through critical thinking, introduce one of seven broad areas of knowledge, and provide initiation into a traditional academic discipline. Most faculty were unfamiliar with the critical thinking movement— its language, knowledge base, and culture. Others who had some familiarity with these concepts simply did not know how to incorporate them all and work toward the goals in a single course. Despite their initial enthusiasm, many faculty felt pedagogically at a loss and wound up paying little or no attention to anything but the disciplinary material. Too little committed to the curriculum's goals, having inadequate expertise in teaching them, and feeling there was too little time in the course for them, they abandoned them. Principles and good intentions had bumped up against the real world of the classroom.

Other faculty—who thought from the beginning that the multiple goals were impossible to achieve in the same course—never had any intention of participating in the program. In short, the core courses were found to be too ambitious. There was little information circulating about what they were supposed to be and how they could be taught. Thus, the program floundered for two years until the problems were addressed by a faculty handbook. By then, however, a fracture between expectations and reality had developed, a fracture that never fully healed and forever hobbled the program.

Antagonism toward the curriculum never abated, so that when another budget crisis hit in the mid-1980s, the new curriculum was easy prey. Another faculty committee, appointed and supported by the dean, chose to make the curriculum more traditional and less skill-based. Most foundation courses were to be taught as if they were introductions to the disciplines. The educational innovators never forgave the dean for pushing this agenda. A number of them said that the results had made them wary about getting engaged in future campus affairs. The early fervor of these faculty was replaced by alienation and anger.

It is fair to say that reforming curriculum was a great deal more complicated at the University of Massachusetts, Boston, than at Plymouth State College. Boston is larger and more organizationally complex. Faculty there are torn between their teaching and research ambitions, while Plymouth State faculty are more comfortable in their teaching roles. The decision at Boston to create a new curriculum was made in the midst of organizational turmoil caused by the state's fiscal crisis; by contrast, the decision to revise Plymouth State's curriculum was an internal one, and the change was made during a relatively tranquil period in the college's history. While turmoil can create an opportunity for curricular change—and, indeed, enrollment or fiscal crisis served as the catalyst for curricular change on several of the campuses we studied—the change process itself tends to be more difficult during such periods due to high levels of fear and uncertainty. Despite the differences in the size and circumstances of these two institutions, we believe the contrasts in their approaches to curricular reform to be noteworthy. Plymouth State undertook reform by defining a clear framework, operationalizing their program in a modest way, paying painstaking attention to process and the inclusion of faculty and administration, and effectively training faculty in the implementation of the new program. Boston mounted an ambitious program without adequate grassroots support, and well-intentioned efforts to train faculty to teach skills-based core courses failed because the program was not well understood.

On the matter of designing a realistic program, we want to note that several campuses in our study failed to fully realize the scope of the curricular innovation envisioned by an ambitious design committee; after the compromising was said and done, the new program was only a minor improvement over the old one it was meant to replace. We have a few thoughts on why such curriculum change can be considered successful. First, at least a few participants on every campus are always energized by a campuswide discussion of educational goals and believe they improve as teachers. Second, administrators are often pleased that something concrete has been done, albeit small. Finally, curriculum change can successfully occur in waves; the innovations that do not make it into the first round of reform may well be adopted the second time around. Thinking back to the economic, cultural, structural, and political constraints described earlier in this chapter, it is no wonder that the garden variety of curriculum change tends to be modest . . . and, under the circumstances, it should be considered quite an accomplishment.

Eleven Suggestions for Good Practice

Life is not linear or simple, and neither is curriculum reform. We are painfully aware of the difficulties of carrying out change in the curriculum, but we have learned from close analysis of campuses that have tried to do so that it can be done, and often successfully. We conclude with eleven suggestions that should increase the odds for success.

- *Be realistic.* A curriculum should not be weighed down with multiple goals that are poorly understood by faculty. This does not mean that imaginative attempts at creating curricula with character and ambition should be discouraged; it does mean that people should not be set up for failure by attempting to do more than a campus's culture, politics, finances, and organizational constraints will realistically allow. Leaders need to know how far a campus can be stretched.

- *Anticipate implementation needs.* Good curriculum reform most often stumbles because no one is paying attention to the details of making it work. Inattention to implementation is almost always the weak link in the change process. Faculty education about the goals of the program and professional development to prepare faculty to teach the program are crucial. So too are financial support and coordination with the administrative offices likely to be affected, typically the offices of the registrar, admissions, advising, and publications.

- *Don't try to do everything in the first try.* Successful institutions tended to think of change as occurring on a continuum. Not everything needs to be accomplished on the first pass. Assessment and revision can be constant. Mistakes made in the first generation of reform can be corrected in the second generation, and so on.

- *Develop an appropriate administrative structure.* Successful programs are coordinated, monitored, assessed, protected, and nurtured by clear administrative structures. Programs that work well have a coordinator drawn from the administration or faculty, typically on release time, who works with a committee. Lack of clear authority for implementing the change is a common problem.

- *Provide rewards and incentives for participating in the program.* These can include public recognition, workload adjustments, release time, consideration of the participation in promotion and tenure decisions, and monetary rewards.

- *Ensure that professional development activities are adequate.* Current and new faculty must understand the goals and, if appropriate, the pedagogies, of the program. Therefore, faculty development activities prior to implementation are critical, especially those having to do with course development. Examples of professional development activities include workshops, retreats, release time to master new materials and teaching techniques, collaborative course development, and ongoing faculty seminars.

- *Actively recruit faculty to teach in the program.* Successful programs recruit qualified faculty to teach in them. They do not draft unwilling and poorly prepared teachers just to satisfy a department's need to staff courses. Qualified faculty can come both from within the institution and from the outside. Examples include recruiting practitioners, interdisciplinary faculty, and faculty representing cultures and backgrounds that may be called for in the new program. Ideally, senior faculty members will be visible participants in the new program.

- *Resources should be adequate and predictable.* Large—and sustained—resources should be allocated to support all phases of the program. Even when outside grants sustain a new curriculum through its first few years (through, for example, professional development activities or the provision of release time for course development), securing long-term funding should be a campus priority. Symbolic resources are important also, specifically the creation by presidents, provosts, and deans of a climate of belief in and support for the program.

- *Develop an assessment timetable.* An ongoing, serious evaluation of the program should begin at implementation, before problems are set in stone. This implies that the program and its implementation should be defined and treated as fluid and subject to modification. An identifiable group—an ad hoc committee, for example—should be given formal responsibility for evaluating the program.

- *Have an open, participatory process.* Critics of higher education often cite faculty autonomy as a major obstacle to reform. Whatever one's view of faculty roles and responsibilities, faculty have a large say in how they spend their time on campus. Successful curriculum change depends on the goodwill and interest of the faculty. While some sectors in the economy can impose unwanted changes on their employees, it makes little sense to implement unwanted changes in higher education, where faculty can choose their level of participation.

- *Pay attention to subtexts but don't let them overwhelm the process.* Conducting a truly open, participatory curriculum change process is not easy. There will be a great deal of territorialism—the desire by faculty and administrators to make changes that protect or enhance their jobs. The art of curriculum change is to walk a tightrope—that is, to stay focused on the educational goals even while making accommodations to multiple interests and broader organizational needs.

Difficult though curricular reform may be, the rewards are many. In addition to improved student outcomes, faculty can benefit from professional development opportunities derived from the new curriculum as well as from the sense of community elicited by discussion of educational mission and curricular goals. Managed well, curricular reform can challenge all campus constituents to transcend individual subtexts for the collective text of serving the educational needs of students.

References

Cohen, M. D., March, J. G., and Olsen, J. P. "A Garbage Can Model of Organizational Choice." *Administrative Science Quarterly,* 1972, *17,* 1–25.

Gamson, Z. F. "The Realpolitik of Reforming General Education." *Proceedings of the Asheville Institute on General Education.* Washington, D.C.: Association of American Colleges, 1992.

Gamson, Z. F., Kanter, S. L., and London, H. B. "General Education Reform: Moving Beyond the Rational Mode of Change." *Perspectives*, 1992, *22*, 58–68.

Hughes, E. C. (ed.). *Education for the Professions of Medicine, Law, Theology and Social Welfare.* Report prepared for the Carnegie Commission on Higher Education. New York: McGraw-Hill, 1973.

Kanter, S. L. "The Buck Stops Here: Outside Grants and the General Education Curriculum Change Process." Working Paper #9. Boston: New England Resource Center for Higher Education, University of Massachusetts, 1991.

Kanter, S. L., Gamson, Z. F., and London, H. B. (eds.). *Revitalizing General Education in a Time of Scarcity: A Navigational Chart for Administration and Faculty.* Needham Heights, Mass.: Allyn & Bacon, forthcoming.

Kanter, S. L., London, H. B., and Gamson, Z. F. "Implementing General Education: Initial Findings." Working Paper #5. Boston: New England Resource Center for Higher Education, University of Massachusetts, 1990.

Kanter, S. L., London, H. B., and Gamson, Z. F. "The Implementation of General Education: Some Early Findings." *The Journal of General Education,* 1991, *40*, 119–132.

Weick, K. E. "Educational Organizations as Loosely Coupled Systems." *Administrative Science Quarterly,* 1976, *21*, 1–19.

CHAPTER THIRTY-THREE

SUPPORTING CURRICULUM
DEVEL~~OPM~~

~~...~~erry

[handwritten note:] Copy pgs 633-660 / on Reserve under Dolinsky - Core Curriculum

...n feel besieged—in every sense of that
...ile forces, importuned with requests,
... cries for greater accountability have
... institutional autonomy. Faculty and
...en overwhelmed by pressures to engage in
outcomes assessment, productivity studies, continuous quality improvement, and
strategic planning. They know these disparate initiatives should be integrated, and
that, if done well, they can have a profound effect on the undergraduate curriculum. Nevertheless, integration is an ideal often perceived, yet rarely achieved.
Instead comes fragmented and begrudged work, committee recommendations at
odds with one another or passing each other in broad daylight, and a general sense
of inadequacy and malaise. The curriculum, meanwhile, often is in a shambles
or remains less than meets the eye.

An answer to these widespread woes may be found in curriculum development and change that are mutually supported by and integrated with *faculty development* and organizational development, as shown in Figure 33.1.

Note: We wish to thank our anonymous reviewers and our colleagues at the University of Northern
Iowa for their comments on this chapter, especially Joan E. Duea, professor of curriculum and instruction, who initiated the idea of a curriculum coordinating council.

FIGURE 33.1. STRATEGIES INFLUENCING AND INFLUENCED BY CURRICULUM DEVELOPMENT AND CHANGE.

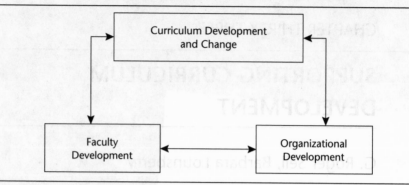

If well conceived and appropriately coordinated, such a multifaceted approach can lead to faculty empowerment, better teaching, stronger institutions, and a high-quality curriculum strategically aimed at clearly defined outcomes and fine-tuned by regular review. From this approach can come faculty, not under siege, but with a firm sense of the institution's mission and how its curriculum works to fulfill its promise. This process can encourage faculty to focus on common concerns, and thus enhance collegiality. Perhaps most important, faculty and organizational development linked with curriculum development can maintain institutional vitality.

The complex tasks of curriculum development and change are undertaken most successfully when they occur in conjunction with faculty development and organizational development. Within our framework, *faculty development* is treated as a set of strategies aimed at the acquisition and refinement of knowledge, skills, and values needed in the professional roles of faculty; *organizational development* as a set of strategies aimed at establishing, maintaining, and enhancing an institution's health and its effectiveness through improved policies, procedures, and practices; and *curriculum development and change* as a set of processes by which curricula—educational experiences in a broad sense—are created, implemented, reviewed, maintained, and modified or eliminated over time. In this sense, curriculum development and change would subsume *instructional development,* which is aimed at the systematic design, production, testing, implementation, and evaluation of materials, methods, and technologies used with learners. Our definitions are quite similar to those used by Gaff (1975) and Bergquist and Phillips (1975, 1977) as well as those endorsed by the Professional and Organizational Development Network in Higher Education. We recognize that some use these terms interchangeably and others might quibble with the specific characteristics or relationships of one or another. However, we have tried to be consistent in using these definitions throughout the chapter. Also, we recognize there is no standard definition of curriculum in higher education (Stark and Lowther, 1986; Wood and Davis, 1978), and there is no single undergraduate curriculum (Levine, 1978; Rudolph, 1977)—even within institutions that have prescribed core curricula. Perhaps ultimately, as Cross (1975) suggests, each student has his or her own curriculum, that is, learning experiences that define a personal program of study.

Faculty Development and Curriculum Improvement

Ensuring faculty support for curriculum improvement is one of the principles identified as vital by the Association of American Colleges (AAC):

> Faculty commitments and capabilities make or break the implementation of curriculum change, and they are central to sustaining program vitality. Faculty design and teach the courses and instruct the students: they are a program's most important resource. That is why strong general education programs continuously provide faculty support. . . . When a new curriculum is implemented, faculty need support to learn new content and new approaches to teaching and learning. . . . They may need to learn new subject matter that allows them to reach beyond their familiar specializations. . . . Although it is important for faculty to see continuous improvement of the curriculum as part of their day-to-day work in the profession, additional support for substantially new curricular initiatives is necessary to ensure successful implementation of major reforms. . . . Often courses of a certain type must be planned, at least in part, by a team to assure that all courses or sections address common goals or follow certain guidelines. It takes time for faculty members to hammer out common understandings and to reach agreement about topics, concepts, texts, and examinations. [1994, pp. 44–46]

Despite the eminent common sense of this AAC declaration, few empirical studies have focused on the relationship between faculty development and undergraduate curriculum improvement. A recent exception is the study by Gaff (1991), which surveyed more than three hundred deans, provosts, and presidents representing the full range of institutions from community colleges to research universities, with a response rate of 74 percent. Gaff found that institutions with major faculty development programs experienced substantial gains in:

- Planning and implementing large-scale changes in general education
- Designing and implementing offerings of required special courses in general education, including freshman seminars, courses using primary sources, interdisciplinary core courses, and senior seminars or projects
- Introducing themes or practices across the curriculum, such as ethics or values, global studies, cultural pluralism, gender issues, writing, and computer literacy
- Developing faculty policies to involve active learning or other pedagogical approaches designed to increase student involvement and decrease student memorization and passivity
- Achieving greater appreciation of general education on the part of students, faculty, and administrators
- Enhancing student admissions and retention, faculty renewal, sense of community, institutional identity, and public relations (visibility)

Based on these findings, Gaff concluded:

> Faculty development is not simply something "nice" to do. The evidence indicates that it is a very important strategy for strengthening general education by changing a curriculum, by improving the nature of teaching and learning within courses, and by keeping the focus on the people at the heart of the enterprise—students and faculty members. Simultaneously, it helps to increase the quality of education for students, to vitalize the institution, and to renew the faculty. As such, it is in everyone's self-interest to operate a substantial program that supports the professional growth of the faculty as teachers of general education. [1991, p. 120]

Eble and McKeachie reached a similar conclusion based on their study of thirty diverse institutions receiving faculty development grants from the Bush Foundation: "We believe that faculty development programs not only enhance student learning but also can maintain and increase [for faculty] the satisfactions of teaching and of belonging to a community of learners" (1985, p. 223).

Organizational Development and Curriculum Improvement

Curriculum development and implementation always occur within organizational contexts, which can provide support for successful curriculum development, or can pose obstacles to it (Gaff, 1980). As Chapter Thirty-Two points out, faculty tend to be more resistant to curricular change at the college and institution-wide levels than at the department level. An important step, therefore, in seeking curriculum improvement is to recognize that our current structures often constitute barriers to that very end. We must begin, in short, to think of organizational development and change as an important foundation for curriculum improvement.

A second challenge to authentic curriculum improvement, in our view, is the general lack of formal ties between the long-standing organizational structures for dealing with curriculum and the relatively new faculty development programs that have sprung up since the 1960s. Typically, curriculum decisions occur through faculty governance structures; that is, curriculum approval generally moves from department to college curriculum committees, then perhaps to a university curriculum committee, the faculty senate, the administration, and then the board of trustees or regents—as noted in Figure 33.2.

This, indeed, is the structure for curriculum review and approval at the University of Northern Iowa, our midsized comprehensive university. (We have approximately 11,500 undergraduates and 1,500 graduate students.) In the spring of 1994, five of the twenty members of the university faculty senate introduced a motion to create a quality in the curriculum committee to examine our university's

FIGURE 33.2. TYPICAL HIERARCHICAL PATTERN OF CURRICULUM APPROVAL IN COLLEGES AND UNIVERSITIES.

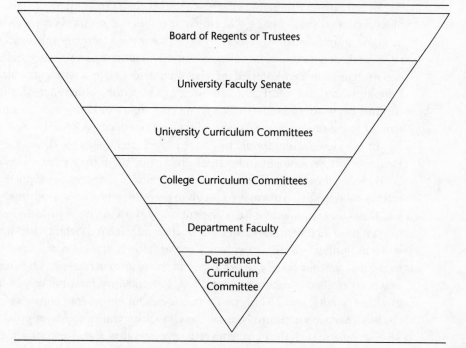

Board of Regents or Trustees

University Faculty Senate

University Curriculum Committees

College Curriculum Committees

Department Faculty

Department Curriculum Committee

undergraduate curriculum and to make recommendations aimed at enhancing its quality. Significantly, three of the five were also members of the university curriculum committee, and they believed the current curricular process simply was not producing a high-quality curriculum.

During the fall of 1994, the quality in the curriculum committee interviewed faculty, students, and administrators regarding our curricular process and came away with a list of problems that may strike a responsive chord with other academics. Committee members observed that our model for curriculum approval was hierarchical and faculty intensive. A new course or program must be endorsed by increasingly larger constituencies, or their representatives, until the sign-off by the regents signals approval at the state governing board level. All 630 of our tenured and pretenure faculty participate in curricular review at the department level; more than 80 then render further service on various college and university curricular review bodies.

This model was designed to provide rigor. One might expect such a faculty-intensive, multilevel process to produce high-quality curricula. Our students, our colleagues, and our administrators tell us it does not. Curriculum proposers find the process redundant. Curriculum reviewers find themselves seeking to exercise wise judgment on a stack of paper that grows ever higher (we have forty undergraduate departments) the higher up in the hierarchy they sit.

Even more distressing was the way—rather than providing rigor—the levels often encourage buck-passing. "Let the next committee stop it" becomes a way of avoiding tough decisions, a way to avoid saying no to proposals from other colleagues, departments, or colleges. "In the final analysis, we must defer to a department's superior knowledge" was often defended as a wise curricular philosophy, with the result that tough questions regarding coherence of a course within a program of study—or its connection to other courses in the curriculum, or to the university's mission—often have not been addressed.

In our view, faculty should not be chastised too harshly for these omissions. Resort to "the department knows best" philosophy stems from what we believe to be the essential weakness of the current hierarchical and summary judgment structure: beyond the department level it fails to prepare faculty adequately to do their job. Disinclination to pass hard judgment might be thought the prudent response to what most faculty acknowledged to be their information deficit when it comes to the institution's entire curriculum. Even with the course catalogue open before them, it is hard for faculty to comprehend the whole curriculum. Our midsized university offers 6 undergraduate degrees, 124 undergraduate majors, 84 undergraduate minors, and 23 program certificates. Our curriculum consists of 2,400 courses—and we are relatively small; the Ohio State University has approximately 10,000 courses. With the current inverted pyramid structure, everyone is involved, but no one is really minding the store (except, perhaps, the chief academic officer or his or her designee, who generally is without a vote).

The quality in the curriculum committee brought to light another problem of our current model. At our university, and we think at many others, there is no actual site where the curriculum can be found—save for the course catalogue, or in the historical files at the provost's office. No wonder it is hard for our faculty to comprehend the curriculum in the root sense of that word (to grasp).

The failure of our curriculum-as-a-whole to be literally present and graspable reinforces another weakness of our current structural model—the fact that the actual cost (in dollars) of curricular decisions has not been sufficiently prominent in campus discussions. Indeed, a common complaint by members of the university curriculum committee and administrators alike has been that, although the new-course or new-program forms ask for the costs of these additions to the curriculum, most curriculum proposers write "none." As a result, chief academic officers often find themselves in the queasy position of defending before the trustees a continuously expanding and less-than-coherent curriculum. At our university, slightly more than 90 percent of the provost's budget is allocated to faculty salaries and benefits in support of the curriculum. However, during the past five years, 139 courses have been added to the curriculum—beyond the number that have been dropped. Hefferlin (1969), from a review of course changes at 110 four-year colleges between 1962 and 1967, estimated an average annual net increase of 4 percent to 5 percent in the number of courses (new courses arriving minus old courses departing).

Where will the funds come from to pay for new courses and programs? What are we sacrificing for this incremental approach to curricular development and choice? At present, curriculum development and review processes that we are aware of do not provide sufficient information or assistance to the faculty to help them become wise stewards of limited resources when making curricular choices.

A final problem we will mention in our current organizational model for curriculum development and review is its cyclical nature. Faculty complained that our present two-year curriculum cycle is driven by the catalogue production schedule rather than focused on the needs of high-quality education. Designed to provide adequate time for thorough curriculum development and review, in practice the cycle's deadlines often have resulted in hasty work as people rush to submit their curriculum proposals. University curriculum committee members acknowledged that they could spend more time on questions of coherence and connectedness of proposals if they were not so bogged down double-checking prerequisites and rewriting course descriptions—matters supposedly dealt with at the initial levels of the hierarchy.

Curriculum Coordinating Council

What, then, is a remedy for these serious structural problems? Our quality in the curriculum committee came to believe the answer lay in a creative reimagining of the entire curricular process. Committee members believed that this would require reducing curricular levels and inverting the process from curricular bodies solely passing summary judgments to bodies actively involved in curriculum at the developmental stage. Their recommendation, which will be voted on by the faculty-as-a-whole in spring 1996, is to transform the present university curriculum committee into a curriculum coordinating council operating at the first stage of curriculum development and review (see Figure 33.3).

For our university, the curriculum coordinating council would consist of five to ten faculty and three to four students. Faculty would serve staggered two-year terms and would receive (as never before) one course reassigned time during each semester of council membership. In this way, studying and developing the university's curriculum would be a recognized part of faculty life. We believe the lack of reassigned time for study and development of the curriculum has been one of the factors leading to the crisis in curriculum quality many institutions face.

If the motion creating the curriculum coordinating council passes, faculty serving on the council next year will be charged with the following responsibilities:

- Keeping abreast of state, regional, national, and international curricular trends
- Comprehending the institution's entire curriculum, its interrelations and potentialities
- Encouraging and providing counsel in the development of quality curriculum proposals initiated by individual faculty, faculty groups, departments, colleges, and students
- Initiating innovative curricular proposals themselves, when and where appropriate (such as interdisciplinary programs making use of existing curricular offerings)
- Ensuring that all affected persons and bodies are consulted and (when appropriate) involved at each stage of new curriculum development
- Ensuring that resources needed for new offerings are identified, available, and committed before new offerings are approved
- Adhering to the highest standards of quality in making recommendations to the faculty senate regarding curriculum proposals
- Planning and sponsoring regular colloquia, focus groups, and reading and discussion groups on curricular issues to engage the academic community (faculty, students, and staff) in an ongoing conversation regarding curricular concerns

FIGURE 33.3. THE PLACE OF A CURRICULUM COORDINATING COUNCIL IN THE DEVELOPMENT, REVIEW, AND APPROVAL OF A CURRICULUM PROPOSAL.

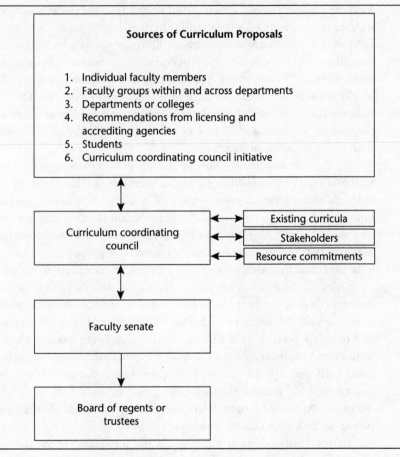

Under this new model, the professor wishing to propose a course—say, "Midwestern Literature"—will not work in isolation and then wait for peers to pronounce judgment. Instead, during the earliest stages of development, the professor will meet in consultative sessions with the curriculum coordinating council. Indeed, a faculty member from the council will be assigned as the special coach or consultant for a proposal.

At these early consultative sessions, council members will listen to the curricular concept, and then explore with the proposer how it might connect with current curricular offerings and the university's mission and priorities. Council members, for example, will be able to turn to their charts and files and provide the proposer not only with the information that "Midwestern History" and "Midwestern Geology" courses are currently being taught but with the actual syllabi for these courses as well. This will lead naturally to suggestions that the professor may wish to consult with these and other colleagues as the new course is being fashioned. Consultative sessions also will involve forthright discussions of library and support services, space, equipment, software, materials, people, and other resources needed for successful implementation of the course, for here the proposer will be invited to imagine the highest-quality course possible. The council consultant will then investigate whether such resources would be available and whether they would be committed to the new offering—taking this often-awkward burden from the curriculum proposer.

Similar discussion and follow-up would occur regarding individuals and bodies that should be consulted as the proposal evolves. To ease the transition from the old to the new curricular process, the quality in the curriculum committee has recommended that departments and colleges retain their curriculum committees if they wish. When "Midwestern Literature" is eventually developed in consultation with the curriculum coordinating council, the proposer's consultant will offer to be present at department or college curriculum presentations with the professor.

Once all the appropriate bodies have discussed and given their support for the new offering, the proposal would come before the entire curriculum coordinating council for discussion. This would be followed by a formal council report and recommendation to the faculty senate. Following its discussion, the senate would vote to approve or not to approve the proposal, taking into account the proposal itself, the report and recommendation from the curriculum coordinating council, and any presentations from the proposer and council at the time of consideration. Approved proposals would be sent to the board of regents for final approval, as under the current practice.

In trouble-shooting curricular scenarios, the quality in the curriculum committee envisioned several benefits from conversations that may arise in the new structure. A curriculum proposer, for example, may see during the first consultations that the new course being proposed is more appropriate as a graduate rather than undergraduate offering, or that the original idea for the new course is unsuited to the university's mission and priorities for undergraduate education. Far better to learn this early, before considerable time and energy are devoted to development of the proposal.

In conflicts that may arise during consultation—for example, students served or course objectives or course title—the council consultant will act as a mediator between the proposer and the objecting department or college, seeking a mutually agreeable outcome while keeping the focus on curriculum quality. The intent is to avoid bitter campus battles while promoting and supporting initiatives that foster a high-quality curriculum. In addition, failure to obtain commitments for the resources needed to support a new course or program becomes a persuasive reason for delaying a course, yet also for considering those resources in future budgets. Whenever the curriculum coordinating council's report and recommendation are negative, the proposer can still take the proposal forward to the faculty senate. Ultimately, the council's success in persuading both proposer and faculty senate of the wisdom of its recommendations will depend on the ethos it creates through campus interactions.

Besides the potential benefits arising from creative tensions in the new process, the quality in the curriculum committee envisioned other benefits of this new organizational structure, including:

- Reduction of ineffectual faculty committee work while at the same time increasing the assurance of: coherence and connection of new courses with present curricular offerings, consultation with and involvement of all affected bodies during curricular development, resource commitment to new curricular proposals, and adherence to consistently high-quality standards in the development of new curricula.

- Provision for support and counsel at the essential developmental stage of curriculum building.

- Creation of a forum in which instructional design and development become natural considerations in curriculum development.

- Creation of a climate of collaboration and support, as opposed to one of fractionation and apprehension.

- Creation of greater collegiality as virtually all members of the academic community at some point participate in colloquia, workshops, focus groups, and reading-discussion groups on issues affecting the curriculum. This structure assumes that developing and maintaining a high-quality curriculum is an ongoing, never-ending effort. It establishes a means for creating the ongoing conversation around curricula.

- Recognition that students are stakeholders in the curriculum and that their voices are important in curriculum review and development.

- Liberation of the curriculum from the restraints of arbitrarily imposed cycles. With the council, curricular proposals develop organically, at their own pace. They are forwarded to the faculty senate only when ready. The faculty senate, in turn, can give each proposal full consideration, rather than as one of hundreds of items in a huge curricular package. This in itself may slow the rampant growth of the curriculum.

- Establishment of a core of faculty with time allocated for keeping abreast of current trends in curriculum development and for providing that expertise to the academic community as a whole. Thus faculty are being developed at the same time the curriculum is being studied and advanced. After serving on the curriculum coordinating council, faculty members will be better future curriculum developers themselves, and can serve as helpful informal consultants in their departments and colleges. Over time, more and more faculty will have this expertise. This will assist the institution not only in maintaining a quality curriculum, but also in advancing the curriculum to even higher levels of excellence.

- Establishment of an ongoing site for the study and development of the curriculum. Our quality in the curriculum committee recommendations calls for the curriculum coordinating council to have office and meeting space in our university's Center for Teaching Excellence, which is located in new space in the library facility. All members of the university community will thus be able to drop in at their convenience to study and discuss our curriculum.

The concept of a curriculum coordinating council thus contributes to synchronous curriculum development, faculty development, and organizational development. When linked to other organizational and faculty development strategies, the curriculum coordinating council can be especially potent in supporting curricular reform.

New Strategies

Three relatively new organizational strategies are also emerging as potentially strong approaches for supporting curriculum and faculty development. These include practice-centered inquiry, outcomes assessment, and strategic planning.

Practice-Centered Inquiry

Offices of institutional research are prevalent on campuses throughout the United States. Formed initially to respond to external requests for institutional information, these offices generally have grown in scope and complexity to include a variety of both internal and external reporting functions. At times, these offices are also involved in various planning and program review activities; however, few are integrally involved with inquiries directly related to curriculum, faculty, or organizational development.

Quite separate from these offices has grown research that can be termed *practice-centered inquiry.* Ranging from the "reflective practitioner" approach of Schön (1983, 1987) and the "action science" methodology of Argyris, Putnam, and Smith (1985) to the "assessment studies" initiated at Harvard University (Light, Singer, and Willett, 1990) and the "Classroom Research" of Angelo and Cross (1993), these forms of practice-centered inquiry show promise of building local knowledge that can contribute to curriculum improvement as well as faculty and organizational improvement.

We recommend expansion of these local research initiatives. When well designed and supported, practice-centered inquiry can provide faculty with data and reasoning systems essential to effective curriculum development and implementation efforts. At the same time, the inquiry process is an excellent vehicle for faculty development and for colleges and universities to learn about themselves and use that knowledge to make instructional improvements. It encourages expansion of knowledge, honing of skills, and clarification of values. In conjunction with a curriculum coordinating council or other organizational strategies mentioned in this section, practice-centered inquiry can provide essential feedback and guidance for successful curriculum review, development, and implementation.

Outcomes Assessment

As of summer 1995, at least twenty states required public colleges and universities to establish programs to assess what students learn ("Almanac Issue," 1995, p. 10). Such mandated outcomes assessment is yet another expression of public demands for institutional accountability. Many institutions, however, are initiating their own programs for assessing student outcomes. While some of these programs are clearly linked to institutional planning and program review (for example, Nichols, 1989), many are not designed to be directly supportive of curriculum development and change (Sell 1989a).

A strongly expressed concern is that outcomes assessment not be designed solely as an accountability mechanism, but rather as a useful approach for the continuous improvement of academic quality (Gray, 1989). Outcomes assessment can lead to improvement in at least four areas of curriculum development and implementation: translating student needs into curriculum goals and objectives (intended outcomes); designing curriculum components so that content, teaching and learning activities, and assessment procedures are mutually supportive and reflect the intended outcomes; collecting and using formative outcomes information in piloting and revising new curricula; and providing students with formative feedback on their attainment of intended outcomes and ways in which their performance can be improved. A synthesis of recommended principles and practices in outcomes assessment that can be adapted to curriculum development and change is found in Sell (1989b).

Strategic Planning

Regrettably, as with outcomes assessment, strategic planning has often failed to focus on the undergraduate curriculum and its improvement. Typically, strategic planning has been undertaken by an institutional, college, or department committee (usually assisted by an internal or external planning expert) without distinct ties to other committees or groups involved in outcomes assessment, program review, curriculum development, or faculty development.

Such inadequate linkages were found in a recent study of "strategic planning councils" at eight institutions (Schuster, Smith, Corak, and Yamada, 1994). These investigators suggested that one or more of four crucial elements—leadership support, shared governance, open communication, and comprehensive planning—are typically bypassed, or are out of sync, in major decisions colleges and universities make. Institutional choices have tended to be made without the kind of broad participation that evokes commitment, without engaging faculty and administrative leaders in effective decision making, without mechanisms for adaptation to change, and without thoughtful resource considerations. By bringing vital organizational elements into the process, and by introducing curriculum priorities as critical elements, strategic planning has high potential for enhancing curriculum development and change.

Strategies for Curriculum and Faculty Development

While new organizational strategies seem to be required to link curriculum and faculty development, existing strategies and mechanisms should not be overlooked. Because of their prevalence throughout postsecondary education, two relatively well-established organizational strategies are here highlighted: faculty development centers and programs, and instructional enhancement grants.

Faculty Development Centers and Programs

In 1962, the Center for Research on Learning and Teaching at the University of Michigan became one of the earliest institutional efforts to provide faculty with a range of support for instructional improvement. Broad-based surveys in the 1970s and 1980s found that approximately one-half of U.S. four-year colleges and universities had established formal centers or programs for faculty development (Centra, 1976; Erickson, 1986). Such centers and programs provide a range of support for instructional improvement. Based on the Erickson survey, which for the most part confirmed the earlier findings of Centra, 50 percent or more of the colleges and universities with centers and programs for faculty or instructional development provided the type of activity or material in the following list, which is arranged by order of frequency within groupings.

- *Workshops or seminars* on various methods or techniques of instruction, academic advising, and counseling
- *Resources to faculty for assessing and improving their teaching,* including student ratings of instruction, classroom observation by peers, instructional technology such as audiovisual aids and computer-assisted instruction, and videotaping and critique of classroom instruction
- *Grants of awards, leaves, and exchanges,* including travel funds for attending professional conferences, sabbatical leaves with at least half salary, unpaid leaves for educational or development purposes, grants for faculty members developing new or different approaches to courses or teaching, temporary teaching load reductions to work on new courses or major course revisions or research, travel grants to refresh or update knowledge in a particular field, and summer grants for projects to improve instruction or courses
- *Other forms of support,* including instructional assessment instruments used for periodic review of all faculty members, annual awards to faculty for excellence in teaching, a campus committee on faculty development, and a visiting scholars program

Many of these activities also could help support and strengthen the curriculum. However, at present, the only formal connection to curriculum development and curriculum change in these various center-provided activities seems to be through grants for course development and revision. Surely more creative linkages between faculty and curriculum development can be established. As noted earlier, centers and programs for faculty development may be natural sites for curriculum coordinating council materials and meetings, which can lead to collaborative curriculum efforts with individual faculty, teams of faculty, and academic units.

Instructional Enhancement Grants

Both Centra (1976) and Erickson (1986) found that a majority of institutions responding to their surveys had some form of grants program for funding instructional innovations. Often, however, instructional enhancement grants programs are not coordinated with curriculum development activities. As a case in point, Davis (1979) identified the criteria for judging instructional grants proposals at Michigan State University: the number of students affected, the experimental or innovative quality of the approach, the generalizability of the approach for other academic areas of the institution, and the capability for evaluation of the project. None of these criteria refer to curriculum development efforts as such.

Others have conducted systematic studies of grants programs and their impact on faculty, students, and curricula. For example, Sell (1990) provided an overview of four different kinds of projects supported by instructional enhancement grants at Ohio State, characteristics of successful projects, and contributions of projects to qualities of effective instruction. In a more detailed fashion, Sell (1992) reported on an extensive evaluation study of 140 instructional enhancement grants awarded over a ten-year period at Ohio State. Based on mail and telephone surveys, in-person interviews, archival data, and project report analysis, this study found new instructional materials and methods implemented in courses and programs, improvements in student learning, new knowledge and skills acquired by faculty, publications and externally funded projects linked to internal grants, and continuation of project-initiated activities beyond the grant period. However, there was little evidence of curriculum effects beyond the course level. While instructional enhancement grants need not be tied to curriculum priorities and new curricula, it would seem prudent for institutions to investigate these possibilities. The curriculum coordinating council might serve as a mechanism for joining instructional enhancement grants with curriculum and faculty development.

Unresolved Problems and Continuing Challenges

Since the early 1820s, colleges and universities have been engaged almost constantly in fiddling with undergraduate curricula (Levine, 1978; Rudolph, 1977). However, at least one historical study suggests that curriculum reform in postsecondary education mostly has been cosmetic in nature and has not significantly changed the teaching-learning process (Veysey, 1973). Yet, as Cross (1976) argues, meaningful reshaping of the curriculum must become a priority if we are to move beyond access concerns (education for all) to concerns for the quality of education individual students experience (education for each). Special reports from the Association of American Colleges (1985), The Carnegie Foundation for the Advancement of Teaching (Boyer, 1987), the National Endowment for the Humanities (Bennett, 1984), and the National Institute of Education (Study Group on the Conditions of Excellence in American Higher Education, 1984) have called for such significant curriculum changes—especially for engaging students in more active and meaningful learning within a coherent undergraduate program characterized by strong teaching and general education.

To accomplish needed development and change in the undergraduate curriculum, we believe that research and practical experience lend support for the importance of faculty development and organizational development. We have identified, however, a number of unresolved problems and continuing challenges for improving curriculum practice and the support provided through faculty and organizational development.

Practice-Centered Inquiry for Curriculum Development

One of the most fundamental problems for the support and advancement of curriculum development in undergraduate education is our incomplete understanding of what is actually entailed in curriculum work, especially the development of new curricula and the change of existing curricula. The design approach to curriculum may be a useful point of departure. Stark and others define curriculum as "an academic plan that is purposefully constructed to facilitate student learning" (1990, p. 2). In a similar but expanded vein, Toombs and Tierney define curriculum as "an intentional design for learning negotiated by faculty in light of their specialized knowledge and in the context of social expectations and students' needs" (1991, p. 21). Both these definitions focus on curriculum as a design problem (see, for example, Simon, 1969) and both definitions can be applied at all levels of the curriculum—student, course, program, or institution.

But are these definitions a useful starting point for describing what faculty actually do in curriculum development? Toombs and Tierney present what they perceive to be the current uncomfortable situation: "Systematic description [of curriculum development], that is, an orderly technical terminology that will enhance insights on practice and that is a means of linking ideas to application, has not developed. . . . Often faculty at work on the curriculum are forced to invent their own labels to describe what they do" (1991, p. 15).

If the concept of curriculum as a design for learning (or a learning plan) is to be useful for describing tasks related to curriculum development, then some additional specifications are required. We would want to know, for example, what the components of curriculum design are, what variables need to be taken into consideration for each component, and what curriculum tasks are associated with particular design components and variables. Considerable formative research has helped to address these questions (for example, Bergquist, Gould, and Greenberg, 1981; Conrad, 1978; Dressel, 1971; Eisner, 1979; Toombs and Tierney, 1991; Tyler, 1950). Many others have also studied curriculum components at the postsecondary level—Boyer (1987), Carnegie Foundation for the Advancement of Teaching (1977), Gaff (1983), Levine (1978), Mayhew and Ford (1971), and Stark and Lowther (1986).

While the curriculum terminology and components vary across frameworks, it seems reasonable to infer from the literature that the following five tasks are common to curriculum planning and development in undergraduate education: establishing needs, goals, and objectives; selecting and organizing content; selecting and arranging instructional strategies; selecting, developing, and allocating resources such as people, materials, equipment, learning environments, and time; and evaluating formative and summative results for students and for the curriculum under development. A focus on tasks such as these could be used to anchor studies of curriculum development in action.

The participant-observer studies reported by Eisner (1979), Grobman (1968, 1970), and Walker (1975) provide a rich description and analysis of precollege curriculum development in action. We are not aware of similar undertakings in postsecondary curriculum development, although the work of Stark and others (1990) in faculty surveys of "course decisions" and the formative evaluation of curricula under development reported by Diamond and others (1975) and Forman, Aversa, Sell, and Brown (1976) suggest some possible approaches for replication.

Where might such inquiry focus attention? Among many possibilities, we suggest five targets of concentration:

•   *An individual course from a structural perspective.* Attention would be given to how a course is designed, developed, implemented, and sustained within a department as part of a course sequence, general education program, major, minor, or undergraduate degree.

•   *An individual course from an interdisciplinary perspective.* Here attention would focus on how a course is designed, developed, implemented, and sustained by faculty representing more than one department or area of academic work.

•   *Multiple courses from a thematic perspective.* These inquiries would center on how themes or priorities (such as learning to learn, collaborative learning, information technologies, or multicultural education) are designed, developed, implemented, and sustained across courses in a core curriculum, general education program, major, or undergraduate degree.

•   *Programs from an intrainstitutional perspective.* These inquiries would explore how institution-wide programs (such as a general education program, major, or undergraduate degree program) are designed, developed, implemented, and sustained within an institution.

•   *Programs from an interinstitutional perspective.* These inquiries would explore how interinstitutional programs (such as teacher education or international study) are designed, developed, implemented, and sustained across two or more postsecondary institutions or between postsecondary institutions and other educational providers (such as public schools) or entities outside formal education (such as business and industry).

If studies such as these produce a more detailed and complete map of curriculum work from various perspectives, the identification of challenges and opportunities for faculty, organizational, and curriculum development would be more firmly grounded and sharply focused.

Practice-Centered Inquiry for Curriculum Implementation

Practice-centered inquiry for curriculum implementation and change could follow a pattern similar to that described for curriculum development. Indeed, the curriculum process should be examined holistically from initial conception to discontinuation or major revision of a course or program. However, several key issues dealing specifically with curriculum implementation and change have not yet been identified and deserve separate attention.

One continuing issue in the change literature is whether new curricula are actually implemented and, if so, to what extent. We may think curricula are fully implemented, but often a close examination of teaching and learning practices after the changeover reveals that this is not the case. To get at implementation concerns, we might ask, for example: Which goals and objectives do students perceive as most important? What directs and sustains their attention to these goals and objectives? Because students are highly concerned about grades and evaluation of their performance, how do testing and grading practices influence student academic work, and is the work students undertake consistent with our intent, evaluation criteria, and evaluation methods? Are the learning activities students engage in meaningful and consistent with our intent and with their personal sense of what is important? Where and how do students allocate their time and attention in academic work, and is the focus of their efforts strategic to the most important accomplishments they expect—and we expect of them? What resources, other than student and teacher time, do students use in their learning activities and how do these other resources contribute to the quality of student effort and the results obtained? A parallel set of questions also could be directed to teachers to get a fuller picture of where and how curriculum implementation has occurred.

As pointed out by Cross (1975), the curriculum that students learn is not necessarily the curriculum that faculty teach or the curriculum described in institutional documents and publications. Future research should identify contextual factors that facilitate or impede implementation of curricula and that have positive (intended and unanticipated) and negative effects on students and teachers.

Another key implementation and change issue is whether a new curriculum is better than an existing or prior one. In assessing curriculum improvement, we might ask: Is a new curriculum more effective in terms of student performance, student satisfaction, or student motivation to continue learning? Is a new curriculum more efficient in the use of resources, including student and teacher time, other personnel resources, physical resources, information resources, and financial resources? What evidence and means of assessment are there to indicate that a new curriculum contributes to student, faculty, or institutional vitality? Do faculty development and organizational development strategies play a significant role in contributing to a better curriculum and, if so, how and why? Acceptable criteria, evidence, and standards of comparison need to be established for both of these issues.

Practice-Centered Inquiry to Support Curriculum Development and Implementation

Earlier in this chapter we suggested some of the possible ways faculty and organizational development can be instrumental in curriculum work. However, we also noted that faculty development and organizational development tend to be separate from the ongoing work of curriculum review, development, and implementation. *Our main thesis is that faculty development strategies, along with organizational development strategies, should be synchronous with and complementary to curriculum development and change.*

Related to this thesis, two other lines of practice-centered inquiry would seem to be most opportune. One would be to locate or create cases where curriculum development and implementation are integrated systematically with faculty and organizational development strategies. While one could argue that virtually all successful curriculum development projects involve some form of faculty and organizational development, with relatively few exceptions this position has not been closely studied or clearly supported in the literature. Some exceptions include studies reported by Gaff (1991), McTighe Musil (1995), and Schmitz (1992) that describe characteristics of selected projects with regard to connections between faculty development and curriculum development and change. Studies reported by Hefferlin (1969), Levine (1978, 1980), and Lindquist (1978) tease out linkages between organizational strategies and curriculum change. However, even with these exceptions, it is not clear why or how these connections work. Typically, strategies discussed in the literature are used to develop, explain, or defend a particular approach to curriculum change and not necessarily to investigate the effects of various faculty or instructional development strategies on curriculum work.

Another line of inquiry to advance professional practice is the careful study of faculty development and organizational development strategies used in specific curriculum development and implementation efforts. A central question for such studies would be: Under what conditions are particular strategies effective in supporting desired curriculum development and implementation outcomes? We must shift our initial focus from generating a model or general theory of curriculum development and change to exploring and anchoring our notions about curriculum development and change within contextualized, ongoing efforts. In this sense, for the advancement of professional practice, we must move beyond declarative knowledge (what we do) and procedural knowledge (how we do it) to conditional knowledge (why, when, where, and with what effects we do it).

The overall intent of the practice-centered inquiries we are proposing is to create, improve, implement, and sustain high-quality curricula. Our specific aim is to uncover, understand, and use strategies for faculty development and organizational development that have beneficial effects for particular kinds of curriculum development projects in particular settings. Such practice-centered inquiry would enable us better to integrate new and existing strategies in the service of undergraduate education. Curriculum coordination councils could be excellent vehicles to conduct such inquiry and to contribute to greater sophistication among faculty members about curricular issues.

References

"Almanac Issue." *Chronicle of Higher Education*, Sept. 1, 1995, p. 10.

Angelo, T. A., and Cross, K. P. *Classroom Assessment Techniques: A Handbook for College Teachers.* (2nd ed.) San Francisco: Jossey-Bass, 1993.

Argyris, C., Putnam, R., and Smith, D. M. *Action Science: Concepts, Methods, and Skills for Research and Intervention.* San Francisco: Jossey-Bass, 1985.

Association of American Colleges. *Integrity in the College Curriculum: A Report to the Academic Community.* Washington, D.C.: Association of American Colleges, 1985.

Association of American Colleges. *Strong Foundations: Twelve Principles for Effective General Education Programs.* Washington, D.C.: Association of American Colleges, 1994.

Bennett, W. J. *To Reclaim a Legacy: A Report on the Humanities in Higher Education.* Washington, D.C.: National Endowment for the Humanities, 1984.

Bergquist, W. H., Gould, R. A., and Greenberg, E. M. *Designing Undergraduate Education.* San Francisco: Jossey-Bass, 1981.

Bergquist, W. H., and Phillips, S. R. *A Handbook for Faculty Development.* Vol. 1. Washington, D.C.: Council for the Advancement of Small Colleges, 1975.

Bergquist, W. H., and Phillips, S. R. *A Handbook for Faculty Development.* Vol. 2. Washington, D.C.: Council for the Advancement of Small Colleges, 1977.

Boyer, E. L. *College: The Undergraduate Experience in America.* New York: HarperCollins, 1987.

Carnegie Foundation for the Advancement of Teaching. *Missions of the College Curriculum: A Contemporary Review with Suggestions.* San Francisco: Jossey-Bass, 1977.

Centra, J. A. *Faculty Development Practices in U.S. Colleges and Universities.* Project Report 76–30. Princeton, N.J.: Educational Testing Service, 1976.

Conrad, C. F. *The Undergraduate Curriculum: A Guide to Innovation and Reform.* Boulder, Colo.: Westview Press, 1978.

Cross, K. P. "Learner-Centered Curricula." In D. W. Vermilye (ed.), *Learner-Centered Reform: Current Issues in Higher Education.* San Francisco: Jossey-Bass, 1975.

Cross, K. P. *Accent on Learning: Improving Instruction and Reshaping the Curriculum.* San Francisco: Jossey-Bass, 1976.

Davis, R. H. "Special Funds for the Improvement of Instruction." In S. C. Ericksen and J. A. Cook (eds.), *Support for Teaching at Major Universities.* Ann Arbor: Center for Research on Learning and Teaching, University of Michigan, 1979.

Diamond, R. M., and others. *Instructional Development for Individualized Learning in Higher Education.* Englewood Cliffs, N.J.: Educational Technology Publications, 1975.

Dressel, P. L. *College and University Curriculum.* (2nd ed.) Berkeley, Calif.: McCutchan, 1971.

Eble, K. E., and McKeachie, W. J. *Improving Undergraduate Education Through Faculty Development: An Analysis of Effective Programs and Practices.* San Francisco: Jossey-Bass, 1985.

Eisner, E. W. *The Educational Imagination: On the Design and Evaluation of School Programs*. New York: Macmillan, 1979.

Erickson, G. A. "Survey of Faculty Development Practices." In M. Svinicki, J. Kurfiss, and J. Stone (eds.), *To Improve the Academy*, Vol. 11. Stillwater, Okla.: New Forums Press, 1986.

Forman, D. C., Aversa, F. M., Sell, G. R., and Brown, L. A. *An Examination of Formative Evaluation in Course Development*. Lincoln, Nebr.: University of Mid-America, 1976.

Gaff, J. G. *Toward Faculty Renewal: Advances in Faculty, Instructional, and Organizational Development*. San Francisco: Jossey-Bass, 1975.

Gaff, J. G. "Avoiding the Potholes: Strategies for Reforming General Education." *Educational Record*, 1980, *61*(4), 50–59.

Gaff, J. G. *General Education Today: A Critical Analysis of Controversies, Practices, and Reforms*. San Francisco: Jossey-Bass, 1983.

Gaff, J. G. *New Life for the College Curriculum: Assessing Achievements and Furthering Progress in the Reform of General Education*. San Francisco: Jossey-Bass, 1991.

Gray, P. J. (ed.). *Achieving Assessment Goals Using Evaluation Techniques*. New Directions for Higher Education, no. 67. San Francisco: Jossey-Bass, 1989.

Grobman, H. *Evaluation Activities of Curriculum Projects: A Starting Point*. Skokie, Ill.: Rand McNally, 1968.

Grobman, H. *Developmental Curriculum Projects: Decision Points and Processes*. Itasca, Ill.: Peacock, 1970.

Hefferlin, J. B. "Changes in Curriculum." In J. B. Hefferlin (ed.). *Dynamics of Academic Reform*. San Francisco: Jossey-Bass, 1969.

Levine, A. *Handbook on Undergraduate Curriculum*. San Francisco: Jossey-Bass, 1978.

Levine, A. *Why Innovation Fails: The Institutionalization and Termination of Innovation in Higher Education*. Albany: State University of New York Press, 1980.

Light, R. J., Singer, J. D., and Willett, J. B. *By Design: Planning Research on Higher Education*. Cambridge, Mass.: Harvard University Press, 1990.

Lindquist, J. *Strategies for Change*. Berkeley, Calif.: Pacific Soundings Press, 1978.

Mayhew, L. B., and Ford, P. J. *Changing the Curriculum*. San Francisco: Jossey-Bass, 1971.

McTighe Musil, C. *Diversity in Higher Education: A Work in Progress*. Washington, D.C.: Association of American Colleges and Universities, 1995.

Nichols, J. O. *Institutional Effectiveness and Outcomes Assessment Implementation on Campus: A Practitioner's Handbook*. New York: Agathon, 1989.

Rudolph, F. *Curriculum: A History of the American Undergraduate Course of Study Since 1636*. San Francisco: Jossey-Bass, 1977.

Schmitz, B. *Core Curriculum and Cultural Pluralism: A Guide for Campus Planners*. Washington, D.C.: Association of American Colleges, 1992.

Schön, D. A. *The Reflective Practitioner: How Professionals Think in Action*. New York: Basic Books, 1983.

Schön, D. A. *Educating the Reflective Practitioner: Toward a New Design for Teaching and Learning in the Professions*. San Francisco: Jossey-Bass, 1987.

Schuster, J. H., Smith, D. G., Corak, K. A., and Yamada, M. M. *Strategic Governance: How to Make Big Decisions Better*. Phoenix, Ariz.: Oryx Press, 1994.

Sell, G. R. "An Organizational Perspective for the Effective Practice of Assessment." In P. J. Gray (ed.), *Achieving Assessment Goals Using Evaluation Techniques*. New Directions for Higher Education, no. 67. San Francisco: Jossey-Bass, 1989a.

Sell, G. R. "Making Assessment Work: A Synthesis and Future Directions." In P. J. Gray (ed.), *Achieving Assessment Goals Using Evaluation Techniques*. New Directions for Higher Education, no. 67. San Francisco: Jossey-Bass, 1989b.

Sell, G. R. *Are the Teaching Methods Used in My Courses Effective?* Notes on Teaching, no. 8. Columbus: Center for Teaching Excellence, Ohio State University, 1990.

Sell, G. R. *The Instructional Enhancement Grant Program at Ohio State: An Analysis of Its Impact.* Unpublished report. Columbus: Center for Teaching Excellence, Ohio State University, 1992.

Simon, H. F. *The Sciences of the Artificial*. Cambridge, Mass.: MIT Press, 1969.

Stark, J. S., and Lowther, M. A. *Designing the Learning Plan: A Review of Research and Theory Related to College Curricula*. Ann Arbor: National Center for Research on Postsecondary Teaching and Learning, University of Michigan, 1986. (ED 287 439)

Stark, J. S., and others. *Planning Introductory College Courses: Influences on Faculty*. Ann Arbor: National Center for Research to Improve Postsecondary Teaching and Learning, University of Michigan, 1990.

Study Group on the Conditions of Excellence in American Higher Education. *Involvement in Learning: Realizing the Potential of American Higher Education*. Washington, D.C.: National Institute of Education, 1984.

Toombs, W., and Tierney, W. *Meeting the Mandate: Renewing the College and Departmental Curriculum*. ASHE-ERIC Higher Education Report No. 6. Washington, D.C.: George Washington University, School of Education and Human Development, 1991.

Tyler, R. W. *Basic Principles of Curriculum and Instruction*. Chicago: University of Chicago Press, 1950.

Veysey, L. "Stability and Experiment in the American Undergraduate Curriculum." In C. Kaysen (ed.), *Content and Context: Essays on College Education*. New York: McGraw-Hill, 1973.

Walker, D. F. "Curriculum Development in an Art Project." In W. A. Reid and D. F. Walker (eds.), *Case Studies in Curriculum Change*. New York: Routledge & Kegan Paul, 1975.

Wood, L., and Davis, B. G. *Designing and Evaluating Higher Education Curricula*. ASHE-ERIC Higher Education Research Report No. 8. Washington, D.C.: American Association for Higher Education, 1978.

CHAPTER THIRTY-FOUR

TENSIONS BETWEEN
TRADITION AND INNOVATION

Jerry G. Gaff

Today's undergraduate curriculum is the cumulative product of actions and events that, during the last century and a half, transformed the old colonial college into colleges and universities as we know them today. Chapters Two and Three discuss this history in some detail, but the most significant developments include:

- *The rise of practical studies.* Encouraged originally by the Morrill Land-Grant Act of 1862, practical studies today include preparation for careers in traditional fields, such as business, engineering, nursing, and teaching; careers in new fields, such as computer science; and worker training and retraining programs.
- *The introduction of the German research university model.* Introduced in the late 1800s, this model became the dominant ideal, and was accompanied by a virtual explosion of knowledge and of the creation of new fields of study.
- *The advent of academic disciplines and departments.* Academic disciplines and departments were created to support and disseminate research and to organize the academy, including the curriculum.
- *The specialization and professionalization of faculty work.* This led to greater authority and autonomy for professors and to the proliferation of courses and programs.
- *The development and expansion of the academic major.* The major became the centerpiece of undergraduate education and of faculty and student life.

- *The elective principle.* Originally pioneered by Eliot at Harvard and now widely practiced in some form at the great majority of institutions, electives give students a wide array of curricular options.
- *The mechanization and credentialization of learning.* So-called Carnegie units now allow credit hours and cumulative grade point averages to make learning comparable and portable within and between institutions and to certify learning.
- *The expansion of access.* The growth in size and numbers of institutions and the creation of different types of colleges and universities with differentiated missions and curricula open higher education to a very large proportion of the population.
- *The diversification of the student body.* Especially since World War II, the proportion of the general population attending postsecondary education has increased and the student population has moved away from the traditional eighteen- to twenty-two-year-old bracket to include more diversity in terms of age, and also of gender, race, ethnicity, ability, interests, and other attributes.
- *The division of learning.* Trends toward increased specialization of knowledge and the curriculum mean that knowledge and curricula are offered to various markets that differ in terms of purposes, people, sites, and delivery systems.
- *The development of an elaborate superstructure.* Education now depends for curriculum support on a variety of state and regional systems, higher education associations, scholarly societies, labor unions, testing agencies, accrediting bodies, publishers of textbooks and journals, and other organizations.
- *The increasing cost.* This large and complex enterprise known collectively as American higher education demands ever-larger amounts of financial and human resources.

This system is so familiar to us today that it is hard to realize that it was created by a series of conscious decisions by countless individuals and groups, often as the result of hard-fought political battles now buried in the past and all but forgotten.

Today's large, multipurpose, complex, and differentiated system of higher education stands in contrast to the monolithic complex of academic values and structures that Jencks and Riesman (1968) called an "academic revolution." During the twentieth century, as knowledge and information became more important to the conduct of the economy and society, the value of advanced education grew; more and higher degree programs were developed. College professors were in great demand to staff new and larger programs, particularly during the expansive years after World War II when federal support for research exploded. Their prestige and salaries went up, and the nature of their work changed. They gradually shed responsibilities for cultivating the character of students and shifted responsibilities for supervising student groups and dealing with students outside of class to newly hired professional student affairs staff. They even reduced their teaching and advising loads, especially of undergraduates. This freed them to concentrate on professional tasks in their disciplines, to conduct research, and to publish the results. In his study of the origins of the research university, Wegener (1978, p. 17) observed, "From the beginning, in fact, it was not always clear why there needed to be students at all." To the extent that students were involved, the purpose of the curriculum was to teach them how to inquire and to conduct studies, that is, to acquire the research skills of their professors. The professor was the central figure of the university, the academic sun around whom all planets and moons revolved.

A new academic pecking order was established, led by the research universities, which most fully embraced these academic values, attracted the largest number of grants, and enjoyed the resources to offer professors more of what the profession desired—autonomy to do their own work, support for research and writing, excellent students, and good working conditions. Because research universities educate and socialize virtually all future faculty members, these values have been extended throughout all types of institutions, even those with very different missions. Although different institutional types continue to have different missions and different definitions of educational programs, we have seen a "mission creep." Two-year colleges have become four-year ones. Comprehensive and liberal arts colleges have aspired to university status, adding master's degree and eventually doctoral degree programs.

In many respects, the values characterized by the academic revolution are the backdrop against which many curricular innovations, not just today but throughout the twentieth century, are set. Educational challenges to this dominant trend also have characterized American higher education. Examples include Alexander Meiklejohn's Experimental College at the University of Wisconsin in the 1920s, Robert Maynard Hutchin's College at the University of Chicago in the 1930s and 1940s, the experimental colleges created at the University of California at Santa Cruz and Michigan State University, among others, in the 1960s and early 1970s, the general education reform agendas at all types of institutions during the 1980s, and the new campuses at San Marcos and Monterey Bay in the California State University system in the 1990s. Whenever champions of effective undergraduate education have challenged traditional philosophies or introduced alternative structures to realize their goals (as discussed in Chapters Four and Five), they have emphasized:

- Defending the value of the liberal arts and sciences, the distinctive mission of the undergraduate college, and the importance of common educational principles and standards
- Providing a broad general education for all students, regardless of their academic major or intended career and in all types of institutions

- Developing interdisciplinary studies to bridge the disciplines and the creation of programs and centers to promote integrative study
- Focusing on the needs, interests, and diversity of students
- Expanding the definition of scholarship, supporting undergraduate teaching, connecting the work of faculty members across specializations, and fostering academic community
- Attempting to counteract the proliferation of specialized courses and fragmentation of the curriculum by creating coherence and promoting common learning, both within and across programs
- Returning to genuine learning and its assessment—through performance, demonstration, or portfolios, for instance—as opposed to mechanical measures of learning and the tendency to focus on the sheer accumulation of credit units as ends in themselves
- Providing for experiential, hands-on, and service learning
- Creating human-scale learning communities
- Inventing experimental programs or colleges, often within traditional universities, to try out alternative structures and practices
- Attempting to streamline and simplify academic complexity and management

These efforts, counterrevolutions perhaps, are as persistent and characteristic of American higher education as the more dominant trends listed earlier.

The undergraduate curriculum today contains continuing tensions between these two poles. If research and doctoral universities embody the values of the academic revolution, the innovative impulse at many other colleges and universities, most vividly in experimental colleges, embrace this alternative vision of undergraduate education. Nonetheless, most institutions embody tensions between these competing notions of what a college education should be. But there is no mistaking what has been the dominant tendency. Rudolph (1977, p. 253) put it succinctly in his classic study of curriculum history: "Concentration was the bread and butter of the vast majority of professors, the style they knew and approved, the measure of departmental strength and popularity. Breadth, distribution, and general education were the hobby horses of new presidents, ambitious deans, and well-meaning humanists of the sort who were elected to curriculum committees as a gesture of token support for the idea of liberal learning."

Today's Challenge: A Historic Reversal of Dominant Trends

When American colleges and universities award over five hundred different types of baccalaureate degrees, it begs the question of the meaning of *a* baccalaureate degree. When psychology, for example, is described as a family of over a hundred disciplines, what does it mean to provide an introduction to the field? When a mid-sized university has 2,400 courses on the books, how can anybody understand and intelligently manage its curriculum? When a Big Ten university awards two hundred different degrees, what happens to the "uni" in university, to the sense of wholeness? Concentration, specialization, and departmentalism have led to a curriculum that is in many respects out of control.

The curriculum is literally out of control for some very understandable reasons. After having seen the instructional program determined variously by the church, boards of trustees, and administrations during most of its history, the faculty—those with essential knowledge—wrested authority over the curriculum early in this century. Arguing that authority ought to reside with those who have expertise rather than with those who have bureaucratic standing, faculty gained legitimate authority over the instructional program, including the curriculum. Working within the contexts of their academic disciplines, professors were eager to create effective curricula as they understood them, that is, to expand, divide, recombine fields, and add more and more specialized courses and programs to the curriculum. At the same time, they had no mandate to manage the curriculum for efficiency. Professors had authority but lacked accountability. Administrators, on the other hand, had accountability but no authority to meddle with the curriculum. The result is proliferation of courses and programs resulting in both fragmentation of the educational experience for students and increases in the cost of the curriculum.

A spate of current analyses by thoughtful leaders (Breneman, 1995; Callan, 1995; Ewell, 1994; Guskin, 1994; Kennedy, 1995; and Zemsky and Massy, 1995) assert that fundamental change is inevitable. Ewell, for instance, states "We are right in the middle of what amounts to a major transformation, visible particularly in the relationship between academic institutions and the wider society." He adds, "About every two generations we seem to experience such a shift," citing the emphasis on access and delivery after World War II, the rise of the research university at the turn of the century, and the Morrill Act before that. The reasons for expecting fundamental changes at this time are primarily fiscal and political. He observes that academics have had an "unquestioning expectation of the continuing, unchecked expansion of higher education in both scale and quality," which is simply no longer possible, given the size and cost of the enterprise and the pressures to finance competing social needs. Further, higher education has become so central to the strategic future of the nation and its states and regions that the traditional autonomy of institutions and efforts to protect them from political interference are no longer possible. Today, government—and the larger public—must redefine what it needs from the academy, and what it will pay for. Ewell says this transition is permanent, and fundamental changes in colleges and universities, including their academic programs, are necessary. We appear to be in the midst of developing a new social contract—the outlines of which are murky—about the role and purposes of postsecondary education.

Callan (1995, p. 4) drew a similar conclusion from an analysis of the state of California. He projected an increase of 450,000 students from 1990 to 2005. Using "the most conservative set of projections that anyone has made so far," he concludes, "There is no scenario under which the *status quo* model can move into the future at its current cost. In other words, the cost of the way we are doing business now is not sustainable if we want to maintain our goals regarding access." That means, "The state of California and its institutions of higher learning must choose between: 1) maintaining the current system at its current cost and serving a much smaller portion of the population, or 2) reducing the overall cost per student."

It is curious that two different arenas of activity that have operated on different tracks for over a decade are now coalescing, and like two weather systems that collide, their combined winds of change are swirling ever more strongly. First is the effort to improve academic programs and the curriculum in particular, the primary subject of this book. On the campuses, this agenda has been led by the faculty and academic administrators, and off campus it has been furthered by association and foundation leaders who support experimentation and innovation. Second is the effort to foster accountability and financial efficiency; these have been led on the campus by presidents, chief financial officers, planners, and often by assessment experts. Off-campus accountability initiatives have come from governors' and legislative offices, coordinating boards, and public policy think tanks. Leading thinkers in curriculum and instruction, such as most authors of this handbook, are typically not credible spokespersons for accountability issues, and vice versa.

But today these two agendas are coming together. The educational improvement agenda is being joined—and strengthened—by the management-fiscal-political agenda. Developing a quality educational program based on shared academic principles is one of the best ways to gain the public's trust and support. As Chapter Twenty-Five points out, it is possible to enhance educational quality, build academic community, and still contain costs. Chapter Twenty-Six shows why traditional behaviors must change so that it is possible to manage the curriculum to achieve both effectiveness and efficiency. The new impetus from the joining together of these previously separate agendas is fueling some of the restructuring that is increasingly being talked about—and actually done in a few places. For the first time in many decades, good education is good politics and good economics.

The fundamental social, economic, and technological trends that have led to reengineering in business, the military, and the federal government are knocking on the door of higher education, as discussed in Chapter Six. Significant change to foster productivity in learning and to lower costs is coming, and it is vital that such changes be informed by sound educational principles. That is the context in which the development of a new social contract between higher education and the public should take place. But how do higher education and society renegotiate a social contract, when forums do not exist to do such a thing? It is done through a plethora of separate decisions by campus leaders dealing with planning, budgeting, admissions, and financial aid, for instance. It is done by actions of state coordinating boards, state and local elected officials, and labor unions. It is done through a large number of political campaigns and media displays. And, yes, it is done by campus faculties and administrators when they make decisions about which learning is most valuable and about how to design a curriculum to cultivate it.

In recent years, campus leaders have often made budget and curricular decisions without a long-term plan and against the backdrop of a prolonged recession and the decline of revenues available for higher education. In most cases spending cuts have been made in what might be called traditional ways. That is, budgets have been reduced, positions frozen, and programs squeezed. If this was not sufficient, across-the-board cuts have been made. Although across-the-board cuts tend to weaken strong and weak programs alike, they are easier to conceive and politically safer to implement than targeted programmatic reductions. The upshot is that many institutions have cut sections of courses, raised class sizes, replaced full-time faculty with adjuncts, and generally protected specialized majors and full-time faculty. Relatively few institutions have taken advantage of the opportunity to become self-conscious about their academic programs, their organizational structures, and the values that they hold most dear, and to use that insight to develop innovative academic programs that are more effective and efficient.

These manifold decisions of policy makers reflect not just educational and political principles, in the best and worst sense of those terms, but the power of the market. Nearly all institutions must be attuned to the market; only a few with high prestige and large endowments have a measure of insulation. And the market today—undergraduate students and their families, as well as potential donors such as governments and foundations—finds the values championed by the academic revolution out of favor. The people paying the price want institutions to put students and learning at the center.

Putting Students and Learning at the Center

Already we are seeing institutions of all types and sizes—major research universities, comprehensive institutions, liberal arts colleges, and community colleges—making innovations in their academic programs because they see them not just as good education but as strategic to their futures. As we have seen in previous chapters, large numbers of institutions are seeking to strengthen the undergraduate curriculum by:

- Introducing university-wide general education curricula that contain higher quality, more purposefulness, greater structure, and more coherence (Chapter Seven)
- Developing academic majors that contain greater focus, sequence, and integrative learning (Chapter Eleven)
- Developing more intentionality in cultivating fundamental academic skills, such as writing and critical thinking, that are often taught across the curriculum (Chapters Eight and Eighteen)
- Devising more holistic, thematic, experiential, and integrative models of learning the liberal arts and sciences, including the humanities, the natural and social sciences, and fine and performing arts (Chapters Twelve through Fifteen)
- Joining theoretical and practical knowledge in the professions (Chapter Sixteen) and in occupational and technical programs (Chapter Seventeen) and connecting such programs to changing social conditions
- Designing interdisciplinary studies that transcend the academic disciplines and build bridges among them (Chapter Nineteen)
- Incorporating cultural diversity and adding new voices and instructional materials into the curriculum (Chapters Nine and Twenty-One)
- Internationalizing the curriculum (Chapter Twenty)
- Developing learning communities by transcending separate courses and tapping the power of group work to increase learning and growth of both students and faculty (Chapter Twenty-Two)
- Using technology to enrich the classroom and incorporate knowledge and information from multiple sources and media (Chapter Twenty-Three)
- Providing supplemental instruction, where necessary, to help at-risk students achieve high standards (Chapter Ten)
- Establishing administrative positions to provide leadership for programs that require coordination of individuals across departments and other units (Chapter Twenty-Four)
- Assessing student learning and academic programs to provide feedback and improve learning (Chapters Twenty-Eight, Twenty-Nine, and Thirty)
- Developing priorities and mechanisms to maintain quality and coherence as students transfer among diverse institutions (Chapter Twenty-Seven)

These are discernible features of a renaissance of undergraduate education. Collectively, they amount to nothing less than a curriculum reform movement and, collectively, they point to directions for change in the future.

Innovations such as those described here are rarely, if ever, directly transferrable. What works in one environment may fail in another due to differences in mission, heritage, people, timing, or resources. Innovation is most often adaptation rather than adoption, and it takes considerable investment of time, people, and resources just to seed change.

The curriculum reform movement is difficult to see, because the innovations appear to be so diverse, scattered, and diffuse. Improvements are taking place in many different areas and in many different institutions, and not every kind of improvement is under way at the same institution or at the same time. Furthermore, these changes are often small-scale and isolated initiatives. They sometimes are taken up by a only few faculty volunteers, and are thus presented as options for students rather than as requirements. Even at institutions where there are multiple initiatives and new requirements, there may be little awareness or interaction between students or faculty in different programs. Nonetheless, institutions are increasingly developing comprehensive efforts to put students and learning at the center. Taken together, there can be little doubt that we are in the midst of a curriculum reform movement designed to improve the quality of undergraduate education, consonant with the changing social, economic, political, and technological environment.

Some of these curricular innovations are found, of course, in the nation's research universities and leading liberal arts colleges. But in reality, most of the elite two hundred or so universities and colleges are not leaders in curriculum change. This is understandable, because prestigious institutions have been the winners under the old game featuring producers and professors. But if the rules of the game are changing so that the quality of undergraduate education is more highly valued and so that consumers and students are in the foreground, then other types of institutions may acquire greater prestige, and even resources.

If we are in the midst of a historic transformation of academic values, as I have argued, then it opens the way for new institutions to become recognized leaders. Whatever the reason, the boldest initiatives and the most fervent spokespersons for them are among the other—over two thousand—nonspecialized institutions. Clark Kerr (1991) talked of "the new race to be Harvard or Berkeley or Stanford" and of the new opportunities to move up on the academic ratings. Citing the projected turnover of faculties, increased competition among institutions, and shifting sources of funding, he explored opportunities for universities to move into the upper ranks in terms of the traditional values of the research university.

But the vast majority of institutions—the ones that educate the majority of undergraduate students—also face projected faculty turnover, stiff competition, and shifting resources. New leaders may be expected among institutions that take their students seriously and place the quality of learning at the center of their missions, strategic plans, marketing, and all their institutional functioning. Indeed, places as diverse as Miami University in Ohio, California Lutheran University, St. Francis College in Pennsylvania, and the community colleges in Minnesota are making their curriculum reforms a centerpiece of their institutional life.

In fact, new exemplars are developing *within* sectors of higher education. Community colleges may not look to Stanford or Harvard for ideas, but they readily recognize developments at Miami-Dade, Maricopa, or LaGuardia Community Colleges. Similarly, the regional state colleges and universities are excited by curricular initiatives among their own members—James Madison, Truman State, and Eastern Washington.

During recent years, various groups of colleges and universities have banded together to define new commitments to undergraduate education and to create new market niches. The New American College (Berberet and Wong, 1995) is a group of small private institutions offering undergraduate programs in liberal arts and sciences and in professional fields as well as small graduate programs. Leaders have organized a new association and are taking in new members to address common concerns of identity and image diffusion and of limited resources by focusing on their centers of excellence, which are responsive to student and community interests.

Another group of institutions has created a new Council of Public Liberal Arts Colleges. These institutions have a liberal arts mission unusual for the public systems in which they are located. They, too, are developing shared academic programs, faculty development, and program review efforts that capitalize on their distinctive qualities.

Yet another forty-five institutions, primarily public, have created the Coalition of Metropolitan Universities. These universities are acutely attuned to the needs of their communities and serve their diverse student constituencies. In teaching, they focus on preparation for citizenship and for practice in professions and occupations; in research, they exploit opportunities to apply research that addresses complex metropolitan problems; and in service, they create partnerships with business, community, and cultural groups and bring intellectual resources to improve the quality of life. These are all newly organized efforts to define and legitimize different kinds of institutions of higher learning with different missions and niches, yet all—in various ways—are emphasizing the vitality of undergraduate education.

But what of the faculty? It would seem that they have everything to lose and nothing to gain by adopting curriculum changes that make the interests of students primary and place their own interests in a supporting role. Actually, faculty members are leading all the curriculum changes cited in this handbook, with

support from administrators. Curriculum reform has always held several benefits for faculty. First, a large majority of faculty members like to teach and enjoy
working with students. A national survey (Carnegie Foundation for the Advancement of Teaching, 1989) found that 71 percent of faculty said their interests were
"primarily in teaching" or "leaning toward teaching," rather than research. A majority in every type of institution except research universities reported their interests were more in teaching than in research. The curriculum and institutional
changes discussed here create an environment that is more supportive of their
work with undergraduates and one in which they can be more effective.

Faculty also very often report a genuine sense of professional and personal
renewal when they work together to fashion and implement stronger instructional
programs (as discussed in Chapters Twenty-Two and Thirty-Three, and in Gaff,
1991). Further, most faculty yearn for something we used to call a community of
scholars. By teaching and working in the context of a broadly shared and clearly
articulated educational philosophy that is operationalized in the life of the institution, faculty members can be connected to such communities of learning. In addition, if such changes are part of a comprehensive initiative focused on a
high-quality education for undergraduate students, that is likely to position the
institution in a favorable competitive position. To the extent that the institution
competes more effectively for students, donors, educational grants, or state
appropriations, these additional resources strengthen the position of the faculty.
Finally, Guskin (1994, p. 16) adds another, more ominous reason for some: "Restructuring the role of faculty members will, at first, prove to be a monumental
undertaking. All of the incentives seem against doing so—except, in the end,
survival." Many will see that these benefits outweigh the alternative of fighting a
rearguard action to retain perquisites, which will be doomed in all but a few exceptional institutions.

There can be no significant change in the curriculum unless it is paralleled by
a change in the faculty role. Here, too, are signs of change. One is the call from
Boyer (1990) and Rice (1991) for the creation of "the new American scholar" as
a new model for faculty work. One aspect is a broader definition of research
that legitimates and honors a wider variety of intellectual work than the traditional one of conducting research in an academic discipline and publishing it in
a refereed journal. That is, while research that advances knowledge in the discipline would still be valued, so also would work that integrates knowledge across
fields, is closely related to application and practice, and illuminates the teaching
and learning of one's knowledge. Further, the new scholar would work in a genuine academic community, making the work of the faculty greater than the sum
of the parts, and various career paths would be available to individual faculty
members.

A second example is the socialization of future faculty in their graduate education to value undergraduate education. Some evidence of this change can be seen in the recent expansion of training and support for graduate teaching assistants, which enhances the quality of their current teaching of undergraduates. Even greater evidence of the transformation is the rapid growth of programs to prepare future faculty, especially those supported by The Pew Charitable Trusts and the Fund for the Improvement of Postsecondary Education (Gaff and Lambert, 1996). These efforts bring academic leaders from diverse institutions, primarily undergraduate, into partnership with graduate universities. They focus on the full range of responsibilities of faculty—not just research and teaching. In addition to formal study of teaching and professional roles, graduate students work with a teaching mentor, teach segments of courses in settings beyond the graduate university, attend faculty and committee meetings, and learn about life in various academic cultures. These programs, designed to prepare future assistant professors, are generating considerable enthusiasm on the part of graduate students, faculty members, and administrators, and point to effective ways to socialize future faculty to the value of undergraduate education. The changing roles and preparation of faculty reinforce the changes in the curriculum, and together they point toward ways to recast the heart of the academic enterprise.

Fragility of the Innovations

Although these trends are very much in evidence, one should not overestimate how deeply rooted any of these new programs are in the lives of institutions. In fact, these new types of programs have a tenuous status in most colleges and universities. The primary reason is that each of these innovations requires change in individuals and institutions, which is inherently a difficult and uncertain process (as discussed in Chapters Thirty-One and Thirty-Two). Promoting interdisciplinary or integrative study in a university organized by academic departments, for instance, runs counter to the usual ways of thinking, behaving, planning, and budgeting. Developing a plan of study that operates across the curriculum requires the collaboration of many individuals and departments and runs counter to the laissez-faire spirit that has pervaded academic culture. Developing a learning community challenges the traditional notion that the individual class is the basic unit of curriculum. In all these cases, innovations go against the grain and constantly encounter the inertia of individual habits, academic traditions, and entrenched bureaucracies.

Because these innovations represent coordinated institutional initiatives—a program rather than the independent work of scattered individuals—they typically depend on the leadership of some central authority. Usually this is the chief academic officer, or in the case of a college within a larger university, a dean. But it can also be the president or a faculty committee, or, within a department, the chair or a respected faculty leader. Ideally, institution-wide initiatives are launched with strong support from *both* administration and faculty leaders. Without such central leadership, curriculum change—beyond the course level—is unlikely to be designed, approved, or implemented.

Translating each of these initiatives from ideas into operational programs of study (as discussed in Chapter Five) requires even more time, energy, and resources. Faculty members must be recruited and supported while they explore common ground and plan new courses. Students must be recruited and oriented to the program and why it is important. Descriptive materials, brochures, and advising guides need to be devised. Organizational supports are necessary, whether that means administrative responsibility, faculty oversight, or library support. This is why new initiatives require an initial investment in people and programs, even though they will often reap rewards in terms of better education or cost savings at some later time. Many innovations are started with support of grants from private foundations, such as the Bush, Ford, and Kellogg Foundations, the Lilly Endowment, and The Pew Charitable Trusts—or their local and regional counterparts. Other innovations are supported by the Fund for the Improvement in Postsecondary Education, the National Endowment for the Humanities, or the National Science Foundation.

Of course, there is a need to provide permanent financing from hard budget sources after grant funds expire. As Chapter Thirty-Two reports, institutions tend to provide a great deal of support to design a curriculum proposal but often fail to support its implementation sufficiently. Strong and continuous leadership to orchestrate all these forces is pivotal if new curricula are to be introduced into traditional institutions. These are some reasons why academic folklore holds that it is easier to move a cemetery than to change a curriculum.

Even if successfully implemented, most new programs face another challenge when they seek to escape their marginal position and become regular and routine features of institutional life. A new program typically has to continually prove itself, and, unlike established programs, it often must be rigorously assessed. That is, faculty and administrators may see it as experimental and as reversible, should events warrant it. Not until it has drawn a good number of individuals into its orbit and developed its own constituencies—including credible and influential spokespersons—can a program be regarded as institutionalized.

And institutionalization has its own vulnerabilities. Even established and proven programs may erode. Time washes away the rationale for the program; new faculty may be less committed to it; administrators may come and go and develop other agendas; student interests and needs may change; and changes may occur in the social and political environment. Any or all of these factors may call for a new curriculum review and more revision. Vital academic programs require continuous attention if their lifeblood is to be sustained.

Renewal of the undergraduate curriculum, therefore, is a constant, never-ending process. That is why curriculum matters can never be cut and dried, settled and set aside. A vital curriculum is one where current practices are critically and reflectively analyzed, ideas from elsewhere are studied and explored for their utility, experiments are tried by both individuals and groups, and evidence of effectiveness is constantly sought. The current period of rethinking the undergraduate curriculum, rather than being perceived as an episodic and unusual event, should presage a continuous practice of academic life.

Supports for the New Curricula

When a phenomenon as broad and significant as the undergraduate curriculum reform movement sweeps the nation, it doesn't just happen *sui generis*. It results from stimulus, guidance, and encouragement from many different sources. It needs vision, leadership, and resources, often from beyond the campus itself. In short, it requires new infrastructural supports. And these have been growing.

Thousands of books and articles have been written to analyze curricular problems and to propose solutions since the *Missions of the College Curriculum* (Carnegie Foundation for the Advancement of Teaching, 1977) proclaimed general education to be "a disaster area," helping to launch the current round of interest in the undergraduate curriculum. Countless conferences, workshops, and institutes have been held to discuss the goals of undergraduate education, explore alternative curricular models, and devise strategies for change.

New standards and principles have been formulated and adopted by state and national organizations, and demonstration projects and experimental programs have been developed, pilot tested, and implemented. In the process, research studies have been conducted on the impact of different aspects of the learning environment on students, and funding agencies have created programs to support faculty and curriculum development. Legislation, system guidelines, and new funding formulas have been devised to advance quality in undergraduate education. The work of educational organizations of all types has established programs that foster innovative thought and practice in the undergraduate curriculum. All these activities have created a hospitable national climate for the colleges and universities that have taken a serious review of their academic programs and made revisions in them.

Further support for improving undergraduate education comes from a wide variety of organizations. Consider the two organizations sponsoring this volume. The group now called the Association of American Colleges and Universities (AAC&U) was created in 1915 as a group of colleges banding together to protect traditional college education from encroachments by the new and growing universities. The 1995 name change (from Association of American Colleges) itself symbolizes the changing environment of higher education in the United States. Throughout most of its years, the organization held an annual meeting and published a journal, *Liberal Education,* both of which relied on initiatives and creativity from its members. The association served as a convening authority to showcase the most important ideas, programs, and concerns from college campuses. Today it serves the needs of all types of colleges and universities; leverages member dues about four times through grants to conduct studies, develop model programs, and prepare publications; publishes not only *Liberal Education* but also newsletters, occasional papers, and a serious series of monographs; puts on not only an annual meeting but also a rich series of working conferences on such topics as sustaining vitality in general education, teaching cultural diversity, and internationalizing the curriculum; and administers the American Academy of Academic Deans, a group that advances the professional development of academic deans. Through these various endeavors, AAC&U involves large numbers of individuals and institutions. A typical letter from a member president states that her college had made a paradigm shift and that it "would not have made nearly as much progress these last few years without the inspiration, resources, and good advice and counsel of AAC&U."

The second sponsor, the National Center on Postsecondary Teaching, Learning, and Assessment, is housed at Pennsylvania State University's Center for the Study of Higher Education. It is a collection of researchers, writers, and disseminators drawn from several major universities to conduct studies leading to improvements in undergraduate education. Supported originally by a five-year grant from the U.S. Department of Education, it focuses its attention on several areas: research into the effectiveness of collaborative learning and various forms of active learning; determination of what works in assessment and how to make assessments more useful; study of how new faculty learn to teach and work with students in different types of institutions; publication of reports on and studies of the implications of its research for improvement; and dissemination of the results and implications of its work through conferences and special sessions at conferences for policy makers.

The point is that these are but two examples of how existing organizations have been mobilized to provide leadership and support for improvements in the curriculum and related aspects of undergraduate education. Organizations of all sorts are now involved in helping to redirect the priorities and energies of colleges and universities.

New relationships and new organizations, too, are being created to support curriculum improvement. Some curriculum changes take place within departments, where they are supported by their staff, leadership, and budgetary resources. Such efforts are also supported by the learned societies that often feature innovative approaches in their national and regional programs—the development of learning communities in science, for instance, or the new approaches to teaching calculus and the experiential learning programs in biology. Many current innovations span disciplines and encourage connections that cross traditional structures, and these draw encouragement from educational associations that cross boundaries and create new relationships, such as the American Association for Higher Education or The Carnegie Foundation for the Advancement of Teaching.

For many campus initiatives, like freshman seminars or writing across the curriculum, institutions are appointing new leaders and giving them staff and budgets to make the new programs work (see Chapter Twenty-Four). Most institutions today are characterized by tensions and continual negotiations between the academic departments and these supradepartmental programs. The fact of the matter is that such innovations are not likely to survive for long unless they are rooted in academic departments and embraced as a central part of faculty and student responsibilities. And someone needs to have the job of seeing that those responsibilities are actually assumed.

Not surprisingly, when individuals—typically faculty leaders—are given leadership responsibility for innovations on their campuses, they look for colleagues who are in comparable positions elsewhere. Since a campus is likely to have only one person serving as director of the general education curriculum or the multicultural affairs program, for example, these leadership positions entail a certain amount of professional loneliness. Leaders tend to look for persons in similar positions elsewhere to share their dreams, opportunities, and struggles; to think through common problems and strategies; to express their excitement, successes, and disappointments; and to share resources. Consequently, they have formed new professional organizations, formal and informal, to support their work.

Typically small, these new groups supplement the work of the scholarly disciplinary societies (such as the American Chemical Society) as professional associations of academics. Although these groups help to support the new courses of study, they serve, also, to lend credibility, visibility, and respectability to innovative campus programs, just as the disciplinary societies have done before them. Table 34.1 lists a number of relatively recently formed—or recently revitalized—small professional organizations that nourish the leaders of curriculum innovations.

TABLE 34.1. NEW PROFESSIONAL ASSOCIATIONS OF ACADEMIC LEADERS.

Name	Purpose
American Academy for Liberal Education	Accredit liberal arts programs
American Association for the Advancement of Core Curricula	Support core curricula
Association for General and Liberal Studies	Support general and liberal studies
Association for Integrative Studies	Promote interdisciplinary studies
Association for Practical and Professional Ethics	Support teaching of ethics
Association for the Study of Afro-American Life and History	Advance Afro-American study
Campus Compact	Encourage service learning
Center for Indian Education	Advance study of Native Americans
Community College General Education Association	Enhance general education
Community College Humanities Association	Enhance the humanities
Council for the Administration of General and Liberal Studies	Support general education leaders
Council of Writing Program Administrators	Advance writing programs
EDUCOM	Enhance use of educational technology
Freshman Year Experience Network	Strengthen freshman year programs
National Association for Chicano Studies	Promote Chicano studies
National Association for Ethnic Studies	Promote ethnic studies
National Association of Scholars	Promote traditional academic values
National Initiative for a Networked Cultural Heritage Association	Guide use of technology in art, culture, and history
National Women's Studies Association	Advance women's studies
Professional and Organizational Network for Higher Education	Conduct faculty development and improve teaching
Teachers for a Democratic Culture	Promote teaching of diversity
The Institutional 50	Promote internationalization at liberal arts colleges

Collectively, the creation of these new organizations is indicative of the scope and significance of the curriculum reform movement. These groups may seem small and marginal, if compared to the mainstream disciplinary societies of faculty, but they are significant players in the current era of reform. In many respects, the very fragility of these new academic associations mirrors the fragility of the campus programs they advocate, but they gain strength in numbers.

It is ironic that the curriculum reform movement—designed in part to counteract fragmentation—is itself fragmented. Writing program directors are unlikely to belong to the Association for General and Liberal Studies, for example, and members of the Association for Integrative Studies are unlikely to be involved with the Association for Practical and Professional Ethics. Leaders of innovations in each area tend to be relatively uninformed about innovations in other areas. The extent to which these new groups diverge from the traditional interests in the disciplines can be illustrated by a colleague who belongs to the Modern Language Association. This year he says he is the only person to both chair an English department, and thereby belong to the Association of Departments of English, and direct a writing program, and thus be a member of the Council of Writing Program Administrators.

Leadership in each area listed in the table calls for both specialized competence and the ability to enlist the support of constituencies from across the campus. The agendas of each of these diverse initiatives can be furthered by connecting the pieces together, combining forces, and working together. Schmitz has commented on the rich source of practical wisdom about changing the curriculum that exists among individuals involved in these various innovations. Writing about the efforts to incorporate cultural pluralism into core curricula, she noted, "[t]he importance of capitalizing on the knowledge and experience of those in writing programs, faculty development programs, area studies, women's studies, and American ethnic studies" (1992, p. 81). Leaders in these curricular initiatives on a campus or within a system can derive a powerful synergy by sharing experiences, linking resources, and working together.

Of course, even as these kinds of changes coalesce across departments, intellectual work and scholarly advances are continuing within the disciplines. New specializations continue to come into being, both by further subdivision of disciplines and more commonly by cross-fertilizing concepts and methods across disciplines (Geertz, 1983). For example, the rich intellectual work being done in the cognitive sciences comes from physiology, biochemistry, psychology, computer science, and other fields. Like the molten mass of radioactive material that forms the core of the earth, only to erupt periodically in a volcano or to shift tectonic plates and change the shape of the crust, scholarship continues throughout all the disciplines and occasionally bursts forth to change the shape of the intellectual landscape. Inevitably, it also finds its way into the constantly shifting curriculum.

Prospects for Continued Reform

It is foolhardy to make forecasts about anything as complex and unpredictable as the future of academic life. But one can make a reasoned guess about whether the current period of innovation, experimentation, and change will continue.

Although some may disagree, I think that the pressures to put students and learning at the center and to make the curriculum both more effective and more efficient will continue until four ends have been achieved.

• *Correct the worst excesses of the academic revolution and restore a better balance between competing values.* If the academic revolution elevated the interests of faculty members, the reform movement gives primacy to the interests of students, as Riesman (1980) himself predicted—although he was too early on its timing. Similarly, the values represented by teaching (as opposed to research), undergraduates (as opposed to graduate students), at least a modicum of common studies (as opposed to entirely free electives), and emphasis on fundamental knowledge, skills, and attitudes (as opposed to a curriculum with no priorities) are on the ascendant. The trend is to counteract the radical proliferation of courses and the supermarket mentality it promotes, thereby combating intellectual fragmentation and helping to bring costs under better control.

• *Create greater self-consciousness and restore a greater sense of purpose in the curriculum.* Boyer was fond of pointing out that we are more confident that a college education should last four years that we are of what its purposes should be. That is because it is very difficult for a group of faculty members, who are trained to "think otherwise," to agree on a common philosophy, educational goals, curriculum structure, graduation requirements, and essential content—even within individual departments, let alone across the entire institution. There are obvious benefits to individual autonomy and laissez-faire administration. Colleges and universities traditionally have minimized conflict by blurring differences of opinion, making compromises, and giving individuals wide latitude to pursue their own interests. Making few demands on either students or faculty, deciding to live and let live, is an easy way to deal with such complexity. But there are times, and today is one, when we need to be self-conscious about our education and purposeful and collaborative about our work. As we have seen, continuing our previous patterns is not possible for any but the most privileged institutions. That is why colleges and universities are tackling the difficult agenda, reaching for wide agreements, and making changes in the undergraduate curriculum.

• *Restore integrity to the curriculum.* The undergraduate curriculum has many faces. It may be seen in terms of philosophy, policy, or practice (Brubacher, 1977) or in terms of its intent, content, or consequences (Ahlgren and Boyer, 1981). There is the hidden curriculum, that collection of expectations, norms, and values through which students learn what is *really* important, regardless of the formal curriculum (Snyder, 1971). To put it succinctly: there is a curriculum as offered by the college, as taught by the faculty, and as learned by the student. For a curriculum to have integrity, these various reflections must emanate from the same reality. Integrity is a key to delivering both effectiveness and efficiency in the curriculum.

- *Bring greater efficiency into the system.* House (1994, p. 29) argues that higher education is facing a severe downsizing or transformation. "Likely policies include elimination of tenure; consolidation of campuses, departments, and programs; cutbacks in staff; more students per faculty member; more teaching contact hours; setting of priorities by politicians; outside interference in internal campus affairs; mandating of campus policies and curricula; outsourcing of services; privatization (e.g., industries deciding which research to support); and the use of productivity indicators to compare higher education institutions with one another for purposes of cost containment. Most reforms aim to increase productivity but they entail reducing autonomy as well."

Although one might quibble with some of the specifics, few observers would quarrel with the tenor of this analysis. Campus leaders can wait for these drastic measures to come at them and mount rearguard defensive actions, or they can regard this as an opportune time to reexamine the basic assumptions of undergraduate education and chart new directions. As Green, Levine, and others (1985) have shown, tough times are when many innovations in undergraduate education occur. Instead of simply shrinking the existing system, wise campus leaders are seeking to transform their courses of study into something different, and arguably better, than the current ones.

The evidence in this handbook is that the academic priesthood, prodded by serious external forces, is in the process of reforming itself. The reformation is proceeding slowly and falteringly, but it is moving. Times are uncertain, the old verities no longer hold, and the vision of what will emerge as the new academic norm is cloudy. Social changes of several sorts are leading to pressure for more and faster academic change. And several exemplary institutions are setting the pace and showing the way. It has taken about a century and a half to create the system we have now, and it will surely take time for this corrective process to run its course.

I believe that we are in the midst of making a historic reversal of the trends that have been dominant in American higher education for over a century. The curriculum has always been a battleground for different interests, and it again is reflecting fundamental societal changes. Although one cannot know with certainty, my best thinking suggests that the forces that have now been set in motion will not end until we see the interests of students and learning more prominent in colleges and universities, more purpose in undergraduate education, more integrity in the curriculum, and lower costs for the entire enterprise. That will be the time we have negotiated a new social contract between society and higher education.

This is not to say that we will reach a state of nirvana or some fixed condition at the end of history. As long as society changes, student backgrounds and interests shift, and scholars create new knowledge, frames of reference, interpretations, and methodologies, it will be necessary to critically examine the best way to educate students. As long as academics can dream of better curricula and experiment with innovative ways of engaging students in learning, the curriculum will remain in a dynamic state of continuous unfolding. In the words of Rudolph (1977, p. 3): "Values change and so does the curriculum, as the more than 300 years since the founding of Harvard College clearly say. Since that time long ago, when a peculiarly self-demanding band of alienated Englishmen got themselves a college almost before they had built themselves a privy, change in the course of study has been constant, conscious and unconscious, gradual and sudden, accidental and intentional, uneven and diverse, imaginative and pedestrian."

In this sense, the future of the undergraduate curriculum promises more of what we have had in the past.

References

Ahlgren, A., and Boyer, C. M. "Visceral Priorities: Roots and Confusion in Liberal Education." *Journal of Higher Education*, Mar.–Apr. 1981, pp. 173–181.

Berberet, J., and Wong, F. "The New American College: A Model for Liberal Learning." *Liberal Education*, winter 1995, pp. 48–52.

Boyer, E. L. *Scholarship Reconsidered: Priorities of the Professoriate.* Princeton, N.J.: Carnegie Foundation for the Advancement of Teaching, 1990.

Breneman, D. W. "Sweeping, Painful Changes." *Chronicle of Higher Education*, Sept. 8, 1995, p. B1.

Brubacher, J. S. *On the Philosophy of Higher Education.* San Francisco: Jossey-Bass, 1977.

Callan, P. M. *Public Purposes and Public Responsibilities.* San Jose: California Higher Education Policy Center, 1995.

Carnegie Foundation for the Advancement of Teaching. *Missions of the College Curriculum: A Contemporary Review with Suggestions.* San Francisco: Jossey-Bass, 1977.

Carnegie Foundation for the Advancement of Teaching. *The Condition of the Professoriate: Attitudes and Trends, 1989.* Princeton, N.J.: Carnegie Foundation for the Advancement of Teaching, 1989.

Ewell, P. T. "A Matter of Integrity: Accountability and the End(s) of Higher Education." *Change*, 1994, *26*(6), 24–29.

Gaff, J. G. *New Life for the College Curriculum: Assessing Achievements and Furthering Progress in the Reform of General Education.* San Francisco: Jossey-Bass, 1991.

Gaff, J. G., and Lambert, L. "Socializing Future Faculty to the Values of Undergraduate Education." July–Aug., 1996, 38–45.

Geertz, C. *Local Knowledge: Further Essays in Interpretive Anthropology.* New York: Basic Books, 1983.

Green, J. S., Levine, A., and Associates. *Opportunity in Adversity: How Colleges Can Succeed in Hard Times.* San Francisco: Jossey-Bass, 1985.

Guskin, A. E. "Reducing Student Costs and Enhancing Student Learning. Part II: Restructuring the Role of Faculty." *Change*, Sept./Oct., 1994, pp. 16–25.

House, E. "Policy and Productivity in Higher Education." *Educational Researcher,* 1994, *16,* p. 29.

Jencks, C., and Riesman, D. *The Academic Revolution.* New York: Doubleday, 1968.

Kennedy, D. "Another Century's End, Another Revolution for Higher Education." *Change,* May–June, 1995, pp. 8–15.

Kerr, C. "The New Race to Be Harvard or Berkeley or Stanford." *Change,* May–June, 1991, pp. 8–15.

Rice, R. E. "The New American Scholar: Scholarship and the Purposes of the University." *Metropolitan Universities,* 1991, pp. 7–18.

Riesman, D. *On Higher Education: The Academic Enterprise in an Era of Rising Student Consumerism.* San Francisco: Jossey-Bass, 1980.

Rudolph, F. *Curriculum: A History of the American Undergraduate Course of Study Since 1636.* San Francisco: Jossey-Bass, 1977.

Schmitz, B. *Core Curriculum and Cultural Pluralism: A Guide for Campus Planners.* Washington, D.C.: Association of American Colleges, 1992.

Snyder, B. R. *The Hidden Curriculum.* New York: Knopf, 1971.

Wegener, C. *Liberal Education and the Modern University.* Chicago: University of Chicago Press, 1978.

Zemsky, R., and Massy, W. F. "Toward an Understanding of Our Current Predicaments: Expanding Perimeters, Melting Cores, and Sticky Functions." *Change,* Nov./Dec., 1995, pp. 40–49.

A GLOSSARY OF TERMS

Analytic Curricular Models   Descriptions of the relationship and interaction between institutional characteristics and student social, economic, and educational characteristics as they affect student learning, personal development, and maturation (Chapter One).

Analytical Thinking   The use of heuristics, theories, or conceptual frameworks to organize the collection and interpretation of data (Chapter Eight).

Anthropological Approach to Evaluation   Assessment technique involving observation, interviewing, journal entry, group discussions, and critical incident reporting to provide the basis for analyzing connections between the process and outcomes of liberal education (Chapter Twenty-Nine).

Articulation Arrangements   Agreements between or among two- and four-year institutions that detail the rules for transferring degrees and credits (Chapter Twenty-Seven).

Assessment   The process of describing and monitoring performance of students or educational programs against a specified set of criteria (Chapter One; see also Chapters Twenty-Eight and Twenty-Nine).

Borderlands   Social or physical areas that occur whenever two or more cultures edge each other, where people of different races occupy the same territory, where under, lower, middle and upper classes touch, and where the space between two individuals shrinks with intimacy (Chapter Nine).

Canon   The body of knowledge that defines particular genres of work as the most legitimate for study (Chapter Fourteen).

Capstone Course   Course illustrating literary or historical developments in dynamic and chronological relationship with one another and providing a final opportunity to master key concepts and procedures (Chapter Eleven; see also Chapter Twenty-Eight).

Cognitive Development   Theory suggesting that all people, regardless of circumstance, progress through identifiable stages of intellectual ability, although not all reach the highest stage of abstract thinking and hypothesizing (Chapter Four).

Cognitive Rationality   The proposition that administrators need to establish more rational research and planning sequences, whether they involve assessment of student learning or preparation of strategic plans (Chapter Thirty-One).

Coherence   Interconnection within a curriculum, allowing students to encounter logical sequences of coursework leading to useful and long-lasting skills and insights about the world; a complex concept, implying much more than mere consistency among demands made and information presented (Chapter Seven).

Collaborative Learning   Pedagogy that encourages the development of individual learning through group learning (Chapter Twenty-Two).

Concentration   Cluster of courses offering in-depth experience in a single field (Chapter Fifteen).

Conceptual Curricular Model   Approach to curricular design that is concerned with the structure, purpose, and process of undergraduate education and with assessing its differential effects (Chapter One).

Connected Learning   Integrative learning within the major, and between the major and general education (Chapter Eleven).

Connoisseurship   Ability to focus on the intrinsic properties of an art object, that is, those properties that give the work its structure, shape, and identity (Chapter Fifteen).

Constructivism   Paradigm suggesting that effective learning (as distinguished from rote learning) consists less in recording information than in interpreting it; and that in order to interpret what is received and is attended to, the learner must personally construct meaning about it (Chapter Thirteen).

Cornerstone Course Courses that follow and reinforce learning in course sequence aimed at specific educational goals in general education, major, or minor (Chapters One and Twenty-Two).

Course Formal unit of undergraduate curriculum (Chapter One).

Course Cluster Group of courses, loosely linked either thematically or through a text (Chapter Eighteen), or as identified through assessment procedures (Chapter Seven).

Credentialism Theoretical position asserting that the primary function served by schooling is to provide school completers with credentials that set them apart from the remainder of the workforce and provide them with the credentials for entry into occupations with status (Chapter Seventeen).

Cultural Literacy The study of Western culture through familiarity with a specific cultural canon (Chapter Fifteen).

Culture Wars Controversy over the focus given to issues of diversity and multi-culturalism on campus and within society (Chapter Six).

Curriculum The process and substance of an educational program, comprising the purpose, design, conduct, and evaluation of educational experiences. It gives shape to an institution's particular intellectual beliefs and aspirations, negotiated by faculty in light of their specialized knowledge and in the context of social expectation and students' needs, and manifested in a body of courses that present the knowledge, principles, values, and skills intended as consequences of an undergraduate education (Chapters One, Six, Twenty-Five, and Twenty-Seven, among others).

Curriculum Development Process of planning an educational program, including the identification and selection of educational objectives, the selection of learning experiences, the organization of learning experiences, and the evaluation of program results (Chapter One).

Deconstructionists Scholars who object to shared intellectual standards, which they view as masks for the will to political power of dominant, hegemonic groups (Chapter Twelve).

Descriptive and Prescriptive Curriculum Curricular models representing the nature and organization of the substantive elements of the manifest curriculum (Chapter One).

Developmental Education   Pedagogy aimed at maximizing the talents and skills of each student rather than at the remedial goal of alleviating deficiencies (Chapter Ten).

Developmental Programs   Academic programs concerned with issues of student self-esteem, personal growth, and feelings of autonomy, with an emphasis on counseling (Chapter Ten).

Discipline   Conceptual framework for understanding a general body of knowledge and how it is acquired (Chapter One).

Discretionary Curriculum   Those courses that are not a requirement for any major and not a part of general education or a prerequisite for any required higher-level courses (Chapter Twenty-Six).

Educational Effectiveness Movement   Term describing people advocating the argument that colleges could reconstruct their curricula, student services, and pedagogy to create inviting and supportive environments for nontraditional students (Chapter Ten).

Efficiency   The distribution of students across courses such that actual enrollments per course taught by a regular member of the faculty equal the ideal class size for the pedagogy used for that course (Chapter Twenty-Six).

Essentialists   Scholars who believe that the classics, especially Plato and Aristotle, are the key to timeless truths of human nature (Chapters Seven and Twelve).

Evaluation   The process followed in rendering judgments regarding the information gathered through an assessment activity (Chapter One).

Faculty Development   A set of strategies aimed at the acquisition and refinement of knowledge, skills, and values needed in the professional roles of faculty (Chapter Thirty-Three).

Formative Evaluation   A nonlinear measurement activity whose purpose is to improve a program rather than to judge its worth (Chapter Twenty-Nine).

Functionalism   Theoretical position that assumes a tight coupling between higher education preparation and occupational competence (Chapter Seventeen).

Gateway Labs   Interactive tutorials on basic concepts (Chapter Thirteen).

General Education   The cultivation of the knowledge, intellectual skills, and attitudes that citizens and workers use throughout their lives (Chapter Twenty-Seven).

Goal-Free Evaluation   Approach to evaluation aimed at discovering and judging the actual effects of a program, including its unintended or accidental effects, based on the concept that unintended side effects of a program may be as important as its intended effects (Chapter Twenty-Nine).

Humanities   Disciplines that study human cultures and expressions (Chapter Twelve).

Hypertext   On-line document that permits nonsequential access to the contents depending upon choices the reader makes at the time the text is being read (Chapter Twenty-Three).

Instruction   The presentation of subject matter to students to carry out curricular goals and objectives (Chapter One).

Integrative Learning   Moving beyond the course format to general open-ended kinds of questions, or applying material learned in one course to issues in other courses (Chapter Eleven).

Intellectual Skills   Mental operations that transform information into knowledge (Chapter Eight).

Intellectual Skills Approach   Pedagogy involved in making expectations explicit for students and consciously addressing them in the design and practice of learning experiences in courses throughout the curriculum (Chapter Eight).

Interdisciplinary Courses   Courses organized around a theme, problem, cultural or historical period, world area or national region, or other unifying principle, rather than a departmental discipline. Faculty from various departments interact in designing such courses by bringing to light and reexamining the topic's underlying assumptions, and then modifying their own disciplinary perspectives in the process (see Multidisciplinary Courses) (Chapter Nineteen).

Interdisciplinary Pedagogy   Innovative teaching techniques that promote dialogue and community, problem-posing and problem-solving capacities, and an integrative habit of mind (Chapter Nineteen).

Interdisciplinary Studies   A process or program designed to answer questions, resolve problems or issues, or examine a topic that is too broad or complex to be dealt with adequately through a single discipline or field of study (Chapter Nineteen).

Internal Evaluation Report   Course or program evaluation based on review of original departmental goals (Chapters Twenty-Nine and Thirty).

Internationalization   The incorporation of the study of foreign peoples, countries, and cultures into the curriculum through language study, study abroad, the education of foreign students, and the creation of interdisciplinary programs examining global issues and topics or separate regions of the world (Chapter Twenty).

Junkyard Curriculum   Curriculum that has grown by accretion in a haphazard fashion—thus taking on the appearance of a junkyard—a process that encourages mediocrity (Chapter Twenty-Five).

Latent Curriculum   Unspoken aspects of a curriculum that teach the way people value time, order, neatness, promptness, and interpersonal relations (see Manifest Curriculum) (Chapter One).

Learning   An exercise of constructing personal knowledge that requires the learner to be mentally active rather than passive; interpreting rather than recording information (Chapters Eleven and Thirteen).

Learning Communities   Conscious curricular structures that link two or more disciplines around the exploration of a common theme, and that can serve as the entire educational experience during a given semester for both the students and the faculty involved (Chapter Twenty-Two).

Learning Webs   Proposed alternative educational system that would replace schools with a collaborative learning process linking the learner to networks providing access to formal educational programs in a variety of settings and learning endeavors (Chapter Four).

Legitimation Theory   View that postsecondary institutions legitimize knowledge areas by identifying them as appropriate for particular fields, structuring college courses and programs that represent them, and providing credentials to practitioners (Chapter Seventeen).

Liberal Education   Program designed to foster capacities of analysis, critical reflection, problem solving, communication, and synthesis of knowledge from different disciplines by providing students with an intellectual and social context for recognizing the continuity between the past and future and for drawing on reason and experience about human nature to develop and question values and to communicate the results of this process of thinking (Chapters Twelve, Sixteen, and Nineteen).

Lyceum Movement   Nineteenth-century lecture program designed to disseminate information about agriculture and other subjects; fostered discussion of the relationship between science and agriculture (Chapter Two).

Manifest Curriculum   Formal aspects of a curriculum, specifying subject matter to be studied as well as behaviors needed for learning these subject matters; includes the written goals, objectives, and rules and regulations of an institution (see Latent Curriculum) (Chapter One).

Master Learner   A faculty member released from usual teaching commitments to take classes with the students, to facilitate the integrating seminar, and to give occasional feedback to the faculty teaching those classes (Chapter Twenty-Two).

Measurement   Measurement is the process of gathering and quantifying information. Assessment occurs when measurements are analyzed according to established criteria and standards of performance (Chapter One).

Models   Theoretical constructs that describe observable behaviors (Chapter One).

Multicultural Education   Course design principle based on the idea that cultural difference has consequences in the classroom, that some differences are privileged over others, and that educational reform is necessary to bring equity into education (Chapter Twenty-One).

Multidisciplinary Courses   Courses designed to present various aspects of a theme by having faculty with different specialties present their individual perspectives in serial, encyclopedic fashion. This approach generally leaves differences in underlying assumptions to be examined and integrated later by the students (see Interdisciplinary Courses) (Chapter Nineteen).

Multimedia   Collective term for types of information including text and images consisting of graphs, charts, drawings, photographs, animation, audio, and video; generally used in connection with computers (Chapter Twenty-Three).

Objectivist   View that it is possible to identify and measure certain aspects of general and liberal education across disciplines, departments, even institutions and systems (Chapter Seven).

Occupational Education   Level of training less complex and theoretical than Professional Education but more so than Vocational Training, designed to prepare students for skilled crafts, usually but not always requiring licensure (Chapter Seventeen).

Pedagogy   Methods of teaching and interaction employed by an instructor; may encourage students either in passive absorption of information or in active construction of meanings for course material (Chapter Thirteen).

Perenialists   Those who hold the philosophy that the value of education is in preserving and transmitting language, knowledge, and values that provide the basis for culture. Perenialists believe that certain ideas and issues have recurrent value and provide the core questions confronted by a civilized society (Chapter Seven).

Pluralism   Approach to curriculum design incorporated into many undergraduate curricula as a way of encouraging the appreciation of differences and sameness among racial and ethnic groups and developing a better understanding of our changing society (Chapter Six).

Professional Education   System of formal education that prepares novices for highly skilled occupations such as law, medicine, and engineering, through a combination of theory and practice culminating in an award of certification, licensure, or other formal credential (Chapter Sixteen).

Queue Theory   Belief that the competition for jobs causes more desirable positions to have a large queue of applicants and less desirable positions have a shorter queue. Aspirants to desirable positions are drawn to higher education as a means to set themselves apart from other applicants in the queue. Higher education responds to market forces and produces programs based on market demand (Chapter Seventeen).

Reflective Practice   Professional activity involving thinking about and learning from one's own practice and the practice of others so as to improve judgment and increase the probability of taking wise action in complex, unique, and uncertain situations as they arise (Chapter Sixteen).

Scholarticism   Study characterized by the use of the dialectic, a form of logic that involves disputation or discrimination of truth from error in matters of opinion or controversy (Chapter Three).

Socratic Method   Pedagogy for teaching logic and analysis by posing new questions prompted by the previous response (Chapter Three).

Summative Evaluation   Form of evaluation conducted for a program that has been in operation for a period of time to determine its success or failure (Chapter Twenty-Nine).

Synthesis   Process of differentiating, comparing, and contrasting different disciplinary and professional perspectives; identifying commonalities and clarifying how the differences relate to the task at hand; and devising a holistic understanding grounded in the commonalities but still responsive to the differences (Chapter Nineteen).

Team-Teaching   Pedagogical practice (useful for Interdisciplinary Courses) where a group of instructors plan and teach a course, interacting with each other during class sessions—an expensive process often superseded by team planning but individuals teaching as team members become familiar with each other's perspectives and contributions (Chapter Nineteen).

Total Quality Management   Strategy to improve quality, reduce costs, increase efficiency, and create a self-renewing organization with high faculty and student satisfaction by simplifying procedures, eliminating bureaucratic structures, creating teamwork, delegating decision making, and gathering information on all parts of the system as a basis for continuous change (Chapter Twenty-Five).

Transfer Initiatives   Measures designed to make it easier for students to move from one institution to another by increasing the similarity in curricular content and standards across institutions, or by providing other incentives either to institutions or to students (Chapter Twenty-Seven).

Transferability   Ability to apply skills independently and creatively to new situations (Chapter Eight).

Virtual Classroom   Courses or entire degree programs delivered in whole or in part electronically via a combination of World Wide Web pages, Internet newsgroups, e-mail, Telnet, and video conferencing (Chapter Six).

Vocational Training   Preparation for jobs that call for extensive practical experience and training but have few requirements for theory, technical knowledge, or liberal arts education (Chapter Seventeen).

Work   A sustained and purposeful activity that enriches or sustains life and through which the purposes and meaning of the worker are expressed. A job becomes work when it includes the "exercise of judgment, sense of style, and the practice of a sense of craft" (Chapter Seventeen).

Writing Across the Curriculum   Pedagogical movement based on the concept that the faculty as a whole, not just one academic department, is responsible for students' writing skills; it encourages combined assignments for classes in writing and discipline-based subject areas (Chapter Eighteen).

NAME INDEX

SUBJECT INDEX